GLOBAL ISSUES

2017 Edition

Sara Miller McCune founded SAGE Publishing in 1965 to support the dissemination of usable knowledge and educate a global community. SAGE publishes more than 1000 journals and over 800 new books each year, spanning a wide range of subject areas. Our growing selection of library products includes archives, data, case studies and video. SAGE remains majority owned by our founder and after her lifetime will become owned by a charitable trust that secures the company's continued independence.

Los Angeles | London | New Delhi | Singapore | Washington DC | Melbourne

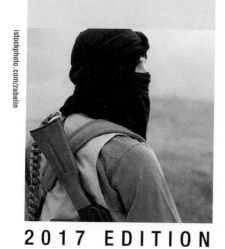

istockphoto.com/zabelin

GLOBAL ISSUES

SELECTIONS FROM *CQ RESEARCHER*

2017 EDITION

$SAGE | CQPRESS

FOR INFORMATION:

CQ Press

An Imprint of SAGE Publications, Inc.

2455 Teller Road

Thousand Oaks, California 91320

E-mail: order@sagepub.com

SAGE Publications Ltd.

1 Oliver's Yard

55 City Road

London EC1Y 1SP

United Kingdom

SAGE Publications India Pvt. Ltd.

B 1/I 1 Mohan Cooperative Industrial Area

Mathura Road, New Delhi 110 044

India

SAGE Publications Asia-Pacific Pte. Ltd.

3 Church Street

#10-04 Samsung Hub

Singapore 049483

Printed in the United States of America

ISBN 978-1-5063-6875-7

This book is printed on acid-free paper.

Senior Acquisitions Editor: Carrie Brandon

Editorial Assistant: Duncan Marchbank

Production Editor: David C. Felts

Copy Editor: Kim Husband

Typesetter: C&M Digitals (P) Ltd.

Cover Designer: Anupama Krishnan

Marketing Manager: Jennifer Jones

17 18 19 20 21 10 9 8 7 6 5 4 3 2 1

Contents

CONFLICT, SECURITY, AND TERRORISM

Annotated Contents

CONFLICT, SECURITY, AND TERRORISM
Defeating the Islamic State

Since emerging from the conflicts in the Middle East, the self-proclaimed Islamic State (ISIS) has become the leading instigator of global terrorism, including deadly bombings in Brussels and Paris. ISIS proclaims devotion to a radical version of Islam, and it has imposed a brutal dictatorship in areas it controls in Syria and Iraq. It also has initiated or inspired terrorist attacks in places as far flung as Indonesia and California. The United States and a coalition of nations have committed themselves to defeating ISIS. However, the Islamic State has proven more resilient than many predicted, leading to a contentious debate over strategy. Some political leaders are calling for an increased U.S. military effort, including use of ground troops. Others believe the approach would increase ISIS's popularity and lead to further attacks in the West. Governments also are struggling to counter ISIS's propaganda and recruiting efforts, both of which rely on a sophisticated use of the Internet.

Far-Right Extremism

The massacre in June of nine African-American worshippers at the historically black Emanuel AME Church in Charleston, SC, was the most lethal in a string of ideologically motivated post–9/11 attacks committed by far-right extremists. They range from white supremacists and anti-government militia members to so-called sovereign citizens, who deny the legitimacy of most U.S. laws. Dylann Roof, the 21-year-old suspect in the Charleston killings, is believed to have written an online manifesto ranting against blacks and

Hispanics and explaining how a white supremacist website inspired him to commit violence. While experts say most adherents of extremist movements are not violent, a recent survey found that police agencies are more concerned about violence by anti-government extremists than by Islamic extremists. The threat of violence has spurred debate about the strength of the government's efforts to fight extremism and whether it should try to prevent far-right radicalization of young people. Meanwhile, Life After Hate, a group founded by former racist skinheads, is working to help former white supremacists find a new path in life.

Modernizing the Nuclear Arsenal

In his first term, President Obama vowed to try to rid the world of nuclear weapons. In his second term, while still hoping for a non-nuclear world, Obama embarked on a vast plan to modernize the U.S. nuclear arsenal, a step he says is needed to keep the weapons reliable and safe. The effort — aimed at upgrading the nation's launch systems and warheads and the missiles, bombers and submarines that deliver them — could run nearly $350 billion in equipment and operational costs over the next decade and up to $1 trillion by 2050. The move comes amid rising tensions with Russia and China, the world's other top nuclear superpowers, as well as continuing skirmishes between nuclear-armed India and Pakistan and the nuclear ambitions of rogue states such as North Korea and Iran. Advocates of nuclear disarmament say the administration's plan will increase the danger of a nuclear holocaust by encouraging other countries to add to their nuclear stockpiles. But advocates of modernizing the U.S. arsenal say up-to-date and powerful nuclear weapons will discourage hostile nations from attacking the United States.

U.S.-Iran Relations

Under an agreement last July with the United States and five other world powers, Iran promised to dismantle its military nuclear facilities and refrain from building a nuclear weapon for at least a decade. In exchange, the United States and other countries lifted stiff economic sanctions placed on Iran because of its nuclear activities. The agreement has raised speculation that Iran might someday join China, Vietnam and Cuba — non-democracies and former U.S. enemies — in cooperating on trade and diplomacy. Indeed, some believe the deal not only could spur trade between the United States and Iran but also unite them in efforts to stabilize the Middle East. Others say, however, that improvement in U.S.–Iran relations is far from certain. Iran continues to antagonize the United States in national security–related incidents. As a result, the United States has imposed new sanctions on Iran unrelated to its nuclear activity. Moreover, pro-engagement leaders in both countries face internal resistance against forming a closer relationship.

INTERNATIONAL POLITICAL ECONOMY
Reforming the U.N.

Seventy-one years after its founding, the United Nations remains a work in progress. Established in 1945 after a murderous world war, the new international organization set out to achieve peace and prosperity around the globe. Its supporters cite a record of success in many areas: The U.N. helped keep the Cold War from turning hot, its peacekeepers routinely monitor post-conflict zones, and it has promoted economic development, education and better health for hundreds of millions of people. But critics say the U.N. is an ineffectual colossus made up of 193 bickering member nations, overseen by a bloated and inefficient bureaucracy whose operations are plagued by corruption. Reform is needed at both the governing and bureaucratic levels, they say, to ensure the organization remains relevant in the new century, and the Security Council — dominated by the United States and four other big powers — needs to expand to include more permanent members representing emerging nations such as India.

Women in Leadership

Women have made huge strides in the United States since the modern feminist revolution began some 50 years ago. Women serve on the Supreme Court and as Federal Reserve chair, and a few run multinational companies like General Motors and PepsiCo. But scholars say women still have a long way to go before they enjoy parity with men. They lead only 21 of the nation's 500 largest corporations, hold fewer than a fifth of congressional seats and earn less on average than men for comparable work. In professional sports, female players are paid far less than men, even when they are more successful.

Women's advocates were looking to Hillary Clinton, the first female presidential nominee of a major party, to win the White House and advance the cause of women's rights. A Clinton victory would end any doubts that women can achieve the highest summits of power and leadership. Some fear, however, that a Clinton loss could set back the

The Obama Legacy

As Barack Obama nears the end of eight years in the White House, he has several major accomplishments to point to but a longer list of unfinished initiatives and unrealized ambitions. Obama started strong in 2009 with a Democratic-controlled Congress that approved, in the face of Republican opposition, a much-needed economic stimulus and later the intensely controversial Affordable Care Act. But he had fewer legislative victories after 2010, when Republicans won a majority in the House. Obama wound down the U.S. role in Afghanistan and Iraq even as the Islamic State posed new dangers to American interests in the region. The economy has improved, but many Americans are pessimistic about the future. And while Obama had hoped to bring Americans together, race relations remain tense, and political polarization persists. In addition, some of Obama's important projects in such areas as immigration, climate change and trade are on hold in the courts or in Congress. His legacy may depend on the outcome of the bitterly divided presidential race between Hillary Clinton and Donald Trump.

RELIGIOUS AND HUMAN RIGHTS
Privacy and the Internet

In decisions with far-reaching implications on both sides of the Atlantic, European courts and regulators have ruled that Google and other search engines must delete links to Europeans' unwanted personal information from the Web, reinforcing a "right to be forgotten" that has a long legal tradition on the Continent. A French regulator's order applying that doctrine to the Google. com search page used by Americans is widely seen as conflicting with the U.S. Constitution's guarantee of free expression. Even so, some privacy advocates say Americans should have a right to erase some information from the Web, such as embarrassing photos or postings

that could damage their reputation or prevent them from getting a job. So far, federal and state laws allow only certain kinds of data, such as bankruptcy records, to be expunged online after a certain period of time. But polls suggest Americans want more control over other kinds of personal information online.

The Dark Web

Millions of people worldwide are using computer technology that allows them to visit websites, communicate with others and conduct business online without leaving a trace of their identity or location. That so-called anonymizing technology has created what experts call the Dark Web, a murky layer of the online world far less visible than the one accessible by Google and other common search engines. Proponents say the Dark Web's ability to mask identities helps protect dissidents in repressive regimes, allows police and military personnel to conduct covert operations and lets human rights activists report atrocities without risking reprisal. But critics say the Dark Web is a pathway for cybercrime, used by child pornographers, drug dealers and sex traffickers to hide their illegal dealings. Some law enforcement officials say the technology cripples their ability to catch criminals. But civil-liberties advocates counter that online anonymity is so valuable for good causes that it must not be curtailed.

Decriminalizing Prostitution

Amnesty International has spurred a global debate on prostitution with a controversial proposal to decriminalize the sex trade worldwide. The human rights organization argues that lifting bans on prostitution would make life safer for prostitutes. But critics say decriminalization would increase global sex trafficking and put many women at greater risk. Policies on prostitution are shifting throughout Europe and the United States. In response to concerns about trafficking and health risks, the German and Dutch governments have proposed tightening existing regulations that have legalized prostitution. New Zealand, on the other hand, has fully decriminalized the sex trade along the lines supported by Amnesty. Sweden has adopted what is known as the "Nordic model," in which only the buyers of sex are prosecuted. Seattle and 10 other U.S. cities are copying Sweden, hoping to stop prostitution altogether by eliminating demand for commercial sex. But critics, arguing that no way exists to halt the world's "oldest profession," say the Nordic approach simply drives the sex trade further underground.

Virtual Reality

Technology that immerses users in artificial but strikingly realistic experiences is poised to move beyond flight simulators and other specialized training applications into games, health care, education and mental health therapy, to name a few uses. Improvements in the technologies that drive virtual reality — computing power for creating virtual worlds, cameras that track and analyze users' movements, sensor-rich devices for processing touch and software allowing multiple users to interact — are behind the advances. Programmers can now create an array of lifelike sensations: flying like a bird, fighting off predators, riding a roller coaster or climbing a mountain. But experts are concerned that virtual reality also could cause disturbing physical or psychological reactions, such as paralyzing terror, motion sickness or injuries caused by disorientation. Meanwhile, others worry that so much can be learned about individuals' personalities from tracking their behavior in virtual-reality environments that personal privacy could be compromised. Some are calling for strict regulation of the technology, while others say voluntary ratings of games and programs would be enough.

Nanotechnology

Scientists are making motors tiny enough to deliver medicine from inside human cells and microfibers that are 20 times stronger than steel. The gee-whiz science of nanotechnology has grown from obscurity in the 1980s into a trillion-dollar industry that already produces ingredients for some 1,800 consumer goods, from sunscreen to baby formula, and could transform such products as computer chips, solar cells and military armor. Some experts say the nanorevolution, which draws billions of dollars in government funding, could reorder the global economy. But other experts worry about the safety of nanomaterials. They argue that government regulators — notably the Food and Drug Administration and the Environmental Protection Agency — are not up to the task of ensuring that nanoparticles are safe for public consumption or exposure. What's more, they fear that enemies eventually could use nanomaterials to make weapons of mass destruction. The nanotechnology industry contends, however, that current regulations are more than adequate and that the field's promise far outweighs its risks.

ENVIRONMENTAL ISSUES
Solar Energy Controversies

The cost of installing a residential or commercial solar energy system has declined rapidly in recent years, aided by federal tax breaks backed by the Obama administration. Solar users say the technology saves them money by allowing them to generate their own electrical power and helps protect the environment by reducing demand on conventional coal- and natural gas–burning power plants. Solar remains a tiny fraction of overall power generation in the United States, but it is growing rapidly. As solar expands, electric utilities all over the country are struggling to integrate it into the existing power system. They argue that the rapid growth in solar threatens the financial stability of the power grid and that solar users should pay to help maintain the vast system of poles, wires and transformers — even if their conventional power needs decline. Meanwhile, the auto industry is looking to solar as an alternative power source, a trend that could add additional pressure to the struggling oil industry.

Arctic Development

As climate change melts the northern polar ice cap, it is opening the sparsely populated and ecologically fragile Arctic region to tourism, shipping, industry and expanded development of oil and other natural resources. The discovery of a major new oil field in Alaskan Arctic waters has stoked some residents' hopes that mineral and industrial development could boost the region's economy and provide more jobs. But others say the environmental consequences of further development, including potential oil spills and other damage to the Arctic ecosystem, outweigh any benefits. Rising seas and eroding coastlines, they say, already are forcing some Native Alaskan villages to abandon their traditional lands. And drilling opponents warn that a warming climate — Arctic ice coverage is at a record low, and temperatures in November spiked 36 degrees Fahrenheit above normal — is harming wildlife, including seals, walruses and migratory birds. Meanwhile, a Russian military buildup has the United States and other Arctic nations bracing for a possible arms race in the geopolitically strategic region.

Fighting Cancer

President Obama has joined a long line of political leaders and patients' advocates calling for a cure for cancer, the nation's second-leading cause of death. But scientists caution that cancer is not just one disease amenable to a single cure but rather more than 100 complex and related diseases, many of which have defied decades of experimental treatments. Congress recently increased federal cancer research funding by $264 million for this year, money scientists say is needed to build on promising treatments that boost the body's immune system or that target molecules on cancer cells. But many new cancer medicines cost more than $100,000 annually, sparking outrage in Congress and among doctors. Drug makers say their charges are necessary to pay for medical research. Meanwhile, some doctors caution against false hope, because many of the drugs don't work for long or treat only certain cancers.

Mosquito-Borne Disease

Bloodthirsty and ubiquitous, the mosquito is a carrier of death and disease. The roster of mosquito-borne illnesses is long: yellow fever, West Nile virus, chikungunya, dengue and the deadliest of all, malaria, which kills more than 400,000 people a year and sickens at least 200 million. The latest scourge is Zika, a fast-moving virus that can cause severe birth defects, including devastating brain damage, in newborns. As mosquitoes spread Zika throughout the Americas, many travelers and athletes plan to avoid next month's Olympics in Brazil, the disease's epicenter. With the mosquito season now underway in the United States, health officials warn that Zika could become endemic in this country, particularly along the Gulf Coast. The outbreak has drawn renewed attention to the weakness of U.S. public health efforts and criticism of Congress's failure to approve funding to combat Zika. Experts say Zika offers the latest evidence that the mosquito threat will grow as Earth's climate warms and the insect's habitat expands.

Preface

In this pivotal era of international policy making, scholars, students, practitioners and journalists seek answers to such critical questions as should the U.S. deploy ground troops to fight ISIS? Does the United Nations need to change to stay relevant? Will tourism and oil drilling worsen climate change? Students must first understand the facts and contexts of these and other global issues if they are to analyze and articulate well-reasoned positions.

The 2017 edition of *Global Issues* provides comprehensive and unbiased coverage of today's most pressing global problems. This edition is a compilation of 16 recent reports from *CQ Researcher*, a weekly policy brief that unpacks difficult concepts and provides balanced coverage of competing perspectives. Each article analyzes past, present and possible political maneuvering, is designed to promote in-depth discussion and further research and helps readers formulate their own positions on crucial international issues.

This collection is organized into four subject areas that span a range of important international policy concerns: conflict, security and terrorism; international political economy; religious and human rights; and environmental issues. All 16 of these reports are new to this edition.

Global Issues is a valuable supplement for courses on world affairs in political science, geography, economics and sociology. Citizens, journalists and business and government leaders also turn to it to become better informed on key issues, actors and policy positions.

CQ RESEARCHER

CQ Researcher was founded in 1923 as *Editorial Research Reports* and was sold primarily to newspapers as a research tool. The magazine was renamed and redesigned in 1991 as *CQ Researcher.* Today, students are its primary audience. While still used by hundreds of journalists and newspapers, many of which reprint portions of the reports, *Researcher's* main subscribers are now high school, college and public libraries. In 2002, *Researcher* won the American Bar Association's coveted Silver Gavel Award for magazine excellence for a series of nine reports on civil liberties and other legal issues.

Researcher writers—all highly experienced journalists—sometimes compare the experience of writing a *Researcher* report to drafting a college term paper. Indeed, there are many similarities. Each report is as long as many term papers—about 11,000 words—and is written by one person without any significant outside help. One of the key differences is that the writers interview leading experts, scholars and government officials for each issue.

Like students, writers begin the creative process by choosing a topic. Working with Researcher's editors, the writer identifies a controversial subject that has important public policy implications. After a topic is selected, the writer embarks on one to two weeks of intense research. Newspaper and magazine articles are clipped or downloaded, books are ordered and information is gathered from a wide variety of sources, including interest groups, universities and the government. Once the writers are well informed, they develop a detailed outline and begin the interview process. Each report requires a minimum of 10 to 15 interviews with academics, officials, lobbyists and people working in the field. Only after all interviews are completed does the writing begin.

CHAPTER FORMAT

Each issue of *CQ Researcher*, and therefore each selection in this book, is structured in the same way. A selection begins with an introductory overview, which is briefly explored in greater detail in the rest of the report.

The second section chronicles the most important and current debates in the field. It is structured around a number of key issue questions, such as "Does decriminalization make the sex trade safer?" and "Can Iranian nuclear activities be accurately monitored?" This section is the core of each selection. The questions raised are often highly controversial and usually the object of much argument among scholars and practitioners. Hence, the answers provided are never conclusive but rather detail the range of opinion within the field.

Following those issue questions is the "Background" section, which provides a history of the issue being examined. This retrospective includes important legislative and executive actions and court decisions to inform readers on how current policy evolved.

Next, the "Current Situation" section examines important contemporary policy issues, legislation under consideration and action being taken. Each selection ends with an "Outlook" section that gives a sense of what new regulations, court rulings and possible policy initiatives might be put into place in the next 5 to 10 years.

Each report contains features that augment the main text: sidebars that examine issues related to the topic, a pro/con debate by two outside experts, a chronology of key dates and events and an annotated bibliography that details the major sources used by the writer.

ACKNOWLEDGMENTS

We wish to thank many people for helping to make this collection a reality. Thomas J. Billitteri, managing editor of *CQ Researcher*, gave us his enthusiastic support and cooperation as we developed this edition. He and his talented editors and writers have amassed a first-class collection of *Researcher* articles, and we are fortunate to have access to this rich cache. We also thankfully acknowledge the advice and feedback from current readers and are gratified by their satisfaction with the book.

Some readers may be learning about *CQ Researcher* for the first time. We expect that many readers will want regular access to this excellent weekly research tool. For subscription information or a no-obligation free trial of *Researcher*, please contact CQ Press at www.cqpress.com or toll free at 1-866-4CQ-PRESS (1-866-427-7737).

We hope that you will be pleased by the 2017 edition of *Global Issues*. We welcome your feedback and suggestions for future editions. Please direct comments to Carrie Brandon, Senior Acquisitions Editor for International Affairs, Public Administration, and Public Policy, CQ Press, an imprint of SAGE, 2600 Virginia Avenue, NW, Suite 600, Washington, DC 20037; or send e-mail to *Carrie.Brandon@sagepub.com.*

— *The Editors of CQ Press*

Contributors

Kevin Begos is a freelance journalist who writes about science, energy and the environment. He is a contributor to *A Field Guide for Science Writers* and a former Associated Press correspondent, Knight Science Journalism Fellow at MIT and Environmental Law Fellow at Vermont Law School. His work has appeared in *Scientific American's 60-Second-Science*, *The New York Times* and many other newspapers.

Marcia Clemmitt is a veteran social-policy reporter who previously served as editor in chief of *Medicine & Health* and staff writer for *The Scientist*. She has also been a high school math and physics teacher. She holds a liberal arts and sciences degree from St. John's College, Annapolis, and a master's degree in English from Georgetown University. Her recent *CQ Researcher* reports include "Search for Life on New Planets" and "Emerging Infectious Diseases."

Sarah Glazer is a London-based freelancer who contributes regularly to *CQ Researcher*. Her articles on health, education and social-policy issues also have appeared in *The New York Times* and *The Washington Post*. Her recent *CQ Researcher* reports include "European Migration Crisis" and "Free Speech on Campus." She graduated from the University of Chicago with a B.A. in American history.

Alan Greenblatt is a staff writer at *Governing* magazine. Previously he covered politics and government for NPR and *CQ Weekly*, where he won the National Press Club's Sandy Hume Award for political journalism. He graduated from San Francisco State University in 1986 and received a master's degree in English literature from the University of Virginia in 1988. His *CQ Researcher* reports include "Gentrification," "Future of the GOP," "Immigration Debate," "Media Bias" and "Downtown Revival."

Kenneth Jost has written 170 reports for *CQ Researcher* since 1991 on topics ranging from legal affairs and social policy to national security and international relations. He is the author of *The Supreme Court Yearbook* and *Supreme Court From A to Z* (both CQ Press). He is an honors graduate of Harvard College and Georgetown Law School, where he teaches media law as an adjunct professor. He also writes the blog *Jost on Justice* (http://jostonjustice.blogspot.com). His earlier reports include "The Bush Presidency" (February 2001) and "The Obama Presidency" (January 2009).

Reed Karaim, a freelance writer in Tucson, AZ, has written for *The Washington Post, U.S. News & World Report, Smithsonian, American Scholar, USA Weekend* and other publications. He is the author of the novel *If Men Were Angels*, which was selected for the Barnes & Noble Discover Great New Writers series. He is also the winner of the Robin Goldstein Award for Outstanding Regional Reporting and other journalism honors. Karaim is a graduate of North Dakota State University in Fargo.

Barbara Mantel is a freelance writer in New York City. She was a 2012 Kiplinger Fellow and has won several journalism awards, including the National Press Club's Best Consumer Journalism Award and the Front Page Award from the Newswomen's Club of New York for her Nov. 1, 2009, *CQ Global Researcher* report "Terrorism and the Internet." She holds a B.A. in history and economics from the University of Virginia and an M.A. in economics from Northwestern University.

Patrick Marshall, a freelance policy and technology writer in Seattle, is a technology columnist for *The Seattle Times* and *Government Computer News*. He has a bachelor's degree in anthropology from the University of California, Santa Cruz, and a master's degree in international studies from the Fletcher School of Law and Diplomacy at Tufts University.

Chuck McCutcheon is an assistant managing editor of *CQ Researcher*. He has been a reporter and editor for *Congressional Quarterly* and Newhouse News Service and is coauthor of the 2012 and 2014 editions of *The Almanac of American Politics* and *Dog Whistles, Walk-Backs and Washington Handshakes: Decoding the Jargon, Slang and Bluster of American Political Speech*. He also has written books on climate change and nuclear waste.

William Wanlund is a freelance writer in the Washington, DC, area. He is a former Foreign Service officer, with service in Europe, Asia, Africa and South America. He holds a journalism degree from The George Washington University and has written for *CQ Researcher* on abortion, intelligence reform and the marijuana industry.

Global Issues,
2017 Edition

1

Defeating
the Islamic State

Reed Karaim

A woman and children mourn for the victims of Islamic State bombings in Brussels on March 23, 2016. As the violent reach of ISIS spreads deep into Western Europe, critics are questioning not only the ability of European intelligence agencies to uncover ISIS plots but also whether the United States should launch boots-on-the-ground military operations against the terrorists.

From *CQ Researcher*,
April 1, 2016

I n the aftermath of the Islamic State's March bombings of the Brussels airport and Metro station that killed more than 30, President Obama acknowledged the "difficult work" of defeating the terrorist group.

"It's not because we don't have the best and the brightest working on it; it's not because we are not taking the threat seriously," Obama said. "It is because it's challenging to find and identify very small groups of people who are willing to die themselves and can walk into a crowd and detonate a bomb."[1]

But as the violent reach of the Islamic State (ISIS) has spread from Iraq and Syria deep into Western Europe — the Brussels attack was preceded by an even deadlier one in Paris in November — the debate over how to stop the group has grown increasingly urgent and sometimes bitterly contentious.

Some argue that the United States and other Western nations have not been doing enough militarily to halt ISIS, while others say current strategies remain the wisest approach in a fight with few good options. Meanwhile, the Brussels and Paris bombings have exposed what critics say are deep flaws in European intelligence gathering.

A key aspect of the debate is whether the United States needs to commit more ground troops to the effort to defeat ISIS. Obama has long resisted doing so, relying instead on a strategic bombing campaign by the United States and its allies, regional diplomacy and the deployment of small groups of military advisers and special forces to help Iraqi and Syrian forces fight the Islamic State, known variously as ISIS, ISIL and the Arabic acronym Daesh.

ISIS Expands Global Influence

The Islamic State (ISIS) occupies territory in Iraq, Libya and Syria, has formed alliances with groups in 12 other countries and has large numbers of supporters who were arrested in four others. ISIS lost an estimated 14 percent of its territory in 2015, much of it along the Turkish-Syrian border and near Tikrit in Iraq. However, the group captured additional areas in central and northeastern Syria and new territory along the Syrian-Lebanese border.

Sources: Lisa Curtis *et al.*, "Combatting the ISIS Foreign Fighter Pipeline: A Global Approach," Heritage Foundation, Jan. 6, 2016, http://tinyurl.com/gujefd2; "Islamic State's Caliphate Shrinks by 14 Percent in 2015," press release, IHS Conflict Monitor, Dec. 21, 2015, http://tinyurl.com/hn7z3x9

Pentagon officials say the bombing campaign, in concert with raids by special operations forces, is seriously undermining ISIS and weakening its morale and fighting capability. Officials cited the recent killing of two top Islamic State leaders — the group's minister of war, Omar al-Shishani and its top commander in Syria, Abd al-Rahman Mustafa al-Qaduli — as evidence the U.S. strategy is working.

"We are systematically eliminating ISIL's Cabinet," Defense Secretary Ashton B. Carter said at a March 25 press conference. "The momentum of this campaign is now clearly on our side." However, he acknowledged that ISIS can replace its leaders and that continued effort is needed to defeat the group.[2]

But critics of Obama's strategy argue that the Brussels and Paris attacks, combined with ISIS's unrelenting atrocities in the Middle East, underscore the need for an all-out military campaign to eradicate the threat.

Alongside the debate over military strategy is a discussion over whether the United States and other Western nations are doing enough to counter ISIS's sophisticated recruiting methods, which include the use of slick social media and "fanboy"-style zealotry aimed at luring disaffected Muslim youths from around the world into the organization. Critics argue that U.S. efforts aimed at undermining ISIS recruiting are too scattered and subtle to be effective.

ISIS proclaims its devotion to a brutal, apocalyptic version of Islam based on a selective reading of parts of the Quran and other Islamic texts — a reading that mainstream Islamic leaders have denounced as a gross misrepresentation of the faith. The group seeks to justify the killing of "kafir," or nonbelievers, including Muslims who do not share its views. ISIS also engages in sexual slavery and the destruction of other cultures' historic landmarks. On March 17, U.S. Secretary of State John Kerry declared that ISIS is committing "genocide against groups in areas under its control, including Yazidis [an ethnic minority], Christians and Shia Muslims."[3]

ISIS, in fact, celebrates its most violent acts with online videos and photographs of its executioners shooting, beheading, blowing up, drowning and setting fire to its captives.[4] Although no country recognizes it as a legitimate nation, ISIS has declared itself a caliphate — an Islamic state whose ruler has authority over all Muslims worldwide.[5]

More than a dozen countries are now battling ISIS on the ground or through the air.[6] These include the Iraqi army and Syrian militants and the military forces of the autonomous Iraqi region of Kurdistan known as the "Peshmerga," whom U.S. special forces troops are advising. The United States and its Western and Middle Eastern allies have conducted thousands of airstrikes against ISIS.[7]

Yet Obama has steadfastly resisted calls to boost the U.S. military presence, believing America risks being sucked into another lengthy ground war in the Middle East. He argues that the United States, working with its allies, can defeat ISIS through a more limited application of U.S. military power. This approach, emphasizing restraint and a determination to avoid overextending American commitments, is part of what has come to be called the "Obama doctrine."[8]

"With coalition training, equipment and support — including our special forces — local forces continue to push ISIL back out of territory that they had previously held," Obama said in February. "ISIL has now lost a series of key Iraqi towns and cities — more than 40 percent of the areas it once controlled in Iraq."[9]

Some observers say the Islamic State is under increasing internal stress and has not recorded a major military victory in months. Critics, however, say Obama's limited response isn't working.

"After more than a year of an indecisive military campaign, the U.S. still does not have the initiative," Sens. John McCain, R-Ariz., chairman of the Senate Armed Services Committee, and committee member Lindsey Graham, R-S.C., said in a joint statement in December, just after ISIS had attacked multiple sites in Paris in November, killing 130. "The threat is growing and evolving faster than the administration's efforts to counter it. What's needed is a comprehensive civil-military strategy to destroy ISIS quickly."[10]

Others argue that even as ISIS has been pushed out of one town or another in Iraq and Syria, it often pops up in other places, including, most recently, by increasing its presence in Libya.[11] An analysis by IHS, a defense research firm in Colorado, found that ISIS lost only 14 percent of its overall territory in 2015.[12]

Moreover, ISIS still controlled more than 30,000 square miles at the end of 2015, notably a large expanse of territory along or near the Turkish border and stretching into northern and central Iraq.[13] ISIS's call for jihad, or a holy war, appears to be gaining support around the world. A recent study on how to defeat ISIS published by the Heritage Foundation, a conservative Washington think tank, found that the group has established a significant presence in 19 nations.[14] The United Nations says 34 countries have ISIS affiliates of some kind.[15]

Part of ISIS's continued support can be explained by the centuries-old schism between the Shia and Sunni branches of Islam and the political situations in Iraq and Syria.[16] In both countries, autocratic Shia-dominated governments rule over large Sunni populations who feel their safety, or even existence, is threatened. Compared with those governments, some say, many consider ISIS's extremist ideology the lesser evil.

"We have a population in the Middle East, especially the Sunni Arabs, who feel they are left with no other alternative," says Nicolas Hénin, a French journalist held hostage by ISIS for 10 months in 2014-15.

The Brussels and Paris attacks were just the latest evidence of ISIS's continued ability to direct or inspire terrorism where it has little or no visible presence. In the last three months of 2015, ISIS followers detonated bombs in Beirut, killing 43, and bombed a Russian airliner as it left Egypt, killing 224. An apparently ISIS-inspired mass shooting in San Bernardino, Calif., on Dec. 2 killed 14 people.[17]

While most ISIS fighters have come from the Middle East, the group has drawn a significant number of

Most Oppose Troop Deployment

More than half of American adults oppose sending U.S. ground troops to Syria and Iraq to fight Islamic State militants. About four in 10 favor deploying troops to the region.

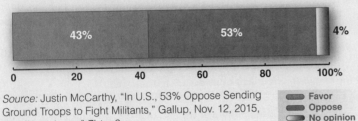

Percentage of U.S. Adults Who Favor or Oppose Sending Troops to Iraq and Syria

Source: Justin McCarthy, "In U.S., 53% Oppose Sending Ground Troops to Fight Militants," Gallup, Nov. 12, 2015, http://tinyurl.com/h7btpz2

Favor
Oppose
No opinion

recruits from the West. Estimates of the total number of foreign fighters vary, but a House Homeland Security Committee study concluded last September that more than 25,000 fighters — including 4,500 Westerners — had traveled to Syria and Iraq to fight. More than 250 Americans have traveled or tried to travel to Syria to help ISIS, according to the report.[18]

Some experts believe ISIS's recruiting success proves it has not lost the war of ideas. Belief in its ideology is "unfortunately getting stronger," says Stuart Gottlieb, an international affairs professor at Columbia University in New York City.

Analysts who have studied ISIS propaganda say brutality is only part of the image the terrorist organization is selling. Using the Internet and social media, the group promotes a vision of life inside its borders where devout Muslims are welcomed, safe and respected. However, first-hand reports from ISIS defectors and escapees point to a far darker vision of life there.

As the United States and other nations struggle to find ways to defeat the Islamic State, here are some of the questions being debated:

Will defeating ISIS militarily destroy the group and discredit its ideology?

The area controlled by ISIS changes with each military advance and retreat. Still, an estimated 6.5 million people live under its authority in a self-proclaimed caliphate, which in Islamic tradition is an area ruled by Sharia or

Islamic law, under the leadership of a caliph — a supreme spiritual and political leader for all Islam.[19]

ISIS's leader, Abu Bakr al-Baghdadi, was declared caliph by his followers in 2014. In an audio recording, the group declared that this made Baghdadi "the leader for Muslims everywhere." The recording also instructed: "Listen to our caliph and obey him. Support your state, which grows every day."[20]

The declaration of a caliphate marks a crucial difference between ISIS and other Islamic jihadist groups, such as al Qaeda, which has viewed such a move as premature. Experts note that al Qaeda did not believe it needed to hold territory and, after it lost its home base in Afghanistan following the U.S. invasion of that country in 2001, operated as a diffuse organization of small cells — common among terrorist groups.[21]

But for a caliph to be declared, he must have a caliphate. A lengthy analysis of ISIS's beliefs in a March 2015 article in *The Atlantic* magazine concluded that the Islamic State "requires territory to remain legitimate, and a top-down structure to rule it."[22] Thus, many analysts of the war on ISIS say destroying it on the ground will largely destroy the group's appeal, effectively ending it as a significant worldwide threat.

ISIS's ability to call itself a caliphate — the one true Islamic state — is crucial to its existence, according to Peter Mansoor, a professor of military history at Ohio State University in Columbus and the former executive officer to Gen. David Petraeus, commander of coalition forces in Iraq in 2007-08.

"You cannot defeat ISIS' ideology unless you destroy the Islamic State," Mansoor says. "They are portraying themselves as being on the right side of history because they've created the caliphate. If they no longer have the caliphate, if they go down to bloody defeat, they're no longer on the right side of history. That would tamp down a lot of the fervor around the world where people want to join ISIS."

But Columbia University's Gottlieb says although ISIS may be the most violent "jihadist" interpretation of

Islam, it is really part of a continuum that includes al Qaeda and several other groups operating in various countries. "Everyone forgets that ISIS is just the latest iteration of an ideology, and if you wipe out ISIS, you don't wipe out that part of it," Gottlieb says. "ISIS is only one component of what is really a broad global jihad [holy war]."

Gottlieb says defeating ISIS on the ground would significantly hurt the group's international recruiting efforts but not destroy its appeal. "You do have to deal them a humiliating blow," he says. "That will take care of 50 percent of the problem — maybe 50 percent of the recruiting gets knocked out by dealing them a fatal blow, but then the other 50 percent you have to deal with is the long-term ideology."

An ideological struggle is going on within Islam, Gottlieb says. On one side, he says, are Muslims who adopt a moderate vision of Islam that can peacefully coexist with the West; on the other is the militant view promoted by ISIS, which analysts say has historical roots in seventh-century Islamic texts. Which side will prevail remains unclear, Gottlieb says. "There's a civil war in the Islamic world," he says. To discredit ISIS's ideology, the West needs to "partner up with the moderate Muslim world. This can't be a Western solution."

Many political analysts agree the Muslim community needs to play a leading or major role in discrediting ISIS's ideology. Already, an overwhelming majority of people in 11 predominantly Muslim countries, including the Palestinian territories, have a negative view of ISIS, according to a 2015 poll by the Pew Research Center, a polling and data analysis organization in Washington, D.C. No more than 14 percent of the population in the countries surveyed had a positive view of ISIS. Pakistanis exhibited the most ambivalence, with 62 percent saying they didn't know how they felt, while the Lebanese registered the strongest disapproval of ISIS, at 99 percent.[23]

Many Muslim leaders reject the idea that ISIS has any legitimate claim to represent Islam and say its vision of jihad against unbelievers is fundamentally incorrect. A more correct translation of the word, jihad, they say is "struggle," which encompasses everything from an internal struggle against evil to efforts to improve society.

"ISIS is little more than a criminal gang that attaches itself like a leech to revered symbols of Islam," wrote Nihad Awad, national executive director of the Council on American-Islamic Relations (CAIR), the nation's largest Muslim civil rights and advocacy organization. "Islam prohibits the extremism exhibited by ISIS. An essential part of the faith is moderation. . . . Muslim scholars around the world have repudiated and rejected ISIS's twisted ideology, calling it not just un-Islamic, but 'anti-Islamic.' "[24]

Others who have studied the region believe ISIS's rise is tied to the political situations in Iraq and Syria as much as it is to dueling visions of Islam. With Shia-dominated governments ruling over large Sunni populations in the two countries, the centuries-old Sunni-Shia theological split has become a matter of political power and security.

"Until we figure out a way to make Sunni Arabs feel protected, feel safe in both Iraq and especially in Syria, another ISIS will rise," says Jessica Stern, a research professor at Boston University's Pardee School of Global Studies and the co-author of *ISIS: The State of Terror*. "The bigger problem is much more political than military."

But the Islamic State's appeal still depends largely on its ability to maintain control in part of the region, says Lisa Curtis, lead author of the Heritage Foundation's study on ISIS.[25]

"We have to deny them the ability to hold territory," she says. "This is critical to stopping the flow of foreign fighters and reducing ISIS' appeal, because we have to show that they're not invincible. The longer they can hold on to territory and claim to have a caliphate, the harder it is to stop the flow of people moving to the region, or even other [jihadi] groups rebranding themselves as ISIS supporters.

"We're seeing this a lot in places like Asia — people are attracted to the brand of ISIS because of their success," she continues. "Denying them territory is critical to stopping their appeal."

Should the United States commit ground forces to defeating ISIS?

At the height of the Iraq War, which killed some 4,500 Americans and up to half a million Iraqis, more than 170,000 U.S. troops were in the country, operating 500 bases.[26] By the end of 2011, only 150 American military personnel remained to train Iraqi fighters. Obama, who had made ending the conflict a signature campaign promise, declared in December of that year: "After nearly nine years, our war in Iraq ends this month."[27]

Demonstrators in New York City's Times Square on Nov. 21, 2015, mourn victims of the ISIS attacks in Paris and condemn the Islamic State's radical interpretation of Islam. ISIS proclaims its devotion to a brutal, apocalyptic version of Islam based on a selective reading of parts of the Quran and other Islamic texts — a reading that mainstream Islamic leaders have denounced as a gross misrepresentation of the faith.

Since ISIS first seized the Iraqi city of Fallujah in early 2014 and began expanding its presence, Obama has continued to insist the group can be defeated without the return of U.S. ground troops, who had left Iraq by Dec. 18, 2011. "It is not just my view, but the view of my closest military and civilian advisers, that that would be a mistake," Obama said shortly after last fall's Paris attacks.[28]

The president made clear he viewed sending a large U.S. force the first step toward a potentially unending commitment. Absent a stable political situation, he said, ISIS or some offshoot would be likely to spring up again "unless we're prepared to have a permanent occupation of these countries."[29]

Nevertheless, U.S. involvement in the battle against ISIS has steadily increased. As of March 15, the United States and other European and Middle Eastern coalition members had conducted 10,962 airstrikes against the Islamic State — about 77 percent of them by the United States.[30]

The United States also has 250 special forces troops, mostly members of the Army's elite Delta Force, operating in Iraq and Syria.[31] Pentagon sources say their mission is largely to raid ISIS targets identified as gathering places for leaders of the terrorist group or individuals thought to have so-called high-value intelligence.[32] The United States has an estimated 3,700 military personnel in Iraq overall, providing logistical and intelligence support for Iraqi government forces.[33] It also has begun to establish a small military presence in Syria, with the arrival of a contingent of about 50 special operations forces working with local Syrian fighters.[34]

But ISIS's continued survival has led some military analysts to call for a more substantial U.S. military commitment, including ground forces. Ohio State's Mansoor says the current strategy isn't uprooting and destroying ISIS. "All we're doing is mowing the grass," he says. "We've killed perhaps 20,000 ISIS fighters or sympathizers, but in that time, at least that many have joined the Islamic State. So we're not destroying ISIS through attrition."

Mansoor says victory requires a force that includes military personnel from regional and Western nations, including the United States. "If we just rely on the Sunni Arab states [such as Saudi Arabia] to do it, they can't project that kind of power," he says. "If we just rely on the local [Iraqi and Syrian forces] to do it, they don't have that kind of capability either, and they're badly divided. It's going to take a multinational campaign, and it's going to take U.S. ground forces."

ISIS fighters have "a quite capable light infantry force," Mansoor points out, "but they have no air force; they have no armor [tanks]." A mechanized military that uses air, armor and infantry in a coordinated fashion can destroy ISIS, he contends. "It won't be painless or bloodless, but it should probably be pretty quick. We should be able to do this in less than a year of fighting, and then stay just long enough to transition into a local force."

Craig Whiteside, a professor of theater security decision-making at the Naval War College in Monterey, Calif., says the United States could undoubtedly defeat ISIS in relatively short order, but that that's not the problem. "The United States military has this incredible mobility, where we could go a lot of places at will and defeat them pretty quickly, just like we did in 2003," says Whiteside, who served as a U.S. Army officer in Iraq during the war there. "But it all goes back to — what do you do afterwards?" he says.

The problem is maintaining the peace, he says, because ISIS has support within the communities it rules. "They really have won the [Sunni] tribes over," he says. "There's significant support for the Islamic State throughout Iraq."

But Mansoor says the question of how to deal with a post-ISIS Iraq and Syria will remain, regardless of how ISIS is finally beaten. "The same issue is at stake whether we defeat ISIS or the locals defeat ISIS," he says, "but it would be much easier for us to train a local force to police and govern the area if we defeat ISIS quickly and decisively."

James Jeffrey, a fellow at the Washington Institute for Near East Policy and a former U.S. ambassador to Iraq, also supports sending U.S. ground troops — and sooner rather than later. "The Islamic State . . . has taken tens of thousands of innocent lives in the region, and now hundreds more civilian lives in Turkey, Egypt, Lebanon and France. At what point does such a growing river of gore justify risking American lives?" Jeffrey asked rhetorically.[35]

But Boston University's Stern says drawing the U.S. military into Iraq and Syria would be doing what the Islamic State wants: "It's a stated objective of theirs to goad us into sending ground forces to attack their state."

The group has contradictory reasons for wanting this to happen, she says. First, they believe it was foretold by the Prophet Muhammad that a huge battle will take place on the plains near the Syrian city of Dabiq that will lead to the defeat of the "crusader armies" — the modern forces of the West. This battle will be an important prelude to the Day of Judgment, the apocalyptic battle between good and evil. In other words, enticing the United States into war fulfills a prophecy that ends this world and brings on a better one.[36]

On a less apocalyptic level, Stern says, ISIS thinks the overwhelming use of Western force will lead Muslims to choose sides, rallying many to the Islamic State's cause by reinforcing the idea that the West continues to oppress and humiliate the Islamic world.

"They're trying to polarize Muslim against Muslim, Muslim against non-Muslim, Sunni against Shiite," Stern says. "That's their strategy, and when we attack them, it encourages [support] beyond their current borders."

Can the West counter ISIS's appeal among disaffected Muslim young people?

The Islamic State's success in attracting recruits has depended largely on persuading younger Muslims to join their cause — mostly men, but also women. More than 4,000 Muslim youths from Western nations have joined ISIS, leaving behind lives of security and relative

Getty Images/John Moore

Suspected ISIS members are detained by Kurdish Peshmerga forces in Sinjar, Iraq, on Nov. 16, 2015. "With coalition training, equipment and support — including our special forces — local [Iraqi] forces continue to push ISIL back out of territory that they had previously held," Obama said in February.

prosperity to live and fight in a war zone. Others have been caught while trying to travel to territory controlled by the Islamic State.[37]

A study by a special House committee task force found that the average age of Americans who have tried to become ISIS fighters in Syria and Iraq was 24, with the youngest 15.[38]

In August 2015, for example, the FBI arrested two native-born Americans — newlyweds at Mississippi State University in Starkville — as they set out on their journey to Syria. Authorities had been tracking Mohammad Oda Dakhlalla, 22, and Jaelyn Delshaun Young, 19, online after they showed interest in the caliphate.[39]

About 80 similar ISIS-related cases have emerged in the United States since March 2014, according to Seamus Hughes, deputy director of the Program on Extremism at George Washington University's Center for Cyber & Homeland Security, which monitors ISIS-related law enforcement cases in the United States. Hughes says it is important to keep the relative size of the problem in mind: That's 80 cases out of 3.3 million Muslims in a country with 322 million people.[40]

However, 61 of those cases occurred last year, Hughes points out — "orders of magnitude larger" than in previous years. "Sixty-one is a small number when you look at the overall population," Hughes says, "but it is unprecedented in terms of what we've been seeing in the past."

The problem is more serious in Europe, which has seen a much larger number of young people travel to the Mideast to fight. In one well-publicized case, three London girls, ages 15 and 16 and considered top students, snuck away together to join ISIS.[41]

Such stories have triggered a debate about what Western countries can do to counter ISIS's appeal and recruiting efforts. The Islamic State's ideology may be rooted in an ancient version of Islam, but analysts say its approach to spreading its message is thoroughly 21st century.

The largest number of Western recruits — more than 1,500 — have come from France, according to a congressional study.[42] Some social scientists say discrimination and the lack of opportunity for Islamic youths in that country and other parts of Europe help to explain why the Islamic State's message has attracted some young Muslims. Poor Islamic neighborhoods in suburban Paris are cited as a fertile recruiting ground for radical Islam.[43]

But counterterrorism experts who have examined the history of Western ISIS recruits note that many were from middle-class or even more successful backgrounds and became radicalized in various ways. Hughes has studied the cases of Americans who have joined or tried to join ISIS. "There is no typical profile for an ISIS recruit," he says. "Their socioeconomic status runs the gamut. Their race runs the gamut."

The Islamic State's Internet presence extends from official ISIS videos, photography and statements to a legion of "fanboys," who advocate for its cause through social media and online chatrooms, says Nikita Malik, a senior researcher with the Quilliam Foundation, an anti-extremist organization in London that has studied ISIS propaganda and recruiting efforts. The fanboys are very Internet savvy, she says. "When their accounts are taken down, they're able to quickly reappear elsewhere."

Last year, the Obama administration expanded efforts by the State Department's Center for Strategic Counterterrorism Communications, created in 2011 to counter the message of ISIS and other extremist Islamic groups.[44] The center seeks to use social media, Twitter and message boards — the same avenues used by ISIS — to challenge the group's propaganda.

> **"ISIS is little more than a criminal gang that attaches itself like a leech to revered symbols of Islam."**
>
> *— Nihad Awad,*
> *National Executive Director,*
> *Council on American-Islamic Relations*

But many analysts worry that anything connected to the United States or other Western governments is tainted in the eyes of the young people drawn to ISIS. For opposition to ISIS to be effective online, "the role of governments will have to be less visible," says Malik. A more effective way for government to aid in the battle against ISIS recruitment, Malik says, might be to support "actors at a much more micro level — a mothers' group combating extremism, for example."

The Heritage Foundation's Curtis says the most effective anti-ISIS message comes from other Muslims. "This is something that has to happen among the Muslim community, because the vast majority of Muslims obviously don't support the ISIS ideology," she says. "They have to point that out, and I think many Muslim leaders are doing just that."

However, Richard LeBaron, a former director of the Center for Strategic Counterterrorism and Communications, said he sees "a legitimate role for an overt U.S. government mechanism that adopts a sharp edge to make prospective terrorists aware of the human consequences of terror. People do listen to that voice, despite the skeptics who contend that only credible Muslim voices resonate."[45]

Hughes also points out that it is difficult for Western Muslims on their own to effectively counter ISIS's online propaganda and recruitment efforts, to which the Islamic State devotes extensive personnel and money and which also has the commitment of its fanboy network.

"ISIS supporters are fervent in their beliefs and are willing to devote endless time to this," Hughes says. "Muslim-Americans who do engage in [countering them online] also have full-time jobs as doctors and lawyers or other positions. There's clearly a lack of resources on one side."

Malik says the West needs to recognize it isn't winning the online battle. "This war cannot be won through military and political means alone," she says. "It is as much a war of information and propaganda as anything else and, currently, it is fatally imbalanced to the advantage of [the] Islamic State."

At the same time, however, Hughes and Malik caution that focusing solely on ISIS's online presence misses the complexity of the path that can lead young people toward extremism. While some are radicalized and recruited simply through online conversation, "what tends to happen is that by the time they get in touch with someone from the Islamic State, they've already been radicalized," says Malik. "The online conversation is for logistical purposes — 'How do I get there? What can I do?' "

Young people can be radicalized through friends or people they look up to, or by their sense that Western society or Middle Eastern governments are treating Muslims unjustly, say scholars who have studied such cases. Altaf Husain, vice president of the Islamic Society of North America, one of the nation's largest Islamic groups, says it is crucial to understand the root causes of alienation that can send a young person searching for answers from ISIS or other extreme ideologies.

Prejudice or feelings of exclusion can have a "toxic" effect on young minds, Husain says. "Are we doing everything possible to help them feel included in society, so they don't feel they have to resort to these other means of critiquing our country?" he asks. "This is our first big challenge."

Countering the appeal of extremist ideologies, Husain says, requires a proactive effort to make sure "our children come out stable and mentally healthy, feeling they can prosper as members of this particular faith here" so they can become "our greatest ambassadors to the Muslim world about what it feels like when democracy works."

BACKGROUND
Birth of ISIS

The Islamic State began as Al Qaeda in Iraq (AQI) — an offshoot of the Qaeda terrorist organization responsible

Getty Images/John Moore

An Iraqi army commando conducts combat training in Baqubah, Iraq, on July 18, 2007. Today, more than a dozen countries are battling ISIS on the ground or via air strikes, including the Iraqi army and the military forces of the autonomous Iraqi region of Kurdistan known as the Peshmerga, whom U.S. special forces troops are advising.

for the 1993 bombing of New York's World Trade Center, the 1998 attacks on two U.S. embassies in Africa, the 2000 bombing of the USS *Cole* destroyer in Yemen and the Sept. 11, 2001, attacks on the United States.[46]

In Iraq, al Qaeda was led by a notoriously ruthless Jordanian street thug, Abu Musab al-Zarqawi, who had begun working with the terrorist group at its headquarters in Afghanistan in the late 1990s even though he had not yet been officially accepted into the organization. From the beginning, al Qaeda's leaders worried that his views were too extreme even for them, particularly his hatred of the Shia and his dismissal of all Muslims who did not share his view of what counted as the true faith.[47]

When al Qaeda had to abandon Afghanistan after the United States invaded in response to the 9/11 attacks, Zarqawi moved to Iraq to establish a terrorist network.[48] He was convinced the United States would invade Iraq and, as Brookings Institution scholar William McCants wrote, "When the Americans showed up in March 2003, Zarqawi's cells in Baghdad were there to greet them."[49] In short order, Zarqawi's group bombed the Jordanian embassy, the U.N. headquarters, both in Baghdad, and the mosque of Iman Ali in Najaf, one of the Shiites' holiest sites. These acts played a significant role in steering Iraq into violent chaos.[50]

CHRONOLOGY

1989-2000 *Al Qaeda organizes.*

1989 Osama bin Laden, from a prominent Saudi family, founds the Sunni Muslim terrorist group al Qaeda with the goal of removing Western influences from Islam.

1993 Bin Laden sets up terrorist training camps in Sudan. Qaeda-trained operatives detonate a truck bomb at the World Trade Center in New York City, killing six and injuring more than 1,000.

1996 Al Qaeda is expelled from Sudan and relocates in Afghanistan.

1998 Qaeda-linked extremists explode bombs at U.S. embassies in Kenya and Tanzania, killing more than 231. United States retaliates with airstrikes against Qaeda terrorist camps in Sudan and Afghanistan.

2000 Suicide bombers believed connected to bin Laden attack Navy destroyer USS *Cole* in Yemen, killing 17 sailors.

2001-2010 *Terrorist attacks plunge United States into war in Middle East.*

2001 Nearly 3,000 people die after Qaeda operatives use three hijacked airliners to attack the World Trade Center in New York and the Pentagon outside Washington. A fourth hijacked aircraft — possibly targeting the Capitol — crashes near Shanksville, Pa., after passengers fight the hijackers. . . . United States goes to war in Afghanistan to destroy al Qaeda. Abu Musab al-Zarqawi, leader of the terrorist group that will eventually become the Islamic State in Iraq and Syria (ISIS), flees Afghanistan for Iraq.

2003 United States and allies invade Iraq, defeat Saddam Hussein's forces and capture the Iraqi president. . . . Zarqawi deploys suicide bombers to destroy United Nations headquarters in Baghdad and kill Shiite Muslim leader Ayatollah Baqr al-Hakim.

2004 Zarqawi terrorist group joins al Qaeda and becomes al Qaeda in Iraq.

2006 A Qaeda bomb attack on a Shia shrine in Samarra, Iraq, unleashes wave of violence. . . . Zarqawi killed in

U.S. airstrike and succeeded by Abu Ayub al-Masri, who renames the group Islamic State in Iraq.

2007 President George W. Bush announces "surge" in U.S. forces sent to Iraq to bring security to the country. U.S. Army works with Sunni tribes to defeat Islamic State in Iraq.

2008 Iraqi parliament approves security pact with the United States that says all U.S. troops will leave the country by 2012.

2010 Masri kills himself when surrounded by U.S. and Iraqi forces. Islamic State in Iraq names Abu Bakr al-Baghdadi its new leader, but the U.S. and Iraqi governments believe the group has been largely defeated.

2011-Present *Islamic State resurfaces amid continued Middle East violence.*

2011 Final U.S. troops leave Iraq as President Obama announces war there is over. . . . U.S. Navy SEALs kill bin Laden, who was hiding in Pakistan. . . . Assortment of groups rebel against Syrian President Bashar al-Assad, leading to civil war.

2012 Violence between Islam's two major sects flares back to life in Iraq. At least 4,612 civilians are killed during the year.

2013 Senior Qaeda leaders escape in mass breakout from two Iraqi prisons.

2014 A reborn ISIS makes gains across Syria and Iraq, capturing Iraqi cities of Fallujah and Mosul. The group declares itself a caliphate, or political-religious state with authority over Muslims worldwide.

2015 ISIS attacks multiple sites in Paris, killing 130. . . . Mass shooting in San Bernardino, Calif., that leaves 14 dead is blamed on couple whom the FBI says were inspired, but not directed, by Islamic extremists. . . . Iraqi army retakes Ramadi from Islamic State with help of U.S. air support.

2016 Islamic State is reported to have affiliated groups in 34 countries, including a rapidly growing presence in Libya.

When analysts look at the sequence of events that led to ISIS's rise in Syria and Iraq, many trace the beginnings to the George W. Bush administration's decision to invade Iraq, which removed Iraqi leader Saddam Hussein and his Sunni-dominated ruling Baath Party, creating a power vacuum and widespread Sunni resentment.

"By far the biggest mistake was the decision to invade Iraq in 2003," David Kilcullen, formerly the chief strategist in the U.S. State Department's Bureau of Counterterrorism, told the BBC recently. "None of this would have happened if we hadn't invaded Iraq in the first place."[51]

In 2004, Zarqawi pledged allegiance to al Qaeda, and his organization formally became Al Qaeda in Iraq. But his eagerness to attack the Shia and his brutal methods still worried Qaeda leaders, who believed they needed to win the support of a broader base of Muslims.[52]

A U.S. airstrike killed Zarqawi in 2006, but his successor, Abu Ayyub al-Masri, deepened the split between al Qaeda and its Iraqi wing when he declared the Islamic State of Iraq in 2006, a move al Qaeda considered premature.

The group's brutality soon turned even the Sunni tribes against it. Working with the U.S. military, which had deployed an additional 30,000 troops to the country in a "surge" intended to quell Islamic State insurgency and restore order, local Sunni militias helped to crush the group. By 2010 when al-Masri blew himself up after being cornered by U.S. and Iraqi troops, the Islamic State in Iraq was considered effectively dead.[53]

ISIS's Rebirth

Only four years after its initial defeat, ISIS not only reappeared in Iraq but swept to a series of victories in Iraq and Syria that gained enough territory for ISIS to proclaim itself the caliphate.

Several former U.S. officials who worked in Iraq say that didn't have to happen. "ISIS was not inevitable," says Emma Sky, a British Middle East expert who served as a political adviser to U.S. Gen. Ray Odierno from 2007 to 2010, when Odierno commanded U.S. and multinational forces in Iraq.

Sky says the surge succeeded in creating a realistic chance for a stable Iraq, one that could overcome the country's Shia-Sunni sectarian differences. She points to

the 2010 Iraqi parliamentary election, in which a secular Iraqi political party that claimed support from both Muslim sects won the most seats.

"The U.S. should have upheld the right of the winning bloc to [have] a first go at trying to form a government," she says. "Iraqi public opinion at the time was against sectarianism, wanted to put the sectarian war behind it. The U.S. should have seized the opportunity to broker an inclusive government."

Instead, the United States allowed Iraqi Prime Minister Nouri Maliki to stay in power as part of a coalition government. That coalition collapsed after Maliki, a Shia, issued arrest warrants for several of the country's high-ranking Sunni politicians. "This created the conditions for ISIS to rise up out of the ashes of Al Qaeda in Iraq and present itself as the defender of the Sunnis against the Iranian-backed sectarian regime of Maliki," Sky says.

According to Kilcullen, the former U.S. State Department Bureau of Counterterrorism chief strategist, the Obama administration failed to see that the sectarian conflict in Iraq had not been resolved. "We conflated leaving Iraq with ending the war," he said. "We did successfully bring American troops out of Iraq; we didn't successfully translate the military progress that had happened in the surge to long-term political stability."[54]

The United States compounded the error in 2013 by not responding forcefully when the Syrian regime of Bashar al-Assad used chemical weapons against the Syrian population during that country's civil war, Kilcullen added. That weakened Assad's secular opponents and faith in the West, and ISIS stepped into the void, he said.[55]

Obama has said he felt a cruise missile attack against Assad — the proposed response to Assad's use of chemical weapons — would not have destroyed the regime's chemical arsenal and could have weakened U.S. standing in the region further. In addition, he said, the United States was able to get Syria's chemical weapons removed through diplomacy by working with the Russians, a traditional Assad ally.[56]

As it re-emerged in Iraq's Sunni territory after the 2010 election, the Islamic State assassinated more than 1,000 Sunni tribal leaders who had opposed it during the surge.[57] In addition, a mass breakout from two Iraqi

Refugees Say ISIS Propaganda Paints a False Picture

"We went back to the Stone Age."

As portrayed in Islamic State (ISIS) online propaganda, life inside perhaps the most brutal terrorist regime on Earth can seem idyllic. The group posts pictures of happy families, playing children and people going about routine life. It touts its health care and schools. Those images can be hard to reconcile with the other videos that the Islamic State shares online of its executions — including beheadings — and mass killings. But analysts who study the group's propaganda say the two approaches have a purpose in recruiting followers.

"The violence can be a red herring that causes us to miss everything they're trying to accomplish [with their online presence]. It's done in a barbaric way to shock the West, but simultaneous with that they release lots of material depicting . . . this utopia that they're supposedly building," says Nikita Malik, a senior researcher with the Quilliam Foundation, an anti-extremist organization based in London.

The Islamic State's approach has proven a powerful draw to thousands of Muslims who have traveled from the United States and numerous other countries to join its cause. But many of those who have lived in the territory controlled by the group paint a far darker picture of life inside its ever-changing boundaries. Far from being the ideal Muslim state, they say, the Islamic State governs as a brutal occupying force, treating the local population harshly.[1]

The free housing, education and health care that the Islamic State touts online are largely reserved for its fighters, according to former residents. For the local population,

exorbitant taxes and fees are levied to support the fighters and pay their salaries, while local schools and many hospitals are often closed.[2]

Some former residents do say ISIS does a better job than previous governments of providing certain services, such as garbage collection, but water and electricity can be shut off for hours or days, and life's basic necessities can be hard to find. "We went back to the Stone Age," Mohammad Ahmed, who lived near Raqqa in northern Syria, told a reporter after fleeing to a refugee camp in Jordan.[3]

Those who have lived under Islamic State rule say what they find most oppressive is the fear of crossing the group's many dictates concerning proper Muslim behavior. In a diary of his experiences smuggled to the BBC, a young man living in Raqqa recorded the nature of ISIS's authority: His boss was beaten for smoking; a friend was arrested because his pants were too long; another was sentenced to death because he missed a compulsory class on Sharia; bystanders were forced to witness beheadings, stonings and even crucifixions. "Many people just don't go out on the streets anymore," he said.[4]

ISIS defectors also have shared their own disillusionment at the reality of life in the Islamic State, saying the group's narrow and unforgiving view of what constituted true Islam meant it was far from the paradise portrayed for Muslims. "Anything that contradicts their beliefs is forbidden," said a defector who wished to remain anonymous. "Anyone who follows what they reject is an apostate [one who doesn't follow the true faith] and must be killed."[5]

---

prisons in 2013 freed some of ISIS's leaders and most experienced fighters.[58] But the Naval War College's Whiteside, who worked with the Sunni tribes while serving in Iraq, says it is a mistake to underestimate the local support the group had. Many Sunnis made a calculated decision that they were better off with ISIS than the Shia-dominated central government and supported a

reborn ISIS as it swept through the area in 2014, capturing major cities such as Mosul and Fallujah.[59]

"You see that at Mosul, because a bunch of guys in pickup trucks doesn't just take over Mosul and defeat three [Iraqi army] divisions," he says. "It just doesn't happen. The Iraqi army knew it wasn't just the guys in pickup trucks they were facing. It was everybody around them."

ISIS devotes part of its propaganda to recruiting young women, claiming they will be welcomed with respect. But the lives of women are highly circumscribed, insiders say. The group's rules specify when and how females are allowed to leave the home and how they must dress and behave. Even small violations can result in public lashings. The Islamic State believes the principal role of a woman is to be a wife, and it pressures single women to marry quickly, including girls as young as 9.[6]

Life is even worse for non-Muslim women. The Islamic State practices sexual slavery, condoning the enslavement, rape and trading of women it considers nonbelievers. Many of the slaves are members of the Yazidis, an ethic and religious minority in Iraq and Syria. At least 3,400 Yezidi women and girls were being held in captivity in late 2015, according to a report in *Time*.[7]

Nadia Murad Taha, a Yazidi who escaped captivity, testified before the United Nations Security Council last December about her life as the slave of an Islamic State fighter. She said the pictures of captive women were posted on a wall at the Islamic Court, along with the phone number of each woman's owner so the men could swap them. When she once complained to her owner about her treatment, he left her to be gang-raped by six men. Basee said several women killed themselves to escape their treatment. She said she also wished for an end to her captivity. "I did not want to kill myself," she said, "but I wanted them to kill me."[8]

— *Reed Karaim*

Nadia Murad Basee Taha, a Yazidi woman abducted from her village in Iraq last August and held for three months by Islamic State militants, speaks with Greek President Prokopis Pavlopoulos in Athens on Dec. 30, 2015.

AP Photo/Yorgos Karahalis

[1] Kevin Sullivan, "Life in the 'Islamic State': Spoils for the Rulers, Terror for the Ruled," *The Washington Post*, Oct. 1, 2015, http://tinyurl.com/qgy4s3r.

[2] *Ibid.*

[3] *Ibid.*

[4] "Life Inside 'Islamic State': Diaries," Entries 3, 4, 5, BBC Radio 4, Feb. 29-March 3, 2016, http://tinyurl.com/ho2xc9d.

[5] "More Islamic State defectors speaking out — report," BBC News, Sept. 21, 2015, http://tinyurl.com/zbhhgcz.

[6] Kevin Sullivan, "Life in the 'Islamic State': Women, 'Till Martyrdom Do Us Part,'" *The Washington Post*, Oct. 1, 2015, http://tinyurl.com/q63trxe.

[7] Charlotte Alter, "A Yezidi Woman Who Escaped ISIS Slavery Tells Her story," *Time*, Dec. 20, 2015, http://tinyurl.com/oevju3c.

[8] *Ibid.*

Global Movement

Several Islamic extremist groups outside of Iraq and Syria have pledged allegiance to ISIS since it re-emerged in 2014. Estimates of how many vary from fewer than 10 to more than 40.

ISIS calls its overseas affiliates "wilayat" — Arabic for province. The Islamic State already has announced wilayats in parts of Afghanistan, Algeria, Egypt, Libya, Nigeria, Pakistan, Saudi Arabia, Yemen and the Caucasus, the region between the Black and Caspian seas.[60]

Other groups proclaiming their loyalty to ISIS are less directly tied to the group. In February, U.N. Secretary-General Ban Ki-moon said 34 militant groups had reportedly pledged allegiance to ISIS as of

Minnesota's Somali-Americans Confront Extremism

At least 50 young people have sought to join Middle Eastern groups.

Those who knew the three young men in the Minneapolis suburb of Burnsville say they liked to shoot baskets and embraced social media. They also seemed somewhat adrift at times, and passionate about the world's injustices. In other words, they were typical American youths in many ways. Except all three would try to join the Islamic State, or ISIS.

In March of 2014, Hanad Mohallim, 18, traveled to Syria, where he told his family he would be serving as a border guard. Some months later, the family received word he had been killed. Abdullahi Yusuf, 18, and Hamza Ahmed, 20 — who attended high school with Mohallim — tried to follow his path to Syria, but federal agents intercepted them before they left the country.[1] They were charged with conspiring to provide support to a foreign terrorist group.[2]

Between 50 and 60 young people of Somali descent in Minnesota either have made it to the Middle East to join extremist groups, been stopped en route or are under investigation for possibly planning to do so, law enforcement officials say. No other state has more young people who have tried to travel to the Middle East to become foreign fighters.[3]

Leaders of the Minneapolis Somali community, estimated at between 30,000 and 100,000 people, are working to understand what has driven some of their young people to embrace extremist ideologies and how to counter that appeal.[4] Most Somali immigrants are relatively new to the United States, having emigrated after the collapse of the Somali government in 1991.

Although many members of the community have risen to positions of success, Somalis have faced the traditional challenges confronting new immigrants, says Hodan Hassan, co-chairwoman of the Somali-American task force in Minnesota, a group that fights the radicalization of disillusioned local youths. "There is going to be poverty. There is high unemployment. There are gangs," she says.

These problems can leave young men, in particular, frustrated and at loose ends. But an even greater challenge, she says, can be the struggle to reconcile two cultures. "I grew up in this country. I know what it feels like not being American enough and not being Somali enough," she says.

The extremist groups promise to provide a strong sense of identity. "These young people are looking for belonging," she says, "and the call they're getting [from the Islamic State and other extremist Islamic groups] is: 'Come and belong to something bigger than you, a cause you can believe in.'"

The Somali community, working with local, state and federal officials, is trying to present better options to its young people. Minneapolis, along with Boston and Los Angeles, is participating in a federal pilot program aimed at

mid-December 2015, a figure he predicted would grow in 2016. Ban said the speed at which ISIS had expanded its "sphere of influence across West and North Africa, the Middle East and South and Southeast Asia demonstrates the speed and scale at which the gravity of the threat has evolved in just 18 months."[61]

Southeast Asia appears to be the newest area of growth. ISIS claimed responsibility for a terrorist attack in Jakarta, Indonesia's capital, in January that killed seven and wounded 23.[62] Extremists groups in the Philippines, a key U.S. ally in the region, have pledged allegiance to ISIS, but the government there dismisses the significance of the claims.[63]

The deadliest ISIS affiliate is Boko Haram, a radical Islamic sect that controls parts of predominantly Muslim northeastern Nigeria. Seeking acceptance by ISIS, the group began emulating the Islamic State's approach to online propaganda and added ISIS's signature black flag and Islamic chants to its videos.[64] Boko Haram pledged allegiance to ISIS in March 2015 and was accepted by the group.

Boko Haram, which loosely interpreted from the local Hausa language means "Western education is forbidden," countering violent extremism by dealing with the root causes. Nearly $1 million has been committed to the effort through a public-private partnership, Building Community Resilience, that will provide mentorship and educational and job support for Somali youths in the Twin Cities through several nonprofit organizations.

The program has come under criticism from some Muslim leaders who say it profiles Muslim youths and, because some of the money came from the U.S. Justice Department, is too closely tied to federal law enforcement. Jaylani Hussein, the Somali-American executive director of the Council on American-Islamic Relations in Minnesota, told Minnesota Public Radio that the program "stigmatizes a community that is already getting backlash and pressure."[5]

Others say $1 million simply isn't enough. "The reality is, there needs to be more funding. There needs to be more resources. There needs to be more opportunities for these kids," says Saciido Shaie, a Twin Cities Somali activist who sits on a state commission on juvenile justice.

Shaie is the founder and president of the Ummah Project, which hopes to build a recreation and community center that she says would give Muslim young people a culturally appropriate place to study, workout or enjoy activities. For example, young men and women would enjoy separate swimming facilities, and the dress code would conform to Islam's standards of modesty. "We want to create a safe haven," she says.

Experts who have studied the cases of young people drawn to the Islamic State caution there is no one route toward radicalization. Not all those drawn to ISIS have been economically disadvantaged or part of recently arrived immigrant communities. But as reported in the news media, the lives of the three young men who attended Burnsville High indicate that they sought a place to fit in.

Mohallim and Yusuf changed schools several times. Ahmed was suspended for fighting while in high school and never graduated. Their online posts and tweets reflect young men trying to figure out who they were and what mattered to them. Ahmed tweeted about his desire to "help and fight for the Muslims in Syria." Mohallim and Yusuf both shared their struggle to become better Muslims.[6]

Shaie says a crucial part of the solution is helping young Somalis understand they can embrace their dual identity as Somali-Americans and take advantage of both their heritage and the opportunities of the country in which they now live.

"We need to talk about the beauty of this community," she says. "We're bringing a rich, beautiful culture to the Twin Cities. We have people working in every sector of society. We came to America for a better life. We need to make sure our young people know they can share in this."

— *Reed Karaim*

[1] Laura Yuen, Mukhtar Ibrahim and Sasha Aslanian, "From MN suburbs, they set out to join ISIS," Minnesota Public Radio, March 25, 2015, http://tinyurl.com/ j237y58.

[2] Joe Kimball, "Ten ISIS suspects have been charged in Minnesota, second most in U.S.," *Minnpost*, Nov. 19, 2015, http://tinyurl.com/ h2p4yws.

[3] Dina Temple-Raston, "Minneapolis Unveiling Plan to Counter Recruiting by ISIS," NPR, Sept. 9, 2015, http://tinyurl.com/pzmfrsa.

[4] Chris Williams, "New census data: Minnesota Somali population grows," Minneapolis *Star Tribune*, Oct. 27, 2011, http://tinyurl.com/ juvuhyd; Teresa Welsh, "Sowing Trust at Home," *U.S. News & World Report*, July 2, 2015, http:// tinyurl.com/h55n35j.

[5] Temple-Raston, *op. cit.*

[6] Yuen, Ibrahim and Aslanian, *op. cit.*

believes Muslims are prohibited from taking part in any activity, dress or customs associated with Western society. To that end, according to Amnesty International, it kills and kidnaps residents as it sweeps through towns and villages, looting, bombing and burning schools, churches, mosques and other public buildings. Like ISIS, it practices sexual slavery. In April 2014 Boko Haram captured more than 200 schoolgirls from the town of Chibok and announced it would treat them as slaves who would be given to its fighters.[65] In all, the group kidnapped 2,000 adults and children during 2014 through early 2015.[66]

Although it has not sought to expand its attacks against nonbelievers into the West as ISIS has, Boko Haram was ranked by the Global Terrorism Index as the world's deadliest terrorist group in 2014, responsible for 6,644 deaths. ISIS, which killed 6,073, was second. Together, the Islamic State and its Nigerian affiliate were responsible for nearly half the deaths attributed worldwide to terrorism that year, according to the index.[67]

The index also found that 78 percent of all the deaths worldwide from terrorism occurred in just five countries — Iraq, Nigeria, Syria, Pakistan and

Afghanistan — underscoring the tremendous human cost of political instability and militant extremism in the Muslim world.[68]

CURRENT SITUATION

Preventing Attacks

In the aftermath of the attacks in Brussels, European Union (EU) officials struggled to see how they could improve their efforts to control ISIS-inspired terrorism across the 28-member union, with a welter of intelligence and law enforcement operations and a tradition of open borders and free assembly.

Many officials said the lack of coordination between authorities in different countries leaves the region vulnerable to attack. President Recep Tayyip Erdogan of Turkey, which is not an EU member, pointed out that his government had warned Belgium and the Netherlands that at least one of the Brussels attackers, Ibrahim el-Bakraoui, was dangerous when Turkey deported him to the Netherlands last year.

"Despite our warnings that this person was a foreign terrorist fighter," Erdogan told a news conference in Ankara on March 23, "the Belgian authorities could not identify a link to terrorism."[69]

Other analysts point out the extreme difficulty of preventing random terrorist attacks in open Western societies, in which individual rights and freedom of movement are essential. After last year's attack in Paris, Obama said, "The truth is that in a free and open society, we will never completely eliminate the possibility of a single terrorist act happening in any given time."[70]

American and European officials warned that the Islamic State remains determined to bring the war to the West. Testifying on Capitol Hill in February, Marine Lt. Gen. Vincent Stewart, director of the Defense Intelligence Agency, said ISIS probably would "attempt to direct attacks on the U.S. homeland in 2016." James Clapper, director of national intelligence, also told Congress that ISIS was inserting operatives into the flood of migrants fleeing Syria and Iraq.[71]

About 20 to 30 percent of the Westerners, mostly young men, who joined ISIS in Syria and Iraq have returned to their home countries, according to a report by the Soufan Group, a security and intelligence consulting firm in New York. About 1,000 returned to the

AP Photo/Yorgos Karahalis

Some 200 Assyrian Christians stage a demonstration in front of the United Nations office in Tehran, Iran, on March 12, 2015, to protest ISIS attacks on Assyrians in Iraq and Syria. The Islamic State targets anyone who does not subscribe to its narrow interpretation of Islam.

U.K., France, Germany and Belgium, while about 40 returned to the United States, the report said.[72]

British officials have warned that the danger posed by foreign-fighter returnees is one of the biggest threats facing the country. London Assistant Police Commissioner Mark Rowley said recent arrests of suspected extremists indicate ISIS is trying to get fighters with weapons and paramilitary training into Northern Europe.[73]

Speaking before the Brussels attack, Columbia University's Gottlieb said the Paris attack last winter serves as a model of how ISIS hopes to strike at the West. "They want to do a major attack," he says. "Their goal would be that we would react hyper-aggressively. They want to draw us back in. If we don't respond, they proclaim it as a sign of weakness. If we do, they've provoked the response they want."

War in Syria, Iraq

In late March, the latest round of negotiations between the various parties involved in the Syrian civil war, which includes the government of Syrian President Assad, most opposition groups and the United States and Russia, concluded without making substantial progress. The groups agreed to meet again later in April. The Islamic State, however, is not a part of the negotiations, and military action against it continues.[74]

AT ISSUE

Are U.S. ground troops needed to defeat the Islamic State?

YES James Jay Carafano
Vice President, Foreign and Defense Policy Studies, Heritage Foundation

Written for *CQ Researcher*, March 2016

The United States should be prepared to send ground troops back to fight in Iraq and help keep the peace. The Middle East is too important to risk the region spiraling into war and chaos.

The Middle East matters. More than just a big gas pump, it is pretty much at the crossroads of global affairs. International routes of sea and air trade, finance and human migration criss-cross the region. As a global power with international interests to protect, Washington cannot afford to ignore what is happening in the Middle East.

Most concerning is the rise of the Islamic State, or ISIS. Despite recent reversals, it still controls nation-size territory in Iraq and Syria, issues its own currency and commands a small army.

The capacity of a terrorist group to act as a state carries grave dangers. The ISIS "brand" as a rising caliphate animates Islamist extremists across the globe. As long as ISIS survives and thrives, it will inspire more terrorist attacks worldwide.

The terrorist state itself could become a global platform for transnational terrorism, just as Afghanistan was until the post-Sept. 11, 2001, invasion by the United States and other Western nations. In some respects, ISIS already has assumed that role. What makes the possibility of terrorists mixing in with legitimate refugees heading to Europe so dangerous is that, once they make it there, they can fall in with existing terror networks.

Danger flows in the opposite direction, too. Nations such as Australia have found that once their radicalized citizens make it to the battlefields of Iraq, they reach back to try to set up terror networks in their homelands.

Beyond the transnational threat, a massive Sunni terrorist state in the center of the Middle East significantly raises the potential for regional war.

The United States thus has every reason to end ISIS' territorial control in Iraq. But what will it take? The Obama administration believes a light touch — supporting the Iraqi military, aerial bombing and selected special operations — will suffice. That plan has not worked yet.

Certainly, by the end of President Obama's term, we'll know if it has a chance. The key is Mosul. If the Iraqis can't take that city back, they can't break the back of ISIS. If ISIS retains Mosul, the only realistic option for rooting them out is to reintroduce substantial U.S. combat forces.

NO Daniel L. Davis
Retired Lieutenant Colonel, U.S. Army; Winner, 2012 Ridenhour Truth-Telling Prize

Written for *CQ Researcher*, March 2015

It seems intuitive to some people: "The battle against the Islamic State, or ISIS, using only airpower has been inconclusive, so if we want to defeat them, as unpalatable as it may be, we're going to have to send in ground troops to finish them off."

A number of counterintuitive facts, however, render that conclusion wrong. Deploying ground combat forces will not defeat ISIS, nor will it safeguard American security. Sending ground troops almost certainly will worsen the situation.

It is true that two years of airstrikes against ISIS targets in Syria and Iraq have proven inconclusive. But our failure to take out ISIS isn't because we've deployed insufficient combat force. We haven't succeeded because we've relied on the wrong instrument. Military power does have a role, but it should be secondary to diplomacy. A national effort relying primarily on diplomacy has a chance to achieve U.S. objectives, whereas a military-first approach does not.

For ISIS to even exist, much less succeed, it must have an effective logistics system. No militant organization can fight unless it has steady deliveries of food, water, clothing, ammunition, weapons, spare parts and fuel for vehicles and generators, plus effective battlefield health care and a constant supply of replacement troops. Render that logistics system inoperative and ISIS dies in the field.

ISIS is landlocked everywhere it controls territory. It can sustain itself only if it has the secret support — either passive or active — of the states surrounding it: Iran, Turkey, Jordan, Saudi Arabia or others. The United States should use its robust intelligence capability to identify all the sources from which ISIS receives its massive logistics, then employ its diplomatic might to pressure those groups or states to cease such support. The military would be used to enforce interdiction efforts.

The 2004 battle of Fallujah against Iraqi insurgents graphically demonstrated that U.S. ground troops can destroy an enemy house by house but also can devastate civil infrastructure and embitter the population. After achieving an unequivocal military victory on the ground, Fallujah was then lost to ISIS almost without a fight. So the battle was a tactical victory but a strategic defeat. If we don't want to repeat the mistake on a much larger scale, we must subordinate the use of the military and unleash our full diplomatic force.

President Obama meets youngsters at the Islamic Society of Baltimore on Feb. 3, 2016. Obama's visit was widely seen as a rebuke to anti-Muslim Republican campaign rhetoric. "We have to reject a politics that seeks to manipulate prejudice or bias and targets people because of religion," Obama said, describing U.S. Muslims as part of "one American family."

Severe differences between the various parties exist — starting with a fundamental disagreement over whether Assad should be allowed to stay in power — and many analysts remain skeptical that the peace talks will succeed.[75] If the negotiations did succeed, however, a peace agreement would allow the Syrian government to turn its attention from fighting domestic opposition groups to defeating ISIS.

In Iraq, ISIS operatives on March 6 reportedly detonated a fuel truck filled with explosives at a police checkpoint in Hilla, a town south of Baghdad, killing at least 60 and wounding 70.[76] The attack was the third suicide bombing in or near Baghdad in two weeks, according to press reports. Such attacks have killed more than 170 in the past month. The campaign, which has hit targets behind Iraqi government lines, is considered an attempt to force Iraqi forces to overextend themselves.[77]

Both Shiite militias and the Iraqi army, backed by heavy U.S. air support, have been striking ISIS forces. Last month the Iraqi army retook the city of Ramadi, which had fallen to ISIS in May 2015 in a humiliating defeat.[78] U.S. military officers in Iraq say they consider the latest battle for Ramadi a sign that parts of the Iraqi military trained by U.S. advisers are gaining confidence on the battlefield.[79]

The small contingent of U.S. special operations forces in Iraq and Syria are also stepping up operations in carefully targeted raids designed to gather intelligence, free hostages or seize key ISIS personnel. Secretary of Defense Carter told reporters the raids are a sign that ISIS must fear "that anywhere, anytime, it may be struck."[80]

Meanwhile, ISIS has expanded its reach in other parts of the Middle East and North Africa. About 6,500 ISIS fighters are believed to be in Libya, where the extremist group has strongholds along 150 miles of the Mediterranean coastline. ISIS is reported to be drawing fighters from across North Africa to the area.[81]

The Pentagon is planning for a possible expansion of U.S. airstrikes or covert special operations forces operating in Libya, according to *The New York Times*, which said clandestine reconnaissance missions to map out possible targets are underway.[82]

Overall, however, the U.S. and Western strategy is to depend on local forces to defeat ISIS on the ground, said an analysis in *Military Times*. American planners reportedly believe the various militias and armies pressing on ISIS can eventually squeeze it out of existence. But they expect the conflict to take years and require more U.S. troops on the ground to provide support, along with stepped-up U.S. air support.[83]

To that end, the U.S. Air Force reportedly is preparing to add B-52 heavy bombers, which have a payload capacity of 70,000 pounds, in the air campaign against ISIS. The bombers, which first saw service in the 1950s, have been used for large-scale bombardment with old-fashioned unguided bombs, but Air Force officials say the planes now can be outfitted with smart weapons that can be guided precisely to their target.[84]

News reports also indicate that a force of 40,000 Syrian, Kurdish and Arab fighters, assisted by a small contingent of U.S. special operations forces and French and British commandos, has been cutting off supply lines to the Islamic State's Syrian capital of Raqqa in preparation for an eventual assault to retake that city. However, no timeline for the operation has been made public.[85]

American Politics

The Brussels attack has heated up the U.S. presidential primary debate about how the United State should respond to the terrorism threat.

Donald Trump, the reality TV star and real estate developer currently leading the Republican race for the nomination, reiterated his earlier call for a ban on allowing Muslims to enter the United States. "At this point, we cannot allow these people to come into our country," he said.[86]

Previously, Trump had urged increased surveillance of U.S. mosques and Muslims. "You have people that have to be tracked," Trump said. "If they're Muslims, they're Muslims."[87] Trump also has said his administration would torture terrorists and kill their families, although he later said his administration would follow U.S. law in each case.[88]

Sen. Ted Cruz of Texas, running second to Trump in the GOP race, responded to the Brussels attack by calling for law enforcement to "patrol and secure Muslim neighborhoods."[89] To deal with ISIS in the Mideast, Cruz has promised to "carpet-bomb them into oblivion," an approach military experts have pointed out would lead to widespread civilian casualties.[90]

On the Democratic side, former Secretary of State Hillary Clinton, leading in the Democratic presidential nomination race, and her rival, Sen. Bernie Sanders of Vermont, have stressed the need to work with Middle Eastern nations and traditional Western allies to defeat ISIS. They also have pledged to bolster security in the United States to prevent terrorist attacks.[91] But both have rejected calls to discriminate against or ban Muslims.[92]

In February, Obama visited a Baltimore mosque in what was widely seen as a rebuke to Republican campaign rhetoric. "We have to reject a politics that seeks to manipulate prejudice or bias and targets people because of religion," Obama said at the Islamic Society of Baltimore mosque. The president described U.S. Muslims as part of "one American family."[93]

OUTLOOK
Fertile Ground

Few, if any, analysts expect a quick defeat of the Islamic State. Nor do they expect a rapid solution to the larger problem of an extreme Muslim ideology that considers itself at war with billions of people worldwide who reject its religious vision.

George Washington University's Hughes points out that the United States and its allies have defeated or decimated other groups holding extremist Islamic ideologies,

such as the Taliban in Afghanistan and al Qaeda, only to see similar ideas resurface in other forms. Defeating ISIS on the battlefield could have the same effect down the road, he says, especially if much of the Middle East remains in political chaos with weak or nonexistent local governments.

"The ideology has the ability to metastasize and adjust to the situation," he says. "It will transform itself and move on to other ungoverned spaces as long as the underlying problems remain."

Boston University's Stern says the current military focus on defeating ISIS on the ground misses the nature of the challenge. "The problem is, . . . the Islamic State is partly a totalitarian state and partly a transnational terrorist organization," she says. Any long-term solution to the problem must address the ideology behind the "whole jihadi movement" that includes al Qaeda and other extremist groups, she adds, and must be led by the Muslim world.

Columbia University's Gottlieb says many Middle Eastern countries likely will remain fertile ground for extremist ideologies until they work out stable political structures that effectively integrate Islamic beliefs and law with the requirements of the modern nation-state. "They're going to have to find their own comfort zones," he says. "They're not going to be Jeffersonian democracy. They could be fundamentalist in nature." But they will have to accommodate some difference, he says, "and not be dedicated to fighting a global war."

A Heritage Foundation report that examined the inspiration for foreign fighters to join ISIS suggested that the West needed to address several fundamental problems in the region to undercut the appeal of extremist Islamic ideology. Among other things, the report recommended pressuring Saudi Arabia to stop exporting Wahhabism, a highly intolerant version of Islam to other countries, insisting that President Assad step down as leader of Syria and working to make the Iraqi and Syrian governments more religiously and ethnically inclusive.[94]

However, given the persistence of the Shia-Sunni divide in Iraq, the Naval War College's Whiteside says partitioning Iraq so that the Sunnis have a semiautonomous region similar to that of the Kurds could be the best solution to the sectarian differences. "This isn't a personal preference," he says, "but if I had to put my money on something, that would be it, because it reflects the reality on the ground."

Sky, the former coalition official, who developed many friends in Iraq during her time there, sees a difficult road ahead for that country. "It is going to take a long time to rebuild the society," she says. "Young people have only ever known war." A better future, she says, will require an end to the civil war in Syria, greater regional stability and "a new generation of leaders in Iraq."

NOTES

1. "Remarks by President Obama and President Macri of Argentina in Joint Press Conference," press release, The White House, March 23, 2016, http://tinyurl.com/hemjwu7.

2. "Department of Defense Press Briefing by Secretary Carter and General Dunford in the Pentagon Briefing Room," U.S. Department of Defense, March 25, 2015, http://tinyurl.com/jq6dbfj.

3. John Bacon, "Kerry: Islamic State committing genocide against religious minorities," *USA Today*, March 17, 2016, http://tinyurl.com/z793nf2.

4. "Timeline: Rise and Spread of the Islamic State," The Wilson Center, March 22, 2016, http://tinyurl.com/gqqupyh.

5. Graeme Wood, "What ISIS Really Wants," *The Atlantic*, March 2015, http://tinyurl.com/ngfwzy8.

6. Ashley Fantz, "War on ISIS: Who's doing what?" CNN, Nov. 27, 2015, http://tinyurl.com/zuth8u9.

7. "Operation Inherent Resolve, Targeted Operations Against ISIL Terrorists, Strikes in Iraq and Syria," U.S. Department of Defense, March 1, 2016, http://tinyurl.com/ot8b6zh. Also see Helene Cooper, "U.S. Special Operations Force in Iraq to Grow, Pentagon says," *The New York Times*, Dec. 1, 2015, http://tinyurl.com/znk9oqd.

8. Jeffrey Goldberg, "The Obama Doctrine," *The Atlantic*, April 2016, http://tinyurl.com/zfzlg5g.

9. "Remarks by the President on Progress Against ISIL," White House, Feb. 25, 2016, http://tinyurl.com/zl5jjs7.

10. Lindsey Graham and John McCain, "How to Defeat ISIS Now — Not 'Ultimately,' " *The Wall Street Journal*, Dec. 7, 2015, http://tinyurl.com/hrb8v96.

11. Jim Sciutto, Barbara Starr and Kevin Liptak, "ISIS fighters in Libya surge as group suffers setbacks in Syria, Iraq," CNN, Feb. 4, 2016, http://tinyurl.com/hp6emq7.

12. Sergio Peçanha and Derek Watkins, "ISIS' Territory Shrank in Syria and Iraq This Year," *The New York Times*, Dec. 22, 2015, http://tinyurl.com/hwt9rcf.

13. "Islamic State's Caliphate Shrinks by 14 Percent in 2015," press release, *IHS Conflict Monitor*, Dec. 21, 2015, http://tinyurl.com/hn7z3x9.

14. Lisa Curtis *et al.*, "Combatting the ISIS Foreign Fighter Pipeline: A Global Approach," Special Report #180 on Terrorism, Heritage Foundation, Jan. 6, 2016, http://tinyurl.com/jx8wrg7.

15. Edith M. Lederer, "UN chief: 34 groups now allied to Islamic State extremists," The Associated Press, Feb. 6, 2016, http://tinyurl.com/jnhfg2h.

16. "Sunnis and Shia: Islam's ancient schism," BBC, Jan. 4, 2016, http://tinyurl.com/lxdfolk.

17. Christopher Harress, "ISIS Timeline Of Major Attacks Since The Caliphate In Iraq And Syria Was Formed," *International Business Times*, Nov. 14, 2015, http://tinyurl.com/ndbrd2w. Also see Michael S. Schmidt and Richard Pérez-Peña, "F.B.I. Treating San Bernardino Attack as Terrorism Case," *The New York Times*, Dec. 4, 2015, http://tinyurl.com/hcm5tl3.

18. "Final Report of the Task Force on Combating Terrorist and Foreign Fighter Travel," U.S. House Homeland Security Committee, September 2015, http://tinyurl.com/nlqedrt.

19. Zachary Laub and Jonathan Masters, "The Islamic State," Council on Foreign Relations, March 22, 2016, http://tinyurl.com/o4rvjol.

20. "Sunni rebels declare new 'Islamic caliphate,' " Aljazeera, June 30, 2014, http://tinyurl.com/nbzvtp9.

21. Wood, *op. cit.*

22. *Ibid.*

23. Jacob Poushter, "In nations with significant Muslim populations, much disdain for ISIS," Pew Research Center, Nov. 17, 2015, http://tinyurl.com/nj2oql6.

24. Nihad Awad, "ISIS is Not Just Un-Islamic, It Is Anti-Islamic," *Time*, Sept. 5, 2014, http://tinyurl.com/nus9huy.

25. Curtis *et al.*, *op. cit.*

26. Dan Vergano, "Half-Million Iraqis Died in the War, New Study says," *National Geographic*, Oct. 16, 2013, http://tinyurl.com/ogdznuu.

27. David Jackson, "Obama campaign touts end of Iraq War," *USA Today*, Dec. 16, 2011, http://tinyurl.com/j68yua3.

28. "Press Conference by President Obama — Antalya, Turkey," The White House, Nov. 16, 2015, http://tinyurl.com/oe5g3ut.

29. *Ibid.*

30. "Operation Inherent Resolve, Targeted Operations Against ISIL Terrorists," *op. cit.*

31. David Ignatius, "The Islamic State is degraded but far from being destroyed," *The Washington Post*, March 8, 2016, http://tinyurl.com/zwfbroe.

32. Barbara Starr, "Army's Delta Force begins to target ISIS in Iraq," CNN, Feb. 29, 2016, http://tinyurl.com/hs3qfe6.

33. Andrew Tilghman, "U.S. troops in Iraq move into region where ISIS just used mustard gas," *Military Times*, Feb. 18, 2016, http://tinyurl.com/hdsdme2.

34. Ignatius, *op. cit.*

35. James Jeffrey, "The U.S. must send ground forces to eliminate the Islamic State," *The Washington Post*, Nov. 16, 2015, http://tinyurl.com/zlx7j5v.

36. Wood, *op. cit.*

37. "Final Report of the Task Force on Combating Terrorist and Foreign Fighter Travel," *op. cit.*

38. *Ibid.* Also see "Terrorism in the U.S., January 2016, Update," Program on Extremism, The George Washington University, http://tinyurl.com/h8ywjwx.

39. Lorenzo Vidino and Seamus Hughes, "ISIS In America: From Retweets to Raqqa," Program on Extremism, The George Washington University, December 2015, http://tinyurl.com/h6w53sa.

40. Besheer Mohamed, "A new estimate of the U.S. Muslim population," Pew Research Center, Jan. 6, 2016, http://tinyurl.com/jg89vsu.

41. Katrin Bennhold, "Jihad and Girl Power: How ISIS Lured 3 London Girls," *The New York Times*, Aug. 17, 2015, http://tinyurl.com/owgvbbk.

42. "Final Report of the Task Force on Combating Terrorist and Foreign Fighter Travel," *op. cit.*

43. Hugh Schofield, "Paris attacks: Can France integrate disaffected suburbs?" BBC, Jan. 23, 2015, http://tinyurl.com/zv58dbn.

44. Eric Schmitt, "U.S. Intensifies Effort to Blunt ISIS' Message," *The New York Times*, Feb. 16, 2015, http://tinyurl.com/gsu7joh.

45. Richard LeBaron and William McCants, "Experts weigh in: Can the United States counter ISIS propaganda," Markaz blog, The Brookings Institution, June 17, 2015, http://tinyurl.com/z3aj9b7.

46. For background, see David Masci and Kenneth Jost, "War on Terrorism," *CQ Researcher*, Oct. 12, 2001, pp. 817-848.

47. William McCants, *The ISIS Apocalypse* (2015), pp. 7-9. Also see Joby Warwick, *Black Flags: The Rise of ISIS* (2015), p. 50.

48. *Ibid.*

49. *Ibid.*, p. 10.

50. *Ibid.*

51. "How we 'stuffed up' in the war on terror: former State Department official," BBC News-hour, March 3, 2016, http://tinyurl.com/gtp2 new.

52. For background, see Barbara Mantel, "Assessing the Threat from al Qaeda," *CQ Researcher*, June 27, 2014, pp. 553-576.

53. McCants, *op. cit.*, pp. 31-45.

54. "How we 'stuffed up' in the war on terror: former State Department official," *op. cit.*

55. *Ibid.*

56. Goldberg, *op. cit.*

57. David Ignatius, "How ISIS Spread in the Middle East," *The Atlantic*, Oct. 29, 2015, http://tinyurl.com/q3cy7yn.

58. Kareem Raheem and Ziad al-Sinjary, "Al Qaeda militants flee Iraq jail in violent mass break-out," Reuters, July 22, 2013, http://tinyurl.com/zmh3ele.

59. Martin Chulov, "Isis insurgents seize control of Iraqi city of Mosul," *The Guardian*, June 10, 2014, http://tinyurl.com/k48hfb7.

60. Daniel L. Byman, "ISIS goes global: Fight the Islamic State by targeting its affiliates," Markaz blog, The Brookings Institution, Feb. 17, 2016, http://tinyurl.com/hawjaj2.

61. Lederer, *op. cit.*

62. Joe Cochrane and Thomas Fuller, "Jakarta Attack Raises Fears of ISIS' Spread in Southeast Asia," *The New York Times*, Jan. 13, 2016, http://tinyurl.com/jmdpl2v.

63. Julia Glum, "ISIS in the Philippines: Islamic State Support Growing Despite Government Claims," *International Business Times*, Jan. 13, 2016, http://tinyurl.com/judf2bj.

64. Sarah Almukhtar, "How Boko Haram Courted and Joined the Islamic State," *The New York Times*, June 10, 2015, http://tinyurl.com/phg 99rn. For background, see Brian Beary, "Terrorism in Africa," *CQ Researcher*, July 10, 2015, pp. 577-600.

65. Farouk Chothia, "Who are Nigeria's Boko Haram Islamists?" BBC, May 4, 2015, http://tinyurl.com/l8ka4tm.

66. "Nigeria: 'Our job is to shoot, slaughter and kill': Boko Haram's reign of terror in North-East Nigeria," Amnesty International, April 2015, http://tinyurl.com/k9dquft.

67. "Global Terrorism Index 2015," The Institute for Economics and Peace, November 2015, http://tinyurl.com/gn3t8zc.

68. *Ibid.*

69. Adam Nossiter, "As Terrorists Cross Borders, Europe Sees Anew That Its Intelligence Does Not," *The New York Times*, March 23, 2016, http://tinyurl.com/z8m223m.

70. David Jackson, "Obama: We can stop 'large scale' terror attacks," *USA Today*, Dec. 2, 2015, http://tinyurl.com/hcptwqx.

71. Ryan Browne, "Top intelligence official: ISIS to attempt U.S. attacks this year," CNN, Feb. 9, 2016, http://tinyurl.com/zro3hvt.

72. Lucy Westcott, "Report: Number of Foreign Fighters in Iraq and Syria Double to 31,000," *Newsweek*, Dec. 7, 2015, http://tinyurl.com/zj37yc9.

73. Michael Holden, "Islamic State looking for spectacular attacks — UK police," Reuters, March 7, 2016, http://tinyurl.com/z6m69zu.

74. Jamey Keaten, " 'No drama, no walkouts' and no progress in Syria peace talks," The Associated Press, March 25, 2016, http://tinyurl.com/gmhkaz6.

75. Patrick J. McConnell, "As Syrian peace talks near, Bashar Assad's future remains a sticking point," *The Los Angeles Times*, March 14, 2016, http://tinyurl.com/grrv6r7.

76. "ISIS Suicide Bomb Attack Kills 60 South of Baghdad," Reuters, *Newsweek*, March 6, 2016, http://tinyurl.com/gt433xm.

77. Rick Hampson, "Latest ISIL bombing kills scores in Iraq," *USA Today*, March 6, 2016, http://tinyurl.com/j4f4xbo.

78. "The fall of Ramadi is a significant defeat for Isis," *The Independent*, Dec. 28, 2015, http://tinyurl.com/gs7wj9u.

79. Jane Arraf, "How Iraqi Forces Drove ISIS From Ramadi," *Newsweek*, Feb. 25, 2016, http://tinyurl.com/jn3q89t.

80. Helene Cooper, Eric Schmitt and Michael S. Schmidt, "U.S. Captures ISIS Operative, Ushering in Tricky Phase," *The New York Times*, March 1, 2016, http://tinyurl.com/j5oamxt.

81. Eric Schmitt, "Obama is Pressed to Open Military Front Against ISIS in Libya," *The New York Times*, Feb. 4, 2016, http://tinyurl.com/zoabtcd.

82. *Ibid.*

83. Tilghman, *op. cit.*

84. Oriana Pawlyk, "The B-52 could rise again, this time to fight ISIS," *Air Force Times*, March 7, 2016, http://tinyurl.com/gotfab4.

85. Ignatius, *op. cit.*

86. David Wright, "Donald Trump: Brussels 'just the beginning," CNN, March 22, 2016, http://tinyurl.com/zno6g7f.

87. David Jackson, "Trump, GOP candidates call for more surveillance," *USA Today*, Dec. 6, 2015, http://tinyurl.com/hjqbcz6.

88. Maggie Haberman, "Donald Trump Reverses Position on Torture and Killing Terrorists' Families," *The New York Times*, March 4, 2016, http://tinyurl.com/jqld9to.

89. Katie Zezima and Adam Goldman, "Ted Cruz calls for law enforcement to 'patrol and secure' Muslim neighborhoods," *The Washington Post*, March 22, 2016, http://tinyurl.com/ja6zt4n.

90. Pamela Engel, "Ted Cruz doubles down on vow to 'carpet bomb' ISIS," *Business Insider*, Jan. 28, 2016, http://tinyurl.com/zlnehqm.

91. Leo Shane III, "In fight over ISIS strategy, Clinton and Sanders debate last Iraq War," *Military Times*, Feb. 12, 2016, http://tinyurl.com/hkvcycg.

92. Matthew Rozsa, "Democratic candidates blast Trump's Muslim ban at debate," *MSNBC*, Dec. 20, 2015, http://tinyurl.com/zogoxcf.

93. Gardiner Harris, "Obama, in Mosque Visit, Denounces Anti-Muslim Bias," *The New York Times*, Feb. 3, 2016, http://tinyurl.com/zcn3ajx.

94. Curtis *et al.*, *op. cit.*

BIBLIOGRAPHY

Selected Sources

Books

McCants, William, *The ISIS Apocalypse: The History, Strategy, and Doomsday Vision of the Islamic State*, St. Martin's Press, 2015.
A senior fellow at the Brookings Institution's Center for Middle East Policy uses Arabic primary sources, including internal Qaeda and ISIS documents, to explore the Islamic State's beliefs and long-term strategy.

Sky, Emma, *The Unraveling: High Hopes and Missed Opportunities in Iraq*, Public Affairs, 2015.
A British expert on the Middle East, who worked in Iraq as part of the governing authority after the U.S.-led invasion and later served as a political adviser to U.S. Army Gen. Raymond Odierno, describes what she sees as U.S. policy failures leading to ISIS's rise.

Stern, Jessica, and J. M. Berger, *ISIS: The State of Terror*, Ecco, 2015.
Two of America's leading experts on terrorism examine the Islamic State, or ISIS, including its methods for enforcing its will and disseminating its message globally.

Warrick, Joby, *Black Flags: The Rise of ISIS*, Doubleday, 2015.
A Pulitzer Prize-winning Washington Post reporter traces the rise of Abu Musab al-Zarqawi, the original leader of al Qaeda in Iraq, from which ISIS emerged.

Articles

Alter, Charlotte, "A Yezidi Woman Who Escaped ISIS Slavery Tells Her Story," *Time*, Dec. 20, 2015, http://tinyurl.com/oevju3c.
A victim of the Islamic State's practice of raping and sexually enslaving non-Muslim women it considers "kafir," or non-believers, recounts her capture and sexual abuse.

Callimachi, Rukmini, "ISIS and the Lonely Young American," *The New York Times*, June 27, 2015, http://tinyurl.com/pyzqxk4.
A journalist chronicles how a young woman in rural Washington state was drawn into the world of Islamic State supporters through social media.

Miller, Greg, and Souad Mekhennet, "Inside the surreal world of the Islamic State's propaganda machine," *The Washington Post*, Nov. 20, 2015, http://tinyurl.com/o5xdrb9.
Two journalists interview former Islamic State workers about the extensive personnel and resources that the group devotes to its online videos and other propaganda.

Tilghman, Andrew, "This is the Pentagon's new strategy to defeat ISIS," *Military Times*, Jan. 14, 2016, http://tinyurl.com/hj8wlco.
A journalist says the Pentagon envisages a conventional ground campaign by local forces against Islamic State strongpoints, aided by U.S. air power and technical support.

Wood, Graeme, "What ISIS really wants," *The Atlantic*, March 2015, http://tinyurl.com/ngfwzy8.
A journalist says the Islamic State's beliefs are deeply rooted in an apocalyptic, seventh-century version of

Islam that sees ISIS playing a key role in bringing about the end of the world.

Studies and Reports

Cordesman, Anthony, "The Human Cost of War in the Middle East: A Graphic Overview," Center for Strategic & International Studies, Feb. 3, 2016, http://tinyurl.com/o28b8ok.
A military expert estimates that tens of millions of people have been displaced or seen their lives devastated by the ongoing wars in four Middle Eastern countries, including areas where the Islamic State has taken control of large swaths of territory.

Curtis, Lisa, *et al.*, "Combatting the ISIS Foreign Fighter Pipeline: A Global Approach," Heritage Foundation, Jan. 6, 2016, http://tinyurl.com/gujefd2.
Counterterrorism and Middle East experts at a conservative think tank propose a wide-ranging approach to counter Islamic State recruiting, which uses social media and well-produced propaganda to try to persuade Muslims to join.

Gambhir, Harleen, "ISIS's Global Strategy: A Wargame," Institute for the Study of War, July 2015, http://tinyurl.com/zbakm4o.
A think tank whose funders include military contractors has studied possible military scenarios against the Islamic State and concludes it is "a brutal, capable enemy" that could require the United States and other nations to form an even stronger coalition to defeat it.

Vidino, Lorenzo, and Seamus Hughes, "ISIS in America: From Retweets to Raqqa," Program on Extremism, George Washington University, December 2015, http://tinyurl.com/h6w53sa.
Researchers who study extremist movements look at Americans who have traveled or attempted to travel to Syria or Iraq to join the Islamic State through late 2015 and how those Americans became radicalized and attracted to the group.

For More Information

Brookings Institution, 1775 Massachusetts Ave., N.W., Washington, DC 20036; 202-797-6000; www.brookings.edu/about/centers/middle-east-policy. The think tank's Center for Middle East Policy conducts research on issues central to the region and promotes discussion and partnerships among the United States and Muslim communities globally.

Center for Strategic & International Studies, 1616 Rhode Island Ave., N.W., Washington, DC 20036; 202-887-0200; http://csis.org. Think tank focused on defense and security issues, including how the United States should deal with international terrorism.

Combating Terrorism Center, U.S. Military Academy, 607 Cullum Road, Lincoln Hall, West Point, N.Y, 10996; 845-938-8495, https://www.ctc.usma.edu. Independent, privately funded education and research institution at the U.S. Military Academy at West Point that studies terrorist groups.

Heritage Foundation, 214 Massachusetts Ave., N.E., Washington DC 20002; 202-546-4400; www.heritage.org. Conservative think tank studying international terrorism, including the Islamic State.

Institute for the Study of War, 1400 16th St., N.W., Suite 515, Washington, DC 20036; 202-293-5550; www.understandingwar.org. Think tank founded by an advocate of President George W. Bush's Iraq War troop surge; works to advance understanding of military affairs.

Islamic Society of North America, 6555 S. County Road 750 E., Plainfield, IN 46168; 317-839-8157; www.isna.net. Muslim organization that condemns religious extremism and terrorism while working to foster the development of the Muslim community and eradicate prejudice.

2

Far-Right Extremism

Barbara Mantel

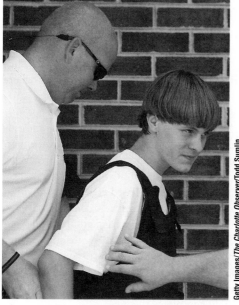

Twenty-one-year-old Dylann Roof was charged with hate crimes, murder and other offenses in connection with the shooting deaths of nine parishioners at the historically black Emanuel AME Church in Charleston, S.C., in June 2015. The massacre is the most lethal of several recent ideologically motivated fatal attacks by far-right extremists.

From *CQ Researcher*, September 18, 2015

After the June [2015] slaying of nine parishioners at the historically black Emanuel AME Church in Charleston, S.C., the motives of 21-year-old suspect Dylann Roof came under intense scrutiny. A blogger tipped investigators to a website, initially registered in Roof's name, containing a 2,500-word manifesto ranting against Hispanics and "Negroes" that Roof's friends said they believe he wrote.[1]

"I chose Charleston because it is [the] most historic city in my state, and at one time had the highest ratio of blacks to Whites in the country," the manifesto reads. "We have no skinheads, no real KKK, no one doing anything but talking on the internet. Well someone has to have the bravery to take it to the real world, and I guess that has to be me."[2]

Roof has been charged with hate crimes and other offenses by federal prosecutors, who have yet to say whether they will seek the death penalty. Until then, Roof's lawyer said he cannot advise his client how to plead, so a judge entered a not guilty plea on the federal charges on his behalf. Roof also faces state murder charges, for which state prosecutors are seeking the death penalty. Roof also has yet to enter a plea on those charges.[3]

The Charleston shooting is the most lethal in a string of ideologically motivated fatal attacks committed since 9/11 by people aligned with far-right extremism, including white supremacy, anti-government militias and the sovereign citizens movement, which denies the legitimacy of most local, state and federal laws. In the 14 years since al Qaeda killed nearly 3,000 people in strikes against the World Trade Center and the Pentagon, far-right extremists

Police: Anti-government Extremists a Top Threat

Nearly three-fourths of 382 local law enforcement agencies surveyed rated anti-government extremism among the top three terrorist threats in their jurisdictions in 2014, far more than those that listed al Qaeda-inspired threats.

Percentage of Law Enforcement Agencies Rating Types of Extremism Among the Top Three Terrorist Threats, 2014

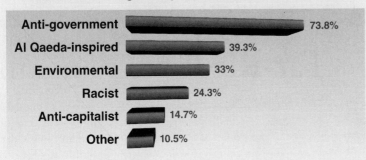

Anti-government	73.8%
Al Qaeda-inspired	39.3%
Environmental	33%
Racist	24.3%
Anti-capitalist	14.7%
Other	10.5%

Source: Charles Kurzman and David Schanzer, "Law Enforcement Assessment of the Violent Extremism Threat," Triangle Center on Terrorism and Homeland Security, p. 4, http://tinyurl.com/pa6333f

have killed 48 people in 19 attacks in the United States, nearly twice the 26 people killed in seven Islamist extremist attacks, according to a study by the New America Foundation, a Washington-based centrist research organization.[4] Far-left animal rights and environmental extremists have caused millions of dollars in property damage but no deaths, according to researchers.

Some terrorism experts say the American public and the federal government should be paying more attention to far-right extremism and its potential for mass-casualty violence. They point to the 1995 truck bombing of the Oklahoma City federal building by two anti-government conspirators, in which 168 people died and hundreds were wounded, and to more recent, disrupted plots.

But federal law enforcement officials say they can nimbly move resources as needed, and are doing everything necessary against the threat.

Meanwhile, there is debate about whether the federal government should broaden its controversial community outreach programs, designed to prevent Islamist extremist groups from radicalizing American Muslim youths, to include prevention of the radicalization of American youth by far-right extremists.

"These programs should be expanded beyond the Muslim community. A lot of the risk factors towards radicalization are common across ideological groups," says Susan Szmania, a senior researcher at the National Consortium for the Study of Terrorism and Responses to Terrorism (START), based at the University of Maryland.

But Michael German, a former FBI agent and a fellow at the New York-based Brennan Center for Justice, a law and policy institute, said anti-radicalization programs are based on the false notion that individuals follow a discernible path to violent extremism. "Instead of wasting resources chasing false leads, police should focus their resources where they have evidence of criminal activity," he said.[5]

Far-right, right-wing or radical-right extremism — all such terms are used — is primarily composed of two spheres, says Mark Pitcavage, investigative research director at the Anti-Defamation League (ADL), a New York-based civil rights organization. One sphere is white supremacy, consisting of neo-Nazis; racist skinheads; Ku Klux Klan groups; a religious sect called Christian Identity; and white supremacist prison gangs. The other sphere is anti-government — the so-called Patriot movement — which includes militias and sovereign citizens. Many, but not all, of its adherents hold conspiracy theories.

According to a prominent conspiracy theory, "the United Nations, which is usually seen as spearheading the 'New World Order,' is imposing a global plan, called Agenda 21, to take away citizens' property rights," according to the Southern Poverty Law Center (SPLC), an advocacy group in Montgomery, Ala., that tracks hate and anti-government groups. Another theory holds that the government has a secret plan to place citizens in concentration camps.[6] This summer, an eight-week, military training exercise across six Southern and Southwestern states prompted some residents' concern about a military takeover of Texas, causing at least some Texans to stock up on ammunition and bury their guns. The exercise passed without incident.[7]

"We're very careful in saying that our listing of hate and anti-government groups has nothing to do with criminality, violence or any kind of estimate we're making for the potential for those things," says Mark Potok, a senior fellow at the center. "It's all about ideology."

In fact, most U.S.-based extremist ideologies do not explicitly call for violence, says Pitcavage. "They tend to present a view in which there is some sort of danger, and only imminent action can solve the problem," he says. "That's OK if you can do the action through legal means or civil disobedience, but some people will say, 'We have to go beyond that.'" He says the majority of extremist movement adherents typically are not violent.

Events of the past seven years have galvanized far-right extremists, say analysts. The 2008 election of Barack Obama, the United States' first African-American president, "greatly upset white supremacists," said an Anti-Defamation League report. "At the same time, anti-government extremists quickly linked Obama to their 'New World Order' conspiracy theories."

Sovereign citizens, in particular, tapped into the desperation that the 2007-2009 recession and mortgage crisis created.

But while "white supremacists became angrier, more agitated and also more violent, they did not appreciably increase in numbers," said the ADL report, largely because of leader deaths and group fragmentation in the previous decade. On the other hand, the number of active militia groups more than quintupled between 2008 and 2010, and the growth of the sovereign-citizen movement, which consists mostly of unaffiliated individuals, "was even more spectacular," according to the report.[8]

While the Southern Poverty Law Center estimates the number of hate and anti-government groups, the Anti-Defamation League tracks individual white supremacists. But, their numbers are best estimates and subject to outside scrutiny and critique.[9]

Increasingly, far-right extremists are finding each other online, making joining an organized group, such as a Ku Klux Klan group, far less relevant. Unaffiliated white supremacists far outnumber those belonging to specific organizations, which these days are often quite small, according to the ADL.[10]

"If people want to meet or have a demonstration, they can do it through us or through social media," says Don Black, a former Alabama Klan leader and the founder of Stormfront, a white nationalist online discussion forum. The number of registered Stormfront users has grown from 5,000 in 2002 to nearly 300,000 today, although many are inactive.[11] The site attracts about 31,000 unique visitors a day, roughly 60 percent from the United States, and takes in from $3,000 to $7,000 a month in dues and donations.[12]

Black, who advocates for a whites-only homeland, says Stormfront does not encourage violence: "People either get banned if they express their intent to conduct illegal violence or they recognize that it is counterproductive."

But Tony McAleer, a former organizer for the neo-Nazi group White Aryan Resistance and now director of Chicago-based Life After Hate, which helps white supremacists leave the movement, says it's necessary to look carefully at hate sites' language. "It's often really the implied threat of violence. By openly advocating violence, you expose yourself to all kinds of legal hot water," he says.

A few Stormfront users have gone on to commit mass murder. They include anti-immigrant extremist Anders Behring Breivik, who killed 77 adults and children in Norway in 2011, and racist skinhead Wade Michael Page, who fatally shot six people at a Sikh temple in Oak Creek, Wis., in 2012. Breivik had visited Stormfront only briefly, says Black. Page "posted 15 times on Stormfront, and he posted other places, too. We're not responsible for him," he says.

As researchers, law enforcement officials and others study the future of extremist groups in the United States, here are some of the issues being debated:

Should the public be worried about violent far-right extremists?

While the FBI maintains a database of hate crimes, which include crimes committed by individuals who aren't followers of any particular movement, it does not maintain a database of ideologically motivated far-right extremist violence. That task is up to researchers, and their estimates vary.

For example, START-funded researchers' estimates in their Extremist Crime Database are higher than the

Ex-skinheads Help Former Racists Rejoin Society

Life After Hate offers counseling and support.

As a young man, Tony McAleer of Toronto managed a racist skinhead rock band, recruited others for a neo-Nazi organization called White Aryan Resistance and became notorious for running a phone service that provided recorded hate messages. After a legal battle, the Canadian government shut the service down in the early 1990s.

McAleer says he was bullied both at school and by his father as a child, and that joining the racist skinhead movement gave him a sense of acceptance and power that he was lacking.

But at age 24, single-parenthood and financial hardship led McAleer to question his choices.

"I was virtually unemployable," says McAleer, who is now 48 and runs his own wealth-management company. "The birth of my daughter was the moment that began my transformation. It was the first time that I thought of somebody other than myself." Having spent years stockpiling weapons and preparing for a coming "race war," McAleer says he fully expected to be dead by age 30 and faced the prospect of leaving his baby daughter an orphan.

But it took six years before he actually started distancing himself from the activities of the white power movement and another eight years before he began to truly shed his commitment to its ideology by entering therapy with a psychologist. In addition, he says, doing business in China as a software developer opened his eyes to other cultures.

Extricating oneself from the extremist far right can be a long and difficult process, McAleer says. In 2011 he joined Life After Hate, a Chicago-based nonprofit founded in 2009 by former racist skinheads as a place for ex-members of the movement, known as "formers," to share their stories and come together. But people still in the white supremacist movement also began to contact the group for help in getting out.

This spring, McAleer, Life After Hate's volunteer president and executive director, started a formal de-radicalization program called Exit USA, modeled after Exit Sweden, which helps neo-Nazis leave the movement. McAleer estimates that Life After Hate, both informally and through Exit USA, has helped 100 individuals so far.

"We know what they are feeling, what their fears are, and we can help them through that," says McAleer. "Most of the time, there are deep emotional wounds. We're not therapists, so we encourage people to get therapy because it's critical to the healing process."

The most challenging part is the initial isolation, he says. "When people leave any extreme group, they get excommunicated from their entire social circle. And if you've been a neo-Nazi or a racist skinhead for a number of years, I'll bet my bottom dollar that the rest of society has excommunicated you as well," McAleer says. "So you get stuck in this void, and there is intense loneliness."

New America Foundation's numbers. START researchers calculate that 134 people were killed in ideologically motivated far-right extremist attacks in the United States between 2000 and 2014, compared to 52 people killed by Islamic extremists, excluding the 9/11 victims.[13]

Yet both sets of data tell a comparable story. Far-right extremists are responsible for more deaths in the United States than Islamic extremists in recent years. Law enforcement concerns reflect those statistics.

"Three quarters of the 382 local law enforcement agencies that we surveyed [in 2014] expressed concern about anti-government violent extremism, nearly double the number who expressed concern about al Qaeda-inspired and other Islamist extremists," says Charles Kurzman, a sociology professor at the University of North Carolina-Chapel Hill and co-author of a working paper about the survey results.

Law enforcement officers' concern makes sense, considering that they often are the target of violent

The "formers" of Life After Hate will travel if necessary to meet with someone, and they rely on a board member with a master's degree in social work to provide guidance. The group also has a private Facebook page, called Formers Anonymous, to provide support.

"Everyone is vetted," McAleer says. "The last thing we want is a 'current' getting in there and finding out who are the 'formers.' "

Life After Hate is working with academic researchers to better understand why and how people join and leave extremist groups. Pete Simi, a criminologist at the University of Nebraska, Omaha, and colleagues have received funding from the U.S. Department of Justice to conduct interviews with former members of primarily white supremacist groups with the help of Life After Hate.

"We will use those interviews as a baseline to try and help inform the development of Life After Hate's intervention efforts," Simi says.

Life After Hate doesn't seek out individual white supremacists and try to persuade them to change.

"We can only help people who want to be helped," says McAleer. "We can make our presence known in those communities, but we can't go beyond that. I think, ethically, we have to wait for people to contact us."

To get its message out through social media, Life After Hate is producing two 30-second public service video announcements as well as banner ads, which will go live sometime this month. McAleer won't discuss their content but did describe how they will work. "For example, someone who did a search for 'white power music videos' on YouTube might see our public service announcement," he says.

Simi says the federal government may want to consider supporting such ground-level efforts. And Life After Hate,

Courtesy of Tony McAleer

Tony McAleer abandoned the white power movement and has started Exit USA, a deradicalization program that helps white supremacists leave the movement.

which relies on donations to finance its work, would consider accepting government funding, says McAleer, even though it could taint the message.

"The government is the enemy to people in the far right," he says. "But what is the alternative? It needs to be a partnership."

— *Barbara Mantel*

anti-government extremists. A July 2014 Department of Homeland Security (DHS) intelligence assessment noted a spike in militia-linked violence against law enforcement, while a February 2015 assessment predicted a continuation of sporadic, unplanned violence by sovereign citizens against law enforcement officers during routine traffic stops and home visits.[14]

One of the more notorious recent examples of such violence occurred in June 2014, when Jerad Miller and his wife, Amanda, ambushed and fatally shot two police

officers eating lunch at a Las Vegas pizza restaurant. A note they left on one officer's body said the murders were "the start of the revolution." And their social media profiles talked about their willingness to "die fighting" to stop government oppression. From the restaurant, the two entered a nearby Walmart, where they killed a civilian and wounded another officer before Jerad Miller died in a shootout with police and Amanda Miller died by suicide.[15]

Such crimes may be shocking, but the number of all kinds of extremist violence, including al Qaeda-inspired,

Extremism's Deadly Legacy

Far-right extremists killed 245 people in the U.S. in ideologically motivated attacks between 1990 and 2014, compared with 62 killed by extremists associated with al Qaeda and affiliated movements.*

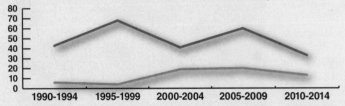

Number of Homicide Victims of Extremist Groups, 1990-2014*

* The data exclude the nearly 3,000 who died in the Sept. 11 terrorist attacks and the 168 killed in the 1995 bombimg of the Alfred P. Murrah Federal Building in Oklahoma City.

— **Far-right extremists**
— **Inspired by al Qaeda and associated movements**

Source: William S. Parkin et al., "Twenty-five Years of Ideological Homicide Victimization in the United States of America," National Consortium for the Study of Terrorism & Responses to Terrorism, August 2015

pales in comparison to the number of overall murders. "With more than 14,000 murders in the U.S. annually, violent extremism counts for less than 1 percent of fatalities in recent years," says Kurzman. "Many Americans have greater fear of extremist attacks than other forms of violence, but the statistics suggest that we should be concerned about mundane violence that doesn't make the national news."

While surveyed law enforcement agencies ranked anti-government extremism a top concern in their jurisdictions, 66 percent gauged that threat to be moderate or low. And 83 percent rated the threat from al Qaeda-inspired violent extremism as moderate or low.[16]

"Of the list of things I lose sleep over at night, terrorism and violent extremism are not at the top of my list, and it's my profession," says William Braniff, START's executive director. "I worry much more about traffic accidents, gangs and other kinds of violence and criminality in the United States. I think something like gang violence is horrifically damaging to communities."

But Potok of the Southern Poverty Law Center (SPLC) says the public "absolutely should be worried about violence from the radical right. All you need is one or two to get through." Some of the plots the FBI has

disrupted over the years have been quite scary, Potok says, including one in which a self-professed member of the Ku Klux Klan was convicted in August of conspiring to use a weapon of mass destruction to kill American Muslims.

Glendon Scott Crawford, a General Electric industrial mechanic in Schenectady, N.Y., took steps to purchase and then weaponize a commercially available industrial X-ray machine that he planned to install in a van or truck, park near the entrance to mosques and an Islamic community center and school and remotely activate, exposing people entering and exiting the facilities to lethal doses of radiation, according to the Department of Justice.[17]

"In terms of lethal violence, there's no doubt. White supremacists rule the roost," says Pitcavage of the Anti-Defamation League. He calculates that in the past 10 years, ideologically motivated killings by white supremacists greatly outnumbered those by all other far-right extremist movements. That conforms with data from the Extremist Crime Database.[18]

Steven Chermak and Joshua Freilich, criminologists at Michigan State University and the John Jay College of Criminal Justice in New York City, respectively, helped to create that database. Two years ago, they published a study exploring the characteristics that distinguish violent far-right hate groups from nonviolent hate organizations. They examined groups from the SPLC's database that had been in existence for at least three years. In a sample of 275 organizations, 21 percent had members who had committed at least one ideologically motivated violent act.[19]

The researchers found that as groups get older or increase in size, "they're more likely to be involved in violence," says Chermak.

But perhaps the most robust variable linked to violence were groups that advocated leaderless resistance, in which everyone serves in an equal position and contacts between individuals and other groups are minimized, says Chermak. Leaderless resistance reduces the chance that an informant or an arrested member would have valuable information to share with law enforcement.

"Interestingly, groups that distributed ideological literature were less likely to be involved in violence," says Chermak. Violence and the resulting attention from law enforcement "might not only harm their propaganda efforts, but it could also hurt their bottom line, because many try to profit by selling literature," he says.

But this study compared only groups. It did not compare non-violent far-right extremists unaffiliated with any groups to violent lone wolves, such as accused Charleston shooter Dylann Roof. Freilich says lone wolves account for about 35 percent of ideologically motivated far-right extremists' homicides in the Extremist Crime Database.

In a way, they are more worrisome than attacks planned by a group, Freilich says. "The general consensus among law enforcement and scholars has been that loner attacks are harder to prevent," says Freilich. "An individual acting alone is flying beneath the radar, not emailing anyone, not calling anyone, planning in secret."

But there is a flip side, says Freilich: "When you act alone, you have less of an infrastructure and may do less damage than a group."

Is the federal government doing enough to fight far-right extremist violence?

A chorus of voices, from members of Congress to advocacy groups, is demanding that the federal government pay greater attention to violent far-right extremists.

"The United States allocates significant resources towards combating Islamic violent extremism while failing to devote adequate resources to right-wing extremism," wrote 20 House Democrats in July to President Obama and Secretary of Homeland Security Jeh Johnson. "When efforts are made to address right-wing extremism, they are often met with significant political backlash."[20]

The reference was to a 2009 Department of Homeland Security (DHS) intelligence assessment, which warned of growing recruitment by "domestic right-wing terrorists" and said that a small percentage of military personnel were joining far-right extremist groups.[21]

The document, meant for state and local law enforcement, was leaked and prompted a swift backlash from

President Obama addresses the White House Summit on Countering Violent Extremism on Feb. 19, 2015. The Obama White House favored a strategy — known as countering violent extremism, or CVE — to prevent violent extremists from recruiting and radicalizing U.S. residents.

conservatives, who called the assessment a slur against veterans. "That was simply not true," says Potok of the Southern Poverty Law Center, adding that the intelligence assessment was accurate. Then-Homeland Security Secretary Janet Napolitano withdrew it and publicly criticized its authors, some of whom quit.

Some conservatives are on guard once again after then-U.S. Attorney General Eric Holder announced in June 2014 that he was reviving the Domestic Terrorism Executive Committee (DTEC), originally established after the 1995 bombing of the Alfred P. Murrah Federal Building in Oklahoma City but abruptly discontinued after 9/11. It's composed of leaders within the Department of Justice who coordinate with federal U.S. attorneys in districts across the country on non-jihadist domestic terrorism cases.[22]

Holder said that while law enforcement must remain vigilant against threats from al Qaeda affiliates and individuals they inspire, "we also must concern ourselves with the continued danger we face from individuals within our own borders who may be motivated by a variety of other causes, from anti-government animus to racial prejudice."[23]

At a hearing days later, Rep. Bob Goodlatte, R-Va., chairman of the House Judiciary Committee, expressed

Ex-supremacists Cite History of Drugs, Abuse

Former members of violent white-supremacist groups said they had dealt with substance abuse, attempted and/or considered suicide or experienced mental health problems, according to interviews with 44 ex-members. Common childhood trauma included neglect, physical abuse and sexual abuse.

Backgrounds of Former Violent White Supremacists
(by percentage of those with each problem)

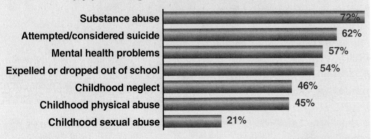

Substance abuse	72%
Attempted/considered suicide	62%
Mental health problems	57%
Expelled or dropped out of school	54%
Childhood neglect	46%
Childhood physical abuse	45%
Childhood sexual abuse	21%

Source: Pete Simi *et al.*, "Trauma as a Precursor to Violent Extremism," National Consortium for the Study of Terrorism and Responses to Terrorism, April 2015, http://tinyurl.com/opz2wcw

reservations. "What and whom does the attorney general really intend to target via the DTEC?" asked Goodlatte. "Would a group advocating strenuously for smaller government and lower taxes be included in the attorney general's definition of a group with 'anti-government animus'?"[24]

But several analysts who track domestic extremism welcomed the task force's resurrection and said that even more should be done. The restoration of the Homeland Security unit that issued the 2009 report should be first on the agenda, says Potok.

"DHS has allowed its non-Islamic domestic terrorism unit, essentially, to go fallow," he says.

Daryl Johnson, a former senior domestic terrorism analyst at DHS who was the primary author of the controversial report, agrees with Potok. "Over the past year or so, they've had a modest effort to publish a few finished intelligence reports related to this topic," says Johnson, now a private consultant on domestic terrorism. "Nevertheless, the number of analysts at DHS's Office of Intelligence and Assessment monitoring this subject is three, compared to nearly 100 looking at Islamic terrorism. There's a clear imbalance of resources." A DHS spokesman would not confirm the figures.

Johnson says the FBI also could be doing more analysis. "The FBI has a very small domestic terrorism analysis unit — 10 analysts — but they don't put out a lot of reports," he says.

The Anti-Defamation League's Pitcavage says, "Some of the complaints about the federal government not doing enough are not quite fair to the many people in law enforcement who deal with right-wing extremism on a regular basis." He praises the work of the FBI's Joint Terrorism Task Forces, which are small teams of investigators, analysts, linguists and other specialists drawn from the FBI and federal, state and local agencies.[25]

The teams are located in each of the FBI's 56 field offices and are divided into domestic and international terrorism squads. The domestic terrorism squads "routinely make cases, and they routinely make arrests of right-wing extremists," says Pitcavage. Still, he would like to see more FBI agents assigned to them, without diminishing the focus on international terrorism.

"It's a zero-sum game. We only have so many agents," says David Gomez, a retired FBI executive, who estimates that about one-quarter to one-third of task force FBI agents are working on domestic terrorism. In any case, he says, "The FBI is pretty good at allocating resources to where they are needed."

A senior U.S. law enforcement official who spoke on condition of anonymity concurred with Gomez. "I can't give you specific numbers," the official says, but "on a regular basis, the FBI looks at the threats and its resources and adjusts accordingly. And we feel comfortable that we are properly resourced."

The FBI cannot surf the Internet looking for troubling posts or begin investigations of individuals based solely on their Internet postings, which are constitutionally protected. Evidence or probable cause must exist to believe that someone is "moving towards criminal activity," says Gomez. That can come from public tips or a confidential source, he says.

For Pitcavage, the biggest concern is that the government is not training enough state and local law enforcement personnel to deal with domestic extremism. He says law enforcement officers need to understand domestic extremists' ideologies and recognize potentially violent far-right extremists through tattoos and other indicators in order to avoid being shot during routine encounters.

The Department of Justice funds the State and Local Anti-Terrorism Training Program (SLATT), which focuses on both domestic and international terrorism. SLATT has trained more than 142,600 state, local and tribal law enforcement officers since its founding in 1996, says a Justice spokeswoman. The Anti-Defamation League is the largest nongovernment provider of such training, reaching 10,000 to 12,000 law enforcement officers a year, says Pitcavage.

"But we're both just a drop in the bucket," he says. "There are nearly a million law enforcement personnel in this country, and there's a lot of turnover."

However, the funding for SLATT may be in jeopardy, say Johnson and others. The congressional ban on earmarks, or items that lawmakers can add to spending bills independently of the executive branch, has limited Congress' ability to appropriate funding directly to SLATT. The Department of Justice was able to find money for SLATT this fiscal year, but next year's funding level is in question.

Should the federal government try to prevent young people from becoming extremists?

The Obama administration has recognized that just disrupting extremist plots and making arrests is not a sustainable strategy, says START's Braniff. "You're constantly reacting and not getting ahead of the issue," he says.

The White House announced an approach in 2011 — known as countering violent extremism, or CVE — to prevent violent extremists from recruiting and radicalizing U.S. residents.[26] The plan called for the Department of Justice, the FBI, Department of Homeland Security (DHS), the National Counterterrorism Center and U.S. attorneys in key regions to partner with communities to develop anti-radicalization programs. Although the plan said that CVE should focus primarily on Islamist extremism, it said it should not ignore "other forms of violent extremism."[27]

Anti-immigrant extremist Anders Behring Breivik, who killed 77 adults and children in Norway in 2011, was known to have visited Stormfront, a white nationalist online discussion forum. The number of registered Stormfront users has grown from 5,000 in 2002 to nearly 300,000 today, although many are inactive.

But that is what happened, said a June report from George Washington University: "Between 2000 and 2013, the vast majority of attacks in the homeland were carried out by non-Islamist extremists. Yet 100 percent of federal CVE efforts are aimed at Muslim communities."[28]

A three-day summit at the White House in February on countering violent extremism is a prime example of misplaced priorities, says Potok of the Southern Poverty Law Center.

"Much fine lip service was given by the president and others to the idea that this summit would cover all kinds of terrorism," he says. "But virtually all of the discussion was about Islamist terrorism."

Asked for examples of how CVE applies to non-Islamist extremism, Justice Department spokesman Mark Raimondi would only say, "CVE programs are designed to counter all violent extremists. They are not limited to any single group or demographic."

The CVE approach is not new; anti-extremism programs have existed sporadically for nearly a decade. They include everything from raising awareness through DHS-led community meetings about radicalization, to building trust through an FBI agent's sharing a meal at a mosque to break the daily Ramadan fast, to improving community resilience through leadership training for American Muslim youths.

The summit highlighted three new pilot programs led by U.S. attorneys in Boston, Minneapolis and Los Angeles that, the George Washington University researchers said, are aimed chiefly at ISIS radicalization.* The Los Angeles program seems to build on existing outreach to the Muslim community. Boston's program would send resources to organizations providing "vulnerable individuals" with mental-health services, educational assistance and transitional job opportunities.[29]

But there are myriad problems with CVE, including no evidence that it works, say critics. It also stigmatizes American Muslims as inherently suspect, says Hina Shamsi, director of the National Security Project at the New York-based American Civil Liberties Union (ACLU), by setting "them apart from their neighbors based on their faith, their race, their ethnicity." In some cases, the FBI has secretly used "community outreach to actually gather intelligence," alienating communities, she says.[30] Several Muslim organizations in pilot cities have refused to participate.[31]

Critics have difficulty imagining the government using the same model to combat far-right radicalization. "You'd have to go to churches in places where there has been white supremacist violence and say, 'Hi, I'm DHS and I want to tell you the 12 signs of racism in your child that lead him or her to violence.' Do you think anybody would stand for that?" says Faiza Patel, co-director of the Liberty & National Security Program at the Brennan Center for Justice.

Szmania of START says the United States could take a page from Europe and emulate Exit Sweden, a non-profit run by former neo-Nazis that helps people leave the movement. Its members also talk to schools "about the negative experience of being part of a violent extremist group," says Szmania. Life After Hate began its own Exit program this past spring.

Braniff says the government could focus on prisons. "We have more white supremacists in the U.S. prison system than we'll ever have jihadists," he says. "Yet there is no formal reintegration and rehabilitation for them."

And, he says, the federal government could help communities concerned about racial violence raise awareness, provide prevention programming and create intervention teams. That way, "if the next Dylann Roof mentions to friends or acquaintances that he's going to shoot black people, there is an intervention team that can talk to him."

People must understand laws that protect behavior and speech and the privacy of students, says Braniff, "but there are also exceptions to those laws, such as when a student talks about shooting other students."

These efforts would depend on continued government funding of organizations like START that conduct violent-extremism research, says Braniff. The research results could be made accessible in one- or two-page summaries "for nongovernmental organizations to hand out to teachers, administrators and counselors," he says. In fact, START produces such bite-size digests.

Pete Simi, a criminologist at the University of Nebraska-Omaha, is the author of a two-page research brief. He and colleagues examined the life histories of 44 violent white supremacists and found that nearly half reported being physically abused as children. Almost two-thirds said they had attempted and/or seriously considered suicide, and nearly three-quarters reported having problems with alcohol and/or illegal drugs. Slightly more than half had either been expelled from school or dropped out. These rates are higher than in the general population.[32]

Simi cautions that there is no way to predict whether someone with these experiences will become a violent extremist. "It is never a simple cause and effect," he says. But there is heightened risk, and he says a young person with such a background is vulnerable to chance encounters. The person may attend a white-power concert, for example, and meet a neo-Nazi skinhead who can "become a mentor of sorts in a very unfortunate way."

Simi's research did not look at nonviolent white supremacists for comparison, which makes the findings of limited utility. But Simi says the research indicates that the nation needs to better provide at-risk youths with mental health services and other supports.

---

* ISIS is a terrorist organization that aims to create an Islamic state across Sunni areas of Iraq and in Syria and tries to radicalize European and North American youths through the Internet and social media.

CHRONOLOGY

1950s-60s *Ku Klux Klan re-emerges amid civil rights movement; neo-Nazi groups form.*

1954 Supreme Court landmark ruling in Brown v. Board of Education declaring segregated public schools unconstitutional spurs Klan growth.

1959 Navy veteran George Lincoln Rockwell founds American Nazi Party.

1961 Klan leaders form United Klans of America, by mid-decade the nation's largest Klan group, with an estimated 26,000 members.

1963 Bombing of 16th Street Baptist Church in Birmingham, Ala., kills four black girls; four Klan members are suspects, but no arrests are made.

1964 Congress passes Civil Rights Act, spurred in part by outrage over the 1963 church bombing. . . . White Knights of the Ku Klux Klan of Mississippi founded; members murder three civil rights workers.

1967 Seven Klan members are convicted of federal conspiracy charges in the 1964 murders of the three civil rights workers. . . . American Nazi Party founder Rockwell is assassinated; the party fractures.

1970s-80s *Ku Klux Klan declines; neo-Nazis organize.*

1970 Rockwell disciple William Pierce founds the National Alliance, the most dangerous and best organized neo-Nazi group to emerge in the next several decades.

1977 One Klan member is convicted of murder in the 16th Street Baptist Church bombing; two others are not convicted for decades; the fourth dies before prosecution.

1979 FBI infiltrates Klan groups, and civil rights movement's victories lead to steep decline in Klan membership.

1980 A Klan grand wizard, David Duke, leaves Klan to form National Association for the Advancement of White People and in 1989 wins a seat in the Louisiana legislature as a Republican; he later loses races for the U.S. Senate and Louisiana governorship.

1989 Hammerskin Nation unifies dispersed, racist skinheads, who hold neo-Nazi ideas and have shaved heads and unique tattoos.

1992-Present *Anti-government extremists bomb federal building in Oklahoma City; al Qaeda kills nearly 3,000.*

1992 Federal agents conduct a much-criticized siege of a white supremacist compound in Ruby Ridge, Idaho. Several people are killed, including a teenage boy.

1993 Federal agents lay siege to Branch Davidian compound in Waco, Texas, resulting in the deaths of more than 80; the raids fuel anti-government militia movements.

1994 Jeff Schoep, a neo-Nazi from Minnesota, founds the National Socialist Movement.

1995 Anti-government militants detonate a truck bomb at Oklahoma City's federal building, killing 168; government cracks down on far-right violent extremists, whose numbers plummet by decade's end.

2001 Al Qaeda operatives kill nearly 3,000 people in attacks on the World Trade Center in New York and the Pentagon and the crash of a hijacked plane.

2002 National Alliance loses most members following Pierce's death; many neo-Nazis remain unaffiliated over the next decades.

2008 Election of Barak Obama, nation's first black president, the 2007-09 recession and the mortgage crisis anger white supremacists and fuel revival of anti-government extremism.

2012 Racist skinhead Wade Michael Page attacks an Oak Creek, Wis., Sikh temple, killing six and wounding four before killing himself.

2015 Dylann Roof is charged with killing nine black parishioners in a church in Charleston, S.C.

Militias Score Successes in Standoffs with Feds

Some criticize government's inaction, but officials cite safety concerns.

In April 2014, Eric Parker stood on an overpass in the Nevada desert, holding a semi-automatic rifle and watching as the crowd below faced off against agents of the federal Bureau of Land Management (BLM).

Parker had traveled from central Idaho, one of hundreds of armed militia members, states' rights advocates, gun rights activists and other protesters who had gathered to support renegade rancher Cliven Bundy. The week before, BLM agents had begun rounding up hundreds of Bundy's cattle that were grazing illegally on federal land. Bundy denies federal authority over the land and refuses to pay federal grazing fees and penalties, which amount to more than $1 million.[1]

Five days after the armed contingent arrived, the BLM halted the roundup and released the cattle. BLM Director Neil Kornze cited "serious concern about the safety of employees and members of the public."[2]

Militia experts, however, say it was an unprecedented retreat by the government. "It's not the groups, it's not their concerns, it's not their anger, all of that is old, but the federal government backing down? I was like, 'wow! Seriously?' " said Catherine Stock, a history professor at Connecticut College in New London who studies rural militias.[3]

The federal agency's stance led Robert Crooks to assert, "BLM no longer exists in this section of Nevada," at a Bundy ranch celebration marking the one-year anniversary of the standoff. Crooks, founder of the Tecate, Calif.-based Mountain Minutemen group opposed to illegal immigration, had spent much of the past year living in his RV on the Bundy ranch.[4]

The FBI is reportedly investigating Bundy's armed supporters, but a year and a half later, authorities have not charged anyone with pointing weapons at federal agents or tried to collect the money Bundy owes, and his cattle continue to roam federal land.[5]

"Our primary goal remains, as it was a year ago, to resolve this matter safely and according to the rule of the law," agency spokeswoman Celia Boddington said in April.[6]

Bundy has become a hero to anti-government activists and met privately in June with Sen. Rand Paul, R-Ky., who is running for president.[7]

"It's clear that the 'victory' of Bundy and his sympathizers has already encouraged a number of similar defiant stands against government authority," said Ryan Lenz, a senior writer with the Southern Poverty Law Center (SPLC), an advocacy group in Montgomery, Ala., that researches antigovernment groups.[8]

In July, inspired by Bundy's resistance, the Filippini ranching family defied the BLM and released hundreds of cattle onto drought-stressed federal land in Nevada that the

"Some of these youth join street gangs, some become runaways, drugs addicts or lead otherwise dysfunctional lives, and some become violent extremists," he says. "I'm not suggesting that CVE is a bad idea, but I am suggesting that we need to think bigger than a CVE-only approach."

Providing needed mental health services, after-school programs and other outreach is a good idea, says the ACLU's Shamsi, but it "shouldn't be done in an effort led by law enforcement agencies, and it shouldn't be done in ways that say to the world at large that these communities are being targeted because we think they are a threat."

BACKGROUND
Extreme Dissatisfaction

The United States has seen multiple extremist movements throughout its history, especially during times of crisis.

"Extremists seek either a radical change in the status quo . . . or the defense of privileges they perceive to be threatened," said Martha Crenshaw, a senior fellow at Stanford University's Freeman Spogli Institute for International Studies. "Their dissatisfaction with the policies of the government is extreme, and their demands usually involve the displacement of existing political elites."[33]

agency had placed off limits to grazing in 2013. The family had sued and protested, but nothing had changed the government's mind.

Nevada ranchers are "pretty close to being extinct," said matriarch Eddyann Filippini, "and they're using the drought as the ax to cut our heads off." A few days later, the government and the family reached an agreement allowing the cattle to graze for three more years in exchange for a $106 fine.[9]

"The BLM really needs to take care of the public's land, needs to regulate the ranchers' exploitation of this privilege to graze on public lands," said Kirsten Stade, advocacy director for the Washington-based Public Employees for Environmental Responsibility. But "they're scared."[10]

In August, more than 20 armed members of Patriot groups that describe themselves as defenders of the Constitution arrived in Lincoln, Mont. Two local miners embroiled in a dispute with the U.S. Forest Service over the legality of their mining operations sought the groups' help. Federal prosecutors have asked a federal judge in Montana to prevent the miners and their supporters from blocking access to public lands and threatening government officials.[11]

The government's caution in the field traces to two seminal events of the early 1990s. In 1992, federal agents laid siege to a compound of white separatists in Ruby Ridge, Idaho, which ended with several people killed, including a teenage boy. The next year, agents raided the Branch Davidian compound in Waco, Texas. The apocalyptic religious sect was believed to be amassing a weapons arsenal. A gun battle between federal agents and the Davidians, in which four agents and six Davidians died, led to a 51-day siege, broken when the FBI fired tear gas and the Davidians then set fire to the compound. When the siege was over, 75 Davidians, a third of them children, had died.[12]

"What they learned from Waco was that a heavy-handed approach risks a major loss of life," said the SPLC in a 2014 report. "Yet allowing the anti-government movement to flout the law at gunpoint is surely not the answer."[13]

— *Barbara Mantel*

[1] Jonathan Allen, "After Nevada ranch stand-off, emboldened militias ask: where next?" Reuters, April 17, 2014, http://tinyurl.com/kwwt9zm.

[2] "Nevada cattle issue stalled," *The Richfield Reaper* (Utah), April 16, 2014, http://tinyurl.com/pj4kkur.

[3] Allen, *op. cit.*

[4] Kirk Siegler, "Year After Denying Federal Control, Bundy Still Runs His Bit of Nevada," NPR, April 14, 2015, http://tinyurl.com/owafag3.

[5] *Ibid.*

[6] Caroline Connolly, "'Liberty Celebration' at Bundy ranch marks one-year since armed confrontation with BLM," Fox 13-Salt Lake City, April 10, 2015, http://tinyurl.com/nj5ow37.

[7] Adam B. Lerner, "Rand Paul Meets With Rogue Rancher Cliven Bundy," *Politico*, June 30, 2015, http://tinyurl.com/pdxjdud.

[8] Ryan Lenz, "Free Radicals," Intelligence Report, Southern Poverty Law Center, June 10, 2015, http://tinyurl.com/ojuct2t.

[9] Julie Turkewitz, "Drought Pushes Nevada Ranchers to Take On Washington," *The New York Times*, July 2, 2015, http://tinyurl.com/p7ksk3a.

[10] *Ibid.*

[11] Matt Volz, "US government seeks ruling against miners, armed protesters," The Associated Press, Aug. 11, 2015, http://tinyurl.com/pe5vxrb.

[12] Clyde Haberman, "Memories of Waco Siege Continue to Fuel Far-Right Groups," *The New York Times*, July 12, 2015, http://tinyurl.com/ns3qeq9.

[13] Haberman, *op. cit.*

Movements considered extreme in one age can, over time, occasionally become part of the mainstream.

"Sometimes, those who take an inflexible, radical position hasten a purpose that years later is widely hailed as legitimate and just," said Michael Kazin, a professor of history at Georgetown University. For instance, "moderate authorities in politics and the media" once lambasted extreme abolitionists, pioneering woman suffragists and militant opponents of Jim Crow.[34]

And sometimes, mainstream movements come to be considered extreme. In the 1920s, the Ku Klux Klan had widespread support. The post-World War I waves of Catholic and Jewish immigration and Prohibition-related crime "brought the Klan millions of recruits," wrote University of Florida historian David Chalmers in *Hooded Americanism: The History of the Ku Klux Klan*.[35]

Here are brief histories of the some of today's far-right extremist movements.

Ku Klux Klan

The Klan was born in 1865 in the wake of the Civil War, quickly becoming a vigilante group intent on intimidating Southern blacks and their white supporters and preventing blacks from exercising basic civil rights.

David Duke, a Ku Klux Klan grand wizard, left the Klan in 1980 to form the National Association for the Advancement of White People. He won a seat in the Louisiana legislature in 1989 before running unsuccessfully for multiple offices, including Louisiana governor and U.S. president.

It became especially infamous for lynchings and burning crosses.[36]

"Outlandish titles (like imperial wizard and exalted cyclops), hooded costumes, violent 'night rides,' and the notion that the group comprised an 'invisible empire' conferred a mystique that only added to the Klan's popularity," according to the Southern Poverty Law Center (SPLC). "Lynchings, tar-and-featherings, rapes and other violent attacks on those challenging white supremacy became a hallmark of the Klan."[37]

After Jim Crow laws enforced racial segregation in the South, Imperial Wizard Nathan Bedford Forrest — a former Confederate general — formally disbanded the Klan in 1869. But during its resurgence 50 years later the Klan "picked up its first genuine Klan senator in Texas," "helped capture the governorship" in Oregon, and "with business support, elected two U.S. Senators and swept the state" in Colorado, wrote Chalmers. From Indiana to Wisconsin to New Jersey and New York, the Klan organized in thousands of localities and influenced local and state elections.[38]

But internal power struggles, sex scandals, newspaper exposés and a growing public revulsion with its terror and violence eventually reduced the Klan's influence. By the beginning of the 1930s, the group that had numbered in the millions in the 1920s had no more than 100,000 members.[39]

The Klan experienced its third surge in the 1960s in response to the civil rights movement. In efforts to preserve segregation, the Klan conducted nocturnal cross burnings and mass meetings that began to draw growing turnouts in Alabama and Georgia. The group returned to its violent ways, according to the SPLC, and its bombings, murders and other attacks "took a great many lives."[40] Bombing targets included the 16th Street Baptist Church in Birmingham, Ala., in September 1963, in which four young girls died and 22 others were injured.[41] The resulting public outrage helped to spur passage of the Civil Rights Act of 1964 and the Voting Rights Act of 1965.

Within a decade, the Klan had waned in the wake of the civil rights movement's achievements. "The black marchers were gone from the city streets but were taking their places in the schools and factories, legislatures, city commissions, and even Southern police forces. Klansmen seemed even more likely to end up in jail," wrote Chalmers.

Since the 1970s, "the Klan has been greatly weakened by internal conflicts, court cases, a seemingly endless series of splits and government infiltration," said the SPLC, which estimates its current membership, divided among competing factions, at no more than 8,000 individuals.[42] One prominent former grand wizard, David Duke, won a seat in the Louisiana state legislature in 1989, before running unsuccessfully for multiple offices, including Louisiana governor and U.S. president.

Neo-Nazis and Skinheads

The modern American neo-Nazi movement is rooted in the late 1930s, when Adolf Hitler's Germany and Benito Mussolini's Italy inspired the proliferation of more than 100 Nazi and fascist groups in the United States. Four had a national impact, wrote Stephen Atkins, a former Texas A&M University librarian, in *The Encyclopedia of Right-Wing Extremism in Modern American History:*[43]

- The Khaki Shirts of America — whose goal was to seize the federal government, abolish Congress, build the world's largest military and kill Jews — had fewer than 200 active members.
- The Silver Shirts, modeled after Hitler's Brown Shirts and Mussolini's Black Shirts, had up to 50,000 members at its peak in 1934.
- The German American Bund, with close ties to Nazi Germany, spread pro-Nazi and anti-Semitic propaganda in public meetings and at youth camps.
- The America First Committee, an alliance of conservatives, fascists and politicians who wanted to keep the United States out of World War II, became increasingly extremist as Fascist and Nazi supporters flocked to it.

Leadership problems, as well as the United States' entry into World War II, ended some groups and significantly reduced the influence of others, wrote Atkins.[44]

The American Nazi Party of the 1950s and '60s was the first significant neo-Nazi group to emerge in the post-war years. Its founder, World War II and Korean War Navy veteran George Lincoln Rockwell, blamed Jews for fomenting the civil rights movement and called for the execution of Jews and blacks. After an expelled member assassinated Rockwell in 1967, the party "fractured into a variety of squabbling small neo-Nazi groups," according to the Anti-Defamation League (ADL).[45]

In 1970, West Virginia physicist and Rockwell disciple William Pierce founded the National Alliance, which the SPLC said was "for decades the most dangerous and best organized neo-Nazi formation in America." The group called for the eradication of the Jews and non-white races as well as creation of an all-white homeland. Pierce's novel, *The Turner Diaries*, described a race war in which Jews and others are slaughtered. It inspired the 1995 bombing of the federal building in Oklahoma City, whose perpetrators had ties to both white supremacy and anti-government extremism, and many other acts of terror.[46]

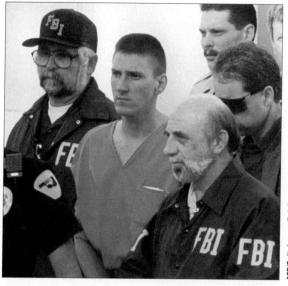

Timothy McVeigh, a supporter of the militia movement, detonated the truck bomb in Oklahoma City that killed 168 people in 1995. He said he was seeking revenge for the government sieges at a white separatist camp in Ruby Ridge, Idaho, in 1992 and an apocalyptic religious sect in Waco, Texas, the next year. McVeigh was executed by lethal injection in June 2001.

The National Alliance reached its peak in the 1990s. "At its height, it had chapters in several European countries, and *The Turner Diaries* was translated and made available free in half a dozen languages," said the SPLC, which estimates that by 2002, the Alliance had 1,400 "carefully vetted, dues-paying members." However, after Pierce's death in 2002, the group lost most of its members.[47]

The resulting power vacuum was filled by the National Socialist Movement, currently the nation's largest neo-Nazi organization, with an estimated 350 members.[48] Led by Jeff Schoep, a neo-Nazi since his teen years in Minnesota, the group has been known for its theatrical protests — in full Nazi uniforms until 2007 and in black uniforms since then.

The movement has set up a youth corps for recruiting teens and women and skinhead divisions. It owns a so-called hate-rock music (also known as white power music) label and a popular white supremacist social networking site. The group idolizes Hitler and believes that only "pure-blood whites" should be U.S. citizens, while everyone else should be deported. Its recent protests have focused on illegal immigrants.[49]

Overall, "the organized portion of the neo-Nazi movement has for some years been in relatively poor health," according to the ADL. "However, there still remains a large number of unaffiliated neo-Nazis in the United States, many of whom could come back 'into the fold' if a group began to experience significant success."[50]

The racist skinhead movement, which first emerged among British youth in the 1970s, also has been stagnant in recent years, according to the ADL. (The two other branches of the skinhead movement are traditional skinheads and anti-racist skinheads.) By the 1980s the racist skinhead subculture had spread across Western Europe and North America, its members sporting shaved heads and unique tattoos and holding essentially the same beliefs as neo-Nazis. They are largely unaffiliated with any organized groups, although there are two prominent racist skinhead gangs, the Hammerskin Nation, a national league of regional crews, and the Midwest-based Vinlanders Social Club.

Page, the racist skinhead who attacked the Sikh temple in Oak Creek, Wis., in 2012, played in several hate-music bands.[51]

Militia Movement and Sovereign Citizens

In 1994 and 1995, hundreds of militias with a total of as many as 100,000 members had formed across the United States, wrote University of Hartford historian Robert Churchill in *To Shake Their Guns in the Tyrant's Face*, a chronicle of the militia movement.[52]

Churchill said the movement grew out of its members' perception "that their government had turned increasingly violent." The government sieges at a white separatist compound in Ruby Ridge, Idaho, in 1992 and of an apocalyptic religious sect in Waco, Texas, the next year — both ending in multiple deaths and later criticized in official reports — "were the most important events driving this perception," said Churchill. "Finally, militia men and women feared that recently passed gun-control legislation would be enforced with the same violence exhibited at Waco and Ruby Ridge."

The militia members argued that popular violence was a legitimate response to a government's denial of fundamental rights or to state-sponsored violence against citizens.[53] Timothy McVeigh, who detonated the truck bomb in Oklahoma City that killed 168 people in 1995, said he was seeking revenge for Ruby Ridge and Waco. McVeigh was executed by lethal injection in June 2001.

The militia movement included some African-Americans, such as J.J. Johnson, the leader of the largest militia group in Ohio in the 1990s. Johnson denounced "the militarization of our law enforcement, those 'peace officers' who can be found clad in their black ninja suits while they storm inner-city neighborhoods indiscriminately shooting and beating residents while fighting their 'war on drugs.' "[54]

Many of these militias were led by constitutional fundamentalists, who argued that the federal government had exceeded its powers. Other militia leaders were more conspiracy-minded, arguing that Waco and Ruby Ridge were "dress rehearsals for an impending invasion by the forces of the New World Order," and that the federal government was stripping citizens of their guns through legislation in advance of the plot, wrote Churchill.[55]

After the Oklahoma City bombing, state and federal law enforcement agencies made "major arrests of militia group members who were engaged in a variety of plots and conspiracies in West Virginia, Georgia, Arizona, Washington, Michigan, Florida and many other states," according to the ADL. By the end of the 1990s, "many anti-government extremists had lost their energy, while a number of them were in prison," and the movement went into a steep decline.[56]

The 2008 election of Democrat Barack Obama, the nation's first African-American president, along with the recession, mortgage crisis and renewed discussion of gun-control legislation, helped to spur a second surge in the militia movement. The number of militia groups tracked by the ADL and the SPLC grew sharply between 2009 and 2010, although the numbers have declined since 2012.

The sovereign citizen movement, in particular, was galvanized by the mortgage crisis. The movement had begun in the 1970s and grew in numbers during the deep recession and farm crisis of the 1980s. Its core belief is that "many years ago an insidious conspiracy infiltrated and subverted the U.S. government, slowly replacing parts of the original, legitimate government (often referred to by sovereigns as the 'de jure' government) with an illegitimate, tyrannical government (the 'de facto' government)," according to a 2012 ADL report.[57]

Sovereign citizens believe they can tear up what they see as the illegitimate government's contracts, such as driver's licenses and Social Security cards, and thus regain their sovereignty and freedom from the illegitimate government's laws. Sovereign citizens typically eschew organized groups but rather are a loosely formed mass of individuals who follow sovereign citizen "gurus."[58]

To try to avoid paying taxes and fines, sovereign citizens resort to what is commonly called paper terrorism. "Paper terrorism involves the use of bogus legal documents and filings, or the misuse of legitimate ones, to intimidate, harass, threaten, or retaliate against public officials, law enforcement officers, or private citizens," said the ADL.

Perhaps the oldest tactic is the filing of false or nuisance liens against the personal properties of law enforcement officials and public officials, who then have to hire lawyers to clear the title at considerable expense.[59]

CURRENT SITUATION

Countering Extremists

Congress is considering legislation aimed at coordinating and funding the federal government's efforts to prevent violent extremism in the United States. In mid-July, the House Committee on Homeland Security approved the Countering Violent Extremism Act of 2015, which defines violent extremism as "ideologically motivated terrorist activities."

The measure would establish an Office for Countering Violent Extremism within the Department of Homeland Security (DHS), to be run by a new assistant secretary, with a budget of $10 million a year.[60]

"In the face of mounting threats, our government is doing far too little to counter violent extremism here in the United States," said Rep. Michael McCaul, R-Texas, the committee chair and the bill's sponsor. "Whether it is the long reach of international terrorists into our communities or the homegrown hate spread by domestic extremist groups, we are ill-equipped to prevent Americans from being recruited by dangerous fanatics."[61]

The new office would coordinate with other federal agencies and manage DHS' activities to counter violent extremism, which the legislation says should include:

- Identifying risk factors that contribute to violent extremism and potential remedies;
- Identifying populations targeted by violent extremist recruitment;
- Managing outreach and engagement programs in communities at risk;
- Assessing the methods used by violent extremists to disseminate propaganda, and
- Establishing a counter-messaging program via the Internet and social media.[62]

All activities would be supported by empirical research and "respect the privacy, civil rights and civil liberties of all Americans," according to the proposed bill.[63]

Conservative opinion on beefing up DHS prevention and de-radicalization efforts is mixed. For example, the Heritage Foundation, a Washington think tank, supports such change, but several grassroots conservative and libertarian bloggers oppose it for what they consider its excessively broad definition of violent extremism.[64]

"We certainly don't need to give the government carte blanche to declare 'ideological' enemies in such a nebulous manner," said the Bastrop County Tea Party in Texas in a blog post. The group is calling for the bill to be killed.[65]

Forty-eight human rights, civil liberties and community-based organizations, including the ACLU, the Council on American-Islamic Relations and the National Association for the Advancement of Colored People (NAACP), also have strong objections to the legislation. In a letter to the House committee before the vote, the organizations outlined their many long-standing objections to CVE programs, including the lack of evidence that such programs help to reduce terrorism, the threats they pose to freedoms of speech, association and religion and their almost exclusive focus on Muslim communities.

"Our organizations believe that this effort is misguided and likely to be harmful," they wrote.[66]

Rep. Bennie Thompson of Mississippi, the Homeland Security Committee's ranking Democrat, said that he could not support the bill as currently written.[67] He introduced an amendment that tried to address some of the concerns. It would have required DHS to analyze the

Should hate speech be regulated in the United States?

YES

Michel Rosenfeld
Professor of Law and Comparative Democracy and Human Rights, Yeshiva University; author of Law, Justice, Democracy, and the Clashes of Cultures: A Pluralist Account

Written for *CQ Researcher*, September 2015

The United States protects hate speech unless it amounts to incitement to violence, whereas Canada and European democracies prohibit hate speech if it incites racial hatred. American exceptionalism regarding hate speech mirrors the country's extraordinary devotion to free speech and has several palpable advantages. The American approach carves out clear boundaries between permissible and impermissible speech while encouraging discussion over suppression of hateful ideas, convinced that reason can best hate. One notorious example was the proposed 1978 neo-Nazi march in Skokie, Ill., a Chicago suburb where many Holocaust survivors live. The courts cleared the way for the march, and the thrust of the marchers' message fell on overwhelmingly deaf ears.

The Skokie case underscores a sharp contrast between the United States and Germany, where hate speech and Holocaust denial are criminalized in vigilance against any resurgence of Nazism. Any comparison centering on the swastika is, however, misleading, as the closest analogy in this country to what the swastika symbolizes in Germany is cross burning. The latter embodies racial hatred, intimidation and a history of extreme violence against the country's African-American minority. Yet in 1992, a unanimous U.S. Supreme Court held in *R.A.V. v. City of St. Paul* that a city's effort to punish the perpetrators of a cross burning on the lawn of an African-American family was unconstitutional. The perpetrators were not intent on violence, but on scaring and intimidating their victims so they would move out of a white neighborhood.

For the German courts, punishing Holocaust denial was imperative to uphold the dignity and cement the communal bonds of postwar German Jewish citizens. Analogously, banning cross burning in the United States would somewhat heal the dignitary wounds stemming from the legacy of U.S. racism — which is far from eradicated, as sadly attested by the recent Charleston church massacre.

Besides demeaning those it targets, hate speech often circumvents reason and fuels prejudice. Most whites living in the neighborhood of the victims in R.A.V. undoubtedly found the cross burning despicable, but several of them nonetheless preferred that their neighborhood not become truly racially mixed.

In the case of African-Americans, just as with German Jews, it is important that the state weigh in against hatred and officially sanction unmistakable hate speech. Such sanction is not likely to eradicate hate, but it will enhance dignity for all.

NO

James Weinstein
Professor of Constitutional Law, Sandra Day O'Connor College of Law, Arizona State University; author of Hate Speech, Pornography and the Radical Attack on Free Speech Doctrine

Written for *CQ Researcher*, September 2015

Free and open discussion of matters of public concern is the lifeblood of democracy. The Supreme Court has accordingly interpreted the First Amendment — properly, in my view — to guarantee each individual the right to participate in this discussion by expressing any viewpoint, even those that the vast majority of Americans finds offensive, disturbing or even morally repugnant.

A "hate speech" exception allowing government to ban speech that demeans people on the basis of race, ethnicity, sexual orientation or similar characteristics would likely undermine this vigorous protection of public discourse. It would be most difficult for the Supreme Court to articulate a principle excluding hate speech from First Amendment protection that would not also apply to other types of expression. A long-standing justification for banning hate speech is that it might persuade others to discriminate against minorities. But by that reasoning, anti-war speech could be punished because it might persuade conscripts to resist the draft, just as radical environmentalist literature could be suppressed lest it lead to acts of eco-terrorism.

More recently, it has been argued that hate speech alienates minorities from society. It can seriously be questioned, however, whether public expression of bigoted ideas significantly contributes to such alienation in America. Indeed, in recent years, hate speech incidents often elicit massive condemnation from all segments of society in ways likely to reassure those vilified by the bigoted expression.

But even if it were possible to identify a rationale for suppressing hate speech that would not lead to a proliferation of other viewpoint-based First Amendment exceptions, banning hate speech would nevertheless likely impede public discussion of important issues. Though hate-speech laws may be intended to suppress only the most virulent forms of bigoted expression, experience in other democracies has shown that their actual reach is not so limited. For instance, under such laws, the leader of a far-right Dutch political party was imprisoned for advocating that guest-workers be removed from the Netherlands; a Catholic bishop in Belgium was arrested for saying that homosexuality was a "blockage in their normal psychological development, rendering them abnormal"; and French actress Brigitte Bardot was fined for protesting on her website the slaughter of sheep during a Muslim festival and complaining that Muslims were destroying France by "imposing their ways."

In a free and democratic society, bigoted ideas should be refuted, not censored.

risk posed by extremist violence based on documented threats and empirical data; to explain its efforts to identify programs whose effectiveness has been validated by independent researchers; to provide safeguards against religious, ethnic and racial discrimination; and to assess the compatibility of all materials and training with constitutionally protected speech, belief and activities. It would have required the DHS secretary to submit this "comprehensive strategy" to Congress within 90 days of the legislation's enactment.[68]

However, the committee voted down Thompson's amendment.

McCaul said at the time that neither the White House nor DHS had expressed any opposition to the bill.[69] It's now up to the full House to consider the legislation.

Convicting Extremists

Three important criminal cases involving far-right extremists involved in violence or conspiracies have been resolved this summer.

A Kansas jury in September sentenced long-time white supremacist and self-described anti-Semite Frazier Glenn Miller Jr. to death for the murder of three people outside two Jewish facilities in the Kansas City suburb of Overland Park, Kan., on April 13, 2014. Miller, 74, the founder and former grand dragon of the Carolina Knights of the Ku Klux Klan, a paramilitary group, shot William Corporon, 69, and Corporon's 14-year-old grandson, Reat Underwood, outside the town's Jewish Community Center. A few minutes later, he killed Terri LaManno, 53, outside the Village Shalom care center, where her mother lived. None of the victims was Jewish.

Representing himself, Miller dared jurors, whom he called "whores of the Jews," to sentence him to death, ending with a Nazi salute and "Heil Hitler."[70]

In late August, a federal judge in Sacramento, Calif., sentenced sovereign citizen Brent Douglas Cole to nearly 30 years in prison for shooting and wounding two law enforcement officers at a campsite on public land. According to their trial testimony, the officers were attempting to impound a stolen motorcycle at the campsite when Cole, 61, admitted to being armed. One of the officers withdrew a pair of handcuffs, prompting Cole to draw his revolver and begin shooting.

"Take the right to bear arms away, and this country will fall like a ripe tomato," Cole said in an interview at the county jail. "You will see genocide."[71]

Getty Images/John Moore

A Ku Klux Klan member shouts racial slurs during a Klan demonstration protesting the removal of the Confederate flag at the statehouse in Columbia, S.C., on July 18, 2015. Controversy over displays of the Confederate flag erupted after the fatal shooting in June of nine black parishioners at a church in Charleston, when images of alleged shooter Dylann Roof holding a Confederate flag showed up on a website.

That same month, a federal judge in Atlanta sentenced three members of a Georgia militia to 12-year prison terms for conspiring to use weapons of mass destruction to attack federal government agencies. A concerned participant in a chat room frequented by militia members notified the FBI in early 2014 after Brian Cannon, 37, Terry Peace, 47, and Cory Williamson, 29, discussed online their plans for attacking federal government facilities in Georgia. The FBI then mounted a sting operation, in which a cooperating witness supplied the three men with inert pipe bombs that they planned to use against a local police department.[72]

Flag Controversy

Controversy over displays of the Confederate flag erupted after the racially motivated massacre in Charleston in June, when images of alleged shooter Roof holding a Confederate flag showed up on a website he is believed to have created. He was wearing a jacket emblazoned with the flags of two former African apartheid nations and displaying his .45 caliber Glock pistol, according to the federal indictment.[73]

Defenders of the flag say it is a symbol of Confederate heritage and honor, while opponents say it represents racism, oppression, and slavery. Less than a week after the murders, South Carolina's Republican Gov. Nikki

Haley urged state lawmakers to pass legislation to remove the flag from state property.

"This flag, while an integral part of our past, does not represent the future of our great state," she said.[74]

A few days later, Alabama Gov. Robert Bentley ordered Confederate flags removed from the grounds of his state capital. "This had the potential to become a major distraction as we go forward," said Bentley, a Republican.[75]

In early July, after several days of emotional debate, South Carolina lawmakers passed, and Haley signed, a bill ordering the flag's removal. On July 10, in the state where the Civil War began in 1861, the flag was permanently lowered from its perch on the grounds of the statehouse in Columbia.[76]

The state's action prompted rallies in support of the flag across the nation. Meanwhile, local governments also are removing Confederate symbols. For example, in early August Albuquerque, N.M., took down the four "Stars and Bars" flags, an earlier version of the Confederate flag, hanging over the city's historic district. And Danville, Va., passed an ordinance to remove the Confederate flag from city-owned flagpoles.[77]

Major retailers were some of the earliest to act. Walmart, Sears, Amazon and eBay removed Confederate flag merchandise from their online marketplaces within a week of the Charleston murders. "We have decided to prohibit Confederate flags, and many items containing this image, because we believe it has become a contemporary symbol of divisiveness and racism," said eBay spokesperson Johnna Hoff.[78]

OUTLOOK
Ebbs and Flows

Far-right extremist activities, including violence, have tended to move in cycles over the past 50 years, and several analysts expect the same ebb and flow over the next decade.

"Since the mid-1980s, right-wing extremism has consistently been the most lethal type of extremism in the United States, and nothing is going to change that in the near future," the ADL's Pitcavage says.

Former white supremacist McAleer, of Life After Hate, says much depends on the economy. "If there is a serious economic downturn, all bets are off, and radical solutions

become more palatable," he says. "Then all it takes is for a charismatic leader to show up and harness that."

Former DHS analyst Johnson predicts that 2016 "will be another active year for right-wing extremist violence." How the country handles polarizing issues, such as immigration and gun control, will help determine what happens during the next administration, he says.

The SPLC's Potok also is pessimistic about the future. "It's very possible that the number of extremist groups will remain very high, as the country continues its transition from a white-majority nation to a truly multicultural one," he says. "I also think that it is entirely possible that we will see attacks on the scale of the Oklahoma City bombing in the years ahead."

Pitcavage doesn't expect much change in the government's response to far-right extremist violence, such as an increase in funding for training law enforcement. "The recent Charleston shooting — the third most-lethal domestic terrorist event in the past five decades — seems to have done nothing at all to motivate the government to increase its resources in combating right-wing violence, so perhaps it would take an even worse tragedy . . . to focus attention on the problem," he says. "That's not a happy prospect."

START's Szmania is optimistic that countering violent extremism programming in the United States will increase across ideologies, including far-right extremism, in the next five to 10 years. "Mostly likely, far-right programs will build on successful examples like Life After Hate and Exit," she says.

The ACLU's Shamsi expects CVE programs to be a thing of the past in a decade. "Key aspects raise significant federal constitutional concerns and are possibly also open to challenge under state constitutions as well as privacy statutes or regulations," she says.

Researchers predict that violent-extremism studies will become more grounded in scientific methods. "In the next 10 years, we will see an increase in studies that compare violent terrorists to nonviolent extremists who share the terrorists' ideologies but don't commit violent acts," says criminologist Freilich.

Szmania says that "research will probably never be able to predict who will become a violent extremist." But, she says, it could lead to "a better understanding of the effectiveness of interventions aimed at supporting youth to stay in school, addressing mental health needs, limiting the availability of weapons, and addressing gateway criminal behavior, such as petty crime leading to involvement in more serious infractions."

NOTES

1. Frances Robles, "Dylann Roof Photos and a Manifesto Are Posted on Website," *The New York Times*, June 20, 2015, http://tinyurl.com/od5che9.

2. *Ibid.*

3. "Not guilty plea in federal court for accused Charleston shooter," CBSNews, July 31, 2015, http://tinyurl.com/pmwfdoe; "S.C. To Seek Death Penalty For Dylann Roof In Charleston Shooting," NPR, Sept. 3, 2015, http://tinyurl.com/ppfapol.

4. "Homegrown Extremists," New America Foundation, http://tinyurl.com/nhsrzxx.

5. Michael German, "Stigmatizing Boston's Muslim Community is No Way to Build Trust," Brennan Center for Justice, Oct. 9, 2014, http://tinyurl.com/o79xgeb.

6. "Antigovernment Movement," Southern Poverty Law Center, http://tinyurl.com/oazpdl2.

7. Manny Fernandez, "As Jade Helm 15 Military Exercise Begins, Texans Keep Watch 'Just in Case,'" *The New York Times*, July 15, 2015, http://tinyurl.com/pjpztol.

8. "Then and Now: Right-Wing Extremism in 1995 and 2015," Anti-Defamation League, March 25, 2015, pp. 3, 5, 7, http://tinyurl.com/o6cs5sa.

9. See J. M. Berger, "The Hate List: Is America really being overrun by right-wing militants?" *Foreign Policy*, March 12, 2013, http://tinyurl.com/ogkjmeu.

10. "With Hate in their Hearts: The State of White Supremacy in the United States," Anti-Defamation League, July 2015, p. 5, http://tinyurl.com/o7ryzzz.

11. "Don Black," Southern Poverty Law Center, http://tinyurl.com/obc9pxw.

12. Stormfront statistics, Aug. 24, 2015, http://tinyurl.com/pg7398d; "Contributions in August 2015," http://tinyurl.com/or825tz.

13. William S. Parkin *et al.*, "Twenty-five Years of Ideological Homicide Victimization in the United States of America," August 2015, unpublished, p. 5.

14. "Domestic Violent Extremists Pose Increased Threat to Government Officials and Law Enforcement," Homeland Security Office of Intelligence and Analysis, July 22, 2014, p. 1, http://tinyurl.com/qy9fvkb; "Sovereign Citizen Extremist Ideology Will Drive Violence at Home, During Travel, and at Government Facilities," Homeland Security Office of Intelligence and Analysis, Feb. 5, 2015, p. 1, http://tinyurl.com/pkx6wo6.

15. "Domestic Violent Extremists Pose Increased Threat to Government Officials and Law Enforcement," *ibid.*; "Terror From the Right: Plots, Conspiracies and Racist Rampages Since Oklahoma City," Southern Poverty Law Center, 2015, http://tinyurl.com/qhp8hkw.

16. Charles Kurzman and David Schanzer, "Law Enforcement Assessment of the Violent Extremism Threat," Triangle Center on Terrorism and Homeland Security, June 25, 2015, p. 3, http://tinyurl.com/pa6333f.

17. "Upstate New York Man Convicted for his Role in Attempting to Develop Lethal Radiation Device," Department of Justice News, U.S. Department of Justice, Aug. 21, 2015, http://tinyurl.com/osj879z.

18. Parkin *et al.*, *op. cit.*, p. 7.

19. Steven Chermak *et al.*, "The Organizational Dynamics of Far-Right Hate Groups in the United States: Comparing Violent to Nonviolent Organizations," *Studies in Conflict & Terrorism*, Feb. 14, 2013, p. 203, http://tinyurl.com/pae4bmr.

20. "Letter to Barack H. Obama and The Honorable Jeh Johnson," U.S. Congress, July 15, 2015, http://tinyurl.com/oobq7ky.

21. "Rightwing Extremism: Current Economic and Political Climate Fueling Resurgence in Radicalization and Recruitment," U.S. Department of Homeland Security, April 7, 2009, http://tinyurl.com/k3ghvbo.

22. "Reestablishment of Committee on Domestic Terrorism: Statement of Atty. Gen. Eric Holder," Department of Justice, June 3, 2014, http://tinyurl.com/otwflbd.

23. *Ibid.*

24. Bob Goodlatte, "Hearing: Oversight of the Federal Bureau of Investigation," House Judiciary Committee, June 11, 2014, http://tinyurl.com/ow3xder.

25. "Protecting America from Terrorist Attack: Our Joint Terrorism Task Forces," FBI, http://tinyurl.com/6f6sddq.

26. "Strategic Implementation Plan for Empowering Local Partners to Prevent Violent Extremism in the United States," Executive Office of the President of the United States, December 2011, p. 1, http://tinyurl.com/d2kavs8.

27. *Ibid.*, p. 2.

28. Lorenzo Vidino and Seamus Hughes, "Countering Violent Extremism in America," Center for Cyber & Homeland Security, The George Washington University, June 2015, p. 11, http://tinyurl.com/ozbw5nw.

29. *Ibid.*, pp. 7-8.

30. Cora Currier, "Spies Among Us," *The Intercept*, Jan. 21, 2015, http://tinyurl.com/p2rq9cc.

31. Bryan Bender, "Islamic leader says US officials unfairly target Muslims," *The Boston Globe*, Feb. 18, 2015, http://tinyurl.com/ouc9o3b.

32. Pete Simi, "Trauma as a Precursor to Violent Extremism," START Research Brief, April 2015, http://tinyurl.com/q8qgwra.

33. Stephen E. Atkins, *Encyclopedia of Right-Wing Extremism in Modern American History* (2011), p. xii.

34. Michael Kazin, "A Kind Word for Ted Cruz: America Was Built on Extremism," *The New Republic*, Oct. 29, 2013, http://tinyurl.com/ngwpaat.

35. David M. Chalmers, *Hooded Americanism: The History of the Ku Klux Klan* (1987), pp. 2-3.

36. Brendan Koerner, "Why Does the Ku Klux Klan Burn Crosses?" *Slate*, Dec. 2, 2002, http://tinyurl.com/mle8o3a.

37. "Ku Klux Klan," Extremist Files, Southern Poverty Law Center, http://tinyurl.com/p3tagdh.

38. Chalmers, *op. cit.*, p. 3.

39. *Ibid.*, p. 5.

40. "Ku Klux Klan," *op. cit.*

41. *Ibid.*

42. *Ibid.*

43. Atkins, *op. cit.*, pp. 65-66.

44. *Ibid.*, pp. 66-68, 72, 74-75.

45. "With Hate in their Hearts: The State of White Supremacy in the United States," *op. cit.*, p. 8; Chalmers, *op. cit.*, p. 91.

46. "National Alliance," Extremist Files, Southern Poverty Law Center, http://tinyurl.com/nnkaq56; "Then and Now: Right-Wing Extremism in 1995 and 2015," *op. cit.*, p. 6.

47. *Ibid.*

48. "With Hate in their Hearts," *op. cit.*, p. 8.

49. "National Socialist Movement," Extremist Files, Southern Poverty Law Center, http://tinyurl.com/nax598q.

50. "With Hate in their Hearts," *op. cit.*, p. 9.

51. *Ibid.*, pp. 9-10.

52. Robert H. Churchill, *To Shake Their Guns in the Tyrant's Face: Libertarian Political Violence and the Origins of the Militia Movement* (2012), p. 2.

53. *Ibid.*, p. 5.

54. *Ibid.*, p. 238.

55. *Ibid.*, pp. 241-242.

56. "Then and Now," *op. cit.*, pp. 6-7.

57. "The Lawless Ones: The Resurgence of the Sovereign Citizen Movement," Anti-Defamation League, 2012, p. 3, http://tinyurl.com/pyd2ujn.

58. *Ibid.*, p. 6.

59. *Ibid.*, p. 16.

60. "Amendment in the Nature of a Substitute to H.R. 2899," U.S. House of Representatives, July 15, 2015, pp. 1, 8, http://tinyurl.com/nc4ev6n.

61. "Bipartisan Support in Congress to Counter Violent Extremism: McCaul's CVE Bill Unanimously Passes Committee," House Committee on Homeland Security, July 15, 2015, http://tinyurl.com/p9syl4p.

62. "Amendment in the Nature of a Substitute to H.R. 2899," *op. cit.*, pp. 3-5.

63. *Ibid.*

64. David Inserra, "Revisiting Efforts to Counter Violent Extremism: Leadership Needed," The Heritage Foundation, April 20, 2015, http://tinyurl.com/nn6khh7.

65. Allen West, "H.R.2899 Countering Violent Extremism Act — Should Not See the Light of Day," Bastrop County Tea Party, July 28, 2015, http://tinyurl.com/p5cct7n.

66. "Re: H.R. 2899, Countering Violent Extremism Act of 2015," July 10, 2015, http://tinyurl.com/nfzdf2r.

67. Rep. Bennie G. Thompson, "No Case for Countering Violent Extremism Office," U.S. House of Representatives, July 13, 2015, http://tinyurl.com/qxdj6gy.

68. "Substitute to the Amendment in the Nature of a Substitute to H.R. 2899 Offered by Mr. Thompson of Mississippi," House Committee on Homeland Security, July 15, 2015, pp. 1-4, http://tinyurl.com/nrjvmsr.

69. Dibya Sarkar, "House panel unanimously OKs bill creating countering violent extremism office within DHS," FierceHomelandSecurity.com, July 16, 2015, http://tinyurl.com/ojkq3h4.

70. Tony Rizzo, "F. Glenn Miller deserves death for killings outside Jewish facilities, jury says," The Kansas City Star, Sept. 8, 2015, http://tinyurl.com/ogh7efk; "Frazier Glenn Miller," Extremist Files, Southern Poverty Law Center, http://tinyurl.com/npv4qw4.

71. Liz Kellar, "'Sovereign citizen' Brent Cole sentenced in shootout," The Union, Aug. 31, 2015, http://tinyurl.com/no4xn52.

72. "Men Sentenced for Conspiracy to Use Weapons of Mass Destruction," U.S. Attorney's Office, Northern District of Georgia, Aug. 28, 2015, http://tinyurl.com/nszq963.

73. Bill Chappell, "Charleston Shooting Suspect Roof Could Face Death Penalty Over Federal Charges," NPR, July 22, 2015, http://tinyurl.com/nk44xsz.

74. Jeremy Diamond and Dana Bash, "Nikki Haley calls for removal of Confederate flag from capital grounds," CNN, June 24, 2015, http://tinyurl.com/nludak9.

75. Amanda Terkel, "Alabama Governor Removes Confederate Flags From State Capital," The Huffington Post, June 24, 2015, http://tinyurl.com/pdeshbz.

76. Richard Fausset and Alan Blinder, "Era Ends as South Carolina Lowers Confederate Flag," The New York Times, July 10, 2015, http://tinyurl.com/nl3qsp3.

77. Dan McKay, "Mayor strikes Confederate flag in Old Town," Albuquerque Journal, Aug. 3, 2015, http://tinyurl.com/p7nlgg5; Shayne Dwyer, "New Danville flag ordinance brings down other flags in city as well," WDBJ7 WDBJ (Roanoke-Lynchburg, Virginia), Aug. 7, 2015, http://tinyurl.com/q4gskns.

78. MJ Lee, "eBay to ban sale of Confederate flag merchandise," CNN, June 24, 2015, http://tinyurl.com/oksu227.

BIBLIOGRAPHY

Selected Sources

Books

Atkins, Stephen E., *Encyclopedia of Right-Wing Extremism in Modern American History*, ABC-CLIO, 2011.
A former Texas A&M University librarian examines the history of right-wing extremism in the U.S.

Churchill, Robert H., *To Shake Their Guns in the Tyrant's Face: Libertarian Political Violence and the Origins of the Militia Movement*, University of Michigan Press, 2012.
A University of Hartford history professor traces the origins of the modern American militia movement.

Articles

Bender, Bryan, "Islamic leader says US officials unfairly target Muslims," *The Boston Globe*, Feb. 18, 2015, http://tinyurl.com/omg5ssm.
A Boston Islamic leader criticizes the federal government's deradicalization program, saying it stigmatizes Muslims and assumes they are predisposed to violence.

Currier, Cora, "Spies Among Us," *The Intercept*, Jan. 21, 2015, http://tinyurl.com/p2rq9cc.
The government's outreach to Muslim communities blurs the line between outreach and intelligence gathering.

Fausset, Richard, and Alan Blinder, "Era Ends as South Carolina Lowers Confederate Flag," *The New York Times*, July 10, 2015, http://tinyurl.com/nl3qsp3.
The Confederate battle flag is removed from the grounds of the South Carolina State House.

Robles, Frances, "Dylann Roof Photos and a Manifesto Are Posted on Website," *The New York Times*, June 20, 2015, http://tinyurl.com/od5che9.
An online racist manifesto is discovered and is presumed written by the accused Charleston church shooter.

"S.C. To Seek Death Penalty For Dylann Roof in Charleston Shooting," NPR, Sept. 3, 2015, http://tinyurl.com/ppfapol.
Prosecutors have not yet decided whether to seek the death penalty for the suspect in the Charleston, S.C., church shooting.

Shapiro, Emily, "Charleston Shooting: A Closer Look at Alleged Gunman Dylann Roof," ABC News, June 18, 2015, http://tinyurl.com/nklm2eo.
Accused Charleston shooter Dylann Roof planned his attack for six months, according to Roof's roommate.

Siegler, Kirk, "Year After Denying Federal Control, Bundy Still Runs His Bit of Nevada," NPR, April 14, 2015, http://tinyurl.com/owafag3.
A renegade rancher continues to refuse to pay federal grazing fees and penalties after armed supporters confronted federal agents a year earlier.

Reports and Studies

Chermak, Steven, *et al.*, "The Organizational Dynamics of Far-Right Hate Groups in the United States: Comparing Violent to Nonviolent Organizations," Studies in Conflict Terrorism, Feb. 14, 2013, http://tinyurl.com/pae4bmr.
Three university criminologists compare the characteristics of nonviolent and violent far right hate groups.

Kurzman, Charles, and David Schanzer, "Law Enforcement Assessment of the Violent Extremism Threat," June 25, 2015, http://tinyurl.com/pa6333f.
Two university terrorism experts ask law enforcement agencies to rank their concerns about violent extremist movements.

Pitcavage, Mark, "With Hate in their Hearts: The State of White Supremacy in the United States," Anti-Defamation League, July 13, 2015, http://tinyurl.com/o7ryzzz.
A researcher at a civil rights organization explains white supremacy movements.

Simi, Pete, "Trauma as a Precursor to Violent Extremism," START Research Brief, April 2015, http://tinyurl.com/q8qgwra.
A criminologist at the University of Nebraska, Omaha, and colleagues examine the life histories of 44 violent white supremacists and conclude that many suffered childhood trauma.

"The Strategic Implementation Plan for Empowering Local Partners to Prevent Violent Extremism in the United States," Executive Office of the President of the United States, December 2011, http://tinyurl.com/d2kavs8.
The Obama administration explains how it plans to work with local communities to prevent the recruitment and radicalization of individuals in the United States by violent extremists.

"Then and Now: Right-Wing Extremism in 1995 and 2015," Anti-Defamation League, March 25, 2015, http://tinyurl.com/o6cs5sa.
A civil rights organization takes stock of right-wing extremism on the 20th anniversary of the bombing of the Oklahoma City federal building and says a recent surge has gone largely unnoticed.

Vidino, Lorenzo, and Seamus Hughes, "Countering Violent Extremism in America," Center for Cyber and Homeland Security, The George Washington University, June 2015, http://tinyurl.com/ozbw5nw.
Two George Washington University experts on extremism assess the U.S. program to prevent violent extremists from recruiting adherents.

For More Information

American Civil Liberties Union (ACLU), 125 Broad St., 18th Floor, New York, NY 10004; 212-549-2500; www .aclu.org. Advocacy group working to preserve legal and constitutional individual rights.

Anti-Defamation League (ADL), 605 Third Ave., New York, NY 10158; 212-885-7700; www.adl.org. National civil rights organization combating bigotry.

Brennan Center for Justice, 161 Avenue of the Americas, 12th Floor, New York, NY 10013; 646-292-8310; www .brennancenter.org. Law and policy institute at New York University School of Law.

Federal Bureau of Investigation, 935 Pennsylvania Ave., N.W., Washington, DC 20535; 202-324-3000; www.fbi .gov. National security and law enforcement agency.

Life After Hate, 917 W. Washington Blvd., Suite 212, Chicago, IL 60607; lifeafterhate.org. Nonprofit helping individuals wishing to leave far-right extremist movements.

National Consortium for the Study of Terrorism and Responses to Terrorism (START), 8400 Baltimore Ave., Suite 250, College Park, MD 20740; 301-405-6600; www .start.umd.edu. Research group that is part of the University of Maryland and that maintains terrorism databases.

Southern Poverty Law Center (SPLC), 400 Washington Ave., Montgomery, AL 36104; 334-956-8200; www.splc .org. Advocacy group fighting hate and bigotry.

U.S. Department of Homeland Security, Washington, DC 20528; 202-282-8000; www.dhs.gov. Government agency charged with keeping America safe.

3

Modernizing the Nuclear Arsenal

William Wanlund

An unarmed Minuteman III intercontinental ballistic missile — capable of delivering an atomic warhead to Russia — is test launched at Vandenberg Air Force Base, Calif. Among the nine nations with nuclear weapons, the United States and Russia, each with about 7,000 warheads, hold approximately 93 percent of the total.

From *CQ Researcher*, July 29, 2016

The B61-12 nuclear bomb is a battlefield commander's dream — and an anti-war activist's nightmare.

The most flexible and most accurate nuclear weapon in the U.S. arsenal, it allows the military to increase the bomb's strength to the equivalent of 50,000 tons of TNT, or lower it to 300 tons. (In comparison, the largest bomb in America's arsenal has a yield equivalent to 1.2 million tons.)*

This "dial-a-yield" capability means that when the B61-12 is operational — it is undergoing testing and scheduled to enter production in 2020 — commanders can use it at its lower setting to largely confine damage to a battlefield. At a higher setting, they can use the bomb to wipe out an industrial complex or even a city.[1]

But it is those attributes of accuracy and flexibility that worry disarmament advocates, who say the bomb's versatility makes it tempting to use and thus more dangerous because the risk of collateral damage to property and of killing noncombatants is lower than with larger, less accurate bombs. Hans Kristensen, director of the Nuclear Information Program of the Federation of American Scientists, said, "It's more likely that a military commander will go to the president with this weapon and say, 'Mr. President, all our other options are out of the question, but we have a good one here that doesn't pollute [the atmosphere with radiation] a whole lot.' "

---

* The atomic bombs dropped on Hiroshima and Nagasaki, Japan, ending World War II delivered the equivalent of 15,000 and 21,000 tons of TNT, respectively.

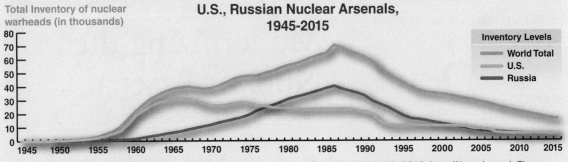

U.S., Russian Nuclear Stockpiles Decline

The world's nine nuclear powers hold about 15,350 warheads, down from a peak of 70,300 in 1986. After the end of the Cold War in 1991, when the Soviet Union imploded, the United States and Russia drastically cut their nuclear stockpiles. France and the United Kingdom have reduced theirs as well, but the other nuclear powers have held steady. The overall pace of reduction has slowed in recent years because of regional rivalries and other factors.

Total Inventory of nuclear warheads (in thousands)

U.S., Russian Nuclear Arsenals, 1945-2015

Inventory Levels
— World Total
— U.S.
— Russia

Source: "Status of World Nuclear Forces," Federation of American Scientists, May 26, 2016, http://tinyurl.com/q7lxnzn

Such a scenario, some argue, could cause a low-level conflict to escalate into a nuclear war.[2] The $8 billion B61-12 program is part of an ambitious, potentially 30-year Obama administration plan to spend up to $1 trillion to operate, maintain and modernize the nation's nuclear warheads as well as the planes, missiles and submarines that deliver them.[3] Modernization supporters say America's aging nuclear arsenal puts the country at risk from aggressive adversaries such as Russia, which also is modernizing its weapons systems, China — the world's No. 4 nuclear power — and North Korea, which is developing and testing nuclear weapons in defiance of global condemnation.

"We are fast approaching the point where [failing to modernize aging nuclear weaponry] will put at risk our . . . nuclear deterrent," Adm. Cecil Haney, who as commander of the U.S. Strategic Command is responsible for the military's nuclear forces, said in January.[4]

But those who oppose the plan say it will lead to a more dangerous world, is irrelevant to the threats facing the country and exacerbates an already dangerous arms race with Russia and perhaps China.

Kingston Reif, director for disarmament and threat reduction policy at the pro-disarmament Arms Control Association, called the modernization plan "overly ambitious and excessively expensive" and said the administration should look for other ways to reshape the nation's nuclear arsenal.[5]

Critics also express disappointment at Obama's apparent policy reversal. Shortly after becoming president, he vowed in a 2009 speech in Prague, Czech Republic, to "seek the peace and security of a world without nuclear weapons."[6] Now, with only months left in his second term, "Obama is on course to leave a legacy that boosts, not busts, America's nuclear arsenal," said Tom Collina, policy director of the Ploughshares Fund, which develops and finances projects that promote reduction and elimination of nuclear weapons.[7]

Advocates of modernization point out that Obama also declared in Prague that as long as other nations have nuclear weapons, "the United States will maintain a safe, secure and effective arsenal to deter any adversary, and guarantee that defense to our allies."

Michaela Dodge, a policy analyst specializing in nuclear issues at the conservative Heritage Foundation think tank in Washington, says it would be "ludicrous" for the United States not to modernize its nuclear arsenal. She says the nation's land, air and sea "triad" — its missiles, bombers and submarines used to deliver nuclear weapons — is too old to be reliable or safe.

For example, she and other modernization proponents point out, the B-52 bomber, the nation's principal aircraft in a nuclear attack, entered service in 1954. The 12 Ohio class nuclear missile-equipped submarines, which carry about half of U.S. nuclear warheads, will begin reaching the end of their 42-year service lives in 2027.[8] The nation's nuclear infrastructure is so outdated, critics say, that computers that would receive a presidential order to launch Minuteman 3 intercontinental nuclear ballistic missiles (ICBMs), rely on data stored on 8-inch floppy discs.[9]

"We have spent almost nothing [on nuclear arms] since the end of the Cold War," says Brad Roberts, a former Defense Department official who is director of the Center for Global Security Research at the Lawrence Livermore National Laboratory, a federal research facility in Livermore, Calif.

These nuclear proponents also say the United States must modernize to keep pace with other nations. The Federation of American Scientists (FAS), which tracks the world's nuclear forces, estimates the world's nine nuclear powers possess 15,350 warheads.* That is down from 70,300 in the peak year of 1986 but still big enough to destroy much of the planet.

Despite the sharp drop, "All the nuclear weapon states continue to modernize their remaining nuclear forces and appear committed to retaining nuclear weapons for the indefinite future," according to Kristensen and Robert S. Norris, a senior fellow for nuclear policy at FAS.[10]

North Korea has test-detonated four nuclear devices and its government has declared it is developing ballistic missiles capable of carrying nuclear warheads to the continental United States.[11] India and Pakistan, neighbors with a history of violent border clashes, have an estimated 120 nuclear weapons apiece, and Pakistan is expected to double its arsenal in the next 10 years, according to a 2015 report in the *Bulletin of the Atomic Scientists*.[12] And China, which has maintained a relatively small arsenal — roughly

260 warheads — has developed a multiple-warhead missile capable of reaching the United States and is expanding its missile-carrying submarine fleet.[13]

The United States and Russia, each with about 7,000 warheads, hold approximately 93 percent of the world's nuclear arms, according to FAS. This equilibrium puts the two nations in a state of "mutual vulnerability," according to the Carnegie Endowment for International Peace, a Washington think tank that promotes peaceful resolutions to international conflicts. "Put simply, both sides have the power to wreak unprecedented destruction on the other through the employment of nuclear weapons even in the face of a determined effort by the other to preempt or defend against it."[14]

The United States and Russia retain their nuclear weapons to keep each other at bay and protect their economic and political interests and those of their allies. The tensions that characterized relations between the two countries during the Cold War lessened considerably after the 1991 breakup of the Soviet Union, thanks largely to arms control treaties and agreements that have reduced arsenals and improved transparency. However, Russian officials say they are modernizing their arsenal partly to counter NATO's installation of anti-ballistic missile (ABM) systems in Eastern Europe. NATO has said the systems are to defend against attacks on Europe from adversaries in the Middle East; Russia disputes that claim, saying the ABMs are intended to counter Russia's nuclear missiles.

Some experts consider a nuclear strike involving the major nuclear powers unlikely. Steven Pifer, a former U.S. ambassador to Ukraine who is now director of the Arms Control and Non-Proliferation Initiative at the Brookings Institution, a Washington think tank, says a nuclear exchange between Russia and the United States, "while not a zero probability, is still way smaller than during the Cold War."

But Keith B. Payne, co-founder and CEO of the National Institute for Public Policy, which analyzes defense and foreign policy issues, says the United States would be mistaken to minimize the threat from modern Russia. "If a threat is measured by probability times consequences," he says, "you can't avoid the conclusion that nuclear conflict between the U.S. and Russia is the greatest threat."

---

* The nine countries with nuclear weapons, listed in the order of the size of their arsenals, are Russia, the United States, France, China, the United Kingdom, Pakistan, India, Israel and North Korea. (Israel has never acknowledged that it has nuclear weapons. North Korea reportedly has enough material to build warheads but it is not clear if it has done so.)

Russia and U.S. Dominate the Nuclear Club

With a combined arsenal of more than 14,000 warheads, Russia and the United States possess approximately 93 percent of the world's nuclear weapons. Of the nine nuclear powers, Russia, the United States and the United Kingdom are slowly reducing their arsenals while China, Pakistan and India are increasing theirs. France and Israel are holding steady. North Korea reportedly has enough nuclear material to build 10 to 12 warheads, but it is unclear whether it has done so.

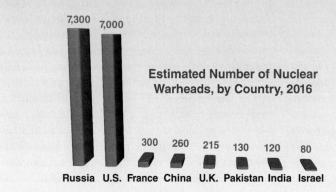

Estimated Number of Nuclear Warheads, by Country, 2016

Russia	U.S.	France	China	U.K.	Pakistan	India	Israel
7,300	7,000	300	260	215	130	120	80

Source: "Status of World Nuclear Forces 2016," Federation of American Scientists, May 26, 2016, http://tinyurl.com/q7lxnzn

Experts also are unsure about the potential for terrorist organizations, such as the self-described Islamic State (ISIS), to obtain and use nuclear materials. "[W]e don't have any publicly available evidence that [ISIS is] pursuing a nuclear weapon," said Matthew Bunn, a professor of practice at Harvard University's Kennedy School of Government who researches nuclear theft and terrorism. "But they have an apocalyptic ideology that calls for a final total war between Islam and the so-called crusader forces, which of course refers to the West and the United States in particular. . . . If [ISIS] did turn toward nuclear weapons, they have more money, more people, more territory under their control, and more ability to recruit globally than al Qaida ever had."[15]

Because of the sophisticated technology needed to manufacture a nuclear weapon, some experts believe terrorists are more likely to detonate "dirty bombs" than nuclear explosives. Dirty bombs are portable devices that detonate conventional explosives to disperse radioactive material stolen from places that use radiological equipment, such as atomic power plants,

hospitals or other civilian facilities. Their potency depends on the size of the explosive and the amount and type of radioactive material; a small dirty bomb could be carried in a suitcase or backpack.[16]

As military officials, foreign-policy experts, disarmament advocates and supporters of modernizing the nuclear arsenal consider the nuclear-weapons outlook, here are some of the questions they are debating:

Are U.S. ballistic missile defenses in Europe hampering arms control?

In May, a U.S. anti-ballistic missile (ABM) defense system to be operated by NATO began operations at an air base in the southern Romanian village of Deveselu. The Aegis Ashore system uses radar to detect and destroy enemy missiles.[17] But a dispute over the stationing of the ABMs has raised tensions between the United States and Russia and may stymie future arms control negotiations, experts say.

The Deveselu installation is NATO's first land-based ABM system in Europe. Until now, four U.S. ships based in Rota, Spain, have been equipped to identify and intercept enemy missiles, aided by a U.S. command-and-control center at Ramstein Air Base in Germany and a radar station in Turkey.[18] A second Europe-based ABM missile battery, similar to that in Deveselu, is under construction in Redzikowo, Poland, and scheduled to be operational in 2018.[19]

The new elements form what the Obama administration calls the European Phased Adaptive Approach (EPAA), which will permit detection and interception of hostile ballistic missile attacks on America's European allies.[20]

The United States said the EPAA system is intended to defend America's NATO allies from short- and medium-range missile attacks by Iran or other "rogue states" or terrorist groups in the Middle East.

But Russian President Vladimir Putin isn't buying that explanation, saying that a 2015 agreement between

Iran and six major powers preventing Iran from developing nuclear weapons has eliminated any Iranian nuclear threat. The defense system's real objective, he contended, is to neutralize Russia's missiles. That, Putin said, would leave Russia without its most important deterrent force, and unable to retaliate against an enemy's first strike.[21]

Another Russian concern is that the ABM systems might also harbor offensive weapons. Foreign Ministry spokeswoman Maria Zakharova said that the Aegis Ashore launchpad was "practically identical" to a system used aboard Aegis warships that can fire Tomahawk cruise missiles. U.S. officials said the Romanian base has no Tomahawks.[22]

The United States also denies that the system is intended to counter a Russian threat. Deputy Secretary of Defense Bob Work, speaking at the inauguration of the Deveselu site, said, "This site, nor the site in Poland, has any capability — none whatsoever — to undermine Russia's strategic deterrent. It is a defensive system."[23]

But Alexei Arbatov, director of the Center for International Security at the Russian Academy of Sciences in Moscow, says Russia simply doesn't trust the United States. Russia believes "there is no reason for that defense to be deployed in Europe, and if it is deployed in Europe, its assigned mission must be against Russia, to undercut Russian strategic deterrence, which is the central pillar of Russian defense and security," Arbatov says.

Putin said Russia could retaliate against Romania and Poland for hosting the NATO ABM facilities, although he did not specify what actions Russia might take.[24]

In March 2013, hoping to overcome Russian resistance to future arms control negotiations, Obama canceled an upgrade to the EPAA system, scheduled to begin in 2022, which Russia suspected would have allowed the missiles to also target Russia's longer-range intercontinental missiles — those capable of reaching the United States.[25]

Russia's initial reaction to the cancellation was cautious. A week after it was announced, Deputy Foreign Minister Sergey Ryabkov said, "There is no unequivocal answer yet to the question of what consequences all this can have for our security. The causes for concern have not been removed, but dialogue . . . is in our interest, and we welcome the fact that the American side also, it appears, wants to continue this dialogue."[26]

A Russian Yars RS-24 intercontinental ballistic missile system rolls through Moscow on May 9, 2016, during the 71st anniversary of the Soviet Union's victory over Nazi Germany in World War II. Cold War nuclear tension between Russia and the United States eased after the 1991 breakup of the Soviet Union, thanks largely to arms control treaties. Today, however, Russian officials say they are modernizing their arsenal partly to counter NATO's installation of anti-ballistic missile (ABM) systems in Eastern Europe.

So far, however, there are no signs that Russia is now more amenable to seeking new agreements.

A 2015 study by Jaganath Sankaran, a researcher at the Center for International and Security Studies at the University of Maryland, concluded that canceling the upgrade "has opened a window for the United States and Russia to come together on additional bilateral nuclear arms reduction measures and missile defense cooperation."

"The restructured EPAA system does not pose a threat to Russian ICBMs," Sankaran wrote. "The interceptors at Deveselu are not capable of reaching Russian ICBMs," nor, under realistic conditions, are those based at Redzikowo, because the interceptors' reaction time would be too great.[27]

The interceptors, Pifer of Brookings explains, would struggle to catch up to the Russian missiles. That's because the ICBM would have a head start, he says. "You have to watch and track the missile for the first couple of minutes of flight to understand where it's going before you launch the interceptor. Most people use the analogy that the interceptor just runs out of gas — it can't catch up."

Heather Williams, a MacArthur postdoctoral fellow who researches nuclear weapons policy at the Centre for

Science and Security Studies at King's College London, says while future talks with Russia may be possible, "right now, there doesn't seem to be a chance for arms control negotiations," with the impasse over ballistic missile defense a chief obstacle.

"Russia's biggest concern is in balance, in strategic stability," she says. "For quite a while the Russians have been saying that a combination of things has been upsetting strategic stability as they see it, and No. 1 is U.S. missile defenses in Eastern Europe. Meanwhile, the U.S. really wants reductions in Russian tactical [short-range battlefield] nukes," which could pose a threat to America's NATO allies.

"We're stuck, because both sides want very different things," Williams says.

Do terrorists pose a nuclear threat?

World leaders including Obama, Putin and United Nations Secretary-General Ban Ki-moon have all called nuclear terrorism one of the greatest dangers facing the world.

The threat is real, said a report in March by Harvard University's Belfer Center for Science and International Affairs: "At least two terrorist groups — al Qaeda and [in the 1990s] the Japanese terror cult Aum Shinrikyo — have made serious efforts to get nuclear weapons, and there is suggestive evidence of Chechen terrorist interest as well," the report said. "Al Qaeda had a focused nuclear weapons program and repeatedly attempted to buy stolen nuclear bomb material and recruit nuclear expertise."[28]

European investigators reinforced these fears earlier this year when they found evidence that ISIS-connected terrorists responsible for suicide bombings in Brussels on March 22 had secretly videotaped the residence of a Belgian nuclear scientist. "The terrorist cell . . . naively believed they could use him to penetrate a lab to obtain nuclear material to make a dirty bomb," according to a French nuclear security expert.[29] It was also reported that Salah Abdeslam, a suspect in the Nov. 13, 2015, terrorist attacks in Paris, had hidden documents pertaining to Germany's Jülich Nuclear Research Center, where nuclear waste is stored, in his Brussels apartment.[30] Belgian federal investigators said they found evidence linking Abdeslam to ISIS.[31]

The Belfer report described the three forms nuclear terrorism could take:

- Detonation of a nuclear bomb, either acquired from a state's arsenal or improvised from stolen weapons-usable nuclear material (most difficult to accomplish but by far the most devastating).
- Use of a "dirty bomb" to spread radioactive material and create panic and disruption (least difficult and lethal, "but could impose billions of dollars in economic disruption and cleanup costs," according to Belfer).
- Sabotage of a nuclear facility causing a large release of radioactivity (somewhere between the other two in difficulty and lethality).[32]

Many nuclear experts largely discount the possibility of terrorists building a nuclear bomb because the necessary materials are difficult to obtain and dangerous to handle. "Terrorists don't have access to highly enriched uranium or plutonium, the key components of a nuclear weapon," Pifer says.

Similarly, illicitly obtaining a so-called loose nuke from a country's stockpile is also difficult to accomplish. However, the possibility of ready-to-use nuclear weapons falling into terrorists' hands came into sharp relief in July 2016 when a violent though short-lived coup attempt in Turkey temporarily left in question control of the Incirlik air base, home to an estimated 50 hydrogen bombs — NATO's largest nuclear stockpile.[33] A modern hydrogen bomb is hundreds of times more destructive than the two atomic bombs dropped on Japan in World War II.

Incirlik is just 68 miles from Turkey's border with Syria, where terrorist groups are participating in that country's civil war. Turkey also is battling Kurdish militants, adding to the precariousness of the security situation, Kristensen of the Federation of American Scientists said, noting that in 2015 the U.S. Air Force initiated security upgrades at Incirlik and at the nuclear facility at Italy's Aviano air base to improve protection for the estimated 50 weapons stored there. The need for the upgrades indicates that "nuclear weapons deployed in Europe have been stored under unsafe conditions for more than two decades," Kristensen said, and calls into question the security for weapons stored at bases in Belgium, Germany and the Netherlands.[34]

Kelsey Davenport, director for nonproliferation policy at the Arms Control Association, worries more about a dirty bomb. "The material that could be used for a dirty bomb is widely available," Davenport says. For example, "hospitals have a lot of radioactive isotopes that are used against cancer and other diseases and which are produced from weapons-usable materials that could be stolen, concealed in a truck or van and detonated in a populated area."

And such materials sometimes go missing. A database maintained by the Vienna-based International Atomic Energy Agency (IAEA) of the United Nations reported 2,889 confirmed incidents of illicit trafficking in nuclear and other radioactive material between 1993 and 2015. Most of the incidents involved small quantities, the agency said, although "a small number of these incidents involved seizures of kilogram quantities of potentially weapons-usable nuclear material."[35]

"As you do research into these illicit incidents, you find it was always small quantities," says Rafael Mariano Grossi, Argentina's ambassador to the IAEA. "One reason is that buyers don't know how much they need [to make a dirty bomb]; in other cases it's buyers going to a bar in Chișinău [in Moldova] or Moscow and asking, 'Where can I buy some uranium?' "

"We should be concerned about nuclear terrorism, but the immediacy, or the urgency, is very difficult to assess," Grossi says. "Who would have expected 9/11? It's much better to err on the side of caution and to be prepared."

Others, while acknowledging the existence of a terrorist nuclear threat, feel it less keenly. "I know I should worry about [nuclear terrorism]; a lot of money's been spent on [preventing] it, and it would be a really, really bad thing if someone got a weapon and somehow detonated it in a populated area," says George Perkovich, vice president for studies at the Carnegie Endowment for International Peace. "But it's not going to end civilization;

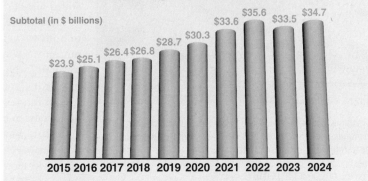

U.S. to Spend $348 Billion on Nuclear Forces

The cost to maintain, operate and modernize the nation's nuclear arsenal will run an estimated $348 billion over the next decade. The projected cost includes upgrading or replacing warheads as well as the airplanes, submarines and missiles that carry them.

Projected Costs of Operating, Modernizing U.S. Nuclear Forces

Subtotal (in $ billions)

2015	2016	2017	2018	2019	2020	2021	2022	2023	2024
$23.9	$25.1	$26.4	$26.8	$28.7	$30.3	$33.6	$35.6	$33.5	$34.7

Source: "Projected Costs of U.S. Nuclear Forces, 2015 to 2024," Congressional Budget Office, January 2015, http://tinyurl.com/z9yjadd

it's not going to be the kind of cataclysm that changes the global environment."

Is U.S. spending to modernize its nuclear arsenal warranted?

The price tag of the Obama administration's modernization plan varies depending on how costs are calculated. According to the Congressional Budget Office (CBO), the United States is proposing to spend $348 billion between 2015 and 2024 to operate, maintain and upgrade its nuclear force, including replacing the planes, submarines and missiles that carry the weapons. The CBO estimates the total will amount to 5 to 6 percent of the national defense budget.[36]

But the James Martin Center for Nonproliferation Studies in Monterey, Calif., looked at a longer time frame, projecting the total cost over 30 years at $872 billion to $1.1 trillion.[37]

Regardless of which estimate is accurate, Roberts of Lawrence Livermore National Laboratory acknowledges that "the raw investments, the dollar investments, are huge," although he adds, "I invite you to be wary of these numbers. They depend on big assumptions on how

Hiroshima, Japan, lies devastated after the United States dropped an atomic bomb on the city of 300,000 on Aug. 6, 1945. When Japan refused to surrender, ending World War II, the U.S. dropped a second atomic bomb, on Nagasaki. The death toll in Hiroshima was 200,000, and 140,000 in Nagasaki.

long one thinks it will take and how much inflation there might be."

Proponents of modernization say the costs should be put in perspective. Retired Lt. Gen. James Kowalski, who was deputy commander of U.S. Strategic Command, said that even the higher estimate represents less than 0.3 percent of gross domestic product (GDP), a measure of national output. "At the end of the day we're talking about something that is foundational to the national security of our country," he said.[38]

Katherine Blakeley, a research fellow at the Center for Strategic and Budgetary Assessments, says costs are so high partly because the bill is coming due for years of neglect. "After a decline in [nuclear weapons] spending in the 1990s and early 2000s," she says, "you are seeing the beginning of a rise now, partly because a lot of these systems that were fielded in the 1970s and '80s are reaching end-of-life, and the recapitalization costs are all bunched into one narrow time frame."

Pifer of Brookings argues that the United States must spend money to keep pace with Russia, which is buying new missile-launching submarines and upgrading its ballistic missiles and nuclear bombers. Although Russia traditionally does not make the details of its defense expenditures public, in 2011 Russia's first deputy minister

of defense, Vladimir Popovkin, said his country planned to spend about $70 billion — 10 percent of the military budget — between 2011 and 2020 to modernize its strategic nuclear triad.[39]

But other analysts believe the Pentagon is asking for more than it needs and that the necessary modernization can be done more cheaply, for example by building fewer replacement submarines or eliminating a class of nuclear-armed missiles.

Some think the high cost will doom the modernization plans. "The military knows they can't modernize nuclear weapons and also modernize their conventional weapons," says Joseph Cirincione, Ploughshares Fund president. "You reach a tipping point where you can't sustain funding the nuclear enterprise, and the whole thing starts to tumble."

In 2015 Sen. Ed Markey, D-Mass., introduced legislation that would significantly reduce U.S. spending on nuclear weapons. Markey said the bill, called the Smarter Approach to Nuclear Expenditures (SANE) Act, would cut $100 billion from the nuclear weapons budget over the next 10 years by reducing the numbers of current and replacement submarines, canceling construction of nuclear weapons processing facilities and other measures. The legislation has three co-sponsors — Democrats Al Franken of Minnesota and Jeff Merkley of Oregon and independent Bernie Sanders of Vermont. Rep. Earl Blumenauer, D-Ore., introduced companion legislation in the House. The independent legislative tracking service GovTrack.us gives the legislation no chance of passing.[40]

A Center for Strategic and Budgetary Assessments report said applying the most frequently proposed cost-cutting measures "would substantially reduce U.S. nuclear forces, with significant [negative] near-term and long-term strategic consequences" while saving only $106 billion by 2030, which one expert called "small potatoes."[41]

Davenport of the Arms Control Association says the cost of maintaining an up-to-date nuclear arsenal should be measured in more than dollars. "We've moved away from the fundamental question of whether or not we'd actually be willing to use a nuclear weapon, and whether it actually provides the deterrence and the security we think it does," she says.

"And is that value, weighed against the risk posed by theft, sabotage or accidental use, and the cost of maintaining these arsenals, worth modernizing and deploying these weapons? I think we've lost the greater understanding of the risks posed by obtaining these weapons."

BACKGROUND

"Most Terrible Bomb"

In a letter dated Aug. 2, 1939, physicist Albert Einstein wrote to President Franklin D. Roosevelt, warning that scientists in Nazi Germany were working to develop "extremely powerful bombs" using "a nuclear chain reaction in a large mass of uranium." Einstein had fled Europe to escape Nazism and feared the consequences if Germany developed a nuclear bomb first.

"A single bomb of this type," Einstein wrote, "carried by boat and exploded in a port, might very well destroy the whole port together with some of the surrounding territory." He urged Roosevelt to support uranium research at U.S. universities.[42]

Eight days after receiving the letter, Roosevelt replied to Einstein that he had created a military-civilian board "to thoroughly investigate the possibilities of your suggestion regarding the element of uranium."[43]

Meanwhile, French and British scientists also had been conducting research; a British report in July 1941 concluded that uranium could be used to produce a powerful explosive.[44]

With France falling under Nazi occupation in 1940 and Great Britain unable to commit resources to full-fledged nuclear weapons research, it fell to the United States to pursue it. Roosevelt approved government involvement on Jan. 19, 1942. The effort, then headquartered in New York City, received the code name "Manhattan Project."[45]

A nuclear bomb requires fissile material "composed of atoms that can be split by neutrons in a self-sustaining chain-reaction to release enormous amounts of energy" to produce the nuclear chain reaction required for a bomb, according to the Institute for Energy and Environmental Research, an environmental advocacy organization.[46]

Manhattan Project researchers, based in Los Alamos, N.M., aimed to develop a bomb by the first half of 1945.[47]

(As it happened, while German scientists had begun nuclear experiments in 1939, developing a bomb hadn't

been a Nazi priority. "Germany . . . made other choices and simply ran out of time," said Mark Walker, who teaches modern German history at Union College in Schenectady, N.Y.[48])

Roosevelt died on April 12, 1945. His successor, Vice President Harry S. Truman, knew little about the Manhattan Project until he was briefed on April 25. The bomb was tested July 16, 1945, in the New Mexico desert, exploding with a force equivalent to about 20 kilotons (20,000 tons, or 20 KT) of TNT.

Germany had surrendered on May 7, so Truman had to decide whether to use the new weapon against Japan. On July 25 he wrote in his diary, "We have discovered the most terrible bomb in the history of the world." But he added, "it can be made the most useful."[49]

Truman decided using it could end the war sooner and avoid risking the lives of hundreds of thousands of U.S. servicemen in an invasion of Japan.[50] On Aug. 6 an American plane dropped a 15 KT atomic bomb on Hiroshima, a military and communications center with a population of about 300,000. Three days later, Nagasaki, home to a Mitsubishi munitions factory and a population of 240,000, was hit with a 21 KT bomb. Japan surrendered Aug. 14.[51]

In his July 25 diary entry, Truman wrote he had "told the secretary of war, Mr. Stimson, to use [the bomb] so that military objectives and soldiers and sailors are the target and not women and children."[52]

Even so, the Hiroshima bomb killed 70,000 civilians outright; five years later, deaths from radiation poisoning had brought the number killed to 200,000. Nagasaki's bomb killed 40,000 immediately, and the final death toll reached 140,000.

Arms Race Begins

The United Nations, founded in late 1945, unanimously passed its first resolution on Jan. 24, 1946: to establish a U.N. Atomic Energy Commission "to deal with the problems raised by the discovery of atomic energy and other related matters."[53]

Six months later, U.S. Ambassador to the U.N. Bernard Baruch proposed to the commission that nuclear-related scientific information be shared among nations; that atomic energy be used only for peaceful purposes; that all nuclear weapons be eliminated and that inspections be carried out to ensure compliance.[54]

CHRONOLOGY

1930s-1940s *The atomic bomb is born.*

1939 With World War II imminent, U.S. physicist Albert Einstein alerts President Franklin D. Roosevelt that Germany could develop an atomic bomb.

1942 Roosevelt establishes Manhattan Project to develop an atomic bomb.

1945 President Harry S. Truman orders atomic bombs dropped on Japan, ending World War II.

1946 United Nations establishes a commission to deal with dangers posed by nuclear weapons.

1949 Soviet Union detonates atomic bomb, ending U.S. nuclear monopoly.

1950s-1960s *Cold War intensifies arms race.*

1952 U.S. tests hydrogen bomb at Eniwetak Atoll in the Pacific. . . . Britain tests atomic bomb.

1955 Soviet Union tests hydrogen bomb.

1958 Soviet Union, Britain and the United States suspend nuclear testing.

1960 France tests an atomic bomb.

1961 American, British and Soviet testing resumes after negotiations for a permanent ban fail. . . . Soviets test a 50-megaton hydrogen bomb, the most powerful weapon in history.

1962 U.S. discovers Soviet missiles in Cuba; the resulting confrontation threatens to escalate to nuclear war before a compromise is found.

1963 U.S., Britain and Soviet Union sign Limited Test Ban Treaty, the first major nuclear arms control agreement.

1964 China tests an atomic bomb, becoming the world's fifth nuclear power.

1970s *New nuclear treaties take effect.*

1970 Nuclear Non-Proliferation Treaty pledges U.S., Soviet Union, United Kingdom, France and China to prevent the spread of nuclear weapons.

1972 U.S. and Soviet Union sign Strategic Arms Limitation Treaty (SALT) and Anti-Ballistic Missile (ABM) Treaty.

1974 India tests a nuclear bomb.

1979 President Jimmy Carter and Soviet President Leonid Brezhnev sign SALT II, limiting the number of multiple-warhead missiles; the treaty never enters into force, but both countries agree to abide by its terms.

1980s-1990s *More nations acquire nuclear weapons.*

1986 Global inventory of nuclear weapons peaks at 70,300.

1987 U.S. and Soviet Union ban medium-range missiles.

1991 Strategic Arms Reduction Treaty (START) makes deep cuts in longer-range missiles. . . . Soviet Union collapses, ending the Cold War.

1998 India and Pakistan declare themselves nuclear powers.

2000s-2016 *North Korea becomes nuclear power.*

2002 U.S. withdraws from ABM Treaty.

2004 Russian President Vladimir Putin authorizes modernization of his country's Cold War-era nuclear arsenal.

2006 North Korea explodes a nuclear device.

2013 Obama administration announces a sweeping modernization of the U.S. nuclear arsenal, potentially costing up to $1 trillion by 2050.

2015 Iran promises to limit its nuclear program; critics doubt Iran's sincerity.

2016 In its fourth nuclear test since 2006, North Korea detonates what it calls a hydrogen bomb; outside observers dispute the claim.

However, under Baruch's proposal the United States would retain its nuclear capability until it was certain the Soviet Union would not be able to develop its own nuclear weapons. The Soviets objected.

Instrumental in formulating the Baruch plan were two wartime U.S. government officials, Vannevar Bush, director of the Office of Scientific Research and Development, which directed national science and technology policy, and James Conant, chairman of the National Defense Research Committee. They had written to Secretary of War Henry Stimson in 1944, calling it "the height of folly" to assume the United States and Great Britain could retain global nuclear superiority.[55] They also warned of possible espionage and a coming arms race.

Bush and Conant proved prophetic: Among British scientists sent to the United States to collaborate on the Manhattan Project was Klaus Fuchs, a German-born physicist, naturalized British citizen and Soviet spy. He began passing nuclear secrets to the USSR soon after his arrival in the United States — including a detailed drawing of "Fat Man," as the Nagasaki bomb had been nicknamed.[56]

On Aug. 29, 1949, the Soviets detonated their first atomic bomb — a 22 KT near-replica of Fat Man — breaking the U.S. monopoly on nuclear weapons.[57]

The United States and the Soviet Union, allies during World War II, had become Cold War rivals. When the Soviets acquired a nuclear weapon, the United States embarked on a crash program to develop a more powerful device, the hydrogen bomb, in order to retain its nuclear advantage. The United States tested the first hydrogen bomb — a 14.8 megaton (MT) weapon 700 times more powerful than the atomic bomb used on Hiroshima — on Nov. 1, 1952, on Eniwetak Atoll in the central Pacific.

Eniwetak was uninhabited, but people living hundreds of miles away soon registered signs of radiation poisoning, although no deaths of these islanders were attributed to the explosion.[58]

Between 1946 and 1958, the United States conducted 67 nuclear tests in the Marshall Islands — 23 on Bikini Atoll and 44 on or near Eniwetak. When the harmful health and environmental effects of the testing became known, the U.S. government established a program to compensate affected islanders, paying them $531 million between 1958 and 2004.[59]

The Soviet Union tested its first hydrogen bomb on Nov. 22, 1955, having developed it with information obtained by Fuchs before his arrest and conviction in Britain for espionage in 1950.[60]

Fears and Hopes

In 1953, in a speech to the U.N. General Assembly, President Dwight D. Eisenhower warned of the consequences of a developing arms race and suggested nuclear power instead be used to "serve the peaceful pursuits of mankind." The address became known as the "Atoms for Peace" speech.[61]

Eventually, the United States created its own Atoms for Peace program, allowing nuclear technology and material to be exported to other nations if they were not used for "atomic weapon design, development or fabrication capability."[62]

Still, planning for a possible nuclear war continued and testing accelerated: Between 1953 and 1958, the three nuclear powers (Britain had tested its first atomic bomb in 1952) conducted 231 tests, prompting growing international concern over health hazards posed by fallout. In March 1958, under growing worldwide pressure to end testing, the Soviet Union announced it was suspending its nuclear tests; the United States and Britain followed suit in August. The three countries began test ban negotiations in Geneva, Switzerland, on Oct. 31.[63]

Meanwhile, France tested its first bomb in February 1960. Continued French testing and escalating Cold War tensions led the Soviets, and then the British and Americans, to resume testing in September 1961.[64]

The Geneva test ban talks ended in January 1962 without a treaty. Then, that October, an American spy plane discovered evidence of Soviet nuclear missile sites in Cuba, from which missiles could reach the United States within minutes. President John F. Kennedy ordered preparations for a nuclear counterattack against the Soviet Union.

The Soviet Union withdrew its missiles on Oct. 28, ending the crisis. For its part, the United States removed missiles based in Turkey which had threatened the Soviet Union and had been "a key reason for [Soviet Premier Nikita] Khrushchev's decision to send nuclear missiles to Cuba," according to historian Philip Nash.[65]

Advocates See a Nuclear Weapons-Free World

But opponents say elimination is unrealistic, even mistaken.

In the tense Cold War 1980s, recalls Joseph Cirincione, "we really thought we were on the brink of thermonuclear war." Cirincione had been a congressional staff member specializing in nuclear issues, but he gradually came over to the anti-nuclear weapons movement. Now president of the Ploughshares Fund, which seeks global elimination of nuclear weapons, he says, "The more I learned about some of these programs and strategy and doctrines, the crazier it seemed."

Derek Johnson, executive director of Global Zero, another anti-nuclear weapons organization, took a different route to the movement. An attorney, he worked for JUSTICE, the British section of the International Commission of Jurists, focusing on human rights and rule of law, before joining Global Zero.

"I'm not a nuclear security expert," Johnson says. "I was initially drawn to the organization because it was full of pragmatic idealists — people who had a vision and a clear plan to make it happen. It was a chance to work for a cutting-edge organization that had a real shot AT advancing big social change." Now, he says, "it's a job that became a calling."

Organized opposition to nuclear weapons is nearly as old as the atomic bomb. In November 1945, a group of scientists and engineers from the Manhattan Project, which had developed the bomb, organized into the Federation of Atomic Scientists (renamed the Federation of American Scientists three months later) to promote disarmament. They worried about nuclear weapons' potential health and environmental risks.[1]

Testing of increasingly powerful nuclear bombs in the 1950s and '60s led to global protests. In the United States, the National Committee for a Sane Nuclear Policy (SANE), founded in 1957, and Womens Strike for Peace, established in 1961, were among early "ban the bomb" organizations.[2]

Some countries, and even some towns and cities, have taken it upon themselves to oppose nuclear weapons and their risks. Eighty-nine nations, including leading economies such as Australia, Brazil and Indonesia, have grouped themselves into five regional nuclear weapon-free zones [NWFZs], whose members have committed themselves not to manufacture, acquire, test or possess nuclear weapons. Taken together, four such NWFZs span the entire Southern Hemisphere.[3]

At least 130 U.S. communities — including Berkeley, Calif.; Takoma Park, Md., and Hoboken, N.J. — have declared themselves "nuclear-weapons free," largely seen as symbolic expressions of political attitude having little or no practical impact.[4]

The movement to eliminate nuclear weapons has some influential supporters. In 2007, four key members of the U.S. national security establishment during the Cold War — former secretaries of State George Shultz and Henry Kissinger, ex-Secretary of Defense William Perry, and former Senate Armed Services Committee Chairman Sam Nunn — formed the Nuclear Security Project, a program of the Nuclear Threat Initiative, to advance the cause of a nuclear weapons-free world."[5]

Johnson is optimistic about getting to a nuclear-free world. "Getting to (global) zero will require a multilateral

The Cuban missile crisis had brought the nuclear powers to the brink of war, convincing the two sides to begin negotiations to reduce the risk of a future conflict. The United States, Britain and Soviet Union reopened test ban negotiations on July 15, 1963, and quickly completed the Limited Test Ban Treaty, which banned all but underground nuclear testing.[66]

In 1964, China became the fifth country to test an atomic bomb, which led to the 1968 Treaty on the Non-Proliferation of Nuclear Weapons (known as the Non-Proliferation Treaty, or NPT) whose signatories pledged to prevent the spread of nuclear weapons beyond the five nations that already had them. Eventually, all U.N. member states except Israel, India and Pakistan signed the treaty. By 1998, all three of those non-signatories had developed and tested nuclear weapons.

In the 1970s the United States — under both GOP and Democratic administrations — negotiated treaties approach: nuclear-armed states acting in concert to proportionately phase out their arsenals, with rigorous verification every step of the way," he says, but adds "There are no insurmountable technical or financial barriers to achieving global zero. The barriers are political, and that's a problem we know how to solve."

Adds Cirincione, "We will get to a world without nukes. These are obsolete weapons that were an accident of history, and history has shown their disutility. We've lost tens of thousands of troops in some major wars in the last 70 years, and yet not once did the president think he had to use a nuclear weapon. We have some risks today, but they pale in comparison to the conflicts we've already fought without using nuclear weapons."

But Keith Payne, president of the National Institute for Public Policy in Fairfax, Va., which researches U.S. foreign and defense policies, thinks history offers a different lesson. "It's not clear to me that nuclear disarmament is a desirable goal now," says Payne, who is also head of the Graduate Department of Defense and Strategic Studies at Missouri State University. "Deterrence remains a key to preventing war. If you liked the first half of the 20th century, which saw something like 100 million deaths in just 12 years of combat, you'll love nuclear disarmament and the elimination of nuclear deterrence.

"Obviously there are dangers associated with maintaining nuclear weapons," Payne says. "But, unless you've instituted a new, cooperative world order that deals effectively with international conflict without the resort to war, the great danger is not having nuclear deterrence."

Michaela Dodge, a senior policy analyst at the Heritage Foundation, a conservative think tank in Washington, says eliminating all nuclear weapons is "unrealistic." "Countries are sovereign,' she says. "There will always be room for nations to pursue their own interests, and one of the most powerful guarantees of national interest, and survival as a state, is having nuclear weapons. There is no room for nuclear zero. And even if we could get rid of all nukes tomorrow, I'm not convinced that a world without them would be more peaceful than one with them."

But Valerie Plame, a Ploughshares board member and former CIA operative, sees global nuclear disarmament as a daunting but vital goal that would require political engagement by the emerging leadership generation — the "millennials" — who reached maturity during a period of relative nuclear tranquility. "How do we get people to understand that this is an existential threat, but that they can do something about it?" Plame says.

"The whole notion of nuclear weapons is so damn intimidating — it's easier just to recycle your garbage if you want to feel good about doing something for the planet," Plame says. "But how do we harness this generation coming up, which has no functional awareness of this existential threat, and put that pressure on politicians? There's a huge reservoir of passion, but we need to tap into it."

— *William Wanlund*

[1] "About FAS," Federation of American Scientists, https://fas.org/about-fas/.

[2] Lawrence S. Wittner, "Disarmament movement lessons from yesteryear," *Bulletin of the Atomic Scientists*, July 27, 2009, http://tinyurl.com/zcdkobh.

[3] "Nuclear-Weapon-Free Zones (NWFZ) At a Glance," fact sheet, Arms Control Association, Dec. 15, 2009, http://tinyurl.com/777pluh.

[4] Adeshina Emmanuel, "Sometimes Fiscal Urgency Tops Desire to be Nuclear Free, Cities Find," *The New York Times*, July 10, 2012, http://tinyurl.com/no2vqcb.

[5] "About NSP," Nuclear Security Project, http://tinyurl.com/hger4cp.

with the Soviet Union designed to reduce the number of nuclear weapons:

- Strategic Arms Limitation Treaty (SALT), limiting the number of nuclear missiles on each side (1972).
- Anti-Ballistic Missile (ABM) Treaty, limiting the Soviet Union and United States to two ABM complexes, each of which could have no more than 100 anti-ballistic missiles (1972).
- SALT II, limiting the number of multiple-warhead missiles; the treaty never entered into force, but both countries agreed to abide by its terms (1979).

Post–Cold War Challenges

On March 23, 1983, concerned that the United States could not protect itself against a Soviet attack, President Ronald Reagan announced the Strategic Defense

Does "Mutual Assured Destruction" Still Prevent Armageddon?

Some experts say the Cold War-era doctrine is outdated.

The doctrine of mutual assured destruction — or MAD — is fundamentally simple: If both sides have big enough nuclear arsenals to survive a first strike from an enemy and retaliate, then neither side will dare to attack at the risk of its own destruction.

The concept took root during the Cold War, when the Soviet Union successfully challenged American nuclear superiority. In a 1967 speech, then-Secretary of Defense Robert McNamara outlined the MAD concept, saying, "[W]e must be able to absorb the total weight of nuclear attack on our country. . . . Deterrence of nuclear aggression . . . means the certainty of suicide to the aggressor, not merely to his military forces, but to his society as a whole."[1]

Today, some experts believe MAD is irrelevant to the unorthodox threats the United States faces from terrorists and "rogue nations," in particular North Korea.

Others argue, however, that Russia — now overhauling the massive nuclear arsenal it inherited from the Soviet Union — remains a menace that can be kept in check only by a modern and reliable U.S. force.

When the Soviet Union dissolved in 1991 and the Cold War ended, the United States reassumed the nuclear dominance it lost in the 1970s to the Soviets, who had the world's biggest arsenal. In 1994, William Perry, secretary of Defense under President Bill Clinton, said America's nuclear strategy was no longer based on MAD. "We have coined a new word for our new posture, which we called mutual assured safety, or MAS," based on reduced arsenals and "improved safety and security for the residual force of nuclear weapons."[2]

But Steven Pifer, a senior fellow at the Brookings Institution, think tank that advises Washington policymakers, says elements of MAD remain. "The one country that poses an existential threat in terms of being able to destroy the United States is Russia, and how do we prevent that? By having the basis to form a strong nuclear capability, that the Russians would understand that if they tried to do something, the result would be the destruction of Russia."

Pifer continues, "I'd like to see more of a move toward MAS, where in a cooperative way you begin to reduce weapons, with greater transparency. But I think it's been derailed by the politics between Moscow and Washington over the last four years."

MAD isn't a one-size-fits-all doctrine, says Brad Roberts, director of the Center for Global Security

Initiative (SDI) to intercept incoming missiles.[67] The controversial plan, which included using space-based weapons, became known derisively as "Star Wars."

If developed, the SDI would have required the United States to withdraw from the ABM Treaty and upset the strategic balance between the United States and the Soviet Union. In any event, the required technology proved too complex and expensive. SDI was abandoned after Reagan left office in 1989, and his successors pursued less ambitious missile defense schemes.[68]

Despite efforts to halt the spread of nuclear weapons, the global inventory peaked in 1986 at 70,300 warheads, with the United States and Soviet Union together holding about 63,000 of them. Meeting in Reykjavik, Iceland, that year, Reagan and Soviet Premier Mikhail Gorbachev discussed eliminating all ballistic missiles, which travel outside the atmosphere before falling back to Earth, and eventually doing away with nuclear weapons altogether. The discussion foundered, mostly over language dealing with SDI.

However, the Reykjavik meeting led to the 1987 signing of the Intermediate-Range Nuclear Forces Treaty, banning nuclear missiles with a range between 300 to 3,400 miles, and laid the groundwork for the first Strategic Arms Reduction Treaty (START I) providing for deep reductions in missiles with a range of more than 3,400 miles.[69]

Research at the Lawrence Livermore National Laboratory. "It's been the policy of every administration since the Cold War to reject a relationship of mutual vulnerability or mutual assured destruction with countries like North Korea." That Asian nation, according to the Congressional Research Service, has at most a handful of nuclear weapons, and the United States maintains clear nuclear superiority over it.[3]

"We had to accept this relationship of MAD with the USSR during the Cold War. There was nothing we could do to escape it," Roberts says. "We accept it today as a matter of principle with Russia, but we reject it as a matter of national policy since the Cold War with states like North Korea."

For George Perkovich, vice president for studies at the Carnegie Endowment for International Peace, a Washington think tank that promotes peaceful resolutions to international conflicts, MAD isn't really a doctrine. Rather, he says, "it's a fact of life. It was stumbled upon as it became a fact.

"But ultimately, when you have an adversary that has a lot of capabilities and resources like the Russians, or now like China," which has the world's third-largest nuclear arsenal, after Russia and the United States, "you can't escape [MAD]," says Perkovich. "As long as the other side has a survivable nuclear force that can destroy some large fraction of your population, that's mutual deterrence."

Some defense policymakers say MAD's value is that it has worked. Despite the Cold War arms buildup and the global and regional tensions among nuclear powers today, no nation has used an atomic bomb since August 1945 when the United States dropped one on Nagasaki, Japan.

"[T]here is no doubt for 70 some years . . . that the United States has deterred great power war against nuclear-capable adversaries" by maintaining a sizable and modern deterrent force, said Adm. Cecil Haney, commander of the U.S. Strategic Command.[4]

Joseph Cirincione, president of the pro-disarmament Ploughshares Fund in Washington, has a different perspective. "Some argue that MAD is pragmatic and has prevented nuclear war, but you can't make the argument that it's just, that it's right, that we should actually launch a thermonuclear war," he says. "No sane person could walk through what it means to launch these weapons and say it's the right thing to do.

"The problem with MAD is, it works until it doesn't — and then it fails catastrophically. The consequences of the failure of this doctrine isn't that your country is invaded or a war starts; it's that civilization is destroyed."

— *William Wanlund*

[1] Secretary of Defense Robert McNamara, "Mutual Deterrence," *Atomic Archive*, Sept. 18, 1967, http://tinyurl.com/ye73nxs.

[2] Secretary of Defense William Perry, press conference, Department of Defense, Sept. 22, 1994, http://tinyurl.com/zqhkymb.

[3] Emma Chanlett-Avery, Ian E. Rinehart and Mary Beth D. Nikitin, "North Korea: U.S. Relations, Nuclear Diplomacy, and Internal Situation," Congressional Research Service, Jan. 15, 2016, http://tinyurl.com/jfahdkl.

[4] Cecil D. Haney, remarks at the Center for Strategic and International Studies, Washington, D.C., Jan. 22, 2016, http://tinyurl.com/gloy2mt.

START I, signed July 31, 1991, was the last arms-control agreement between the United States and Soviet Union, which within six months had disintegrated into 15 countries. The fall of the Soviet Union ended the Cold War and left nuclear weapons in Russia, Ukraine, Belarus and Kazakhstan, all eventually brought under Russian control.[70]

India declared itself a nuclear weapons state in 1998, after conducting five more nuclear tests, followed quickly by Pakistan, which became the world's eighth nuclear power.[71]

After the Sept. 11, 2001, terrorist attacks in the United States, President George W. Bush declared that the United States and Russia no longer had to fear missile attacks from one another. The United States pulled out of the ABM treaty, Bush said, so it could reinforce its missile defenses to protect against attacks by terrorists or "rogue states."[72]

In 2010, Obama and Russian President Dmitry Medvedev signed the New START pact, which replaced the expired START I and further reduced the numbers of missiles and launchers on both sides.[73] New START became operative in February 2011.

Russia and the United States also collaborated on nine-year-long talks that in 2015 produced the Joint Comprehensive Plan of Action, which restricted Iran's nuclear development to peaceful objectives in exchange for the lifting of economic sanctions on that nation.[74]

But the relative cordiality of the U.S.-Russian nuclear relationship had already begun to break down. In July 2014, the United States accused Russia of violating the Intermediate-Range Nuclear Forces Treaty by testing a ground-launched cruise missile, which, unlike ballistic missiles, are guided, jet-powered weapons that fly low over land and water. Russia called the accusation "baseless" and in February 2015 said the United States had itself violated the treaty by installing cruise missile launchers in Eastern Europe.[75] Relations worsened in 2014 when Russian forces entered eastern Ukraine, leading to U.S. support for international economic sanctions being placed on Russia.[76]

The cooling in the relationship coincided with what some observers perceived as a newly threatening tone in the rhetoric of Russian officials in discussing nuclear weapons.[77]

CURRENT SITUATION
Russian Saber-Rattling

Some experts think the tough, recent Russian rhetoric on nuclear weapons reflects the Putin government's efforts to regain international respect it believes was lost when the former Soviet Union broke up. "Russia's goal is to be recognized as a great power, a nuclear superpower, equal to the United States," says Arbatov of the Russian Academy of Sciences.

Williams of Kings College says the Russian saber-rattling "is primarily for domestic consumption." Still, she says, "that doesn't make it any less risky.

"Russia still wants to be in the great-power business, and nuclear weapons remain their No. 1 tool for portraying themselves that way," she says. "That's why we're seeing this increased reliance on nuclear weapons and modernization and this nuclear saber-rattling."

Kristensen of the Federation of American Scientists says the Russian tough talk is meant mainly to camouflage the country's conventional military shortcomings. "When the Putin leadership is saying these things, one has to be careful not to automatically interpret it as an increased willingness to use nuclear weapons," he says.

Others suspect a deeper reason for the Russian rhetoric. The National Institute for Public Policy's Payne says

Putin is trying to regain influence or even control over the other countries of the former Soviet Union. One example is Georgia, which Russia invaded in 2008, ostensibly on behalf of separatists there.

"Russia reportedly went to nuclear alert status during its 2008 move into Georgia, and Putin has said . . . he was considering going to a nuclear alert during Russia's 2014 military occupation of Crimea. That seems to signal that Putin believes the threat of using nuclear weapons can help Russia regain hegemony over [former Soviet territory]. If that really is Russian planning, we have an enormous and unprecedented deterrence challenge on our hands."

South Asian Arsenals

India and Pakistan, two nuclear-armed enemies, remain a flashpoint. Currently the two countries' nuclear arsenals are about equal. The Federation of American Scientists estimates India's inventory at 100 to 120 nuclear weapons and Pakistan's at 110 to 130. But C. Christine Fair, an associate professor at Georgetown University's Peace and Security Studies Program, believes "Pakistan has the [world's] fastest-growing nuclear arsenal and, within the next five to ten years, it is likely to double that of India, and exceed those of France, the United Kingdom, and China. Only the arsenals of the United States and Russia will be larger."[78]

Nadeem Hotiana, spokesman for Pakistan's embassy in Washington, says that, once India had tested a nuclear weapon in 1974, Pakistan felt it needed to develop a nuclear capability to defend itself. "Unresolved conflicts with India . . . required that Pakistan take necessary steps to maintain strategic stability in South Asia," Hotiana says.

India enjoys substantial conventional-weapon superiority over Pakistan and has adopted what it calls the "Cold Start" doctrine, which could allow the Indian military to invade Pakistan with little warning. That puts Pakistan "under increasing pressure to rely on its nuclear arsenal for self-defense," said Oxford University international relations scholar Walter Ladwig III.[79]

Pakistan, which has had numerous coups through the years and has Taliban in its northwest frontier, is falling "farther and farther behind India on nearly all other attributes of national power," including economic strength, according to nuclear scholars Toby Dalton, co-director of the Nuclear Policy Program at the Carnegie Endowment, and Michael Krepon, co-founder and senior associate of the Stimson Center, an international affairs think tank in Washington. And "the weaker Pakistan becomes, the more the dangers associated with its growing stockpiles of nuclear weapons and fissile material will be compounded," they said.[80]

One of those dangers is uncertain command and control of Pakistan's battlefield weapons, says Davenport of the Arms Control Association. "When you consider an India-Pakistan border clash, and escalation in the fog of war, it's not inconceivable that a Pakistani commanding general might choose to use a tactical nuclear weapon in response to [Indian] conventional superiority," Davenport says.

North Korean Secrecy

In January, North Korea tested a nuclear device — its fourth test since 2006 — which it described as a hydrogen bomb. The secrecy surrounding North Korea's nuclear weapons program makes it difficult to verify the claim. Many Western nuclear experts were skeptical, noting that seismic reports indicated the blast wasn't powerful enough for a hydrogen bomb, although some said the explosion could have been "a partial, failed test."[81]

While few doubt North Korea can produce nuclear weapons, experts are uncertain whether it has an arsenal. The Congressional Research Service, which provides nonpartisan policy reports to federal lawmakers, estimated in January that North Korea has enough fissile material to build "at least half a dozen nuclear weapons."[82]

David Albright, president of the Institute for Science and International Security, a Washington think tank that promotes nuclear nonproliferation, estimated North Korea could produce 20 to 100 nuclear weapons by 2020.[83]

North Korea also has test-fired ballistic missiles capable of reaching South Korea and Japan, 650 miles away. U.S. military analysts say North Korea is working to perfect longer-range missiles, but believe it will be years before they will be able to reach the U.S. mainland. Experts debate whether the North Koreans have the ability to miniaturize a nuclear weapon for use as a missile warhead; a 2015 Defense Department report stated they may have overcome that obstacle.[84]

AFP/Getty Images/Niklas Halle'n

Demonstrators in London protest the proposed renewal of Britain's Trident submarine-launched nuclear weapon system on Feb. 27, 2016. Britain has the world's fifth-largest nuclear arsenal behind Russia, the United States, France and China. In 1963 Britain, along with the United States and Soviet Union, signed the Limited Test Ban Treaty, the first major nuclear arms control agreement.

New Arms Race?

On May 27, in the last full year of his administration, Obama again called for the world to rid itself of its nuclear arsenals. Speaking in Hiroshima, Japan, target of the world's first atomic bombing, Obama said, "[A]mong those nations like my own that hold nuclear stockpiles, we must have the courage to escape the logic of fear, and pursue a world without them."[85]

In July *The Washington Post* reported that Obama is considering several strategies to fulfill this promise, including scaling back plans for modernizing the U.S. nuclear arsenal without jeopardizing national security. Another is renouncing the first use of nuclear weapons during a conflict, a policy known as "no first use." A third would be to push the U.N. Security Council to affirm its ban on testing nuclear weapons.[86]

But many feel a nuclear-free world is still a long way away. Former U.S. Defense Secretary William J. Perry has said that "far from continuing the nuclear disarmament that has been underway for the last two decades, we are starting a new nuclear arms race."[87]

Stephen Rademaker, an assistant secretary of State during the George W. Bush administration, said the disarmament goals Obama set in his 2009 Prague speech were never realistic. "Of course, he continues to articulate the abolition of nuclear weapons as a goal,"

Should abolishing nuclear weapons be the chief goal of U.S. nuclear policy?

YES   Derek Johnson
Executive Director, Global Zero

Written for *CQ Researcher*, July 2016

Over an area equivalent to a thousand football fields, a fireball forms a mile out in every direction. Temperatures exceed 20 million degrees Fahrenheit — hotter than the sun's surface. Every living thing and human structure vanishes.

The subsequent blast demolishes everything within two miles. Beyond that range, the heaviest concrete buildings still stand, but barely. Everything else within three miles crumples.

Roughly 1.5 million people die in that first flash of light. Another 1.5 million — men, women and children living or working within seven miles of the epicenter — spend agonizing hours or days dying from burns, crush wounds and radiation.

Meanwhile, thousands of fires ignited by the blast coalesce into a massive firestorm that consumes the city. Above, radioactive fallout stretches hundreds of miles, poisoning everything in its path.

That is a single — and comparatively modest-sized — nuke detonated in downtown Manhattan. The world is bristling with 15,000 of these weapons, some with far greater destructive force.

The terrible prospect that these weapons will be used has driven every American president since Dwight D. Eisenhower to reduce global nuclear arsenals. It is the clear-eyed understanding of what these weapons do that drove President Ronald Reagan's quest for "the total elimination one day of nuclear weapons from the face of the Earth," and compelled President Barack Obama to swing for the fences in 2009 when he announced America's commitment to seek the same.

"Nuclear security" is an absurd proposition so long as nuclear weapons exist. Every day, we risk their use — by accident, by unauthorized action, by mistaken launch on false warning, by deliberate decisions stemming from crisis or conflict, or by terrorists who acquire them. And nuclear-armed nations, including our own, are spending lavishly to upgrade, expand and/or further operationalize their arsenals, increasing that risk.

Perversely, these risks are being accepted in the name of deterrence and security. But deterrence cannot prevent the unintended use of nuclear weapons, and in fact may not prevent intentional use. Its core premise is to threaten, at all times, the use of nuclear weapons. That is not security. The only way to eliminate the risk is to eliminate the weapons. That is an international effort the United States is uniquely suited to spearhead, not unilaterally or "by example," but through relentless leadership, diplomacy and pressure. The alternative is to accept the inevitability of their use — and all that entails.

NO   Keith B. Payne
President, National Institute for Public Policy

Written for *CQ Researcher*, July 2016

The chief goal of U.S. nuclear policy should not be to abolish nuclear weapons. That goal involves extreme dangers that typically go unspoken but are critical to its serious consideration.

Since World War II, U.S. nuclear deterrence capabilities have, without a doubt, helped to prevent and limit wars. The evidence is overwhelming. Correspondingly, since the establishment of nuclear deterrence after World War II, there has been a dramatic reduction in the percentage of combat deaths worldwide from the relatively high levels that had prevailed for centuries. That is a historic accomplishment.

For example, during the first half of the 20th century, absent nuclear deterrence to prevent war, two world wars caused 80 million to 100 million deaths in a dozen years of combat. Another world war fought with modern conventional, chemical and biological weapons would lead to far greater death and destruction. It must be deterred.

Proponents of nuclear disarmament appeal for a new, more cooperative world order that would no longer need nuclear deterrence to prevent world war. But such appeals have never created a cooperative world order, and there is no evidence they ever will. In response to earlier activism for nuclear abolition, Winston Churchill said, "Be careful above all things not to let go of the atomic weapon until you are sure and more than sure that other means of preserving peace are in your hands."

The inconvenient truth is that no plausible alternative to nuclear deterrence for preserving peace is foreseeable, much less in hand. Yet, nuclear abolition would eliminate this existing tool known to have moved human history away from its bloody past.

Another reason for not prioritizing nuclear abolition is that numerous countries that would have to agree instead reject it as a serious goal. Moscow, for example, deems it an American "trick" to deny Russia its most critical weapons. Indeed, Russia now, more than ever, emphasizes its nuclear forces for coercion and wartime employment.

At the same time, U.S. allies place high priority on maintaining the U.S. nuclear deterrence "umbrella" for their security. As former French Ambassador to NATO François de Rose observed wryly, "It will be time to think about general and complete nuclear disarmament when human nature has changed."

Precisely so. Prioritizing nuclear abolition now, rather than effective nuclear deterrence, ignores international realities and would undercut the means we know support what must be our highest priority, preventing and limiting war.

Rademaker said, "but . . . unlike in 2009, when I think he was sincere and he really thought this was achievable, I think today he wants to abolish nuclear weapons in the same way that other politicians say they want to abolish poverty or eliminate drug addiction. It's an aspiration, but . . . something we all understand is not going to be achieved anytime soon."[88]

As Obama's presidency winds down, other observers see a mixed nuclear legacy. "On [nuclear] funding, strategy, arms control policy, the Obama administration has come across as a surprisingly traditional presidency," Kristensen of the Federation of American Scientists says. "There's an inherent reluctance in any administration to do too much, too fast. Maybe that's sound, but there's a disconnect in the public impression of what this administration was thought to be about as opposed to what it has actually accomplished."

Some disarmament supporters feel let down. Derek Johnson, executive director of Global Zero, which, like Ploughshares, advocates total nuclear disarmament, says, "We could not have predicted that President Obama — the man who won a Nobel Peace Prize [in 2009] for his commitment to nuclear disarmament — would embark on a $1 trillion nuclear spending spree of his own, one that threatens to lock in a new nuclear arms race."

Some, however, doubt that Obama's successors will follow through on the modernization plan. "Insiders don't believe it will ever happen," said Philip E. Coyle III, a former head of Pentagon weapons testing.[89] Neither presidential candidate has commented at length on the plan, but GOP nominee Donald J. Trump said that "our nuclear arsenal doesn't work" and is obsolete. Democratic nominee Hillary Clinton has vowed to maintain the world's "strongest military," but said at one campaign stop that expanding and modernizing the nuclear force "doesn't make sense to me." She added she will study the issue.[90]

Other observers see pluses on Obama's nuclear ledger. Harvard's Bunn praised the New START pact with Russia and the recent agreement to prevent Iran from developing nuclear weapons, which he described as a "breakthrough."

On the other hand, Bunn said, "we have a nuclear arms race in South Asia between India and Pakistan. . . . We have North Korea expanding its nuclear arsenal in a very dangerous way," and tensions with Russia have increased.

"The successes are real and important," Bunn said, "but the world has proven to be more resistant to change in nuclear postures than Obama expected when he came to office."[91]

OUTLOOK
Uncertain Future

"Twenty years down the road," says Cirincione of Ploughshares, "the disarmament agenda will be advancing significantly, with fewer nuclear weapons, no new nuclear states and Russian and U.S. weapons levels going down considerably. The weapons become less and less relevant to our threats and become more and more expensive. I think that's the future."

But he cautions, "The question is whether we can get there without a nuclear catastrophe, like a terrorist threat or a nuclear war in South Asia or an accident or a miscalculation."

Payne of the National Institute for Public Policy says "you would have to be omniscient" to know precisely what America's future nuclear weapons deterrence requirements will be. "You would have to know opponents' values, will and decision-making processes so well that you could determine the number and types of weapons necessary to deter them from whatever you're hoping to deter them from," he says. But, he adds, "we still must try to deter war."

Some are optimistic about the possibilities for disarmament. Johnson of Global Zero envisions a four-step scenario that will bring the world to nuclear zero around 2030. The first would see the United States and Russia negotiate to reduce their warheads to 1,000 each, he says. "Once that's ratified, every other nuclear-armed country would agree to freeze its own arsenal and pledge to join multilateral talks."

Then, the United States and Russia would further cut their warheads to 500 each, and other countries would reduce their inventories proportionally. After that, all nuclear countries would sign and implement an accord.

But Thomas Schelling, emeritus distinguished professor in the University of Maryland School of Public Policy, who shared the 2005 Nobel Prize in Economics for research on conflict and cooperation, is skeptical. "Any state with fissionable material would cheat on an agreement and keep a stock of weapons-grade material in the belief that every other nation would do the same thing," he says. "A nuclear-zero world would be a nervous world. It cannot be guaranteed to be a world without war, and if nuclear powers go to war, they will develop nuclear weapons as fast as they can."

It also will be important to keep an eye on China's nuclear development, according to Robert Farley, an assistant professor at the University of Kentucky's Patterson School of Diplomacy and International Commerce. China, he noted, is developing a land-mobile intercontinental ballistic missile, which "suggests that China is moving definitively away from [its traditional policy of] minimal deterrence and toward a more robust, survivable second-strike capability." China is also doubling the size of its missile-carrying submarine fleet from four to eight.

Farley said, "For four decades, the key nuclear arms control agreements have been conducted in bilateral terms between Washington and Moscow. The increasing size and sophistication of the Chinese arsenal may make this approach obsolete."[92]

The dynamic between Russia and the United States, however, remains key to any nuclear future, many observers say. The Carnegie Endowment's Perkovich sees a possible opening for future negotiations. "Arms control treaties make predictable the threat you have to deal with," he says. "The Russians don't want to be without that kind of predictability, and I don't think we do."

However, he adds, "Nuclear disarmament won't be possible unless the major relationships among the states that have nuclear weapons are fundamentally secure. . . . It's very difficult to see all of those relationships being resolved, but, gee, we try to work on them anyway."

NOTES

1. Kyle Mizokami, "Why the Pentagon's New Nukes Are Under Fire," *Popular Mechanics*, Jan. 12, 2016, http://tinyurl.com/j7k8726.

2. "America's nuclear bomb gets a makeover," "PBS Newshour," Public Broadcasting Service, Nov. 5, 2015, http://tinyurl.com/zjha865.

3. Jon B. Wolfsthal, Jeffrey Lewis and Marc Quint, "The Trillion Dollar Nuclear Triad," James Martin Center for Nonproliferation Studies, January 2014, http://tinyurl.com/ozhzqrx.

4. Adm. Cecil Haney, remarks, Center for Strategic and International Studies, Jan. 22, 2016, http://tinyurl.com/jggnkj2.

5. Aaron Mehta, "Work: Russia Will Not Gain Nuclear Advantage," *Defense News*, June 25, 2015, http://tinyurl.com/hg8zjgl.

6. "Remarks by President Obama in Prague, as delivered," the White House, April 5, 2009, http://tinyurl.com/h6evchz.

7. Tom Z. Collina, "Obama's Shop-'til-You-Drop Nuclear Spending Spree," *The Huffington Post*, Feb. 11, 2016, http://tinyurl.com/hpk4ph7.

8. Phillip Swarts, "Air Force prolongs the life of the venerable B-52," *Air Force Times*, Feb. 22, 2016, http://tinyurl.com/jdhq4lf; Jon Harper, "Plan to Fund Ohio Replacement Submarine Reaches Tipping Point," *National Defense*, August 2015, http://tinyurl.com/h5t5bb5.

9. Leslie Stahl, "Who's Minding the Nukes?" "60 Minutes," April 27, 2014, http://tinyurl.com/nykown7.

10. Hans M. Kristensen and Robert S. Norris, "Status of World Nuclear Forces," Federation of American Scientists, May 26, 2016, http://tinyurl.com/q7lxnzn.

11. Anna Fifield, "North Korea claims it could wipe out Manhattan with a hydrogen bomb," *The Washington Post*, March 13, 2016, http://tinyurl.com/hbcjo5l.

12. "Nuclear Weapons: Who Has What at a Glance," fact sheet, Arms Control Association, October 2015, http://tinyurl.com/6ovpr2v; Hans M. Kristensen and Robert S. Norris, "Pakistani nuclear forces, 2015," *Bulletin of the Atomic Scientists*, 2015, http://tinyurl.com/phdqk4w.

13. Robert Farley, "Should America Fear China's Nuclear Weapons?" *The National Interest*, Aug. 10, 2014, http://tinyurl.com/zt5lpxh.

14. Eldridge Colby, "The Role of Nuclear Weapons in the U.S.-Russian Relationship," Carnegie Endowment for International Peace, Feb. 26, 2016, http://tinyurl.com/jxvulfv.

15. Michael Moran, "Q&A: Matthew Bunn on the Nuclear Security Summit," Carnegie Corporation, Feb. 29, 2016, http://tinyurl.com/z4cbbrw.

16. "Fact Sheet on Dirty Bombs," U.S. Nuclear Regulatory Commission, updated Dec. 12, 2014, http://tinyurl.com/aqy8wlh.

17. Ryan Browne, "U.S. launches long-awaited European missile defense shield," CNN, May 12, 2016, http://tinyurl.com/zlay548.

18. *Ibid.*

19. Andrew Kramer, "Russia Calls New U.S. Missile Defense System a 'Direct Threat,' " *The New York Times*, May 12, 2016, http://tinyurl.com/z66qdom.

20. "The European Phased Adaptive Approach at a Glance," fact sheet, Arms Control Association, May 2013, http://tinyurl.com/7gpwjno.

21. "Putin: Romania 'in crosshairs' after opening NATO missile defense base," RT, May 27, 2016, http://tinyurl.com/zq7qysp.

22. Kramer, *op. cit.*

23. Lisa Ferdinando, "Work Helps to Inaugurate Ballistic Missile Defense Site in Romania," DoD News, U.S. Department of Defense, May 12, 2016, http://tinyurl.com/j9q4yog.

24. Susanna Capelouto, "Russian President Vladimir Putin warns he'll retaliate against NATO missiles," CNN, May 28, 2016, http://tinyurl.com/hwgbfhn.

25. Tom Z. Collina, "Pentagon Shifts Gears on Missile Defense," *Arms Control Today*, April 2, 2013, http://tinyurl.com/jm76jes.

26. *Ibid.*

27. Jaganath Sankaran, "The United States' European Phased Adaptive Approach Missile Defense System: Defending Against Iranian Threats Without Diluting the Russian Deterrent," RAND Corp., 2015, http://tinyurl.com/znzhj2z.

28. Matthew Bunn *et al.*, "Preventing Nuclear Terrorism: Continuous Improvement or Dangerous Decline?" Project on Managing the Atom, Belfer Center for Science and International Affairs, Harvard Kennedy School, March 2016, http://tinyurl.com/hfrt7ex.

29. Nancy Ing and Alexander Smith, "Brussels Attacks: Bombers Filmed Nuclear Researcher, Expert Says," NBC News, March 16, 2016, http://tinyurl.com/h2m744l.

30. Lizzie Dearden, "Paris attacks Isis suspect Salah Abdeslam had nuclear files stashed in his flat," *The Independent*, April 14, 2016, http://tinyurl.com/zjwcx57.

31. "Paris attacks: Salah Abdeslam arrested in Brussels," Al Jazeera, March 19, 2016, http://tinyurl.com/jo6s3m7.

32. Bunn *et al., op. cit.*

33. Eric Schlosser, "The H-Bombs in Turkey," *The New Yorker*, July 17, 2016, http://tinyurl.com/h47hvv8. For background, see Brian Beary, "Unrest in Turkey," *CQ Researcher*, Jan. 29, 2016, pp. 97-120.

34. Hans Kristensen, "Upgrades At US Nuclear Bases In Europe Acknowledge Security Risk," Federation of American Scientists, Sept. 10, 2015, http://tinyurl.com/zm6cq4r.

35. IAEA Incident and Trafficking Database (ITDB) 2016 fact sheet, International Atomic Energy Agency, 2016, http://tinyurl.com/gplfh2j.

36. Michael Bennett, "Projected Costs of U.S. Nuclear Forces, 2015 to 2024," Congressional Budget Office Report, January 2015, http://tinyurl.com/z9yjadd.

37. Wolfsthal, Lewis and Quint, *op. cit.*

38. Aaron Mehta, "Is the Pentagon's Budget About To Be Nuked?" *Defense News*, Feb. 5, 2016, http://tinyurl.com/gr5cu8h.

39. Steven Pifer, "Pay Attention, America: Russia Is Upgrading Its Military," *The National Interest*, Feb. 3, 2016, http://tinyurl.com/j4ohvb9; "Russia to spend $70 billion on strategic forces by 2020," Russian Strategic Nuclear Forces, Feb. 24, 2011, http://tinyurl.com/j79hsu5.

40. "Sen. Markey & Rep. Blumenauer Introduce Bicameral Legislation to Cut $100 Billion from Wasteful Nuclear Weapons Budget," press release, Office of Sen. Ed Markey, March 23, 2015, http://tinyurl.com/z2spzdb; "S. 831: Smarter Approach to Nuclear Expenditures Act," http://tinyurl.com/hfbg2z4.

41. Todd Harrison and Evan Montgomery, "The Cost of U.S. Nuclear Forces: From BCA to Bow Wave and Beyond," Center for Strategic and Budgetary Assessments, Aug. 4, 2015, http://tinyurl.com/z7nqqkr.

42. Albert Einstein letter to Franklin D. Roosevelt, Aug. 2, 1939, http://tinyurl.com/gnoj78z.

43. President Franklin Roosevelt letter to Albert Einstein, Oct. 19, 1939, http://tinyurl.com/hzvkrjf.

44. "The Maud Report," Manhattan Project — an Interactive History, U.S. Department of Energy Office of History and Heritage Resources, http://tinyurl.com/gtefj6g.

45. F. G. Gosling, "The Manhattan Project: Making the Atomic Bomb," U.S. Department of Energy, January 2010, http://tinyurl.com/ht3cgrb.

46. "Fissile Material Basics," fact sheet, Institute for Energy and Environmental Research, April 2012, http://tinyurl.com/gsk4q6f.

47. Gosling, *op. cit.*, pp. 30-37.

48. Mark Walker, "Nazis and the Bomb," "Nova," Public Broadcasting Service, Nov. 8, 2005, http://tinyurl.com/hpcfoz4.

49. "Entries from President Truman's Diary, July 25, 1945," "American Experience," Public Broadcasting Service, http://tinyurl.com/o5r9hjp.

50. Nathan Donohue, "Understanding the Decision to Drop the Bomb on Hiroshima and Nagasaki," Center for Strategic and International Studies, Aug. 10, 2012, http://tinyurl.com/n2pnq5g.

51. Gosling, *op. cit.*, pp. 96-97.

52. Truman Diary, *op. cit.*

53. "Establishment of a Commission to Deal with the Problems Raised by the Discovery of Atomic Energy," "Resolutions Adopted on the Recommendations of the First Committee," United Nations Security Council report, Jan. 24, 1946, http://tinyurl.com/z7vgtdy.

54. "The Baruch Plan," remarks by Bernard Baruch presented to the United Nations Atomic Energy Commission, June 14, 1946, http://tinyurl.com/bo45fgl.

55. V. Bush and J. B. Conant, "Memorandum to the Secretary of War," George Washington University National Security Archive, Sept. 30, 1944, http://tinyurl.com/zy9bhbg.

56. "Klaus Fuchs, (1911-1988)," "American Experience," Public Broadcasting Service, http://tinyurl.com/7v65dac.

57. "Cold War: A Brief History, The Soviet Atomic Bomb," Atomic Archive, http://tinyurl.com/gotzllz.

58. "Cold War: A Brief History, The BRAVO Test," http://tinyurl.com/gotzllz.

59. "Republic of the Marshall Islands Changed Circumstances Petition to Congress," Congressional Research Service, May 16, 2005, http://tinyurl.com/z7jzwh4.

60. "Klaus Fuchs," *op. cit.*

61. Dwight D. Eisenhower, "Atoms for Peace" speech, United Nations, Dec. 8, 1953, http://tinyurl.com/zs3sfcb.

62. Public Law 83-703, The Atomic Energy Act of 1954, http://tinyurl.com/zwvxhnq.

63. William Burr and Hector L. Montford, "The Making of the Limited Test Ban Treaty, 1958-1963," George Washington University National Security Archive, Aug. 8, 2003, http://tinyurl.com/gvgh2gh.

64. "Treaty Banning Nuclear Weapon Tests in the Atmosphere, in Outer Space and Under Water," U.S. State Department Bureau of Arms Control, Verification, and Compliance, http://tinyurl.com/ofncs4q.

65. Benjamin Schwarz, "The Real Cuban Missile Crisis," *The Atlantic*, January-February 2013, http://tinyurl.com/arl7clh.

66. "Nuclear Test Ban Treaty," John F. Kennedy Presidential Library and Museum, http://tinyurl.com/gs7qqnl.

67. Interim Agreement Between the United States of America and the Union of Soviet Socialist Republics on Certain Measures With Respect to the Limitation of Strategic Offensive Arms, www.nti.org/media/pdfs/aptsaltI.pdf; Ronald Reagan, "Address to the Nation on Defense and National Security," March 23, 1983, http://tinyurl.com/7595bo9.

68. Treaty Between the United States of America and the Union of Soviet Socialist Republics on the Limitation of Anti-Ballistic Missile Systems, http://tinyurl.com/3w6yfn5; Steven Pifer, "The Limits of U.S. Missile Defense," *The National Interest*, March 30, 2015, http://tinyurl.com/znpq2d8.

69. Treaty Between the United States of America and the Union of Soviet Socialist Republics on the Limitation of Strategic Offensive Arms, Together With Agreed Statements and Common Understandings Regarding the Treaty; James E. Goodby, "Looking Back: The 1986 Reykjavik Summit," *Arms Control Today*, Sept. 1, 2006, http://tinyurl.com/822eul5.

70. Russia country report, Nuclear Threat Initiative, March 2015, http://tinyurl.com/jzdrbrx.

71. Pakistan country report, Nuclear Threat Initiative, April 2016, http://tinyurl.com/hz2j6lw.

72. George W. Bush, "Remarks by the President on National Missile Defense," Dec. 13, 2001, http://tinyurl.com/zjuux5d.

73. Macon Phillips, "The New START Treaty and Protocol," White House blog, April 8, 2010, http://tinyurl.com/hffquby.

74. Kelsey Davenport, "Timeline of Nuclear Diplomacy With Iran," Arms Control Association, January 2016, http://tinyurl.com/z5ebah8.

75. "Adherence to and Compliance with Arms Control, Nonproliferation, and Disarmament Agreements and Commitments," U.S. State Department, Bureau of Arms Control, Verification and Compliance, July 2014, http://tinyurl.com/l4e5ngn; "Russia Accuses US of Violating Nuclear Arms Treaty," *Sputnik News*, Feb. 12, 2015, http://tinyurl.com/jg9yoa4.

76. Dan Roberts, "Obama suggests further sanctions against Russia over Ukraine incursion," *The Guardian*, Aug. 28, 2014, http://tinyurl.com/z84laca.

77. David M. Herszenhorn, "Russia Warns Denmark on Joining NATO Missile Defense," *The New York Times*, March 22, 2015, http://tinyurl.com/h4vwppd.

78. Kristensen and Norris, *op. cit.*; C. Christine Fair, "Pakistan's army is building an arsenal of "tiny" nuclear weapons — and it's going to backfire," *Quartz*, Dec. 21, 2015, http://tinyurl.com/hv9bqh4.

79. Walter C. Ladwig III, "A Cold Start for Hot Wars? The Indian Army's New Limited War Doctrine," *International Security*, Winter 2007/ 08, p. 169, http://tinyurl.com/ms3ok9.

80. Toby Dalton and Michael Krepon, "A Normal Nuclear Pakistan," The Stimson Center and the Carnegie Endowment for International Peace, 2015, http://tinyurl.com/j5v65yg.

81. Barbara Starr, "First on CNN: North Korea may have tested components of a hydrogen bomb," CNN, Jan. 29, 2016, http://tinyurl.com/z7gskn3.

82. Emma Chanlett-Avery, Ian E. Rinehart and Mary Beth D. Nikitin, "North Korea: U.S. Relations, Nuclear Diplomacy, and Internal Situation," Congressional Research Service, Jan. 15, 2016, http://tinyurl.com/jfahdkl.

83. David Albright, "Future Directions in the DPRK's Nuclear Weapons Program: Three Scenarios for 2020," US-Korea Institute, Johns Hopkins University School of Advanced International Studies, February 2015, http://tinyurl.com/zcjsfrs.

84. David Sanger and Choe Sang-Hun, "As North Korea's Nuclear Program Advances, U.S. Strategy Is Tested," *The New York Times*, May 6, 2016, http://tinyurl.com/hquyytb; "Military and Security Developments Involving the Democratic People's Republic of Korea," U.S. Department of Defense report to Congress, 2015, http://tinyurl.com/hf7hcb4.

85. "Remarks by President Obama and Prime Minister Abe of Japan at Hiroshima Peace Memorial," White House Press Office, May 27, 2016, http://tinyurl.com/zafyuts.

86. Josh Rogan, "Obama plans major nuclear policy changes in his final months," *The Washington Post*, July 10, 2016, http://tinyurl.com/hobwtu4.

87. William J. Perry, *My Journey at the Nuclear Brink* (2015), p. 190.

88. "A look at world's nuclear reality, 70 years after Hiroshima," "PBS News Hour," May 27, 2016, http://tinyurl.com/gnvthp6.

89. William J. Broad and David E. Sanger, "As U.S. Modernizes Nuclear Weapons, 'Smaller' Leaves Some Uneasy," *The New York Times*, Jan. 11, 2016, http://tinyurl.com/jefq9xz.

90. Lawrence Wittner, "The Trillion Dollar Question," *Counter Punch*, March 16, 2016, http://tinyurl.com/zp58rbf.

91. Christopher Woolf, "Obama's mixed record on fighting nuclear weapons," "The World," PRI International, May 26, 2016, http://tinyurl.com/zvuhsnx.

92. Farley, *op. cit.*

BIBLIOGRAPHY

Selected Sources

Books

Perry, William J., *My Journey at the Nuclear Brink*, Stanford University Press, 2015.
A former secretary of Defense in President Bill Clinton's administration describes his participation in Cold War nuclear security decisions and how he became an advocate of a nuclear weapons-free world.

Roberts, Brad, *The Case for U.S. Nuclear Weapons in the 21st Century*, Stanford University Press, 2015.
The director of the Center for Global Security Research at Lawrence Livermore National Laboratory and a former Defense Department official describes today's nuclear challenges and argues that unilateral disarmament by the United States would damage the country's interests.

Schlosser, Eric, *Command and Control: Nuclear Weapons, the Damascus Accident, and the Illusion of Safety*, Penguin Press, 2013.
An investigative journalist documents safety and security risks at nuclear weapons sites and how the nuclear warfighting doctrine involving more and cheaper weapons exacerbates the problems.

Sokolski, Henry D., *Underestimated: Our Not So Peaceful Nuclear Future*, Nonproliferation Policy Education Center, 2015.
The executive director of an organization supporting nuclear disarmament discusses the risks of maintaining large nuclear stockpiles.

Articles

Birch, Douglas, and R. Jeffrey Smith, "Israel's Worst-Kept Secret," *The Atlantic*, Sept. 16, 2014, http://tinyurl.com/mecqbra.
The authors discuss the history, significance and possible consequences of Israel's unacknowledged nuclear weapons arsenal.

Broad, William J., and David E. Sanger, "As U.S. Modernizes Nuclear Weapons, 'Smaller' Leaves Some Uneasy," *The New York Times*, Jan. 11, 2016, http://tinyurl.com/h9apxtp.
Some observers fear that the trend toward smaller and more "usable" nuclear weapons increases the danger of nuclear conflict.

Mehta, Aaron, "Is the Pentagon's Budget About To Be Nuked?" *Defense News*, Feb. 5, 2016, http://tinyurl.com/gr5cu8h.
Budget pressures threaten the planned renovation of the Pentagon's nuclear deterrence force.

Williams, Heather, "Russia Still Needs Arms Control," *Arms Control Today*, January-February 2016, http://tinyurl.com/zmvapsd.
A researcher of U.S. and Russian nuclear policies, deterrence theory and trust building in international relations says that, despite Russian saber-rattling, reducing weapons can increase Russia's credibility as an international leader and make it more secure.

Reports and Studies

Bunn, Matthew, et al., "Preventing Nuclear Terrorism: Continuous Improvement or Dangerous Decline?" Harvard Kennedy Center, Belfer Center for Science and International Affairs, March 2016, http://tinyurl.com/hfrt7ex.
Harvard University nuclear researchers assess the threat of nuclear terrorism and suggest ways to reduce it.

Dalton, Toby, and Michael Krypon, "A Normal Nuclear Pakistan," Stimson Center and Carnegie Endowment for International Peace, 2015, http://tinyurl.com/j5v65yg.
Researchers at two Washington think tanks examine nuclear competition in South Asia.

Gosling, F. G., "The Manhattan Project: Making the Atomic Bomb," United States Department of Energy, Office of History and Heritage Resources, January 2010, http://tinyurl.com/j7jzk4s.
The origins and development of the American atomic bomb program during World War II are chronicled.

Harrison, Todd, "Defense Modernization Plans through the 2020s: Addressing the Bow Wave,"

Center for Strategic and International Studies, January 2016, http://tinyurl.com/jt2mgm5.
A defense budget analyst urges the Pentagon to match strategic and budget priorities more closely.

Pifer, Steven, "The Future of US-Russia arms control," Brookings Institution/Carnegie Endownment Task Force on U.S. Policy Toward Russia, Ukraine and Eurasia, Feb. 26, 2016, http://tinyurl.com/zjpz5ka.
The director of the Brookings Institution's arms control and nonproliferation initiative and former U.S. ambassador to Ukraine outlines the differences in U.S. and Russian arms control objectives and how they hinder future agreements.

Wertz, Daniel, and Michael McGrath, "North Korea's Nuclear Weapons Program," The National Committee on North Korea, January 2016, http://tinyurl.com/h2vklh7.
The authors summarize what's known about North Korea's nuclear program and the directions it might take.

For More Information

Arms Control Association, 1330 L St., N.W., #130, Washington, DC 20005; 202-463-8270; https://www.armscontrol.org/. Promotes nonproliferation policies.

Brookings Institution, 1775 Massachusetts Ave, N.W., Washington, DC 20036; 202-797-6000; www.brookings.edu/. Research organization that analyzes arms control and other public policy issues.

Carnegie Endowment for International Peace Nuclear Policy Program, 1779 Massachusetts Ave., N.W., Washington, DC 20036; 202-483-7600; http://carnegieendowment.org/programs/npp/. Promotes nuclear disarmament.

Center for Strategic and International Studies, 1616 Rhode Island Ave., N.W., Washington, DC 20036; 202-887-0200; https://www.csis.org/. Research organization that conducts programs and disseminates information on national security.

Federation of American Scientists Nuclear Information Project, 1725 DeSales St., N.W., Suite 600 Washington, DC 20036; 202-546-3300; https://fas.org/. Disseminates information on nuclear weapons developments.

Global Zero, 1436 U St., N.W., Suite 401, Washington, DC 20009; 202-525-5964; www.globalzero.org/. Promotes the worldwide elimination of nuclear weapons.

International Atomic Energy Agency, Vienna International Centre, P.O. Box 100 A-1400, Vienna, Austria; (+431) 2600-0; https://www.iaea.org/. United Nations body that opposes the spread of nuclear weapons.

National Institute for Public Policy, 9302 Lee Highway, Suite 750, Fairfax, VA 22031-1214; 703-293-9181; www.nipp.org. Researches defense policy issues.

National Nuclear Security Administration, U.S. Department of Energy, 1000 Independence Ave., S.W., Washington, DC 20585; 800-342-5363; https://nnsa.energy.gov/. U.S. government agency that maintains America's nuclear weapons stockpile.

Nuclear Threat Initiative, 1747 Pennsylvania Ave., N.W., Seventh Floor, Washington, DC 20006; 202-296-4810; www.nti.org/. Promotes global cooperation to reduce threats from nuclear, biological and chemical weapons.

Ploughshares Fund, 1100 Vermont Ave., N.W., #300, Washington, DC 20005; 202-783-4401; www.ploughshares.org/. Advocates elimination of nuclear weapons.

4

U.S.-Iran Relations

Chuck McCutcheon

Graffiti on a building in Tehran, Iran's capital, says "Down with the USA." Despite Iran's bellicose attitude toward the U.S. government, 53 percent of Iranians have positive feelings about Americans in general, though nearly 90 percent view the U.S. government negatively.

From *CQ Researcher*,
March 4, 2016

For years, a nuclear reactor complex near Arak, Iran, stirred global fears that World War III could be looming. The Iranian government claimed the complex had a peaceful purpose — conducting research that could benefit hospitals and businesses.[1] Western experts thought differently, however.

Antiaircraft guns and missiles protected the complex, and Iran refused to allow outside inspectors inside. Finally, the world's worries were confirmed: Experts declared in 2014 that the facility was on the verge of being able to produce weapons-grade uranium that could be used to make an atomic bomb.[2]

Now, after years of international pressure, including the imposition of onerous U.S. economic sanctions, Iran has stepped away from its nuclear program in a highly controversial deal with far-reaching global-security implications. Under pressure from the United States, China, France, Russia, the United Kingdom and Germany, Iran said it removed the core of the Arak reactor, pledged to let inspectors visit the site and put other nuclear research on hold for up to 15 years. In return, the other countries lifted many — though not all — economic sanctions against Iran in January, providing some relief to its struggling economy.

The deal does not limit Iran's development of civilian nuclear sites.

"We have a rare chance to pursue a new path — a different, better future that delivers progress for both our peoples and the wider world," President Obama said in announcing Iran's reactor removal and the lifting of sanctions.[3] The agreement has raised speculation in political and foreign-policy circles about whether

A Neighborhood of Turmoil

About the size of Alaska, Iran sits in one of the world's most unsettled regions. It borders the Persian Gulf and Strait of Hormuz — both militarily strategic and vital for crude-oil transportation. Surrounding Iran are war-torn Iraq and Afghanistan, plus Turkey and Pakistan — both wracked by civil unrest. Saudi Arabia, a key U.S. ally and longtime nemesis of Iran, lies just across the Persian Gulf. Most Iranians are Shiites, creating racial and religious tension with Iran's predominantly Arab and Sunni Muslim neighbors. More than a dozen civilian nuclear facilities operate in Tehran or elsewhere in Iran.

* Being repurposed to produce non-uranium materials

Sources: "The World Factbook, Iran," CIA, http://tinyurl.com/yoex73; "World Development Indicators, Iran, Islamic Rep.," The World Bank, http://tinyurl.com/y3kcemn; "From the Sky," Institute for Science and International Security, http://tinyurl.com/zpu4xbt

Iran at a Glance

Population: 81.8 million (2015)

Ethnicity: 60 percent are Persian. Others include Azeri, Kurd, Lur, Arab, Turkmen.

Area: 636,372 sq. miles

GDP: $396.9 billion (2015)

Per Capita Income: $16,900 (2013)

Life Expectancy: 71 years (2015)

Adult Literacy Rate: 86.8% (2015)

Legislature: Islamic Consultative Assembly, 290 members

Religions: Shia Islam (the national religion) (90-95%); Sunni Muslim (5-10%); others include Zoroastrian, Jewish, Christian and Bahá'í.

Key Trading Partners:
- **Exports** — China (29%), India (11.9%), Turkey (10.4%)
- **Imports** — United Arab Emirates (30.6%), China (25.5%), Algeria (8.3%)

Iran can someday join China, Vietnam and Cuba — formerly staunch U.S. enemies that now cooperate on trade, diplomacy and other matters, even as their political systems remain far from American-style democracy.

But any uptick in relations that could bring a flood of U.S. products to Tehran, unite the two countries in stabilizing the Middle East or yield other large benefits is far from imminent — if it occurs at all. Many U.S. sanctions remain in place. And despite some diplomatic cooperation, Iran recently antagonized the United States in several national security-related incidents. What's more, the pro-engagement leaders of both nations face deep skepticism over the nuclear deal at home.

Obama has worked to improve relations with Iran since the deal was clinched last July, but he has less than a year left in office. Many lawmakers and presidential candidates — as well as Prime Minister Benjamin Netanyahu of Israel, a stalwart U.S. ally — remain highly suspicious of Iran, which the State Department says supports terrorists and critics say wants to eradicate Israel. Some in Congress as well as several candidates running for the White House want tougher penalties on Iran but must contend with Obama and his veto pen as they await the outcome of November's U.S. elections. On the other hand, many U.S. allies are likely to be reluctant to jettison the deal because they see big trade opportunities with Iran.

Tense talk over nuclear weapons has dominated U.S.-Iranian relations for years, to the dismay of some who say it has overshadowed other areas. Obama's predecessor, George W. Bush, in 2002 labeled Iran part of an "axis of evil" (along with Iraq and North Korea) for its alleged pursuit of atomic weapons despite Iran's insistence that its nuclear development was for peaceful purposes only.[4]

"We used to have a wide-ranging and often well-informed debate about Iran," Suzanne Maloney, deputy director of the foreign policy program at the Brookings Institution, a centrist think tank in Washington, said at a forum last fall before the International Atomic Energy Agency (IAEA) certified Iran's early fulfillment of its nuclear commitments. "Our conversations on Iran have been afflicted with an almost obsessive focus on one question, the nuclear issue."[5]

On foreign policy, Iran shares the United States' opposition to the Islamic State and al-Qaeda terrorist groups. Economically, Iran is enticing to foreign companies. It has a population of 80 million — second only to Egypt among Middle East countries and almost as large as California, Texas and Florida combined.[6]

Iranian President Hassan Rouhani, a moderate, has taken a wait-and-see stance on the nuclear deal, saying that if it is implemented to Iranian leaders' satisfaction, "we can put other topics on the table for discussion" with the United States.[7] Rouhani can seek a second term in 2017, and experts say his chances of re-election could hinge on whether he has sufficiently bolstered Iran's economy after the easing of sanctions.

But Rouhani, like Obama, is constrained. Rouhani is the civilian leader of an authoritarian theocracy led by Ayatollah Ali Khamenei, who has a lifelong position, final word on Iranian policy and a penchant for using the slogan "Death to America."[8]

Khamenei is the "supreme leader" of Iran's predominantly non-Arab Shiite Muslim population, which is surrounded by Sunni Muslim-dominated Arab countries that — along with Israel — generally have better relations with the United States. Long-standing racial and religious animosity between Iran and its neighbors complicates U.S. diplomacy in the region. America's Arab allies deeply distrust Iran and accuse it of seeking to destabilize the Middle East by backing armed terrorist groups from Lebanon to Iraq.[9] The U.S. State Department has listed Iran as a state sponsor of terrorism since 1984.

In January, Iran pleased supporters of closer relations with the United States by concluding a controversial prisoner swap negotiated separately from the nuclear talks. Under the agreement, Iran released *Washington Post* reporter Jason Rezaian, an Iranian-American, and two other Americans. In return, the United States legally cleared seven Iranians charged or imprisoned for violating economic sanctions and dismissed legal charges against 14 others outside the United States.[10]

But Iran has refused to release Siamak Namazi, an Iranian-American businessman arrested last fall under mysterious circumstances.[11] Iran also has provoked U.S. anger recently by:

- Displaying renewed hostility toward U.S. ally Saudi Arabia. A January mob attack on the Saudi embassy in Tehran led the Saudis and several of their allies to cut formal ties with Iran.[12]
- Launching non-nuclear ballistic missiles last fall, leading Obama in January to impose new sanctions — separate from those lifted as part of the nuclear deal — on people and companies involved with Iran's missile program.[13]
- Hacking computer systems at U.S. banks and other entities. Experts say those attacks have risen since the nuclear agreement was reached. Moreover, Iran "may be preparing" larger cyberattacks, said Martin Libicki, a senior management scientist at the RAND Corp., a think tank specializing in national security.[14]

Although Khamenei accepted Rouhani's request to pursue the nuclear deal, he has said Iran should not negotiate with the United States about anything else.[15] But Middle East experts question how long the 76-year-old — reportedly ailing — will remain in power.[16]

"Iranians voted on Feb. 26 to elect members of Parliament and the Assembly of Experts, a clerical council with the power to name Khamenei's eventual replacement. Moderates and reform-minded politicians who back the nuclear deal won majorities in both bodies.[17] But some experts say those gains are unlikely to have a significant effect on U.S. relations as long as Khamenei remains in power.

Americans and Iranians harbor deep suspicions about one another. A Gallup poll in February showed that only

Americans, Iranians Eye Each Other Warily

An overwhelming majority of U.S. adults view Iran unfavorably, according to a February Gallup poll. Another poll found nearly 90 percent of Iranian adults view the U.S. government negatively, but 53 percent of Iranians had positive feelings about Americans.

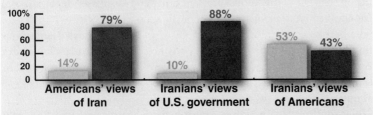

Views of One Another's Governments and People

Sources: Andrew Dugan, "After Nuclear Deal, U.S. Views of Iran Remain Dismal," Gallup Poll, Feb. 17, 2016, http://tinyurl.com/jdaaggy; Ebrahim Gallagher, Nancy Mohseni and Clay Ramsay, "Iranian Attitudes in Advance of the Parliamentary Elections: Economics, Politics, and Foreign Affairs," Center for International and Security Studies, University of Maryland, January 2016, p. 33, http://tinyurl.com/zxrs4kk

14 percent of Americans have a favorable view of Iran, just slightly above the 11 percent average since 1989.[18] A telephone poll of more than 1,000 Iranians found that 53 percent had positive feelings about the American public, but 88 percent felt unfavorably toward the U.S. government.[19] (*See graph, above.*)

As politicians, scholars, diplomats and others assess whether U.S.-Iran relations will improve or worsen, here are some questions being debated:

Should the United States seek closer ties with Iran?

The United States severed diplomatic relations with Iran after the 1979 revolution, when supporters of Ayatollah Ruhollah Khomeini — Khamenei's predecessor — stormed the U.S. embassy in Tehran and took 52 Americans hostage for 444 days. Since then, neither country has had an embassy in the other, so contacts are severely restricted.

Advocates of improved ties cite improved U.S. relations with two former adversaries as guides for gradually making up its rift with Iran: Vietnam, where the United States waged a 21-year war in a failed bid to stop the spread of communism in Southeast Asia, and communist

Cuba, which has been shut off from U.S. commerce and diplomatic ties until an easing this year by the Obama administration.[20]

"If the United States and Vietnam could reconcile after America's Vietnam fiasco, and if the U.S. is able to restore relations following some six decades of enmity with Cuba, a similar development with Iran is not to be viewed as insurmountable," says Amin Saikal, a professor of political science at Australian National University and author of the 2015 book *Iran at the Crossroads*.

Democratic presidential candidate and Vermont Sen. Bernie Sanders, often described as a "socialist independent," said at a January debate that the United States should not open an embassy in Tehran immediately. "But I think the goal has got to be, as we've done with Cuba, to move in [the direction of] warm relations with a very powerful and important country," he said.[21]

The National Iranian American Council, a group in Washington that seeks better U.S.-Iran relations, says the United States should follow former Republican President Richard M. Nixon's example of reaching out to communist China on trade. Nixon's move in 1972 lessened three decades of U.S.-Chinese hostility. The two countries restored diplomatic relations in 1979. Two council members called for "a new [U.S.] outlook towards Iran — one in which economics facilitates an evolution of political relations."[22]

Some advocates say closer U.S.-Iran relations would build on diplomatic ties forged by the nuclear deal. For instance, last October Iran agreed to participate in multination talks aimed at ending the violent, years-long rebellion in Syria against President Bashar al-Assad's government.[23] Then, in January, Iran captured 10 U.S. sailors and accused them of illegally straying into its waters in two small patrol boats. Secretary of State John Kerry, who played a leading role in negotiating the nuclear deal with Iran, worked with his counterpart, Foreign Minister Javad Zarif, with whom he had forged a partnership during the nuclear talks. Iran released the sailors within 16 hours, defusing what Kerry said would have been a major crisis had it occurred a few years earlier.[24]

Kerry and Zarif "have reshaped the relationship between Iran and the U.S. at least on the diplomatic level, and that is something to look at" in building better relations, says Vera Eccarius-Kelly, a professor of political science at Siena College in Loudonville, N.Y. "Now we have staffers at the State Department and Iran Foreign Ministry who know each other. It's not just individuals, but entire structures . . . that have the element of more familiarity and trust."

Some Iranian business leaders embrace an opportunity for closer ties. They say 60 percent of the country's population is under age 35 and is far more interested in improving its standard of living than adhering to the ayatollah's dictates. "This generation is worldly. . . . They have a different range of thinking," said Said Rahmani, the CEO of Iran's first venture-capital fund.[25]

Stephen Kinzer, a senior fellow in international and public affairs at Brown University, said Iran's opposition to the Islamic State and al Qaeda — terrorist movements based on extreme interpretations of Sunni Islam — separates it from other Middle Eastern countries and offers potential for cooperation in trying to stabilize the Middle East.

"Our perception of Iran as a threat to vital American interests is increasingly disconnected from reality," Kinzer said in a January op-ed column. His 2010 book *Reset: Iran, Turkey and America's Future*, argued that Iran should join Turkey — another Muslim country struggling to modernize — as a crucial U.S. ally.[26]

But critics of Iran say it remains unreliable and dangerous and should be kept at arm's length. After Sanders' remarks about Iran, his Democratic rival Hillary Clinton responded that the lifting of sanctions and prisoner swap should not cloud U.S. judgment.

"We've had one good day over 36 years, and I think we need more good days before we move more rapidly" toward better relations, she said. Her top foreign policy adviser, Jake Sullivan, later said Iran "seeks the destruction of Israel" and is "flouting international law with its ballistic missile threats."[27]

Republican presidential candidates share Clinton's skepticism. Before the sailors' release in January, current GOP frontrunner Donald Trump called the incident "an indication of where the hell we're going" with Iran.[28]

Iran's computer hacking also worries U.S. critics. Administration officials said they detected a surge in cyberattacks by Iran's Revolutionary Guards — an elite branch of the military enforcing internal security — coinciding with the arrest of Namazi, who had advocated closer relations.

As of mid-February, Iranian officials had provided no reason for his arrest. They subsequently arrested Namazi's father, also an Iranian-American, in what some experts said was a possible attempt to pressure a confession from his son about being a spy.[29]

Experts say the computer attacks and arrests of Namazi and his father are the Revolutionary Guards' warning against closer ties. "If there's a warming of relations, the reason for existing that unites hard-liners will dissipate and wither away — it's their biggest fear," says Nader Hashemi, director of the Center for Middle Eastern Studies at the University of Denver's Josef Korbel School of International Studies.

Iran's hard-liners have discouraged the smallest appearances of U.S. influence. In November they shut down an Iranian fast-food store that mimicked Kentucky Fried Chicken; an Iranian news agency contended the knockoff company's red-and-white décor too closely resembled the American flag.[30]

Some experts also suspect Iran may be holding Robert Levinson, a retired FBI agent who vanished in the country in 2007. Iranian leaders have denied knowing anything about his whereabouts, but in January *The New York Times* reported that an Iranian official had acknowledged in 2011 that Levinson was being used as a bargaining chip in nuclear negotiations at the time.[31]

And the hard-liners would much rather sully the reputation of the United States, some observers say. Iran released images of the captured U.S. sailors kneeling on deck with their hands clasped behind their heads, called by Senate Armed Services Committee Chairman John McCain, R-Ariz., "one of the great propaganda triumphs that the Iranians have ever had."[32]

Despite anti-U.S. attitudes in some Iranian circles, "Moving forward, Iran's leadership is likely to exploit this channel [of closer contacts] with the United States whenever doing so suits its own interests," said Aaron David Miller, a vice president at the Woodrow Wilson Center for International Scholars, a foreign-policy think tank in Washington.[33]

Getty Images/*The Washington Post*/Bill O'Leary

Israeli Prime Minister Benjamin Netanyahu urges U.S. lawmakers not to negotiate the nuclear deal with Iran during an address to Congress made at the invitation of congressional Republicans. The State Department says Iran supports terrorists, and critics of Iran say it wants to eradicate Israel, a stalwart U.S. ally.

Within Iran, at least one prominent onetime advocate of closer relations now is more skeptical of the idea. Former Iranian diplomat Sadegh Kharrazi was the author of a 2003 memo sent to the State Department proposing a broad dialogue between the two nations, but the Bush administration rejected the offer.[34] Kharrazi last year said the outcome of November's U.S. presidential elections remains too uncertain for his country to commit to anything.

"We need more positive gestures from the Americans" before Iran reciprocates, said Kharrazi. "We do not have high confidence in what will happen after President Obama leaves office."[35]

Should better U.S.-Iranian relations depend on whether Iran improves its human-rights record?

Human-rights groups consider Iran one of the world's worst countries on the issue. Its execution rate per capita is the highest of any U.N. member: In the last two years, more than 2,000 people are believed to have been put to death for drug use or other crimes, or more than in any similar period in the last quarter-century.

Amnesty International says the punishment is imposed "either for vaguely worded or overly broad offenses, or acts that should not be criminalized at all," such as speaking out against the government.[36]

An Iranian female cartoonist who depicted members of Iran's parliament as animals was sentenced last year to more than 12 years in prison.[37] The government also is accused of discriminating against Baha'is, the country's largest non-Muslim religious minority, by imprisoning its followers, restricting their ability to worship and shutting down Baha'i-owned businesses.[38]

The situation has led human-rights activists and others to argue that the United States and other countries should demand improvements as a precondition of conducting more trade or forming ties in other areas. Western countries "should remember that increasing economic, financial and diplomatic integration with Iran will give them greater leverage not only to make lucrative business deals but to speak out strongly against rights abuses," said Faraz Sanei, a researcher for Human Rights Watch's Middle East and North Africa division.[39]

The nuclear talks led to a "de-prioritization" of human rights that must be reversed, said Mark Lagon, president of Freedom House, a U.S.-based human rights and democracy advocacy group. "In dealings with Iran, the United States should address the serious human-rights concerns with at least the same energy as it did in negotiating a nuclear accord," he said.[40]

Rep. Dana Rohrabacher, R-Calif., who chairs a House Foreign Affairs Committee panel on emerging threats, agreed. "History teaches that it is not necessarily wrong to parley with the world's bad actors, but that doesn't mean ignoring the evil nature of those on the other side of the table," he said. "If a regime is based on beating its people into submission, how can we count on its good faith with us?"[41]

But many experts say if the United States uses human rights as a condition of better relations it risks further antagonizing Iran. In addition, they note, Iranian officials are quick to cite what they contend are U.S. human-rights abuses, such as supporting the Saudi government, which tightly restricts women's rights.

"We don't expect the West to impose its assumptions on human rights and human dignity to all societies," said Sadeq Amoli Larijani, chief of Iran's judiciary.[42]

Such assertions show why "it will take generations for the United States to gain some measure of trust with the Iranians" about human rights, says Christopher Dolan, a professor of politics and director of global studies at Pennsylvania's Lebanon Valley College. In the meantime, he and other experts say the United States should let the U.N. continue to assume the lead on monitoring and demanding progress on human rights, given its established mission in that area.

"We should support that U.N. role of holding Iran accountable so it's not a bilateral, tit-for-tat in terms of who's more guilty" on human rights, the University of Denver's Hashemi says.

Secretary of State Kerry has maintained the United States should monitor how well Iran lives up to its commitments in the nuclear deal before further sanctions are imposed to punish it for human-rights abuses.[43] He and other officials have stressed that, despite the lifting of economic sanctions over nuclear weapons, the United States can still penalize Iran for committing violations in that area.

Obama issued executive orders in 2010 and 2012 barring U.S. companies from doing business with Iranian officials responsible for serious human-rights abuses. In addition, a 2012 executive order freezes the U.S. bank accounts of anyone found guilty of providing computers or other technology used by Iran to abuse human rights, adding to the existing sanctions on providing computers for military purposes.[44]

The biggest public misconception about the nuclear deal is that "there has been comprehensive sanctions relief to all the things like terrorism sanctions and human-rights sanctions," said Chris Backemeyer, the State Department's deputy coordinator for sanctions policy. "That's absolutely not the case."[45]

Can Iranian nuclear activities be accurately monitored?

Backers of the nuclear deal say it addresses all the ways in which Iran could cheat to pursue a bomb. But critics are unpersuaded.

Details of Iran's Nuclear Deal

The nuclear deal that Iran struck in January 2015 with the United States and five other world powers limits Iran's uranium enrichment for 15 years. Some limits on Iran's nuclear research and development loosen in about 10 years, but other restrictions will remain for up to 25 years.

Components of Nuclear Deal

Most American trade with Iran remains banned by other long-standing sanctions imposed by the U.S. government, but sales of American commercial aircraft are permitted while luxury Iranian goods such as carpets and caviar, along with nuts, can be imported by the United States.
U.S. sanctions were lifted on foreign companies involved in Iran's automobile or energy sectors that conduct business with most major Iranian banks. American companies in those sectors still cannot do business with Iran without being penalized.
The European Union ended its ban on oil and gas purchases from Iran and a ban on the use of an electronic payments system, enabling Iran to move money among international banks.
The deal requires a future American president to ask Congress within eight years to lift virtually all U.S. sanctions still in place. All remaining U.N. sanctions are to end within 10 years.

Sources: William J. Broad and Sergio Pecanha, "The Iran Nuclear Deal — A Simple Guide," *The New York Times*, Jan. 15, 2015, http://tinyurl.com/njnl4mh; Kenneth Katzman and Paul K. Kerr, "Iran Nuclear Agreement," Congressional Research Service, Jan. 19, 2016, http://tinyurl.com/hwhso9m

---

The deal commits Iran to what the Obama administration calls "extraordinary and robust monitoring, verification and inspection." Inspectors from the International Atomic Energy Agency (IAEA) — an arm of the U.N. — have authority to verify that Iran has not hidden any weapons-grade materials.

If the IAEA learns of possible suspicious sites, Iran has agreed to allow its inspectors to assess them. The agency will search for sites that could be uranium mines, along with any unexplained international purchases of potential bomb-making materials. It will rely on intelligence gleaned from U.S. and other foreign sources.[46]

"I come away pretty confident" in the U.S. spy network's ability to "observe and monitor what the Iranians are doing," said Director of National Intelligence James Clapper, who oversees the CIA and other intelligence agencies.[47]

Getty Images/Scott Peterson

Iranians vote on Feb. 26, 2016, to elect members of Parliament and the Assembly of Experts. Moderates and reform-minded politicians who back the nuclear deal won majorities in both bodies, dealing a blow to hard-liners. But those gains may not have a significant effect on U.S. relations as long as Ayatollah Ali Khamenei, the anti-American supreme leader of Iran's theocracy, remains in power.

If Iran is found to have cheated, the deal calls for re-imposition of international economic sanctions. The deal establishes a formal process in which the IAEA and Iran have up to 24 days to resolve any disputes over inspection.[48] Supporters of the agreement say 24 days are plenty of time: In 2003, they said, it took six months for Iran to grant the U.N. the access it sought to one facility, but testing still uncovered nuclear activity, despite Iran's attempt to cover it up.[49]

"If Iran should decide to start producing weapon-grade highly enriched uranium, it would take about a year before it could accumulate enough for a first bomb," said deal supporter Frank von Hippel, senior research physicist and professor of public and international affairs emeritus at Princeton University's Program on Science and Global Security.[50]

But some lawmakers, arms-control experts and critics of Iran remain unconvinced that all cheating can be detected. And they predict the country will seek to drag the inspections process past 24 days.

"There is a lot the regime can do [to hide material] in a few hours, let alone days," said Charles Duelfer, who led the Iraq Survey Group that searched for evidence of chemical, biological and nuclear weapons in that country a decade ago. "So this allows room for Iran to maneuver

and potentially hide much of what it is doing regarding weapons design or component testing."[51]

Other skeptics say that for all of the attention the agreement pays to places where Iran was known to have done nuclear work, they are not as certain that inspectors will be able to ferret out work at new secret sites. That includes any that Iran might choose to establish in other nuclear-capable countries, such as North Korea.[52]

"In the previous cases of nuclear proliferation over the past two decades . . . the issue was the use of undeclared material, primarily at undeclared facilities," said a report by Olli Heinonen, a former IAEA deputy director general who is now a senior fellow at Harvard University's Belfer Center for Science and International Affairs.

The inspections process is "unclear and leaves unanswered questions," Heinonen said. Inspectors cannot simply visit any Iranian site unannounced; they must first give the Iranians evidence of suspected wrongdoing. Moreover, Heinonen questions whether the process allows inspectors to protect highly confidential spying sources and methods. And he worries the United States and other monitoring countries may not agree on what constitutes conclusive proof of cheating, such as suspicious work that Iranians contend is for non-nuclear purposes.

"What happens when . . . the evidence provided does not meet the standards of all [U.S. allies]?" Heinonen asked. "In other words, the bar will be set very high to begin with and may not allow for gray areas where intelligence is not foolproof."[53]

The Government Accountability Office (GAO), Congress' investigative arm, said in a February report that the IAEA will need an extra $10 million each year for the next 15 years to police the nuclear deal. Some members of Congress who opposed the deal said the report raises concerns about the IAEA's ability to do a thorough job.[54]

Even some nuclear deal supporters wonder how the United States will respond if it encounters relatively minor, yet punishable, evidence of possible nuclear activity. The United States could come under pressure from allies not to impose penalizing economic sanctions because doing so could erode future leverage if evidence of even bigger cheating emerges later.

"We can detect and enforce this if we find an egregious violation," says Ross Harrison, a nonresident scholar at the Middle East Institute, a Washington think tank, and a faculty member at Georgetown University's School of Foreign Service. "The bigger issue is, what constitutes a real breach of the deal? If we impose [sanctions], they might cheat even more."

BACKGROUND
Hot and Cold Relations

For much of the 20th century, the United States and Iran were on friendly terms and partners in some areas. But since 1979, relations have been marked by demonization on both sides, with a few less tense periods in between.

"Iran's attitude toward the United States is like someone pining for a former, perhaps abusive, lover," said Banafsheh Keynoush, who served as an interpreter for four Iranian presidents. "It has declared its contempt but also longs again to be a partner."[55]

The tension can be traced to Mohammed Reza Pahlavi, the "shah" or ruler of the country from 1941 to 1979. His father, Reza Khan Pahlavi, a military officer, had become shah in 1921 after launching a coup against the royal family that had ruled the country since 1794.

In 1935 Reza Shah's government began asking other countries to refer to it as Iran, which in Farsi means "land of the Aryans," instead of its traditional name of Persia. Britain and Russia accused him of supporting Nazi Germany and forced him from power during World War II, but those countries permitted his son, Mohammed Reza, to succeed him.[56]

As with other Middle Eastern countries, Iran's vast oil reserves sparked U.S. and British interest in the country. In 1951, nationalist Prime Minister Mohammad Mosaddeq — whom Shah Pahlavi appointed under pressure from members of Iran's parliament — nationalized the oil industry, removing it from British control. The shah tried to dismiss Mosaddeq, but his followers started an uprising, and Pahlavi fled the country in 1953.

The United States and Great Britain were in the midst of a Cold War with the communist Soviet Union, and American and British leaders felt that "while Mosaddeq was certainly not a communist, . . . the things he was doing might give the Communist Party of Iran an opportunity to strengthen itself and perhaps eventually take over," said Mark Gasiorowski, a professor of political science at Tulane University and author of a book on the shah.[57]

Pahlavi was restored to power within several days in a CIA-backed coup, leading to Mosaddeq's surrender and imprisonment. U.S. officials hailed it as a triumph. But author Tim Weiner wrote in a history of the spy agency: "A generation of Iranians grew up knowing that the CIA had installed the shah."[58]

Seeking to bring Iran closer to the United States, Pahlavi instituted the "White Revolution," a series of development reforms — such as land redistribution — and moved to liberalize women's rights.[59] The two countries worked together on oil extraction, education and nuclear energy. The United States in 1957 signed a civilian nuclear-cooperation deal that provided Iran with technical assistance.[60]

But the program alienated religious Iranians and the Shiite clergy, who felt such Westernization was antithetical to Islam.[61] And the shah's SAVAK spy service was loathed for torturing dissidents.

In 1964 the autocratic Pahlavi government exiled Ayatollah Khomeini, a religious leader without formal political power who passionately argued that Iran had ceded its sovereignty to the United States.[62] The shah never listened to the public, *Reset* author Kinzer said, imposing his policies "by decree or through acts of Parliament, which he corrupted and used like a toy."[63]

But successive U.S. presidents remained loyal. At a 1977 state dinner in Tehran, Democratic President Jimmy Carter lauded the expanded economic cooperation between the two countries. "Iran, because of the great leadership of the shah, is an island of stability in one of the more troubled areas of the world,"[64] Carter said.

The exiled Khomeini continued to demand a revolution, however, triggering rioting and turmoil in Iran. On Jan. 16, 1979, the shah left Iran to seek medical treatment, and in February Khomeini returned, declaring a new Islamic Republic with himself as supreme leader. The country adopted a new constitution through a referendum.

The biggest rupture between the countries came that November, when a group of Khomeini's followers seized the U.S. Embassy in Tehran and took 52 Americans hostage. Carter cut diplomatic ties in April 1980, two weeks before his administration staged a failed military mission to rescue the hostages.[65]

Carter imposed what became "perhaps the most comprehensive sanctions effort ever marshaled by the

CHRONOLOGY

1950s–1980s *U.S. and Iran forge ties; Revolt in Iran forces out shah and sours U.S. relations.*

1951 Prime Minister Mohammed Mosaddeq nationalizes the oil industry, negating Britain's majority interest.

1953 CIA directs coup that ousts Mosaddeq and returns shah to power.

1977 President Jimmy Carter, on visit to Tehran, toasts Shah Mohammed Rezi Pahlavi as a key ally.

1978 Civil unrest against shah's rule erupts, inflamed by Ayatollah Ruhollah Khomeini's taped sermons.

1979 Shah leaves Iran. . . . Khomeini returns and establishes Islamic republic following referendum. . . . Militants storm U.S. embassy and take 52 Americans hostage.

1980 Iraq attacks Iran, triggering eight-year war. . . . U.S. breaks off diplomatic relations and begins imposing economic sanctions on Iran.

1981 Iran frees the hostages on the day Carter leaves office.

1983 Iranian-backed Hezbollah terrorists attack U.S. Embassy and Marine barracks in Lebanon, killing 304.

1984 President Ronald Reagan's administration designates Iran a state sponsor of terrorism.

1986 Reagan admits his administration illegally sold weapons to Iran and funneled profits to "contra" guerrillas in Nicaragua.

1989 Ayatollah Khomeini dies. . . . Conservative Ayatollah Ali Khamenei replaces Khomeini as supreme leader.

1990s *U.S.-Iran relations deteriorate further.*

1992 Iran restarts nuclear program begun under shah's rule.

1995 U.S. imposes oil and trade embargo because of Iran's alleged efforts to acquire nuclear weapons and its hostility toward Israel.

1997 Reformist cleric Mohammed Khatami elected Iranian president.

2000–2008 *Iran steps up nuclear activities in defiance of United States.*

2001 Iran helps U.S. military during its invasion of Afghanistan.

2002 President George W. Bush calls Iran part of the "axis of evil," along with North Korea and Iraq, for its alleged pursuit of nuclear weapons.

2005 Hardliner Mahmoud Ahmadinejad elected Iranian president, declares United States an international bully.

2006 U.N. Security Council imposes sanctions on Iran's trade in nuclear materials and technology.

2009–Present *Iran reaches nuclear deal with U.S. and other world powers.*

2009 Newly elected President Obama sends negotiator to meet with Iranian counterpart on nuclear issues.

2011 Iran denies International Atomic Energy Agency (IAEA) report warning of its increasing nuclear weapons capabilities.

2013 Moderate Hassan Rouhani is elected Iranian president by pledging to get sanctions lifted and improve the economy. . . . Iran reaches interim nuclear deal with the United States and five other powers.

2015 At the invitation of U.S. House Republican leaders, Israeli Prime Minister Benjamin Netanyahu argues against the deal in address to Congress. . . . Iran and other countries finalize the agreement. . . . Congressional opponents fail to override threatened presidential veto, leaving deal intact. . . . Iran launches ballistic missiles in defiance of international ban.

2016 IAEA certifies Iran has fulfilled initial commitments under the deal, leading to lifting of many sanctions. . . . Iran releases *Washington Post* reporter Jason Rezaian and two other Americans as part of a prisoner swap with the United States. . . . Iran holds 10 U.S. sailors captive for 16 hours after they cross into Iranian waters.

international community," according to a Harvard Belfer Center report. The initial executive orders froze Iranian assets in U.S. banks and restricted financial transactions between the countries.

The 28-country European Union (EU) and the U.N. followed suit, imposing separate but related sanctions on Iran. The EU and U.N. joined in threatening harsh fines or other penalties on member countries that sold Iran weapons or any nuclear- or military-related equipment. They also imposed further restrictions on their member countries' banks doing business with Iranian banks and severely limited trade and investment with Iran's energy, telecommunications and transportation industries.[66]

Iran's inability to do business with other countries sharply constricted its economy. A Gallup poll conducted in Iran in 2012 found that 31 percent of Iranians rated their lives poorly enough to be considered "suffering," one of the highest rates of any country in the Middle East or North Africa. The polling company said countries with comparable suffering levels either were at war, such as Afghanistan, or experiencing severe instability, such as Tunisia.[67]

Iran approached the Carter administration in September 1980 about ending the crisis, but an agreement could not be reached. Iranians ended up freeing the hostages within minutes of Republican Ronald Reagan's inauguration as president in January 1981, in what some historians say was intended as a final insult to Carter.[68]

Reagan designated Iran a state sponsor of terrorism in 1984 in response to Iran's funding and training of Hezbollah, a militant Islamist group based in Beirut, Lebanon, which was blamed for a 1983 suicide bombing at a Marine barracks in Beirut that killed 241 U.S. military personnel. During the 1980s, Iran was drawn into a bloody eight-year war with Iraq, after that country's leader, Saddam Hussein, attacked Iran with, among other things, nerve and mustard gas. Iraq's use of those deadly agents led the United States, two decades later, to invade Iraq on the suspicion that it might again deploy such weapons.[69]

During the Iran-Iraq War (1980-1988), the United States tilted its support toward Iraq and became entangled in several incidents as it sought to protect international oil shipments in the Persian Gulf. For example, in 1988 a U.S. warship shot down an Iranian commercial jet that the Pentagon later said had been mistaken for a military plane, killing 290 people aboard. Outraged Iranians labeled the incident a "barbaric massacre."[70]

Nevertheless, the two sides talked secretly about the release of seven U.S. hostages held in Lebanon by Iranian-backed militants. The Reagan administration also secretly sold weapons to Iran — in violation of U.S. and international sanctions — using the profits to fund anti-government "contra" rebels in Nicaragua in what became known as the "Iran-Contra affair."[71] The sale of arms to Iran did little to improve relations between Iran and the United States: When Reagan left office, several Americans remained in captivity in Beirut.

When President George H. W. Bush succeeded Reagan in 1989, he tried to defuse U.S.-Iran tensions. In seeking Iranian help for getting the hostages in Lebanon released, in exchange for easing sanctions, Bush said that "goodwill begets goodwill." But even the presidency of centrist Hashemi Rafsanjani (1989-1997), who advocated closer U.S.-Iranian ties, could not bridge differences because of the ayatollah's grip on power.[72]

Bush's successor, Democrat Bill Clinton, wanted to prevent either Iraq or Iran from interfering with his broader goal of reaching an Israeli-Palestinian peace agreement. His administration initially imposed tougher bans on trade and investment with Iran.

The 1997 election of moderate Iranian President Mohammad Khatami, who called for eroding the "wall of mistrust" between the two countries, raised hope of better relations.[73] The United States agreed to lift some sanctions and by 2014 was annually exporting to Iran about $180 million in humanitarian goods, such as medical instruments and pharmaceuticals.[74]

"Axis of Evil"

After the November 2000 election of Republican George W. Bush and the Sept. 11, 2001, terrorist attacks by al Qaeda, U.S.-Iranian relations took a far rockier course. Khatami publicly condemned the attacks and sought to help the United States defeat the Taliban in Afghanistan, which was sheltering al Qaeda leader Osama bin Laden.[75]

But two days after the president's "axis of evil" speech, Bush's national security adviser, Condoleezza Rice, criticized Iran's "direct support of regional and global terrorism" and "its aggressive efforts to acquire weapons of mass destruction," including nuclear weapons.[76]

An exiled opposition group in 2002 revealed the existence of two previously unknown Iranian nuclear sites.[77] The resulting international criticism helped spur Khatami's government to reach agreement with France,

Sanctions Continue to Limit U.S.-Iran Business

Trade supporters hope more American products can be sold to Iran.

The recent easing of economic sanctions against Iran permits U.S. companies to sell it commercial planes and aircraft parts — but hardly anything else.

Backers of closer relations, however, hope that someday American consumer goods ranging from iPhones to Marlboros might legally be exported to the long-standing U.S. enemy.

The nuclear deal among the United States, Iran and five other countries continues to prohibit a variety of U.S. companies from doing business with Iran. While it did lift U.S. sanctions related to Iran's nuclear work, it did not affect other U.S. sanctions, such as those imposed after the 1979 Iran hostage crisis or others implemented after the State Department designated Iran a state sponsor of terrorism in 1984. Under the 1984 sanctions, for instance, U.S. companies cannot export products to Iran that could have both commercial and military purposes, such as computer equipment.[1]

Suzanne Maloney, deputy director of the foreign policy program at the Brookings Institution, a centrist Washington, D.C., think tank, said it could be difficult to ease future sanctions, in part because U.S. policymakers have come to depend on them as a tool to punish the country.

"The sanctions are now a semi-permanent fixture of American policy" towards Iran, Maloney wrote in a 2015 book on Iran's economy.[2]

The recent deal allows American aircraft to be sold to Iran, and it also allows certain Iranian products into the United States: Those include so-called "luxury items" such as carpets and caviar, along with pistachio nuts, one of Iran's biggest exports.[3]

Experts say conservatives in Iran's government who control many industries are wary of the impact of trade with the West. They cite iBridges, a nonprofit international technology consortium that held meetings in Berkeley, Calif., and Berlin to discuss future investment possibilities in Iran. Hardline media in Iran accused the group of seeking a "soft overthrow" of the Iranian government by trying to supplant home-grown companies.[4]

American groups supporting greater U.S.-Iranian engagement, such as the National Iranian American Council in Washington, D.C., say the United States is the biggest loser of all sanctions-enforcing nations, having sacrificed between $134.7 billion and $175.3 billion in potential export revenue to Iran from 1995 to 2012 alone.[5]

However, the Washington-based Iran-American Chamber of Commerce, an association of Iranian-American business executives, is optimistic that Iran's eagerness to improve its economy eventually could pave the way for U.S. investment.

"There is a vast area for expanding the two countries' future trade relations [because] the demands and resources of the two countries are abundant and, in Iran's case, untapped," according to the group.[6]

Supporters of greater engagement say if U.S. sanctions against Iran are ever lifted, attention should be paid to the potential trade benefits. Meanwhile, companies like Apple are watching to see if things are likely to change. Here are some areas in which American companies see potential for U.S.-Iranian trade:

Airplanes: Under the terms of the nuclear agreement, U.S. aircraft firms can sell commercial aircraft to Iran, which needs up to 600 new planes for its aging fleet, and in February the government cleared Boeing Co. to begin selling in Iran.[7]

Even if Boeing doesn't sell Iran any planes, it could still provide parts and maintenance, said Richard Aboulafia, an analyst with the Teal Group aerospace consulting firm in Fairfax, Va.[8] In 2014, Boeing sold manuals, drawings, navigation charts and data to Iran Air, the national airline — its first transaction with the country since 1979. Because the sales were aimed at improving commercial aircraft safety, they were not prohibited under U.S. sanctions.[9]

Oil and gas infrastructure: Iranian officials said they want to invest upward of $100 billion to modernize aging oil pipelines and other parts of the industry.[10]

U.S. companies are best-positioned to provide oil pipeline and drilling technology, according to Amin Saikal, a professor of political science at Australian National University and author of the 2015 book *Iran at the Crossroads.* However, Russia already is working with Iran on the issue and would be a competitor.[11]

Consumer electronics: *The Wall Street Journal* has reported that Apple has approached Iranian distributors about selling iPhones and other products if U.S. sanctions eventually are lifted on consumer products. However, the technology giant has declined to comment.[12]

Currently, Iran's 50 million cellphone users rely on Chinese technology.[13] However, Apple and Dell computer products are smuggled into Iran, where they are resold.[14] China will continue to be a U.S. competitor in consumer electronics: In January, Chinese president Xi Jinping signed 17 agreements with Iran on technological and economic cooperation.[15]

Cars: Iran is the Middle East's biggest automobile market, with 900,000 passenger cars and trucks — mostly Chinese imports — purchased in 2014. But the National Iranian American Council says U.S. manufacturers could sell cars in Iran, where they were once popular and where Chinese cars are seen as low-quality.[16]

Tobacco: Western cigarette brands such as Marlboro were popular during the 1970s in Iran, where the number of smokers reportedly has risen in recent years and a pack of cigarettes costs about 50 cents. The state-owned Iranian Tobacco Company controls just over one-third of the market, and British and Japanese companies share the rest.[17]

— *Chuck McCutcheon*

AFP/Getty Images/STR

Pipelines for oil exports stretch along the shore of the Persian Gulf. Iranian officials have promised to spend as much as $100 billion to upgrade aging pipelines and other infrastructure.

[1] Kenneth Katzman, "Iran Sanctions," Congressional Research Service, Jan. 21, 2016, http://tinyurl.com/hq2vgbe.

[2] Suzanne Maloney, *Iran's Political Economy Since the Revolution* (2015), p. 487.

[3] Steven Mufson, "For U.S. firms, the Iran deal means pistachios, airline parts and carpets," *The Washington Post*, July 14, 2015, http://tinyurl.com/gst8d6h.

[4] Saeed Kamali Dehghan, "From Digikala to Hamijoo: the Iranian startup revolution, phase two," *The Guardian*, May 31, 2015, http://tinyurl.com/pzngcyv; David Ignatius, "Despite the nuclear deal, Iran continues its economic sabotage," *The Washington Post*, Dec. 29, 2015, http://tinyurl.com/h86wbsf.

[5] Jonathan Leslie, Reza Marashi and Trita Parsi, "Losing Billions: The Cost of Sanctions to the U.S. Economy," National Iranian American Council, July 2014, http://tinyurl.com/gsnvaub.

[6] "About Us," United States-Iran Chamber of Commerce, undated, http://tinyurl. com/zgggug5.

[7] Jon Ostrower, "Boeing Secures Iran License," *The Wall Street Journal*, Feb. 19, 2016, http://tinyurl.com/zn4q3lm.

[8] Jackie Northam, "Boeing Can Sell Planes To Iran, But Does Iran Want Them?" NPR, Feb. 7, 2016, http://tinyurl.com/zax8bjj.

[9] "Boeing books first sales to Iran since 1979," Reuters, Oct. 22, 2014, http://tinyurl.com/zhrnrfm.

[10] Najmeh Bozorgmehr, "Iran eyes $100bn of western investment in oil industry," *Financial Times*, July 1, 2015, http://tinyurl.com/h8us5k9.

[11] Andy Tully, "Russia To Help Iran Reboot Oil Industry," OilPrice.com, Jan. 3, 2016, http://tinyurl.com/z9knnrt.

[12] Benoit Faucon, "Apple in Talks to Sell iPhone in Iran," *The Wall Street Journal*, Oct. 29, 2014, http://tinyurl.com/ohl69fq.

[13] "Losing Billions," *op. cit.*

[14] Garrett Nada, "If sanctions are lifted, here's what trade between Iran and the US could look like," *Quartz*, April 24, 2015, http://tinyurl.com/m4vht25.

[15] Steve Mollman, "Iran plans to boost trade with China by about 1,000% over the next 10 years," *Quartz*, Jan. 24, 2016, http://tinyurl.com/jqdhpb6.

[16] "Losing Billions," *op. cit.*; Andy Sharman, "Carmakers eye golden Iranian opportunity in wake of nuclear deal," *Financial Times*, July 15, 2015, http://tinyurl.com/j7awtwk; Mathieu Rosemain and Golnar Motevalli, China Carmakers Will Challenge West in Iran When Sanctions Lift," *Bloomberg*, April 15, 2015, http://tinyurl.com/ong249x.

[17] Elizabeth Whitman, "Iran Nuclear Deal: Big Tobacco Sees Opportunity For Cigarette Market Amid Lagging Revenues Elsewhere," *International Business Times*, Oct. 27, 2015, http://tinyurl.com/gtboxjz.

Iran President a "Loyalist of the System"

Rouhani watching nuclear deal before committing to better U.S. relations.

When it comes to dealing with the United States, Iranian President Hassan Rouhani is no Mahmoud Ahmadinejad, his antagonistic predecessor who accused America of trusting the devil.[1] But he's also no Mikhail Gorbachev, the former Soviet leader who helped end the Cold War and ushered in better U.S.-Russian relations.

Rouhani, elected in 2013, is a sophisticated, Western-educated politician who pushed for last year's nuclear deal with the United States and five other nations. He is vastly different from Ahmadinejad, who was reviled worldwide for his scathing criticisms of the United States and Israel and stout defense of his country's nuclear program.

Many foreign-policy experts say, however, that Rouhani should not be mistaken for Gorbachev, who, upon becoming the Soviet Union's president in 1990, oversaw the dismantling of communism to spur more trade with the United States and other nations. Unlike Gorbachev, they say, Rouhani is a careful political insider unwilling to upend his country's entrenched power structure for the sake of improving its standing in the world.

"Rouhani is a loyalist of the system," says Nader Hashemi, a professor at the University of Denver's Josef Korbel School of International Studies and director of its Center for Middle East Studies. "To the extent he can bring about change within it, he'll try to do so by making speeches and appeals within the corridors of power. But he's not going to rock the system."

Rouhani showed his cautiousness when asked about the prospects for U.S.-Iranian relations after Iran agreed to curtail nuclear work in exchange for the West lifting numerous economic sanctions on Iran. Without providing specifics, he said he first wants to see whether the deal is carried out to his satisfaction, such as ensuring sanctions are not reimposed for what he considers unfair reasons.

"If it is well implemented, it will lay the foundations for lesser tension with the U.S., creating the conditions for a new era," he told an Italian newspaper. "But if the Americans don't meet their nuclear deal commitments, then our relationship will certainly be the same as in the past."[2]

Rouhani, 67, who was born with the last name Feridoun, studied religion and changed his name in his youth to the Persian word for "cleric." He received a Ph.D. in law from Glasgow Caledonian University in Scotland in 1995.[3]

Rouhani became a supporter of Ayatollah Ruhollah Khomeini in the 1970s before the Khomeini-led Islamic Revolution toppled the U.S.-backed shah, whom hard-liners reviled for his use of torture. But Rouhani also became close with Hashemi Rafsanjani, Iran's centrist former president (1989-1997) who advocated repairing ties with the United States.[4]

"Rouhani's pragmatic policy approach on issues such as the nuclear issue and relations with the United States approximate Rafsanjani's views," the Congressional Research Service, which studies issues for Congress, said in an analysis published in January.[5]

Rouhani's long background in government posts has given him credibility with Iranian conservatives loyal to Ayatollah Ali Khamenei, Khomeini's successor and current "supreme leader." In 1986, as deputy speaker in parliament, Rouhani took part in secret talks with U.S. officials as part of what became known during the Ronald Reagan administration as the Iran-Contra "arms-for-hostages" affair. Administration officials defied an arms embargo on Iran and sold it weapons to obtain the release of hostages held in Lebanon by a group with Iranian ties. The money then was funneled to the "contra" guerrillas fighting Nicaragua's left-wing government.[6]

Rouhani drew attention last November when he accused Iran's hardline, anti-Western media of being too closely

Germany and the U.K. to temporarily suspend some aspects of its program and invite inspections of the facilities, which Khatami claimed were for non-military work. The United States joined in the negotiations in 2005, but talks sputtered after Iran insisted on resuming uranium enrichment before continuing to try to strike a deal.[78]

Khatami's elected successor, Mahmoud Ahmadinejad, ratcheted up the tension with the United States by labeling it an international bully and offending Israel by proclaiming the Holocaust — in which Nazi Germany exterminated 6 million Jews — a "myth."[79] Many outraged U.S. and Israeli officials said Ahmadinejad had aligned with the ayatollah-controlled Revolutionary Guards Corps, which enforces internal security.[7] Before the February 2016 parliamentary elections in Iran, Rouhani also rebuked an internal election committee's attempt to limit the number of moderate candidates.[8]

For now, Rouhani is popular in Iran. A recent telephone poll of more than 1,000 Iranians by the University of Maryland with the University of Tehran and Canadian firm IranPoll.com found he had a favorability rating of 82 percent, with 42 percent of those surveyed regarding him "very favorably."[9]

Rouhani has succeeded in cutting Iran's annual inflation rate from about 40 percent to less than 13 percent over the past two years and ending three straight years of economic downturns.[10] But experts say he needs to achieve more economic progress by 2017, when he would be eligible to seek re-election.

If the sanctions-unburdened economy doesn't dramatically improve by then, they agree, impatient voters may be more willing to back a challenger less inclined to work with the United States. At the same time, they say, a new U.S. president might try to undo the nuclear deal and reimpose sanctions.

"Rouhani does not have a lot of time on his hands," says Amin Saikal, a professor of political science at Australian National University and author of the 2015 book *Iran at the Crossroads*. "He will have to move really fast to show evidence of the nuclear agreement not only to the public, but the hard-liners."

— *Chuck McCutcheon*

Moderate President Hassan Rouhani says that if the nuclear deal is implemented to Iranian leaders' satisfaction, "we can put other topics on the table for discussion" with the United States.

[1] Dana Hughes and Amy Bingham, "Iran's Ahmadinejad Says America Entrusted Itself to the Devil," ABC News.com, Sept. 12, 2012, http://tinyurl.com/bt8j9dc.

[2] Viviana Mazza and Paolo Valentino, "Rouhani: 'A New Era Between Iran and the World,'" *Corriere della Sera* (Italy), Nov. 12, 2015, http://tinyurl.com/h5qay2o.

[3] Ian Black and Saeed Kamali Dehghan, "Hassan Rouhani, 'ultimate insider' who holds key to a more moderate Iran," *The Guardian*, June 20, 2013, http://tinyurl.com/hfrsrw3.

[4] Robin Wright and Garrett Nada, "Latest on the Race: Rafsanjani Redux?" U.S. Institute of Peace Iran Primer, May 20, 2013, http://tinyurl.com/zgrxpeh.

[5] Kenneth Katzman, "Iran, Gulf Security and U.S. Policy," Congressional Research Service, Jan. 14, 2016, http://tinyurl.com/gw2ca94.

[6] Shane Harris, "When Rouhani Met Ollie North," *Foreign Policy*, Sept. 28, 2013, http://tinyurl.com/jgxqurv.

[7] Thomas Erdbrink, "Iran's President Suggests Link Between Hard-Line Media and Arrests," *The New York Times*, Nov. 8, 2015, http://tinyurl.com/j2mykab.

[8] "Rouhani Enters Iran Election Row Over Barred Candidates," Agence-France Press, Yahoo News, Jan. 21, 2016, http://tinyurl.com/z67a4mz.

[9] Nancy Gallagher, Ebrahim Mohseni and Clay Ramsay, "Iranian Attitudes in Advance of the Parliamentary Elections: Economics, Politics, and Foreign Affairs," University of Maryland Center for International & Security Studies, January 2016, http://tinyurl.com/zowabqs.

[10] Najmeh Bozorgmehr, "Iran desperate for nuclear deal dividend as economy stagnates," *Financial Times*, Sept. 20, 2015, http://tinyurl.com/gnu4zdd.

vowed that Israel should be "wiped off the map," but experts say he was incorrectly paraphrasing Khomeini, who consistently has said "the cancerous tumor called Israel must be uprooted from the region."[80]

At a 2007 Democratic presidential debate, Obama — then a U.S. senator from Illinois — said that if elected, he would seek to talk to Iran's leader and those from other hostile countries.[81] Once in office, Obama sent a senior official to meet with Iran's chief nuclear negotiator. But Iran continued to expand its nuclear program and in 2011 refused to make concessions. International negotiations broke off for more than a year.[82]

Young women chat at a coffee shop in Tehran. Some experts on Iran see bright potential for improved U.S.-Iran relations over the long term, given the greater influence they say Iran's youthful, well-educated population will exercise over the country's politics.

Meanwhile, the U.N. Security Council in 2010 had imposed even tougher sanctions, including a tightening of the arms embargo and a ban on international travel for those involved in Iran's nuclear program.[83]

The IAEA warned the country had sought to learn how to put a nuclear payload onto an intermediate-range missile capable of reaching Israel, but Iran said the allegations were based on false Israeli and U.S. information. Nevertheless, Ahmadinejad agreed to restart negotiations.[84]

The Obama administration continued a program, begun during the second Bush administration, to use an Israeli-developed computer virus to shut down computer-driven nuclear-processing machines.[85]

Nuclear Negotiations

As the number of Iranian families living in poverty reached 40 percent of the population by 2013, Rouhani won election that year by promising to lift Iran's economy.[86]

The same year Rouhani spurned a chance to meet Obama while visiting New York City for a U.N. meeting, but he did speak with his White House counterpart by telephone. The gesture was the highest-level contact between the two countries in decades and was widely interpreted as underscoring Tehran's seriousness about wrapping up nuclear negotiations.[87]

The deal was finalized in July 2015 over the vehement objections of Israel's Netanyahu, whom congressional

Republicans had invited earlier to address a joint session of Congress to make his case against negotiating with Iran.[88] The agreement was not a formal treaty requiring U.S. Senate ratification, but negotiators gave Congress the opportunity to consider a "resolution of disapproval." Congressional opponents had enough votes to pass such a measure but not enough to override a threatened presidential veto, leaving the deal intact.[89]

The two sides continued talks even after Rezaian, a dual U.S.-Iranian citizen and *The Post*'s Tehran bureau chief, was abducted in July 2014 and charged with spying. He was tried behind closed doors and sentenced to prison. Obama resisted calls from journalism organizations, human-rights groups and politicians to make the reporter's release a condition of the nuclear deal, saying he did not want to set a precedent or complicate negotiations.[90]

In January Obama announced he had resolved a separate dispute with Iran dating back to the shah's era, when Iran demanded more than $400 million in payments for U.S. military equipment sold to the shah but never delivered after his overthrow. The Iranians received the money in January, plus $1.3 billion in accumulated interest.

But in response to Iran's missile tests last fall, Obama imposed new sanctions on a handful of Iranian business officials and some foreign companies accused of shipping crucial technologies to Iran, including missile parts. Because the new sanctions were focused on those individuals and firms — not the government — the penalties are small compared to the nuclear-based sanctions and not expected to affect most Iranians.[91]

CURRENT SITUATION
Iranian Elections

In the Feb. 26 election for Parliament, reformist candidates, who advocate expanding social freedoms in Iran as well as greater engagement with the United States and other Western countries, won at least 85 seats. Moderate conservatives, who also support the nuclear deal but whose views are not quite as far to the left politically as those of the reformists, won 73 seats. Those combined gains are enough to give both camps a majority in the 290-seat assembly over hard-liners who oppose the nuclear deal.

Moderates also won a 59 percent majority in the Assembly of Experts, an 88-member group charged with

AT ISSUE

Should the United States seek closer ties with Iran?

YES

Trita Parsi
Founder and President, National Iranian American Council

Written for *CQ Researcher*, March 2016

The idea of improving relations with Iran has spread panic among both U.S. and Iranian hard-liners. The latter fear that improved U.S.-Iran relations will open a window for Washington to regain influence in Iran and bring about its "cultural subversion." The former fear that a U.S.-Iran thaw will cause the United States to betray its security commitments to historical allies in the Middle East — and jeopardize military contracts worth billions of dollars.

Clearly, a wide gulf separates U.S. and Iranian interests, particularly if viewed from a narrow and immediate security perspective. But it is a profound mistake to reduce Iran to its current regime and discount Iran's vibrant society. That perspective led to the West consistently being surprised by Iranian presidential elections.

If we study Iran's society, however, we will quickly notice that it holds one of the region's most modern, well-educated and liberally oriented populations. In fact, Iranian society tends to share far more values with Western liberal democracies than do the societies of most of America's Middle Eastern allies.

Consider: Among 15- to 24-years-olds in Iran, literacy rates are near universal for men and women. Primary school enrollment is at 99.9 percent. Most Iranians (69 percent) live in cities and have adopted both an urban lifestyle and the values that come with it. Astonishingly, women represent one-third of Iran's doctors, 60 percent of its civil servants, 60 percent of its university students and 80 percent of its teachers. Compare that to Saudi Arabia — American's chief Arab ally — where the question of whether women should drive continues to be debated.

Moreover, according to economist Djavad Salehi-Isfahani of Virginia Tech, 60 percent of Iran's population is middle class. If Iran grows a moderate 5 percent a year for 10 years as a result of the nuclear deal, its middle class will constitute 85 percent of the population by 2025. A country with such a large middle class is more likely to pursue moderate, status-quo policies, both internally and externally, than promote radicalism. Clearly, engagement with Iran would benefit Iran's moderate society.

Granted that the U.S. interest in the region is stability and not domination, then the long-run compatibility of U.S. and Iranian interests are clear. But to gain a friend in the long run, American must look beyond Iran's current regime in the short run.

NO

Sen. Dan Sullivan, R-Alaska
Member, Senate Armed Services Committee

Written for *CQ Researcher*, March 2016

When President Obama and Secretary of State John Kerry were selling the Iranian nuclear deal to Americans, implicit in their appeal was that it would mark the beginning of a more transparent and cooperative Iran, as it shed its pariah-state identity and re-entered the community of nations. However, since its signing, we have seen no evidence of this hoped-for transformation, only an escalation of provocations by an emboldened regime.

Since the deal was negotiated, Iran has captured U.S. sailors in the Persian Gulf and used their detention for propaganda, conducted ballistic missile tests in violation of U.N. Security Council resolutions, launched rockets near a U.S. aircraft carrier and used innocent Americans as bargaining chips for the release and clemency of Iranian criminals. The regime continues to hold rallies where leaders chant "death to America." It also refuses to renounce its sponsorship of terrorism by continuing to finance groups such as Hezbollah, whose long history of activities includes the 1983 bombing of a U.S. Marine barracks in Beirut and the dispatch of troops and weapons to fight Americans in the Iraq War.

This is a regime with the blood of thousands of American soldiers on its hands, for which it refuses to take responsibility.

Might Iran change in the future? We hope so. Data suggest that Iranian youths are as open to change as any similar Middle Eastern demographic. More than 60 percent of Iran's population is under 30. The possibility that a future U.S. administration could strike an understanding with a more democratic and peaceful Iran — if its politics moderate — shouldn't be discounted, but it is not likely to occur with the current Iranian president, nor in the next decade. Indeed, the regime most recently barred thousands of pro-reform candidates from running in the February elections — seen as the largest suppression of human rights in Iran since 2009.

The Islamic Republic's revolutionary identity is tied to advancing an agenda that seeks the destabilization of the Middle East and complete hegemony in the region. Even so-called political moderates are more pragmatists than reformists. This presents a challenge. There is no incentive for political change because the nuclear deal, which should have been a reward for good behavior, was offered before such good behavior transpired.

The regime, as it is, is no friend of the United States, our policies or our people, and until reformation replaces radicalism, we should remain vigilant.

choosing Khamenei's eventual successor. Two extremely prominent hard-liners lost their seats in the assembly.[92]

Experts say the results mean Rouhani will have more political support as he seeks to conduct more trade with other countries to improve Iran's economy. But they say Khamenei's opposition to negotiating anything with the United States beyond the nuclear deal still matters more than the election results.

"The elections will have little direct or immediate effect on U.S.-Iran relations, in large part because the supreme leader has the full and final say on this matter," the University of Denver's Hashemi says.

Iranian political analyst Hamidreza Taraghi, who is close to Iran's leadership, predicted the moderate faction "will quickly face division among themselves" because of differences in their political backgrounds. "To write off the hard-liners would be a major mistake," Taraghi said.[93]

Avoiding Sanctions

The lifting of sanctions after Iran was judged to have met its initial commitments under the nuclear deal has sparked a flood of international investment interest. But the United States has promised to penalize any domestic companies or foreign countries whose companies conduct business with the Revolutionary Guards, who control many industries through front companies.

As a result, European and Asian businesses are scrambling to ensure that the companies they do business with are not fronts.[94] The Treasury Department has begun issuing guidelines about what foreign companies must do to avoid penalties, but experts say the Commerce and State departments need to provide more clarity.

Besides the Revolutionary Guards, other parts of Iran's government directly own and operate hundreds of enterprises and indirectly control others. Within the first few weeks after the sanctions were lifted, all of the major international deals involved industries in which Iran's government is somehow involved.

One of the largest agreements was with Iran's national airline, Iran Air, which signed a deal with the European consortium Airbus to buy more than 100 planes. An Italian steelmaker, Danieli, began a $2 billion joint venture with the Iranian Mines and Mining Industries Development and Renovation Organization.[95]

Meanwhile, Iran, which hopes to ship more oil overseas, is jostling with two oil-producing U.S. allies — Saudi Arabia and the United Arab Emirates — for control over an oil market in which prices have plummeted because of worldwide oversupply. After Saudi Arabia's state oil company announced it would sell oil at discounted prices, Iran said it would follow suit.[96] That followed a November 2014 move by those countries to oppose Tehran's call for a cut in oil production to boost plummeting oil prices.

The Saudis and their allies have sought to use their dominance in the 13-member Organization of Petroleum Exporting Countries (OPEC) "to limit Iran's income from its oil and thus restrain its military spending," Australian National University's Saikal wrote.[97]

U.S. Politics

Congressional lawmakers who opposed the nuclear deal have passed or are considering legislation intended to punish Iran for its recent ballistic missile tests.

Some senators from both parties said Obama's sanctions imposed after the missile tests did not go far enough. They are crafting bills that impose harsher, broader-ranging penalties, along with legislation to beef up sanctions for Iran's human-rights violations.

"I think Congress can be bolder" in dealing with Iran, said Sen. Benjamin Cardin of Maryland, the Senate Foreign Relations Committee's top Democrat and a staunch supporter of Israel. Cardin was one of four Senate Democrats to oppose the nuclear deal, citing Israel's security concerns, but he said he wants to make sure it is successfully implemented.[98]

In February the House passed, along party lines, a bill to restrict a president's ability to lift economic sanctions.[99] The White House said the bill would undo the progress made in the nuclear deal and threatened a veto.[100]

In the U.S. presidential race, all major candidates except Sanders have taken tougher public stances toward Iran than Obama.

Republican contenders Marco Rubio and Ted Cruz have been especially vocal in vowing to revoke the nuclear deal immediately upon taking office. Rubio, a Florida senator, said he would demand that Iran permanently forsake any pursuit of nuclear weapons and would back up the demand with "a credible threat of military force," along with tougher economic sanctions for terrorism and human-rights violations.[101] Cruz, a Texas senator, said the deal "will facilitate and accelerate" Iran's pursuit of a nuclear weapon.

But many experts refute Cruz's assertion. Iran's pledges under the deal "would slow and impede any nuclear weapons effort, not facilitate and accelerate it," said Matthew Bunn, a specialist in nuclear issues at Harvard's John F. Kennedy School of Government.[102]

Republican front-runner Trump has joined Cruz and Rubio in harshly criticizing the deal. But Trump has not called for its abandonment, instead pledging stringent enforcement to deter cheating. "I would police that contract so tough that they [Iran] don't have a chance," he said.[103]

Clinton has expressed strong support for the deal but said she would consider military action if Iran is found to have cheated. And she has outlined several other hawkish measures, including increasing support for Israel's military to protect itself against Iranian threats, strengthening ways to keep Hezbollah from acquiring weapons and considering expanding current human-rights sanctions against Iran.[104]

OUTLOOK
Uncertain Relations

Because the nuclear deal is not a formal treaty, foreign-policy experts say the next U.S. president could use executive authority to negate the agreement, re-imposing suspended sanctions and ordering federal agencies not to implement it. But they predict those moves would face tremendous opposition from abroad.

U.S. allies that signed the deal would put significant pressure on a new chief executive to keep it intact to avoid what the experts agree would be an extremely messy international dispute.

"If we try to reimpose sanctions on Iran and no one follows, then we have the worst of all worlds," said Robert Einhorn, a former Iran nuclear negotiator at the State Department.[105]

Australian National University's Saikal agrees a U.S. pullout could leave the new administration "very much isolated by other world powers" while accelerating the potential for Iran to pursue bomb making. Senate Foreign Relations Committee Chairman Bob Corker, R-Tenn., said he is frustrated by what he predicts will be the unwillingness of those countries to get tougher with Iran if it breaks the nuclear deal.

"It's going to be difficult — very, very difficult — in the future to push back in any meaningful way against the violations that take place," Corker said.[106]

But Saikal and other experts say the flourishing business ties between Iran and other countries are likely to create an incentive for Iran to fulfill its commitments under the deal. If that happens, they say, U.S. hostility toward Iran eventually could lessen — depending on how long Khamenei is in control.

"As long as the supreme leader remains in power, I don't think Iran and America will normalize relations," said Karim Sadjadpour, a senior associate for the Middle East program at the Carnegie Endowment for International Peace, a Washington think tank.[107] RAND Corp. researchers said Khamenei's departure "will mark a fundamental change" in how Iran deals with the world, since a successor could be more willing to engage the United States.[108] Khamenei suggested in September that he may be gone within a decade.[109]

Other experts see bright potential for U.S.-Iran relations over the longer term, given the greater influence they say Iran's youthful, well-educated population will exercise over the country's politics. "It's a young, dynamic, incredibly well-positioned society for the future," Brookings' Maloney said. "If I were to place a bet on the long-term democratic opportunities in the region, Iran is it, by a long shot."[110]

The Middle East Institute's Harrison says while it's difficult to predict what will happen in the region, it could remain highly unstable, which could compel a closer U.S.-Iran partnership on fighting terrorism.

"Given the challenges Iran and all the major players [in the Middle East] are going to have in the next 10 years, I would expect a more pragmatic relationship to evolve" between Iran and the United States, he says. But he expects that on some "deeply ideological" issues such as human rights, "We are going to cross swords."

The recent University of Maryland poll conducted with the University of Tehran and IranPoll.com found a split among Iranians about the future of relations between the two countries. Thirty-eight percent said relations would improve in the next three years, while 36 percent predicted they would stay the same. Just over one-fifth speculated that relations would worsen.[111]

Because of the persistent ideological constraints between Iran and the United States, Trita Parsi, the

National Iranian American Council's founder and president, is pragmatic about how much can be achieved over the short term.

"I don't think they're going to be best friends anytime soon," Parsi said. "But I think they can stop being worst enemies."[112]

NOTES

1. "Iran Fact File: Arak Heavy Water Reactor," U.S. Institute of Peace, April 28, 2014, http://tinyurl.com/zo9vt5y.

2. William J. Broad, "Plutonium Is Unsung Concession in Iran Nuclear Deal," *The New York Times*, Sept. 7, 2015, http://tinyurl.com/gmpqt9m.

3. "Statement by the President on Iran," White House Office of the Press Secretary, Jan. 17, 2016, http://tinyurl.com/j5p9y2o.

4. "How Iran Entered the 'Axis,' " PBS Frontline, undated, http://tinyurl.com/zbfehph.

5. "Understanding Iran Beyond The Deal," panel discussion, The Brookings Institution, Oct. 15, 2015, http://tinyurl.com/zfkqqby.

6. "Florida Passes New York to Become the Nation's Third Most Populous State, Census Bureau Reports," news release, U.S. Census Bureau, Dec. 23, 2014, http://tinyurl.com/jq8trzm.

7. "Transcript: Iranian President Hassan Rouhani's Full NPR Interview," NPR, Sept. 28, 2015, http://tinyurl.com/jhmtclt.

8. For background, see Roland Flammini, "Rising Tension Over Iran," *CQ Global Researcher*, Feb. 7, 2012, pp. 57-80; Peter Katel, "U.S. Policy on Iran," *CQ Researcher*, Nov. 16, 2007, pp. 961-984.

9. "Country Reports on Terrorism 2014," U.S. Department of State, http://tinyurl.com/plvrsfz.

10. Carol Morello *et al.*, "Plane leaves Iran with Post reporter, other Americans in swap," *The Washington Post*, Jan. 17, 2016, http://tinyurl.com/h2mkdvc.

11. Jessica Schulberg, "Siamak Namazi's Friends Thought He'd Be Freed From Iranian Prison, But The Media Had It Wrong," *The Huffington Post*, Jan. 19, 2016, http://tinyurl.com/hm7gyxm.

12. Thomas Erdbrink, "Iran's Supreme Leader Condemns Mob Attack on Saudi Embassy," *The New York Times*, Jan. 20, 2016, http://tinyurl.com/hjmbeao.

13. Gregory Korte, "U.S. Sanctions Iran's Ballistic Missile Program," *USA Today*, Jan. 17, 2016, http://tinyurl.com/zwxctqx.

14. Martin C. Libicki, "Iran: A Rising Cyber Power?" RAND.org blog, Dec. 16, 2015, http://tinyurl.com/je95d4l.

15. "Khamenei says Iran will not negotiate with U.S. beyond nuclear talks," Reuters, Sept. 9, 2015, http://tinyurl.com/jp83n6y.

16. Teresa Welsh, "Supreme Leader's Poor Health Injects Instability Into Iranian Politics," *U.S. News & World Report*, March 10, 2015, http://tinyurl.com/mj4jqtv.

17. "Iranian Hard-liners Losers In Parliament, Clerical Body," The Associated Press, *The New York Times*, Feb. 29, 2016, http://tinyurl.com/je42m4c.

18. Andrew Dugan, "After Nuclear Deal, U.S. Views of Iran Remain Dismal," Gallup.com, Feb. 17, 2016, http://tinyurl.com/jdaaggy.

19. Nancy Gallagher, Ebrahim Mohseni and Clay Ramsay, "Iranian Attitudes in Advance of the Parliamentary Elections: Economics, Politics, and Foreign Affairs," University of Maryland Center for International & Security Studies, February 2016, http://tinyurl.com/zowabqs.

20. For background see Peter Katel, "Restoring Ties With Cuba," *CQ Researcher*, June 12, 2015, pp. 505-528.

21. "Transcript of the Democratic Presidential Debate," *The New York Times*, Jan. 17, 2016, http://tinyurl.com/h8espoy.

22. Tyler Cullis and Amir Handjani, "US should forge economic ties with Iran," *The Hill*, Oct. 8, 2015, http://tinyurl.com/gsqhmgo.

23. Thomas Erdbrink, Sewell Chan and David E. Sanger, "After a U.S. Shift, Iran Has a Seat at Talks on War in Syria," *The New York Times*, Oct. 28, 2015, http://tinyurl.com/ntjqaq4.

24. Karen DeYoung, "Intense diplomacy between Secretary of State Kerry and his Iranian counterpart

to secure sailors' release," *The Washington Post*, Jan. 13, 2016, http://tinyurl.com/gsakfm6.

25. Robin Wright, "Tehran's Promise," *The New Yorker*, July 27, 2015, http://tinyurl.com/omnvsdk.

26. Stephen Kinzer, "Is Iran Really So Evil?" *Politico Magazine*, Jan. 17, 2016, http://tinyurl.com/z9o7r9n. For background on Turkey, see Brian Beary, "Unrest in Turkey," *CQ Researcher*, Jan. 29, 2016, pp. 97-120.

27. Leigh Ann Caldwell, "Clinton Expands Her Attacks Against Sanders Over Foreign Policy," NBCNews.com, Jan. 21, 2016, http://tinyurl.com/hcredzg.

28. Barbara Starr *et. al.*, "10 U.S. Sailors in Iranian Custody," CNN.com, Jan. 12, 2016, http://tinyurl.com/zpwdkqv.

29. Jay Solomon, "U.S. Detects Flurry of Iranian Hacking," *The Wall Street Journal*, Nov. 4, 2015, http://tinyurl.com/nkwwmae; Yeganeh Torbati and Bozorgmehr Sharafedin, "Iranian-American businessman detained in Iran denied access to lawyer," *Business Insider*, Feb. 21, 2016, http://tinyurl.com/zpouqce; Haleh Esfandiari, "Iran Arrests 80-Year-Old Father of Dual-Citizen Already in Custody," *The Wall Street Journal*, Feb. 24, 2016, http://tinyurl.com/guph95f.

30. Tim Craig, "In Islamic countries, Kentucky Fried Chicken isn't always 'finger-lickin' good,'" *The Washington Post*, Nov. 4, 2015, http://tinyurl.com/jto3mc8.

31. Dugald McConnell and Brian Todd, "Despite Iran prisoner swap, Robert Levinson's family still seeks answers," CNN.com, Jan. 18, 2016, http://tinyurl.com/z3x8hgn; Barry Meier, "Clues Emerge on Robert Levinson, C.I.A. Consultant Who Vanished in Iran," *The New York Times*, Jan. 22, 2016, http://tinyurl.com/j5ypj5b.

32. Sarah Mimms, "The GOP's Iran Frustration," *National Journal*, Jan. 20, 2016, http://tinyurl.com/zh8lagr.

33. Aaron David Miller, "America's awkward Iran dance," CNN.com, Feb. 2, 2016, http://tinyurl.com/je75hxn.

34. Glenn Kessler, "In 2003, U.S. Spurned Iran's Offer of Dialogue," *The Washington Post*, June 18, 2006, http://tinyurl.com/rt9lb.

35. Karl Vick, "Is Iran Finally Ready for Change?" *Time*, Nov. 5, 2015, http://tinyurl.com/h7fyhry.

36. Ivan Sascha Sheehan, "An Opportunity to Focus on Human Rights in Iran," Al Jazeera, Sept. 28, 2015, http://tinyurl.com/zcdyrfv; "Iran's 'staggering' execution spree: nearly 700 put to death in just over six months," Amnesty International, July 23, 2015, http://tinyurl.com/j69pnnc.

37. Michael Cavna, "Iranian artist, sentenced to 12 years for cartoon, wins CRNI's Courage award," *The Washington Post*, Aug. 14, 2015, http://tinyurl.com/zwqqjry.

38. "Situation of Baha'is In Iran," Baha'i International Community, Feb. 5, 2016, http://tinyurl.com/ztjn78d.

39. Faraz Sanei, "Dispatches: Time to Prioritize Human Rights With Tehran," Human Rights Watch, July 14, 2015, http://tinyurl.com/jsl6acl.

40. "U.S. Interests in Human Rights: Leveraging Prudent Policy Tools," testimony, Mark P. Lagon before the Senate Foreign Relations Committee, July 16, 2015, http://tinyurl.com/zxwcuoy.

41. Dana Rohrabacher, "Obama and Iran's human rights record," *The Washington Times*, Oct. 28, 2015, http://tinyurl.com/jv2lhed.

42. "Judiciary Chief: US Human Rights Allegations Against Iran 'Ridiculous,' " FARS News Agency, Dec. 14, 2015, http://tinyurl.com/h844wqq.

43. Richard Lardner, "Kerry Advises Against Hitting Iran With More Sanctions Now," The Associated Press, ABCNews.com, Feb. 24, 2016, http://tinyurl.com/jf3mb4b.

44. "Frequently Asked Questions Relating to the Lifting of Certain U.S. Sanctions Under the Joint Comprehensive Plan of Action (JCPOA) on Implementation Day," U.S. Treasury Department, Jan. 16, 2016, http://tinyurl.com/jy6qasr.

45. Darren Samuelson, "The Debrief: What's Next for the Iranian Sanctions," *Politico*, Sept. 29, 2015, http://tinyurl.com/jq6o3at.

46. "Member States," International Atomic Energy Agency, undated, http://tinyurl.com/z4eeu6v; "The Historic Deal That Will Prevent Iran From

Acquiring a Nuclear Weapon," White House Briefing Room, February 2016, http://tinyurl.com/qbotkze.

47. Jamie Crawford, "U.S. spy chief: We can catch Iran if it cheats on nuclear deal," CNN.com, Sept. 9, 2015, http://tinyurl.com/jkwov7g.

48. Glenn Kessler, "Schumer's claims about '24 days before you can inspect' in Iran," *The Washington Post*, Aug. 17, 2015, http://tinyurl.com/gmpuhlz.

49. John Kerry and Ernest Moniz, "John Kerry and Ernest Moniz: The Case for a Nuclear Deal With Iran," *The Washington Post*, July 22, 2015, http://tinyurl.com/ohmro78.

50. John Mecklin, "The experts assess the Iran agreement of 2015," *Bulletin of the Atomic Scientists*, July 14, 2015, http://tinyurl.com/h7oauys.

51. "The Iranian Inspections Mirage," *The Wall Street Journal*, July 22, 2015, http://tinyurl.com/zne7r6m.

52. Bill Gertz, "Verifying Iran Nuclear Deal Not Possible, Experts Say," *Washington Free Beacon*, April 6, 2015, http://tinyurl.com/h727f23. For background on North Korea see Robert Kiener, "North Korean Menace," *CQ Global Researcher*, July 5, 2011, pp. 315-340.

53. Olli Heinonen, "Strengthening the Verification and Implementation of the Joint Comprehensive Plan of Action," Foundation for the Defense of Democracies, Nov. 25, 2015, http://tinyurl.com/hqfcewy.

54. Julian Pecquet, "Will IAEA be able to verify Iran's nuclear program?" Al-Monitor.com, Feb. 23, 2016, http://tinyurl.com/jx3w4ut.

55. Banafsheh Keynoush, "The secret side of Iran-US relations since the 1979 revolution," *The Guardian*, July 10, 2015, http://tinyurl.com/owq3bna.

56. Kenneth Katzman, "Iran, Gulf Security and U.S. Policy," Congressional Research Service, Jan. 14, 2016, http://tinyurl.com/gw2ca94; Ehsan Yarshater, "When 'Persia' Became 'Iran,' " "Iranian Studies," Iran Chamber Society, 1989, http://tinyurl.com/87srszs.

57. "U.S. Comes Clean About The Coup In Iran," CNN transcript, April 19, 2000, http://tinyurl.com/gp8yksj.

58. Tim Weiner, *Legacy of Ashes: The History of the CIA* (2007), p. 105.

59. "Mohammed Reza Shah Pahlavi," *Encyclopaedia Brittanica*, undated, http://tinyurl.com/z2x6wsv.

60. Ishaan Tharoor, "The key moments in the long history of U.S.-Iran tensions," *The Washington Post*, April 2, 2015, http://tinyurl.com/zq7h24b.

61. "Mohammed Reza Shah Pahlavi," *op. cit.*

62. Katzman, *op. cit.*

63. Stephen Kinzer, *Reset: Iran, Turkey and America's Future* (2010), p. 113.

64. President Jimmy Carter, "Tehran, Iran Toasts of the President and the Shah at a State Dinner, Dec. 31, 1977," University of California-Santa Barbara American Presidency Project, http://tinyurl.com/jb38ttz.

65. Katzman, *op. cit.*

66. Gary Samore, ed., "Sanctions Against Iran: A Guide to Targets, Terms and Timetables," Harvard University Belfer Center for Science and International Affairs, June 2015, http://tinyurl.com/jaxf68r; Zachary Laub, "International Sanctions on Iran," Council on Foreign Relations, July 15, 2015, http://tinyurl.com/hlle mbb.

67. Mohamed Younis, "Iranians Feel Bite of Sanctions, Blame U.S., Not Own Leaders," Gallup.com, Feb. 7, 2013, http://tinyurl.com/cqj7v4o.

68. Louis Jacobson, "Mitt Romney says the Iranians released hostages in 1981 because they feared Ronald Reagan's approach to foreign policy," *PolitiFact*, March 7, 2012, http://tinyurl.com/893j9ao.

69. "Saddam's Iraq: Key Events: Chemical warfare, 1983-88," BBC News, undated, http://tinyurl.com/pgz5ozs.

70. Katzman, op. cit.; George C. Wilson, "Navy Missile Downs Iranian Jetliner," *The Washington Post*, July 4, 1988, http://tinyurl.com/baooj.

71. "General Article: The Iran-Contra Affair," "American Experienc," PBS.org, undated, http://tinyurl.com/3djty9z; Robin Wright, "The Iran Deal's 'Argo' Moments," *The New Yorker*, Jan. 19, 2016, http://tinyurl.com/jxszf7m.

72. Maureen Dowd, "Iran Is Reported Ready for a Deal to Recover Assets," *The New York Times*, Aug. 9, 1989, http://tinyurl.com/j8w4ngf.

73. Tharoor, *op. cit.*

74. Garrett Nada, "If sanctions are lifted, here's what trade between Iran and US could look like," *Quartz*, April 24, 2015, http://tinyurl.com/z5l63kc.

75. Amin Saikal, *Iran at the Crossroads* (2015), p. 62.

76. "How Iran entered the Axis," *op. cit.*

77. Tharoor, *op. cit.*

78. Kenneth Katzman and Paul K. Kerr, "Iran Nuclear Agreement," Congressional Research Service, Jan. 19, 2016, http://tinyurl.com/hwhso9m; Molly Moore, "Iran Restarts Uranium Program," *The Washington Post*, Feb. 15, 2006, http://tinyurl.com/co3eyc.

79. Karl Vick, "Iran's President Calls Holocaust 'Myth' In Latest Assault on Jews," *The Washington Post*, Dec. 15, 2005, http://tinyurl.com/ckvug.

80. Glenn Kessler, "Did Ahmadinejad really say Israel should be 'wiped off the map'?" *The Washington Post*, Oct. 5, 2011, http://tinyurl.com/ht49sak.

81. "Fact check: Would Obama meet 'unconditionally' with Iran?" CNN.com, Sept. 25, 2008, http://tinyurl.com/zwtda96.

82. "Iran nuclear agreement — a timeline," CBS News, July 14, 2015, http://tinyurl.com/jmr8ra4.

83. Katzman, *op. cit.*

84. *Ibid.*

85. David E. Sanger, "Obama Order Sped Up Wave of Cyberattacks Against Iran," *The New York Times*, June 1, 2012, http://tinyurl.com/d264zk4.

86. Beheshteh Farshneshani, "In Iran, Sanctions Hurt the Wrong People," *The New York Times*, Jan. 22, 2014, http://tinyurl.com/hal6uan.

87. Jeff Mason and Louis Charbonneau, "Obama, Iran's Rouhani hold historic phone call," Reuters, Sept. 28, 2013, http://tinyurl.com/zpsokq8.

88. "5 Things to Know About Netanyahu's Speech to Congress," CBS News, March 3, 2015, http://tinyurl.com/gstfbyh.

89. Jordain Carney, "Senate Dems stonewall Iran resolution, handing victory to Obama," *The Hill*, Sept. 17, 2015, http://tinyurl.com/owxghqm.

90. Gregg Zoroya, "Timeline: From Jason Rezaian's arrest to release in Iran," *USA Today*, Jan. 16, 2016, http://tinyurl.com/hklevth.

91. David E. Sanger, Rick Gladstone and Thomas Erdbrink, "3 Freed Americans Leave Iraq; U.S. Places New Sanctions," *The New York Times*, Jan. 17, 2016, http://tinyurl.com/jt68l7r.

92. "Iranian Hard-liners Losers in Parliament, Clerical Body," *op. cit.*

93. Thomas Erdbrink, "Iranian President and Moderates Appear to Make Strong Gains in Elections," *The New York Times*, Feb. 29, 2016, http://tinyurl.com/zbdxjyf.

94. Hannah Murphy, "Iran is back in business," *Financial Times*, Jan. 29, 2016, http://tinyurl.com/jf7jquy.

95. Thomas Erdbrink, "In Iran, State-Backed Companies Win From Lifted Sanctions," *The New York Times*, Feb. 5, 2016, http://tinyurl.com/hkkkjf6.

96. Murphy, *op. cit.*

97. Saikal, *op. cit.*, p. 132.

98. Karoun Demirjian, "With Iran nuclear deal in place, key senators look to slap new sanctions on country," *The Washington Post*, Feb. 2, 2015, http://tinyurl.com/zzowr7n.

99. "House passes bill again to restrict Obama lifting Iran sanctions," Reuters, Feb. 2, 2016, http://tinyurl.com/jk8ra9o.

100. "Statement of Administration Policy — HR 3662, Iran Terror Finance Transparency Act," White House Office of Management and Budget, Jan. 11, 2016, http://tinyurl.com/zdzf8zr.

101. "As President, I'll Reimpose Sanctions On Iran On Day One," Marco Rubio campaign website, undated, http://tinyurl.com/zuco5xs.

102. Louis Jacobson, "Ted Cruz says deal will 'facilitate and accelerate' Iran getting a nuclear bomb," *PolitiFact*, Sept. 10, 2015, http://tinyurl.com/pwwmkmo.

103. "Meet the Press transcript — Aug. 16, 2015," NBCNews.com, Aug. 19, 2015, http://tinyurl.com/ju6l3v7.

104. "Hillary Clinton: Consistent, Tough, and Effective Leadership to Counter Threats from Iran," Hillary Clinton campaign, http://tinyurl.com/hqvtnpu.

105. Nahal Toosi, "How a Republican president could kill the Iran deal," *Politico*, July 14, 2015, http://tinyurl.com/htlahov.

106. Mimms, *op. cit.*

107. Isaac Chotiner, " 'Iran is the Arsonist and the Fire Brigade,' " *Slate.com*, Jan. 6, 2016, http://tinyurl.com/jghn89p.

108. Alireza Nader, David E. Thaler and S. R. Bohandy, "The Next Supreme Leader: Succession in the Islamic Republic of Iran," RAND Corp., 2011, http://tinyurl.com/hpkmqqd.

109. Welsh, *op. cit.*; Rick Gladstone, "Iran's Ayatollah Suggests He May Not Be Around in 10 Years," *The New York Times*, Sept. 16, 2015, http://tinyurl.com/nu27zr6.

110. Suzanne Maloney and Fred Dews, "Suzanne Maloney talks U.S.-Iran relations, the Iran nuclear deal, and the future of Iran," Brookings Cafeteria podcast, Brookings Institution, Sept. 11, 2015, http://tinyurl.com/hokw789.

111. Gallagher, Mohseni and Ramsay, *op. cit.*

112. "Arena: What is the future of U.S.-Iran relations?" "Upfront," Al Jazeera, Sept. 19, 2015, http://tinyurl.com/ovy296w.

BIBLIOGRAPHY

Selected Sources

Books

Berman, Ilan, *Iran's Deadly Ambition: The Islamic Republic's Quest for Global Power*, Encounter Books, 2015.
A vice president at a foreign-policy think tank details what he says are conflicts between Iran's ambitions and those of Israel and the United States.

Edwards, Brian T., *After the American Century: The Ends of U.S. Culture in the Middle East*, Columbia University Press, 2015.
A Northwestern University professor of Middle Eastern studies examines how Iran and neighboring countries have interpreted American popular culture through comic books, social networking sites and other means.

Maloney, Suzanne, *Iran's Political Economy Since the Revolution*, Cambridge University Press, 2015.
The deputy director of the Brookings Institution's foreign policy program explores the changing nature of Iran's economy and future foreign investment.

Saikal, Amin, *Iran at the Crossroads*, Polity, 2015.
An Australian National University professor of political science and author of several books on the Middle East contends closer U.S.-Iranian ties would benefit both countries as well as the region.

Secor, Laura, *Children of Paradise: The Struggle for the Soul of Iran*, Riverhead Books, 2016.
A journalist who frequently writes about Iran chronicles the efforts of several people pressing for greater Iranian engagement with the United States and the West.

Articles

"The Iranian Inspections Mirage," *The Wall Street Journal*, July 22, 2015, http://tinyurl.com/zne7r6m.
The newspaper's conservative editorial page argues that Iran's nuclear program cannot be adequately inspected.

Kinzer, Stephen, "Is Iran Really So Evil?" *Politico Magazine*, Jan. 17, 2016, http://tinyurl.com/z9o7r9n.
The author of several books on Iran and the Middle East contends the threat Iran poses to the United States is greatly overstated.

Libicki, Martin C., "Iran: A Rising Cyber Power?" RAND.org, Dec. 16, 2015, http://tinyurl.com/je95d4l.
A researcher for a think tank specializing in national security assesses recent Iranian cyberattacks.

Miller, Aaron David, "America's awkward Iran dance," CNN.com, Feb. 2, 2016, http://tinyurl.com/j3s72us.
A former Middle East negotiator who is now at the Woodrow Wilson International Center for Scholars think tank examines why improved U.S-Iran relations could be difficult.

Nada, Garrett, "If sanctions are lifted, here's what trade between Iran and the US could look like," *Quartz*, April 24, 2015, http://tinyurl.com/m4vht25.
A writer for a business website provides an overview of areas most likely to benefit from future U.S.-Iranian trade.

Tharoor, Ishaan, "The key moments in the long history of U.S.-Iran tensions," *The Washington Post*, April 2, 2015, http://tinyurl.com/gkokj2g.
A journalist looks at the events that have formed the basis for hostile relations between the United States and Iran since 1979.

Wright, Robin, "Tehran's Promise," *The New Yorker*, July 27, 2015, http://tinyurl.com/omnvsdk.
A journalist specializing in the Middle East visits Iran and interviews residents who want improved relations with the United States.

Reports and studies

Gallagher, Nancy, Ebrahim Mohseni and Clay Ramsay, "Iranian Attitudes in Advance of the Parliamentary Elections: Economics, Politics, and Foreign Affairs," University of Maryland Center for International & Security Studies, February 2016, http://tinyurl.com/zowabqs.

American and Iranian universities, together with a Canadian firm, present the results from a poll of more than 1,000 Iranians on the United States, President Hassan Rouhani and the February parliamentary elections.

Heinonen, Olli, "Strengthening the Verification and Implementation of the Joint Comprehensive Plan of Action," Foundation for the Defense of Democracies, Nov. 25, 2015, http://tinyurl.com/j7kekhk.
A former International Atomic Energy Agency official critiques the implementation of the nuclear deal.

Katzman, Kenneth, "Iran, Gulf Security and U.S. Policy," Congressional Research Service, Jan. 14, 2016, http://tinyurl.com/gw2ca94.
An analyst for the agency researching background issues for Congress provides an overview of Iran's politics.

Samore, Gary, ed., "Sanctions Against Iran: A Guide to Targets, Terms and Timetables," Harvard University Belfer Center for Science and International Affairs, June 2015, http://tinyurl.com/jrr3vrf.
The university's scientific and foreign policy research group provides an overview of economic sanctions.

For More Information

Belfer Center for Science and International Affairs, Harvard University, 79 John F. Kennedy St., Cambridge, MA 02138; 617-495-1400; http://belfercenter.ksg.harvard.edu. Conducts research on international security issues and sanctions.

Brookings Institution, 1775 Massachusetts Ave., N.W., Washington, DC 20036; 202-797-6000; www.brookings.edu. Centrist think tank that studies U.S.-Iran relations.

Foundation for Defense of Democracies, P.O. Box 33249, Washington, DC 20033; 202-207-0190; www.defenddemocracy.org. Conservative think tank focusing on national security and foreign policy.

International Atomic Energy Agency, P.O. Box 100, A-1400 Vienna, Austria; 431-2600-0; www.iaea.org. UN agency charged with overseeing international nuclear research and development.

National Iranian American Council, 1411 K St., N.W., Suite 250, Washington, DC 20005; 202-386-6325; www.niacouncil.org. Nonprofit advocating for improved U.S.-Iran relations.

U.S. Department of State, 2201 C St., N.W., Washington, DC 20520; 202-647-4000; www.state.gov. Oversees diplomatic relations between Iran and the United States.

5

Reforming the U.N.

Reed Karaim

AFP/Getty Images/Abd Doumany

Food and other emergency supplies are unloaded after a U.N. aid convoy entered the rebel-held Syrian town of Douma, near the capital of Damascus, on June 10, 2016. Critics say corruption, bureaucracy and other problems have slowed the U.N. response to recent international crises, including the flood of Middle Eastern refugees trying to enter Europe.

From *CQ Researcher*,
June 24, 2016

To many observers, it was the United Nations at its finest — and its most controversial. A 2015 U.N. report catalogued the many ways in which war had harmed children that year and which countries were to blame, an account that one activist described as "a list of shame." Near the top was Saudi Arabia.[1]

The Saudis and a coalition of Arab partners are supporting the Yemeni government in its ongoing civil war by bombing insurgents' military targets. But the aerial campaign also has struck schools and hospitals, leading the U.N. report to blame Saudi Arabia and its partners for 60 percent of the nearly 2,000 children killed and injured in the conflict in 2015.[2]

But this June, U.N. Secretary-General Ban Ki-moon removed Saudi Arabia and its coalition partners from an annex to the report that listed countries violating children's rights. Ban acknowledged he made the decision in response to threats by unnamed countries that the report could cost the U.N. crucial funding, saying he had to consider "the very real prospect that millions of other children would suffer grievously if, as was suggested to me, countries would defund many U.N. programs."[3]

Saudi Arabia denied that it had tried to intimidate the secretary-general, but observers said it was clear Ban had come under pressure from the Saudis and other coalition members.[4]

The episode highlights the crosswinds buffeting the United Nations as it enters its eighth decade of existence — trying to do right, but facing blowback nearly every step of the way. To its critics, the United Nations is an ineffectual colossus, hamstrung by bickering membership, ineffective leadership and a slow-moving

U.N. Oversees 16 Peacekeeping Operations

The 16 ongoing United Nations peacekeeping operations, primarily in Africa and the Middle East, involve about 103,000 uniformed personnel from 123 countries. Nearly 1,700 peacekeepers have died in those operations, with more than half of the deaths occurring in Lebanon, Darfur (Sudan), Cyprus and Haiti (not shown). That death toll represents about half of the nearly 3,500 peacekeepers killed during all of the 71 peacekeeping missions begun by the U.N. since 1948.

Locations of Current Peacekeeping Operations

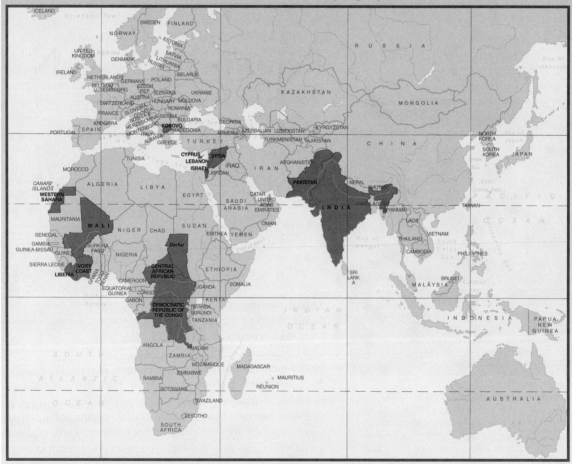

Sources: "Current peacekeeping operations," http://tinyurl.com/44cgkku, and "Peacekeeping Fact Sheet," http://tinyurl.com/5tzmet7, United Nations Peacekeeping

bureaucracy. More fundamentally, many question whether the 193-member organization, founded in 1945 to foster global peace and promote human rights, remains relevant in today's world.

But to its supporters, the U.N. is still essential and effective, especially in its promotion of economic development and social justice. The organization has more than 30 specialized agencies and funds, staffed by 44,000 people worldwide, dealing with everything from peace-keeping and vaccinations to maritime regulations and international refugees. The agencies are involved in a wide range of development, health, education and social welfare activities across the globe. And the organization remains central to negotiations on many of the world's most pressing issues, from global climate change to violent regional conflicts, supporters say.[5]

But critics say the U.N.'s management has become so inept and its bureaucracy so inefficient that it cannot react swiftly enough to today's challenges. "If you locked a team of evil geniuses in a laboratory, they could not design a bureaucracy so maddeningly complex," Anthony Banbury, a former U.N. assistant secretary-general, wrote recently, explaining his resignation from the organization.[6]

Under the 1945 charter, member nations meet in a General Assembly where they debate issues and pass resolutions calling for action in areas of concern. But the real authority is largely reserved to the 15-member Security Council, which can make binding decisions that the U.N. charter requires member countries to follow. Ten seats on the council are held for two-year terms by nations representing different regions. Five countries — the United States, Russia, China, France and Great Britain — have permanent seats on the council and have veto power over U.N. resolutions, enabling any one of them to block action.[7]

The secretary-general — the chief administrative officer of the U.N. — is appointed by the General Assembly to renewable five-year terms, but the Security Council nominates the candidates, so the five veto-wielding permanent members of the council effectively select the secretary-general. The secretary-general supervises all U.N. staff at the organization's New York City headquarters and in offices and missions around the world. The General Assembly annually elects a president who oversees that body.[8]

But critics note that many U.N. agencies operate as autonomous fiefdoms and fill senior positions based on patronage rather than competency. And many agencies or other entities operating within the U.N. duplicate effort, they say, wasting money and diluting the organization's focus.[9]

This flawed governing structure, critics say, means the United Nations has struggled to respond to recent international crises, such as Africa's Ebola outbreak and the flood of Middle Eastern refugees now trying to enter Europe.

Scandals are another serious problem: U.N. peacekeepers from France and the Democratic Republic of the Congo have been accused of sexually exploiting and abusing women and children during the ongoing peacekeeping mission in the Central African Republic.[10] And charges of corruption among senior U.N. officials have led to calls for the organization to become more transparent and democratic.

Conservative critics in the United States, meanwhile, have raised concerns that U.N. treaties and initiatives could supersede U.S. national authority, although the organization's supporters dismiss the possibility as exaggerated.

Others who have worked closely with the U.N. say it operates more effectively and accomplishes more than it's given credit for. "The U.N. isn't a perfect organization, but it still provides enormous net benefits to the world and the United States," says Esther Brimmer, a former U.S. assistant secretary of State for international organization affairs and a professor of international affairs at George Washington University in Washington.

Among the U.N.'s most important work, she says, is economic and social development. In 2000, the U.N. committed itself to an ambitious agenda — the so-called Millennium Development Goals — which aimed by 2015 to eliminate extreme poverty and hunger, achieve universal primary education, reduce child mortality, promote gender equality, improve maternal health, combat diseases, promote environmental sustainability and boost aid donations to developing countries.[11]

A 2015 U.N. assessment found that impressive gains had been made in all key areas, including lifting more than 1 billion people out of extreme poverty, increasing from 83 percent to 91 percent the percentage of primary-school-age children in developing countries who are attending school and cutting under-5 child mortality by more than half. The report also noted that global HIV/AIDS cases have fallen by about 40 percent and malaria by more than a third. Malaria is being conquered in part due to a massive U.N.-coordinated effort to deliver more than 900 million insecticide-treated mosquito nets to African countries between 2004 and 2014.[12]

Nongovernmental organizations (NGOs) and national aid agencies, such as the U.S. Agency for International Development (USAID), have worked in concert with the U.N. in all these areas. But the organization's supporters say it has played a central role by establishing global priorities and helping to coordinate activities.

Former Slovenian President Danilo Türk is interviewed by video by U.N. officials on April 13, 2016. He is among the 10 candidates being considered to replace Secretary-General Ban Ki-moon, whose term expires in December. Observers hope his successor will bring new energy to the position and implement needed improvements to U.N. operations.

"It helped create a single conversation among the major players in development," says Brimmer. The U.N. has continued leading that conversation by adopting a new set of "sustainable development goals" for 2030, which aim to further promote peace, prosperity and responsible environmental stewardship.[13]

Many international affairs experts also credit the United Nations for shining a spotlight on human rights. In 1948, the U.N. adopted a "Universal Declaration of Human Rights" that called on nations and people everywhere to recognize that "all human beings are born free and equal in dignity and rights," with the right to "freedom of thought, conscience and religion," as well as "freedom of opinion and expression."[14] In recent years, the U.N. has devoted significant attention to the rights of women and promoted equal treatment of gay, lesbian, bisexual and transgender people.[15]

But critics say the makeup of the U.N.'s 47-member Human Rights Council, responsible for promoting human rights, reflects the subversion of some U.N. programs by including several autocratic regimes. And the council recently chose Saudi Arabia to head a key council panel. "Saudi Arabia has arguably the worst record in the world when it comes to religious freedom and women's rights," said Hillel Neuer, executive director of U.N. Watch, an independent watchdog organization based in

Geneva.[16] A conservative strain of Islam, Wahhabism is the state religion in Saudi Arabia, which bans the public practice of any other religion, and strictly limits women's rights. Saudi Arabia insists it is an active defender of human rights.[17]

Critics further complain that, even accounting for inflation, U.N. program costs are 40 times higher than in the early 1950s. The organization's core budget has more than doubled in the last two decades to $5.4 billion biannually.[18] Yet some of the organization's humanitarian programs are on the verge of bankruptcy as they struggle to deal with the refugee crisis stemming from conflicts in Syria and other parts of the Middle East.[19]

The United Nations High Commissioner for Refugees, an agency commonly known as UNHCR, provides humanitarian relief to refugees and helps them find new homes. At the start of the year, the agency and other refugee-aid groups called for an additional $550 million in aid to help deal with the flood of immigrants fleeing the Middle East and trying to get into Europe.[20]

U.N. supporters say the budget remains relatively modest, given the scope of its efforts. In comparison, the United States spent 10 times as much — roughly $40 billion — on international affairs in 2015.[21] And the European Union and United States are also struggling to find solutions to the refugee crisis, they note.

"It's easy to make the U.N. a scapegoat for the world's challenges," says Peter Yeo, president of the Better World Campaign, which works to foster a strong relationship between the United States and the U.N.

As the United Nations selects a new secretary-general and its members consider how the organization can continue promoting global peace and prosperity, here are some of the questions being debated:

Does the U.N. need major reforms to remain relevant?

Calls to reform the United Nations are a constant, with critics complaining that the organization has too many agencies pursuing similar goals and that its bureaucracy is too insular and unresponsive.

The problem of multiple agencies tasked with overlapping responsibilities, such as in water and energy, resulted because the United Nations often responds to perceived needs by adding initiatives similar to existing efforts, analysts say. "We have 70 years' accretion of various organizations, funds, programs, special entities etc., etc.," says Thomas Weiss, a distinguished scholar of international relations at City University of New York. "More and more of them are doing the same things."

Because each initiative develops its own constituency within the U.N., it becomes almost impossible to get rid of them once they've been established, Weiss explains, leading to a maze of competing, largely independent bureaucracies. While the core U.N. budget is supported through assessed contributions from each member nation based on its wealth, many programs are supported by voluntary, direct contributions from countries or NGOs, he continues, which means agencies are competing for the same resources.

The bureaucratic overlap, Weiss says, combined with what he characterizes as weak leadership at the top under current Secretary-General Ban, has created a U.N. often at odds with itself. "There used to be something that might be characterized as a [U.N.] 'system' " when the organization was new and smaller, he says, "but now I use the word family — because like most of our families, this one is terribly dysfunctional."

If the United Nations continues on its present path, he says, "it's not going to disappear, but it is going to become a kind of relic and diminished presence on the world stage."

Weiss, the author of *What's Wrong With the United Nations and How to Fix It*, says greater centralization, including greater authority over spending, would help end the problem of overlapping missions and competition for resources. This would also require member-nations to be focused more on the greater global good, rather than on protecting pet programs, he adds.

But Erin Graham, an assistant professor of politics specializing in international relations at Drexel University in Philadelphia, said the United Nations already has made changes in response to criticism that its agencies operate too independently. "There are new funding mechanisms designed to reward U.N. agencies if they coordinate," she said.

In 2003 the U.N. established the Multi-Partner-Partner Trust Fund Office, which was "designed to distribute money across multiple agencies and facilitate coordination between them," she said. The U.N. also has made the budgetary process more transparent, she said, allowing donors to better track how money is spent.[22]

Moreover, member nations support a system whereby various U.N. agencies compete for financial resources from individual countries, because it increases the countries' leverage over U.N. activities, Graham said. While reformers want increased centralization to make the U.N. more efficient, the current approach makes agencies accountable to the countries and NGOs that are paying for much of their work, she said. "U.N. agencies know that donors can give more or less," she said, "depending on how happy they are with performance."[23]

But Banbury, the former U.N. official, said the organization's administrative bureaucracy remains unresponsive in key ways, most notably in staffing up quickly to respond to rapidly unfolding crises such as pandemics or natural disasters. "The United Nations needs to be able to attract and quickly deploy the world's best talent. And yet, it takes on average 213 days to recruit someone," he said, adding that recent changes in hiring policies by the U.N.'s Department of Management increased the delay even further.[24]

In addition, Weiss notes, U.N. staff appointments often are made to satisfy different countries or constituents. "The leadership at the top, . . . the senior and junior posts, are often very politicized appointments," he says, so competency and expertise are not top priorities.

Making matters worse, Banbury said, operational leaders on the ground cannot hire their own staff or reassign incompetent personnel. "Short of a serious crime, it is virtually impossible to fire someone in the United Nations," Banbury said. While he acknowledges the U.N. is still doing valuable work in some areas, thanks to "colossal mismanagement, the United Nations is failing," he said.[25]

But Stanley Meisler, author of *United Nations: A History*, who has covered the organization over a 30-year career as a foreign policy journalist, says calls for an operational overhaul are overstated. The U.N. bureaucracy must deal with people from many different nations and cultures, and the process of learning how to work together can sometimes be cumbersome and slow, Meisler says. But the slow pace doesn't strike him as significantly worse than other governmental entities, he says.

"In my experience, I found [the U.N.] was just as efficient as the U.S. State Department," he says. "I think reform is a phony issue."

Other experts believe improvements in hiring procedures and accountability could be helpful, but in most cases the problems haven't kept the U.N. from getting the job done. "You have some dead wood there, no question, and it can be slow and cumbersome as all bureaucracies are, but I would say that the secretary-general has learned to work around it," says David Forsythe, an emeritus professor of political science at the University of Nebraska, Lincoln, and co-author of *The United Nations and Changing World Politics.* "It's a problem, but it's not the major problem at the U.N."

Yeo, of the Better World Campaign, says the United Nations is streamlining operations. The campaign reports that the U.N.'s 2016-17 budget was down slightly and eliminated 150 redundant staff posts, while reducing equipment and travel expenses by 5 percent.[26] "The U.N. is reforming, but it needs to reform much more deeply and quickly," Yeo says. "Number one is finding a way to sunset programs that no longer serve a purpose. There's a real opportunity for the new secretary-general to insist that programs that aren't working be shuttered."

But other analysts say the United Nations has proven largely impervious to reform. Kelly-Kate Pease, an international relations professor at Webster University in St. Louis, an expert on international organizations, says the complexity of the U.N.'s operations and the fact that its member-nations have different priorities make it extremely difficult to impose real reform.

"It's like punching a featherbed," Pease says. "You can punch it all day long, and at the end, it's going to look pretty much the same."

Can U.N. peacekeepers be effective in today's armed conflicts?

For more than half a century, the blue helmets and berets worn by U.N. peacekeepers have been a highly visible sign the United Nations was on the ground in the world's trouble-spots. Secretary-General Ban has called peacekeeping "the flagship of the United Nations enterprise." The U.N. currently has 16 missions underway in countries as different as Haiti and Cyprus. Twelve missions are in the Middle East or Sub-Saharan Africa.[27]

But peacekeeping has only become "more and more dangerous," Ban said in May. "In some areas, . . . our blue flag has gone from being a shield to a target."[28]

Radical Islamic groups such as the Islamic State (also known as ISIS and ISIL) and al Qaeda reject the underlying notions that give the U.N. authority, says Michael Boyle, an associate professor of political science at La Salle University in Philadelphia whose research focuses on international relations and terrorism.

"If you reject nation states and groups that represent nation states, then the U.N. means nothing to you," Boyle says. "They see the U.N. as an institution representing the West. They see it as representing the United States," a secular, Western democracy they consider contrary to the wishes of God.

In Mali, where drug smugglers, arms dealers and jihadists have created a chaotic and violent situation, the U.N says 86 peacekeepers have died since the U.N. mission began there in 2013, currently making it the U.N.'s deadliest peacekeeping mission. Other missions have resulted in more deaths, but over longer periods of time.[29]

Throughout the organization's history, U.N. troops most often were not sent to fight but to help preserve a tentative peace between warring parties and to shield vulnerable civilian populations. Analysts note the effectiveness of such missions largely depended on a willingness by combatants to see an end to conflict and a respect for the United Nations as a neutral arbiter. It also depended on an acceptance of the U.N.'s legitimacy as a representative of world order.

Elizabeth Cousens, deputy chief executive officer of the United Nations Foundation, a nonprofit advocacy group for the U.N. based in Washington, D.C., that works to build partnerships between the organization and groups around the world, says U.N. personnel, both peacekeeping forces and other staff, still play a unique role that allows them to step into many conflicts in a way others cannot. "The U.N. is still understood to have a degree of impartiality, and that's not to be underestimated," she says. "The U.N. mediator in Syria, he's still seen as trying to broker a peace between all parties, and that's a huge advantage."

In Syria, however, several of the principal actors, including ISIS and the local affiliate of al Qaeda, are transnational terrorist groups. Battling these groups presents a challenge to the United Nations, which was set up to deal with member states, says Sue Eckert, a senior fellow at the Watson Institute for International and Public Affairs at Brown University in Providence, R.I.

"These nonstate actors are entirely different, and how you deal with them is different," Eckert says. "It's hard because the U.N. was not set up to deal with these threats, but I think [the U.N.] is evolving and has taken some innovative approaches."

Those approaches include non-military options, such as imposing targeted economic sanctions against terrorist groups to cripple their financing capabilities and helping member nations increase security along their borders.[30]

But U.N. peacekeeping forces increasingly have pursued "coercive action," abandoning neutrality and taking offensive military action against local militias or insurgent forces in an effort to protect civilians or restore order.

"You get into 'second-generation' peacekeeping, which tends toward combat. You have these military operations which are not neutral operations at all," says the University of Nebraska's Forsythe. "They are really efforts to coerce militias and other groups into not attacking civilians . . . and you've got to have some real capability to carry these out."

Some analysts doubt the United Nations can carry out more aggressive missions, given that its annual peacekeeping budget is a relatively modest $8.27 billion.[31] Moreover, the U.N. does not have its own military. It borrows troops and equipment from member nations for each mission. Many troops come from developing countries and are not considered as well trained as more professional armies.

"Even though these international security deployments have been around since 1956, they're still put together with duct tape and chewing gum," Forsythe says. "The secretary-general has to go around and ask for countries to volunteer forces and equipment, and sometimes the equipment sent is cast-off stuff that doesn't work, so it's very hard for international forces to prove themselves against these very nasty guys."

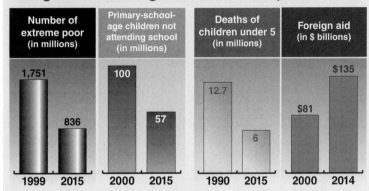

Significant Progress Made on Development Goals

The United Nations has made impressive strides toward reaching the eight Millennium Development Goals it adopted in 2000, such as eliminating extreme poverty and cutting child mortality, according to a 2015 U.N. assessment. The report found that both extreme poverty and under-5 child mortality have fallen by more than half, while the number of primary-school-age children not attending school has dropped by almost half. Foreign aid, meanwhile, rose by 66 percent between 2000 and 2014.

Progress in Reaching Millennium Development Goals

Number of extreme poor (in millions)		Primary-school-age children not attending school (in millions)		Deaths of children under 5 (in millions)		Foreign aid (in $ billions)	
1,751	836	100	57	12.7	6	$81	$135
1999	2015	2000	2015	1990	2015	2000	2014

Source: "The Millennium Development Goals Report 2015," United Nations, pp. 4-5, http://tinyurl.com/p92xdd3

Last September, President Obama chaired a U.N. summit of more than 50 world leaders to discuss bolstering the U.N.'s peacekeeping capacity. Countries pledged 40,000 new troops and more equipment, including 10 field hospitals. China made the biggest pledge, promising up to 8,000 soldiers. The United States, which provides only a handful of troops but pays a quarter of the peacekeeping budget, has been pushing for a more aggressive use of peacekeeping forces.[32]

Some experts believe that's a mistake. "We may be stumbling into an enormous strategic trap because, if we have learned over the last decade that very highly capable NATO forces, U.S. forces, actually can't suppress Islamic extremist groups, why on Earth do we think slightly strengthening U.N. missions is going to give us a tool that allows us to fight terrorists?" said Richard Gowan, a non-resident fellow at the Center on International Cooperation at New York University.[33]

But Yeo, of the Better World Campaign, says U.N. peacekeepers, with the proper support and training, can

U.N. peacekeepers carry the coffins of seven Guinean soldiers killed on Feb. 12, 2016, during a jihadist attack against their camp in Mali, where 86 peacekeepers have died since the U.N. mission began there in 2013. The U.N. currently has 16 missions underway, including 12 in the Middle East or Sub-Saharan Africa.

A Syrian war refugee is sheltered in a camp near Aleppo, Syria, run by the U.N. High Commissioner for Refugees and Turkish humanitarian organizations. At the start of the year, the agency and other aid groups called for an additional $550 million to help deal with the immigrants fleeing the Middle East.

effectively share some of the burden the United States has shouldered to maintain world order. The United Nations, he says, "allows us to avoid going it alone." Peacekeeping operations are also less expensive than comparable U.S. military operations, which cost eight times as much, according to a study by the U.S. Government Accountability Office.[34]

Should the U.N. Security Council be enlarged to expand participation?

The United Nations may have 193 members in the General Assembly, but the 15-member Security Council has most of the institution's power. The council can block any resolution by a majority vote, and any one of the council's five permanent members can veto any resolution.

The 10 nonpermanent council members serve two-year terms. The seats are parceled out by region: five for Africa and Asia, one for Eastern Europe, two for Latin America and the Caribbean and two for Western Europe and other states.

The Security Council has expanded once since 1945, going from 11 members to 15 in 1965. But the five permanent members — the United States, Russia, China, France and Great Britain — have essentially remained the same since the end of World War II, with Communist China's government replacing Taiwan in 1971 and Russia taking the former Soviet Union's seat after it dissolved in 1991.

Critics say the choice of the permanent members is a relic of the immediate postwar era, favoring nations that defeated the Axis powers. With three European nations and the United States as four of the five members, they note, it also reflects the dominant Western power when many of today's developing nations were still European colonies.

Members of the General Assembly repeatedly have called for expanding the number of permanent council seats to make it more reflective of the global community. But while the United States, Russia and China have publicly expressed openness to adding new members, they have quietly worked behind the scenes to prevent expansion, analysts say.[35]

Calls for expansion grew stronger during the U.N.'s 70th anniversary in 2015.[36] Several proposals were put forward. One would add Germany and Japan, the former Axis powers that now have two of the world's largest economies and are among the biggest financial contributors to the U.N., along with Brazil and India, two emerging powers. Another proposal would add a representative from Africa, with South Africa and Nigeria considered the strongest possibilities. Other ideas include adding up to eight new seats.[37]

The Elders, a group of former world leaders that includes former Secretary-General Kofi Annan, have proposed a compromise that would add a new class of members to the Security Council that would serve for longer than two-years and could be re-elected, giving them de facto permanent status. The Elders' plan would leave veto power with the five original permanent members but ask those nations to pledge not to use it to block U.N. action in certain crises, especially threats of mass genocide or atrocity.[38]

Some analysts believe change makes sense. "There's a case for expanding the Security Council — I think in the five- to six-[nation] category," says George Washington's Brimmer. "There are gaps in the council. One of those gaps is that there's no permanent member from Africa.

"But you have to get it right," she adds. "We've expanded the Security Council once since 1945, so this is not something to be taken lightly." She adds that "a modest increase into the low 20s would be possible — too large, and it won't function."

But other experts say disagreements between members with veto power, particularly the United States and Russia, often deadlock the Security Council already. "In terms of the big important issues, the Security Council has rarely been able to act, and I don't see that expanding it and allowing more participation is going to help matters," says Webster University's Pease. "Part of the problem with the Security Council as an effective governing institution is that nations have real disagreements about what is causing specific problems, and because you have a disagreement about what's causing the problem, your solution is going to be different."

Other observers say the challenge in expanding the council is not just the concerns of the five permanent members but the divisions between other nations. "Everybody agrees the Security Council needs to be reformed. This isn't 1945. You've got very important states that are not permanently on the council, such as India, Brazil or South Africa or Nigeria," says the University of Nebraska's Forsythe. "The problem is, nobody can agree on the specifics. How do you add India without Pakistan jumping ship? Which African state do you add — South Africa or Nigeria? When it comes to Latin America, should it be Mexico or Brazil? The regional caucuses can't agree. So nothing happens."

Brimmer, however, says the objections can probably be overcome. "I think it will take several more years to work this out, but I think enough member states want it that it could happen," she says "I think it could be good for the institution if done well with serious intent."

She says India, the world's most populous democracy, seems to have the most support for being added as a permanent member, an idea President Obama endorsed during a visit to New Delhi in 2010.[39]

But Yeo, of the Better World Campaign, doubts expansion will happen anytime soon. "It would require the [five permanent] members of the council to give up some of their powers, and they don't want to do that," he says. "I think Security Council reform is long overdue and highly unlikely in the foreseeable future."

BACKGROUND
Postwar Idealism

On June 25, 1945, delegates from 50 nations met in the San Francisco Opera House. It was the final session of a two-month conference to work out the basic structure of a new international body that organizers hoped could create lasting global peace out of the ashes of World War II.[40]

Lord Halifax, the British ambassador to the United States, presided. As he placed the final draft of the organization's charter before the delegates, he said, "The issue upon which we are about to vote is as important as any we shall ever vote in our lifetime."[41]

One by one, the delegates from each nation stood to signify their support. The crowd gathered to witness the historic moment broke into applause as the U.N. charter was adopted unanimously.[42]

The vote and signing ceremony the next day did not immediately bring the U.N. into existence. It took until Oct. 24, four more months, before enough signatories had ratified the agreement and the United Nations was officially created. But the international attention given the San Francisco conference signified the great hopes for the new organization.

Author and journalist Meisler says the hope was that, through the United Nations, the United States, Great Britain and Russia — who had spearheaded the Allied victory in World War II — along with China and France, could work together as "policemen" who would keep global peace.

Even before the war had ended, President Franklin D. Roosevelt had forcefully pressed the concept of creating an international organization where countries could resolve their differences, hoping to extend the cooperation of the

CHRONOLOGY

1945-1950 *The United Nations is founded.*

1945 Delegates from 50 nations gather in San Francisco to draw up the U.N. charter, which becomes effective in October.

1946 The first General Assembly meets in London; U.N. moves to New York City later in year.

1950 North Korea invades South Korea. With the Soviet Union boycotting the Security Council, the council's other members authorize an armed intervention by U.N. states to defend South Korea in the first significant conflict of the Cold War.

1956-1968 *U.N. peacekeepers begin operating, but hopes the world's great powers could work in concert are dashed by the Cold War.*

1956 First armed U.N. peacekeeping force replaces British, French and Israeli troops who invaded Egypt after it nationalized the Suez Canal.

1960 A record 17 newly independent states join U.N. as colonialism winds down in Africa.

1964 U.N. dispatches peacekeepers to Cyprus to prevent a recurrence of fighting between Greek and Turkish communities. The mission, still ongoing, is U.N.'s longest peacekeeping effort.

1967 Security Council adopts Resolution 242, which calls for Israel to return territory seized in the Six-Day War in return for recognition and peace from its Arab neighbors.

1968 General Assembly approves first treaty on nuclear weapons.

1972-1987 *U.N. treaties and agencies extend the organization's global influence.*

1972 First U.N. environmental conference meets in Stockholm.

1975 U.N. holds its first world conference on the status of women in Mexico City.

1987 Forty-six nations sign landmark U.N. global environmental agreement.

1990-2000 *Cold War's end brings hope that a more unified and influential United Nations can emerge.*

1990 U.N. approves U.S.-led intervention to drive Iraqi troops out of Kuwait.

1992 U.N. sends peacekeepers to the Balkan republics, beginning an involvement in the ethnic conflict that will lead to U.N.-authorized airstrikes.

1997 U.N. ban on chemical weapons takes effect.

2000 U.N. adopts the Global Millennium Development Goals, to reduce poverty over the next 15 years.

2001-Present *Terrorist attacks on U.S. mark a new era of conflict that tests U.N. capabilities.*

2001 In the wake of al Qaeda's Sept. 11 attacks that killed nearly 3,000 in the United States, U.N. declares right of member states to defend themselves against terrorism.

2005 U.N. adopts the Responsibility to Protect (R2P) doctrine, which declares that the U.N. has the responsibility to intervene if a nation fails to protect its population from crimes against humanity.

2010 U.N. creates UN Women to support gender equality and the empowerment of women.

2013 First U.N. Youth Assembly is held. Malala Yousafzai, a Pakistani schoolgirl shot by the Taliban for attending classes, urges the delegates to use education as a weapon against extremism.

2015 U.N. turns 70 and establishes a new global development goals. . . . UN-led effort culminates in historic international accord to fight climate change.

2016 Ten candidates vie to replace Ban Ki-moon, whose term as secretary-general expires in December.

Allied nations once Germany, Italy and Japan were defeated. "It was a vision of Franklin Roosevelt that the powers that were going to the win the Second World War would unite and prevent any further aggression by future Hitlers," Meisler says.

The power and authority Roosevelt envisioned for the United Nations was to stand in contrast to the League of Nations, an earlier attempt following World War I to create an international body of nations to keep the peace. The League, which was headquartered in Geneva, was hampered by the refusal of the U.S. Senate to ratify American membership and by an unwillingness of members to take action to stop aggression by powerful nations.[43]

Roosevelt hoped for different results for the United Nations. A series of meetings during and immediately after World War II fleshed out his idealistic concept. But it quickly ran into difficulties. Behind-the-scenes negotiations between the Soviet Union and the United States over several issues were intense.[44]

The main sticking point was the veto power of the Security Council's five permanent members. The Soviet Union wanted the permanent members to have the authority to veto even the discussion of a dispute. The United States wanted the veto restricted to decisions, not debate. The disagreement was serious enough that Harry S. Truman, who had become president when Roosevelt died in April 1945, sent a special envoy to Soviet leader Joseph Stalin to plead the U.S. position, to which Stalin finally agreed.[45]

That disagreement, although patched up, foreshadowed the split that would soon emerge between the Americans and the Soviets. As the Cold War began, pitting the U.S.-led alliance of Western democracies against the communist bloc led by the Soviet Union, the idea that the world's great powers would work in concert to police the globe evaporated.

"With the onslaught of the Cold War, it all got thrown out the window," says City University's Weiss. "It totally disappears in a matter of months."

Cold War Era

The Korean War, which began on June 25, 1950, when North Korea invaded South Korea, marked the first time the United Nations authorized member states to use military force to defend a country. A coalition of 16 U.N. countries led by the United States fought on behalf of South Korea.[46]

Ironically, the first conflict of the Cold War was one of the few times the United Nations was able to react to aggression in a manner close to its founding vision. The Security Council decision to authorize force was possible because the Soviet Union was boycotting the council in protest over the U.N.'s decision to seat the government of the Republic of China in Taiwan instead of the communist government led by Mao Zedong that had taken control of mainland China.[47]

The Soviet Union soon ended its boycott, however, and would use its veto frequently in the years ahead. In 1956, after the Soviet army invaded Hungary to topple an anti-communist government that had taken power, the Soviet Union vetoed a U.S. resolution calling for Soviet forces to withdraw.[48] During the height of the Cold War, from the mid-1950s through the mid-1980s, vetoes by Andrei Gromyko, Soviet foreign minister, were so familiar that he became known as "Mr. Nyet" (Mr. No).[49]

While the United States or the Soviet Union blocked U.N. action in many Cold War disputes, the organization still provided a forum for the two sides to air their disagreements, says Cousens, the United Nations Foundation official. "Through the long period of the Cold War, the U.N.'s biggest security job was to take the edge off the tensions between the big powers — in the U.S.-Soviet rivalry," she says.

The United Nations, Cousens says, also helped manage the decolonization of Africa and Asia, providing technical assistance to new governments as they assumed power in countries previously controlled by Western powers. In 1960, 17 newly independent nations, a record number, would join the United Nations.[50]

The U.N.'s first armed peacekeeping mission came in 1956 when the United Nations objected to a military incursion by British, French and Israeli troops in Egypt. The three countries had sent troops into Egypt after it nationalized the Suez Canal Company, which operated the key Middle Eastern waterway.[51]

The three nations had acted without U.N. authority, and the backlash was swift, with both the Soviet Union and the United States demanding the troops withdraw. The three countries finally agreed to allow a U.N. force to replace their soldiers. Secretary-General Dag Hammarskjöld hastily assembled a U.N. peacekeeping

Americans Remain Wary of U.N.

They generally support it — with qualms.

Americans long have had a love-hate relationship with the United Nations. The international organization was founded under U.S. leadership, and the United States remains its most powerful member and biggest financial contributor, providing 22 percent of its core budget.[1] The United States works within the U.N. framework on many international issues, including climate change and the fight against terrorism.

But polling indicates the American public has mixed feelings about the United Nations. Since the 1950s, Gallup has regularly asked Americans whether they thought the U.N. was doing a good or bad job. In most years, less than half have chosen good job, and in the last 10 years, a majority annually said they thought the U.N. was doing a bad job.[2]

Yet at the same time, Gallup polling shows very little support for a U.S. withdrawal from the U.N.[3] And other polling finds that Americans consistently have had an overall favorable opinion of the United Nations.[4]

The United Nations also has been a target of harsh criticism, particularly within conservative circles. "For those on the right side of the political spectrum, there is a strong belief in unilateralism, and there is part of the Republican Party that disdains the U.N. and multilateralism," says David Forsythe, emeritus political science professor at the University of Nebraska, Lincoln, and co-author of *The United Nations and Changing World Politics.*

John Bolton, former U.S. ambassador to the U.N. under Republican President George W. Bush and one of its more vocal critics, has proposed that the United States should only pay for U.N. programs it supports.[5]

The far-right John Birch Society has been campaigning to get the United States out of the United Nations for more than half a century, arguing the U.N. is an effort to create a "socialistic global government" that would strip the United States of its sovereignty.[6]

In the last 25 years, suspicions that the U.N. is superseding national authority have moved from fringe views into more mainstream discourse.

Conservative distrust of the United Nations — inflamed by false rumors that U.N. "black helicopters" were scouting America's national parks for a possible takeover — grew strong enough in the 1990s that the Clinton administration vetoed a traditional second term for Secretary-General Boutros Boutros-Ghali in an effort to appease Republican critics.[7]

During the current presidential campaign, several Republican candidates criticized the United Nations and voiced fears it was being used to undermine U.S. independence. Presumptive GOP presidential nominee Donald Trump, the billionaire real estate developer and reality TV star, has dismissed the U.N. as "a political game" and indicated he will dramatically cut support for the organization."[8]

The United Nations has not been an issue on the Democratic side of the presidential race, and presumptive nominee Hillary Clinton and her opponent, Sen. Bernie Sanders of Vermont, support multinational approaches to solving global problems.

Still, liberal politicians and groups also have been frustrated with the United Nations, most recently in the area of human rights. The U.N. Human Rights Council has been criticized for passing resolutions viewed as limiting free speech. The rights of gay and lesbian people also have been a point of contention, with Russia and several Islamic countries recently uniting to pass a council resolution that critics felt favored traditional marriage and family structures.[9]

---

force from troops volunteered by 10 nations. The peacekeepers supervised the gradual withdrawal of Israeli forces and monitored the border between Egypt and Israel, setting a template for future missions.[52]

The U.N.'s actions and the subsequent retreat by Britain and France were widely seen as signaling the passing of the colonial era.[53] Since that first operation in Egypt, the United Nations has operated 70 other peacekeeping missions, and U.N. Peacekeeping Forces won the 1988 Nobel Peace Prize in recognition of their work.[54]

Economic Development

The dissolution of the Soviet Union in 1991 following reforms implemented by Soviet President Mikhail Gorbachev and the emergence of a more democratic Russia marked the end of the Cold War.[55]

Both Democrats and Republicans have been sharply critical over the years of several U.N. resolutions concerning Israel, most particularly a 1975 statement equating Zionism with racism — a statement that the U.N. General Assembly repealed in 1991.[10]

Yet despite all these concerns, the United States has remained a central player in the United Nations, with no administration seriously suggesting leaving. Despite the frequently stark divide in rhetoric between the two parties, Peter Yeo, president of the Better World Campaign, a nonprofit effort to strengthen U.S.-U.N. ties, points out that Republicans and Democrats both have supported the U.N. on Capitol Hill.

"Seven years running, the U.S. Congress, led by Republicans in both the House and Senate, has fully paid our dues to the U.N.," he says. "And that's significant."

— *Reed Karaim*

[1] "Assessment of Member States' advances to the Working Capital Fund for the biennium 2016-2017 and contributions to the United Nations regular budget for 2016," United Nations Secretariat, Dec. 28, 2015, http://tinyurl.com/h66vp77.

[2] "United Nations," Gallup, April 18, 2016, http://tinyurl.com/7m95wrw.

[3] *Ibid.*

[4] "The U.S and the U.N. in 2016, Congressional Briefing Book," Better World Campaign and United Nations Association of USA, p. 14, http://tinyurl.com/h99dvlv.

[5] John Bolton, "The U.N. doesn't work. Here's a fix," American Enterprise Institute, Oct. 15, 2015, http://tinyurl.com/hg6hukp.

[6] "Get Us Out! of the United Nations," The John Birch Society, http://tinyurl.com/m9nrwxf.

[7] John Goshko, "U.N. becomes lightning rod for rightist fears," *The Washington Post*, Sept. 23, 1996, http://tinyurl.com/j7qwjee.

[8] Ashley Parker, "Donald Trump Says NATO is 'Obsolete,' UN is 'Political Game,' " *The New York Times*, April 2, 2016, http://tinyurl.com/j5hdu2d.

[9] "A new global force is fighting liberal social mores," Erasmus blog, *The Economist*, July 11, 2015, http://tinyurl.com/gn86sku.

[10] Paul Lewis, "U.N. Repeals Its '75 Resolution Equating Zionism With Racism," *The New York Times*, Dec. 17, 1991, http://tinyurl.com/gw2wluu.

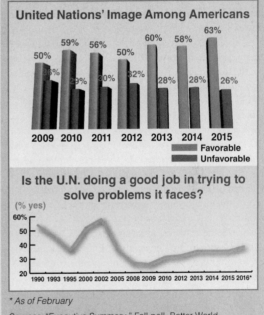

Americans Have Mixed Views on the U.N.

In 2015, more than six in 10 voters had a favorable opinion of the United Nations, the highest since 2009, according to bipartisan polling sponsored by the pro-U.N. Better World Campaign (top). But an annual Gallup poll has found sharply fluctuating opinions since 1990 on whether the U.N. has done a good job at solving problems (bottom).

United Nations' Image Among Americans

	2009	2010	2011	2012	2013	2014	2015
Favorable	50%	59%	56%	50%	60%	58%	63%
Unfavorable	%	29%	30%	32%	28%	28%	26%

Is the U.N. doing a good job in trying to solve problems it faces?
(% yes)

* As of February

Sources: "Executive Summary," Fall poll, Better World Campaign, http://tinyurl.com/zd7jfgb; "United Nations," Gallup, April 18, 2016, http://tinyurl.com/7m95wrw

The conclusion of decades-long tensions between the United States and Russia sparked a burst of optimism that the United Nations would be able to play a larger role in maintaining the new order. In 1992 the leaders of the 15 nations on the Security Council met to adopt "an agenda for peace," later adopted by the Security Council.

The new secretary-general, Boutros Boutros Ghali, who laid out the U.N.'s renewed ambitions, started by acknowledging that "the adversarial decades of the Cold War made the original promise of the [U.N.] impossible to fulfill." But with the end of tensions, he said, "an opportunity has been regained to achieve the great objectives of the Charter — a United Nations capable of maintaining international peace and security, of securing justice and human rights and of promoting, in the words of the Charter, 'social progress and better standards of life in larger freedom.' "[56]

Peacekeepers Accused of Sexual Assault

"It's a real problem that stems from the fact that the U.N. does not have its own troops."

The distinctive blue helmets worn by United Nations peacekeeping forces are supposed to herald the arrival of an outside force that will protect civilians and restore order. But in Central Africa over the last couple of years, they have been connected to reports of the horrific sexual exploitation of women and children.

The claims involve some French troops, but most commonly peacekeeping forces from the Democratic Republic of Congo. The troops have been accused of paying girls and women in refugee camps as little as 50 cents for sexual acts and of sexually assaulting under-age girls. A *Washington Post* report included interviews with several girls who had born "peacekeeper babies."[1]

The case is one of several over the past 20 years in which U.N. peacekeepers have been accused of exploiting and mistreating the people they were supposed to be protecting. Charges of rape, sexual abuse and even collaboration with local human traffickers have been made against U.N. forces operating in Eastern Europe, Haiti and several African nations. Some incidents have involved children as young as 6.[2]

"It's a serious problem," says David Forsythe, emeritus professor of political science at the University of Nebraska, Lincoln, who has co-authored a book on the U.N. "It's a real problem that stems from the fact that the U.N. does not have its own troops."

When the United Nations puts together a peacekeeping force, it essentially has to beg for troops and equipment from member nations who agree to participate. "Some of these national forces, not only in Africa but elsewhere, are not very well trained," says Forsythe. "They're not well versed in the laws of war and the Geneva Conventions [rules of wartime conduct]. They have abused civilians."

A study by Transparency International, an anti-corruption monitoring group based in Berlin, found that the militaries of the 30 countries that provide the most personnel to U.N. peacekeeping are among those that have the biggest problems with corruption within the ranks. Three countries — Bangladesh, Ethiopia and India — contribute almost one-quarter of the troops used in U.N. peacekeeping, and all scored poorly in the study.[3]

U.N. Secretary-General Ban Ki-moon has acknowledged the severity of the problem, calling sexual abuse by peacekeepers "a cancer in our system."[4] The United Nations has removed nearly 1,000 troops connected to the abuse from Central Africa, including an entire battalion — about 800 soldiers — from the Democratic Republic of Congo.[5]

But punishment of U.N. peacekeepers is left to the military command of the individual nations providing troops, and observers say penalties are often insufficient. In countries with less professional militaries, it means soldiers know they have a good chance of escaping punishment when on peacekeeping missions.

The problem, however, has included peacekeeping forces from Western nations with highly trained personnel. In the 1990s, U.N. peacekeepers and aid workers, including police and staff from several European nations, were accused of collaborating with Bosnian prostitution rings in the trafficking of young women into sexual slavery, even helping to bribe officials and forge documents as part of the criminal operations. The scandal attracted so much attention that it later served as the basis for a 2010 movie "The Whistleblower," starring Rachel Weisz.[6]

Yet the number of peacekeepers accused of abuse are only a small portion of the more than 121,000 U.N.

The U.N.'s new confidence showed in both the number and size of peacekeeping missions in the 1990s. "In the first four decades, the Security Council authorized only 13 peacekeeping missions. In the fifth decade, another 20 were launched," wrote Meisler in his history, *The United Nations: The First Fifty Years*.[57] Three of the missions deployed more than 20,000 troops each, significantly larger than most prior peacekeeping forces.[58]

But in Somalia and Bosnia, U.N. forces found themselves in the middle of complicated and violent conflicts in which the peacekeepers struggled to assert their authority. In Bosnia in the early 1990s, peacekeepers were accused of standing by while Serbian soldiers killed Muslims. And in Somalia in 1993, U.S.-led U.N. forces withdrew after 18 Americans were killed in a failed mission that became the basis for the book and movie "Black Hawk Down."[59]

peacekeeping personnel currently serving in 16 different operations around the world.[7]

Still, the U.N. Security Council was concerned enough about the sexual abuse cases that it passed a resolution in March authorizing the secretary-general to replace all troops or other peacekeeping forces sent from a particular country if that nation fails to properly investigate or hold its forces accountable. The council also emphasized its concern over the "continuing and serious allegations" of sexual exploitation by U.N. peacekeepers in the Central African Republic.[8]

Forsythe says that until the U.N. gains more direct control over peacekeeping forces, including the ability to punish those who commit crimes while serving, the problem is likely to continue. "The whole thing stems from the weakness and lack of authority of the personnel who are supposedly in charge," he says.

But other observers say the U.N. already has the authority to act more forcefully. Anders Kompass, a senior U.N. aid official in Africa, was suspended and placed under investigation by the United Nations after he brought French peacekeepers' alleged abuse to the attention of French officials.[9] U.N. administrators said he had not followed official channels, but Miranda Brown, Kompass's former assistant, says he only spoke out after U.N. officials failed to act despite repeated reports about the abuse. "His sole reason for taking action was to stop this abuse," she says.

Brown, who also spoke out, was reassigned to Fiji and dismissed when she refused the transfer. She is seeking reinstatement. She says the United Nations needs to reform its procedures to respond more aggressively to reports of wrongdoing. "Unless you have recognition that you are responsible . . . you're not going to fix the problem," she says. "And from what I can see at this point, there isn't recognition that the U.N. has to fix its own mess."

— *Reed Karaim*

Hervé Ladsous, U.N. undersecretary-general for peacekeeping operations, briefs reporters at U.N. headquarters on his trip to the Central African Republic to investigate possible rapes by peacekeepers from France and the Democratic Republic of the Congo.

Getty Images/LightRocket/Luiz Rampelotto

[1] Kevin Sieff, " 'Sometimes when I'm alone with my baby, I think about killing him. He reminds me of the man who raped me,' " *The Washington Post*, Feb. 27, 2016, http://tinyurl.com/jrv4vzy.

[2] Elsa Buchanan, "UN Peacekeeping: Allegations of sexual exploitation and abuse — a 20 year history of shame," *International Business Times*, March 7, 2016, http://tinyurl.com/z3bwr8q.

[3] Rick Gladstone, "Armies used by U.N. Fail Watchdog Group's Test," *The New York Times*, April 3, 2016, http://tinyurl.com/hsj7nvw.

[4] Sieff, *op. cit.*

[5] *Ibid.*

[6] Ed Vulliamy, "Has the UN learned lessons of Bosnian sex slavery revealed in Rachel Weisz film?" *The Guardian*, Jan. 14, 2012, http://tinyurl.com/h5la9fm.

[7] "Peacekeeping Fact Sheet," United Nations, March 31, 2016, http://tinyurl.com/5tzmet7.

[8] "Security Council endorses steps to combat sexual exploitation by UN peacekeepers," UN News Centre, April 30, 2016, http://tinyurl.com/h89ruzm.

[9] "UN whistleblower resigns over French peacekeeper 'child abuse,' " BBC News, June 8, 2016, http://tinyurl.com/jmggf65.

The following year, the U.N. faced intense criticism after peacekeepers stood by while Hutu militia slaughtered about 800,000 Tutsis in Rwanda.[60] Kofi Annan, who was in charge of U.N. peacekeeping at the time, later expressed personal regret at the U.N.'s failure to take stronger action. "I realized after the genocide that there was more that I could and should have done to sound the alarm and rally support," he said.[61]

"There were a lot of what looked like failures," says Meisler, "so the U.N. became skittish about these kinds of missions."

But others say the U.N.'s effort yielded meaningful results. "From the 1990s to the 2000s, we saw a dramatic decline in the number of wars, the lethality of wars and the number of deaths," says Cousens. "It's a tremendous success story that's rarely told . . . and a huge contribution to that came from the United Nations."

Peacekeeping was only part of the U.N.'s ambitious program. In 1994, the United Nations also adopted an agenda for development, which sought to boost sustainable economic development around the world and called on U.N. member states to embrace the effort.[62]

The agenda stressed the need for coordinating the efforts of nations, NGOs and other international donors, a role Webster University's Pease says the U.N. increasingly plays in the developing world. "I liken it to a cop directing traffic, trying to get the aid to where it needs to be. Without the cop, people would still sort it out, but it wouldn't operate as smoothly."

The U.N.'s emphasis on helping nations develop their own capabilities is key to sustainable development, she adds. "Where the U.N. is really valuable is in its education function, its training function," says Pease. "They're helping states to build the capacity to do these things for themselves, and I think that's really important."

Taken together, the agenda for peace and the agenda for development were an attempt to refocus the U.N. on its historic missions in the post-Cold War era. But as the 20th century ended, the global picture was about to be redrawn by the emergence of a new threat: radical Islamic terrorism.

Post-9/11 Era

The terrorist attacks on Sept. 11, 2001, that killed 2,977 people in New York City, at the Pentagon and outside Shanksville, Pa., when Qaeda terrorists hijacked four jetliners marked a new era of international conflict.[63]

"Terrorism is a global menace. It calls for a united global response," Secretary-General Annan said after the attack. "To defeat it, all nations must take counsel together and act in unison. That is why we have the United Nations."[64]

In the past, the United Nations had struggled to define terrorism, with some nations believing that violent, nongovernmental resistance could be legitimate if it was against an occupying foreign force or a dominating power.[65]

But after 9/11, the Security Council moved to support the United States, unanimously approving a resolution declaring that a "terrorist attack on one country was an attack on all humanity" and recognizing the right of nations to defend themselves against terrorist groups.[66] The council also passed a wide-ranging measure targeting

terrorist financing and calling on members to share intelligence to combat terrorism.[67]

U.N. support for U.S. actions, however, would founder as the United States went to war against Iraq, which wasn't involved in the 9/11 attacks. In 2003, then-Secretary of State Colin Powell infamously told the Security Council that Iraq was hiding weapons of mass destruction. But U.N. inspectors found no such weapons, and the Security Council opposed the U.S. invasion.[68] Annan would later call the war "illegal" because it did not conform to the U.N. charter.[69]

Despite the discord over Iraq, the United Nations has taken a more aggressive stance on terrorism since 9/11, analysts say, and has been essential in imposing international sanctions on terrorist groups and their supporters.

"The U.N., in a way that isn't well noticed, provides technical assistance to over 60 countries to help them comply with these international sanctions," says the Better World Campaign's Yeo. "That's an important contribution because it's one thing for the Security Council to say, 'We're going to freeze the assets of al Qaeda affiliates,' but if you're a nation without the technical skills to do that, you can ask the U.N. for help, and the U.N says here's what you do."

In 2005, a U.N. sponsored summit of world leaders for the first time condemned terrorism and approved a doctrine called "the responsibility to protect," or R2P. Under the doctrine, nations were obligated to protect their population from war crimes, genocide and other harms.[70]

The U.N. helps countries improve their ability to battle terrorism in other ways, Cousens says, including through improved border controls and counterterrorism skills. Terrorists find harbor in politically unstable or economically ravaged countries, Cousens adds, and the U.N.'s experience with economic and political development are important parts of the "U.N. toolkit" in the battle against terrorism.

CURRENT SITUATION
Leadership Battle

In December [2016], Ban Ki-moon is expected to step down as secretary-general when his second term expires. Observers say they hope his successor will bring new energy to the position and, with the supporters of the United States and other key nations, make needed improvements to U.N. operations.

Is the U.N. still an effective agency for international change?

YES
Peter Yeo
President, Better World Campaign

Written for *CQ Researcher*, June 2016

Seventy years after its creation, the United Nations is more relevant and needed than at any time in its history to advance U.S. national security priorities while fostering burden-sharing among nations.

Peace and stability remain at the core of the institution's efforts as they did when President Harry S. Truman signed its charter, with peacekeepers constituting the world's largest deployed military force. However, the kinds of conflict they take on are much different than the brutality the world feared after World War II.

Today's peacekeepers operate in terrorist hotbeds like Mali and in nations wracked by civil war like South Sudan. Their presence often means the difference between life and death. A 2013 study found that deploying large numbers of U.N. peacekeepers "dramatically reduces civilian killings." A Columbia University study found that, in the post-Cold War era, deploying U.N. peacekeepers reduces by half the hazard that a country will slide back into all-out war. As former Joint Chiefs of Staff Chairman Mike Mullen noted, peacekeepers "help promote stability. . . . Therefore, the success of these operations is very much in our national interest."

Yet some of the U.N.'s value is hidden in the stories that don't make the front pages — or perhaps the stories it prevents from happening. Take its delivery of vaccines: They are one of the most cost-effective ways to save the lives of children, improve health and ensure long-term prosperity in developing countries.

Immunizations have saved more children than any other medical intervention in the last 50 years. The U.N. is a leader in this field, vaccinating 58 percent of the world's children. As a result, polio is close to being eradicated, and vaccines for measles, diphtheria, tetanus and pertussis save some 2.5 million lives each year.

Similarly, as the Zika virus affects thousands of pregnant women throughout the Americas, the U.N. is on the front lines: The World Health Organization is coordinating the international response; the U.N. Population Fund is providing voluntary contraception and family planning; UNICEF is helping affected families.

The U.N. is not a perfect institution, and U.S. involvement will remain essential to continue reforms and ensure improvement. Yet, as global crises become more complex, so too do the work and reach of the U.N. Today more than ever, no single country can resolve the world's most pressing challenges. By working with the U.N., we don't have to go it alone.

NO
U.S. Rep. Mike Rogers, R-Ala.
Sponsor, Restore American Sovereignty Act

Written for *CQ Researcher*, June 2016

According to its charter, the United Nations can take action on a wide range of issues confronting humanity in the 21st century, from peace and security, climate change, sustainable development, human rights, disarmament and terrorism to gender equality and food production. As noble as its mission sounds, the U.N. has lost its way and become an ineffective and bloated international organization.

The United States funds 22 percent of the U.N.'s operations, significantly more than any other member state. Despite relying on American taxpayer dollars, recent U.N. actions go directly against the interests and values of our nation. The proposed U.N. Arms Treaty is a threat to our Second Amendment rights, and the Law of the Sea Treaty directly infringes upon American sovereignty. Recently, the U.N. Human Rights Council condemned Israel with five resolutions, but human rights abusers like China were never mentioned. The United Nations cannot balance its broad mission with so many member nations.

Another aspect the U.N. fails in is as an international peacekeeper. The world is more dangerous than ever. With North Korea, China and Iran provoking America and its allies, national security is at the forefront of my mind. We need a deliberative body that acts quickly and forcefully to neutralize threats across the world.

However, the United Nations Security Council, tasked with this exact job, remains gridlocked. Its sanctions against North Korea after that country's most recent provocations amount to nothing more than a slap on the wrist.

When Syrian President Bashar al-Assad began using chemical weapons against his owns citizens, the Security Council was inactive in a response. Russia, led by President Vladmir Putin, continues to ignore internationally recognized nuclear treaties. Yet, as one of the five permanent council members, Russia remains unpunished.

Many people have tried to prescribe a fix for the U.N. I won't do that. Former U.N. Ambassador Jeane Kirkpatrick was once asked why the United States didn't leave the U.N. She responded that it's not worth the trouble.

I disagree. I have introduced H.R. 1205, the Restore American Sovereignty Act, that would remove the United States from the United Nations. When American taxpayers pay for an organization that actively works against them, I think it's time we step up and move on.

Getty Images/COP21/Anadolu Agency/Arnaud Bouissou

In Paris in December 2015, U.N. and French officials — including. U.N. Secretary General Ban Ki-moon, center, and French President François Hollande, far right — raise their arms in celebration of the adoption of the pact committing 195 nations to fight climate change. Unlike previous agreements, the pact requires all nations to act regardless of their economic status.

"We have something that has not happened since 1952. We're going to have a new secretary-general and a new [U.S.] president at the same time. It's an exciting opportunity to embrace U.N. reform," says the Better World Campaign's Yeo.

The contest to replace Ban is spirited. In May, Susana Malcorra, Argentina's foreign minister, became the 10th declared candidate for secretary-general.[71]

Overall, the five men and five women seeking to become the ninth secretary-general have a wide variety of experience on the world stage. For example, Helen Clark, a former prime minister of New Zealand, leads the U.N. Development Programme; Danilo Türk is a past president of Slovenia and former assistant secretary-general. Most of the candidates are from Eastern Europe. The Security Council, which makes the final choice, traditionally assigns the post to people from different regions, and Eastern Europe is widely considered to be next in line.[72]

Pressure is mounting for the council to select the first female secretary-general in the U.N's history. The Campaign to Elect a Woman U.N. Secretary General, an independent lobbying effort formed by a group of prominent women, lists qualified candidates from different global regions on its website.[73]

At the United Nations, at least 44 nations have signed on to an initiative, organized by Colombia, to promote

women for the job. "Gender equality is one of the world's most serious challenges, an unfulfilled goal that remains critical to advance towards an inclusive and sustainable future," María Emma Mejía, the Colombian ambassador to the U.N., wrote in a letter promoting the idea of a female secretary-general.[74]

The Elders, the organization of former world leaders, has called for the Security Council to submit more than one candidate to the U.N. General Assembly for final approval.[75] But the Security Council's five permanent members are considered unlikely to agree.

Climate Change

On Earth Day this past April, world leaders gathered at the United Nations to sign a landmark accord committing 195 nations to fight climate change by limiting the greenhouse gases that are warming the planet.[76]

Previous climate change pacts required developed countries such as the United States and European nations to cut greenhouse gas emissions, while largely exempting developing countries such as China and India. The agreement reached in Paris in late December requires countries to act regardless of economic status.[77]

"This is truly a historic moment," Secretary-General Ban said. "For the first time, we have a truly universal agreement on climate change, one of the most crucial problems on Earth."[78]

Global warming has been on the U.N. agenda since at least 1988, when the General Assembly created the Intergovernmental Panel on Climate Change. Two years later, the panel released its first scientific assessment on climate change, saying human activity was warming the planet.[79]

U.N. diplomats worked on the latest accord for nine years.[80] But even if the plan is fully implemented, scientists caution that it will only slow, not reverse, global warming. Some analysts also doubt whether developed countries, including the United States, can live up to their obligations under the agreement.[81]

However, the Union of Concerned Scientists hailed the United Nations pact as historic. "The unprecedented number of countries signing the Paris agreement confirms there's strong global will to act urgently to limit the dire impacts of climate change," said Alden Meyer, the union's director of strategy and policy and an expert on climate negotiations.[82]

Corruption and Reform

Corruption among senior officials remains an embarrassment to the United Nations. The most recent scandal involved bribery charges against John Ashe, a diplomat from Antigua and Barbuda who served as General Assembly president from September 2013 to September 2014.

This March, a task force appointed by Secretary-General Ban to look at reforms in the wake of Ashe's bribery scandal recommended greater transparency in the financial operations of the president's office. The task force also recommended that future General Assembly presidents make annual financial disclosures.[83]

In October 2015, the U.S. Attorney's Office in Manhattan indicted Ashe on charges he accepted more than $1 million in payments from Ng Lap Seng, a Chinese businessman. In return, according to the indictment, Ashe helped Ng obtain "potentially lucrative investments in Antiqua."[84]

Authorities said Ashe spent some of the money on luxury goods, including $59,000 worth of hand-tailored suits and two Rolex watches worth $54,000. Ashe has denied the charges.[85] Francis Lorenzo, deputy permanent representative to the U.N. from the Dominican Republic, was also charged in the case.[86]

The limited nature of the task force's recommendations highlights the difficulty of achieving reform in the complicated U.N. structure. The General Assembly president does not report to the secretary-general. Presidents receive a $326,000 annual budget but are free to raise money from outside sources, including private companies. In its report, the task force noted this creates "significant loopholes and blindspots" when it comes to tracking the office's finances.[87]

Another case highlights a further challenge to U.N. reforms: Those who expose corruption can face retaliation. A senior U.N. aid official, Anders Kompass, was suspended and faced possible dismissal after he reported sexual abuse of children by peacekeepers from France and the Democratic Republic of Congo, serving in the Central African Republic (CAR). The U.N. has removed nearly 1,000 troops connected to the abuse from the CAR.

Kompass was later cleared of charges that he went outside established channels to leak a U.N. report on the abuse to French officials. Still, he resigned in June, saying he did not feel senior U.N. officials had been held accountable for their failure.[88] Miranda Brown, a former assistant to Kompass, says the case illustrates the need for greater protection for whistleblowers who speak out about U.N. abuses. Brown backed him publicly and was transferred to Fiji, a move she contested, leading to her dismissal. A Freedom of Information Act that allows the media to request internal U.N. documents would be an important step toward greater accountability, she says.

Without those changes, Brown says, corruption and cover-ups will continue at the United Nations "and people will suffer, and those that will suffer the most are the people the United Nations is supposed to protect, such as children suffering from sexual abuse."

OUTLOOK
Relevance Debated

For all the challenges facing the United Nations, no one expects it to disappear anytime soon. After all, the 71-year-old organization has survived the Cold War; the birth of dozens of new nations following the collapse of colonialism and communism; the emergence of new economic powers in China, India and Brazil; the transformation of the global economy through free trade and the rise of the Internet age.

But opinions differ sharply on how significant the U.N. will remain in the changing world.

As global prosperity grows and developing nations gain confidence and security, George Washington's Brimmer predicts a U.N. no longer as dominated by the traditional powers. "We might find some countries that have not been as active beginning to play a larger role — Indonesia, Mexico, for example — which would be good for all of us," she says. "I think you'll see more countries with candidates for leading offices or running for the Security Council."

Brimmer says Canada, which has been active in peacekeeping, is an example of how a middle-power country can play a critical role at the U.N. "The role these middle or emerging powers can play is really important. They can help with mediation. They can take areas of specialty and drill down and become specialists, and that's really helpful for the globe as a whole."

City University's Weiss sees a bleaker outlook for the U.N., believing it must make fundamental changes in how it operates — by centralizing power and reining in the bureaucracy — if it hopes to be a remain an effective player on the world stage. Absent significant changes, Weiss says, "it's going to become more and more marginal. And at least the way I read the conversations . . . there's a kind of complacency that there's really no urgency to change."

Other U.N. observers say big-power conflicts — as occurred during the Cold War — once again define and limit the U.N.'s ability to act. Author Meisler notes that the re-emergence of fundamental disagreements between the United States and Russia over how the international community should react to trouble spots in the Middle East and elsewhere, along with increased tension between the United States and China over several issues, have put three of the five permanent members of the Security Council at odds.

"The only evolution that can occur is if Russia and the United States" stop opposing each other again, Meisler says. "And then you have the question of how China and the U.S. get along. Otherwise, I see the [U.N's role in the world] being pretty much as it is right now."

Webster University's Pease also believes that the U.N. is probably going to "continue business as usual." But even with its flaws, she says, the United Nations provides an essential platform for global discussion and action that helps to avert some global crises and prevents others from getting worse.

"There's an old saying from [the second U.N. Secretary-General] Dag Hammarskjöld: The purpose of the U.N. is not to get us into heaven, but to save us from hell," Pease says. "I think what it's designed to do is provide a forum for states and other actors to be heard. It provides that forum and tries to address collective problems, and it's always going to be messy, and people aren't going to agree. But it's the only game in town. There is no other place to go."

NOTES

1. Michele Kelemen, "Saudi Arabia Dropped From List Of Those Harming Children; U.N. Cites Pressure," National Public Radio, June 9, 2016, http://tinyurl.com/jht2jyc.

2. *Ibid.*

3. *Ibid.*

4. *Ibid.*

5. "Funds, Programmes, Specialized Agencies and Others," United Nations, 2016, http://tinyurl.com/nffg4jd; "Where we are," United Nations careers, 2016, http://tinyurl.com/hrzobke.

6. Anthony Banbury, "I Love the U.N., but It Is Failing," *The New York Times*, March 18, 2016, http://tinyurl.com/z57x2ev.

7. "About the UN," The United Nations, http://tinyurl.com/jnug35l.

8. *Ibid.*

9. Chris McGreal, "70 years and half a trillion dollars later: what has the UN achieved?" *The Guardian*, Sept. 7, 2015, http://tinyurl.com/nc8nsd6.

10. Kevin Sieff, " 'Sometimes when I'm alone with my baby, I think about killing him. He reminds me of the man who raped me,' " *The Washington Post*, Feb. 27, 2016, http://tinyurl.com/jrv4vzy.

11. "The Millennium Development Goals Report 2015," The United Nations, 2015, http://tinyurl.com/p92xdd3.

12. *Ibid.*

13. "Transforming our world: the 2030 Agenda for Sustainable Development," United Nations, Sept. 25, 2015, http://tinyurl.com/q9k2rk9.

14. "The Universal Declaration of Human Rights," United Nations, http://tinyurl.com/pnjck5h.

15. "UN Women," United Nations, Dec. 10, 1948, http://tinyurl.com/hvhnc5q; "Free and Equal," the United Nations, http://tinyurl.com/ow2umgm.

16. Christopher Ingraham, "Why one of the world's worst human rights offenders is leading a U.N. human rights panel," *The Washington Post*, Sept. 28, 2015, http://tinyurl.com/jo9tzu2.

17. Alexandra Sims, "Saudi Arabia issues extraordinary defence of human rights record in speech to UN council," *The Independent*, March 9, 2016, http://tinyurl.com/hrbrfeu.

18. McGreal, *op. cit.*

19. Harriet Grant, "UN agencies 'broke and failing' in face of ever-growing refugee crisis," *The Guardian*, Sept. 6, 2015, http://tinyurl.com/paoaa6s.

20. "As refugee and migrant flood into Europe continues, UN and partners seek $550 million for 2016," UN News Centre, Jan. 26, 2016, http://tinyurl.com/j6vtdmb.

21. "Federal Spending: Where does the money go," National Priorities Project, http://tinyurl.com/kakej6h.

22. Erin Graham, "Ignore the old complaints about U.N. funding. Here are some new ones," *The Washington Post*, Sept. 30, 2015, http://tinyurl.com/zhnfuyr.

23. *Ibid.*

24. Banbury, *op. cit.*

25. *Ibid.*

26. "The U.S. and the U.N. in 2016, Congressional Briefing Book," Better World Campaign and United Nations Association of USA, p. 35, http://tinyurl.com/h99dvlv.

27. "Peacekeeping Fact Sheet," United Nations, April 30, 2016, http://tinyurl.com/5tzmet7; "Peacekeeping 'flagship of the UN enterprise,' Ban says ahead of Day honouring 'blue helmets,' " U.N. News Centre, May 19, 2016, http://tinyurl.com/j5xu8jz.

28. "Peacekeeping 'flagship of the UN enterprise,' Ban says ahead of Day honouring 'blue helmets,' " *op. cit.*

29. "World's most dangerous peacekeeping mission," BBC News, Nov. 20, 2015, http://tinyurl.com/j6j6jka; "Peacekeeping Fact Sheet," *op. cit.*

30. "Themes and Priorities," United Nations Counterterrorism Center, 2016, http://tinyurl.com/h4engh8.

31. "Peacekeeping Fact Sheet," *op. cit.*

32. Michelle Nichols, "Countries pledge 40,000 U.N. peacekeepers at U.N. summit," Reuters, Sept. 28, 2015, http://tinyurl.com/jdglglp.

33. Chris McGreal, "What's the point of peacekeepers when they don't keep the peace?" *The Guardian*, Sept. 17, 2015, http://tinyurl.com/nchbqeu.

34. "The U.S. and the U.N. in 2016, Congressional Briefing Book," *op. cit.*, p. 17.

35. Lydia Swart and Cile Pace, "Changing the Composition of the Security Council: Is There a Viable Solution?" Center for U.N. Reform Education, March 1, 2015, http://tinyurl.com/zujx2m8.

36. "General Assembly Adopts, without Vote, 'Landmark' Decision on Advancing Efforts to Reform, Increase Membership of Security Council," The United Nations, Sept. 14, 2015, http://tinyurl.com/zq6ty9a.

37. "Membership Including Expansion and Representation," Global Policy Forum, http://tinyurl.com/jxf9xvp.

38. "Strengthening the United Nations," *The Elders*, Feb. 7, 2015, http://tinyurl.com/zm48lrv.

39. Sheryl Gay Stolberg and Jim Yardley, "Countering China, Obama Backs India for U.N. Council," *The New York Times*, Nov. 8, 2010, http://tinyurl.com/3867ru4.

40. "1945: The San Francisco Conference," United Nations, http://tinyurl.com/zm76eq8.

41. *Ibid.*

42. *Ibid.*

43. Charles Townshend, "The League of Nations and the United Nations," BBC History, Feb. 17, 2011, http://tinyurl.com/avzb896.

44. Stanley Meisler, "United Nations: The First Fifty years," *Atlantic Monthly Press*, 1995, pp. 16-18.

45. *Ibid.*

46. C. N. Trueman, "The United Nations and the Korean War," History Learning Site, March 3, 2016, http://tinyurl.com/hfspa7t.

47. *Ibid.*

48. "Hungary, 1956," U.S. Department of State Archive, http://tinyurl.com/zvhgppv.

49. Tarik Kafala, "The veto and how to use it," BBC News, Sept. 17, 2003, http://tinyurl.com/6lhnnp.

50. "Milestones, 1951-1960," History of the United Nations, http://tinyurl.com/guwbjad.

51. Meisler, *op. cit.*, pp. 94-114.

52. *Ibid.*

53. Derek Brown, "1956: Suez and the end of empire," *The Guardian*, March 14, 2001, http://tinyurl.com/h9tcr6v.

54. "The Nobel Peace Prize 1988," Nobelprize. org, May 23, 2016, http://tinyurl.com/jaemshl.

55. "The Collapse of the Soviet Union," Office of the Historian, U.S. Department of State, http://tinyurl.com/hyj94f2.

56. Boutros Boutros Ghali, "An Agenda for Peace, Preventative Diplomacy, peacemaking and peace-keeping, Report of the Secretary General pursuant to the statement adopted by the Summit Meeting of the Security Council on 31 January 1992," United Nations, http://tinyurl.com/zlrjosq.

57. Meisler, *op. cit.*, p. 287.

58. *Ibid.*, p. 288.

59. Paul Alexander, "Fallout from Somalia still haunts US policy 20 years later," *Stars and Stripes*, Oct. 3, 2013, http://tinyurl.com/z5rocmn.

60. McGreal, *op. cit.*

61. "UN chief's Rwanda genocide regret," BBC News, March 26, 2004, http://tinyurl.com/ d783pfo.

62. "Boutros Boutros Ghali, Development and International Economic Cooperation, An Agenda for Development, Report of the Secretary General," United Nations, May 6, 1994, http://tinyurl.com/h6d6u2p.

63. "September 11th Fast Facts," CNN, Sept. 7, 2015, http://tinyurl.com/pvhfoh9.

64. Thomas Weiss *et al.*, *The United Nations and Changing World Politics* (2007), p. 95.

65. *Ibid.*, p. 96.

66. "Security Council Condemns, 'In Strongest Terms', Terrorist Attacks on United States," United Nations, Sept 12, 2001, http://tinyurl.com/k6t4jy7.

67. "Security Council Unanimously Adopts Wide-ranging Anti-terrorism Resolution; Calls for Supressing Financing, Improving International Cooperation," United Nations, Sept. 28, 2001, http://tinyurl.com/pkmqp4c.

68. Elaine Sciolino, "France to Veto Resolution on Iraq War, Chirac Says," *The New York Times*, March 11, 2003, http://tinyurl.com/hkzb3ff.

69. Ewen MacAskill and Julian Borger, "Iraq war was illegal and breached UN charter, says Annan," *The Guardian*, Sept. 15, 2004, http://tinyurl.com/l3vv2vh.

70. For background, see Tom Price, "Assessing the United Nations," *CQ Researcher*, March 20, 2012, pp. 129-152.

71. Somini Sengupta, "Susana Malcorra of Argentina Becomes Candidate for U.N. Secretary General," *The New York Times*, May 20, 2016, http://tinyurl.com/jbw75yo.

72. "The Race to Run the United Nations," *The New York Times*, April 9, 2016, http://tinyurl.com/jga5gfz.

73. Campaign to Elect a Woman U.N. Secretary General, 2016, http://tinyurl.com/z5aauwq.

74. "The Push for a Woman to Run the U.N.," *The New York Times*, Aug. 22, 2015, http://tinyurl.com/noybaok.

75. "A U.N. Fit for Purpose," *The Elders*, 2016, http://tinyurl.com/go9fjoo.

76. Doyle Rice, "175 nations sign historic Paris climate deal on Earth Day," *USA Today*, April 22, 2016, http://tinyurl.com/zk8oeer; Coral Davenport, "Nations Approve Landmark Climate Accord in Paris," *The New York Times*, Dec. 12, 2015, http://tinyurl.com/na2wpgp.

77. Davenport, *op. cit.*

78. *Ibid.*

79. Karl Ritter, "Timeline of key events in international effort to combat climate change," *U.S. News & World Report*, Nov. 30, 2015, http://tinyurl.com/h7nn3o2.

80. Davenport, *op. cit.*

81. Justin Gillis and Coral Davenport, "Leaders Roll Up Sleeves on Climate, but Experts Say Plans Don't Pack a Wallop," *The New York Times*, April 21, 2016, http://tinyurl.com/hdps9hg.

82. "What's Next Following the Historic Signing of Paris Agreement?" Union of Concerned Scientists, April 21, 2016, http://tinyurl.com/gt5nyru.

83. Somini Sengupta, "U.N. Panel's Call for Transparency Highlights Limits of Oversight," *The*

New York Times, March 29, 2016, http://tinyurl
.com/z5nwcjx.

84. Marc Santora, Somini Sengupta and Benjamin Weiser, "Former U.N. President and Chinese Billionaire Are Accused in Graft Scheme," *The New York Times*, Oct. 6, 2015, http://tinyurl.com/hoe2egc.

85. *Ibid.*

86. Rebecca Davis O'Brien, Christopher M. Matthews and Farnaz Fassihi, "Former United Nations General Assembly President Charged in Bribery Scheme," *The Wall Street Journal*, Oct. 6, 2015,. http://tinyurl.com/nf36xyp.

87. Sengupta, *op. cit.*, March 29, 2016.

88. "UN whistleblower resigns over French peacekeeper 'child abuse,' " BBC News, June 8, 2016, http://tinyurl.com/jmggf65.

BIBLIOGRAPHY
Selected Sources
Books

Fasulo, Linda, *An Insider's Guide to the UN: Third Edition*, Yale University Press, 2015.
An NBC News correspondent who covers the United Nations provides a guide to the U.N.'s different bodies and programs, along with a review of how the organization addresses terrorism, climate change and other key issues.

Meisler, Stanley, *United Nations: A History*, Grove Press, 2011.
A veteran foreign affairs journalist who wrote about the U.N. looks at its origins in World War II, including the hopes the founders had for the organization, and how it has evolved in the years since.

Weiss, Thomas, *What's Wrong With the United Nations and How to Fix It*, 2nd ed., Polity, 2012.
The director of the Ralph Bunche Institute for International Studies at City University of New York examines the institutional ills he believes leave the U.N. poorly equipped to deal with today's problems, and suggests ways to reform it.

Weiss, Thomas, *et al.*, *The United Nations and Changing World Politics*, Westview Press, 2013.

Four foreign policy scholars examine the U.N.'s role in three areas: building international peace and security; human rights and humanitarian relief; and promoting peace through sustainable economic development.

Articles

Banbury, Anthony, "I Love the U.N., but It Is Failing," *The New York Times*, March 18, 2016, http://tinyurl.com/z57x2ev.
A longtime U.N. official says the international organization's "colossal mismanagement" leaves it unable to achieve its mission in key areas, including protecting world health and keeping the peace.

Brady, Dennis, "Why outgoing U.N. chief Ban Ki-moon was willing to bet big on a climate change deal," *The Washington Post*, May 6, 2016, http://tinyurl.com/jo2nklg.
U.N. Secretary-General Ban Ki-moon explains why he felt the United Nations could play an important role in bringing the nations of the world together to limit global climate change.

Buchanan, Elsa, "UN Peacekeeping: Allegations of sexual exploitation and abuse — a 20 year history of shame," *International Business Times*, March 7, 2016, http://tinyurl.com/z3bwr8q.
A review of sexual abuse charges against U.N. peacekeeping forces finds that accusations have reoccurred repeatedly for 20 years.

Charbonneau, Louis, Nate Raymond and Michelle Nichols, "Exclusive: U.N. audit identifies serious lapses linked to alleged bribery," Reuters, April 3, 2016, http://tinyurl.com/glxh6q7.
An internal U.N. investigation faults officials' lack of oversight in a bribery case involving a former president of the U.N. General Assembly.

McGreal, Chris, "70 years and half a trillion dollars later: what has the UN achieved?" *The Guardian*, Sept. 7, 2015, http://tinyurl.com/nc8nsd6.
On the 70th anniversary of the U.N.'s founding, a review of the organization's history finds real accomplishments — saving lives and boosting health and education in much of the world — but also a bloated and undemocratic structure.

Sengupta, Somini, "At U.N., Ambassadors Hold Auditions for Next Secretary General," *The New York Times,* **April 15, 2016, http://tinyurl.com/hk2hjwz.**
Nine candidates vying to become the next U.N. secretary-general face the ambassadors of various nations to answer questions about the future of the international organization.

Reports and Studies

"Confronting the Crisis of Global Governance: The Report of the Commission on Global Security, Justice & Governance," The Hague Institute for Global Justice and the Stimson Center, June 2015, http://tinyurl.com/hg36mmd.
A commission of former senior diplomats concludes that a range of global challenges — from international terrorism to climate change — calls for a strengthening of international organizations, including the United Nations.

"The Millennium Development Goals Report 2015," United Nations, 2015, http://tinyurl.com/p92xdd3.
A U.N. report assesses the progress made toward reducing world poverty and hunger, improving health and education and other goals set by nations of the United Nations and at least 23 other international organizations at the start of the new millennium.

Troszczynska-van Genderen, Wanda, "Reforming the United Nations: State of Play, Ways Forward," European Parliament, Directorate-General for External Policies, Policy Department, March 2015, http://tinyurl.com/o28ycsb.
A study sponsored by the European Union's Parliament looks at proposed U.N. reforms in a variety of areas, including budgeting and management, and assesses where the proposals stand.

"Uniting Our Strengths for Peace — Politics, Partnership and People," Report of the High-Level Independent Panel on United Nations Peace Operations, United Nations, June 2015, http://tinyurl.com/jot68lo.
A panel appointed by U.N. Secretary-General Ban Ki-moon to assess the relevance and effectiveness of U.N. peacekeeping operations calls for greater clarity in the use of force and a greater emphasis on conflict prevention and mediation.

For More Information

American Enterprise Institute, 1150 17th St., N.W., Washington, DC 20036; 202-862-5800; https://www.aei .org. Conservative think tank that seeks to make the United Nations more responsive to Western interests.

Brookings Institution, 1775 Massachusetts Ave., N.W., Washington, DC 20036; 202-797-6000; www.brookings .edu. Liberal think tank that conducts studies and analysis of global development, foreign aid and world health issues.

Council on Foreign Relations, The Harold Pratt House, 58 E. 68th St., New York, NY 10065; 212-434-9400; www .cfr.org. Nonpartisan think tank that promotes debate on major foreign policy issues.

The Elders Foundation, PO Box 67772, London W14 4EH, United Kingdom; +44-0-207-013-4646; http:// theelders.org. Organization of retired world leaders that promotes peace and human rights and has proposed several U.N. reforms.

United Nations, 405 E. 42nd St., New York, NY 10017; 212-963-9999; www.un.org/en/index.html. Organization of 193 member nations that works on issues of international importance, including peace, disarmament, climate change, sustainable development, terrorism, global health and humanitarian aid.

United Nations Foundation, 1750 Pennsylvania Ave., N.W., Suite 300, Washington, DC 20006; 202-887-9040; www.unfoundation.org. Philanthropy begun in 1988 with a $1 billion gift from media mogul Ted Turner to support the U.N.

United Nations Watch, Case Postale 191, 1211 Geneva 20, Switzerland; +41-22-734-1472; www.unwatch.org/en/. Nongovernmental organization that monitors the performance of the United Nations.

6

Women in Leadership

Alan Greenblatt

AFP/Getty Images/Paul Faith

Theresa May, Britain's second female prime minister, above, is one of a handful of female heads of state in major Western democracies. Studies show that women often face doubts about their leadership and are judged more harshly than men. However, a Pew Research Center study last year found that most Americans agree women are as qualified as men to hold leadership positions.

From *CQ Researcher*,
September 23, 2016

For women's rights advocates who have long dreamed of seeing a woman in the Oval Office, Hillary Clinton is on the precipice of history.

If she wins in November, advocates say, her victory would signify something far more important than the election of a Democratic president or defeat of a conservative political rival. It would be an event that shatters the highest glass ceiling.

"It will be symbolically overwhelming," says Bonnie Dow, a professor of communications and women's and gender studies at Vanderbilt University. "People like me are going to sob for days."

But a Clinton loss would mean something quite different, say her supporters: a setback for women's rights, no less at the hands of Republican presidential candidate Donald Trump, whom critics have accused of spouting sexist rhetoric and unleashing misogynistic behavior among his followers.[1]

"Women's rights are going to be trampled on even worse than they already have been," declared blogger Allen Clifton, co-founder of Forward Progressives, a liberal political website.[2]

Clinton's bid for the nation's most powerful office comes amid an important inflection point for women's rights in the United States. While women have achieved huge advances in politics, business and other professions in recent decades, they still have far to go in achieving parity with men, say rights advocates and social scientists who study gender trends. American women, they say, often face obstacles that men do not, including sexism, sexual harassment and a pay gap based on gender.

Women Scarce in Top Corporate Jobs

Women are the CEOs of only 22 S&P 500 companies. Experts say that while many companies are hiring more women into executive positions, women often face obstacles when seeking top leadership posts. Among those serving as CEOs of major corporations are General Motors' Mary Barra, Yahoo's Marissa Mayer and PepsiCo's Indra Nooyi.

Gender of CEOs of S&P 500 Companies

478

22

— Male
— Female

Source: "Women CEOs of the S&P 500," Catalyst, http://tinyurl.com/oxc43te

Women's leadership roles have expanded greatly since Clinton graduated from Wellesley College in 1969. She herself was the third female secretary of State. Today, women commonly serve in the Cabinet, three women sit on the Supreme Court and the chair of the Federal Reserve is a woman. If elected, Clinton would join female heads of state in two other major Western democracies: Theresa May, Britain's second female prime minister, and Angela Merkel, Germany's chancellor since 2005. French lawyer and politician Christine Lagarde became the first female managing director of the International Monetary Fund in 2011.

But studies show that women in the United States often face doubts about their leadership and are judged more harshly than men. Alice Eagly, who teaches management and psychology at Northwestern University, points to studies showing that female college presidents and police chiefs face additional criticism when they fail. "If a person's in a role that their group is not usually doing, when they fail they get a double-whammy, because stereotypes whip back," she says.[3]

A Pew Research Center study released last year found that most Americans agree women are as qualified as men to hold leadership positions. But women were much more likely than men to believe that society holds female leaders to higher standards in business and politics.[4] "We may see some changes going forward, but it seems like we're a little bit stuck," said Kim Parker, lead author of the study.[5]

A 2015 study by McKinsey & Co., a management consulting firm, found that most men — 88 percent — believe women enjoy equal opportunities to advance within their organizations, even when evidence shows otherwise.[6] "Over and over and over again, the women are viewed more negatively than men, even when the résumés are identical," says Andrea Baran, regional director of the Equal Employment Opportunity Commission (EEOC) in St. Louis.

Besides professional barriers, many women face misogyny and sexism, as illustrated by the numerous accusations of sexual harassment from former Fox News host Gretchen Carlson that led to a $20 million settlement and the ouster of Roger Ailes in July as head of Fox News.[7]

While women have made strides in business — companies such as General Motors and PepsiCo are headed by women — they remain sorely underrepresented as CEOs of large American corporations. Only about 11 percent of executive officers in Silicon Valley are women, and just 4.4 percent at S&P 500 companies.[8] This year only 21 of *Fortune* magazine's top 500 companies have female CEOs — three fewer than last year.[9] (*See graphic, above.*)

And while half the nation's doctors are women, they account for only 5 percent of surgeons, among the most highly paid doctors.[10] Similarly, women make up 36 percent of the lawyers in the United States but only about 21 percent of law firm partners.[11] And about three-fourths of college and university presidents are male.[12]

Moreover, while numerous women have achieved "firsts" to hold leadership positions in many fields, it is still not the norm for a second or third woman to hold a high office or take charge of a major company. That has held true not only in the United States, but internationally.

For example, a long list of countries — including Australia, Brazil, Canada, Ecuador, India, Pakistan, Poland and Panama — have had one female head of state but never a second.[13]

A critical mass of successful women, rather than just a solitary breakthrough, is needed for women to gain true equality and lasting power, says Debbie Walsh, who directs the Center for American Women and Politics at Rutgers University. While pioneers are great, she says, female leaders must become the norm.

"Substantial research — sociological, political, economic — showed that whether it was a legislative body, a corporate board, an appellate court or a Navy ship, if numbers of women were lower than 20 percent, women's voices weren't heard," writes Jay Newton-Small, a *Time* reporter and the author of *Broad Influence*, a book on female leaders. "Either they didn't speak up, or men didn't listen."[14]

The good news, say advocates, is that women today have access to education and employment in numbers that were nearly inconceivable when the women's rights revolution began to take hold in the 1960s. Women now constitute a majority of college students and about half of the students in law and medical schools.[15]

Yet, as women have progressed in the work world, experts say, they have tended to fall behind their male peers, not just in career advancement but also in salary. At the start of their careers, women are paid slightly less than men, but the gap widens as time goes by and they miss out on promotions that offer bigger salaries. Some studies have found that women are paid on average less than 80 percent of what men make.[16]

Researchers have found that some women trail men because they choose to take time off or limit their working hours to spend more time with their families. "One of the reasons many women earn less is they're not willing to work more hours because they're taking care of their kids," says Claudia Goldin, an economist at Harvard University.

Still, women sometimes are passed over for promotions and penalized for having children, even as their male colleagues' salaries rise when they become dads, researchers have found. A 2014 study by University of Massachusetts sociologist Michelle J. Budig found that women's earnings decrease by an average of 4 percent with every child, while men receive a 6 percent fatherhood "bonus."[17]

Efforts to push for greater pay equity have had mixed results in Congress, where women hold fewer than 20 percent of the seats, and in state legislatures, where women make up less than a quarter of lawmakers.

Indeed, women's advocates say the political arena has been one of the most difficult for women. "The fact that there are less than 20 percent of Congress who are women is testament to the fact that there are unique challenges women face in running for office," says Rachel Thomas, press secretary for EMILY's List, a political action committee that works to elect Democratic women.

Currently, only six governors are women, and there have never been more than nine serving at any one time. "For women, the executive office — whether for president, governor, mayor or CEO — remains the broadest hurdle to jump," writes Newton-Small.[18]

While Clinton's election would be a tremendous breakthrough, many women say they don't expect barriers to suddenly start tumbling down. "For the most part, people are not pinning all their hopes on one woman candidate," says Kathryn Pearson, a political scientist at the University of Minnesota.

In fact, some analysts predict that electing a female president will unleash a new age of misogyny, just as the election of a black president unlocked pent-up racism. Misogyny "will probably become even more overt," said Farida Jalalzai, a political scientist at Oklahoma State University, because the more power she wields, the more threatening she will seem. "People will have no problem vilifying her and saying the most misogynistic things imaginable."[19]

As female leaders take stock of their gains and analysts ponder the obstacles that remain, here are some of the questions under debate:

Are women better leaders than men?

Having women at the top can pay dividends. After examining the results from nearly 22,000 publicly traded companies around the world, the nonpartisan Washington-based Peterson Institute for International Economics found that having at least 30 percent of women in top leadership positions in the "C-suite" (CEO, chief financial officer, etc.) adds 6 percent to profits.[20]

Other studies have found that companies with more women on their corporate boards perform better than those where women are underrepresented.[21] "Study after study shows that including more women at the executive level is good for bottom lines," author Newton-Small writes.[22]

In addition, a 2012 survey of more than 7,000 business executives, published in the *Harvard Business Review*, stated: "At every level, more women were rated by their peers, their bosses, their direct reports, and their other associates as better overall leaders than their male counterparts — and the higher the level, the wider that gap grows."[23]

"There is research that shows women are better managers," says Nancy Modesitt, who teaches law at the University of Baltimore. "There's no research that shows women are worse managers, yet we don't have a corporate culture that can recognize that."

Academic studies have found differences in leadership styles between men and women.[24] Newer studies confirm earlier findings that female leaders or managers tend to be better listeners, less hierarchical and better at team-building than men in similar or identical positions.[25]

Of course, leadership styles among women, as with men, vary widely. "We're looking at a whole spectrum of individual differences, even though there do tend to be group differences between the masculine type of leadership and the feminine leadership style, which is more communicative," says Fanny M. Cheung, co-author of the 2008 book on leadership *Women at the Top.*[26]

Several women were selected in recent years to turn around crisis-plagued companies, where the new CEOs faced formidable obstacles to success, some observers say. Marissa Mayer, Yahoo's CEO, was ranked the 16th most-powerful businesswoman in the world in 2014 but one of the world's most disappointing leaders by *Fortune* in 2016 after she failed to stop the company's decline and made several heavily criticized management decisions.[27]

A decade ago, two British researchers identified the phenomenon of putting women in leadership roles during a crisis when the chance of failure is highest and called it the "glass cliff," a term that has gained traction in business circles.[28] Between 2004 and 2013, a higher percentage of female CEOs were forced out of their jobs

Women Far Outnumbered in Congress

The number of women serving in Congress has doubled over the past two decades, but women hold only 20 percent of Senate seats and 19 percent of House seats. California Democrat Nancy Pelosi served as the nation's first and only female House speaker. A woman has never been Senate majority leader.

Number of Women in Congress

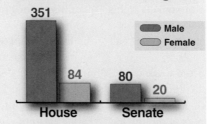

Sources: "Women in the Senate," U.S. Senate, http://tinyurl.com/jrt279e; "Women in the U.S. House of Representatives 2015," Center for American Women and Politics, Rutgers University, http://tinyurl.com/jo4vus3

than their male counterparts — 38 percent of women, compared with 27 percent of men.[29]

Of course, not all female leaders are set up for failure. But the obstacles they face may lead them to develop different leadership styles than men.

"Women incur backlash for being directive and assertive in leadership, so they cope by becoming more participative," says Northwestern's Eagly. In addition, "at least for some audiences, women can lack legitimacy as leaders, especially in powerful positions. That problem is made worse, no doubt, by women 'coming on strong.'"

Therefore, some female leaders play to expectations by being less assertive. In other words, women change their leadership styles to fit their organizations, says Kathy Krendl, the president of Otterbein University in Ohio, who leads a seminar on women in leadership. "Context is very important," she says. "If a woman is in a highly male-dominated company or industry, her approach is more in line with traditional male leadership."

Female leaders also sometimes play to gender stereotypes, says Samantha Paustian-Underdahl, a management professor at Florida International University in Miami. "A woman has to demonstrate the competence and the vision," she says, "but at the same time she really has to play up those feminine characteristics of being caring and empathetic.

"In order to be seen as just competent, they have to be seen as double-amazing," Paustian-Underdahl adds. "When they make it into their leadership roles, it's not surprising that they're seen as effective, because they have to be in order to get there."

A group of female senators demonstrated effective leadership in 2013 when they helped negotiate an end to a partial government shutdown. In part because they made up a minority within the Senate, female senators met regularly on a bipartisan basis — a rarity in Congress, but a practice among the female senators that gave them the edge.[30]

Because women are viewed as effective leaders, Krendl says, more male leaders are imitating them by focusing on building relationships.

In a globalized economy, with companies becoming more interdependent, Cheung says, qualities such as team building and collaboration have become a must-have leadership skill, along with attributes such as intelligence and decisiveness.

"There is a changing model of leadership that is more consistent with our cultural model of femininity," Cheung says. CEOs and managers "are expected to provide mentorship to their teams and not just be autocratic leaders."

Would greater transparency reduce the gender pay gap?

Women working full time earn, on average, 79 percent of what men in equivalent positions make. The gap is larger for women of color and grows as careers continue.

"Women typically are paid about 90 percent of what men are paid until around the age of 35," according to the American Association of University of Women. "After that, median earnings for women are typically 76 to 81 percent of what men are paid."[31]

That's a broad average looking at all jobs. The pay gap is larger for women of color and for mothers and grows with age. It's not the same across all professions or job categories, but even when factors such as education and experience are taken into account, a salary gap between men and women persists.

A recent *Wall Street Journal* examination of 446 occupations found that women earn much less than men, with the widest gaps in professions such as medicine (doctors) and finance (compensation managers and personal financial advisers).[32]

Top professional positions aren't forgiving when women become mothers and put their families first by taking time off or limiting their working hours, says Harvard's Goldin.

Other economists suggest that women typically don't negotiate as hard as men when offered a job.

Some experts say women would be in a stronger negotiating position if wage transparency was greater. A

A supporter of Republican presidential candidate Donald Trump protests against Hillary Clinton at a Trump rally in Manchester, N.H., on Aug. 25, 2016. Critics have accused Trump of spouting sexist rhetoric and unleashing misogynistic behavior among his followers. "The only thing she's got going is the women's card," Trump said of Clinton in April, a comment widely viewed as sexist.

growing number of policymakers believe that if women knew what their male colleagues were making, they would have a better chance of earning the same wages. The Obama administration in January began requiring large federal contractors to report pay scales by race, ethnicity and gender. The number of states that require some form of pay transparency has doubled in the past three years, to a dozen.[33]

Last fall, California enacted a law prohibiting employers from firing or sanctioning workers who ask questions about what their colleagues who are doing "substantially similar" work are making. California companies do not have to publish what wages they pay but must justify why men and women with similar responsibilities are paid differently. In August, Massachusetts passed a bill that protects workers from punishment if they ask about salaries, while forbidding companies from asking prospective workers about their salary history before offering them jobs.

Where salaries are publicly disclosed — for CEOs of publicly traded companies, or for many types of federal jobs — the gender wage gap for comparable positions is substantially smaller than the overall average, says Ariane Hegewisch, program director for employment and earnings at the nonprofit Institute for Women's Policy Research in Washington. "The evidence we have is that where there's transparency, there's less of a wage gap," she says.

Some other countries have begun mandating greater transparency. Beginning in 2018, British companies with more than 250 employees will have to disclose salaries and bonuses for male and female employees.[34] Other European countries, such as Austria, Denmark and France, have implemented limited pay reporting requirements.[35]

But Gowri Ramachandran, a professor at Southwestern Law School in Los Angeles, warns that disclosing information about broad job categories or median salaries would not be "fine-grained" enough to allow individual women to demand more money. She advocates a requirement that companies disclose, internally, exactly who is making what.

Disclosure, she says, is a necessary tool to help determine exactly why a certain man is making more than a woman in the same position.

However, aside from the new legal requirements, salaries are becoming more transparent because of websites such as Glassdoor that give people information on what peers within their industry are making. "Increasingly, people put in their salaries and check others," Hegewisch says. People can then walk up to their boss and ask why they are making much less than someone who holds a similar position. "It's not just pressure through the statutes; it's coming through the technology."

Not everyone is convinced that greater transparency is a panacea, however. The University of Baltimore's Modesitt says women are often paid less because they are on the "mommy track" and less willing than men to work long hours or relocate for a job. But even women who are not taking time out to have or raise children are often paid less. Salary disclosures may not cure that problem, Modesitt says, because women face a catch-22 when it comes to negotiating.

Women who try to hold out for higher salaries are sometimes punished for doing so, she says. "If you don't negotiate, you get what whatever you're offered," Modesitt says. "If you do negotiate, you're seen as pushy" and thus might not get the job or the raise.

Just like some home or car buyers try never to pay the asking price, in some circumstances it would help women negotiate better if they have more information about salaries, says Harvard economist Goldin. "Managers who

have tight budgets will take advantage of certain workers who do not shop around," she says.

That won't work for everyone, she cautions. Many people are hourly workers at large retailers or other outlets that don't typically negotiate hourly rates. Disparities exist in such jobs, but transparency won't raise women's pay, Goldin says.

"The vast majority of Americans are not doing a lot of negotiation over their salaries," she says. "The person who is working at Jamba Juice is not negotiating over salary."

And even in professional settings where salary negotiations take place, transparency is no bonanza for women, according to Buffer, a social media startup that pledged "radical transparency" in pay, disclosing all its salaries and the formulas used to calculate them. Although the company drew considerable attention, it found that the experiment did not equalize pay. In fact, on average, Buffer is paying women about $10,000 less than men since men at the company tended to have started earlier, and thus earned more raises.[36]

Are single gender institutions still valuable?

In May, Harvard University announced a change in policy regarding unregistered single-gender social groups known as final clubs. In an email to students, Harvard President Drew G. Faust said that beginning with the class entering in fall 2017, the university will bar members of final clubs from holding leadership positions in officially sanctioned groups such as student government and will not recommend members for prestigious fellowships and scholarships.

In part, the move aims to address the issue of sexual assault on campus, after a university task force said the clubs incubate "deeply misogynistic attitudes."[37]

"[T]he discriminatory membership policies of these organizations have led to the perpetuation of spaces that are rife with power imbalances," Dean of the College Rakesh Khurana said in a letter accompanying Faust's May 6 announcement. "The most entrenched of these spaces send an unambiguous message that they are the exclusive preserves of men. In their recruitment practices and through their extensive resources and access to networks of power, these organizations propagate exclusionary values that undermine those of the larger Harvard College community."

Faust said the groups interfere with student preparation for life after college, in which sex discrimination is "understood as unwise, unenlightened and untenable."[38]

The Harvard move cuts against the grain of recent trends with regard to single-sex institutions. Male- and female-only instruction has been on the rise in recent years at the K-12 level. The number of public schools offering single-sex instruction has soared from 34 in 2004 to 850 a decade later.[39] Many coed schools offer single-sex classrooms as well.

Supporters of single-sex education say it makes it easier for girls to learn when they don't have to jockey for position against boys and can learn and experiment without worrying about whether they're acting appropriately girlish. Advocates cite studies indicating that girls who attend all-female schools are more likely to continue on to college.[40]

"A selling point for a lot of the women-only institutions is that women tend to do better in environments that people characterize as safe spaces," says Krendl, the Otterbein University president. "Certainly those institutions feel that one of their major contributions is giving women a safe place to be unafraid and to build their confidence." Confidence-building and safety are big selling points outside of school, too. Several female-only sites and online communities have sprung up in recent years where women are not subject to the stalking and threatening harassment that have plagued some women online.

"Communities are fundamentally different when they're just women," said Susan Johnson, founder of the website Women.com. "It's this safe environment where everyone can express herself without being trolled all the time."[41]

The apparent benefits of being surrounded by members of one's own sex — as well as the lack of distraction from having the opposite sex around — also have led to an increase in boys-only education. So-called leadership academies for boys have been set up in most major cities.

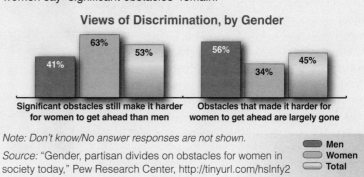

Men, Women Split on Hurdles Facing Women

As Hillary Clinton seeks to become the first female U.S. president, the public remains divided over the persistence of sex discrimination in American life. Far more men than women believe obstacles to women's advancement are "largely gone," while a large majority of women say "significant obstacles" remain.

Views of Discrimination, by Gender

Significant obstacles still make it harder for women to get ahead than men — Men 41%, Women 63%, Total 53%	**Obstacles that made it harder for women to get ahead are largely gone** — Men 56%, Women 34%, Total 45%

Note: Don't know/No answer responses are not shown.

Source: "Gender, partisan divides on obstacles for women in society today," Pew Research Center, http://tinyurl.com/hslnfy2

■ Men ■ Women ■ Total

Still, many experts question the value of separating students or other groups by gender. Discussions about single-sex schooling too often are based on anecdotal experience, says Diane Halpern, a psychologist emerita at Claremont McKenna College in California. Someone who thrived at an all-girls school will understandably insist that single-sex education is superior, she says. "A lot of the studies that report benefits, very few of them control for differences," such as income levels or other demographic differences between students, Halpern says.

Most studies showing benefits cherry-pick the data to present a misleading picture, says Lise Eliot, a neuroscientist at Rosalind Franklin University in Chicago. Some studies have found that girls at single-gender schools show more interest in subjects such as physics and math, she says, but there's no evidence that they sustain greater interest over time.

"There's a lot of myth that same-sex education is superior," Eliot says. "But academically, there doesn't seem to be an advantage."

The total number of all-female colleges has dropped from a few decades ago. The women who grew up to be leaders in Hillary Clinton's generation might have gone to single-sex institutions because that was often the best option available to them. "Back in the day, Ivies [Ivy League schools] were not even accepting women," says Eliot. "The punch line is that Wellesley may have been a great place for Hillary, but they sent [daughter] Chelsea to [top-rated] Stanford."

Like Harvard's Faust, Eliot says the very idea behind single-gender institutions cuts against the contemporary insistence on the values of diversity and inclusion. "It just seems to be very hypocritical to be segregating on the basis of sex when we're trying to prepare people for a corporate and civic culture where we want them to have respect for gender and race," Eliot says. "It's a great opportunity to learn this really important life skill of learning to work with people who are different from you."

Socialization is a key part of school. Young women may find it harder to speak up and claim space in class or in business meetings, particularly in certain male-dominated areas such as technology, says Hegewisch, the Institute for Women's Policy Research scholar. But at a time when women are being advised to "lean in" and become more assertive, rather than remaining in the background, it might be better for them to learn to do so during formative stages, she says.

"It's almost developing the capacity to train yourself to be more proactive in a mixed-gender setting," Hegewisch says.

BACKGROUND

Addressing Discrimination

Hillary Clinton has noted that her family history marks some of the milestones in the women's rights movement. After clinching the Democratic Party's nomination for president in June — becoming the first woman ever nominated for the White House by a major political party — she recalled that her mother was born on June 4, 1919, the day Congress passed the 19th Amendment to give women the right to vote.

"Tonight's victory is not about one person," Clinton said. "It belongs to generations of women and men who struggled and sacrificed and made this moment possible."[42]

Securing the right to vote had been the goal of women's rights activists — known as suffragettes around the turn of the 19th century — for decades. Suffragettes and other activists in what has since been dubbed the "first wave" of feminism were focused on eliminating legal barriers to women's equality, such as winning the right to vote.

Well into the 20th century, women in prominent leadership positions were scarce. With eight women

AP Photo/Supreme Court/Steve Petteway

Three members of the U.S. Supreme Court are women: From left, Justices Sonia Sotomayor, Ruth Bader Ginsburg and Elena Kagan. American women commonly serve in the Cabinet, and the head of the Federal Reserve is a woman. While the number of women serving in Congress has doubled over the past two decades, women remain a minority in both chambers.

serving in his Cabinet, President Obama has more female secretaries than were appointed by all presidents from 1932 to 1976 combined.[43] President Franklin D. Roosevelt appointed the first female Cabinet member in 1933 — Frances Perkins as Labor secretary.

Well into the 1960s, only a dozen women served in Congress at any given time. When 67-year-old Sen. Margaret Chase Smith of Maine in 1964 became the first woman to seek the GOP presidential nomination, her candidacy was treated mainly as an oddity, with news coverage focusing on her gender and age. "There are those who make the contention that no woman should ever dare to aspire to the White House — that this is a man's world and that it should be kept that way," she said.[44] She ended up receiving fewer than 3,000 votes in the first-in-the-nation New Hampshire primary.

In 1968, Democrat Shirley Chisholm of New York became the first African-American woman elected to Congress. Four years later, she became the first woman to seek the Democratic presidential nomination. Chisholm famously told The Associated Press, "I've always met more discrimination being a woman than being black."[45]

In the years just after World War II, it was unusual for women — particularly white middle-class women — to work outside the home, especially after marrying or having children. It was even more unusual for women to attain leadership positions in business, academia and other professions. When Katharine Graham took over the Washington Post Co. in 1972, she became the first female CEO of a *Fortune 500* company.

Equal Rights Amendment

Some women's rights advocates began pushing in 1923 for an Equal Rights Amendment (ERA) to the Constitution that would protect women against discrimination, which was prevalent in the workplace. To cite one example, a number of states barred women from bartending unless they were related to the owner of the establishment. The Supreme Court upheld such laws in 1948.[46]

Others worried that the ERA would eradicate laws passed in the late 19th and early 20th centuries designed to protect women, such as requirements that companies provide pregnancy benefits, safety requirements and mandated work breaks. "The more moderate . . . feminists were more interested in preserving protections they had got for women in the workplace," says Carolyn Wheeler, an employment discrimination attorney in Washington.

In 1963, President John F. Kennedy's Commission on the Status of Women released an influential report noting that women faced workplace discrimination and relative lack of access to training and education. It called for the government to offer paid maternity leave and universal child care.[47] The report helped prod Congress to pass the Equal Pay Act in 1963, calling for women to be paid the same as men for doing the same jobs. But the bill was amended to cover only "equal" work, not "comparable" work, meaning only women holding the same job titles as men would be protected. It was also aimed primarily at hourly workers; professional, executive and administrative positions were exempted.[48]

Also in 1963, Betty Friedan's *The Feminine Mystique* spoke to the frustrations of educated women forced to stay at home who felt they were working essentially as servants. Three years later Friedan helped found the National Organization for Women, which became a leading women's rights organization. In

India's only female prime minister, Indira Gandhi, served from 1966 to 1977 and then again from 1980 until her assassination in 1984. While numerous women have achieved "firsts" to hold leadership positions in many fields, it is still not the norm for a second or third woman to hold the same high office or take charge of a major company. Many countries — including Australia, Brazil, Canada, Ecuador, India, Pakistan, Poland and Panama — have had one female head of state but not a second.

1964, employment protections for women were included as part of the Civil Rights Act.

Meanwhile, an expanding economy — accompanied by the growing financial struggles of families — was bringing more women into the workforce or keeping them working after they married and had children. Large employers such as IBM and Texas Instruments sought to recruit stay-at-home women as employees.[49] "It seemed that overnight, everything that America had taken for granted about a woman's role was being called into question," *New York Times* columnist Gail Collins wrote in *When Everything Changed*, a history of postwar American women. "The fact that the percentage of married women in the workforce kept quietly going up was really the key to women's liberation."[50]

There were other changes as well. The birth control pill had become available in 1960, allowing women to more easily control their pregnancies and leading many to delay marriage and childbirth. In 1965, the Supreme Court overturned a state law that blocked married women from access to contraception and other birth control methods.[51] (The court extended the right to unmarried couples in 1972 in *Eisenstadt v. Baird*.)

C H R O N O L O G Y

1920-1945 *Women push for voting rights.*

1920 States ratify 19th Amendment, giving women the right to vote.

1941-1945 Nearly 6 million women enter the workforce during World War II.

1960s-1970s *Women's rights expand in the workplace.*

1960 Birth control pill is approved.

1963 Congress approves Equal Pay Act, requiring equal pay for the same work for women but exempts women in professional, executive and administrative positions. . . . Betty Friedan's *The Feminine Mystique* crystallizes the frustration of women forced to abandon careers to stay home.

1964 Congress passes Civil Rights Act including protection against job discrimination on the basis of gender. . . . Sen. Margaret Chase Smith, R-Maine, becomes first woman to run for a major party's presidential nomination.

1966 National Organization for Women is founded. Indira Gandhi becomes India's first female prime minister.

1968 Shirley Chisholm becomes first African-American woman elected to Congress.

1969 Israel elects Golda Meir as its first female prime minister.

1972 Congress passes Equal Rights Amendment (ERA), banning sex discrimination. . . . Amendment to the Civil Right Act (Title IX) guarantees equal funding for girls' sports.

1979 Margaret Thatcher becomes Britain's first female prime minister.

1980s-1990s *Professional opportunities improve for women.*

1980 Democratic Party guarantees half of national convention delegates will be women. . . . GOP drops support for the ERA from its platform.

1981 Sandra Day O'Connor becomes first female Supreme Court justice.

1982 ERA falls three states short of the three-quarters necessary for adoption.

1983 Astronaut Sally Ride is the first American woman in space.

1984 Rep. Geraldine Ferraro, D-N.Y., becomes the first woman on a major-party presidential ticket.

1992 Forty-seven women are elected to the House, increasing their ranks from 28; number of female senators triples to six.

1996 Seventy percent of married women with children under 18 are working, up from 18 percent in 1950.

1997 Madeleine Albright becomes first woman secretary of State.

1999 Carly Fiorina of Hewlett-Packard Co. becomes first woman CEO of one of the nation's 20 largest companies.

2000s *Women reach the top of many professions but trail men overall.*

2007 Rep. Nancy Pelosi, D-Calif., becomes first female House speaker.

2009 Lilly Ledbetter Act enhances female workers' ability to sue for pay discrimination.

2013 Facebook executive Sheryl Sandberg argues in her best-selling book *Lean In* that women need to push themselves to become leaders.

2015 Number of women in Congress exceeds 100 for the first time. . . . California requires employers to pay women the same as men for "substantially similar" work.

2016 Obama proposes new rules for big companies to report salary data by race, ethnicity and gender (January). . . . Members of the women's national soccer team sue U.S. Soccer, claiming pay discrimination (March). . . . Obama designates the first women's equality national monument (April). . . . Air Force Gen. Lori Robinson becomes the first female combatant commander (May). . . . Hillary Clinton becomes the first female major-party presidential nominee (July).

Using the civil rights movement as a model, women began demanding changes not only in law but in societal norms. Although sometimes criticized as a "white woman's movement," so-called second-wave feminism questioned many of the assumptions about male and female roles. "Women were learning by questioning all the conventions of gender and male dominance," said historian Linda Gordon of New York University.[52]

And reformers had plenty of conventions to overcome. When Hillary Clinton applied for law school in the late 1960s, a Harvard professor told her the law school didn't need any more female students. She instead went to Yale, although even there a male applicant objected, saying if she took "his" spot, it would be "her" fault if he were drafted and killed in the Vietnam War.[53]

Striving for Equality

In the 1970s and '80s the number of working women continued to climb. So did their educational levels and their prospects of achieving greater white-collar professional and managerial responsibilities.

By 1985, women's share of management jobs had increased to 36 percent, from 20 percent in 1972. The percentages of women in fields such as law and banking were also increasingly rapidly, albeit from a very low base.[54]

But such changes prompted a backlash. Congress finally approved the ERA in 1972 and states began ratifying it almost immediately. But conservative activist and author Phyllis Schlafly led the opposition to the measure, contending that "women's liberation is a total assault on the role of the American woman as a wife and mother and on the family as the basic unit of society."[55] (Schlafly died on Sept. 5 at age 92.)

The struggle for equal rights for women became conflated with debates about abortion, gay rights and family values. By 1980 the Republican Party, which since 1940 had formally supported the ERA, no longer supported the amendment in its platform. Two years later, 10 years after Congress had approved it, the amendment fell three states sort of the three-quarters majority needed for ratification.[56]

Even without the amendment, however, laws that blocked women from holding certain types of jobs had begun to fall by the wayside, thanks to the 1964 Civil Rights Act and actions in the states. In 1988, Congress passed the Women's Business Ownership Act, which ended legal discrimination in lending and abolished state laws that required married women to have their husbands co-sign for loans.

By that time, the number of female entrepreneurs was growing rapidly.[57] In 1982, for example, Barbara Bradley, then a stay-at-home mom, borrowed $250 from her husband and, with the help of co-founder Patricia Miller, started the luggage company Vera Bradley, which now has annual sales in excess of $500 million.[58]

During his four years in office, Democratic President Jimmy Carter appointed 40 women to the federal judiciary — five times the number of all his predecessors combined. And during his first year in office in 1981, Carter's successor, Republican Ronald Reagan, selected Sandra Day O'Connor as the first female Supreme Court justice.[59]

O'Connor's career illustrates the dramatic changes that were occurring with regard to women's professional opportunities. Although O'Connor had graduated near the top of her class from Stanford Law School in 1952, more than 40 law firms had rejected her applications for a job.[60] She had to work for free before eventually being hired as a deputy county attorney.

During the 1980s, women debated whether "supermoms" could "have it all," successfully balancing the demands of high-powered careers with family obligations. As it turned out, most working women felt they had to do so, because male incomes were sliding.

Women struggled with continuing expectations that they would bear primary responsibility for child-rearing and domestic chores even while working full time. At work, their bosses often passed them over for top opportunities, even when they were well qualified. Meanwhile, women remained underrepresented in elective office. That began to change after the polarizing confirmation process in 1991 for Supreme Court nominee Clarence Thomas, whose former aide Anita F. Hill accused him of sexual harassment. Thomas was narrowly confirmed after riveting hearings that divided the nation, but many women felt the all-male Senate Judiciary Committee had failed to ask the right questions.[61]

The following year was dubbed the "Year of the Woman" because of a spike in the number of female congressional candidates. The number of women in the

Female Athletes Losing the Pay Game

"It's going to take a few generations before we get equity."

Female athletes are celebrated for their achievements at the Olympics and in professional sports. But, like their peers at the top of other professions, they generally are paid far less than male athletes.

Consider Jazmine Reeves. The former Virginia Tech soccer star had a great year in 2014, scoring the second-most goals of any Boston Breakers player and was named the team's rookie of the year.

Nevertheless, she quit after one season in the National Women's Soccer League. The reason: money. During her year on the team, Reeves earned just $11,000.

That was nearly double the league's minimum salary, but by comparison, the minimum salary in the men's Major League Soccer was $36,500 in 2014. Thanks to a contract renegotiation between the league and the players' union, that figure jumped to $60,000 last year.[1]

The women's league and players' union have been trying to negotiate a new contract since November. In June, a judge ruled that a no-strike clause from 2013 was still in effect, blocking female players from sitting out the Olympics.[2]

Pay in women's professional soccer is so low that the Breakers and other teams arrange for players to stay at fans' homes to save on rent. "My host family was great, but at the same time, as an adult, you want to be able to pay for your own apartment," Reeves said.[3]

In March, five players from the women's national soccer team filed a complaint with the Equal Employment Opportunity Commission (EEOC), accusing, U.S. Soccer, the sport's governing body, of wage discrimination.[4]

U.S. Soccer in June asked the EEOC, which enforces federal anti-discrimination laws, to dismiss the complaint, saying there is no evidence the league has a "discriminatory motive" or is breaking the law.[5]

The women's national team is a perennial powerhouse, having won three World Cups and four Olympic championships, while the men's team has been mediocre. Nevertheless, the women are paid far less than men, particularly when accounting for factors such as victory bonuses and per diems.[6]

"On its face, it seems like a huge inequity," says Michael Sagas, who chairs the University of Florida's Department of Tourism, Recreation and Sport Management.

Soccer is not the only sport with gender disparities. At the collegiate level, each win in the men's NCAA basketball tournament is worth more than $1.5 million to the winning team's conference. Victories in the women's conference are rewarded with zero.[7]

Among the pros, players in the Women's National Basketball Association receive less than a third of the league's revenue, while male NBA players receive half.[8]

Days before the women's soccer players filed their EEOC complaint, Raymond Moore — the director of a woman's professional tennis tournament — resigned his position following remarks that provoked an outcry. Female players "ride on the coattails of the men," Moore said. "If I was a lady player, I'd go down every night on my knees and thank God that Roger Federer and Rafa Nadal were born because they have carried this sport. They really have."[9]

Among professional sports, tennis, in fact, comes closest to parity, with the four major Grand Slam tournaments offering men and women equal purses. But other tournaments typically offer women less than 70 cents on the dollar earned by men. Serena Williams, the highest-paid female player, earned $29 million last year, which sounds pretty good, but it was less than half the $68 million that Roger Federer, the highest-paid male player, earned.[10] Similar disparities exist among other top male and female players.

House jumped from 28 to 47, and tripled in the Senate, from two to six.[62]

"It is very hard to think of any legal proceedings that had the effect of the Anita Hill hearings, in the sense that women clearly went to the polls with the notion in mind that you have to have more women in Congress," said Democrat Eleanor Holmes Norton, Washington, D.C.'s House delegate.[63]

Many female candidates received assistance from the political action committee EMILY's List, founded in 1985 to help elect Democratic women who support abortion rights. "Young women today can't possibly

Officials with various sports leagues offer similar rationales when asked to explain why female athletes are paid less. Women's sports usually are less lucrative in terms of TV revenue and ticket sales than men's, so it makes sense that their compensation is lower, they say.

In 2013, the Women's National Basketball Association signed a six-year extension of its television contract with ESPN worth $72 million — or $12 million per year.[11] By contrast, the following year, the NBA agreed to a nine-year extension with ESPN and TNT worth $24 billion — or $2.6 billion per year.[12]

"The marketplace is why the average NBA player makes several million dollars annually, while in the WNBA, it's probably $100,000 or $150,000," says Edward Kian, a sports media professor at Oklahoma State University.

But Kian sees a chicken-and-egg situation. Less interest in women's sports may largely occur because they receive a fraction of the media attention given to men's sports. "There's no doubt that if the media covered women's sports more, [those sports] would receive more interest," he said.

It will take many years for women's sports in general to be considered worthy of the same level of media attention and remuneration that men's sports receive, Sagas says. "It's going to take a few generations before we get equity," he says. "It's an evolution, just a really slow one."

— *Alan Greenblatt*

Serena Williams, the world's highest-paid female tennis player, earned $29 million last year, far less than the $68 million made by top earner Roger Federer. Similar disparities exist among other top male and female players.

[1] Jonathan Tannenwald, "MLS, players agree to free agency and raises in new CBA," *The Philadelphia Inquirer*, March 4, 2015, http://tinyurl.com/h8u8ebj.

[2] Matt Bonesteel, "Judge rules that U.S. women's soccer team can't go on strike before Olympics," *The Washington Post*, June 3, 2016, http://tinyurl.com/zvzto74.

[3] Maggie Mertens, "Women's Soccer Is a Feminist Issue," *The Atlantic*, June 5, 2015, http://tinyurl.com/qgazqr3.

[4] Andrew Das, "Top Female Players Accuse U.S. Soccer of Wage Discrimination," *The New York Times*, March 31, 2016, http://tinyurl.com/j6gzldw.

[5] "U.S. Soccer asks EEOC to dismiss U.S. women's wage complaint," *Sports Illustrated*, June 1, 2016, http://tinyurl.com/ztrz8v8.

[6] Karen Yourish, Joe Ward and Sarah Almukhtar, "How Much Less Are Female Soccer Players Paid?" *The New York Times*, March 31, 2016, http://tinyurl.com/h5eghl3.

[7] Andrew Zimbalist, "The NCAA's Women Problem," *The New York Times*, March 25, 2016, http://tinyurl.com/juvs5l7.

[8] Bill Littlefield, "No Matter The Sport, Women Athletes Are Always Paid Less," WBUR, April 16, 2016, http://tinyurl.com/j4fxdae.

[9] "Indian Wells CEO: 'lady' players should 'thank God' for Federer and Nadal," *The Guardian*, March 20, 2016, http://tinyurl.com/jcfr8qx.

[10] Kerry Close, "These Are The Highest Earning Male and Female Tennis Players," *Money*, July 1, 2016, http://tinyurl.com/z7btknv.

[11] Terry Lefton and John Ourand, "ESPN Signs Six-Year Extension With WNBA That Is Worth $12M Per Year," *SportsBusiness Daily*, March 28, 2013, http://tinyurl.com/gls795l.

[12] Anthony Riccobono, "NBA TV Deal 2014: What The $24 Billion New Agreement Means For The League," *International Business Times*, Oct. 6, 2014, http://tinyurl.com/goynta4.

imagine how quixotic the goal of getting women elected to political office seemed 30 years ago," the group's founder, Ellen R. Malcolm, wrote in her recent memoir.[64]

In 2007, Rep. Nancy Pelosi, D-Calif., became the first female House speaker, and in 2015, the number of women in Congress exceeded 100 for the first time.

Outside of Congress, more women are assuming top leadership positions, whether at the helm of a *Fortune* 500 company or serving as a Cabinet secretary. Many young women, as a result, take basic gender equality for granted, some observers say. Since the 1970s, *Times* columnist Collins noted, American women have gone "off

Women Often Face a Gender Backlash in Politics

"They're vastly underrepresented in elected office."

If Democrats win control of the Senate in November, it will be because of women. Female nominees are running in many of the states where the Democratic Party is hoping to pick up seats, including Arizona, Illinois, New Hampshire, North Carolina and Pennsylvania.

The number of female senators next year could break the current record of 20, which has held constant since the 2012 elections. As recently as 1992, only two women served in the Senate. But even with two or three more females, the 100-member body would remain a long way from gender parity.

The same is true for other offices. Currently, 84 women serve in the House, less than one-fifth of total members. (The current Congress is the first to have more than 100 women serving in total in both chambers.)[1]

Six women are governors, down from a peak of nine a decade ago. And women make up just under one-quarter of state legislators — roughly their proportion over the past 20 years.

"Women are 53 percent of the electorate, and they're vastly underrepresented in elected office," says Ellie Hockenbury, a spokeswoman for the Republican State Leadership Committee, which assists GOP candidates running for state offices.

Some political scientists assert that more women are not officeholders because parties and interest groups don't do enough to encourage them to run. Women often take a lot more encouraging than men to decide to put themselves forward, says Debbie Walsh, who directs the Center for American Women and Politics at Rutgers University.

"Women do need to be recruited more than men," Walsh says. "In our surveys, men were much more likely to say it was largely their own idea, that nobody had to ask them."

A 2013 report from American University indicated that women are less likely to seek political office than men even if they have similar resumes.[2] Parents are more likely to encourage their sons to think about politics as a career than their daughters, according to the report, while young women tend to be exposed to less political information and discussion.

A 2009 report from the Rutgers center said party leaders, activists and elected officials are less likely to recruit female candidates. "Many political gatekeepers believed that women did not belong in politics and that voters would be less likely to vote for female than for male candidates," wrote Susan J. Carroll and Kira Sanbonmatsu, the study's authors.[3]

to college thinking about what work they wanted to do, not what man they wanted to catch."[65]

CURRENT SITUATION
Barriers Remain

Women continue to make both symbolic and substantive breakthroughs in the workforce and in politics.

But while some women have reached the top in nearly every profession and overt discrimination is seen by many as largely a thing of the past, women continue to face obstacles both in their professional and personal lives.

"Very few people are explicitly saying that women can't do these things," such as run for office or serve in executive positions, says Melissa Blair, a historian at Auburn University who studies women and politics. "It's more subtle, but it still very much happens."

And in some cases the double standard is still overt, such as comments widely viewed as sexist that Republican presidential candidate Trump has made. "The only thing she's got going is the women's card," he said of Clinton in April.[66] He also made widely derided comments about Fox News host Megyn Kelly and Carly Fiorina, his one-time GOP rival for the presidential nomination.

Women who might run for Congress or state legislatures are sometimes put off by what still appear to be double standards and even outright misogyny when it comes to female candidates, researchers and political observers say. Women may think twice about running if they see other women, from Democratic presidential nominee Hillary Clinton on down, subject to attacks that appear to be driven by sexism.[4] "There can almost be a gender backlash," says Jason Windett, a political scientist at St. Louis University who has studied women in politics. "Women looking at the political landscape think, if they didn't like the governor, why would they like another woman on the town council?"

As a result, say political scientists, the women who do run tend to have both a certain sense of themselves and considerable professional credentials. "I've published research that shows women who run as challengers in House general elections are more qualified, more likely to have previous electoral experience than their male counterparts," says Kathryn Pearson, a University of Minnesota political scientist.[5]

Women already in elected office make the best recruiters, says Andrea Dew Steele, founder and president of Emerge America, a San Francisco group that recruits and trains female candidates. Once a core group of women achieves power, it's easier for nervous neophytes to see themselves achieving success, Steele says. "We've seen that when we get one or two women in, they bring the others in," she says.

That has been the case in the handful of states, such as Arizona, Colorado, New Hampshire and Oregon, where women have played leadership roles for a while. Once women started getting elected to office in Oregon in the 1970s and 1980s, Democrats did their best to bring other women along, establishing a political action committee to support women candidates and a "campaign school" to recruit and train them, says state Rep. Val Hoyle, a Democrat.

"We've set up an infrastructure on the Democratic side," Hoyle says.

In Oregon, the governor, attorney general and secretary of state are women, as are the state House speaker and three other top legislative leaders. Hoyle says she was proud that after she gave up her post as House majority leader this year to run unsuccessfully for statewide office, another woman replaced her. She says that showed "my being there was not an anomaly."

— *Alan Greenblatt*

[1] Judith Warner, "104 Women in Congress. Does It Matter?," *Politico*, January-February, 2015, http://tinyurl.com/h7hk3ml.

[2] Jennifer L. Lawless and Richard L. Fox, "Girls Just Wanna Not Run: The Gender Gap in Young Americans' Political Ambition," American University, March 2013, http://tinyurl.com/hm926bg.

[3] Susan J. Carroll and Kira Sanbonmatsu, "Gender and the Decision to Run for the State Legislature," Center for American Women and Politics, April 2009, http://tinyurl.com/jl62haw.

[4] Clare Malone and Julia Azari, "Thinking They're 'Unqualified' Is A Big Reason More Women Don't Run For Office," *FiveThirtyEight*, April 8, 2016, http://tinyurl.com/z8tscbj.

[5] Kathryn Pearson and Eric McGhee, "Should Women Win More Often than Men? The Roots of Electoral Success and Gender Bias in U.S. House Elections," *Politics and Gender*, April 29, 2013, http://tinyurl.com/hn5vvww.

Meanwhile, vendors at his rallies sell merchandise emblazoned with phrases such as "Life's a Bitch — don't vote for one" and "KFC Hillary Special: Two fat thighs, two small breasts . . . left wing."[67]

Society continues to hold women to different standards than men, Blair says. Female candidates and those seeking top professional jobs are judged by their appearance more than men are, political scientists note. News coverage of Clinton often focuses on her wardrobe, hairstyle, appearance, expressions of emotion or the "shrillness" of her voice in ways that don't usually occur with male candidates.[68] Clinton herself has sought to deflect attention from such matters, making occasional jokes about her hair — and the media's focus on it.

Some scholars say a woman running for president would never be able to get away with some of the shortcomings seen among male candidates, such as Wisconsin GOP Gov. Scott Walker's lack of a college degree or Bernie Sanders' disheveled hair and rumpled clothing.

"The idea that a woman could look as sloppy as Sanders — that's just laughable," says Kathryn Pearson, a University of Minnesota political scientist.

Female candidates also must be far more qualified than their male counterparts, Pearson suggests. "The women who run for office will continue to accrue more experience, be more ready, dot all the i's and cross [more] t's than men," she says. Trump continues to be dismissive of Clinton's qualifications, as was Sanders at points during the primaries. In September, Trump said Clinton doesn't have "a presidential look."[69]

Corporate Challenges

Women also continue to lag in the professions. At this year's World Economic Forum in Davos, Switzerland, a prestigious gathering of business and political leaders, women made up just 18 percent of delegates.[70] A 2015 University of California, Davis, study of the 400 largest companies headquartered in California found that women hold only 13.3 percent of the seats on corporate boards and make up just 10.5 percent of the highest-paid executives.[71]

But although those numbers don't look good, there's another way of looking at them. The Davis study showed women recorded some gains, with the number of women in top positions up 6.5 percent over the previous year, while the number of companies without any top female leaders fell below 100, or 25 percent of the total, for the first time.

Nationwide, "a small but growing number of U.S. companies have intensified their push to increase the ranks of women on their boards as businesses pay greater attention to gender parity at all levels," *The Wall Street Journal* reported in August.[72]

Some high-profile women in Hollywood — including actors, directors, writers and others — have pushed back against pay and opportunity gaps in the entertainment field, with male stars often making millions of dollars more than their female counterparts and women being significantly underrepresented in top management and leadership positions. The discrepancy is particularly evident for directors: Women made up only 1.9 percent of the directors in the 100 top-grossing films in 2013 and 2014. The EEOC is investigating the gender imbalance among directors in Hollywood.[73] A recent academic study found a significant gender pay gap in the arts in general.[74]

Elsewhere in the business world, academia and the professions, the numbers are discouraging. A 2014 study by the National Academies of Sciences looking at pitches made by entrepreneurs at competitions found that investors are more receptive to those made by men,

even when women are presenting identical information.[75] Women make up just 6 percent of partners at venture capital firms.[76]

Women also face more obstacles in achieving tenure at universities: They are not published as often in prestigious journals, tend to receive less credit than their male co-authors and are called on to do more service work for their universities, according to a group of female professors who wrote a piece in *Foreign Policy* last April. "Letters [of recommendation] about women tend to be shorter and focus on their personality traits, whereas letters about men typically feature superlatives about their aptitudes and abilities," the professors said. "Moreover, hiring committees . . . tend to view women who are parents as less serious scholars."[77]

Male undergraduates also are prone to underrate their female peers, according to a recent study of undergraduate biology students by researchers at the University of Washington and other institutions. It found that male students consistently ranked their fellow males as more knowledgeable than women, even when the women were better-performing students. "Our work implies that the chilly environment for women may not be going away any time soon," the researchers wrote.[78]

In some scientific disciplines, women hold only one-tenth of full professorships, while the share of women earning doctorates in such fields is declining, according to the National Science Foundation.[79] Women are much more likely to perform the experiments associated with scientific studies, but men are "more likely to be associated with all other authorship roles," conclude researchers from Indiana University and the University of Quebec.[80] (Male researchers are also more likely to cite their own prior publications than women.[81])

Women earn more bachelor's degrees than men but hold only 12 percent of computer science degrees.[82] At major technology companies such as Google, Facebook and Apple, only about 30 percent of employees are women, and only 10.8 percent of executive officers in Silicon Valley are women.[83] A wide range of organizations, from professional associations of women in scientific fields to the Girl Scouts of America are running programs encouraging girls to stick with science and technology studies.[84]

But the EEOC's Baran has another explanation. "Tech companies are testing applicants not just for

Should Congress pass the Paycheck Fairness Act?

YES Lisa Maatz
Vice President, Government Relations,
American Association of University Women

Written for *CQ Researcher*, September 2016

Both major political parties have said they support equal pay for equal work, and polls have shown voters clearly care about the issue. Yet the gender pay gap has barely budged over the past decade. Indisputable evidence shows the gap exists and that it harms working families.

Our research reveals that just one year out of school, college-educated women earn 7 percent less than their male peers, even when controlling for academic major, occupation and hours worked. As workers become parents, the gap grows wider. Studies detail that when men become dads, they get a financial boost, but women's earnings decrease when they have children. Along with moms, women of color also face a larger pay gap.

That's why women need the Paycheck Fairness Act. Women can't rely on outdated laws such as the Equal Pay Act of 1963. The proposed measure would provide a vital update to the Equal Pay Act, bringing its principles and practices in line with the nation's other civil rights laws. It takes meaningful steps to create incentives for employers to follow the law, empower women to negotiate and strengthen federal outreach and enforcement efforts.

The bill also would strengthen penalties for equal-pay violations and prohibit retaliation against workers who inquire about wage practices or disclose their own salaries. Without the Paycheck Fairness Act, many women are prohibited from talking about wages with their coworkers without the fear of being fired. This forced silence keeps women from discovering discriminatory salary practices. The fear of being fired is strong enough to keep employees from broaching the subject.

The recovery of the American middle class begins and ends with good-paying jobs, but that cannot happen if women continue to earn less than they deserve. There is no higher priority for the American public than continuing to rebuild the economy and creating good-paying jobs. Achieving equal pay is a critical step in that direction. In fact, a poll commissioned by a coalition of groups backing the law showed 84 percent of voters support such a law.

Women represent half of the paid workforce and increasingly are the primary breadwinners of their families. Equal pay is not just a moral issue; it's an economic one. Without legislative remedies, the pace of change has been glacial. At this rate, the pay gap won't close in our lifetimes. Our nation's economy and working families can't wait.

NO Christina Hoff Sommers
Resident Scholar, American Enterprise Institute

Written for *CQ Researcher*, September 2016

The Paycheck Fairness Act will do little to help women, but much to create havoc in the workplace. The bill is based on the premise that the 1963 Equal Pay Act has failed. As proof, proponents point out that women are still paid 77 cents on the dollar for doing the same work as men. But the 23-cent wage disparity is simply the difference between the average earnings of all men and all women working full time. It does not account for differences in occupations, positions, education, job tenure or hours worked per week. When these factors are taken into account the unexplained gap narrows — to the point of vanishing.

Take nursing, for example. Proponents of the bill find it unacceptable that even in this traditionally female field, men are better compensated. Male nurses do tend to earn more, but they also work longer hours, gravitate to the best-paid specialties and pursue jobs in cities with the highest levels of compensation. Career choices and educational differences thus explain most of the gender gap.

Some of the bill's supporters will concede that the pay gap is largely explained by men's and women's choices, but they argue those choices are skewed by sexist stereotypes and social pressures. Those are interesting points worthy of continued debate. But why enact a law that targets employers and demands they correct gaps over which they have little control?

The bill would make employers liable not only for sex discrimination — banned long ago — but also for the "lingering effects of past discrimination." What does that mean? Universities, for example, typically pay professors in the business school more than those in the school of social work. This is a result of market demand. But according to the gender theory behind this bill, the market is tainted by "past discrimination." Expert witnesses from activist groups will testify that sexist attitudes led society to place a higher value on male-centered fields such as business than on female-centered fields such as social work. Faced with multimillion-dollar lawsuits, innocent employers will settle. They will soon be begging for the safe harbor of federally determined occupational wage scales.

The Paycheck Fairness Act rests on a foundation of false statistics and misguided employer-vilifying theories. It would not advance equality but instead unleash a torrent of litigation that hampers job growth. That could explain why it has languished in Congress for nearly 20 years.

Few top executives of S&P 500 companies are women, among them Sheryl Sandberg, Facebook's chief operating officer, left, and Mary Barra, CEO of General Motors. In her best-selling book *Lean In*, Sandberg argues that rather than holding themselves back, women need to "lean in" to take advantage of leadership opportunities and demand a seat at the table.

coding skills but cultural fit," she says. "They're looking for a unicorn, the one-in-a-million person who comes from a different racial, ethnic or gender background but is identical to the white men who work there."

Some tech companies are establishing quotas for hiring more women. Last year, the chipmaker Intel surpassed its goal of having women as well as underrepresented minorities make up 40 percent of its new hires. This year, it's shooting for 45 percent.[85]

In the legal field, women made up 44 percent of associates, the junior position for attorneys, in 2015 — about where they were a decade earlier, according to a survey by the advocacy group National Association of Women Lawyers. But women made up only 18 percent of equity partners, those who share in the profits at law firms, and women of color fared even worse: less than 2 percent of equity partners.[86]

"After 12 years of practice, we find that 52 percent of the women and almost 69 percent of the men are now reporting that they are partners," says Joyce Sterling, associate dean of the University of Denver College of Law.

There are firms that are hiring more women and promoting them to partner. Hogan Lovells, one of the largest firms in the country, has made an effort to promote women into management positions. Women make up a third of the firm's board and lead 19 of its 46 offices.

"The women coming out of law school pay attention to whether there are women in management, whether there are women who are the leads in their practice groups, whether there are women with significant client relationships who are getting in the pitch rooms and landing the business," said Catherine Stetson, a member of the Hogan Lovells board.[87]

Lara Setrakian, co-founder of the media firm News Deeply, says women lag behind men in some cases because they are not as good as men at promoting themselves. "I call it the swagger gap," she said. "We really seem to put market value on swagger, and I do think that men are better at swaggering than women are."[88]

"Make Yourself Heard"

Sheryl Sandberg, the chief operating officer of Facebook, has advised women to "lean in," which is her catchphrase to encourage women to put themselves forward and act as advocates for themselves in their own careers. She worries that too many women undersell their abilities. Rather than holding themselves back, they should "lean in" and demand a seat at the table — whatever the table is where important discussions are happening and decisions are being made.

U.S. Attorney General Loretta Lynch advises something similar. "I think sometimes women face the very real risk of not being seen and not being heard," she told *The Washington Post*. "So that's why I always tell young women, make yourself seen and make yourself heard — this is your idea. . . . Own it, express it, be the voice that people hear."[89]

At the White House, in an attempt to increase the influence of women in the president's inner circle, female staff members are pursuing a strategy of assertiveness that entails attending more meetings and speaking up more forcefully once there. They have dubbed this strategy "amplification." When a woman makes a point, other women repeat it, so that Obama will take notice of their contributions. Female aides say it is working.[90]

Yet women are often penalized when they do "lean in" by making their ambitions clear or demanding greater compensation, point out psychologists Corinne Moss-Racusin and Laurie Rudman. "[P]rofessional women face a catch-22: They must overcome negative stereotypes about women by 'acting like men,' yet when they do so they risk being penalized for violating gender prescriptions," they write. "Self-promoting women are seen as more dominant and arrogant than self-promoting men, whose behavior is consistent with stereotypic expectations."[91]

Some women seeking to advance in their careers also continue to face sexual harassment. The most notorious recent example was outlined in a lawsuit by Carlson, the former "Fox and Friends" anchor, who alleged that Ailes had verbally harassed her when he was CEO of Fox News. More than two dozen women soon came forward to allege that Ailes had told them that sexual favors were expected in return for career advancement. "If you sleep with me, you could be a model or a newscaster," a woman who had been an accounting intern told *The Washington Post*.[92]

And in a long-running case, more than 60 women have accused comedian Bill Cosby of drugging and raping or otherwise assaulting them, often after luring them to a meeting to discuss how he could further their careers in show business. Harassment and sexism can be particularly intense for female pioneers moving into male roles. For example, Nicole Mittendorff, a firefighter in Fairfax County, Va., killed herself last spring after facing intense cyberbullying and harassment from her male colleagues.[93]

"What really sets off the haters is when women do things that men have traditionally done: Firefighter, sportswriter, Army Ranger, video game designer, commander in chief," wrote *Washington Post* columnist Petula Dvorak.[94]

OUTLOOK
Changes and Backlash

Women are enjoying levels of success that their mothers and grandmothers could scarcely have dreamed of. But women in leadership roles, while no longer uncommon, remain exceptional. Women are underrepresented at the top of nearly every field, whether politics, the law, medicine or business.

For that to change, scholars say, society has to evolve further. As long as caring for children is seen primarily as a mother's responsibility, it will remain difficult for many women to take on the most challenging — and financially rewarding — jobs, they say. And the expectation will persist among many employers that women will be sidelined on the "mommy track."

Many people still associate the very idea of being a leader with men. A phenomenon known as Think manager, think man "creates a problem for women who aspire to leadership roles," writes Raina Brand, an assistant professor of organizational behavior at the London Business School.[95]

A Clinton presidency could help change expectations among many Americans about what a top leader looks like. But it also could make some people uncomfortable. Just as racial tension, distrust and debates about racism increased during the nation's first African-American presidency, scholars predict that dissension over women's place in society and the workplace will get a thorough airing under the nation's first female president.

"These are huge societal changes," says Georgia Duerst-Lahti, a political scientist at Beloit College in Wisconsin. "We're going to see both — the awareness that women can do these things, and virulent attacks on women and continued attempts to control them."

"It will probably go to both extremes," says Otterbein University President Krendl. "Women will feel empowered. Girls will feel they can be president for the first time in reality in our history. But there will also be a backlash, just as there has been with our first African-American president."

But other scholars say a Clinton presidency wouldn't be as contentious as Obama's, because gender-based schisms don't run as deep as those surrounding race. Women don't live in different neighborhoods, says Duerst-Lahti, but share their beds with men and are perceived by most heterosexual males, however critically, as partners and helpmates.

However, says Julie Lawson, executive director of the Women's Foundation of Greater St. Louis, which supports programs for at-risk women, "you won't be able to hide the misogyny anymore. I don't know if it will get any worse, [but] you'll see it's there because people will blame things on her being a woman."

Others say that a Clinton presidency might actually discourage women from seeking office because of the criticism the first female president will inevitably receive.

"You can't get women to step up to the plate at any [political] level because they see this viciousness," says Liz Berry, president of the National Women's Political Caucus of Washington, which seeks to get more women elected or appointed to office. "It's just nasty."

If Clinton is elected, the sense of triumph also could be leavened with nervousness among women about how she will perform in office. "There's this sense among women that they want her to be perfect," says Walsh, the Rutgers professor, referring to Clinton. "There's the notion that if she makes mistakes, it will be a reflection on women in high-level leadership positions."

NOTES

1. Demetri Sevastopulo, "Trump battles media over sexism claims," *Financial Times*, May 16, 2016, http://tinyurl.com/zkhz3gf; Matea Gold and Jenna Johnson, "Republicans warn that Trump's critique of Clinton's 'look' fuels accusations of sexism," *The Washington Post*, Sept. 9, 2016, http://tinyurl.com/gummghg.

2. Allen Clifton, "Here Are 6 Truly Awful Things That Will Happen if Republicans Win the White House in 2016," Forward Progressives, Aug. 17, 2015, http://tinyurl.com/hkqehrz.

3. Victoria L. Brescoll, Erica Dawson and Eric Luis Uhlmann, "Hard Won and Easily Lost: The Fragile Status of Leaders in Gender-Stereotype-Incongruent Occupations," *Psychological Science*, Sept. 28, 2010, http://tinyurl.com/z222ye4.

4. "Women and Leadership," Pew Research Center, Jan. 14, 2015, http://tinyurl.com/kmtylw9.

5. Emily DeRuy, "4 out of 10 people say the country is 'not ready' for women in power," *Fusion*, Jan. 14, 2015, http://tinyurl.com/z3y8sc5.

6. "Women in the Workplace," McKinsey & Company, Sept. 2015, http://tinyurl.com/jzm8qkq.

7. Rajini Vaidyanathan, "Bill Cosby: Why is there a time limit on bringing sexual assault cases to US courts?" BBC News, Sept. 9, 2016, http://tinyurl.com/jtfddzx; Gabriel Sherman, "The Revenge of Roger's Angels," *New York*, Sept. 2, 2016, http://tinyurl.com/hrjtdjf; and Paul Fahri, "$20 million settlement and a host's abrupt exit add to Fox's summer of discontent," *The Washington Post*, Sept. 6, 2016, http://tinyurl.com/hk3oy73.

8. Thomas Ricker, "How do tech's biggest companies compare on diversity?" *The Verge*, Aug. 20, 2015, http://tinyurl.com/pbhfale; "Women CEOs of the S&P 500," Catalyst, http://tinyurl.com/oxc43te.

9. Valentina Zarya, "The Percentage of Female CEOs in the Fortune 500 Drops to 4%," *Fortune*, June 6, 2016, http://tinyurl.com/gt6bhp3.

10. Jay Newton-Small, *Broad Influence: How Women are Changing the Way America Works* (2016), p. 187.

11. "A Current Glance at Women in the Law," American Bar Association, May 2016, http://tinyurl.com/hxy9stn.

12. Bryan J. Cook, "The American College President Study: Key Findings and Takeaways," American Council on Education, Spring 2012, http://tinyurl.com/la52xxs.

13. "The Lady Vanishes," *Revisionist History*, June 15, 2016, http://tinyurl.com/hck9qrs.

14. Newton-Small, *op. cit.*, p. 6.

15. For law students, see "A Current Glance at Women in the Law," *op. cit.* For medical students, see Diana M. Lautenberger *et al.*, "The State of Women in Academic Medicine: the Pipeline and Pathways to Leadership 2013-2014," Association of American Medical Colleges, 2014, http://tinyurl.com/z9gc5a5.

16. "The Simple Truth (about the Gender Pay Gap)," American Association of University Women, 2016, http://tinyurl.com/ce6qus3.

17. Michelle J. Budig, "The Fatherhood Bonus & the Motherhood Penalty: Parenthood and the Gender Gap in Pay," Third Way, September 2014, http://tinyurl.com/zz49qfp.

18. Newton-Small, *op. cit.*, p. 60.

19. Michelle Cottle, "The Era of 'The Bitch' Is Coming," *The Atlantic*, Aug. 17, 2015, http://tinyurl.com/jhudvsy.

20. Marcus Noland, Tyler Moran and Barbara Kotschwar, "Is Gender Diversity Profitable? Evidence from a Global Survey," Peterson Institute for International Economics, February 2016, http://tinyurl.com/hf7tzsp.

21. Corinne Post and Kris Byron, "Women on Boards and Firm Financial Performance: A Meta-Analysis," *Academy of Management Journal*, Oct. 1, 2015, http://tinyurl.com/zqnlb62.

22. Newton-Small, *op. cit.*, p. 7.

23. Jack Zenger and Joseph Folkman, "Are Women Better Leaders Than Men?" *Harvard Business Review*, March 15, 2012, http://tinyurl.com/jxbybfz.

24. For example, see Alice H. Eagly, Mary C. Johannesen-Schmidt and Marloes L. Van Engen, "Transformational, Transactional and Laissez-Faire Leadership Styles: A Meta-Analysis Comparing Women and Men," *Psychological Bulletin*, 2003, http://tinyurl.com/zlmse7t.

25. Alice H. Eagly, "Gender & Work: Challenging Conventional Wisdom," Harvard Business School, Feb. 28, 2013, http://tinyurl.com/pjn6gwd.

26. Diane F. Halpern and Fanny M. Cheung, *Women at the Top: Powerful Leaders Tell Us How to Combine Work and Family* (2008).

27. Seth Fiegerman, "Why Marissa Mayer couldn't save Yahoo," CNN Money, July 25, 2016, http://tinyurl.com/h348zan; Vindu Goel and Michael J. de la Merced, "Yahoo's Sale to Verizon Ends an Era for a Web Pioneer," *The New York Times*, July 24, 2016, http://tinyurl.com/j8f95o3.

28. Michelle K. Ryan and S. Alexander Haslam, "The Glass Cliff: Evidence that Women are Over? Represented in Precarious Leadership Positions," *British Journal of Management*, June 2005, http://tinyurl.com/zzqqpm4.

29. Ken Favaro, Per-Ola Karlsson and Gary L. Neilson, "The 2013 Chief Executive Study: Women CEOs of the last 10 years," Strategy & and PwC, April 29, 2014, http://tinyurl.com/hmzv36a.

30. Newton-Small, *op. cit.*, p. 37.

31. "The Simple Truth (about the Gender Pay Gap)," *op. cit.*

32. Janet Adamy and Paul Overberg, "Women in Elite Jobs Face Stubborn Pay Gap," *The Wall Street Journal*, May 17, 2016, http://tinyurl.com/gujwodt.

33. Shan Li, "What you need to know about California's new wage-equality law," *Los Angeles Times*, Oct. 8, 2015, http://tinyurl.com/h7zbo3r.

34. Rowena Mason, "Gender pay gap reporting for big firms to start in 2018," *The Guardian*, Feb. 12, 2016, http://tinyurl.com/hzvetoe.

35. "Pay transparency: What have we got to hide?" *The European*, March 15, 2016, http://tinyurl.com/hsflb78.

36. Lydia Dishman, "Why Salary Transparency Didn't Eliminate The Gender Wage Gap At This Startup," *Fast Company*, March 31, 2016, http://tinyurl.com/gtq2jxf; Emily Peck, "Even At A Company Obsessed With Fair Pay, Women Make Less Than Men," *The Huffington Post*, March 21, 2016, http://tinyurl.com/hm2fl7n.

37. C. Ramsey Fahs, "Sexual Assault Report Lambasts Final Clubs," *The Harvard Crimson*, March 9, 2016, http://tinyurl.com/zcbmjeb.

38. Melissa Korn, "Harvard to Bar Members of Single-Gender Clubs From Leadership in Official Groups," *The Wall Street Journal*, May 6, 2016, http://tinyurl.com/gv8ncd4.

39. Mokoto Rich, "Old Tactic Gets New Use: Public Schools Separate Girls and Boys," *The New York Times*, Nov. 30, 2014, http://tinyurl.com/zxven5g.

40. Hyunjoon Park, Jere R. Behrman and Jaesung Choi, "Causal Effects of Single-Sex Schools on College Entrance Exams and College Attendance: Random Assignment in Seoul High Schools," *Demography*, April 2013, http://tinyurl.com/pjmd3oz.

41. Caitlin Dewey, "How do you stop online harassment? Try banning the men," *The Washington Post*, April 14, 2016, http://tinyurl.com/jrmg98o.

42. Emily Atkin, "The Most Memorable Moment From Hillary Clinton's Historic Victory Speech," ThinkProgress, June 7, 2016, http://tinyurl.com/j632ccl.

43. "Women Appointed to Presidential Cabinets," Center for American Women and Politics, 2015, http://tinyurl.com/zh2xpnm.

44. Ellen Fitzpatrick, "The Unfavored Daughter: When Margaret Chase Smith Ran in the New Hampshire Primary," *The New Yorker*, Feb. 6, 2016, http://tinyurl.com/jqkreyx.

45. See James Barron, "Shirley Chisholm, 'Unbossed' Pioneer in Congress, Is Dead at 80," *The New York Times*, Jan. 3, 2005, http://tinyurl.com/zvazudj.

46. Eric Felten, "Women Behind Bars," *The Wall Street Journal*, April 25, 2009, http://tinyurl.com/h4eop6h.

47. Dorothy Sue Cobble, Linda Gordon and Astrid Henry, *Feminism Unfinished: A Short, Surprising History of American Women's Movements* (2014), p. 50.

48. Gail Collins, *When Everything Changed: The Amazing Journey of American Women From 1960 to the Present* (2009), p. 68.

49. *Ibid.*, p. 98.

50. *Ibid.*, p. 99.

51. *Griswold v. Connecticut*, 381 U.S. 479 (1965).

52. Cobble, *op. cit.*, p. 82.

53. Ellen R. Malcolm, *When Women Win: EMILY's List and the Rise of Women in American Politics* (2006), p. 8.

54. George Gilder, "Women in the Work Force," *The Atlantic*, September 1985, http://tinyurl.com/on8k72m.

55. Malcolm, *op. cit.*, p. 17.

56. Jo Freeman, "Whatever Happened to Republican Feminists?" JoFreeman.com, 1996, http://tinyurl.com/c7f8nwe.

57. Debrah Lee Charatan, "30 Years of Female Entrepreneurship: From Anomalies To Assets," *Entrepreneur*, May 4, 2016, http://tinyurl.com/jbj2a4a.

58. Dinah Eng, "How Vera Bradley's founder bagged success," *Fortune*, Sept. 12, 2015, http://tinyurl.com/hmznso7.

59. Malcolm, *op. cit.*, p. 19.

60. Newton-Small, *op. cit.*, p. 82.

61. Irin Carmon, "Senator Patty Murray on women in power," MSNBC, April 1, 2014, http://tinyurl.com/zvhojxu.

62. Collins, *op. cit.*, p. 343.

63. Cobble, *op. cit.*, p. 150.

64. Malcolm, *op. cit.*, p. ix.

65. Collins, *op. cit.*, p. 241.

66. Jose A. DelReal and Anne Gearan, "Trump: If Clinton 'were a man, I don't think she'd get 5 percent of the vote,' " *The Washington Post*, April 27, 2016, http://tinyurl.com/h8bbjqy.

67. Cottle, *op. cit.*

68. Dustin Harp, Jaime Loke and Ingrid Bachmann, "Hillary Clinton's Benghazi Hearing Coverage: Political Competence, Authenticity, and the Persistence of the Double Bind," Women's Studies in Communication, June 13, 2016, http://tinyurl.com/zh324xv.

69. Tessa Berenson, "Donald Trump: Hillary Clinton Doesn't Have a 'Presidential Look,' " *Time*, Sept. 7, 2016, http://tinyurl.com/zpfqauf.

70. Alexandra Stevenson, "A Push for Gender Equality at the Davos World Economic Forum, and Beyond," *The New York Times*, Jan. 19, 2016, http://tinyurl.com/hx3tgd7.

71. Amanda Kimball, "UC Davis Study of California Women Business Leaders: A Census of Women Directors and Executive Officers, 2015-2016," University of California, Davis, Nov. 17, 2015, http://tinyurl.com/h3vzrkn.

72. Joann S. Lublin, "Some Firms Intensify Push for Gender Parity at Board Level," *The Wall Street Journal*, Aug. 16, 2016, http://tinyurl.com/z3pc566.

73. For background, see Christina Hoag, "Diversity in Hollywood," *CQ Researcher*, Aug. 5, 2016, pp. 649-672.

74. Danielle J. Lindemann, Carly A. Rush and Steven J. Tepper, "An Asymmetrical Portrait: Exploring Gendered Income Inequality in the Arts," *Social Currents*, March 15, 2016, http://tinyurl.com/z3vnhc3.

75. Alison Wood Brooks *et al.*, "Investors prefer entrepreneurial ventures pitched by attractive men," Proceedings of the National Academies of Science, March 25, 2014, http://tinyurl.com/hnnxovl.

76. Claire Cain Miller, "What It's Really Like to Risk It All in Silicon Valley," *The New York Times*, Feb. 27, 2016, http://tinyurl.com/h2xqhl2.

77. Erica Chenoweth *et al.*, "How to Get Tenure (If You're a Woman)," *Foreign Policy*, April 19, 2016, http://tinyurl.com/jj4oj8x.

78. Daniel Z. Grunspan *et al.*, "Males Under-Estimate Academic Performance of Their Female Peers in Undergraduate Biology Classrooms," PLOS One, Feb. 10, 2016, http://tinyurl.com/jhda54h.

79. Paul Voosen, "The Subtle Ways Gender Gaps Persist in Science," *The Chronicle of Higher Education*, March 6, 2016, http://tinyurl.com/jyklc7r.

80. Benoit Macaluso *et al.*, "Is Science Built on the Shoulders of Women? A Study of Gender Differences in Contributorship," *Academic Medicine*, Aug. 2016, http://tinyurl.com/gsd4m4c.

81. Christopher Ingraham, "New study finds that men are often their own favorite experts on any given subject," *The Washington Post*, Aug. 1, 2016, http://tinyurl.com/hkvdu6u.

82. Penny Pritzker, "Celebrating Women Entrepreneurs," Commerce Department, March 4, 2016, http://tinyurl.com/jcpqe92.

83. Ricker, *op. cit.*

84. Karen D. Purcell, "5 Ways to Get Girls into STEM," *Edutopia*, Oct. 21, 2015, http://tinyurl.com/jys6wot.

85. Aarti Shahani, "Intel Discloses Diversity Data, Challenges Tech Industry To Follow Suit," NPR, Feb. 3, 2016, http://tinyurl.com/zf3b64s.

86. Lauren Still Rikleen, "Women Lawyers Continue to Lag Behind Male Colleagues," National Association of Women Lawyers, 2015, http://tinyurl.com/jcaaqty.

87. Karen Sloane, "Women Lawyers Face a Steep Climb to Partner," *The National Law Journal*, June 27, 2016, http://tinyurl.com/jd6crdh.

88. Jason Abbruzzese, "Break the News," *Mashable*, March 21, 2016, http://tinyurl.com/zal68hr.

89. Matt Zapotosky, "Loretta Lynch says women face 'risk of not being seen.' She speaks from experience," *The Washington Post*, Sept. 13, 2016, http://tinyurl.com/jh7rlc4.

90. Juliet Eilperin, "White House women want to be in the room where it happens," *The Washington Post*, Sept. 13, 2016, http://tinyurl.com/zhhvy6h.

91. Corinne A. Moss-Racusin and Laurie Rudman, "Disruptions in Women's Self-Promotion: The Backlash Avoidance Model," *Psychology of Women Quarterly*, May 2010, http://tinyurl.com/gnzk9rq.

92. Manuel Roig-Franzia *et al.*, "The fall of Roger Ailes: He made Fox News his 'locker room' — and now women are telling their stories," *The Washington Post*, July 22, 2016, http://tinyurl.com/jsfebo4.

93. Nina Golgowski, "Female Firefighter's Suspected Suicide Sparks Cyberbullying Probe," *The Huffington Post*, April 25, 2016, http://tinyurl.com/jfnolu7.

94. Petula Dvorak, " 'Ghostbusters,' the bros who hate it and the art of modern misogyny," *The Washington Post*, July 14, 2016, http://tinyurl.com/z4ou9ff.

95. Raina Brands, " 'Think manager, think man' stops us seeing woman as leaders," *The Guardian*, July 15, 2015, http://tinyurl.com/htaevzk.

BIBLIOGRAPHY
Selected Sources
Books

Cobble, Dorothy Sue, Linda Gordon and Astrid Henry, *Feminism Unfinished: A Short, Surprising History of American Women's Movements*, Liveright, 2014.
A trio of historians traces how women have made gains in politics and culture over the past century.

Malcolm, Ellen R., with Craig Unger, *When Women Win: EMILY's List and the Rise of Women in American Politics*, Houghton Mifflin Harcourt, 2016.
The founder of a prominent political action committee dedicated to electing Democratic women looks back on her career and the strides women have made in politics since the 1970s.

Newton-Small, Jay, *Broad Influence: How Women Are Changing the Way America Works*, Time Books, 2016.
Examining politics, law, technology, the military and other fields, a *Time* correspondent finds that the cultures in such organizations change once women represent a "critical mass" of about 20 percent to 30 percent.

Thomas, Gillian, *Because of Sex: One Law, Ten Cases and Fifty Years that Changed American Women's Lives at Work*, St. Martin's Press, 2016.
A senior staff attorney for the American Civil Liberties Union examines how anti-discrimination protections for

women under the 1964 Civil Rights Act have had long-term legal consequences that are "nothing short of revolutionary."

Articles

Cain Miller, Claire, "What It's Really Like to Risk It All in Silicon Valley," *The New York Times*, Feb. 27, 2016, http://tinyurl.com/h2xqhl2.
A journalist finds that within Silicon Valley's venture capital culture, where white males are prevalent, women receive only 8 percent of funds from private investors.

Cottle, Michelle, "The Era of the Bitch Is Coming," *The Atlantic*, Aug. 17, 2016, http://tinyurl.com/jhudvsy.
Just as President Obama's term ushered in heated discussions about race, a Hillary Clinton presidency would likely trigger misogyny and a backlash against women, a journalist argues.

Dishman, Lydia, "Why Salary Transparency Didn't Eliminate The Gender Wage Gap At This Startup," *Fast Company*, March 31, 2016, http://tinyurl.com/gtq2jxf.
After several tech companies made salaries more transparent, a journalist finds that the move did not equalize pay between women and men.

Johnson, Stefanie K., David R. Hekman and Elsa T. Chan, "If There's Only One Woman in Your Candidate Pool, There's Statistically No Chance She'll Be Hired," *Harvard Business Review*, April 26, 2016, http:// tinyurl.com/jeht248.
University of Colorado business professors conclude in an experiment that when only one woman or person of color is up for a job, that person has almost no chance of being hired.

Kliff, Sarah, "The Truth About the Gender Wage Gap," *Vox*, Aug. 1, 2016, http://tinyurl.com/zxhv2xf.
A reporter summarizes a study by three economists that found top-paying jobs disproportionately reward those who can work long, mostly inflexible hours and penalize those with responsibilities outside the workplace, who tend to be women.

McCain Nelson, Colleen, and Janet Adamy, "Hillary Clinton's Historic Moment Divides Generations of Women," *The Wall Street Journal*, July 27, 2016, http://tinyurl.com/zd3juny.
Two reporters find professional progress for women has been so widespread that many younger voters appear indifferent to the prospect of a female president.

Mertens, Maggie, "Women's Soccer Is a Feminist Issue," *The Atlantic*, June 5, 2015, http://tinyurl .com/qgazqr3.
A journalist contends that feminists largely have ignored gender disparities in sports salaries.

Reports and Studies

Hegewisch, Ariane, and Asha DuMonthier, "The Gender Wage Gap by Occupation 2015 and by Race and Ethnicity," Institute for Women's Policy Research, April 2016, http://tinyurl.com/gvczqfl.
Two researchers find that on average, women earn 81.1 cents for every $1 earned by men and that their median earnings are lower than men's in nearly all occupations.

Lawless, Jennifer L., and Richard L. Fox, "Girls Just Wanna Not Run: The Gender Gap in Young Americans' Political Ambition," American University, March 2013, http://tinyurl.com/hm926bg.
Political scientists at American University (Lawless) and Loyola Marymount University (Fox) find young women are less likely than young men to consider running for office because they receive less encouragement and consider themselves less qualified.

Noland, Marcus, Tyler Moran and Barbara Kotschwar, "Is Gender Diversity Profitable? Evidence from a Global Survey," Peterson Institute for International Economics, February 2016, http://tinyurl.com/ hf7tzsp.
Researchers at an economic think tank who surveyed 21,890 firms in 91 countries found that companies with more women board members or in top executive positions were more profitable.

For More Information

American Association of University Women, 1310 L St., N.W., Suite 1000, Washington, DC 20005; 202-785-7700; www.aauw.org. Nonprofit advocacy and research group that promotes policies to empower women.

Catalyst, 120 Wall St., 15th Floor, New York, NY 10005; 212-514-7600; www.catalyst.org. Nonprofit that conducts research and promotes policies on workplace inclusivity for women.

Center for American Women and Politics, Rutgers University, 191 Ryders Lane, New Brunswick, NJ 08901; 848-932-9384; www.cawp.rutgers.edu. Conducts research and education programs on women in politics.

Clayman Institute for Gender Research, Stanford University, 589 Capistrano Way, Stanford, CA 94305; 650-723-1994; gender.stanford.edu. Conducts research aimed at promoting gender equality, including a program on women's leadership.

Institute for Women's Policy Research, 1200 18th St., N.W., Suite 301, Washington, DC 20036; 202-785-5100; www.iwpr.org. Think tank that conducts research aimed at addressing women's needs.

U.S. Women's Chamber of Commerce, 700 12th St., N.W., Suite 700, Washington, DC 20005; 888-418-7922; uswcc.org. Association that works to influence policy and help women start and build successful careers and businesses.

7

The Obama Legacy

Kenneth Jost

President Obama delivered an upbeat account of his accomplishments during the Democratic National Convention in Philadelphia on July 27, 2016, saying the country was "stronger and more prosperous" than when he took office in 2009. The Republican Party's platform blamed Obama for below-average economic growth and said national security is "at great risk" because Obama has "placed strategic and ideological limitations and shackles on our military."

From *CQ Researcher*, November 4, 2016

With just under six months left in his presidency, Barack Obama strode onto the stage at the Democratic National Convention in Philadelphia in July, ready to rouse the party's faithful with an upbeat account of his accomplishments in office. With his approval ratings in the midrange, Obama also hoped to transfer some of his popularity to Hillary Clinton, the Democrats' choice to win election as his successor in November.

The country is "stronger and more prosperous" than when he took office in 2009, Obama assured the delegates, in a valedictory delivered 12 years to the day after he had catapulted to national prominence with a stirring 2004 speech about national unity. "There is not a liberal America and a conservative America," Obama had famously told the Democratic convention in Boston. "There is the United States of America."

As the nation's first African-American president, Obama has spent nearly eight years trying to unify the country on the strength of twice winning popular-vote majorities — only the third Democratic president to do so, after Franklin D. Roosevelt and Andrew Jackson.[1] But he has confronted determined opposition from congressional Republicans, conservative groups and commentators and a wide and irreconcilable swath of the American public.

This year, however, the country remained deeply divided as the general election campaign got underway between Clinton — the former first lady, U.S. senator and secretary of State — and Republican nominee Donald Trump, the name-brand real estate developer and former reality TV star. Trump's campaign slogan, "Make America Great Again," demeaned the Obama years as part

Blacks, Whites Differ on Obama's Impact on Race

Americans are sharply divided along racial lines on how President Obama has affected race relations in the United States. A majority of black respondents said Obama had "made progress toward improving" race relations. A comparable number of whites said either that Obama had made progress or had tried but failed, but nearly one-third of whites said Obama had made relations worse.

Views on Obama's Handling of Race Relations*

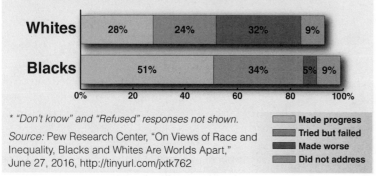

* "Don't know" and "Refused" responses not shown.

Source: Pew Research Center, "On Views of Race and Inequality, Blacks and Whites Are Worlds Apart," June 27, 2016, http://tinyurl.com/jxtk762

- Made progress
- Tried but failed
- Made worse
- Did not address

of a long-term decline in U.S. prestige in world affairs and in economic vitality and social values at home.

Obama has rejected what he called Trump's "pessimistic vision" that he said played to Americans' fears. "America is already great," he said. "America is already strong. And I promise you, our strength, our greatness, does not depend on Donald Trump."[2]

Obama's legacy was the backdrop for Clinton's campaign, as she moved to shore up the coalition of Democratic constituencies and Trump worked to expand on his core strength among white, male, non-college-educated working-class voters. Despite the political divisions, president watchers and partisans across the ideological spectrum agreed that Obama has had a record of significant achievements — some said for the better, some said for the worse.

Obama has won praise for withdrawing U.S. troops from combat roles in Afghanistan and Iraq even as critics said the drawdowns sacrificed hard-won gains by U.S. service members. He also has been credited with the recovery from the 2008-09 recession yet blamed for a decade of slow economic growth. His signature domestic policy achievement, the Affordable Care Act, has been praised for expanding access to health care but denounced

for driving up premiums and adding to bureaucratic red tape. And the renewed attention to race-related issues has been seen by one side as improving race relations and by the other as heightening racial tensions.

Michael Days, editor of the *Philadelphia Daily News* and author of the celebratory book *Obama's Legacy*, calls Obama "a transformative" president. He cites the Affordable Care Act, the auto industry bailout and other economic revitalizations, criminal justice reforms and advances for LGBT rights, including marriage equality. From the opposite side, Matthew Margolis, a political blogger and author of *The Worst President in American History*, says Obama's presidency was "transformative . . . in the sense that America ceased to be the world's beacon of freedom and opportunity."

Steven Schier, a professor of political science at Carleton College in Northfield, Minn., and editor of *Debating the Obama Presidency*, calls Obama a "consequential" president. "He will not be simply a placeholder," Schier says. "He came in and wanted to change Americans in a substantial way, and he's had some substantial success."

Obama, who campaigned in 2008 on the promise of "hope" and "change," "has been a change agent," Schier adds, "but he has fallen far short of his ambitions."

George C. Edwards III, a professor of political science at Texas A&M University in College Station, says Obama overestimated his ability to initiate change through public persuasion. "He thought he could create opportunities for change by taking his case to the American public," says Edwards, author of *Overreach*, a study published during Obama's first term. "That was their theory of governing, and they were wrong. They couldn't get the public on their side."

The string of successes in Obama's first two years, including passage of the Affordable Care Act "led to a political disaster in 2010," Edwards says, referring to the Republican takeover of the House in the midterm elections. "He lost the ability to govern effectively through Congress for the rest of his tenure."

Others say Obama has been hampered by GOP obstructionism, voiced by presumptive House Speaker Rep. John Boehner, a Republican from Ohio, on the cusp of the 2010 midterms. Referring to Obama's agenda, Boehner said, "We're going to do everything — and I mean everything we can do — to kill it, stop it, slow it down, whatever we can."[3]

Frustrated by Republican opposition in Congress, Obama turned toward greater use of executive powers to institute policy changes without legislation. The practice prompted Republicans and legal conservatives to accuse Obama of circumventing constitutional limits on presidential power and to challenge some of those moves in court. In some cases the Supreme Court agreed. Some of those regulatory moves, Republicans said, hurt employment and economic growth.

Andrew Rudalevige, a professor of political science at Bowdoin College in Brunswick, Maine, and co-editor of a forthcoming volume of essays on Obama's presidency, calls Obama "an important figure" in presidential history, partly because of his race and partly because of the generational shift he represented as the first president to have been born after 1960. "He certainly won't be seen as a failed president," Rudalevige says. "Whoever follows him is going to be less successful. He will benefit from the comparison."

Obama won election by assembling Electoral College majorities from states in the East and mid-Atlantic region, the West and Northwest and some key battleground states in between. With the presidential campaign in its final week, Clinton is leading in most polls by an average of just under 2 percent.* She is seen as the odds-on favorite to win an Electoral College majority with virtually all of those same states and possibly others.

As the election nears, Obama's approval rating is holding steady at 55 percent. From a high of 67 percent after his first inauguration, Obama's rating has never fallen below 40 percent. In comparison, President George W. Bush peaked at 90 percent after the Sept. 11, 2001, terrorist attacks and sank to 30 percent as the country fell into recession in fall 2008.

Obama's approval ratings have inevitably been capped by the residual distrust fueled by false but ineradicable insinuations that he was not qualified to be president because he was not actually "a natural born" U.S. citizen as the Constitution requires or that he was a Muslim. For years, Trump was one of the chief proponents of the so-called "birther" controversy, but he acknowledged in mid-September that Obama "was born in the United States. Period."[4]

Mixing the presidential and the political, Obama is treating the Nov. 8 election as a referendum on his legacy. "I will consider it a personal insult, an insult to my legacy, if this community lets down its guard and fails to activate itself in this election," Obama said in a Sept. 17 address to the Congressional Black Caucus's annual dinner. He repeated the thought later to the African-American radio talk show host Steve Harvey. "My legacy is on the ballot," Obama said in the Sept. 28 broadcast.[5]

One part of Obama's legacy is the appointment of a record number of women and racial and ethnic minorities to the federal bench. "One of the president's greatest achievements has been the remarkable progress in increasing diversity in the judiciary," says Nan Aron, president of the Alliance for Justice, a liberal judicial advocacy organization. The Supreme Court now includes three women for the first time in history after Obama's appointment of Justices Sonia Sotomayor and Elena Kagan. But Senate Republicans have refused to hold hearings on Obama's third Supreme Court nominee, federal appeals court judge Merrick Garland, saying the vacancy should be filled by the next president.

With early voting on Obama's successor well under way, here are questions being debated about his eight years in the White House:

---

* Eleven days before the election, Clinton's lead appeared to be threatened after FBI Director James Comey announced a new development in the investigation of Clinton's use of a private email server while secretary of State. Comey sent members of Congress a letter on Oct. 28 notifying them that FBI agents, during an unrelated investigation, had found emails "that appear to be pertinent" to the earlier investigation on a computer used by former Rep. Antony Weiner, D-N.Y., the estranged husband of key Clinton aide, Huma Abedin. In a report on that probe on July 5, Comey criticized Clinton's use of the private server but recommended no criminal charges be brought. In response to the new inquiry, Clinton again acknowledged a mistake in using the private server but expressed confidence that no criminal charges were warranted. "There is no case here," she said in an Oct. 31 rally in Kent, Ohio.

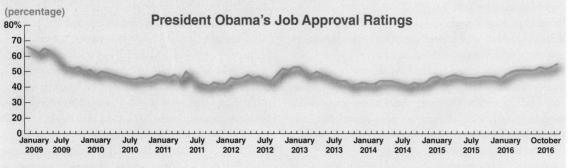

Obama's Approval Hits Second-Term High

President Obama's approval rating stood at 55 percent in late October, its highest point since June 2009. Compared with other two-term presidents at corresponding points in their terms, Obama's approval rating is most similar to Ronald Reagan's, higher than those of George W. Bush and Harry Truman and lower than Bill Clinton's and Dwight D. Eisenhower's.

President Obama's Job Approval Ratings

(percentage)

Source: "Presidential Approval Ratings — Barack Obama," Gallup, October 2016, http://tinyurl.com/yj3bjw3

Has Obama strengthened the U.S. position in global affairs?

The Democratic Party platform adopted at its national convention in late July confidently declared the United States "stronger abroad and safer at home" because of President Obama's moves to strengthen alliances and reduce the U.S. role in "two costly wars." At their convention two weeks earlier, however, Republicans adopted a platform that found national security to be "at great risk" because Obama had "frequently placed strategic and ideological limitations and shackles on our military."[6]

Vice President Joe Biden made the administration's case in a valedictory overview written for *Foreign Affairs*, maintaining that the United States is "stronger and more secure" than when he and Obama took office. Biden credits the administration with "disciplined application of military force" and success in "expanding and modernizing the United States' unrivaled network of alliances and partnerships and embedding them within a wider international order of rules and institutions."[7]

Foreign policy experts differ sharply in assessing Obama's record along ideological lines that parallel the partisan divisions.

"He has basically done a marvelous job in enhancing Americans' security," says Lawrence Korb, a senior fellow with the liberal Center for American Progress think tank

who served as assistant secretary of Defense in the Reagan administration. Danielle Pletka, senior vice president for defense and foreign policy studies at the American Enterprise Institute, a conservative think tank, disagrees. "Look at the old election question, 'Are you better off than you were eight years ago?'" says Pletka, a Republican staffer on the Senate Foreign Relations Committee in the 1990s. "The obvious answer to that is no," she says.

Margolis, the blogger critic, sees U.S. influence around the world in decline. "When America does not represent its own values with confidence on the global stage, freedom fighters throughout the world turn to despots, radical extremists or strongmen for aid," he says. "That is exactly what we have seen on Obama's watch." But Rudalevige, the Bowdoin professor, praises the administration's "restraint" in foreign affairs. "The United States was probably overextended," he says. "I'm sympathetic to the idea that President Obama did not want to expand our footprint and didn't want to start another war with Russia or China or start a massive expansion in Syria."

Much of the debate over Obama's foreign policy surrounds his reduction in the U.S. combat role in Bush-era wars in Afghanistan and Iraq, his use of drone strikes to help curb the rise of the so-called Islamic State (also known as ISIS and ISIL) and his decision to minimize America's role in aiding rebels in Syria's bloody, five-year civil war.[8]

In Afghanistan, Obama increased the number of U.S. troops in 2009 but promised to start a "drawdown" by mid-2011; he now plans to leave a minimal U.S. force there. Korb, who has also been affiliated with the Council on Foreign Relations and the Brookings Institution, both middle-of-the-road think tanks, says the strategy has worked. "We were losing when he came in," Korb says. "He turned the tide there and has now given the Afghan government a chance to hold on."

Again, Pletka flatly disagrees. "The Taliban is more active now than when he came into office, and al Qaeda is on the rise," she says. "We've had to increase troops and have not been able to draw down on the schedule suggested by the president."

On Iraq, Korb and Pletka agree that Obama's decision to fulfill Bush's commitment to pull out U.S. troops by the end of 2011 opened opportunities for the Islamic State to gain influence and territory. But Korb says Obama had no choice. "We had to leave," he says.

"The reality is that if President Obama had not pulled our troops back from Iraq in 2011, we would likely not be in this situation," Pletka says. She insists that the administration could have negotiated a new agreement with the Iraqi government that could have permitted U.S. troops to stay.

In their platform, Republicans blame the rise of ISIS on the destabilization of the Middle East, which they say resulted from Obama's mishandling of the so-called Arab Spring that emerged in 2011.[9] The Democratic platform vows to "continue to lead a broad coalition of allies and partners to destroy ISIS' stronghold in Iraq and Syria."

Korb credits Obama for containing the Islamic State. "We've killed 45,000 members," he says. But, he adds, "You're not going to defeat ISIS militarily. What you want to do is to undermine its ideology so that it doesn't keep attracting followers."

James Mann, a veteran journalist and author in residence at Johns Hopkins University's School of Advanced International Studies in Washington, faults Obama for a slow response to ISIS. "He did not do enough at first," Mann says. But Mann thinks ISIS may have reached its peak. "They seem to be having trouble getting recruits," he says.

Getty Images/Anadolu Agency/Ibrahim Ebu Leys

Children seek shelter as bombs fall in Aleppo, Syria, on Oct. 11, 2016. During the Syrian civil war, President Obama approved only limited aid to the rebels fighting President Bashar al-Assad, which some critics have called a major foreign policy failure of the administration.

The author of a generally favorable book on the formation of the Obama foreign policy team, Mann joins other critics of the administration's handling of the Syrian civil war. Obama has provided limited assistance to moderate rebels opposed to the dictatorial president Bashar al-Assad and failed to act after Assad crossed Obama's self-declared "red line" by using chemical weapons against civilians. "I think he has taken nonintervention too far," Mann says.

Pletka is indignant about the administration's hesitancy in Syria. "The death of a half million people . . . is a stain on President Obama's reputation that should make him forever ashamed," she says, referring to the estimated total death toll in the five-year conflict.

But Korb doubts that the United States could have changed the course of events in Syria. "We've seen regime change," he says, "and it basically doesn't work."

Critics also complain that Obama has not halted what Pletka calls the "adventurism" of Russia in Ukraine and Crimea and China in the South China Sea, which she sees as "more evidence of the decline of American power and prestige."

Korb counters that the administration helped organize broadly backed economic sanctions against Russia and is working to strengthen ties with allies in the Asia Pacific region.

Health Care Law Expanded Coverage

But can it survive insurance company defections?

In 2008, Democratic presidential nominee Sen. Barack Obama of Illinois laid out his vision for extending health care coverage to millions of uninsured Americans, a plan he hoped would earn bipartisan support.

"The American people are too often offered two extremes — government-run health care with higher taxes," which many Democrats favor, or a very loosely regulated free-market approach in which private, mostly for-profit insurers provide the coverage, as Republicans generally recommend, Obama said. "Both of these extremes are wrong."[1]

Obama proposed including both a government-run insurance program — Medicaid — and a government-managed marketplace in which private insurers would sell health coverage. In 2010, after a bitter struggle, his centrist vision prevailed in Congress, although it was enacted with no Republican votes in support. On March 23, 2010, he signed into law his signature achievement — the Patient Protection and Affordable Care Act, called the Affordable Care Act (ACA) or, simply, "Obamacare."[2]

Today, the White House points with pride to 20 million Americans who are newly insured under the ACA. This year, though, some big insurers have lost money in some states and are leaving the system. That's triggering concerns about whether the ACA's private health insurance markets — called "exchanges" — can work long term.

Politically, the law has brought Obama little but bitter criticism for a too-partisan approach.

From the beginning, ACA's implementation has been "plagued by a widespread belief" that Obama unfairly jammed the law through Congress "without any Republican input or efforts to find common ground," said Norman Ornstein, a resident scholar at the conservative American Enterprise Institute (AEI) think tank. But in fact, Obama asked congressional committees to draft the law, Ornstein said. And in the Senate, he added, Finance Committee Chairman Max Baucus, D-Mont., "deliberately started the talks with a template" based on a plan created by Republicans in 1993-94.[3]

Some high-ranking Senate Republicans entered talks on Baucus' draft. But Kentucky Republican Mitch McConnell, then Senate minority leader, told the lawmakers they could be demoted if they produced "legislation to be signed by Barack Obama," said Ornstein. With the discussions clearly going nowhere, if the president was being unfairly partisan he would simply have asked Baucus to abandon the talks, Ornstein said. Instead, Obama allowed the "faux negotiations" to go on for months, in hopes of drawing some GOP support, Ornstein said.[4] In the end, the legislation passed both houses of Congress, despite GOP opposition.

Today, the White House touts Obamacare's achievements. This year, only 10.8 percent of American adults are uninsured, down from 11.7 percent in late 2015, according to the Gallup polling organization. The rate is down a full 6.5 percentage points from late 2013, just before the ACA took effect. Furthermore, 15.5 percent of U.S. adults reported having trouble paying for needed health care in the past year — down from 18.6 percent in late 2013.[5]

Supporters say the law is working well in states where public officials and insurers have worked together to implement it. California, for example, "followed the blueprint. They did it right," said Dr. J. Mario Molina, chief executive of Long Beach, Calif.-based Molina Healthcare, an insurer that sells ACA coverage in several states.[6] Between 2013 and 2015, the uninsured rate for California adults dropped from 23.7 percent to 11.1 percent. Californians also have seen relatively low insurance-premium increases, and most continue to have a choice of several insurers.[7]

Critics, however, point out that while 20 million people are newly insured, about 9 million of them are covered through Medicaid, the joint federal-state program for poor and disabled individuals and families. That means only 11 million have coverage through the exchanges, a disappointing total compared to initial estimates that 21 million people would be covered by now, says Robert Moffit, a senior fellow in health policy at the conservative Heritage Foundation think tank in Washington.

The exchanges "were supposed to function as real marketplaces" whose insurers would enroll both those who are ill — and thus in dire need of insurance — and younger and healthier people, Moffit says. (A diverse population is necessary so low spenders in any given year can help cover the costs of that year's high spenders.) But few healthy people are finding the exchange coverage attractive, he says.

When people are healthy today, they often forego insurance coverage and pay the penalty if they see it as too expensive, said AEI Resident Scholar Joseph Antos and

Resident Fellow James C. Capretta. For example, a Virginia family of four, earning $60,000 a year, would have paid $4,980 in premiums for coverage in 2016, for a health plan with a $5,000 deductible, they noted. When compared with the mere $725 tax penalty the ACA imposes for not having coverage, many such families simply choose not to carry insurance, they said.[8]

In 2017, the premium-cost dilemma will worsen. Partly because the average ACA enrollee is sicker than originally anticipated, premiums for midlevel ACA insurance plans will soar by 25 percent over current levels. That's compared to average annual premium increases of only 2 percent from 2014 to 2015, and 7 percent for 2015 to 2016.[9]

In addition, some major insurers are leaving the markets, arguing that they can't make enough money. For example, Hartford, Conn.-based Aetna will leave 11 of the 15 exchanges it has served, and Minnetonka, Minn.-based United Healthcare will leave 31 of 34 exchanges, says Sabrina Corlette, project director at the Center on Health Insurance Reform at Georgetown University's Health Policy Institute.

Many conservatives say the ACA's rules — such as strictly limiting the premium hikes that can be imposed on people as they age — cripple insurers. "Exchanges are collapsing because of federal mandates and a lack of flexibility," said Sen. Lamar Alexander, R-Tenn., chairman of the Committee on Health, Education, Labor and Pensions.[10]

But others argue that problems are mainly early-stage glitches of the sort that afflict any complicated system. The exchanges "will stabilize in two or three years," said John Rowe, a physician and a former Aetna CEO.[11]

Most Senate Democrats now endorse a plan to add a public option — a government-run insurance plan — to compete with the private insurers. Both Obama and Democratic presidential nominee Hillary Clinton have endorsed the idea, which was discussed but ultimately dropped when the law was drafted. Including a public plan in the exchanges "is critical to bringing more competition and accountability to the insurance market," said Sen. Jeff Merkley, D-Ore., a chief proponent.[12]

But that's "false advertising," says Heritage's Moffit. While private insurers would continue to be on the hook for their financial losses, a public plan would have taxpayer backing and would therefore risk nothing. That disparity would eventually "destroy competition" and drive all private insurers out of the ACA, Moffit says.

— Marcia Clemmitt

Supporters and opponents of the Affordable Care Act rally at the Supreme Court during oral arguments over President Obama's controversial health care law. The court largely upheld the law on June 28, 2012.

[1] "Barack Obama on Health Care," *WebMD Expert* Blogs, Oct. 24, 2008, http://tinyurl.com/5m5xfu.

[2] For background, see "Health Reform Implementation Timeline," Kaiser Family Foundation, http://tinyurl.com/hrcmlpv; and "Summary of the Affordable Care Act," Kaiser Family Foundation, http://tinyurl.com/zl5srg8.

[3] Norman Ornstein, "The Real Story of Obamacare's Birth," *The Atlantic*, July 6, 2015, http://tinyurl.com/jptw5lo.

[4] *Ibid.*

[5] Nader Nekvasil, "Uninsured Down Since Obamacare; Cost, Quality Still Concerns," Gallup.com, Aug. 29, 2016, http://tinyurl.com/hkttxee.

[6] Noam M. Levey, "So you think Obamacare is a disaster? Here's how California is proving you wrong," *Los Angeles Times*, Oct. 7, 2016, http://tinyurl.com/zoc3l94.

[7] *Ibid.*

[8] Joseph Antos and James Capretta, "The Future of the ACA's Exchanges," *Health Affairs* blog, Oct. 11, 2016, http://tinyurl.com/z2ozwfe.

[9] Robert Pear, "Some Health Plan Costs to Increase by an Average of 25 Percent, U.S. Says," *The New York Times*, Oct. 24, 2016, http://tinyurl.com/gnbrthx.

[10] Robert Pear, "Ailing Obama Health Care Act May Have to Change to Survive," *The New York Times*, Oct. 2, 2016, http://tinyurl.com/h7hmryx.

[11] *Ibid.*

[12] Peter Sullivan, "Merkley: 33 Senate Dems now back ObamaCare Public Option," *The Hill*, Sept. 16, 2016, http://tinyurl.com/zrfr5p6.

The two also clash on the administration's signature diplomatic event of Obama's last year in office: the nuclear agreement with Iran. Korb expects history to remember that Obama "stopped Iran from getting nuclear weapons," but Pletka says the accord gives Iran "free rein to create an arsenal of nuclear weapons in 10-15 years."

Pletka argues that overall the administration's policies have weakened confidence in the United States among allies in Europe and elsewhere. Mann dismisses the criticism. "Every party out of power claims that the party in power is screwing up relations with our allies," he says.

Have Obama's domestic policies improved Americans' lives?

The Democratic platform opens by crediting Obama with lifting the economy out of a deep recession but acknowledges that "too many Americans have been left behind" with wages that have "barely budged" and costs that have "continued to rise." The Republican platform, on the other hand, blames Obama for below-average economic growth, slow growth of private-sector jobs and low labor-force participation.

In mid-September, with the presidential campaign in its final two months, however, economic statistics were generally positive. Unemployment fell to a pre-recession level below 5 percent, according to the Census Bureau, while median household income rose 5.2 percent — the highest annual increase since record-keeping began in 1967 — although it was still below the pre-recession figure in 2007.

Economy watchers saw the news as generally bullish. "It has been a long slog from the depths of the Great Recession, but things are finally starting to improve for many American households," Chris G. Christopher Jr., director of consumer economics at the financial planning firm IHS Global Insight, told *The New York Times*.[10]

Obama took a victory lap of sorts on the campaign trail as the statistics were being released in Washington. Speaking to a Clinton rally in Philadelphia, Obama recited the improved performance in jobs and wages along with health insurance for 20 million more people under the Affordable Care Act. "Thanks, Obama," he added, adopting the sarcastic phrase used by Republicans to denigrate his record.[11]

Gary Burtless, a senior economics fellow with the Brookings Institution, credits Obama and the Democratic-majority Congress that existed during his first two years in office. "The country is in vastly better shape in 2016 than in 2008 or early 2009," he says. The recession "came to an end as early as it did because of the measures passed by Congress in the first two months," he says, citing in particular the fiscal stimulus signed by Obama less than a month after the inauguration.

Burtless, who has been at Brookings since 1981 after holding positions as an economist in two Cabinet-level departments under Democratic President Jimmy Carter, also credits Obama with strengthening the economy by bailing out the U.S. automobile industry. "Without the U.S. government intervention, those companies would have failed," he says. Obama also restored confidence in the U.S. banking industry in those initial months, he says. "By May or June most participants in the financial markets thought the banks were going to survive," he says.

In their platform, Republicans correctly stated that Obama will leave office as the first post-World War II president without a single year of at least 3 percent economic growth. "The recession was very steep and the recovery was slow," Burtless acknowledges. But the economy grew at a rate of 2.9 percent in the third quarter of 2016, the highest rate in two years, according to the government's regular report released on Oct. 28, 10 days before the election.[12] Economic policy experts from different political perspectives offer different reasons for the slow post-recession growth.

Lawrence Mishel, president of the liberal, labor-backed Economic Policy Institute think tank in Washington, gives Obama "high marks" for the fiscal stimulus. But he says that the follow-up was "hampered by an unwillingness to argue for further stimulus," especially after Republicans gained control of the House of Representatives in 2010 and economic policy debates shifted to debt reduction. "That helped undermine the ability to get as good a recovery as we could have," he says.

James Pethokoukis, a columnist and blogger on economics for the business-backed American Enterprise Institute, agrees that the post-recession recovery has been "the weakest ever" by historical standards, but he blames economic conditions more than Obama's policies. "The weight of the evidence is that the recovery has been weak

Unemployment Rate at Pre-recession Level

Joblessness was down in September to the pre-recession rate of 5 percent. During President Obama's two terms, unemployment has declined steadily since peaking at 10 percent during October 2009, in the midst of a deep recession.

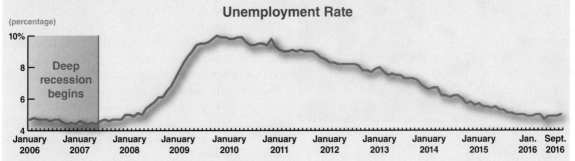

Unemployment Rate

(percentage)

Source: "Labor Force Statistics from the Current Population Survey," Bureau of Labor Statistics, September 2016, http://tinyurl.com/3gss8qd

because of the nature of the recession," Pethokoukis says. "It was a recession accompanied by financial shock," he explains. "Those downturns are followed by slow recoveries, both in terms of income and jobs."

Still, Pethokoukis says Obama's policies were "not optimal for growth." He faults Obama for allowing Bush-era tax cuts for high-income taxpayers to expire at the end of 2012. "I would not have been raising taxes in a period of very slow growth," he says. He also says the Dodd-Frank Act, the Wall Street reform law that Obama signed in July 2010, restricted lending. But Pethokoukis also says the independent Federal Reserve has been too slow to join in stimulating the economy. "They should have started bond buying earlier," he says.[13]

Mishel praises the administration for various actions aimed directly at helping workers. "We have had a terrific, proactive Department of Labor," Mishel says, citing policies expanding overtime for some salaried workers and reclassifying "independent contractors" as employees. He also points to an executive order requiring federal contractors to report violations of labor and employment laws. "It's important to set the moral and legal tone that labor laws have to be adhered to," he says.

Burtless says workers have fared well in the recovery. "We've had a sustained period of employment growth, and there have been improvements in real wages," he says. But he also says business has done well in the recovery. "The profitability of American business has been extraordinarily high," he says.

Public discontent with economic conditions, however, is both wide and deep. A Gallup survey in September found that 58 percent of respondents saw the economy as getting worse compared to 37 percent who thought it was getting better. Gallup's so-called "Economic Confidence Index" has been negative since March 2015.[14]

Despite those surveys, Burtless is bullish on the U.S. economy. "The recovery went better in the United States than in most other countries," he says.

Has Obama helped improve race relations in the United States?

Eight years after Obama's election as the United States' first black president, Democrats adopted a platform pledging to end "systemic and institutional racism" in the country but without citing any specific accomplishments under his administration. In contrast to the detailed planks in the Democratic charter, the Republican platform includes only a brief paragraph endorsing "the opportunity to pursue [the] American dream free from discrimination" while it criticizes a half-century of Democratic-backed anti-poverty programs.

Recent surveys indicate that most Americans, black and white, believe race relations have worsened over the

Demonstrators in El Cajon, Calif., protest on Sept. 30, 2016, after the fatal police shooting of an unarmed black man. Most Americans believe race relations have worsened over the past eight years, but President Obama said they "have improved dramatically in my lifetime."

past eight years, a period punctuated by rising racial tensions over repeated videos showing shootings of unarmed black men by police.

But Obama takes the long view. "Race relations have improved dramatically in my lifetime," Obama remarked at a memorial service for slain Dallas police officers on July 12. "Those who deny it are dishonoring the struggles that helped us achieve that progress."[15]

Race is "the defining feature of our forty-fourth president's two terms in office," Michael Eric Dyson, an African-American professor of sociology at Georgetown University in Washington, writes in his book *The Black Presidency.* Obama has been torn, Dyson writes, between "demands from blacks to be blacker, and the wish of many whites to whitewash the story of American race and politics."[16]

In his book, Dyson lists 37 statements or speeches by Obama on race, including the president's comments following the shooting deaths of black teenagers Trayvon Martin by a white neighborhood security guard in Sanford, Fla., and Michael Brown by a white police officer in Ferguson, Mo. Obama linked the two deaths, two years apart, to racial profiling of black youths and later sought to counter disappointment among African-Americans and others after failed prosecutions in both cases.[17]

Earlier, Obama had tried to serve as peacemaker-in-chief by hosting a "beer summit" at the White House

between the prominent African-American Harvard professor Henry Louis Gates Jr. and the white Cambridge, Mass., police officer who mistook him for an intruder at Gates' own home. Obama used the July 24, 2009, get-together to repeat his earlier description of Gates' arrest as an "overreaction," but he added that Gates had "probably overreacted as well."[18]

Newspaper editor Days agrees that racial issues have gotten more attention during Obama's presidency. "We're talking about racial issues a lot more," he says, while acknowledging that some of Obama's comments — such as those on the Gates episode and following Trayvon Martin's death — triggered backlashes. But, he adds, "You'll see a lot of black folks who say he hasn't talked enough about race."

Political blogger Margolis sees many of Obama's comments as divisive. Obama "used pretty much every opportunity to divide Americans by race or ethnicity, not unite them," Margolis says. "He has had many opportunities to start a real dialogue on race relations and chose, without fail, to lecture Americans instead." The conservative columnist Victor Davis Hanson agrees. "Too often Obama has gratuitously aroused racial animosities with inflammatory rhetoric . . . or injected himself into the middle of hot-button controversies," writes Hanson, a senior fellow with the conservative Hoover Institution think tank at Stanford University, citing the Gates episode and the aftermaths of the deaths of Martin and Brown.[19]

Eddie Glaude Jr., chair of the Center for African American Studies at Princeton University, says Obama's election and presence, along with his family, in the White House are "symbolically significant" but that the effects have differed along racial lines. "He has had an enormous impact on the way in which we think about race, particularly from the vantage point of African-Americans," Glaude says. But, he adds, "There's been a group of folks who've never conceded his legitimacy." Obama's "very presence makes the tensions explicit," Glaude says.

Polls by *The Washington Post*-ABC and *The New York Times*-CBS both found the numbers of white and black Americans who described race relations as "generally bad" to be the highest figures recorded since May 1992, shortly after the videotaped beating of the African-American taxi driver Rodney King by Los Angeles police officers. "This is certainly the worst political climate that I've seen in my lifetime," Peniel Joseph, the founding director of the Center for the Study of Race and Democracy at the University of Texas's Lyndon B. Johnson School of Public Affairs, remarked to *The Washington Post.*[20]

Besides the racial divide on whether Obama has made race relations better or worse, a Pew Research Center survey also found a sharp partisan divide on whether racial issues are getting too much or too little attention. A majority of Republicans — 59 percent — said too much, while a near-majority of Democrats — 49 percent — said too little. Among independents, 42 percent said too much, 25 percent too little and 30 percent "about the right amount."[21]

Days gives Obama generally good marks on policies affecting African-Americans. "If you look at things black people care about, he's done pretty well," he says. He notes as examples two of Obama's early successes — the automobile bailout and Obamacare — that benefited minorities without being presented and advocated in racial terms.

Glaude is less impressed. "He hasn't put forward policies that would actually tackle the issue of racial inequality," Glaude says. Black unemployment is more than twice the figure for whites, he notes. "The fundamentals are deep and abiding inequality."

Obama got high marks across the board for his comments in June 2015 after the mass shooting of a minister and nine parishioners at an African-American church in Charleston, S.C., by a white supremacist-influenced youth. "For too long, we've been blind to the way past injustices continue to shape the present," Obama said before leading mourners in singing the beloved spiritual "Amazing Grace."[22]

"I think he touched all of America with what he said," says Days. "I don't think we've had a president who was able to talk about race and be as effective."

BACKGROUND

A Fast Start

Barack Obama campaigned for the presidency under the slogan "Yes, we can," and took office with a Democratic-majority Congress on his side and his can-do confidence at its height. Quickly, he began reversing policies adopted by his Republican predecessor, George W. Bush, on topics ranging from the war on terror to stem cell research. And after being in office for less than three weeks, he signed into law a $787 billion fiscal stimulus aimed at lifting the economy out of the worst recession since the Great Depression.[23]

Obama outlined an ambitious agenda in an inaugural address that tempered the day's celebratory atmosphere with passages both determined and sober. On economic policy, he promoted his plan to use tax cuts and federal spending to get the country out of what he called the "winter of our hardship." On national security, he drew a contrast with Bush administration policies by vowing to "reject as false the choice between our safety and our ideals." He offered to the Muslim world "a new way forward, based on mutual interest and mutual respect" but defiantly warned terrorists, "You cannot outlast us, and we will defeat you."[24]

On his second full day in office Obama put his stamp on counterterrorism policies by ordering the closure of once-secret CIA prisons used to detain suspected terrorists outside the United States and the repeal of a Justice Department memo authorizing coercive interrogation techniques. Obama also vowed to close within a year the Guantanamo prison camp in Cuba that the Bush administration had opened in 2002 to hold suspected terrorists. His promise remains unfulfilled, thwarted by restrictions imposed by Congress, even though the administration reduced the number of prisoners at Guantanamo from 241 in 2009 to 60 in October.[25]

Congress also acted quickly to approve a package of tax cuts and federal spending introduced on Jan. 26, 2009, passing it on mostly party-line votes within less than three weeks. The 1,100-page American Recovery and Reinvestment Act included $288 billion in tax cuts and nearly $500 billion in federal spending, including $105 billion for infrastructure investments. In signing the bill into law, Obama called it "the beginning of the end" of what was needed to restore the country's economic health. Tellingly, no House Republicans and only three Republican senators voted for the bill.[26]

The money went not only to infrastructure — roads, bridges and the like — but also to initiatives in such areas as education and health care. In education, the bill created the "Race to the Top," competitive grants for states to seek based on adopting various education

CHRONOLOGY: 2009-2012

First Term *Obama takes office as first African-American president; wins important legislative victories; vows to wind down U.S. role in Afghanistan, Iraq.*

January-June 2009 Obama outlines ambitious agenda in inaugural address (Jan. 20) . . . vows to close Guantanamo prison within one year (Jan. 21) . . . signs $787 billion fiscal stimulus (Feb. 17) . . . sets 18-month deadline to end combat operations in Iraq (Feb. 27) . . . announces plan to buy toxic assets from financially troubled banks (March 23) . . . takes first step to broaden auto industry bailout (March 30) . . . nominates Sonia Sotomayor for Supreme Court (May 26); Senate confirms her on Aug. 6.

July-December 2009 Obama meets with Harvard professor Henry Louis Gates Jr. and Cambridge police officer in "beer summit" at White House (July 24) . . . is awarded the Nobel Peace Prize (Oct. 9) . . . announces increase of 30,000 troops to Afghanistan while vowing to begin withdrawals in 2011 (Dec. 1).

January-June 2010 Obama criticizes Supreme Court's *Citizens United* campaign finance decision in State of the Union address (Jan. 27) . . . signs Affordable Care Act after partisan fight in Congress (March 23); opponents challenge law in court . . . nominates Elena Kagan for Supreme Court (May 10); Senate confirms her on Aug. 5.

July-December 2010 Obama signs Dodd-Frank Wall Street reform law (July 22). . . . Republicans gain control of House, narrow Democrats' majority in Senate (Nov. 2). . . . Obama signs prospective repeal of military's "don't ask, don't tell" policy on gay service members (Dec. 22).

January-June 2011 "Arab Spring" revolts test U.S. policy in Middle East; administration backs "regime change" in Egypt, Libya; civil war breaks out in Syria. . . . Navy SEALs kill Osama bin Laden in raid (May 1).

July-December 2011

Obama pushes Congress to pass jobs bill, without success . . . says U.S. combat troops to be out of Iraq by end of year (Oct. 21).

January-June 2012 Obama signs agreement with Afghan president Hamid Karzai to transfer security to Afghan forces (May 2) . . . announces "deferred action" for immigrants who entered illegally before age 13 (June 15). . . . Supreme Court largely upholds Affordable Care Act (June 28).

July-December 2012 Obama re-elected to second term with modest gains for Democrats in House, Senate (Nov. 6) . . . appeals for gun laws after Sandy Hook Elementary School mass shooting (Dec. 16); later institutes some changes by executive actions, including strengthened background checks for gun owners.

---

reforms long favored by public-education critics but resisted by teachers' unions. Other money went to improving energy efficiency, modernizing health information technology systems and providing new equipment for law enforcement and port security.

Despite the pump priming, unemployment rose in Obama's first two years, peaking above 10 percent early in 2010 before steadily declining for the rest of his time in office. In March 2009, however, Obama stepped in to save two troubled U.S. industries. He announced a plan on March 23 to use public and private funds to buy so-called toxic assets from financially strapped banks, setting the stage for stabilizing the banking

industry.[27] A week later, on March 30, he began the intervention that effectively forced troubled General Motors and Chrysler into bankruptcy reorganization before accepting government aid.[28]

By summer 2009, Obama turned to health care, touching off the fierce struggle that culminated in enactment of the Affordable Care Act in March 2010. The massive and intricate bill included the controversial mandate requiring everyone to have health insurance. It also authorized funds for states to expand Medicaid for the poor and provided subsidies for the near-poor to buy insurance through so-called health exchanges, new insurance markets to be established either by states or

CHRONOLOGY: *2013-2016*

Second Term *Obama presses policy goals despite weakened position in Congress.*

January-June 2013 Bush-era tax cuts expire (Jan. 1), but are extended for low- and middle-income taxpayers (Jan. 2). . . . Obama sketches liberal agenda in second inaugural address (Jan. 21).

July-December 2013 Obama pleads for calm after acquittal of security guard in shooting death of Florida teen Trayvon Martin (July 19). . . . Federal government shuts down for two weeks after spending bill impasse (Oct. 1-16). . . . Senate confirms Obama nominees for District of Columbia Circuit Court judgeships, creating a Democratic majority on the court (December).

January-June 2014 Obama directs Labor Department to widen eligibility for overtime pay (March 13); final rule is published two years later, challenged in court.

July-December 2014 Obama notes "mistrust" between police and minorities after shooting death of black teenager Michael Brown in Ferguson, Mo. (Aug. 18) . . . announces "deferred action" policy for illegal immigrant parents of children who are U.S. citizens, lawful residents (Nov. 20); so-called DAPA plan is challenged in court, later blocked. . . . Obama orders restoration of diplomatic relations with Cuba (Dec. 17); visits Havana in March.

January-June 2015 White House is lit in rainbow colors to celebrate Supreme Court's same-sex marriage ruling (June 26).

July-December 2015 Iran nuclear deal is finalized (July 14). . . . Trans-Pacific Partnership trade agreement is signed in Atlanta (Oct. 5); Senate opponents stall vote.

January-June 2016 Supreme Court puts administration's Clean Power Plan on hold pending appeal (Feb. 9). . . . Merrick Garland is nominated for Supreme Court (March 16), but denied hearing by Senate Republicans. . . . U.S. joins 170 nations in climate change agreement (April 22). . . . Supreme Court 4-4 deadlock leaves DAPA immigration policy blocked (June 23).

July-December 2016 Obama gives valedictory address to Democratic National Convention (July 27). . . . Chicago's Jackson Park is selected as site for Obama Presidential Center (July 29). . . . Voters to choose between Democrat Hillary Rodham Clinton and Republican Donald J. Trump to succeed Obama (Nov. 8).

2017 Obama to leave office (Jan. 20); will live in Washington until daughter Sasha completes high school. . . . Obama Presidential Center and museum expected to open in 2021.

---

the federal government. No Republican voted for the final version of the bill. Opponents filed the first of many legal challenges the day after Obama signed the measure on March 23, 2010.

Against the backdrop of domestic policy successes, Obama also took initial steps to bringing U.S. troops back home from Afghanistan and Iraq. For Afghanistan, he announced on Dec. 1, 2009, a surge-like increase of 30,000 U.S. troops to fortify the government's efforts to put down a continuing insurgency, coupled with plans to start withdrawing troops by 2011. Obama also committed to making good on the Bush administration's decision to withdraw U.S. troops from Iraq by 2011.

The plans allowed Republicans to attack Obama as retreating from operations that they said were still needed to defeat al Qaeda and buttress U.S.-friendly governments in both countries.

The Democratic filibuster-proof supermajority of 60 votes in the Senate enabled Obama to make his mark on the Supreme Court by replacing two retiring liberal justices, David H. Souter and John Paul Stevens, with two nominees expected to join the court's liberal wing. Sonia Sotomayor and Elena Kagan won confirmation in 2009 and 2010, respectively, with more than 60 votes but with all but a few Republicans voting no. The appointments cheered women's groups by bringing the number of

Diversity Marks Obama's Judicial Legacy

He has appointed record numbers of women and LGBT individuals.

President Obama leaves a lasting imprint on the federal judiciary with the most diverse pool of judicial nominees ever, but he is being blocked by Senate Republicans from giving the Supreme Court a liberal-leaning majority for the first time in more than 40 years.

Obama's nomination of veteran federal appeals court judge Merrick Garland has gone nowhere since the president announced his selection on March 16. A month earlier, immediately after Justice Antonin Scalia's death on Feb. 13, Senate Majority Leader Mitch McConnell had vowed to block a hearing or vote for any Obama nominee.

Senate Republicans also have slowed action on Obama's nominees to federal district and circuit courts over the past eight months, but Obama still leaves a legacy of a record number of women, African-Americans, Hispanics, Asian-Americans and LGBT individuals appointed to lifetime federal judgeships.

Obama also has changed the political orientation of the nation's federal circuit courts of appeals, the intermediate courts immediately below the Supreme Court. When Obama entered office in 2009, Republican appointees were in the majority on 11 of the 13 courts; Democratic appointees dominated the Ninth Circuit in the West, and Republican and Democratic appointees were evenly balanced on the New York-based Second Circuit.

As he leaves office, Democratic appointees are in the majority on nine of the courts. Republicans still outnumber Democratic appointees but by narrower margins on four circuits: the Fifth, Sixth, Seventh and Eighth, which cover 17 states in the nation's heartland from Ohio westward to the Dakotas in the north and Texas in the south.[1]

Nan Aron, founder and president of the liberal Alliance for Justice, says the federal circuit courts are important because they "are often the last word on important issues relating to civil rights and civil liberties." She says Obama's nominees overall have been "moderate," "fair" and "open-minded," in contrast to what she describes as "agenda-driven" judges named by President George W. Bush. But Curt Levey, former president of the now defunct Committee for Justice and now a legal fellow with the conservative group FreedomWorks, complains that Obama has appointed "more liberal activists" than previous presidents.

The White House touts Obama's record on a website page with the headline, "This Is the First Time Our Judicial Pool Has Been This Diverse." The Alliance for Justice has an interactive, up-to-date "dashboard" that lists all of Obama's judicial nominees and counts them by gender, racial or ethnic background and sexual orientation.[2]

In all, Obama has nominated 172 women for lifetime federal judgeships, more than either of his two predecessors. Of Obama's female nominees, 138 have been confirmed, including two Supreme Court justices — Sonia Sotomayor and Elena Kagan — giving the court three female justices for the first time in history. Of Obama's 34 female nominees who have not been confirmed, seven have been blocked, and 27 are awaiting Senate action. By comparison, Republican President George W. Bush nominated 71 women for judgeships, and Democratic President Bill Clinton, 111, according to the Alliance for Justice.

The alliance also counts a record number of racial or ethnic minorities among Obama's nominees, with 62 African-Americans confirmed, 36 Hispanics and 22

female justices to three for the first time in history. Both quickly began fitting in with the court's liberal wing but were unable to prevent significant setbacks for the administration at the hands of the court's conservative majority — most notably, the so-called *Citizens United* ruling in January 2010 freeing corporations and unions to spend unlimited amounts on federal elections.[29]

Obama's popularity had started to fall because of sharp partisan attacks on the health care reform that was being

pejoratively labeled Obamacare. The issue combined with the slow economic recovery to produce what Obama described as the "shellacking" in the November 2010 midterm elections. Republicans regained control of the House of Representatives by adding 63 seats and cut the Democrats' majority in the Senate from 59 to 53.[30]

Despite the setback, Obama achieved one more victory in the lame-duck session, winning enactment of a bill to abolish the military's "don't ask, don't tell" policy nominees of Asian or Pacific Islander ancestry. Obama has nominated 14 openly LGBT individuals to federal judgeships, 11 of whom have been confirmed. Before Obama took office, there was only one openly LGBT federal judge, Deborah Batts, nominated by Clinton in 1993 after the Senate failed to approve her nomination by President George H.W. Bush two years earlier.

Garland has had a reputation as a moderate liberal during his 19 years on the federal court of appeals for the District of Columbia circuit. McConnell has public or tacit support from all but two of his 53 Republican colleagues in refusing to allow a hearing on the nomination. McConnell says the position should be held for the next president to fill so "the American people" have a voice in the selection. Obama, Democratic senators and liberal groups have criticized what they call an unprecedented and unjustified tactic.

The Supreme Court has had a generally conservative majority since William H. Rehnquist, the fourth of President Richard M. Nixon's four appointees, took the bench in January 1972. Before Scalia's death, the court included five Republican and four Democratic appointees. In many of the most closely divided decisions, the justices divide along partisan lines, but Justice Anthony M. Kennedy often breaks with his GOP-appointed colleagues to join the bloc of liberal Democratic appointees.

Obama has criticized the current court after several of its high-profile decisions, including the so-called *Citizens United* decision in January 2010, which allows unlimited corporate spending in federal election campaigns. During his State of the Union address two weeks later, with six of the justices seated in the House chamber just below him, Obama said the ruling opened the door for campaign spending by foreign corporations. Justice Samuel A. Alito Jr. was seen on camera to mouth the words, "Not true."

Getty Images/*The Washington Post*/Melina Mara

House Minority Leader Nancy Pelosi, D-Calif., takes a selfie with Associate Supreme Court Justices Elena Kagan, Ruth Bader Ginsburg and Sonia Sotomayor. With President Obama's appointment of Sotomayor and Kagan, the Court for the first time now includes three women.

Aron calls the increased diversity on the federal bench "one of Obama's greatest achievements." Diversity is important, she says, because it "builds confidence among a very diverse population of Americans that the courts are open and available to everyone. It's critically important in both the perception and the reality of justice."

— *Kenneth Jost*

[1] Jeremy W. Peters, "Building Legacy, Obama Reshapes Appellate Bench," *The New York Times*, Sept. 13, 2014, http://tinyurl.com/qgrzj97. The article includes a graphic attributed to Russell K. Wheeler, a senior fellow at the Brookings Institution; Wheeler confirmed in an interview that Republican appointees continue to hold majorities on the four circuit courts as shown in the graphic.

[2] White House: http://tinyurl.com/k8tdafd; Alliance for Justice: http://tinyurl.com/zw86khm.

on gay and lesbian service members, subject to a Defense Department review to be completed within six months.[31]

Middle Innings

With Republicans in a stronger position on Capitol Hill, Obama faced stalemates and roadblocks for the rest of his presidency even after winning re-election in 2012. With the House under GOP control, Obama scored few legislative victories and faced constant second-guessing

on foreign policy and national security. Political conditions in Afghanistan and Iraq continued to be unsettled even as the Syrian civil war and the rise of ISIS posed new and intractable difficulties for the United States and its allies.

Obama dropped the Bush administration's phrase "war on terror" as unnecessarily inflammatory, but he and his national security team achieved the single most dramatic victory in the conflict with al Qaeda on May 1,

Obama Presidential Library to Rise in Chicago

"It seems as though they're saying we want things to happen here."

Four years or so after President Obama leaves office, a monument to his presidency will open on the south side of Chicago, his adopted home town. The Obama Presidential Center will be sited in Jackson Park, an urban, lakefront greenspace that already houses Chicago's famed Museum of Science and Industry.

The center will join the 13 other presidential museums and libraries largely financed by private donations but administered by the National Archives and Records Administration. The museums, all celebratory in general tone, attract history-curious tourists and visitors, while the libraries serve as research repositories for presidential papers after they are organized, catalogued and released by archivists.[1]

Expected to cost at least $500 million, the complex will rise in a 500-acre park designed by the noted landscape designers Frederick Law Olmsted and Calvert Vaux and created for the 1893 World's Columbian Exposition. The Obamas picked Jackson Park despite some concerns from local preservationists and despite the hopes of the adjacent Woodlawn neighborhood that the center would be built in Washington Park and help revitalize that area.[2]

Back in 2009, when approached by the University of Chicago about housing his library, Obama "mused to a friend" about "an online library, not bricks-and-mortar," according to author Jonathan Alter in his book *The Promise: President Obama, Year One*. But Alter rightly predicted that the demand for "a splashy museum" would be too great to resist.[3] When Jackson Park was selected as the site for the center, Obama said he was "proud that the center will help spur development in an urban area."

The National Archives, an independent federal agency, gained responsibility for preserving presidential papers under a law passed in 1955 that followed President Franklin D. Roosevelt's precedent-setting decision to donate his papers for public use. In two post-Watergate enactments, Congress

2011, when Navy SEALS killed 9/11 mastermind Osama bin Laden in a compound near Pakistan's military academy in Abbottabad.[32] Obama announced the successful raid in a quickly arranged, late-night television appearance from the White House. The administration later released photos showing Obama and his key national security advisers, including Clinton, in the White House situation room awaiting word on the outcome of the mission.

Bin Laden's death produced a short-lived bump in Obama's approval ratings, but the president had already turned his principal attention to extricating United States troops from what had turned into difficult nation-building missions in Afghanistan and Iraq. In October, Obama announced that the last U.S. combat troops would leave Iraq by the end of the year. The move came despite continuing turmoil between the country's Shiite-dominated government and Sunni majority and was criticized by Republicans, including Obama's eventual 2012 opponent Mitt Romney.[33]

In Afghanistan, the surge of U.S. troops Obama approved in late 2009 was being credited with blunting the momentum of the Taliban insurgency, but Obama persevered with plans announced in June 2011 to draw down the U.S. troop commitment. In a televised address, Obama said the graduated reductions would culminate in a complete transfer of security operations to the Afghan government by 2014. The plan was formalized in an agreement signed by Obama and Afghan president Hamid Karzai on May 2, 2012.

By then U.S. attention had shifted to the bloody civil war that had broken out in Syria in March 2011. The rebellion against Assad's regime had been part of a wave of revolts dubbed the Arab Spring that eventually fell far short of the hopes engendered among democracy advocates in the region and beyond. With his advisers divided, Obama approved only limited U.S. aid to the rebels and rejected calls for a U.S.-imposed no-fly zone to keep Assad from bombing his own people.

passed a law in 1974 taking custody of President Richard M. Nixon's papers and four years later ruled that the papers of all subsequent presidents were public property.

The papers have provided researchers and journalists a treasure trove of materials once becoming public five years after a president leaves office. Anthony Clark, author of *The Last Campaign*, a critical study, says that over time the museums' roles in telling about and celebrating the presidents' careers have relegated the research and archive functions to a distant second place.

"The presidential libraries are not about getting the record out," he says. "They are about memorializing the past."

The newly renovated Nixon library in Yorba Linda, Calif., was originally administered by a private foundation and was forced to redo the Watergate exhibit after the National Archives took it over. Clark notes that the Bill Clinton library tells the story of his impeachment in an exhibit entitled "The Fight for Power." The Obama museum exhibits, he says, are likely to be "as celebratory, conflict-free and hagiographic as his predecessors.'"

The National Archives administers 13 libraries covering the terms of presidents from Herbert Hoover through George W. Bush. Two of them serve in part as bases for the active post-presidencies of Clinton and Jimmy Carter. The Clinton Foundation, headquartered in New York City with offices also at the Clinton Presidential Center in Little Rock, Ark., works on a variety of global issues. The Carter Center in Atlanta supports the former president's work in election monitoring and international mediation.

Clark expects the Obama Center will similarly be the base for an active public life for Obama after he leaves office. "It seems as though they're saying we want things to happen here, not just be launched here," Clark says. "They're looking to physically create an environment that would foster the kind of work they want to do in the post-presidency."

— *Kenneth Jost*

[1] For background, see Kenneth Jost, "Presidential Libraries," *CQ Researcher*, March 16, 2007, http://tinyurl.com/zx4v5lc.

[2] See Kathy Bergen, Patrick M. O'Connell and Katherine Skiba, "Obama library chief vows to grow Washington Park; Parks group won't contest winning Jackson Park site," *Chicago Tribune*, Aug. 4, 2016, http://tinyurl.com/jt2h7c5.

[3] Jonathan Alter, *The Promise: President Obama, Year One* (2010), p. 154.

In a press conference in August 2012, however, Obama stated that the United States would consider the use of chemical weapons by the Assad regime as a "red line." U.S. intelligence agencies confirmed Assad's use of chemical weapons in August 2013. Obama first asked Congress to approve the use of military force. But with public and political support lacking, Obama withdrew the request. The embarrassment was mitigated only somewhat in November by a U.S.-brokered deal with Russia's help for Assad to destroy the stockpile of chemical weapons.[34]

On the domestic front, Obama's signature achievement, the Affordable Care Act, was surviving managerial bungling, partisan attacks and legal challenges. The Supreme Court upheld the bulk of the law in June 2012 by a sharply divided 5-4 vote but allowed states, on a 7-2 vote, to opt out of the act's planned expansion of Medicaid coverage.

Many Republican-governed states did exactly that, reducing what the administration had hoped to achieve in expanding health insurance coverage. The administration's rollout of the new health care exchanges was marred by computer problems that further stoked political attacks. And the Supreme Court dealt the administration another setback in 2014 by allowing employers to claim religious objections to avoid covering contraceptives in their health benefit plans. But the court dealt opponents a more important setback in 2015, with a 6-3 decision largely upholding the financial structure of the law.[35]

Obama was having less success in budget politics. Despite his re-election, Republicans retained solid control in the House. Obama had set his sights since 2011 on negotiating some kind of "grand bargain" on taxes and spending with the Republican speaker of the House, Ohio's John Boehner. But Boehner proved unable to bring along the hard-line Tea Party conservatives in his party's caucus. The negotiations failed most dramatically in October 2013, when the government shut down all but essential operations for 16 days with no spending bill approved for the start of the fiscal year. An interim spending bill allowed the government to reopen until a full-year measure could be enacted in December.[36]

The impasse over spending reinforced Obama's growing resort to executive action to achieve his most contentious policy goals. Earlier in the year, Obama had responded to a December 2012 mass shooting at the Sandy Hook elementary school in Connecticut with a detailed package of gun control measures. He offered four major proposals on Jan. 16 for Congress to consider but also instituted some 23 executive actions aimed at strengthening background checks and bolstering mental health services.[37]

Even earlier, before his re-election, Obama had responded to Congress's inaction on immigration in mid-June by instituting a program, known as Deferred Action for Childhood Arrivals, to give renewable work permits and exemption from deportation to immigrants who had come to the United States illegally before the age of 13.[38]

With the public blaming Republicans more than Democrats for the government shutdown, Democrats approached the November 2014 midterm elections with hopes of defying the normal losses for the incumbent president's party. But Republicans made a modest gain of 13 seats in the House, and Democrats lost an historically high number of nine Senate seats, yielding the upper chamber to Republicans.

Boehner responded by promising "a new start" when the new Congress assembled, but on specifics he renewed the Republicans' previous calls to repeal Obamacare and threats to stall immigration reform if the president took any unilateral action.[39]

"Fourth-Quarter" Politics

Obama rebounded from the 2014 midterm elections with determination to keep pushing an ambitious policy and political agenda at home and abroad. "My presidency is entering the fourth quarter," the nation's No. 1 basketball fan told an end-of-year news conference on Dec. 19. "Interesting stuff happens in the fourth quarter."[40]

His fourth-quarter strategy came to encompass four major diplomatic initiatives, all sharply criticized by Republicans, and continued efforts in signature domestic policy areas, including health care and immigration.

The first of the foreign policy ventures had come just two days earlier when Obama made the surprise announcement on Dec. 17 that the United States would restore full relations with Cuba after more than 50 years of diplomatic isolation.[41] Cuban President Raul Castro, brother of the nation's ailing former longtime leader Fidel Castro, made a similar announcement the same day in Havana.

Republicans criticized the decision, which did not require congressional approval, and signaled they would block repeal of the legislatively imposed trade embargo. Many Americans took advantage of the new freedom to travel to the island nation, including Obama himself, who paid a well-received state visit in March.

Obama faced significantly stronger criticism after the United States and six other nations signed an agreement with Iran on July 14, along terms previously agreed to on April 2, aimed at blocking that nation from developing nuclear weapons. The accord lifted international financial sanctions against Iran.

Republicans warned that the agreement to permit international inspections was incomplete and allowed Iran an opening to resume its nuclear program down the road. Despite the criticism, Obama thwarted efforts by Republicans to require congressional approval.[42]

The administration completed another protracted negotiation in October, when 12 Pacific Rim nations signed a trade-expanding, tariff-lowering pact called the Trans-Pacific Partnership (TPP).[43] Obama depicted the accord, signed in Atlanta, as benefiting the U.S. economy and cementing relations with Asian and other Pacific Rim countries. It would also counter China's assertive use of its own economic and diplomatic influence, he said.

The completion of the trade deal came against the backdrop of growing concern about free trade from politicians in both parties and the general public. Many blamed free trade policies for the steep decline in manufacturing jobs that began in 2000, even though many economists saw technology and automation as more important factors. On Capitol Hill, McConnell, the Senate majority leader, said he would not bring the TPP up for a vote this year. On the campaign trail, both Trump and Clinton opposed the agreement as harmful to the U.S. economy but without citing specific provisions they object to.

With presidential politics in a crescendo, Secretary of State John Kerry joined representatives of 170 nations at the United Nations in New York City on April 22, 2016, to sign an agreement to curb greenhouse gas emissions in hopes of warding off further climate change.[44] With congressional approval required to implement the agreement, Republicans in their party platform vowed to reject the accord and Obama's separate action aimed at reducing greenhouse gas emissions from U.S. fossil fuel power plants. The Environmental Protection Agency's so-called Clean Power Plan had been stalled by the Supreme Court in February while awaiting a federal appeals court hearing on legal challenges brought by 27 states and an array of private utility companies.[45]

The diplomatic initiatives came to fruition as the administration was dealing, less successfully, with an array of other vexing challenges. Russia had effectively annexed Crimea in 2014, carving the strategic peninsula out of the former Soviet republic Ukraine, and continued to back pro-Russian separatists in their conflict with the pro-U.S. government in Kiev. China was pressing island maritime claims in the South China Sea even as the United States engaged in naval operations aimed at supporting allied countries' view of the sea as an international waterway. And the Islamic State continued to hold broad swaths of territory in Iraq and Syria although Obama claimed progress in containing its spread.

On the domestic front, Obama basked in the glow of two successive gay rights rulings by the Supreme Court, each significantly backed by the administration's top lawyer at the high court. The administration had joined with gay rights forces in 2013 in urging the justices to invalidate the so-called Defense of Marriage Act (DOMA), the 1996 law that barred federal marriage-based benefits to legally married same-sex couples.

A year later, Solicitor General Donald Verrilli again argued for the administration in urging the court to guarantee same-sex couples a constitutional right to marry nationwide. Obama, who had first backed same-sex marriage in 2012, hailed the June 2015 ruling; the White House was lit up in rainbow colors on the night of the decision.[46] In their 2016 platform, however, Republicans vowed to reverse the decision.

The administration fared less well in the courts on other domestic issues. Obama had announced a new immigration initiative in November 2014 to lift the

Getty Images/*The Miami Herald*/Al Diaz

In December 2015 President Obama opened the way for full restoration of relations with Cuba after more than 50 years of diplomatic isolation. Republicans criticized the decision and signaled they would block repeal of the Cuban trade embargo. Many Americans took advantage of the new freedom to travel to the island nation, including Miriam Turner, above. Obama himself paid a state visit in March 2016.

threat of deportation from immigrants who were parents of U.S. citizens or legal permanent residents. Texas led a coalition of 26 states in challenging the program, known as Deferred Action for Parents of Americans and Lawful Permanent Residents or DAPA, in federal court. A federal judge in Brownsville blocked the program nationwide, and his ruling was then upheld by the Fifth U.S. Circuit Court of Appeals.

The administration appealed to the Supreme Court and defended the program s in April 2016 before eight justices following the death of Justice Antonin Scalia. As the term ended, the court deadlocked 4-4 along liberal-conservative lines, leaving the injunction against the program in place.[47]

Obamacare was also at the Supreme Court again in a challenge brought by religious charities and schools over procedures for gaining an exemption from the mandate that company insurance policies cover the cost of contraceptives. The administration had won in six of the seven federal appeals court challenges. The justices skirted what appeared to be a 4-4 deadlock in the cases by unanimously sending them all back to the appellate courts in hopes that the government and religious groups would reach a compromise.[48]

Meanwhile, the administration's figures showed enrollment as of March of about 11.1 million people in the health insurance exchanges, numbers that were far short of projections and that threatened financial viability for participating insurers.

Obama was unreservedly upbeat, however, when he addressed the Democratic national convention on its penultimate night in late July. One by one, he ticked off the achievements of his administration: a recession ended; deficits down; unemployment down; health care a right for all; troops home from abroad; and diplomatic initiatives toward Cuba, Iran and climate change.

"By so many measures," Obama said in summarizing, "our country is stronger and more prosperous than it was when we started."[49]

CURRENT SITUATION
Legacy Eyed

With his time in the White House running out, President Obama continues to try to add to his legacy but with the same mix of successes and disappointments from the previous seven years.

Obama returned from what is likely to be his last major international summit in early September with a formal commitment from Chinese President Xi Jinping to support a global climate change agreement. A month after the Group 20 meeting in Hangzhou, China, Obama hailed the news that the pact was set to go into effect in another month because a sufficient number of countries had signed.

"This gives us the best possible shot to save the one planet we've got," Obama said in the Oct. 5 appearance in the White House Rose Garden.[50]

Separately, Obama left the summit with no apparent help from Russian President Vladimir Putin on securing a ceasefire in the Syrian civil war. Secretary of State Kerry later brokered a deal, but it collapsed. Kerry responded on Oct. 4 by angrily breaking off talks with Russia on the issue.[51]

The administration also suffered a setback of sorts when voters in Colombia rejected an agreement the United States had helped broker in the South American nation's protracted civil war. Voters in the Oct. 2 referendum apparently disapproved of the agreement's concessions to the Marxist Revolutionary Armed Forces of Colombia, known as FARC. The administration responded by dispatching a special envoy to join a meeting between the government and the rebels in an effort to salvage the truce.[52]

Meanwhile, U.S. troops deployed in Afghanistan, numbering fewer than 10,000, and the Taliban appeared to be gaining ground. In Iraq, U.S. and Iraqi forces were involved in a major assault to retake Mosul, the nation's second-largest city, from ISIS. The former commander of the U.S. operations against ISIS was voicing confidence in the fight based on the group's reported difficulty in recruiting new militants.

"Their backs are against the wall," Lt. Gen. Sean MacFarland told *The New York Times* in a telephone interview in early October.[53]

On domestic issues, Obama once again criticized the Republican-controlled Congress for failing to act on a range of issues, including his nomination of Judge Garland to the Supreme Court. "Every day that GOP Senate leaders block this nomination, they hamstring the entire third branch of government," Obama wrote in a signed op-ed in *The Huffington Post* on Oct. 4, the day after the court had begun a new term.[54] But Senate Republicans were showing no signs of relenting on their refusal to convene a hearing on the nomination.

Obama went on in the article to criticize congressional Republicans more broadly for refusing to approve job-creating investments on infrastructure, failing to move on tax reform and delaying "serious funding" to combat the opioid epidemic. "On countless priorities," Obama concluded, "Republicans in Washington have traded progress for partisanship."

Meanwhile, critics were depicting the president's health care reform program as failing, citing rising premiums and the withdrawal of some private health insurers from the insurance exchanges created under the law. Obama himself had conceded some "problems" with the law in an article written for a medical journal over the summer, but Republican opposition through the years had killed any chance for legislative fixes. The administration was moving in October to try to shore up the marketplaces by trying to boost enrollment and by increasing some payments to insurers.[55]

Other economic news was also inauspicious for the administration: Although employment increased during September, the unemployment rate rose one-tenth of

1 percent — to 5.0 percent — because of an increase in the number of people looking for work. Republicans had long cited the declining workforce participation rate as a sign that the jobs picture was less rosy than the administration depicted.

In early October, the International Monetary Fund (IMF) significantly lowered its prediction for the U.S. economy's growth over the next year to 1.6 percent, more than half a percentage point below the figure it had projected in July. An IMF official blamed what he called "sub-par" growth on lagging investment and isolationist sentiment in Europe and the United States. Republicans have blamed Obama.[56]

On other fronts, Obama was adding to the record number of commutations issued during his presidency by pardoning 98 nonviolent federal offenders on Oct. 27, bringing to 872 the total number of Obama commutations — more than the previous 15 presidents combined.[57]

Other Obama initiatives remained stalled in the courts, likely preventing any significant action while he is still in office. The federal appeals court for the District of Columbia heard arguments on the Clean Power Plan on Sept. 27 but gave no indication when the 10-judge panel would rule. The federal judge in Texas hearing the challenge to the "deferred action" immigration policy told lawyers in the case to agree by Nov. 11 on a schedule for further proceedings in the case.[58]

Policies Debated

Hillary Clinton and Donald Trump are clashing sharply over President Obama's domestic and foreign policies as the two major party nominees, burdened by personal unpopularity, wage an acrimonious contest to succeed him.[59]

Clinton is seeking to win the White House for a third consecutive Democratic term by generally promising to continue and improve Obama's domestic policies, including the Affordable Care Act, while distinguishing her position on some issues, such as the Trans-Pacific Partnership.

Trump is harshly criticizing Obama's policies across the board. He promises to repeal Obamacare, cut off illegal immigration, reverse Obama's climate change policies and strengthen the war against ISIS.

Clinton and Trump also clashed at length over the Affordable Care Act on Oct. 10, in the second of their

The effort by Navy SEALS to track and kill al Qaeda leader Osama bin Laden in Abbottabad, Pakistan, made for a tense vigil in the White House Situation Room during the successful operation on May 1, 2011. Officials joining President Obama included Vice President Joe Biden, then-Secretary of State Hillary Clinton and members of the president's national security team.

three televised debates. Clinton listed various benefits of the law, including expanded health care coverage. "I want very much to save what works," she said. But she acknowledged that premium costs, deductibles and copays were "too high" and promised steps to "get costs down," including "help to small businesses."[60]

In his turn, Trump bluntly called Obamacare "a disaster." The solution, he said, was "to repeal it and replace it with something absolutely much less expensive." He specifically mentioned eliminating "artificial lines" that limit insurers' abilities to offer policies in different states. But he made no mention of tax-sheltered health savings account, a step prominently listed on the campaign web site that would principally benefit middle- and high-income taxpayers.

On immigration, Trump promises to build "an impenetrable physical wall" on the U.S.-Mexico border and triple the number of immigration control agents. Clinton says she would focus resources on "individuals who pose a violent threat to public safety." Trump's website also says he would immediately terminate Obama's "two illegal executive amnesties." Clinton says she would "defend" the two deferred action policies — DACA for so-called "dreamers" and DAPA for parents of citizens or legal permanent residents — "against partisan attacks."

AT ISSUE

Has President Obama been successful in office?

YES

John Kenneth White
Professor of Politics, Catholic University

Written for *CQ Researcher*, October 2016

Obama's has been a consequential presidency. Of course, that's not saying much. James Buchanan also had a consequential presidency that ended with secession and the onset of civil war. Then again, there are the consequential presidencies of George Washington, Thomas Jefferson, Abraham Lincoln and Theodore Roosevelt that are immortalized on Mount Rushmore. While Barack Obama's visage is unlikely to be placed on Mount Rushmore, his presidency is consequential nonetheless.

Obama rescued an economy on the brink of disaster; instituted health care reform that eluded every prior president since Theodore Roosevelt; facilitated major social and cultural changes (especially in the area of gay rights); largely disentangled the United States from disastrous wars in Iraq and Afghanistan; and killed Osama bin Laden. He also extended diplomatic recognition to Cuba; successfully negotiated the Iran nuclear deal and a Trans-Pacific Partnership trade agreement and ordered restrictions of carbon emissions. Although each will require further action, they all are important beginnings.

This is nothing short of miraculous. When Obama assumed the presidency in January 2009, the United States lost nearly 600,000 jobs in that month alone. To fight the Great Recession, Obama needed congressional passage of a $787 billion stimulus package, a Dodd-Frank bank reform bill and a rescue package for the auto industry.

Obamacare occurred despite unanimous Republican opposition and challenges that survived Supreme Court review. Some 11 million Americans are enrolled in Obamacare, many receiving subsidies to purchase health insurance. Political scientist Paul Pierson writes, "On domestic issues, Obama is the most consequential and successful Democratic president since LBJ. It isn't close."

Of course, there are regrets. Syria is one. Failing to obtain comprehensive immigration reform is another. So, too, is Obama's inability to reform the nation's gun laws following numerous mass killings. And his failure to bridge a widening partisan divide belies his promise to restore the nation's motto, *E Pluribus Unum* — "Out of many, one" — to its full meaning.

But Obama's accomplishments outweigh the regrets. If voters knew in 2008 that the economy would recover; the dream of universal health care would edge closer to reality; the wars in Iraq and Afghanistan would taper off; Osama bin Laden would die; and Bill Clinton's "Don't Ask, Don't Tell" military policy would be repealed and gay marriage would become legal, they would be astonished. Barack Obama's presidency can be summed up in one word: consequential.

NO

John J. Pitney Jr.
Roy P. Crocker Professor of American Politics, Claremont McKenna College

Written for *CQ Researcher*, October 2016

During the 2008 presidential campaign, candidate Barack Obama invoked the themes of "hope" and "change," raising high expectations about what he could accomplish. As president, he fell short.

Consider economic growth, the heart of domestic policy. Between 1946 and 2008, real gross domestic product grew at an average yearly rate of 3.3 percent. Between 2009 and 2015, that figure was just 1.5 percent, or less than half. Supporters of the administration try to paint a brighter picture by highlighting a drop in the official unemployment rate. But a good part of that change happened because so many adults are outside of the workforce. Among developed nations, reports the president's own Council of Economic Advisers, the United States now has the third-lowest labor force participation rate for prime-age men.

Next to "hope" and "change," Obama's most famous promise involved his health care law. "If you like the plan you have, you can keep it," he pledged. "If you like the doctor you have, you can keep your doctor, too. The only change you'll see are falling costs as our reforms take hold." But by 2016, the law's online marketplaces were grappling with double-digit premium hikes, the collapse of nonprofit co-ops and the exit of major insurance companies. Meanwhile, health plans shrank provider networks and raised deductibles. Former Rep. Barney Frank (D-Mass.) said in 2014: Obama "should never have said as much as he did, that if you like your current health care plan, you can keep it. That wasn't true. And you shouldn't lie to people. And they just lied to people."

In 2009, Obama accepted the Nobel Peace Prize. The award was not for his accomplishments — he had served for only a few weeks — but instead reflected the hope that he would make a real difference for the cause of world peace. The data suggest otherwise. Between 2010 and 2015, fatalities in armed conflicts around the globe more than tripled, from 49,000 to 167,000. Obviously, the president was not to blame for all of this bloodshed, but in some places he bore at least some responsibility. *New York Times* columnist Nicholas Kristof writes that "allowing Syria's civil war and suffering to drag on unchallenged has been his worst mistake, casting a shadow over his legacy."

Proverbs 25:14 provides an epitaph for the Obama presidency: "Like clouds and wind without rain is one who boasts of gifts never given."

Regarding climate change, Clinton promises to support Obama's policies, including new fuel efficiency standards for cars, trucks and appliances and the Clean Power Plan. "I won't let anyone take us backward," she says on her website. Trump's website does not address climate change specifically but says he will "[r]escind all job-destroying Obama executive action," and "reduce and eliminate all barriers to responsible energy production," specifically mentioning "anti-coal" regulations.

Clinton and Trump are on opposite sides of Obama administration policies on a range of other issues. Clinton supports steps to stem "gun violence," while Trump says he will support Second Amendment rights and has criticized Obama for taking "baby steps" to eliminate the Second Amendment.[61] Asked during the second debate what kind of nominee she would propose for the Supreme Court, Clinton said she wanted the court to continue to support abortion rights and marriage equality for same-sex couples, in line with administration positions. Trump said he would appoint justices "very much in the mold" of Justice Antonin Scalia, who dissented consistently on abortion-rights decisions and in the marriage case.

On foreign policy, Trump blames the rise of ISIS on the decision that he attributes to Obama and Clinton to withdraw U.S. combat troops from Iraq. "That's why ISIS formed in the first place," he said in the Oct. 10 debate. Clinton answered only indirectly. "I hope by the time I am president that we will have pushed ISIS out of Iraq," she said.

Paradoxically, Clinton has taken a more hawkish position on the Syrian civil war than either Obama or Trump. In the debate, Clinton called the situation in Syria "catastrophic" and noted that as secretary of State she unsuccessfully advocated establishing a no-fly zone in rebel-controlled areas. In his turn, Trump rejected a position taken by his vice presidential running mate, Indiana Gov. Mike Pence, in favor of using military force against the Syrian regime. "He and I haven't spoken," Trump said, "and I disagree."

In another paradox, both Clinton and Trump oppose the Trans-Pacific Partnership trade agreement. "We have to renegotiate our trade deals," Trump said in the first of the presidential debates on Sept. 26. He went on to take credit for what he depicted as Clinton's changed stance in opposing the agreement. Clinton insisted she came out in opposition only after seeing the final agreement. "I was against it once it was finally negotiated and the terms were laid out," she said.[62]

In a contest already dominated by issues of temperament and character, policy issues receded even further when an audio tape surfaced on Oct. 7 of lewd comments that Trump made to the "Access Hollywood" host Billy Bush in 2005. Trump was heard on the tape boasting of grabbing women's genitals and of unsuccessfully attempting to force himself on a married woman.[63]*

Obama addressed the comments in a campaign-trail appearance the day after the Oct. 10 debate. "You don't have to be a husband or a father to have heard what we heard a few days ago and say, 'That's not right,'" Obama told a rally in Greensboro, N.C., on Oct. 11. "You just have to be a decent human being."[64]

OUTLOOK
The Partisan Divide

In the final months of his presidency, Obama remains surprised, disappointed and chagrined at the unbridled, gridlock-producing partisanship that he found in Washington and that he now expects will outlast his time in the White House.

In a candid interview with *New York* magazine writer Jonathan Chait, Obama recalls how the Republican opposition to the administration's fiscal stimulus in the first month of his presidency led to his realization that the GOP had decided on a strategy of opposition rather than cooperation.

"It established the dynamic for not just my presidency," Obama told Chait, "but for a much sharper party-line approach to managing both the House and the Senate that I think is going to have consequences for years to come."[65]

The scant support that Obama got for the fiscal stimulus from a handful of Republican senators and the total GOP boycott of the Affordable Care Act set the stage for

---

* In the succeeding two weeks, 11 women accused Trump of unwanted sexual conduct in various settings and at various times dating from the 1980s to as recently as 2013. Trump strongly denied all the accusations. Those accusations are beyond the scope of this report.

the rest of his presidency. "Obama received less support from Republicans than any other Democrat in modern times," according to Edwards, the Texas A&M professor, who has published data on presidential support for 40 years.

Rudalevige, the Bowdoin professor, agrees. "It became clear that the new Republican Congress just wasn't going to work with him," he says.

The partisan divide that Obama describes is not confined to Washington, but appears to be increasing among Americans nationwide, according to polling by the Pew Research Center in spring 2016. The survey of self-identified Democrats and Republicans, conducted in April and May, found majorities of partisans in each party holding "very unfavorable" views about the rival party for the first time since 1992.

Among Democrats, 55 percent of those surveyed said the Republican Party made them "afraid," 47 percent said it made them "angry" and 58 percent said it left them "frustrated." Among Republicans, 49 percent said the Democratic Party made them "afraid," 46 percent "angry" and 57 percent "frustrated." Percentages were higher in each category among partisans with "high engagement" in politics, such as people who make campaign contributions or volunteer in campaigns.[66]

Obama "has been one of the most polarizing presidents in the history of public opinion polls" along with George W. Bush, according to Schier, the Carleton political scientist. "What is distinctive is the bitterness of the opposition."

Edwards notes that the Republicans' opposition to Obama is based in part on misinformation. "Large percentages of Republicans think that unemployment hasn't come down," he says. "They think illegal immigrations are pouring across the border, and yet we've had net outmigration." They are "entirely wrong," he explains. "It's just crazy."

Margolis, the anti-Obama author and blogger, disputes the picture of a president completely thwarted by a Congress controlled by Republicans. "It is difficult to claim that Obama didn't get most of what he wanted, Margolis says.

On the eight-year balance sheet, Obama can list on the positive side the fiscal stimulus, Obamacare, two Supreme Court appointments and a generally free hand in Afghanistan, Iraq, Syria and elsewhere in foreign affairs despite frequent partisan second-guessing. Through executive actions and regulatory initiatives, he also has tightened fuel efficiency standards, expanded protections for workers and adopted rules to limit anti-LGBT discrimination. On the negative side are such steps as immigration reform, the Clean Power Plan, a third Supreme Court appointment and an array of legislative initiatives that were dead on arrival on Capitol Hill and dozens of pending judicial nominees.

In the interview, Obama recalled that some of his critics, including talk radio host Rush Limbaugh, cheered when the International Olympics Committee, in his first year as president, rejected the bid by his adopted home town of Chicago to host the 2016 summer Olympics. "It was really strange," Obama remarked.

As he leaves office, Obama worries that the partisan divide will continue for the foreseeable future, but he hopes that it will not. "If there's one wish that I have for future presidents, it's not an imperial presidency, it is a functional, sensible majority-and-opposition being able to make decisions based on facts and policy and compromise," he told Chait.

"That would have been my preference for the majority of my presidency," he continued. "It was an option that wasn't always available. But I hope the American people continue to understand that that's how the system should work."

NOTES

1. Obama defeated Republican John McCain in 2008 with 365 electoral votes to 173 for McCain; his popular vote margin was slightly over 9.5 million: 69,456,897 to 59,934,814. Obama defeated Republican Mitt Romney in 2012 with 332 electoral votes to 206 for Romney; his popular vote margin was approximately 4.9 million: 65,446,032 to 60,589,084. See "Historical Timeline: 270 to Win," http://tinyurl.com/nzfxfhh. For background on the start of Obama's time in office, see Kenneth Jost, "The Obama Presidency," *CQ Researcher*, Jan. 30, 2009, pp. 73-104.

2. For coverage, see Julie Hirschfeld Davis and Michael Davis, "Obama, at Convention, Lays Out Stakes for a Divided Nation," *The New York Times*, July 27, 2016, http://tinyurl.com/hhlyz54. "Full

text: President Obama's DNC speech," *Politico*, July 27, 2016, http://tinyurl.com/zx7xyz7. A video of the 44-minute address can be found here: www.youtube.com/watch?v=aip0BAWrdLw.

3. Andy Barr, "The GOP's no-compromise pledge," *Politico*, Oct. 28, 2010, http://tinyurl.com/zekepwx.

4. Maggie Haberman and Alan Rappeport, "Trump Drops False 'Birther' Claim but Offers New One: Clinton Started It," *The New York Times*, Sept. 16, 2016, http://tinyurl.com/hgoupsv.

5. See Ian Schwartz, "Obama: I Will Consider It An Insult To My Legacy If You Do Not Vote; Want to Give Me A Good Send Off? Go Vote," *Real Clear Politics*, Sept. 17, 2016, http://tinyurl.com/zovjjvt; talk show quoted in Aaron Blake, "Obama's sweet 'on the ballot' revenge," *The Fix*, *The Washington Post*, Sept. 28, 2016, http://tinyurl.com/jgk9k7g.

6. See "The 2016 Democratic Platform," https://www.democrats.org/party-platform; "Republican Platform 2016," https://www.gop.com/platform/.

7. Joseph R. Biden Jr., "Building for Success: Opportunities for the Next Administration," *Foreign Affairs*, September/October 2016, http://tinyurl.com/jb86q9c.

8. For background, see Reed Karaim, "Defeating the Islamic State," *CQ Researcher*, April 1, 2016, pp. 289-312.

9. For background, see Kenneth Jost, "Unrest in the Arab World," *CQ Researcher*, Feb. 1, 2013, pp. 105-132.

10. Quoted in Binyamin Appelbaum, "U.S. Household Income Grew 5.2 Percent in 2015, Breaking Pattern of Stagnation," *The New York Times*, Sept. 14, 2016, http://tinyurl.com/zzdvhgq. See also Jim Tankersley, "U.S. household incomes soared in 2015, recording biggest gain in decades," *The Washington Post*, Sept. 13, 2016, http://tinyurl.com/j3o42ep.

11. See Julie Hirschfeld Davis, "Obama Condemns Trump in Full-Throated Pitch for Clinton," *The New York Times*, Sept. 13, 2016, http://tinyurl.com/zwhq284.

12. Nelson D. Schwartz, "U.S. Economy Grew 2.9% in 3rd Quarter, Picking Up the Pace," *The New York Times*, Oct. 28, 2016, http://tinyurl.com/zgkxqud.

13. For background see Peter Katel, "The Federal Reserve," *CQ Researcher*, Jan. 3, 2014, pp. 1-24.

14. "U.S. Economic Confidence Index Lingers at -12," Gallup, Sept. 27, 2016, http://tinyurl.com/z9722wl.

15. Quoted in Philip Bump, "The unusual split in perceptions of race relations between Donald Trump and Barack Obama," *The Fix*, *The Washington Post*, July 12, 2016, http://tinyurl.com/js4kcsc.

16. Michael Eric Dyson, *The Black Presidency: Barack Obama and the Politics of Race in America* (2016), pp. x, 258.

17. Jackie Calmes and Helene Cooper, "A Personal Note as Obama Speaks on Death of Boy," *The New York Times*, March 23, 2012, http://tinyurl.com/hpftak7 (Trayvon Martin); Mark Landler and Michael D. Shear, "President Offers a Personal Take on Race in U.S.," *The New York Times*, July 19, 2013, http://tinyurl.com/l9wxgx2 (George Zimmerman acquittal); Julie Hirschfeld Davis, "Calling for Calm in Ferguson, Obama Cites Need for Improved Race Relations," *The New York Times*, Aug. 18, 2014, http://tinyurl.com/znuugcq (Michael Brown death); Monica Davey and Julie Bosman, "Protests Flare After Ferguson Police Officer Is Not Indicted," *The New York Times*, Nov. 24, 2014, http://tinyurl.com/oahkcjx (no indictment of Officer Darren Wilson).

18. Peter Baker and Helene Cooper, "President Tries to Defuse Debate Over Gates Arrest," *The New York Times*, July 25, 2009, http://tinyurl.com/j6d39w9.

19. Victor Davis Hanson, "The legacies of Barack Obama," *The St. Augustine* (Fla.) *Record*, Sept. 15, 2016, http://tinyurl.com/hogb6ju.

20. Krissah Thompson and Scott Clement, "Poll: Majority of Americans think race relations are getting worse," *The Washington Post*, July 16, 2016, http://tinyurl.com/jtt9fth.

21. Renee Stepler, "5 key takeaways about views of race and inequality in America," Pew Research Center, June 27, 2016, http://tinyurl.com/hnbahpk.

22. See Kevin Sack and Gardiner Harris, "President Obama Eulogizes Charleston Pastor as One Who Understood Grace," *The New York Times*, June 26, 2015, http://tinyurl.com/ppuj5ac.

23. Some background drawn from Chuck Todd, The Stranger: Barack Obama in the White House, 2014, and Michael I. Days, Obama's Legacy: What He Accomplished as President, 2016, . . .

24. For the text and video, see "President Barack Obama's Inaugural Address," The White House, Jan. 21, 2009, http://tinyurl.com/zsfv my8. For coverage, see Peter Baker, "Obama Takes Oath, and Nation in Crisis Embraces the Moment," *The New York Times*, Jan. 20, 2009, http://tinyurl.com/hw7e3d5; Michael D. Shear and Anne E. Kornblut, "A Historic Inauguration Draws Throngs to Mall," *The Washington Post*, Jan. 21, 2009, http://tinyurl.com/bzv9mt.

25. Scott Shane, "Obama Orders Secret Prisons and Detention Camps Closed," *The New York Times*, Jan. 22, 2009, http://tinyurl.com/hsk2yl2. For current population, see "The Guantanamo Docket," *The New York Times*, updated Oct. 20, 2016, http://tinyurl.com/6h8xka. For background, see Patrick Marshall, "Closing Guantanamo," *CQ Researcher*, Sept. 30, 2016, pp. 793-816.

26. For coverage of the bill signing, see Michael A. Fletcher, "Obama Leaves D.C. to Sign Stimulus Bill," *The Washington Post*, Feb. 18, 2009, http://tinyurl.com/cp362s. The House passed the bill on Jan. 28 by a vote of 244-188, the Senate on Feb. 10 by a vote of 61-37.

27. See Edmund L. Andrews and Eric Dash, "U.S. Expands Plan to Buy Banks' Troubled Assets," *The New York Times*, March 23, 2009, http://tinyurl.com/car786.

28. See David Espo, "Obama puts GM, Chrysler on short leash," The Associated Press, March 31, 2009, http://tinyurl.com/hkug44w.

29. The decision is *Citizens United v. Federal Election Commission* (Jan. 21, 2010). For an account, see Kenneth Jost, *Supreme Court Yearbook 2009-2010*. For general background, see Kenneth Jost, "Supreme Court Controversies," *CQ Researcher*, Sept. 28, 2012, pp. 813-840.

30. See William Branigin, "Obama reflects on 'shellacking' in midterm elections," *The Washington Post*, Nov. 3, 2010, http://tinyurl.com/mr8g2ql. Republicans increased their numbers in the House from 193 to 256; the Democrats' 53-47 majority in the Senate included two independents who caucused with the Democrats.

31. Sheryl Gay Stolberg, "Obama Signs Away 'Don't Ask, Don't Tell,' " *The New York Times*, Dec. 22, 2010, http://tinyurl.com/27rajpd.

32. Peter Baker, Helene Cooper, and Mark Mazzetti, "Bin Laden Is Dead, Obama Says," *The New York Times*, May 1, 2011, http://tinyurl.com/6d7p9o6. SEAL is the Navy's acronym for specially trained Sea, Air and Land teams.

33. Mark Landler, "U.S. Troops to Leave Iraq by Year's End," *The New York Times*, Oct. 21, 2011, http://tinyurl.com/3brltd7.

34. See Todd, *op. cit.*, pp. 432-449.

35. The Supreme Court decisions are *National Federation of Independent Business v. Sebelius*, June 28, 2012; *Burwell v. Hobby Lobby Stores*, June 30, 2014; *King v. Burwell*, June 25, 2015. For accounts, see respective editions of Jost, *Supreme Court Yearbook*.

36. See Jonathan Weisman and Jackie Calmes, "Two Parties Start Work to Avoid Repeat Crisis," *The New York Times*, Oct. 17, 2013, http://tinyurl.com/lzjjp7v.

37. See Peter Baker and Michael D. Shear, "Obama to 'Put Everything I've Got' Into Gun Control," *The New York Times*, Jan. 16, 2013, http://tinyurl.com/adxooln. For a complete list of actions, see "What's in Obama's Gun Control Proposal," *The New York Times*, Jan. 16, 2013, http://tinyurl.com/bqqql2v.

38. For background, see Christina L. Lyons, "Presidential Power," *CQ Researcher*, March 6, 2015, pp. 217-240.

39. See Ed O'Keefe and Sean Sullivan, "Top Republicans openly gloat about their midterm election wins," *The Washington Post*, Nov. 6, 2014, http://tinyurl.com/zpgnwnzl.

40. See Zeke Miller and Alex Altman, "Obama Looks to the '4th Quarter' of His Presidency," *Time*, Dec. 19, 2014, http://tinyurl.com/jubrnb2.

41. Peter Baker, "U.S. Will Restore Full Relations With Cuba, Erasing a Last Trace of Cold War Hostility," *The New York Times*, Dec. 17, 2014, http://tinyurl.com/olk6aky.

42. Michael R. Gordon and David E. Sanger, "Deal Reached on Iran Nuclear Program; Limits on Fuel Would Lessen With Time," *The New York Times*, July 14, 2015, http://tinyurl.com/o54nzl2.

43. David Nakamura, "Deal reached on Pacific Rim trade pact in boost to Obama economic agenda," *The Washington Post*, Oct. 5, 2015, http://tinyurl.com/qgg7g2m; Kevin Granville, "The Trans-Pacific Partnership Trade Accord Explained," *The New York Times*, Oct. 6, 2015, http://tinyurl.com/jmff39o.

44. Darryl Fears, "U.S. and 170 other nations sign historic climate agreement," *The Washington Post*, April 22, 2016, http://tinyurl.com/jf24vk2.

45. For background, see Jill U. Adams, "Air Pollution and Climate Change," *CQ Researcher*, Nov. 13, 2015, pp. 961-984.

46. The decisions are *United States v. Windsor* (June 26, 2013); *Obergefell v. Hodges* (June 26, 2015). For accounts, see respective editions of Jost, *Supreme Court Yearbook*.

47. The decision is *United States v. Texas* (June 23, 2016). See Jost, *Supreme Court Yearbook 2015-2016, op. cit.* The Court does not specify the votes of individual justices in 4-4 decisions, but observers uniformly assumed on the basis of oral arguments that the four conservatives voted to uphold the injunction against the administration policy, and the four liberals votes to reverse it.

48. The decision is *Zubik v. Burwell* (May 16, 2016). See *ibid.*

49. See "President Obama's speech at the Democratic convention," *The Washington Post*, July 28, 2016, http://tinyurl.com/zmoz26p. For coverage, see Jonathan Martin and Patrick Healy, "Championing Optimism, Obama Hails Clinton as His Political Heir," *The New York Times*, July 28, 2016, http://tinyurl.com/z7cxq8c.

50. See Nancy Benac, "Obama hails climate change deal as potential turning point," The Associated Press, Oct. 5, 2016, http://tinyurl.com/z2md66o; Mark Landler and Jane Perlez, 'Rare Harmony as China and U.S. Commit to Climate Deal," *The New York Times*, Sept. 3, 2016, http://tinyurl.com/hl3a789.

51. Rod Nordland, "John Kerry Criticizes Russia, Saying It 'Turned a Blind Eye' on Syria," *The New York Times*, Oct. 4, 2016, http://tinyurl.com/zoavorl; Mark Landler, " 'Gaps of Trust' With Russia Bar New Effort to Broker Syrian Cease-Fire, Obama Says," *The New York Times*, Sept. 5, 2016, http://tinyurl.com/zrchl66.

52. Karen DeYoung, "U.S. envoy to Colombia's peace process to join talks on salvaging agreement," *The Washington Post*, Oct. 5, 2016, http://tinyurl.com/jkvetaw.

53. See "Voices From a Worsening Afghan War," *The New York Times*, Oct. 7, 2016, http://tinyurl.com/hdayoga; MacFarland is quoted in Helene Cooper, Eric Schmitt, and Michael R. Gordon, "U.S. Set to Open a Climactic Battle Against ISIS in Mosul, Iraq," *The New York Times*, Oct. 7, 2016, http://tinyurl.com/jrl3kje.

54. Barack Obama, "Republican Obstruction Is Undermining Supreme Court, Enough Is Enough," *The Huffington Post*, Oct. 4, 2016, http://tinyurl.com/zuqv6dv.

55. See Robert Pear, "Ailing Obama Health Care Act May Have to Change to Survive," *The New York Times*, Oct. 2, 2016, http://tinyurl.com/h7hmryx.

56. See Ylan Q. Mui, "International Monetary Fund slashes prospect for U.S. growth," *The Washington Post*, Oct. 4, 2016, http://tinyurl.com/js2v7dn.

57. Gregory Korte, "Obama grants 98 more commutations, setting single-year clemency record," *USA Today*, Oct. 27, 2016, http://tinyurl.com/jyhm6m4.

58. Anne E. Marimow and Brady Dennis, "Appeals court considers Obama's Climate Change Plan," *The Washington Post*, Sept. 29, 2016, http://tinyurl.com/jlaq7db; judge's order tweeted by Josh Blackman, associate professor, Houston Law School (@joshblackman: http://tinyurl.com/zo3zyn4), Oct. 6, 2016.

59. Policy positions drawn in part from campaign web sites: Hillary Clinton 2016: www.hillaryclinton.com; Make America Great Again: www.donaldjtrump.com.

60. For a transcript of the second presidential debate, as prepared by CQ Transcriptswire, see http://tinyurl.com/zdq6n5x.

61. Quoted in Mark Hensch, "Trump: Obama taking 'baby steps' to eliminate Second Amendment," *Ballot Box* blog, *The Hill*, Jan. 4, 2016, http://tinyurl.com/huprgcs.

62. See Aaron Blake, "The first Trump-Clinton presidential debate transcript, annotated," *The Washington Post*, Sept. 26, 2016, http://tinyurl.com/zlxdw34.

63. David A. Fahrenthold, "Trump recorded having extremely lewd conversation with women in 2005," *The Washington Post*, Oct. 8, 2016, http://tinyurl.com/jok7bph. Fahrenthold's scoop resulted in massive coverage and commentary in print, broadcast and social media. The comments were the topic of the first line of questions in the second presidential debate.

64. Julie Hirschfeld Davis, "Obama, in North Carolina, Lashes Trump as He Urges Blacks to Back Clinton," *The New York Times*, Oct. 11, 2016, http://tinyurl.com/jn72sqz.

65. See Jonathan Chait, "Five Days That Shaped a Presidency," *New York*, Oct. 2, 2016, http://tinyurl.com/zjjgxul.

66. "Partisanship and Political Animosity in 2016," Pew Research Center, June 22, 2016, p. 51, http://tinyurl.com/zcwlezw.

BIBLIOGRAPHY

Selected Sources

Books

Chait, Jonathan, *Audacity: How Barack Obama Defied His Critics and Transformed America*, **HarperCollins, forthcoming January 2017.**
The liberal politics columnist for *New York* magazine argues in a compact overview that Obama has had a successful presidency despite some foreign policy failures, disappointment among some supporters and staunch opposition from Republicans in Congress.

Days, Michael I., *Obama's Legacy: What He Accomplished as President*, **Center Street, 2016.**
The editor of the *Philadelphia Daily News* admiringly details Obama's accomplishments as president subject by subject. Includes chronology, detailed notes.

Dyson, Michael Eric, *The Black Presidency: Barack Obama and the Politics of Race in America*, **Houghton Mifflin Harcourt, 2016.**
The Georgetown University sociology professor and one-time Obama campaign surrogate finds that Obama has brought new light to racial issues in the United States while diminishing the role of traditional black power-brokers. Includes detailed notes and list of 50 statements and speeches by Obama on racial issues.

Margolis, Matt, and Mark Noonan, *The Worst President in History: The Legacy of Barack Obama*, **Victory Books, 2016.**
Two political bloggers present what they call 200 reasons why Obama is the "worst president" in U.S. history, compiled in 10 separate chapters on such areas as the economy, Obamacare, foreign policy, civil liberties and radical Islam, among others. Includes 60 pages of sources.

Savage, Charlie, *Power Wars: Inside Obama's Post-9/11 Presidency*, **Little, Brown, 2015.**
The Pulitzer Prize-winning *New York Times* correspondent comprehensively examines how the Obama administration dealt with the legal issues posed in post-9/11 counterterrorism and national security policies. Includes detailed notes.

Schier, Steven E. (ed.), *Debating the Obama Presidency*, **Rowan & Littlefield, 2016.**
Ten essays by contributors representing a range of views and backgrounds provide differing perspectives on Obama's record in foreign policy, economic policy and governance. Schier is a professor of political science at Carleton College. Each essay includes sources.

Todd, Chuck, *The Stranger: Barack Obama in the White House*, **Little, Brown, 2014.**
The former chief White House correspondent for NBC News, now political director and moderator of "Meet the Press," provides a widely praised journalistic account of Obama's presidency through his first six years in office. Includes illustrations, notes.

Articles

Appelbaum, Binyamin, and Michael D. Shear, "Once Skeptical of Executive Power, Obama Has Come to Embrace It," *The New York Times*, **Aug. 4, 2016, http://tinyurl.com/jfpb8ja.**

Reporters describe Obama as "one of the most prolific authors of major regulations in presidential history."

Biden, Joseph R. Jr., "Building for Success: Opportunities for the Next Administration," *Foreign Affairs*, **September/October 2016, http://tinyurl .com/jb86q9c.**
The vice president argues that the United States is "stronger and more secure" than when President Obama took office and describes Obama's foreign policies in the context of challenges for the next administration.

Chait, Jonathan, "Five Days That Shaped a Presidency," *New York*, **Oct. 2, 2016, http://tinyurl.com/zjjgxul.**
President Obama reflects in a lengthy and candid interview with the writer and commentator for *New York* magazine on five critical events in his presidency, including the passage of the fiscal stimulus in 2009 and the Affordable Care Act in 2010. The issue includes an illustrated eight-year timeline of events in Obama's presidency.

Goldberg, Jeffrey, "The Obama Doctrine," *The Atlantic*, **April 2016, http://tinyurl.com/zfzlg5g.**
Goldberg, recently elevated to editor in chief of *The Atlantic*, critically describes President Obama as "feckless" and depicts him as a supporter of "foreign policy realism" and skeptic of "liberal interventionist" policies.

Sorkin, Andrew Ross, "President Obama Weighs His Economic Legacy," *The New York Times Magazine*, **April 28, 2016, http://tinyurl.com/heg5jvn.**
The Times's financial columnist describes Obama's economic policies and quotes the president as taking credit for a successful recovery but blaming shortcomings on lack of "political capital."

Obamacare

For sharply contrasting perspectives on the Affordable Care Act, see **Josh Blackman**, *Unprecedented: The Constitutional Challenge to Obamacare*, **Public Affairs**, **2013**, and **Ezekiel J. Emmanuel**, *Reinventing American Health Care: How the Affordable Care Act Will Improve our Terribly Complex, Blatantly Unjust, Outrageously Expensive, Grossly Inefficient, Error Prone System*, **Public Affairs**, **2014**. Blackman is an associate professor at South Texas College of Law; Emmanuel is a physician and a senior fellow at the Center for American Progress.

For More Information

Alliance for Justice, 11 Dupont Circle, N.W., Washington, DC 20036; 202-822-6070; www.afj.org. A liberal advocacy group that works to ensure the federal judiciary advances core constitutional values and adheres to the even-handed administration of justice.

American Enterprise Institute, 1789 Massachusetts Ave., N.W., Washington, DC 20036; 202-862-5800; www.aei .org. Nonpartisan, nonprofit think tank, partly funded by business interests, that advances ideas rooted in a belief in democracy, free enterprise and American strength and global leadership.

Cato Institute, 1000 Massachusetts Ave., N.W., Washington, DC 20001; 202-842-0200; www.cato.org. Public policy research organization dedicated to individual liberty, limited government and free markets that has played a prominent role in the debate over the Affordable Care Act.

Center for American Progress, 1333 H St., N.W., Washington, DC 20005; 202-682-1611; www.americanprogress.org. Liberal organization that says it promotes a strong, just and free America.

Center on Budget and Policy Priorities, 820 1st St., N.E., Suite 510, Washington, DC 20002; 202-408-1080; www .cbpp.org. Nonpartisan think tank that promotes policies to reduce poverty and inequality and to restore fiscal responsibility that has played an important role in the debate over the Affordable Care Act.

(Continued)

(Continued)

Economic Policy Institute, 1225 I St., N.W., Suite 600, Washington, DC 20005; 202-775-8810; www .epi.org. Nonprofit, nonpartisan think tank, partly funded by labor organizations, that addresses the needs of low- and middle-income workers in economic policy discussions.

FreedomWorks, 400 North Capitol St., N.W., Suite 765, Washington, DC 20001; 202-783-3870; www.freedomworks .org. Conservative organization, formerly Citizens for a Sound Economy, that advocates on legal issues and judicial appointments as part of promoting free enterprise and limited government.

Heritage Foundation, 214 Massachusetts Ave., N.E., Washington, DC 20002; 202-546-4400; www.heritage.org. Seeks to promote conservative policies based on free enterprise, limited government and a strong national defense.

Here are the national committees for the two major political parties:

Democratic National Committee, 430 South Capitol St., S.E., Washington, DC 20003; 202-863-8000; www .democrats.org.

Republican National Committee, 310 1st St., S.E., Washington, DC 20003; 202-863-8500; www.gop.com/

8

Privacy and the Internet

Sarah Glazer

Max Schrems, a 28-year-old Austrian law student, argued in the European Union's highest court that Facebook should not be allowed to transfer his and other European users' data to its American servers because the information would be subject to U.S. government spying. In October 2015, the court agreed, declaring an international agreement on data transfer invalid on the grounds that the United States does not sufficiently protect citizens' personal information.

From *CQ Researcher*,
December 4, 2015

In 2010, Spanish lawyer Mario Costeja González was disturbed to find that when he Googled his name, a 12-year-old newspaper item appeared at the top of the search results announcing that his house was for sale to pay his unpaid taxes. The debt had been settled long ago. When Costeja González asked Google to eliminate the links from the search engine's Spanish domain, the company refused.

He took Google to court, arguing that, under a European legal principle known as "the right to be forgotten," he could demand the removal of data that besmirched his reputation. Last year, the European Union's (EU) highest court agreed.

The Court of Justice in May 2014 upheld an order from the Spanish data-protection agency saying that Google must eliminate the links. The court went on to say that for individuals in the EU, the rights to privacy and to control of their personal data "override" the public's interest in finding out the information by searching a name.[1]

The ruling has had far-reaching consequences and is at the heart of a growing debate spanning multiple countries about how much of an individual's personal information should remain private — and for how long. The debate pits bedrock free-speech protections against privacy rights and increasingly is being played out in the courts and across federal and state governments trying to determine how Google and other technology companies should operate.

Many legal experts say a European-style right to be forgotten will never take hold in the United States because it would violate

France Leads in Link-Removal Requests

Google has removed 42 percent of links that European Union Internet users have asked to be deleted from the company's search results (top). Google began accepting such requests in May 2014, after the EU's highest court ruled that Internet users have the right to ask search engines to remove links with personal information about them under certain conditions. More than 175,000 removal requests have originated in France, Germany and the United Kingdom, with most coming from France (middle). Links from Facebook were the most removed (bottom).

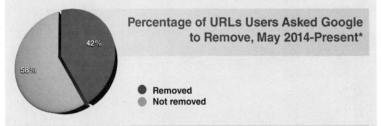

Percentage of URLs Users Asked Google to Remove, May 2014-Present*

- Removed
- Not removed

Number of Removal Requests, by Country, May 2014-Present

Most-Removed Websites, by Number of Link Removals, May 2014-Present

* Excludes removal requests Google is still reviewing.

Source: "European privacy requests for search removals," Google, updated Nov. 24, 2015, http://tinyurl.com/ptypu56

the Constitution's free-speech protections. But in a digitally linked world, it is drawing increasing attention in this country. Some U.S. privacy advocates who favor the idea claim public sentiment is with them: 69 percent of Americans who use the Internet think they should have the right to delete personal information online, according to a recent poll by the market-research firm Ipsos.[2]

"If we are to have an Internet that protects the freedom of its users, we must place fundamental rights of users before the commercial interests of companies," wrote Marc Rotenberg, president of the Electronic Privacy Information Center, a nonprofit research group in Washington.[3]

Under the EU court decision, Google, and all other search engines doing business in Europe, must remove links from an Internet user's name search upon request if the information is "inadequate," "irrelevant," "excessive" or out of date. Google said it had received requests to remove more than 1 million links and deleted 42 percent of them. Most requests originated in France, and Facebook was the most affected website.[4]

Google did not respond to a request for comment on this story.

Journalists and civil libertarians both here and in Europe have criticized the EU court decision as an infringement of free speech. Search engines "must censor their own references to publicly available information in the name of privacy, with little guidance or obligation to balance the needs of free expression," said Danny O'Brien, international director of the Electronic Frontier

Foundation, a San Francisco-based nonprofit defending digital civil liberties.[5]

Defenders of the ruling say the court defended freedom of expression when it affirmed that the Spanish newspaper in question, *La Vanguardia*, was not obliged to erase the original announcement of the house sale from its archives, as Costeja González had originally requested. The court also said search engines should not remove links if the general public has a clear public interest in retaining access to the information, such as when public figures request removal of information about themselves that would inherently be of public concern.

Further heating up the issue, France's data-protection regulatory agency (CNIL) this past June interpreted the Google Spain ruling as applying to all country domains in Europe and to Google's global network. The agency ordered Google to eliminate requested links not only on its French search page but also on its Google.com search engine which the company considers its American site.[6] Most Europeans using Google access search results through their country's Google domain, such as Google.fr in France. But one click on that Google page can instantly bring up Google.com.

Google has complied with delisting requests on its European domains but has refused to extend this service to Google.com. If implemented, the CNIL order also would limit search results that American Internet users could view on Google.com, potentially forcing the company to violate the U.S. Constitution's free-speech guarantees.

The French agency's order "creates an ominous new precedent for Internet censorship that jeopardizes speech

Most in U.S. Back "Right to Be Forgotten"

Nearly seven in 10 American adults who use the Internet say the freedom to remove links containing certain personal data from search engine results should be a human right.

Percentage of American Adults Who Say the Right to be Forgotten . . .

69% — Should be a human right
29% — Allows for censorship
16% — Is impractical

Source: "Majority of Americans Think It Should Be a Human Right to Be Able to Delete or Remove Personal Information Online," press release, TRUSTe and Ipsos, Aug. 26, 2015, http://tinyurl.com/nvejtt8

and press freedoms worldwide," the Washington, D.C.-based Reporters Committee for Freedom of the Press wrote in a Sept. 14 letter to CNIL signed by 29 other major news organizations including *The New York Times* and Reuters.[7]

It's unclear how this standoff with French regulators will be resolved. Many legal experts believe the order violates First Amendment free-expression rights as well as principles of territorial sovereignty. Moreover, the conflict is likely to heat up even more when the EU unveils sweeping new legislation, currently being drafted, establishing new rights for Internet users to erase content about themselves.

For American consumers, the differences are stark in terms of how the United States and Europe approach the issue. After false claims popped up in the Google search for New York City hedge-fund manager Jeffrey Ervine in 2009, it took a $2 million court judgment to persuade Google to remove the links. Costeja González, in contrast, got a negative link removed even though the information was true.

In America, it's much harder to get information removed if it is accurate, as Californian Christos Catsouras discovered when he tried to remove gory photos of a fatal car crash in which his daughter Nikki, 18, was decapitated. The photos showed up on thousands of websites after California Highway Patrol employees emailed them to family and friends. The family asked that the photos be removed, and many websites did, but the photos remain easy to find on Google. With no right to be forgotten in American law, the family had no way to force Google to remove the photos.[8]

Consumer Watchdog, a consumer advocacy group based in Santa Monica, Calif., filed a complaint with the

Executive Wages a Painful Fight to Erase a Slur

"Everything I'd worked for, my reputation, was destroyed."

The seeds of Jeffrey Ervine's digital nightmare go back to 2005, when the New York hedge fund manager was asked to manage the family fortune of a 21-year-old Turkish college student who claimed to be running another hedge fund.

"Something didn't smell right," Ervine says. So he did a deep background check and discovered evidence of a Ponzi scheme, which he turned over to the FBI.* He never managed the student's money, he says.

Later that year, the student, Hakan Yalincak, was arrested on charges of bilking investors out of more than $7 million for a fake hedge fund and passing $45 million in bad checks. He pleaded guilty to bank and wire fraud in 2006 and spent nearly three years in federal prison before being deported to Turkey in 2009.[1]

That should have been the end of the story. But around that same time, Ervine suddenly discovered a mysterious headline, "Con v. Con," appearing at the top of his search page when he Googled himself. It linked to Yalincak's website, which claimed Ervine had sought to "con" the young man and implied that Ervine had committed fraud. It also claimed Ervine's financial situation had deteriorated badly and that he could not manage money.[2]

Each time Ervine met with prospective investors, he was forced to spend the first 15 minutes explaining the accusatory search result, he says. "But it didn't matter because people weren't going to take any career risk by investing with you," he says, especially at a time when the headlines

were filled with news about New York investor Bernard Madoff, who had defrauded thousands of investors out of billions of dollars with a giant Ponzi scheme.[3]

"I felt hopeless at 42," Ervine says. "What could I do? Everything I'd worked for, my reputation, which was now primarily digital, was destroyed."

Ervine asked Google to take down the search result. But Google responded that it would eliminate the link only if it had been the subject of a court order determining the content to be defamatory or unlawful — part of its standard policy, according to Charles Lee Mudd Jr., a Chicago lawyer specializing in Internet law, who represented Ervine.

It took Ervine three years to track down the operators of Yalincak's website and thousands of dollars in legal fees to sue them for defamation over the course of 13 months, he says. He finally won a $2 million judgment in 2012 in federal court in Chicago against the operators, whom the court found responsible for publishing "false and defamatory" accusations.[4]

The court ordered the operators to take down the Web page and request that Google, Bing, Yahoo! "and all other search engines" remove the page from their search and cached results.[5] "The most important part was getting the search engines to pull it," since most people wouldn't have found an obscure website like Yalincak's otherwise, says Mudd.

Under American law, search engines are legally protected from lawsuits for hosting content created by someone else. Seeking to allow young Internet services to flourish, Congress in 1996 added Section 230 to the Communications Decency Act, providing search engines and other intermediaries, such as Facebook, immunity from civil suits for hosting bloggers' or others' information.[6]

---

* A Ponzi scheme is a fraudulent investment operation that pays quick returns to initial investors using money from subsequent investors rather than from profit. Named for Charles Ponzi, who perpetrated such a scheme in the United States (1919-1920).

Federal Trade Commission (FTC) arguing that Google's failure to extend its European delisting right to U.S. consumers is an "unfair and deceptive" practice.[9]

Before the Internet existed, embarrassing acts, such as being photographed drunk at a party, could be forgotten over time unless one searched through old newspaper

clippings or photo albums, observes John M. Simpson, Consumer Watchdog's Privacy Project director. "This right to be forgotten would restore that natural privacy-by-obscurity," he says, noting that today such records are likely to come up every time a prospective employer searches for someone's name.

Ervine's court order doesn't compel the search engines to remove the links — but it "strongly encourages" them to do so.[7]

That's a sharp contrast from European law, which requires search engines to remove someone's search results upon request unless the information is in the public interest or meets some other legal exception.

If a similar right had existed in the United States, Ervine says, it would have saved him years of time, money and personal stress when his name, and by extension his family's, was defamed.

During those difficult years, Ervine started reading about other cases of cyberbullying, particularly those targeting children and teens. He says he was shocked to learn of cases where children were driven to cutting themselves in despair or to suicide.

Like Ervine, parents of a child who is being harassed must track down the Internet service provider where the material originates and be prepared to sue to get the material taken down.

That takes time and money. "If you're rich, you get it done faster than if you're poor," Ervine says. That's an inequity he says he would like to fix.

Ervine went on to found a for-profit company, Bridg-it, aimed at helping schools, parents and children fight bullying, including persecution online. His program is now being used in 10 New York City public schools.[8] For children, bullying often starts off face-to-face. But, as Ervine says he learned from his own painful experience, "The Internet is the largest megaphone of prejudice in the world."

— *Sarah Glazer*

Courtesy of Jeffrey Ervine

New York City hedge fund manager Jeffrey Ervine needed a $2 million court judgment to persuade Google to remove false and defamatory links about him that popped up in a Google search on his name.

---

[1] Alison Leigh Cowan, "An Inmate and a Scholar," *The New York Times*, Feb. 7, 2014, http://tinyurl.com/ok47ac9. Also See, Lisa W. Foderaro, "Former NYU Student Pleads Guilty to Fraud," *The New York Times*, June 7, 2006, http://tiny url.com/pja78wk.

[2] United States District Court, Northern District of Illinois Eastern Division, *Jeffrey Ervine v. S. B. et al.*, Findings of Fact, Conclusions of Law, Default Judgment and Permanent Injunction, March 9, 2012.

[3] "Bernard Madoff Fast Facts," CNN, April 24, 2015, http://tinyurl.com/nlbemdh.

[4] United States District Court, *op. cit.*

[5] *Ibid.*

[6] "Section 230 of the Communications Decency Act," Electronic Frontier Foundation, http://tinyurl.com/ka6gkjj, and "CDA 230 Legislative History," http://tinyurl.com/o2y8nvx, both undated.

[7] United States District Court, *op. cit.*

[8] See "Building a Bridge to Better Behavior," Bridg-it, undated, www.bridgit.com.

Unlike Europe, the United States does not have an explicit constitutional right to privacy. So, the Constitution's right to freedom of expression probably would trump privacy rights in a court challenge, many legal experts say. Laws in selected areas of American life parallel the right to be forgotten, but they tend to involve personal data — such as an individual's credit information.

Constitutionally, the press "has a nearly absolute right to publish accurate, lawful information," *New Yorker* legal writer Jeffrey Toobin has noted.[10] And, says Paul Alan Levy, an attorney with the legal arm of the consumer advocacy group Public Citizen, "Our system gives much greater countervailing weight to the right to speak about other people."

In California, a new Internet "eraser button" law gives children under 18 the right to request removal of information they have posted about themselves, such as an embarrassing social media post, but it does not affect what others write about them. Similar measures have been introduced in other states and in Congress to extend to children the right to delete their online personal information.[11]

It's unclear how the clash of free speech vs. privacy values will be resolved between Europe and the United States. The most likely compromise, some experts predict, will be technological: Under pressure from French regulators, Google could block French users from seeing the search results on Google.com. That, some critics say, would mean a "balkanized" Internet — a far cry from the original vision of a World Wide Web in which information would be "free" and available to everyone on the planet. Already, civil liberties groups have expressed alarm at governments — including Russia and Brazil — that have cited the European right to be forgotten in considering legislation that could further censor the press.[12]

As consumers, regulators and tech companies weigh the implications of the European decisions, here are some of the questions being debated:

Does the "right to be forgotten" violate free-speech principles?

Journalists and free-speech advocates in the United States and Europe say the EU court's ruling allowing the removal of personal data suppresses free expression.

By limiting a search engine's ability to select the most vital news stories and blog postings out of billions of websites and bring them to public attention, the European court "has straitjacketed the librarian," declared Peter Noorlander, CEO of the London-based Media Legal Defense Initiative, which helps journalists and bloggers worldwide defend their rights.[13]

However, defenders of the ruling have disputed the idea that Google's search function acts like a neutral "library" or a "card catalogue," as Google has maintained.[14] Although Google's algorithm for its search results is a trade secret, EU antitrust investigators have accused the company of giving preference to its own

products in shopping search results.[15] And Google already removes millions of links a year after being told they violate copyrights, notes Paul Bernal, a lecturer in information technology, intellectual property and media law at England's University of East Anglia Law School.

"This is not about free speech; it's about privacy and dignity," Michael Fertik, the founder of Reputation.com, a Redwood City, Calif., company that helps people improve their search results, told *The New Yorker*. "If Sony or Disney wants 50,000 videos removed from YouTube, Google removes them with no questions asked. If your daughter is caught kissing someone on a cell-phone home video, you have no option of getting it down. That's wrong. The priorities are backward."[16]

Much of the debate reflects the different values Europeans and Americans have historically placed on freedom of expression versus privacy. In Europe, the right to privacy is considered a fundamental right and "is co-equal with your right to freedom of expression," notes First Amendment lawyer Marc Randazza, who practices in Las Vegas. By contrast, the European Convention requires freedom of expression to be balanced against "the reputation or rights of others."[17]

To Europeans, says Bernal, "Privacy underpins freedom of speech. If you know that the stuff you do on the Internet will come back to bite you, you'll feel less free to act on the Internet. If you know that every move is watched by the government, you will be less likely to act freely on the Internet."

In the Costeja González ruling, the court said search engines, in deciding whether to grant a delisting request, should consider the public's right to know the information, especially if the person involved was a public figure, such as a politician.

But some critics say the court emphasized an individual's right to privacy as the overriding right.[18] The court "did not undertake any kind of balancing between privacy and data protection on the one hand, and freedom of expression and access to information on the other," the Reporters Committee for Freedom of the Press said.[19]

In contrast, in the United States, the First Amendment guarantee of freedom of speech generally trumps privacy rights, many legal experts agree.[20] If challenged in an American court, "It's hard to see how the Google Spain ruling could possibly proceed in the United States given the First Amendment," says Public Citizen attorney Levy.

But Randazza sees the Google Spain ruling as protecting free speech. "The EU says the original article about Costeja González is sacred and you can't get rid of it," he says. "But the links can and should be removed from search results, because he was in a foreclosure 16 years ago, and there's more to him than that."

Ironically, Costeja González and his past debts have become more famous than ever as a result of the publicity surrounding the court's ruling. Links to news stories and blogs about the case now show up at the top of his search results.

Costeja González recently asked Spanish regulatory authorities to remove a link to negative comments about his case that show up in his name search. The Spanish Data Protection Authority refused, saying the Google Spain ruling creates a "preponderant interest of the public" in the now-famous case.[21]

That decision demonstrates that European regulators are protecting the right of free expression and the public's right to know, once someone such as Costeja González becomes a public figure, argues Randazza.

Following the Google Spain court ruling, Google released examples of requests it had received that troubled free-speech advocates — ranging from removing mentions of past criminal activities to a pianist's bad reviews to a past scandal involving a sports referee. Some links were later reinstated after reporting on the deletions by the British newspaper *The Guardian* caused a furor.[22]

However, *The Guardian* later found that fewer than 5 percent of removal requests involved public figures, politicians or convicted criminals, and Google was far less likely to grant requests involving politicians, public figures or serious crimes. Of the 218,000 requests Google had received up to March 2015, the paper reported, more than 95 percent were made by individuals who were not famous but wanted their private data removed, and almost half of those requests were granted.[23]

Nevertheless, critics and journalists say the system established by the European court neglects any kind of role for reporters or their publishers to protest the removal of links to their work. Journalists, if informed, can try to influence a search engine's removal decision, but they don't have a recognized role in the decision-making process.

That is likely to be a continuing problem under new EU-wide data-protection legislation expected to be

Google chairman Eric Schmidt, left, and chief legal officer David Drummond visited Spain and other European countries last year to discuss Web privacy issues after a landmark ruling by the European Union's Court of Justice. The court upheld an order from Spain's data-protection agency saying that Google must eliminate personal Web links that sullied the reputation of Spanish lawyer Mario Costeja González.

approved later this year or early next year, says Daphne Keller, director of intermediary liability at Stanford Law School's Center for Internet and Society, who has been studying the draft legislation. The legislation (known as the General Data Protection Regulation) would replace the EU's existing data-protection rules and give Internet users broader rights to erase content posted about them, according to Keller and others who have seen the drafts.

If Google rejects a request for removal of a link, the requestor can appeal to his or her country's regulators or the courts, Keller says. "But there's no role for the publisher, who put the speech up in the first place and is being silenced" to protest, Keller says. "In terms of due process, it's extremely lopsided."

Should nations regulate Internet privacy beyond their borders?

When Danish-born lawyer Dan Shefet, who practices in Paris, became the subject of defamatory articles accusing him of professional malpractice and fraud, he asked Google to remove the links from searches for his name. Google took down the links, but only from its French domain, Google.fr.

That didn't solve the problem, Shefet says, because his clientele is international, and prospective clients elsewhere could still see the defamatory links. Then last year, after the Google Spain ruling, Shefet took the case to a Paris court, arguing that the links should be removed not just from Google.fr but from all the company's domains, including Google.com. He cited a little-noticed phrase of the EU high court's ruling, saying that Google, Inc. and its Spanish subsidiary Google Spain were "inextricably linked." In a precedent-setting decision, the French judge interpreted that to mean that Google's local subsidiary in one country — in this case France — could be liable for the activities of its parent.

The Paris court's decision was the first to interpret the Google Spain ruling as having a worldwide scope. It concluded that because Internet users in France could still access the information through Google.com, Google's delisting should have global reach. In September 2014, it ordered the company to pay daily fines of 1,000 euros ($1,073) unless links to a defamatory article were removed from Google's entire global network.[24]

Then, last June, the French data-protection agency, CNIL, went further: Every time Google responds to a delisting request in France, the company also must remove the link from its global search network including Google.com, the regulators ordered. Although someone doing a Google search in France is automatically directed to Google's French search engine, it takes merely one click on the bottom right corner of the page to reach Google.com.

Google so far has acceded to removal requests only on its EU domains, such as Google.fr and Google.uk, but not on Google.com.

"If the CNIL's proposed approach were to be embraced as the standard for Internet regulation, we would find ourselves in a race to the bottom," Google global's privacy counsel, Peter Fleischer, wrote in a July 30 blog post. "In the end, the Internet would only be as free as the world's least-free place."[25]

He cited instances where content that is illegal in one country is legal in another: Russia outlaws speech that government officials deem "gay propaganda," while Thailand criminalizes speech the government considers critical of the king.[26] If the French regulator's order extended to the Google.com searches that Americans typically use on U.S. soil, it would prevent Americans from seeing content that is legal in the United States.

"That is extremely worrisome to me," said Jonathan Zittrain, who teaches digital law at Harvard Law School.

"France is asking for Google to do something that if the U.S. government asked for, it would be against the First Amendment."[27]

The order "sends a cue to repressive and autocratic regimes around the world to impose their own local restraints on free expression extraterritorially," the Reporters Committee on Freedom of the Press said.[28]

Jules Polonetsky, who heads the Future of Privacy Forum, a Washington, D.C., think tank, agrees. "Imagine China telling Google that Google.com shouldn't have this disparaging stuff about Tiananmen Square globally . . . truly a scary notion," says Polonetsky.

Opponents also raise concerns that rulings such as CNIL's violate legal standards of territorial sovereignty. An advisory council of outside technology and legal experts appointed by Google endorsed the company's decision to remove links only from domains in Europe, citing the EU Court's limited "authority across Europe as its guidance."[29]

In a dissenting opinion to the Google Advisory Council report, Germany's former minister of justice, Sabine Leutheusser-Schnarrenberger, said, "Since EU residents are able to research globally the EU is authorized to decide that the search engine has to delete all the links globally."[30]

Legal experts are divided, however, over whether French regulators can legally order an American company to edit its searches globally. Viktor Mayer-Schönberger, a professor of Internet governance and regulation at Oxford University and an early champion of the right to be forgotten in his 2009 book *Delete: The Virtue of Forgetting in the Digital Age*, thinks the regulators can do so.

"It is not just the stupid crazy French" who have attempted to stretch the long arm of jurisdiction outside its borders, he says. The United States has prosecuted overseas gambling websites that have U.S.-based customers, he points out. An obvious compromise would be technological, Mayer-Schönberger and other experts say: Google could block Internet users sitting in France from accessing the .com search page by sensing their location — a technology known as "geo-blocking."

But others say the answer is not so simple. As the Electronic Frontier Foundation's O'Brien observes, "The history of geolocation on the Internet is all about people getting around it." For example, an Internet user in

Europe can circumvent geo-blocking by using a "proxy" server in the United States to watch an American TV show that is blocked in Europe by copyright law.

Trying to enforce virtual geographic walls just makes governments more repressive, O'Brien suggests: "What courts are effectively demanding is that the Internet develop its own set of international borders. Not only is that defeating the purpose of the Internet as a global communication system, the more you try to enforce that, the more restricted and balkanized the Internet becomes."

With countries so divided in their views on privacy and free speech, and with their courts likely to come up with clashing decisions, the result will be "legal chaos," says Shefet, the Paris lawyer. As founder of the newly formed Association for Accountability and Internet Democracy, he advocates an international treaty to require search engines and servers to swiftly remove false and defamatory content.

International data experts are skeptical, however, that consensus could be reached on a treaty anytime soon, given cultural and historical divides. For example, the intergovernmental Council of Europe, a human rights organization including 47 member countries, promulgated a data-protection convention in 1981 that all EU member states have signed and that is open to signature from other countries. But the United States has never signed it.[31]

"Even that very loose law — with no teeth in terms of what to do if a country doesn't implement it — has almost no ratifiers from outside Europe," says David Erdos, who teaches data-protection law at England's University of Cambridge.

Should the United States adopt a "right to be forgotten"?

Before the Internet, finding the records of a teenager's arrest for selling drugs or a divorcing couple's accusations in court of infidelity involved tediously digging through paper files in a courthouse basement.

If a right to be forgotten were introduced into the United States, it simply would restore the situation Americans had in the pre-Internet era, when those deeds faded into oblivion, University of Chicago law professor Eric Posner has argued.

"You can beg people to take down offending images and text. If you really work at it and spend money on a lawyer, you might be able to get a court order. But all of the effort will be wasted if the telltale content has already been copied and pasted elsewhere and then swept into Google's servers," according to Posner. "Shouldn't new laws and rulings" — such as the one in the Google Spain case, "give people back the privacy that technology has taken away?"[32]

Consumer Watchdog echoes Posner's argument in its complaint asking the Federal Trade Commission (FTC) to make Google extend the right to be forgotten to American consumers. The group said that in the pre-Internet era, "people tended to forget whatever embarrassing things someone did in their youth." In a formal complaint, it argued that Google is engaging in "deceptive behavior" by describing itself as "championing users' privacy while not offering a key privacy tool," namely the right to be forgotten, that it is implementing in Europe.[33]

But other public-interest advocates say a European-style right to erasure would hamper consumers' ability to make an informed choice. Take the case of Costeja González, the Spanish lawyer. Shouldn't the prospective client know "that 10 years ago, this guy was so irresponsible with his money that he had to have his house sold to pay unpaid taxes?" asks Levy of the Public Citizen Litigation Group.

"The danger of the right to be forgotten is it hides negative information," Levy says. "Why should Costeja González get to hide his past problems when his competitors in the bar have been squeaky clean for the past 20 years?"

The Association of National Advertisers, a marketers' trade group representing 670 companies including Google, has urged the FTC to dismiss Consumer Watchdog's complaint. The hundreds of thousands of delisting requests Google is receiving from Europeans "clearly show that expanding this type of program to the United States would be time-consuming, expensive, burdensome and difficult for Google or any other company," the association said in a July 31 letter to the FTC.[34]

Google's position as judge and jury — operating behind closed doors determining whether information people ask to be erased is relevant, excessive or inadequate — also provokes criticism from American privacy experts. "Those are decisions that ought to be made by courts, not by companies," says Polonetsky of the Future of Privacy Forum.

Moreover, he says, this kind of law puts pressure on Google to block links when in doubt, simply to avoid future legal challenges. As evidence, critics cite copyright law, which is America's closest parallel to Google's European personal-data takedown orders. It exempts search engines from liability if they swiftly take down material after being told it violates copyright.[35]

As a result, the law has led to excessive removal of content from the Internet on spurious grounds, according to several studies, and has been abused to suppress speech.[36] In a famous 2002 case, the Church of Scientology succeeded in getting Google to remove search links to Web pages criticizing the church by claiming that they violated the church's copyright.[37]

Such instances are "absolutely a warning sign" of what could happen in Europe under the right to be forgotten, says Stanford's Keller, who worked as a lawyer for Google and is a specialist in liability issues faced by Google, Facebook and similar Web hosting companies. "By far the easiest thing for these companies is to say, 'We'll remove it. Because if we don't, we might face liability and an expensive process.'"

Under American law, an important distinction is made between personal "data," such as health or credit information already protected by privacy laws, and "expressive content," such as an article someone else writes about someone, which is protected by the First Amendment.

"It's hard to imagine" importing a right to be forgotten to the United States, Posner has conceded. "The First Amendment will protect Google, or any other company, that resurfaces or publishes information that's already public."[38]

In two lower-court cases, Google has argued successfully that its search results are First Amendment-protected speech.[39] However, Google's argument has never been tested in an appellate court or the Supreme Court. Randazza, the lawyer who favors a U.S. right to be forgotten, says he is "not 100 percent convinced" that such courts would say Google's practice of putting search results in a certain order rises to the level of protected speech. "That's a new theory."

In the United States, tentative steps have been taken toward an erasure right, but only for minors, such as California's eraser button law, which took effect Jan. 1.[40] However, the California law is "very different from the

right to be forgotten because it doesn't give you any right to take down something your friend has reposted" or anything that someone posts about you, explains Ariel Fox Johnson, policy counsel for Common Sense Media, a San Francisco advocacy group that pushed for the legislation.

That may explain why no First Amendment challenges have been filed against the law. However, the law would let someone delete their postings of public interest, such as a teenager writing online about a newsworthy event, according to David Greene, who teaches First Amendment law at the University of San Francisco School of Law.

"Any law that requires speech to be removed, without an exception for speech that is a matter of public interest, is going to be problematic" from a First Amendment viewpoint, he says.

BACKGROUND
Legacy of Fascism

The two sides of the Atlantic feature "two different cultures of privacy, which are home to different intuitive sensibilities, and which have produced two significantly different laws of privacy," wrote James Q. Whitman, a Yale University professor of comparative and foreign law.[41]

Whitman explains that in Europe privacy means the protection of one's dignity, dating back to 19th-century "laws of insult" governing duels over honor. In the United States, where the laws of insult never took hold, privacy means the protection of liberty from the government, with a constant wariness of restrictions on speaking freely.

While Europe has developed comprehensive laws protecting privacy, the United States has developed a far more piecemeal approach but with a particularly high value on press freedom.

In the 1930s, the Dutch government compiled a comprehensive registry of its population, which included the names, addresses and religions of all citizens. At the time, the registry was praised as helping the government with its welfare planning. But when the Nazis invaded the Netherlands, they used the registry to track down Jews and Gypsies.[42]

Author Mayer-Schönberger cites that example to explain why Europeans are so protective of their private

CHRONOLOGY

1890-1950s *Right to privacy fails to gain recognition as constitutional right in the United States, but Europe recognizes it as a fundamental human right.*

1890 Louis D. Brandeis argues for a right to privacy in landmark law review article.

1928 Brandeis, as a Supreme Court justice, argues for a constitutional right to privacy in dissent in *Olmstead v. United States.*

1948 U.N. Universal Declaration of Human Rights establishes privacy as fundamental human right.

1950 European Convention on Human Rights adopted; protects right to "private and family life."

1960s-1970s *Supreme Court recognizes right to privacy in some areas, but First Amendment trumps privacy in landmark broadcasting case.*

1967 In *Griswold v. Connecticut,* justices strike down Connecticut law against contraception as invasion of privacy.

1970 Congress passes Fair Credit Reporting Act, preventing old bankruptcies from appearing in credit reports.

1973 In *Roe v. Wade*, Supreme Court recognizes right to privacy in a woman's decision to have an abortion.

1974 Federal Privacy Act bars federal agencies from disclosing personal information without the person's consent.

1975 Supreme Court rejects invasion-of-privacy suit against Cox Broadcasting Corp. for disclosing name of rape victim, saying First Amendment protects true information.

1980s-1990s *After collapse of communism, Europe adopts sweeping privacy laws, while United States protects privacy in specific areas.*

1989 Fall of Berlin Wall marks collapse of East Germany and leads to revelations about how its secret police spied on individuals.

1990 Virtually all U.S. states recognize a right to privacy in civil suits.

1995 European Union (EU) adopts Data Protection Directive, a framework for EU countries' privacy laws, including right to erase personal data.

1996 Section 230 of Communications Decency Act grants websites and search engines immunity from lawsuits for information they host. . . . President Bill Clinton signs Health Insurance Portability and Accountability Act, protecting personal health information.

1998 Congress passes Children's Online Privacy Protection Act giving parents control over information websites can collect from their children.

2000s *EU strengthens "right to be forgotten" online; "eraser" rights allowing children to delete material they post online passes in California.*

2003 Supreme Court recognizes privacy right in homosexual relations in *Lawrence v. Texas.*

2009 EU Treaty of Lisbon grants constitutional stature to right to data protection.

2011 Sen. Edward Markey, D-Mass, and Rep. Joe Barton, R-Texas, introduce "eraser button" bill for children's online data, but Congress does not act on it; similar bill dies in 2013.

2012 EU introduces new legislation to supersede 1995 personal-data directive, to be approved in 2015 or early 2016.

2013 California passes children's "eraser" bill.

2014 In landmark ruling in *Google Spain v. Mario Costeja González,* EU court declares search engines must remove results on request. . . . EU regulators say Google must remove search links from Google.com.

2015 California children's "eraser" bill goes into effect. . . . French regulator orders Google to extend search-result removals requested by French beyond its French search page to include Google.com. . . . French regulator denies Google's appeal. . . . EU "Safe Harbor" decision blocks transfer of personal data from Europeans to U.S.-based servers.

'Revenge Porn' Victims Seek to Be Forgotten

"3,000 people know where I live and what I look like."

In 2011, Annmarie Chiarini, an English professor at a Maryland community college, Googled her name and found herself on a pornography site. "Hot for Teacher? Well, Come Get It!" said her profile, which featured naked images of her, along with her address and the name of her employer.

An ex-boyfriend had posted the information and nude photos he had taken of her, according to Chiarini.[1]

In a genre known as "revenge porn," at least 3,000 websites specialize in purveying sexually explicit photos of women (and sometimes men) without their consent, typically posted by vengeful ex-lovers or ex-husbands.[2]

Images of a typical victim can be posted on up to 2,000 websites, according to Chiarini, who went public with her experience and now serves as victim services director of the Cyber Civil Rights Initiative (CCRI), which advocates criminalizing revenge porn. Removed from one site, the images often reappear on another, reposted by avid revenge-porn aficionados.

Many victims worry most about their search results, says Carrie Goldberg, a Brooklyn attorney and CCRI board member, because that's how prospective employers, landlords or romantic interests are most likely to discover the link to a pornography site.

"If the first three pages of your Google results are monopolized by links to porn sites, you just won't get the job" you're applying for, Goldberg says. "You won't even get asked to the interview. The same is true if you're dating or searching for an apartment."

When Google announced on June 19 that it would honor requests to remove search results involving revenge porn, CCRI rejoiced, having worked with the technology giant to set up a request-and-removal system.[3] Other big online companies —Twitter, Reddit, Facebook and Microsoft's Bing search engine — have followed suit.[4]

"People are saying now there's a 'right to be forgotten' for revenge-porn victims," says Goldberg, referencing Europeans' legal right to request the removal of objectionable results from one's name search.

Chiarini says she never thought to contact Google when she found her photo on a porn site. By then, her profile had been up for 14 days and viewed 3,000 times. It was "absolutely terrifying," she says, to realize that "3,000 people know where I live and what I look like and think I'm open for casual sex."

In several horrific cases, online harassment has stepped off the screen into a person's home.

In 2009 a Craigslist ad featured a woman's picture next to her "interest" in "a real aggressive man with no concern for women." Her ex-boyfriend, Jebidiah James Stipe, who had posted the ad, according to prosecutors, masqueraded as his former girlfriend and sent Ty Oliver McDowell her home address. McDowell broke into the house and raped her at knifepoint, later insisting he was responding to the ad.[5] McDowell and Stipe were convicted of sexual assault, aggravated kidnapping and aggravated burglary and received identical sentences of 60 years to life.[6]

Chiarini eventually got her profile removed by contacting the porn site's Web host and server operators. She also contacted police about an earlier posting in 2010 and again in 2011, but each time officers told her there was no law under which they could prosecute her ex-boyfriend. The experience turned her into an advocate for a Maryland law to criminalize revenge porn.

Today, 26 states, including Maryland and the District of Columbia, have such laws. Rep. Jackie Speier, D-Calif., said she would introduce legislation to make the posting of revenge porn a federal crime. "With our patchwork of current laws, people victimized by 'revenge porn' often have no recourse, and their images can continue to circulate on the Internet indefinitely," Speier says. "The only sufficient solution is to criminalize these destructive acts at the national level."

Civil liberties advocates have opposed some state revenge-porn laws. The American Civil Liberties Union

(ACLU) sued Arizona last year on behalf of booksellers and publishers, claiming a just-passed state law, which would have made it a felony to post a nude photo of someone without the person's consent, violated the First Amendment. A court settlement blocked the law from going into effect.[7]

"In many states this is a new felony that targets the sharing of nudity — something that is frankly a very common American pastime," says Lee Rowland, senior staff attorney at the ACLU. "And whatever you think of sharing pornography or nudity, it's fully protected by the First Amendment."

The ACLU says such laws should be narrowly drawn to apply only to someone who "knowingly and maliciously" posts a revenge-porn photo.

Moreover, Rowland says, some revenge porn already violates existing civil and criminal laws. Indeed, in what experts believe is the first case involving a revenge porn website operator, Kevin Bollaert, was convicted in April under California's identity theft and extortion laws. Bollaert, who was sentenced to 18 years in prison, was convicted of uploading 10,000 photos of women without their consent, then redirecting women to another site where he charged them $300 to $350 to have a photo removed from his website.[8]

Mary Anne Franks, a professor at the University of Miami School of Law who has been helping Speier draft her legislation, says a federal law would eliminate one of the biggest obstacles to shutting down the revenge-porn industry. The federal Communications Decency Act exempts website owners from civil suits and state criminal prosecution for hosting revenge-porn photos posted by others, but it does not prevent prosecution under a federal criminal statute.

Franks says proposed legislative language she drafted for Rep. Speier "would allow for prosecution of websites and other platforms that actively and knowingly engage in the promotion and solicitation" of revenge porn.

— Sarah Glazer

Courtesy of Annmarie Chiarini

Annmarie Chiarini, an English professor at a Maryland community college, Googled her name in 2011 and found herself on a pornography site. She got her profile removed by contacting the porn site's Web host and server operators.

[3] Amit Singhal, " 'Revenge Porn' and Search," Google Public Policy Blog, June 19, 2014, http://tinyurl.com/oe4syb7.

[4] Ruth Reader, "Microsoft Joins Facebook, Google, Twitter, and Reddit in Fight Against Revenge Porn," *VB* (VentureBeat.com), July 22, 2015, http:// tinyurl.com/qhlhbne.

[5] Danielle Keats Citron, *Hate Crimes in Cyberspace* (2009), p. 6.

[6] Caroline Black, "Ex-marine Jebidiah James Stipe Gets 60 Years for Craigslist Rape Plot," CBS News, June 29, 2010, http://tinyurl.com/p3us2hg; Ben Neary, "Second Man Gets 60 Years in Wyo. Internet Rape Case," *Ventura County Star*, June 29, 2010, http://tinyurl.com/olxl7wg.

[7] "Federal Judge Blocks Enforcement of Arizona's 'Revenge Porn' Law," *The Range, Tucson Weekly*, July 10, 2015, http://tinyurl.com/na87ykk.

[8] Liberty Zabala and R. Stickney, "'Revenge porn' Defendant Sentenced to 18 Years," NBC San Diego, April 3, 2015, http://tinyurl.com/o35ezsz.

[1] Annmarie Chiarini, "I was a victim of revenge porn," *The Guardian*, Nov. 19, 2013, http://tinyurl.com/nadwv5z.

[2] "Misery Merchants," *The Economist*, July 5, 2014, http://tinyurl.com/lvakqqc.

data. "We may feel safe living in democratic republics, but so did the Dutch," he writes.[43]

The European experience, with the Nazis' obsessive — often fatal — record-keeping and later with communist secret police spying in Eastern Europe, helps to explain why protecting privacy is seen as such a fundamental right on the continent.

In 1948, following World War II, the United Nations adopted the Universal Declaration of Human Rights, which established privacy as a fundamental human right, a model widely adopted in constitutions around the world but never ratified by the United States Senate.[44]

In 1950, the Council of Europe adopted the European Convention on Human Rights, which has since been embraced by all 28 members of the European Union. Article 8 protects the right to "private and family life." The European Court of Human Rights — an international court that rules on allegations of human rights violations — has interpreted that right to include the protection of personal data. The convention requires member states to ensure their national laws adhere to its principles.[45]

In 1989, with the fall of the Berlin Wall, East German citizens learned that the secret police had compiled extensive files on them, often fed by spying from their neighbors. The new democracies that replaced the communist governments rewrote their laws to prevent the return of such privacy invasions.

In subsequent years, the EU has promulgated a detailed series of laws designed to protect privacy, most significantly under the EU's umbrella regulation known as the Data Protection Directive. It was adopted by the EU in 1995 and became effective in 1998.[46]

The Right to Be Forgotten

Traditionally, some European countries, including France and Italy, had a form of the right to be forgotten in statutes aimed at expunging criminal records after a certain number of years. In the United States, state "expungement" laws may permit minor crimes to be removed from a criminal record after a period of years or if the crime was committed by someone under age 18.[47]

The EU's Data Protection Directive contained a "right to erasure" of one's personal online data and the "right to object" to a website publishing or storing it. Together those provisions became popularly known as

the right to be forgotten, explains Jef Ausloos, a legal researcher in information technology at the University of Leuven in Belgium.

Technically, the directive allowed Europeans to demand that the publisher of a website remove their personal data if it did not comply with strict data-protection rules. But Cambridge University's Erdos, who has studied data regulation across Europe, says, "There's quite a gap between what the law says and what often goes on."

For example, the directive required member states to make some exceptions for news published by journalists — a form of protection for the press. But, in laws adopted by EU member countries, Erdos says, "That's been implemented totally differently across Europe, ranging from making no explicit provision at all to the complete exemption of journalists."

In 2009, the Treaty of Lisbon, which granted constitutional stature to the EU Charter, came into force. It recognized the right to data protection as a separate fundamental right along with the right to respect for one's private and family life.

The concept of a right to be forgotten gained prominence in 2010, when Vivian Reding, the European commissioner responsible for justice and fundamental rights, pushed for a right to remove unwanted information on social media sites such as Facebook. "With more and more private data floating around on the Web — especially on social networking site[s] — people should have the right to have their data completely removed," she said in a speech.[48]

In May 2014, the EU Court of Justice issued its landmark ruling in *Google Spain v. Mario Costeja González*, declaring that Google, and all other search engines, were considered data "controllers" subject to the 1995 Data Protection Directive and were obliged to act on requests to have links deleted from the requestor's name search.

In November 2014, an EU advisory body of data-protection officials from member countries issued recommendations on how the Google Spain ruling should be carried out by each country's data-protection regulatory authority. Any delisting of search links must be made not just on EU search sites but "on all relevant domains," including .com, for the ruling to be effective, the group said.[49]

The group also said search engines should not routinely inform publishers that links to their material were being deleted. Doing so, according to several commissioners, would encourage republication of the material.[50]

The group's statements, intended only as advisory guidelines, were widely interpreted as predicting how data-protection agencies would implement the new ruling.

U.S. Privacy Rights

In an 1890 *Harvard Law Review* article, 34-year-old Boston lawyer Louis Brandeis lamented how new portable cameras and the spread of yellow journalism* were invading individuals' privacy.

"Recent inventions . . . call attention to the next step which must be taken for the protection of the person, and for securing to the individual . . . the right 'to be let alone,'" he wrote. "[N]umerous mechanical devices threaten to make good the prediction that 'what is whispered in the closet shall be proclaimed from the house-tops.'"[51]

Brandeis and co-author Samuel D. Warren proposed that invasions of privacy be classified as a tort — a social wrong for which someone can sue and obtain economic damages in court.

In 1928, the growing popularity of other new technology — the telephone and wiretapping — led Brandeis, who by then was a Supreme Court justice, to argue for a constitutional right to privacy in a dissenting opinion in *Olmstead v. United States*. Brandeis became the first Supreme Court justice to recognize such a right under the Fourth Amendment's prohibition against "unreasonable searches and seizures" and to recognize the threat that technology posed to citizens.[52]

Nevertheless, Brandeis' view of privacy received a "cold reception" in American law, since it drew on aristocratic European ideas of the law of insult, wrote Yale's Whitman.[53] In the years following the Brandeis-Warren article, some lower-court judges recognized a right to privacy while "others refused to recognize such a right merely because two disgruntled legal scholars had written about it," privacy law expert Robert Ellis Smith wrote in *The Law of Privacy Explained*.[54]

Future Supreme Court justice Louis D. Brandeis, shown in about 1900 when he was a young lawyer, argued in a landmark law review article in 1890 that Americans had a right to privacy. In 1928, when he was on the court, he argued for a constitutional right to privacy, becoming the first Supreme Court justice to recognize the threat that technology posed to citizens.

In the early 1900s several states, starting with New York and continuing with Virginia and Utah, recognized a right to privacy by statute when someone's image or persona was misappropriated without consent for commercial purposes. By 1990, all states except Minnesota recognized, either by statute or common law, a right to privacy in a tort action.[55]

The right to privacy has been among the most controversial areas of constitutional law during the past half century, according to Erwin Chemerinsky, a University of California-Irvine law professor.[56] The Supreme Court cited a right to privacy in decisions establishing a right to use contraception (*Griswold v. Connecticut*, 1965), to have an abortion (*Roe v. Wade*, 1973) and to engage in private homosexual relations (*Lawrence v. Texas*, 2003).[57]

While a right to privacy is not mentioned explicitly in the Constitution, Justice William O. Douglas, writing for the majority in *Griswold v. Connecticut*, found that privacy was a "penumbral right," meaning it was implicit in the Bill of Rights. For example, he wrote, the Fourth Amendment, protecting against "unreasonable searches and seizures," created a zone of privacy in the bedroom.

---

* Yellow Journalism, popular during the 19th century, was practiced by newspapers that emphasized sensationalism over factual reporting. The term derived from a popular New York newspaper comic strip that featured a character known as the Yellow Kid.

"Would we allow the police to search the sacred precincts of marital bedrooms for telltale signs of the use of contraceptives?" he asked.[58]

Free Speech vs. Privacy

Despite these Supreme Court rulings upholding a right to privacy, Chemerinsky said, there has been little judicial protection for "informational privacy," the right to prevent one's private information from public dissemination when that information is true.

"[A]lthough there is a strong argument that the Constitution should be interpreted to protect the right to control information, there has been little support for such a right from the Supreme Court," he writes.[59]

In a string of landmark cases, the court consistently has ruled against a right to informational privacy in First Amendment challenges to lawsuits over the public disclosure of private, personal facts.[60] For example, in *Cox Broadcasting Corp. v. Cohn* (1975), a television reporter disclosed the name of a rape and murder victim. The victim's father sued for invasion of privacy, but the Supreme Court ruled against him, saying the information had been obtained from court records and truthfully reported and that the First Amendment protects the publication of such information.[61]

While interpretations of a constitutional right to privacy remain controversial, the United States has mandated privacy rights in specific areas of law. For example:

- The 1970 Fair Credit Reporting Act, which regulates information included in credit reports, stipulated that after seven years — and 10 years for bankruptcy — information about debt collections, civil lawsuits, tax liens and arrests for criminal offenses must be taken out of such reports.[62]
- The 1974 Privacy Act prohibits federal agencies from disclosing personal information about an individual without the person's consent, except for purposes such as law enforcement, census statistics and congressional investigations.[63]
- The 1996 Health Insurance Portability and Accountability Act protects personal health information and established standards for the security of electronic health records.[64]

Congress protected children's privacy rights in 1998, when it passed the Children's Online Privacy Protection Act giving parents control over information that websites collect from children under age 13. Websites and online services must give parents the choice of consenting to the collection of their children's personal information — such as name, address, phone number and screen name — and also provide parents with the opportunity to have the information deleted.[65]

Updated Federal Trade Commission rules in 2013 widened the definition of children's personal information to include geolocation data that could identify a child's street address; photos, videos, audio recordings that contain the child's image or voice; and "persistent identifiers" such as Internet cookies that track a child's activity online.[66]

CURRENT SITUATION
Conflict Ahead

No one is sure how the current standoff between French regulators and Google will turn out.

Google appealed the French regulator's order to erase worldwide the links requested by French consumers, including on Google.com. But in September, when the French data-protection agency, CNIL, denied that appeal, it said Google "must now comply with the formal notice" or it would consider sanctions against the company.[67]

It remains unclear whether Google will try to fight that order in court.

The current dispute "is just a skirmish" in preparation for "the real end-game" — sweeping new data-protection legislation the European Union is expected to enact later this year or early next year, according to Oxford's Mayer-Schönberger. Google's stance is partly aimed at influencing the EU's drafting of that new right-to-be-forgotten legislation, known as the General Data Protection Regulation, he says.[68]

With numerous drafts floating around, it's unclear how strict the final provisions will be. Moreover, EU member states themselves are divided, and some European media conglomerates share Google's views, Mayer-Schönberger says. However, some American experts are already sounding the alarm about the wide-ranging consequences the new legislation could have on American companies.

As Stanford's Keller interprets the current drafts, removal requestors will be able to ask not only for removal of a link from a search engine but also for the erasure of underlying content — such as a post on Facebook, a tweet on Twitter or possibly a news article that someone else has posted about them.

Moreover, the legislation appears to "apply to tons of Internet companies that are small and never even heard of it," she says. Noting the conflict with American-style free-speech rights, she adds, "it's not something Americans are going to like at all." And since American companies will be reluctant to fight requests in court or face steep fines for disobeying regulators, the new right to be forgotten "will be the easiest tool at hand for someone who would like some online content to disappear," Keller predicts.

American businesses are nervously eyeing Europe's data-protection stance, ever since October, when the European Union Court of Justice said American companies could no longer transfer data from Europe to America under the long-standing Safe Harbor agreement, a U.S.-EU accord regulating how U.S. companies handle European citizens' data. EU privacy law forbids the transfer of European citizens' data outside the European Union unless the receiving country has rules in line with EU privacy-protection laws.[69]

Recognizing that the United States lacks such laws, the Safe Harbor pact allowed U.S. companies like Facebook to self-certify that they would protect Europeans' data transferred to and stored in U.S. data centers.

Max Schrems, a 28-year-old Facebook user and Austrian law student, went to the EU's highest court to argue that the social networking site should not be allowed to transfer his and other European Facebook users' data to its American servers. Schrems argued that the transfer would subject his data to the risk of U.S. government snooping revealed in 2013 by former National Security Agency contractor Edward Snowden.[70]

In October, the court agreed, declaring the agreement invalid on the grounds that the United States does not sufficiently protect citizens' data from government spying.[71]

U.S. Privacy Legislation

Some privacy advocates hope the European Court's Safe Harbor decision will nudge the United States towards strengthening data privacy, but they're also realistic about

Californian Christos Catsouras, shown with family, tried to remove gory photos of a fatal car crash in which his daughter Nikki, 18, was killed. The photos showed up on thousands of websites after California Highway Patrol employees emailed them to family and friends. At the family's request, many websites removed the photos, but they remain easy to find on Google. With no "right to be forgotten" in American law, the family had no way to force Google to remove the photos.

Getty Images/*Los Angeles Times*/Allen J. Schaben

the lack of political momentum. The decision is "a reminder that American privacy law needs to be updated," privacy advocate Rotenberg told a November hearing of a House Energy and Commerce subcommittee, citing "skyrocketing identity theft, data breaches and financial fraud."[72]

In an interview with *CQ Researcher*, Rotenberg says the EU court's recent rulings, including Google Spain, show that, "The EU is moving forward with new protections, and the United States is still stuck in the mud; and there's no meaningful progress in the United States."

"Now it's easy for other countries to say to the United States, 'You're wild, lawless actors . . . because you have no privacy legislation," says Polonetsky of the Future of Privacy Forum. "It will be helpful if the U.S. does pass its own privacy legislation."

The most comprehensive recent privacy legislation, President Obama's Consumer Privacy Bill of Rights, unveiled Feb. 27 in draft form, was "dead on arrival," according to Jeff Chester, executive director of the Center for Digital Democracy, a Washington advocacy group for greater consumer Internet privacy. The draft

Should the United States adopt Europe's "right to be forgotten"?

YES
John M. Simpson
Privacy Project Director, Consumer Watchdog

Written for *CQ Researcher*, December 2015

The failure of Internet search engines such as Google, Yahoo and Bing to honor the so-called "right to be forgotten" in the United States is not an abstract issue. Their callous decision hurts real people.

Consider the case of Nikki Catsouras, the 18-year-old daughter of Christos and Lesli Catsouras. Nine years ago she died in a horrific automobile wreck in California. Graphic police photos of her remains were leaked and posted on the Internet. Today those gruesome images are still linked to her name and the names of other Catsouras family members in Internet search results.

"The right to be forgotten is the only chance for my family to find closure and to finally grieve," says Christos Catsouras.

In Europe, the right to be forgotten — perhaps more accurately called the right of relevancy — allows individuals to request the removal of search-engine links to personal information that is "inadequate, irrelevant or no longer relevant, or excessive."

It is not censorship. The original published item is not removed or altered. The link to a person's name may be removed, but the original item can still be accessed using other search terms.

Google's announcement this year that it would honor requests to remove links to "revenge porn" — nude or explicit photos posted without the subject's consent — makes it clear that Google could also easily honor right-to-be-forgotten requests in the United States.

Indeed, U.S. law already recognizes that certain information should become irrelevant after the passage of time has demonstrated that an individual is unlikely to repeat the mistake. The Fair Credit Reporting Act says that debt collections, civil lawsuits, tax liens and even arrests for criminal offenses in most cases should be considered obsolete after seven years and must be excluded from credit reports. The government should extend the same principle to the online world.

Before the Internet, personal privacy was largely protected by the difficulty of gathering information as well as the tendency of humans to forget. Search-engine algorithms don't allow that now. We need to focus on what this sea change means to society and how we can deal with it.

The right to be forgotten offers a clear path forward to help protect our privacy in the digital age. Companies like Google that claim to care about users' privacy should be ashamed that they are not treating people on both sides of the Atlantic the same way.

NO
Samantha Bates
Research Associate, Berkman Center for Internet & Society, Harvard University

Written for *CQ Researcher*, December 2015

Imagine that 10 years after graduating from college you are still explaining to potential employers why the first Google search result under your name is a photo of you passed out drunk at a party. What if you could ask that this photo be permanently removed from Google search results after explaining why it's both embarrassing and not something the public particularly needs to know?

European regulators have granted their citizens the "right to be forgotten," which allows them to request that Google and other search engines remove links from their search results in these types of circumstances.

If Europeans have the power to shape their online reputations, shouldn't Americans be accorded the same right? Although a noble cause in theory, an American version of the right to be forgotten is a bad idea.

First, the right to be forgotten raises genuine First Amendment concerns. In comparison to European nations, the U.S. Constitution places stricter limitations on what the government can order a company to say or not say. Europe's right-to-be-forgotten decision, which orders Google to evaluate removal requests and remove links to content deemed "inadequate, irrelevant or no longer relevant, or excessive," would likely violate the First Amendment by allowing governments to determine what links appear on a Google search-results page. This isn't merely limiting Google's speech. Europeans can request the removal not only of content they personally have posted but also links to content posted by a third party.

Second, the European Court of Justice has left it to Google to judge whether search results should be removed, pressuring Google to abandon neutrality and alter its search results. Worse, Google faces legal action and a fine if it fails to comply with a removal request that the court deems sufficient — but no one can challenge a removal that is in fact in the public interest. With such vague guidelines to follow, Google is likely to remove results in ambiguous cases rather than risk fines.

In a time when people rely on search engines as one of their main sources of information, do we want Google to control the searchability of online content? What will prevent Google from manipulating the search algorithm to suit its own purposes? The United States has a strong tradition of charting its own course — and in this case, doing so is amply justified.

bill was opposed by Internet services companies as well as consumer-privacy activists such as Chester.

The draft called for companies to let consumers see, correct and delete personal information held about them — like credit card numbers, passwords and Social Security numbers.[73] Chester's group said it would weaken privacy by allowing the industry to self-regulate, while industry groups condemned it as too onerous.[74]

The draft has no congressional sponsor, and no congressional action is scheduled. To overcome congressional inaction and to find common ground, U.S. and European data experts have formed the "Privacy Bridges Project," recommending that regulators and industry representatives from both continents try to agree on basic values and policies relating to privacy without changing laws.

"I spent a lot of the last six years trying to get Congress to pass a consumer-privacy bill, and I still hope that will happen, but I don't want to wait around and just hope that will happen," explains Daniel J. Weitzner, former deputy chief technology officer in the Obama White House, who co-chaired the trans-Atlantic Privacy Bridges Project.[75]

Weitzner, who now directs the Internet Policy Research Initiative at the Massachusetts Institute of Technology, would like to see U.S. and European regulators draft privacy notices that are easier to understand than the dense privacy language that Internet users often agree to without reading. In its report describing possible areas of compromise, the Bridges Project does not mention a right to be forgotten. However, Weitzner says, "had our 'bridges' been in place, perhaps the right to be forgotten discussion might have turned out differently."

Eraser Buttons

In Congress, Sen. Edward J. Markey, D-Mass., and Rep. Joe Barton, R-Texas, have proposed the Do Not Track Kids Act, which would give parents and children nationwide an "eraser button" similar to California's but would apply it to a more limited age range and category of personal information. Markey and Barton say the current federal children's online protection law should be updated to recognize that data-collection companies are tracking children's locations and creating detailed profiles about them for marketing purposes.[76]

While existing law requires parental consent for collection of personal information for children up to

A woman identified in court as "Chantal," shown with her lawyer at a courthouse in Amsterdam, Netherlands, sued Facebook last year after a video was posted on the social-networking site showing her in a sex act with her boyfriend; both were minors at the time. A Dutch court ordered Facebook on June 26, 2015, to reveal the identity of the person who posted the so-called revenge porn video on the site or face having its servers opened to outside investigators.

AFP/Getty Images/Robin van Lonkhuijsen

age 13, the Markey-Barton bill would extend protection to age 15. It also would allow children, as well as parents, to request deletion of publicly available personal information.

"Industry sees teens as a digital gold mine," says Chester, whose Center for Digital Democracy supports the measure. He is concerned about the vast amount of data that marketing companies collect about teens. "The Markey bill is a major step forward in making sure America's youth don't daily confront a wholesale invasion of their personal information," he says.

However, Facebook and other large online companies argued when California's eraser button law was being debated that it was unnecessary because they already provide deletion options. And according to Barton's communications director Daniel Rhea, "some large industry stakeholders" oppose the Markey-Barton proposal because, they say, "they are able to self-regulate."

The Markey-Barton bill has been introduced twice before — in 2011 and 2013 — but failed to gain legislative momentum either time. "We are hopeful it will move this Congress," says Rhea. As of mid-November, the measure had only three co-sponsors in the Senate and 14 in the House.[77]

With Congress currently gridlocked, children's advocates say, states may be more receptive to protecting children's privacy. Several states including New York are considering legislation similar to the California bill, according to the advocacy group Common Sense Media. "Congress doesn't have the appetite for addressing difficult privacy rules at the leadership level," says Danny Weiss, vice president for national policy at Common Sense Media, which pushed for the California bill.

OUTLOOK

Fragmented Internet?

Some privacy advocates argue that Americans and Europeans may not be as far apart as their legal systems currently suggest. For example, a Pew Research Center poll earlier this year found that 74 percent of Americans believe control over personal information is "very important," yet only 9 percent believe they have such control.[78]

Even so, says former White House adviser Weitzner, "The likelihood is [that] over time EU law will evolve on the trajectory it's on, and U.S. law will evolve on the trajectory it's on, but they won't magically converge." He doubts that "there will be some grand interglobal treaty on privacy and all these problems will be solved" anytime soon.

Meanwhile, he argues, the United States and Europe can take practical steps to devise common privacy policies by having informal discussions between regulators and industries on both sides of the Atlantic. American corporations that do business in Europe often adopt European privacy guidelines voluntarily, he points out, simply because the Internet works better when common practices cross national borders.

The pressure on U.S. companies operating in Europe to comply with EU laws is likely to increase as the world's information system becomes increasingly global. And that leaves companies like Google in a bind when ordered to do something by the French government that would violate the U.S. constitution.

"All of these businesses [Google, Twitter, Facebook] have a major part of their business in Europe, and they have employees who could be arrested and assets that could be seized," points out Stanford's Keller, a former Google lawyer. "The need to comply with the law of European countries where they operate is significant."

The result could be an increasingly fragmented Internet, or "splinternet," divided by national laws, she warns.

That day is already here, maintains author Mayer-Schönberger, who, in his book *Delete*, extolled the virtues of "oblivion" as preferable to the online world's tendency toward eternal remembering. With its right to be forgotten, the EU has succeeded in putting up "speed bumps" to casual surfers doing name searches of someone who has successfully delisted disparaging links, he says — even if computer geeks can find ways around them. "This speed-bump approach gives people a chance to grow and get beyond these incidents in their pasts."[79]

In *Delete*, Mayer-Schönberger proposed expiration dates for online personal information. Already some apps address the concern that everything will be preserved online. The mobile phone app Snapchat, hugely popular with teens, lets users take photos that last only a few seconds after they're sent to a friend.[80] However, Snapchat last year admitted that the photos don't "disappear forever" after a Federal Trade Commission investigation found the claim deceptive. The app has introduced a new feature this year to let recipients keep the photos long-term, which could surprise some senders who are still counting on Snapchat to make their embarrassing photos disappear quickly.[81]

So-called ephemeral applications — those that are intended to expire — show that technology is evolving to reflect "more nuanced" responses to how we communicate, says Polonetsky of the Future of Privacy Forum. "Why should I expect that yakking to my friends should be enshrined forevermore?"

As online storage has become cheaper and more spacious in the cloud, online platforms have tended to retain more and more information. But Polonetsky says, "Why shouldn't the default shift to: 'Hey, this is really old; do you want to keep it?' Technology should empower me to live better. I think that's the phase that we're going to enter now."

NOTES

1. "Judgment of the Court, Google Spain SL and Google Inc. v AEPD and Mario Costeja González," Court of Justice of the European Union, May 13, 2014, http://tinyurl.com/mjd6hru. The court upheld the order of the Spanish Data Protection Agency (AEPD) saying that the newspaper *La Vanguardia* could leave the items about Costeja González on its website, but that Google must remove the links.

2. "Majority of Americans Think it Should be Human Right to Delete or Remove Personal Information Online," PR Newswire, Aug. 27, 2015, http://tinyurl.com/okroxo2.

3. Marc Rotenberg, "EU Strikes a Blow for Privacy, Opposing View" *USA Today*, May 14, 2014, http://tinyurl.com/qhvsqaf.

4. "Google Transparency Report," Google, updated Nov. 20, 2015, http://tinyurl.com/oghquhn.

5. Danny O'Brien and Jillian York, "Rights That Are Being Forgotten," Electronic Frontier Foundation, July 8, 2014, http://tinyurl.com/qams 66g.

6. "CNIL orders Google to apply delisting on all domain names of the search engine," CNIL, June 12, 2015, http://tinyurl.com/o6e2wvh. Also see "Right to delisting: Google informal appeal rejected," CNIL, Sept. 21, 2015, http://tinyurl.com/ohettz6.

7. "Letter to Commission nationale de l'informatique et des libertés (CNIL)," Reporters Committee for Freedom of the Press, Sept. 14, 2015, http://tinyurl.com/pbgxp2a. Text of letter: http://tinyurl.com/qdloddb.

8. Jeffrey Toobin, "The Solace of Oblivion," *The New Yorker*, Sept. 29, 2014, http://tinyurl.com/neo4qyu.

9. Letter of complaint to FTC, Consumer Watchdog, July 7, 2015, http://tinyurl.com/nkarduu.

10. Toobin, *op. cit.*

11. Ronnie Cohen, "California Law allows kids to erase digital indiscretions," Reuters, Sept. 26, 2013, http://tinyurl.com/pg5jffq.

12. See Danny O'Brien, "Brazil's Politicians Aim to Add Mandatory Real Names and a Right to Erase History to the Marco Civil," Electronic Frontier Foundation, Oct. 14, 2015, http://tinyurl.com/o688pek. For Russia, see Tarun Krishnakumar, "Russian Roulette and the Right to be Forgotten," Chilling Effects, Lumen, June 16, 2015, http://tinyurl.com/o5myt35.

13. Peter Noorlander, "Google Spain Case," LSE Media Policy Project Blog, May 14, 2014, http://tinyurl.com/pu9v4bb.

14. Toobin, *op. cit.*

15. European Commission press release: "Antitrust," April 15, 2015, http://tinyurl.com/oxusos8.

16. Toobin, *op. cit.*

17. Section 1 Rights and Freedoms, Article 10, European Convention on Human Rights, Council of Europe, undated, http://tinyurl.com/qywhyns.

18. David Erdos, "Mind the Gap," Open Democracy, May 15, 2014, http://tinyurl.com/nff2fc7.

19. "Reporters Committee leads Coalition urging French data regulator to reconsider "right to be forgotten" delisting order," Reporters Committee for Freedom of the Press, Sept. 15, 2014, http://tinyurl.com/pkbku2d. Also see text of Sept. 14, 2015 letter at: http://tinyurl.com/qjykmp8.

20. Toobin, *op. cit.* The First Amendment states, "Congress shall make no law . . . abridging the freedom of speech or of the press."

21. Miquel Peguera, "No More Right to be Forgotten for Mr. Costeja," CIS blog, Oct. 3, 2015, http://tinyurl.com/olc8drw. Note: The court papers did not reveal which article link Costeja Gonzalez was protesting.

22. Marc Scott, "Google Reinstates European Links to Articles from *The Guardian*," *The New York Times*, July 4, 2014, http://tinyurl.com/n3enf4w.

23. Sylvia Tippmann and Julia Powles, "Google accidentally reveals data on 'right to be forgotten' requests," *The Guardian*, July 14, 20015, http://tinyurl.com/ne8ns9o.

24. Owen Bowcott and Kim Willsher, "Google's French arm faces €1,000 daily fines over links to defamatory

article," *The Guardian*, Nov. 13, 2014, http://tinyurl.com/owyljur.

25. Peter Fleischer, "Implementing a European, not global, right to be forgotten," Google Europe blog, July 30, 2015, http://tinyurl.com/pfl7rvr. Also see "Russian Parliament Approves 'right to be forgotten' law," *Deutsche Welle*, July 3, 2015, http://tinyurl.com/pzpmmtc.

26. *Ibid.*

27. Farhad Manjoo, "Right to be Forgotten' Online Could Spread," *The New York Times*, Aug. 5, 2015, http://tinyurl.com/o8yasrf.

28. "Reporters Committee leads Coalition urging French data regulator to reconsider "right to be forgotten" delisting order," *op. cit.*

29. "The Advisory Council to Google on the Right to be Forgotten," Google.com, Feb. 6, 2015, http://tinyurl.com/p8jjcov.

30. Natasha Lomas, "Google faces fight in Europe on search delisting," *Tech Crunch*, Feb. 6, 2015, http://tinyurl.com/q8fyc6l.

31. "Convention for the Protection of Individuals with regard to Automatic Processing of Personal Data," Council of Europe, http://tinyurl.com/ng7cmqf.

32. Eric Posner, "We all have the right to be forgotten," *Slate*, May 14, 2014, http://tinyurl.com/mc6ttwx.

33. Consumer Watchdog letter to FTC, *op. cit.*

34. ANA letter to FTC, July 31, 2015, http://tinyurl.com/q8qhmly.

35. "Digital Millennium Copyright Act," Summary, U.S. Copyright Office, 1998, http://tinyurl.com/6u7hf.

36. Daphne Keller, "Empirical Evidence of 'Over-Removal' by Internet Companies under Intermediary Liability Laws," CIS blog, Oct. 12, 2015, http://tinyurl.com/q4r7oxy.

37. Evan Hansen, "Google pulls anti-Scientology links," CNET, April 22, 2002, http://tinyurl.com/pzd6z72.

38. Posner, *op. cit.*

39. Greg Sterling, "Another Court Affirms Google's First Amendment Control of Search Results," *Search Engine Land*, Nov. 17, 2014, http://tinyurl.com/npcrbea.

40. Cohen, *op. cit.*

41. James Q. Whitman, "The Two Western Cultures of Privacy: Dignity versus Liberty," *Yale Law Journal*, Jan. 1, 2004, pp. 1151-see p. 1160, http://tinyurl.com/q4gd9nu.

42. Viktor Mayer-Schönberger, *Delete* (2009), p. 141.

43. *Ibid.*

44. The Universal Declaration was absorbed into the International Bill of Rights, consisting of four treaties, only one of which the United States has ratified. See University of Minnesota Human Rights Library, "Ratification of International Human Rights Treaties-USA," http://tinyurl.com/opk937y. Also see United Nations, "Fact Sheet No. 2, International Bill of Human Rights," http://tinyurl.com/nu6uk7g.

45. European Convention on Human Rights, *op. cit.*

46. See "EU Data Protection Directive," search security.co.uk, http://tinyurl.com/9p4xka5.

47. Sharon Dietrich, "New Ruling Highlights Why We Need REDEEM Act," *Talk Poverty*, June 3, 2015, http://tinyurl.com/qxeeqer.

48. Vivian Reding, "Privacy Matters," European Union, Nov. 30, 2010, http://tinyurl.com/qgyumag.

49. Article 29 Data Protection Working Party, European Commission, press release, Nov. 26, 2014, http://tinyurl.com/ocwgbec.

50. Toobin, *op. cit.*

51. Samuel D. Warren and Louis D. Brandeis, "The Right to Privacy," *Harvard Law Review*, Dec. 15, 1890, pp. 193-220, p. 195, http://tinyurl.com/qavzf2b.

52. Leah Burrows, "To Be Let Alone: Brandeis foresaw privacy problems," *Brandeis Now*, July 24, 2013, http://tinyurl.com/pyhcqgg.

53. Whitman, *op. cit.*

54. Robert Ellis Smith, *The Law of Privacy Explained* (1993), pp. 5-8, http://tinyurl.com/pgr9n5g.

55. *Ibid.*

56. Erwin Chemerinsky, "Rediscovering Brandeis's Right to Privacy," *Brandeis Law Journal*, vol. 45, 2006-2007, pp. 643-657, http://tinyurl.com/pyg5slp.

57. *Ibid.*

58. *Griswold v. Connecticut* (1965) opinion, *Justia*, U.S. Supreme Court, http://tinyurl.com/orrrxc4.

59. Chemerinsky, *op. cit.*, p. 653.

60. *Ibid.*

61. *Ibid.*, p. 654.

62. "A Summary of your Rights under the Fair Credit Reporting Act," Federal Trade Commission, 2014, http://tinyurl.com/narqyf8.

63. "Privacy Act of 1974," Department of Justice, updated July 17, 2015, http://tinyurl.com/nox2xpf.

64. Health Information Privacy, U.S. Department of Health and Human Services, updated, http://tinyurl.com/pydcvt.

65. "Complying with COPPA," Federal Trade Commission, http://tinyurl.com/okd9e5k.

66. Kristin Cohen and Christina Yeung, "Kids apps disclosures revisited," Federal Trade Commission, Sept. 3, 2015, http://tinyurl.com/pb6k586.

67. "Right to delisting: Google informal appeal rejected," CNIL, Sept. 21, 2015, http://tinyurl.com/ohettz6.

68. See "Reform of the Data Protection legal framework in the EU," *op. cit.*

69. For background see Julia Powles, "Tech companies like Facebook not above the law, says Max Schrems," *The Guardian*, Oct. 9, 2015, http://tinyurl.com/oy5crtn.

70. Mark Scott, "Data Transfer Pact Between U.S. and Europe is Ruled Invalid," *The New York Times*, Oct. 6, 2015, http://tinyurl.com/o469wa4. For background, see Chuck McCutcheon, "Government Surveillance," *CQ Researcher*, Aug. 30, 2013, pp. 717-740.

71. "Max Schrems: the lawyer who took on Facebook," Reuters, Oct. 7, 2015, http://tinyurl.com/qg9gesc.

72. Testimony of Marc Rotenberg, hearing on "Examining the EU Safe Harbor Decision and Impacts for Transatlantic Data Flows," United States House of Representatives Energy & Commerce Subcommittees on Commerce, Manufacturing, and Trade and Communications and Technology, Nov. 3, 2015.

73. "Administration Discussion Draft: Consumer Privacy Bill of Rights Act of 2015," White House, undated, http://tinyurl.com/oydmctk.

74. Elizabeth Dwoskin, "White House Proposes Consumer Privacy Bill of Rights," "Digits," *The Wall Street Journal*, Feb. 27, 2015, http://tinyurl.com/m9mflja. The Information Technology Industry Council, a group supported by Microsoft, Facebook and Google, said, "The U.S. has a robust legal framework of privacy protections" that permits the industry to innovate and that "any efforts to modify this framework must be carefully considered."

75. See "EU-US Privacy Bridges," report released Oct. 21, 2015, http://tinyurl.com/o5jwvcu.

76. Sen. Edward J. Markey, press release, "Markey, Barton . . . Reintroduce Bipartisan, Bicameral Legislation to Protect Children's Online Privacy," June 11, 2015, http://tinyurl.com/q3juroo.

77. Do Not Track Kids Act of 2015, "S1563," Congress.gov, http://tinyurl.com/p8cxyhq; Congress.gov, "H.R. 2734," http://tinyurl.com/np56avl.

78. Mary Madden and Lee Rainie, "Americans' Views About Data Collection and Security," Pew Research Center, May 20, 2015, http://tinyurl.com/oj83fb9.

79. Toobin, *op. cit.*

80. "FTC Approves Final Order Settling Charges against Snapchat," Federal Trade Commission, Dec. 31, 2014, http://tinyurl.com/o6w3cln.

81. Helena Horton, "Will Snapchat's New Update stop people from sexting using the app?" *The Telegraph*, Sept. 16, 2015, http://tinyurl.com/pft6ayr.

BIBLIOGRAPHY
Selected Sources
Books

Bamberger, Kenneth A., and Deirdre K. Mulligan, ***Privacy on the Ground: Driving Corporate Behavior in the United States and Europe,*** **MIT Press, 2015.**
U.S. privacy law remains more fragmented than in Europe, but American corporations often have more robust privacy practices than their European counterparts, according to two professors at the University of California's Berkeley Center for Law and Technology.

Citron, Danielle Keats, *Hate Crimes in Cyberspace*, **Harvard University Press, 2014.**
A University of Maryland professor reviews the state of the law for cyber-harassment victims and argues that those who engage in "revenge porn" should be criminally prosecuted.

Mayer-Schönberger, Viktor, *Delete: The Virtue of Forgetting in the Digital Age*, **Princeton University Press, 2009.**
A person's online information should have an expiration date, a professor of Internet governance and regulation says in this seminal book.

Articles

Ausloos, Jef, and Aleksandra Kuczeraway, "From Notice-and-Takedown to Notice-and-Delist: Implementing the Google Spain Ruling," **ICRI Research Paper 24, forthcoming in** *Colorado Technology Law Journal*, **Oct. 5, 2015, http://tinyurl.com/qhyanmm.**
Two researchers at the University of Leuven, Belgium, analyze legal controversies over the recent Google Spain ruling in the European Union saying search engines have a duty to remove someone's search results upon request.

Chemerinsky, Erwin, "Rediscovering Brandeis' Right to Privacy," *Brandeis Law Journal*, **2006-07, pp. 643-657, http://tinyurl.com/pyg5slp.**
Tracing Supreme Court decisions on privacy, a University of California-Irvine law professor concludes that there is little judicial protection for individuals trying to prevent their private information from being publicly disseminated.

Keller, Daphne, "The GDPR's Notice and Takedown Rules: Bad for Free Expression, but Not Beyond Repair," **Center for Internet and Society, Oct. 29, 2015, http://tinyurl.com/nko8vzt.**
Pending European Union legislation could hamper free expression by imposing new erasure requirements, an Internet expert warns.

O'Brien, Danny, and Jillian York, "Rights That Are Being Forgotten: Google, the ECJ, and Free Expression," **Electronic Frontier Foundation, July 8, 2014, http://tinyurl.com/pq5gvsm.**
Two members of a civil liberties advocacy group criticize the Google Spain ruling as forcing search engines to "censor publicly available information" without properly balancing free expression.

Posner, Eric, "We all have the right to be forgotten," *Slate*, **May 14, 2014, http://tinyurl.com/mc6ttwx.**
A University of Chicago law professor says adopting a "right to be forgotten" in the United States would simply return individuals' privacy to the way it was before the Internet.

Rosen, Jeffrey, "The Right to be Forgotten," **Feb. 13, 2012,** *Stanford Law Review*, **http://tinyurl.com/7cwjwvn.**
In this widely quoted article, a George Washington University law professor called pending EU data-protection legislation the "biggest threat to free speech on the Internet in the coming decade."

Tippmann, Sylvia, and Julia Powles, "Google accidentally reveals data on 'right to be forgotten' requests," *The Guardian*, **July 14, 2015, http://tinyurl.com/ne8ns9o.**
The vast majority of requests to Google to remove search results came from people who were not famous.

Toobin, Jeffrey, "The Solace of Oblivion," *The New Yorker*, **Sept. 29, 2014, http://tinyurl.com/neo4qyu.**
A *New Yorker* writer and lawyer presents a sympathetic portrayal of a family that tried to remove gory photos of their daughter's fatal car crash from the Internet, but says Europe's right to be forgotten would "never pass muster under U.S. law."

Reports and Studies

"The Advisory Council to Google on the Right to be Forgotten," Google, Feb. 6, 2015, http://tinyurl.com/qg4uhuu.
Experts appointed by Google to advise it on how to implement the "right to be forgotten" agreed with the company that it should not remove search results outside of Europe.

"Google Transparency Report: European Privacy Requests for Removals," Google, updated Nov. 11, 2015, http://tinyurl.com/ptypu56.
In this report, updated periodically, Google provides information about requests it has received for search removals in Europe by country, and examples of its decisions about whether to remove search results.

Humphries, Daniel, "U.S. Attitudes towards the 'Right to be Forgotten,' IndustryView 2014," **Software Advice, Sept. 5, 2014, http://tinyurl.com/pjrkkhp.**
A software industry poll of 500 Americans found 61 percent want some version of the right to be forgotten.

For More Information

Association of National Advertisers, 2020 K St., N.W., Washington, DC 20006; 202-296-1883; www.ana.net. Industry group representing 670 companies that opposes implementing a "right to be forgotten" in the United States.

Center for Digital Democracy, 1621 Connecticut Ave., N.W., #500, Washington, DC 20009; 202-986-2220; www .democraticmedia.org. Consumer group advocating online consumer privacy.

Common Sense Media, 650 Townsend, Suite 435, San Francisco, CA 94103; 415-863-0600, www.commonsense media.org. Research and advocacy group that works to protect children's online privacy.

Consumer Watchdog, 2701 Ocean Park Blvd., Suite 112, Santa Monica, CA 90405; 310-392-8874; www.consumer watchdog.org. Consumer advocacy group that favors imple-menting a "right to be forgotten" in the United States.

Court of Justice of the European Union, Palais de la Cour de Justice, Boulevard Konrad Adenauer, Kirchberg, L-2925

Luxembourg, Luxembourg; +352-4303-1; http://curia.europa .eu. The European Union's high court that interprets E.U. law to make sure it is applied the same way in all countries.

Electronic Frontier Foundation, 815 Eddy St., San Francisco, CA 94109; 415-436-9333; www.eff.org. Membership organization that defends civil liberties in the digital world.

Electronic Privacy Information Center, 1718 Connecticut Ave., N.W., Suite 200, Washington, DC 20009; 202-483-1140; www.epic.org. Research center that works to protect privacy and provide a public voice in decisions concerning the future of the Internet.

Federal Trade Commission, 600 Pennsylvania Ave., N.W., Washington, DC 20580; 202-326-2222; www.ftc.gov. Federal consumer protection agency.

Future of Privacy Forum, 1400 Eye St., N.W., Suite 450, Washington, DC 20005; 202-642-9142; https://fpf.org. Think tank that seeks to advance responsible data practices.

9

The Dark Web

Marcia Clemmitt

Chinese author and free-speech activist Murong Xuecun says access to the Dark Web through Tor enables citizens to find information their governments try to block. He warns that China's censorship program — known as "the great firewall" — creates "a Chinese information prison where ignorance fosters ideologies of hatred and aggression."

From *CQ Researcher*,
January 15, 2016

Getty Images/Ulf Andersen

The Kilton Public Library in tiny Lebanon, N.H., stirred controversy this past year when it became the first U.S. library to join a global volunteer computer network that helps people surf the Internet anonymously.

The network, a vast system of linked computers that use identity-masking software, helps protect political dissidents and journalists in repressive regimes from revealing their location, communications or website browsing habits and risking government surveillance or reprisal.

Libraries typically support privacy and free-expression rights, including the rights of patrons to read, communicate and surf the Web without fear of prying eyes.

But identity-hiding software — including the most widely used version, Tor, the one used by Kilton — has a darker side as well, and that is where the library ran into problems. Child pornographers, drug dealers and other criminals seeking to hide their identity also use it. When the Department of Homeland Security warned Lebanon city officials about Tor's potential for criminal use, the library put its groundbreaking project on hold.[1]

But that wasn't the end of it. When officials asked citizens to weigh in through a survey and public meeting, the responses heavily favored rejoining the network. Ending participation, said Lebanon resident Raymond Hood, would threaten freedoms gained in the American Revolution. "What would our forefathers think?" he asked. Soon, the library's Tor hook-up was running again.[2]

How Tor Works

Tor software creates a circuit of multiple computers that connects the user anonymously to any Internet destination. The software encrypts the user's location data at each computer link so the pathway cannot be traced. The final computer sends the user's message to its destination bearing the final computer's location data, not the user's.

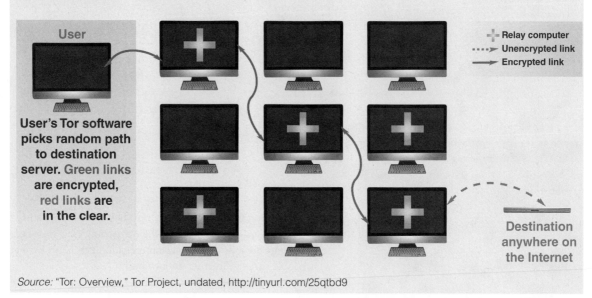

User

User's Tor software picks random path to destination server. Green links are encrypted, red links are in the clear.

Relay computer
Unencrypted link
Encrypted link

Destination anywhere on the Internet

Source: "Tor: Overview," Tor Project, undated, http://tinyurl.com/25qtbd9

The episode underscores an intense debate over Tor and other so-called anonymizing technology, which emerged in the early 2000s and now counts several million daily users across the globe. Users of the technology include military personnel conducting covert operations from overseas safe houses and whistleblowers or dissidents in countries with heavy government censorship. But sex traffickers, arms dealers, terrorists and other criminals also use anonymizing technology, helping earn it the moniker of "Dark Web," a phrase that many law enforcement officials embrace but that free-speech and privacy advocates say obscures its merits as a tool to protect online civil liberties.

The Dark Web has "so much potential, both good and bad," says Joseph Nedelec, an assistant professor of criminology at the University of Cincinnati. "The problem is, how do we allow for the freedom of expression, the opportunity to be private, but at the same time manage the nefarious activity?"

Tor performs several functions, such as:

- Preventing websites from tracking Internet users who utilize the software;
- Allowing users to visit websites blocked by their local Internet service providers;
- Allowing users to set up secret websites accessible only to other Tor users.[3]

The anonymized Internet originally was called the Dark Web because websites carried on it didn't show up in ordinary search engines such as Google. They could be reached only with special software, says Andrea Forte, an assistant professor at Drexel University's College of Computing and Informatics in Philadelphia. "Then 'dark' got to be a value judgment," she says, "and that precludes rational arguments" about the technology's value. While "Dark Web" mainly refers to the network of secret websites accessible only to those using special identity-hiding software, the term sometimes describes any use of Tor or other anonymizing software to surf the Internet without being tracked.

Dark Web pages make up the newest and likely smallest of the Internet's three parts, each accessible by different means. They are:

- The Surface Web — the most familiar — which includes all Web pages indexed and accessible by standard search engines such as Google or Bing.
- The so-called Deep Web, made up of a vast number of Web pages such as university student directories and court or bank-record databases, which standard search engines cannot reach and often require visitors to log in or use a site-specific search engine. The Deep Web is far larger than the Surface Web — perhaps 500 times bigger, according to one oft-cited scholarly analysis.[4]
- The Dark Web, whose sites are reachable only with special anonymizing software that hides their physical locations. Different anonymizing software versions access separate Dark Web sites, but Tor is the most prominent.

The Dark Web's size is harder to determine than the other two parts of the Internet. Its websites are hidden by design, notes the Tor home page. However, "based on popularity it would appear reasonable to guess that, in total, the size of dark networks combined is far smaller [than the Deep Web], and highly likely to be smaller" than the Surface Web, according to analysts at the Massachusetts-based nonprofit Tor Project, which develops and maintains the Tor software.[5]

Some 7,000 volunteers worldwide operate the Tor network, allowing their computers to be used as "relay" computers — like the one at Kilton Public Library, says Katie Krauss, director of communications and public policy for the Tor Project. Project researchers estimate that, in 2014, about 2.5 million people worldwide used Tor browser software every day.[6] The overwhelming

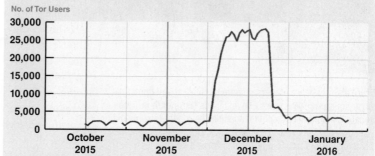

Tor Use Soars Amid a Speech Crackdown

In an example of the Dark Web's use by people fighting for free speech, the number of Bangladeshis connecting directly to Tor rose sixfold in late November after the government blocked social media and mobile messaging in the wake of a high-court ruling up- holding the death penalty for two opposition leaders. Tor use began falling in December after authorities eased the restrictions.

No. of Tor Users

Sources: Data from Tor Metrics, http://tinyurl.com/pfk3yty; caption information from Patrick Howell O'Neill, "Tor use skyrockets in Bangladesh after government bans social networks," *The Daily Dot*, Nov. 23, 2015, http://tinyurl.com/po7xtkg; and Shaikh Azizur Rahman, "Bangladesh Lifts Ban on Facebook," Voice of America, Dec. 10, 2015, http://tinyurl.com/h5qcy8x

majority, however, used the browser to anonymously visit Surface Web sites, not Dark Web sites.[7]

Tor's Dark Web sites — called hidden services — offer the same kinds of functions as other Internet sites, such as file storage, news, archives and discussion forums.[8] Since all their users are anonymous, no one knows who uses the hidden sites' services and why. Many of the reasons people use Tor to surf the Internet, though, are well understood, says Peter Swire, a professor of law and ethics at the Georgia Institute of Technology's Scheller College of Business in Atlanta.

Investors, for example, may want to keep Web surfing patterns private to avoid revealing investment strategies, and police agencies use Tor to protect confidential informants, Swire says. And the State Department strongly supports the Tor network as a way for human-rights workers in dangerous regions to report abuses anonymously, says Susan Landau, a professor of cybersecurity policy at Worcester Polytechnic Institute and former senior staff privacy analyst at Google.

Because anonymizing technology obscures website locations, Tor users can access information their

New York City police officers prepare to patrol against potential terrorism during New Year's Eve festivities last month in Times Square. While law enforcement agencies have scored some major takedowns of Dark Web criminal venues, U.S. intelligence officials say anonymizing technology such as Tor is a key barrier to tackling terrorism and cybercrime.

governments censor and block, wrote Chinese author Murong Xuecun.[9] For instance, China's censorship program — known as "the great firewall" — creates "a Chinese information prison where ignorance fosters ideologies of hatred and aggression," he wrote. "If the firewall exists indefinitely, China will eventually revert to what it once was: a sealed off, narrow-minded, belligerent, rogue state."

Murong downloaded anonymizing software after a friend told him that Tibetans were setting fire to themselves to protest Chinese occupation. He had lived in Tibet for several years just before the self-immolation protests began but had not heard about them in China's censored news.[10]

In November 2015, the government of Bangladesh, in South Asia, temporarily blocked many Internet communication channels on the day it announced it would uphold death sentences for two prominent politicians earlier convicted of war crimes. The number of Bangladeshi Tor users quickly soared from 2,000 to around 12,000 as residents presumably sought ways to read about and discuss the event.[11]

At the same time, anonymizing technology offers criminals new opportunities to hide.

Online activities on the Surface Web "are easy to trace," wrote Marc Goodman, author of the 2015 book *Future Crimes* and chairman for policy, law and ethics at

Santa Clara County, Calif.-based Singularity University, a company that provides educational programs and business-incubator services in Silicon Valley. "Bad guys don't like this; it makes them easy to catch. So instead, they obfuscate and route their traffic through services like Tor. This way, the cops can't see that gangsters are selling AK-47s online using the Comcast server in Chicago," he wrote.[12]

Like legitimate big businesses, organized crime today has much digital infrastructure, some of which it now houses on the Dark Web, Goodman says. "Crime Inc. really is Crime Inc." today, he says. Some criminal organizations have hundreds of employees, including some who perform such familiar business roles as human resource management and research and development on cutting-edge crime techniques, and bases of operation are on all three parts of the Web, Goodman says.

The Dark Web also facilitates sales among criminals, Goodman says. "This is where they actually trade stolen credit-card information" and "buy things to run criminal sites" on the Surface Web, such as "bulletproof" web-hosting services that promise to retain "no information about their clients so they can't give information to law enforcement" if police come knocking, according to Goodman.

The cybercrime known as "ransomware" is making more people aware — and leery — of Tor, says Joseph Lorenzo Hall, chief technologist at the Center for Democracy and Technology, a group in Washington that promotes Internet freedom and innovation. In a ransomware attack, a hacker remotely encrypts files on a computer, making them temporarily unusable, Hall explains. When the computer starts up, a message appears demanding the user pay a ransom, such as $5,000 in bitcoin — the difficult-to-trace currency used on the anonymized Web — before being able to access his data.[13]

To make the ransom payment, the user must download the Tor browser, Hall says. Ransomware crimes are "hitting tens of thousands of people," giving them "a very negative reaction to this anonymizing tool," he says.

Terrorists also can hide on the Dark Web. In early 2015 Ido Wulkan, a senior analyst at S2T, a cybersecurity company in Singapore, said the company had found the first evidence that some Dark Web sites raise money for ISIS, the militant Islamic jihadist group, as some security analysts had long theorized.[14]

Wulkan tracked down what looked to be a Dark Web ISIS fundraising site, apparently operated mainly by Americans, after reading about it on forums. An account number for the digital currency bitcoin was also found, showing that the site had raised five bitcoins, worth about $1,000 at the time. The FBI seized the account. Wulkan acknowledged that the site could simply be a one-off fundraising effort or even a hoax rather than clear evidence of a real and growing ISIS fundraising presence on the Dark Web. But he noted that Internet forum chatter and a blog have previously suggested that ISIS was interested in both the Dark Web and fundraising with bitcoin. "There was smoke, and now we have found the fire," said Wulkan.[15]

As law enforcement agencies, privacy advocates and computer scientists debate whether to support or curb anonymizing technologies, here are some of the questions being asked:

Is the Dark Web driving up crime?

The anonymized Web is so new — and so hard to research — that no solid evidence demonstrates whether it is driving an increase in crime or whether it might be primarily changing the venue of some crimes, such as drug sales and child-pornography distribution.

Anecdotal evidence suggests that the Dark Web may be hosting some new drug dealers, according to Jamie Bartlett, author of the 2014 book *The Dark Net* and director of the Centre for the Analysis of Social Media at Demos, a London-based, nonpartisan social policy think tank. His research on Silk Road, an anonymous black market for drugs shut down by the FBI in 2013, turned up sellers who said they were new to the trade. For example, Ace, a 24-year-old, told Bartlett he filled 10 to 20 orders a day for "homegrown weed" on Silk Road in 2012. And Bartlett found that some scientists who study the effects of prescription drugs had begun illegally selling those drugs out of their laboratories using Dark Web markets.[16]

Future Crimes author Goodman says the proliferation of Dark Web markets is helping lead to "crime as a service," a new, ominous development in which highly skilled cybercriminals package their tech knowhow in software so nontechies can also commit cybercrimes.

In the past, would-be cybercriminals had to be technically savvy to hack into websites to steal credit card information, for example, Goodman says. Today, technologically savvy criminals are creating "point-and-click crimeware in a box," providing "a whole new category of software that actually commits crime," he says. "So you don't need to be a hacker to be a cybercriminal. You just need to buy the software in an anonymous online market." This development multiplies the number of people who can commit cybercrimes, Goodman says.

Moreover, the Internet has facilitated the trading of child pornography, and some researchers think the Dark Web will likely drive further increases in such image-sharing.

"A leading law enforcement expert advised us that child pornography producers are using Tor hidden services for the creation and dissemination of child pornography and bitcoin for payment," although much of the evidence for that is admittedly anecdotal, said Ernie Allen, the recently retired president of the International Centre for Missing & Exploited Children, in Alexandria, Va. The expert also advised Allen's group that the development is significant because the crimes observed in these venues suggest an expansion of the problem, tending "to involve new victims whom law enforcement has not seen before," Allen said.[17]

In December 2014, Gareth Owen, a senior lecturer in computing at England's University of Portsmouth, released a study finding that more than four out of five visits to Tor hidden services were to sites with child pornography, even though such sites are far outnumbered by those dealing with other matters. "Before we did this study, it was certainly my view that the Dark Net is a good thing," said Owen. "But it's hampering the rights of children and creating a place where pedophiles can act with impunity," he said.[18]

Tor Project representatives, though, have argued that the finding isn't as alarming as it appears. For one thing, visits to Tor hidden services account for less than 4 percent of traffic on the Tor network overall.[19] The Tor Project also noted that many visitors to child pornography sites are members of law-enforcement and anti-child-abuse groups that also use the Tor browser to regularly patrol the sites and in some cases hackers have conducted massive so-called denial of service attacks, in which multiple computers access a site at once to crash it.[20]

"People doing cybercrime aren't necessarily doing crime offline" and may therefore represent an entirely new batch of criminals, according to some studies, says the University of Cincinnati's Nedelec. "The studies are few and often are self-reporting, but they point to the idea that maybe there are some individuals who wouldn't do these things without the Dark Web."

Nevertheless, Nedelec says he is not sure whether the Dark Web will lead to an increase in crime. For one thing, he says, few people are comfortable with Dark Web technology. "The average street criminal probably won't go on," Nedelec says. Over time, he continues, as more people become more computer literate, "more will check it out, but I doubt that it will have a real spike effect in terms of crime."

Analyses implying that the Dark Web is greatly increasing the incidence of crime generally ignore how much crime takes place on the Surface Web, said technology and crime reporter Joseph Cox. For example, the Internet Watch Foundation, a charity in Cambridgeshire, England, that works to minimize child pornography, in 2014 found 31,266 Internet URLs with child porn images, said Cox. Of those, only 51 — 0.2 percent — were on the Dark Web.[21]

Similarly, "the volume of [drug] transactions on online anonymous marketplaces is infinitesimal compared to the overall drug trade," says Nicolas Christin, an assistant research professor of computer engineering at Pittsburgh's Carnegie Mellon University, who has conducted some of the most extensive research on anonymous markets. "In terms of the impact of online anonymous marketplaces on the overall drug trade, speaking purely in economic terms, I would say it is negligible" at this point.

While the Dark Web is clearly the best anonymizing option for noncriminals such as whistleblowers, it is seldom the most effective choice for criminals, making its role in driving significant crime increases doubtful, says Cooper Quintin, staff technologist at the San Francisco-based nonprofit Electronic Frontier Foundation, which advocates for civil liberties in the digital world. For most kinds of crime, "criminals have many options that can make them much more anonymous than Tor can," he says. For example, unlike a law-abiding person, a criminal can create a virtually impenetrable false online identity by stealing a credit card or hacking into someone else's computer and hiding behind that stolen identity to commit other cybercrimes, he notes.[22]

Georgia Tech's Swire is skeptical about claims that The Dark Web is helping terrorists plan more attacks. When terrorist attacks killed 130 people in Paris in November 2015, "people speculated that the Dark Web" had aided the planning, Swire says, but it was later shown that most of the attackers' communication had been through everyday channels such as emails.

"A terrorist can use advanced technology to hide communications," he explains. But, he says, employing a very widely used mainstream technology such as Gmail and using simple code words such as referring to a terrorist act as a "birthday party" can actually be more effective against surveillance. "With hundreds of millions of users, your Gmail using vague or common terms gets lost in a sea of messages," exactly the result that terrorists choosing widely used code words hope for.

Some intelligence officers say the mainstream Internet — using common and general language — remains one of the most effective ways for terrorists to communicate. If a "message reads only one word 'tomorrow,' or even 'the weather is good,' how does that help us?" said a U.S. intelligence officer. "We might be warned that something is happening, but we don't know where or when."[23]

Is the Dark Web increasing the illegal sale of drugs?

The Internet has long been used to make illegal drug sales.

As far back as 1971 or 1972, the first commerce ever conducted on the fledgling Internet was a marijuana transaction between computer science students from Stanford University in Palo Alto, Calif., and the Massachusetts Institute of Technology (MIT), wrote technology journalist John Markoff.[24] Through the years, all kinds of online forums and communications channels have facilitated illegal sales of both recreational and prescription drugs.[25]

In 2009, a new drug market — The Drugstore — was the first online drug market to be established as a Tor hidden service.[26] Of the 40,000 to 60,000 hidden websites operated on Tor today, Dark Web researchers estimate that about 15 percent are for illegal drug sales.[27]

With so little evidence yet accumulated, though, drug-policy analysts remain uncertain how the Dark Web may be changing drug use.

The growth of Dark Web markets may have slightly increased illegal drug use in 2014, according to the 2015

Global Drug Survey, an annual international survey by a U.K.-based independent research team. The survey of the substance-use habits of more than 100,000 people in 50 nations found that 4 percent who bought drugs on the Dark Web said they had not consumed illegal drugs before buying them through that means. In addition, 30 percent said the availability of Dark Web markets had increased the variety of drugs they used. Worldwide, the number of drug users buying on the Dark Web rose by 1.2 percent between 2013 and 2014, according to the survey.[28]

"Dark net markets make drugs available more easily," which is "nothing to celebrate," wrote Bartlett of the Centre for the Analysis of Social Media. "It will tend towards higher levels of use, and drug use — legal or illegal — creates misery."[29]

U.S. Leads in Tor Use

Nearly 370,000 people directly connected daily to Tor, an anonymous computer network, from the United States in 2015. Germany ranked second with an average of more than 200,000 daily direct users, followed by Russia (186,000), France (135,000) and the United Kingdom (92,000).

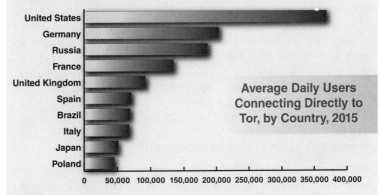

Average Daily Users Connecting Directly to Tor, by Country, 2015

Source: "Top-10 countries by directly connecting users," Tor Metrics, accessed Jan. 6, 2016, http://tinyurl.com/j4c2u8q

At the same time, unique features of Dark Web markets could reduce some harms of the drug trade, Bartlett and others argue. For one thing, in traditional illegal drug sales, the supply chain includes many middlemen, said Bartlett. The longer the supply chain, the more opportunities exist for violent confrontations between rival drug sellers and for dangerous and fraudulent adulteration of drugs by middlemen trying to boost profits, he wrote.[30]

Dark Web markets greatly shorten the supply chain and thus reduce the potential for such harms, said Bartlett. Because payments are exchanged online using anonymous electronic currency such as bitcoin, and because drugs are shipped by mail, drug sellers and individual buyers in Dark Web markets can interact from anywhere, and few middlemen are needed.[31]

Dark Web markets also use customer ratings and reviews, just as Amazon and other online sellers and e-commerce sites do, which helps buyers avoid untrustworthy sellers or sellers of bad drugs, said Bartlett.[32]

"All my fears about quality are gone," thanks to customer ratings and reviews, a Dark Web drug customer told researchers at the Global Drug Policy Observatory

at Swansea University, in Wales. "I know what I'm getting, and I know that it's good."[33]

"I think the notion of harm reduction [for drug sales] is really critical," says Christin. "If a crime is going to be committed, you want to make sure that, as much as possible, you minimize collateral damage from this crime."

Still unanswered is the question of whether Dark Web markets will significantly increase drug availability. At present, they don't appear to be doing so, Christin says.

"Online anonymous marketplaces so far are just a novel, different retail distribution channel," he says in an email interview. "They do not change anything from the bulk side. Basically they are competing with the street corner dealer, not with the Zetas" — a Mexican drug cartel.

Some drug-policy analysts say the Dark Web is a relatively small contributor to drug-abuse problems today but eventually may significantly drive an increase in abuse of at least some drugs.

Prescription-drug abuse, for example, is a substantial problem in countries including the United States, Canada and Australia, but despite availability of prescription drugs for illegal sale on the Dark Web, only a small fraction of the trade currently happens there, said

Ann Roche, director of Australia's National Centre for Education and Training on Addiction, at Flinders University, in Adelaide. It's still cheaper and easier for most people abusing prescription drugs to "doctor shop" for friendly physicians willing to write unwarranted prescriptions or buy leftover prescription pills that "regular mums and dads in the suburbs" may be hawking for side income, said Roche.[34]

However, as countries such as Australia clamp down on such means of procuring the drugs, there is "good reason" to think that Dark Web markets will play a much bigger role in illegal prescription-drug buying, said Roche, the chief architect of Australia's National Pharmaceutical Drug Misuse Strategy.[35]

Is the Dark Web hurting law enforcement's ability to apprehend criminals?

Some crime analysts argue that anonymizing technologies are part of a computer revolution that's changing the nature of crime so drastically that traditional police methods may soon be helpless against crimes with an online component, such as child pornography.

Others, however, say police agencies' success so far in shutting down large Dark Web criminal venues shows that traditional investigative methods can still be effective.

When it comes to drug crimes, "the conclusion of our newest paper is that traditional policing does work" on the Dark Web, says Carnegie Mellon's Christin. "Undercover operations in particular are easier to conduct in an anonymous marketplace, if anything. We have seen several sellers being arrested because they started to engage in business with undercover agents and revealed information they should not have."

Furthermore, drugs are a physical product, so "online anonymous marketplaces do not help when the time comes to actually ship it," says Christin, because the dealer can be spotted on a post office camera making repeated visits to the post office, for example.

Some other criminal activities, such as money laundering, present police with the same issues online and off, Christin says. "Transactions may be a bit easier to conceal if one is using bitcoin currency, but ultimately, those bitcoins have to be converted into actual currency if people want to use them" for regular transactions, such as depositing earnings into a bank account or buying something on Amazon.com, which does not now accept

bitcoins. And converting bitcoins into regular currency involves real-world transactions that produce identifying information accessible to police, he says.

"With enough resources you can go after anybody," regardless of what technologies they use, says cybersecurity expert Landau. Although "anonymizing techniques and encryption make it harder" for law enforcement, she says, "you still can't move through modern society without leaving traces" that police can track. Privacy-enhancing technologies such as anonymizing software actually provide law enforcement with "some enormous new advantages along with some new disadvantages," says Swire of Georgia Tech.

"I call this a Golden Age of Surveillance," says Swire, who was chief counselor for privacy for the Clinton administration. "Almost everybody carries a tracking device" in the form of a mobile phone, he says. "Never before in history have police been able to get the location of every suspect. In the old days, people talking to each other left no records," he says. "So law enforcement's concerns need to be understood in the context of this new situation, in which it's much harder for anyone to hide."

Some Dark Web observers, however, say the barriers to effectively policing the anonymized Internet are increasing. "Law enforcement leaders embrace the broadest possible privacy protections for individuals but emphasize that absolute Internet anonymity is a prescription for catastrophe," said child exploitation expert Allen.[36]

"What I hear most from law enforcement worldwide is frustration," he said. The main investigative technique police use today on the Dark Web is infiltration, but getting undercover officers into the online underworld as operatives is "expensive, time-consuming and often ineffective," he said. Moreover, said Allen, most arrests have mainly been of "less sophisticated users who make mistakes and leave a trail. . . . Our concern is that most often we are apprehending the less sophisticated offenders, not the serious, sophisticated organized criminals who represent the greatest threat and do not make these kinds of mistakes."[37]

Some technology and crime analysts also argue that systemic changes created by the Internet, as well as some soon-to-arrive technological developments related to the Dark Web, could make it nearly impossible to capture and prosecute cybercriminals.

For one thing, although exchanging bitcoins is the main means of buying and selling on the anonymized Web today, using the so-called crypto currency only partly conceals users' identities. But emerging currency innovations, notably one called "Zerocoin," will allow transactions in which both the amount exchanged and who made and received payment will be completely untraceable, says the Center for Democracy and Technology's Hall. Such currency, which will exist "within a year or two," will be "like real-world cash, only even more obscure," he says.[38]

Such a currency would allow virtually untraceable arms sales, for example, Hall says. Online anonymity has great value, he adds, "but are we going to know when we create something too powerful, something that allows completely unregulated commerce?"

Cybercriminals already are figuring out how to make even better use of the anonymized Internet, wrote Michael Chertoff, a security consultant in Washington who served as former President George W. Bush's Homeland Security chief, and Tobby Simon, president of Synergia Foundation, a research group in Bangalore, India.[39]

Chertoff and Simon said new, large Dark Web marketplaces will likely emerge soon that will force government agencies to expend more resources to track increasingly dispersed traffic. Increased use of temporary websites — those that "come online at specific times, have a brief window of trading, then disappear" — may also increase the difficulty for investigators, they wrote.[40]

Many anonymizing technologies are possible, at least theoretically, so "it would not be surprising to see the criminal underbelly becoming more fragmented into alternative dark nets or private networks, further complicating the job of investigators," Chertoff and Simon wrote.[41]

Meanwhile, *Future Crimes* author Goodman warns that before law-enforcement officials and legislators even begin to tackle the specific problems the Dark Web creates, most need to come to terms with a frightening truth. The Internet itself already has "fundamentally broken policing" simply because it is completely international — and virtual rather than built of bricks and mortar, Goodman says.

"Congress can pass whatever laws it wants to make online enforcement easier" or provide more resources, he says, "but New York City policemen can't make arrests in

Moscow. . . . It takes two or three years just to get information" in some international investigations, he says. And even before the identity-hiding Dark Web made cybercriminals even tougher to trace, Internet criminal enterprises could instantly move operations and records from nation to nation.

Furthermore, laws work only in the regions or enterprises over which they have jurisdiction, Goodman says. "If you call your police department to report a drive-by shooting, they're interested. But if you call to report a bad computer virus, they say, 'Don't call us.' Whose jurisdiction is the Internet?"

BACKGROUND
Cypherpunks

Dubbing themselves "Cypherpunks," a loosely affiliated group of computer scientists, mathematicians, programmers, cryptologists and cryptographers — devisers and analyzers of codes — announced a new project in 1992. They would develop technology to allow anyone to navigate the Internet without revealing their locations, the websites they visited or the content of their communications.[42]

"We the Cypherpunks are dedicated to building anonymous systems," said a 1993 manifesto written for the group by Eric Hughes, a young libertarian from Virginia who had studied math at the University of California, Berkeley.[43] "We are defending our privacy with cryptography, with anonymous mail forwarding systems, with digital signatures, and with electronic money."[44]

Big changes in the online world that began in the late 1980s motivated the Cypherpunks. The world's global computer network, formerly operated by universities and government-run laboratories primarily for researchers' use, was handed over to private companies — ISPs, or Internet service providers — in preparation for opening the network to the public. Cypherpunks were leery of ISPs' potential commercial motives for spying on Internet traffic and their potential for facilitating government surveillance.

From computer networks' earliest days in the 1970s, technology experts worried that whoever controlled a network's infrastructure could easily spy on its users, spurring some computer scientists to devise new technologies to protect privacy.

One of the first breakthroughs came in 1976, when American mathematicians Whitfield Diffie and Martin Hellman described an innovative method for keeping encoded messages private.

To encode and then decipher a message, the sender and recipient both needed access to the "key" to the code being used. But sending the key over a computer network posed the same risk as sending an unencoded message. The key could be read by anyone with access to the network's infrastructure. Diffie and Hellman devised an elegant solution — public-key encryption — which remains the basis of much encryption today.[45]

But keeping prying eyes from reading messages isn't the only Internet privacy problem. Online privacy also requires navigating the Internet while remaining anonymous — that is, surfing the Web and sending messages without revealing one's identity or location, which websites one visits and with whom one communicates. Achieving such "anonymization" proved even tougher than finding an effective way to encode online messages.

To send an email, visit a website or join a video conference, a computer or other Internet-connected device exchanges "packets" of data with the computer at the desired destination. To route the packets correctly, each device is assigned a unique number — an IP (Internet Protocol) address — and each data packet carries the IP addresses of both its origin and its destination in a "header."

This so-called metadata includes not only the "to-from" information but also the times and dates of Internet activity. And, just like unencoded messages, metadata can be viewed by others.[46]

American cryptographer David Chaum, founder of the International Association for Cryptologic Research based at the University of California, Santa Barbara, was among the first to tackle this problem. Steven Bellovin, a computer network and security researcher at Columbia University in New York City, says that Chaum came up with a relay system in 1981 that worked to anonymize email traffic — that is, to hide the header information from eavesdroppers. But, Bellovin says, the system didn't work for Internet browsing.

Anonymizing Technology

From the 1990s to the present, cypherpunk philosophy has driven development of most anti-eavesdropping technology. That philosophy holds that technology can better protect individual online privacy than legal or legislative means or business contracts guaranteeing protection of private information.

In general, developers of today's Dark Web have distributed nearly all of the technology for free to whoever wants it. Most is so-called open-source technology — software code published openly for anyone to see and tinker with.

Founding cypherpunk Hughes laid the philosophy out in his 1993 manifesto. "We cannot expect governments, corporations, or other large, faceless organizations to grant us privacy out of their beneficence," he wrote. "We must defend our own privacy if we expect to have any. . . .

"We don't much care if you don't approve of the software we write," he continued. "We know that software can't be destroyed and that a widely dispersed system can't be shut down."[47]

Using technological rather than legal means to protect privacy is simply the only reliable way to do it, wrote the pseudonymous blogger phobos, a member of the Tor Project. "A business promises not to give up your identity unless forced to do so via court order. This is anonymity by policy." But "if a business doesn't have your identity, then there is nothing to divulge. This is anonymity by design."[48]

In the 1990s, work began on several anonymity projects. One of the earliest was software called Freenet, which originated as the 1999 senior thesis of Irish computer science student Ian Clarke at the University of Edinburgh in Scotland. Clarke's thesis earned a B. His tutors thought "the project was a bit wacky" and that he didn't cite enough sources, he said.[49]

Undaunted, a year later Clarke publicly released his "distributed, decentralized information storage retrieval and software system" for free. By 2009, at least 2 million copies had been downloaded from his website.[50]

In 1995, the U.S. Naval Research Laboratory — federal government centers studying technology with military applications — had begun studying anonymizing technology. Their innovation was called "onion routing," named because it protected data packets' headers by wrapping them in multiple layers of encryption, similar to the layered skins of an onion.[51]

"It may seem odd that this was a [Department of Defense] effort," said cybersecurity expert Landau. However, "members of the military are often stationed overseas in situations where it is better that their affiliation not be known."[52]

CHRONOLOGY

1970s-1980s *Communication via networked computers emerges, sparking privacy worries.*

1976 American mathematicians Whitfield Diffie and Martin Hellman publish the "public-key encryption" method of keeping eavesdroppers from deciphering coded online messages.

1981 American cryptographer David Chaum devises a way to keep eavesdroppers from reading email locations, destinations and time information.

1990s *Public floods onto the Internet.*

1992 Cypherpunks, a loosely affiliated group of technology experts, vow to develop software to allow anonymous Web browsing.

1995 U.S. Naval Research Laboratory begins developing anonymizing browser software based on an idea called "onion routing."

1999 Irish computer science student Ian Clarke develops a method to keep Web surfers' locations private.

2000s *First anonymizing technologies for online traffic come into use.*

2000 Ian Clarke offers his anonymizing software, Freenet, to the public at no cost.

2001 U.S. Naval Research Laboratory enlists civilian computer scientists to help develop onion routing for military and civilian use.

2003 After a limited experimental release, the anonymizing technology Tor — an acronym for "the onion router" — becomes publicly available for free.

2008 China blocks Tor website to keep residents from using the software to access censored information.

2009 Using the pseudonym Satoshi Nakamoto, an inventor introduces bitcoin, a currency for online sales that makes financial transactions extremely difficult to trace. . . . The Drugstore Market becomes the first online

marketplace for illegal drug sales, established as a so-called Tor hidden service.

2010s *Anonymizing Internet networks — now widely known as the "Dark Web" — proliferate.*

2010 The Farmer's Market, one of the largest drug markets on the non-anonymized Internet, moves to the Tor network.

2011 Iranian government blocks and slows traffic for various anonymizing technologies during protests over a controversial election.

2012 *Foreign Policy* magazine honors Tor developers Roger Dingledine, Nick Mathewson and Paul Syverson for protecting the rights of people such as corporate whistleblowers "who otherwise might be silenced online."

2013 FBI shuts down Freedom Hosting, a large Dark Web hosting service, and charges its operator with dealing in child pornography. . . . FBI shuts down the largest Tor-based marketplace, Silk Road, and arrests its operator on multiple drug trafficking-related charges.

2014 After a brief decline following Silk Road's closing, Dark Web illegal drug sales increase as new markets open. . . . Each day about 2.5 million people worldwide use the Tor browser software to move about online. . . . British researcher finds that four of five visits to Tor hidden-service websites were to child-pornography sites. . . . Facebook, a longtime advocate of using only real-world identities online, opens a Tor hidden-services site to help people reach Facebook from countries that block the social network.

2015 The first Tor computer node at a U.S. public library opens in Lebanon, N.H., after a brief early shutdown when the Department of Homeland Security warned town officials about criminals using Tor. . . . In an international survey, 4 percent of Dark Web drug buyers said they had not consumed illegal drugs before their Dark Web purchase. . . . Belarus government asks Internet service providers to block access to Tor. . . . Convicted of all charges, Silk Road operator Ross Ulbricht is sentenced to life imprisonment without the possibility of parole.

Who Wants Anonymity?

Whistleblowers, small-time drug dealers, Facebook skeptics use Dark Web.

The Dark Web's anonymizing technology provides a sense of security to people who don't want their online activities watched, tracked or recorded. The many reasons for seeking to avoid surveillance range from the high-minded to the skittish to the criminal.

The Dark Web is popular with law enforcement officials communicating with tipsters, small-time drug dealers trying to avoid the police and everyday Internet users leery of having personal information sold by social-media companies. It can be especially useful for journalists seeking tips from whistleblowers, working on investigative projects or operating in regions where free speech is suppressed and sources face harm for providing information.

"There's a growing technology gap: phone records, email, computer forensics and outright hacking are valuable weapons for anyone looking to identify a journalist's source," said Kevin Poulsen, an American journalist and former computer hacker who served prison time for his hacking exploits. In 2011 Poulsen contacted a young programming whiz — political activist Aaron Swartz — to create software to make it safer for journalists and their anonymous sources to communicate.[1]

The New Yorker, a magazine with "a long history of strong investigative work, emerged as the right first home for the system," said Poulsen. The magazine debuted its pilot version of the anonymous-submission app, which it calls Strongbox, in May 2013.[2] Today, the app — known as SecureDrop at most organizations — offers protection to whistleblowers who reach out to the press or to nonprofit watchdog groups such as the Washington-based Project on Government Oversight. *The Washington Post*, *The Toronto Globe and Mail* and Gawker Media are among the media outlets that use the app, which runs on the popular Tor anonymizing network.[3]

Those selling and buying illegal goods and services — mostly drugs — also have reasons to use the Dark Web. Illegal drugs have long been sold online, via Craigslist, for example, said Nicolas Christin, an assistant research professor of computer engineering at Pittsburgh's Carnegie Mellon University. But the combination of the Tor network and Bitcoin, a digital currency invented in 2009 that makes money exchanges close to anonymous, has created a boom in illegal Dark Web commerce.[4]

Early on, Silk Road became the dominant Dark Web market, selling mainly drugs — which made up about 70 percent of its listings — but also items such as erotica and fake IDs.[5] About 1,000 vendors were using the site, which had opened in February 2011, when the FBI shut it down in October 2013. Business only accelerated after the shutdown, however, wrote New York-based economist Allison Schrager. Dozens of new markets appeared, offering "an exhilarating and terrifying array of products: prescription pills, meth, heroin, speed, crack, guns, stolen identities, gold and erotica," she said.[6]

Small sellers dominate Dark Web markets, according to Carnegie Mellon graduate student Kyle Soska and Christin, who gathered data on Dark Web drug markets from 2013 through 2015. About 70 percent of sales were cannabis, ecstasy and cocaine, they said, and the "vast majority" of dealers grossed less than $10,000 over the period.[7]

Anonymity may not be the only draw for dealers, one seller told Schrager. Ordering drugs online is safer because buyers no longer have to meet suppliers on the street. In addition, more varieties of drugs are available, and the quality is more consistent, the dealer said.[8]

The Dark Web doesn't eliminate all dangers associated with drug dealing, however. Online dealers still

Separate, smaller computer networks within the larger Internet carry out the anonymization process, and a network with heavy and varied traffic works best, since users' data can get lost in the crowd.[53] To create such a network for the military, Naval Research Laboratory scientists joined with civilian researchers led by Roger Dingledine, a young MIT-educated computer scientist, to implement an onion-routing network for joint military and civilian use.

Named Tor — an acronym for "The Onion Router" — the system was deployed experimentally in 2002 and released to the public as free, open-source Web-browser software in October 2003.[54]

must receive large shipments in the real world without arousing suspicion, requiring ruses such as having the drugs shipped to an empty house that the dealer has groomed to look lived in by periodically mowing the lawn and having junk mail delivered, dealers told Schrager.[9]

Some people use the Dark Web for fairly mundane reasons. One is to avoid what they view as today's forced oversharing of personal information online, says Robert Gehl, an associate professor of communication at the University of Utah in Salt Lake City. For instance, participants in the Dark Web Social Network mingle the same way members of social networks such as Facebook and Twitter do — customizing their member pages, "friending" other people and "liking" their posts — but with a twist, says Gehl.

"While that other world of Facebook is making sure that people use their real identities, this is a space where you can be anonymous and private," he says. Before Facebook, online discussion and socializing forums left it up to users whether to use their "real-world" identities, Gehl says. As a result, the use of pseudonyms and the guarding of personal details were often the norm.

Today, the Dark Web Social Network is a refuge for those who want privacy. The network's creator told Gehl that he created it because he was "deeply upset" about Facebook sharing and selling personal information and with the Internet's "general lack of privacy."[10]

— *Marcia Clemmitt*

Ross Ulbricht, shown in a courtroom artist's sketch, was convicted last year of running Silk Road, a Dark Web drug market, and sentenced to life in prison without the possibility of parole.

[1] Kevin Poulsen, "Strongbox and Aaron Swartz," *The New Yorker*, May 14, 2013, http://tinyurl.com/j3usw2j. Swartz, who completed the software near the end of 2012, killed himself in January 2013 while facing a federal criminal indictment for data theft he committed to protest the widening scope of copyright laws.

[2] *Ibid.*; "The Official SecureDrop Directory," SecureDrop, Freedom of the Press Foundation, http://tinyurl.com/hetpx5b.

[3] *Ibid.*, "The Official SecureDrop Directory."

[4] Cited in Allison Schrager, "The safe, user-friendly way to be a little drug lord: economic secrets of the dark web," *Quartz*, Sept. 16, 2015, http://tiny url.com/qdj2k5s.

[5] James Ball, "Silk Road: the online drug marketplace that officials seem powerless to stop," *The Guardian*, March 22, 2013, http://tinyurl.com/narz2og.

[6] *Ibid.*

[7] Kyle Soska and Nicolas Christin, "Measuring the Longitudinal Evolution of the Online Anonymous Marketplace Ecosystem," *Proceedings of USENIX Security Symposium*, Aug. 12-14, 2015, http://tinyurl.com/gq5mgnp.

[8] Schrager, *op. cit.*

[9] *Ibid.*

[10] Robert W. Gehl, "Power/freedom on the dark web: A digital ethnography of the Dark Web Social Network," *New Media & Society*, Oct. 15, 2014, http://tinyurl.com/z78avfc.

Beyond Tor

Tor and Freenet are not the only anonymizing networks. The Invisible Internet Project (I2P) — a "peer to peer" network where users mainly share material such as computer games with one another — also has gained in popularity.[55]

Theoretically any number of such networks are possible, says Columbia's Bellovin. Getting enough people to volunteer their computers to form a network is another matter, though, he says. When it comes to anonymization, "the software is easy. But building up the infrastructure is hard."

Special Technology Helps Users Cover Their Tracks

Secret codes and decentralized networks keep cyber-spies guessing.

Since the earliest days of networked computing, computer analysts have been preoccupied with how to create technology to ward off online spying. Early excitement about computers' communication potential was tempered by the knowledge that online messages would pass through multiple computers, increasing the likelihood that they would be intercepted and spied upon.

Solving the spying problem meant tackling two issues. The first: how to encrypt — or encode — a message securely enough to keep spies at intermediate computers from reading it. The second: devising ways to hide the so-called metadata that accompanies all online activity.

Every action over the Internet, including sending emails and visiting websites, involves exchanges of data between computers. All data exchanges carry "headers" stating the originating computer's location, the destination computer's location and the date and time of contact — this information is the metadata. Although a single metadata capture might not jeopardize privacy much, analysis of metadata patterns captured over time can reveal an Internet user's associates as well as a detailed timeline of online activity.

In 1976, American mathematicians Whitfield Diffie and Martin Hellman solved the message-eavesdropping problem with an insight that remains the basis of most encryption methods. The obvious way to send a private message is to encode it, but doing so online only pushes the spying problem back one step. The sender and recipient of a coded message both need a "key" to the code. And computers can spy on a key just as easily as they can spy on an unencoded message.[1]

Diffie and Hellman solved this dilemma with "public key encryption." This system gives each user two different but mathematically related keys to a personal code. A system user's "public key" encrypts messages into the user's code. The public key can travel online safely because even if the public key is intercepted, it can't decipher the code. A mathematically related "private key," which the code owner keeps secret, does that job.

To receive a coded message, the recipient sends the "public key" to the sender, who encodes the message. Once the message is encoded, only the recipient's private key can decipher it.[2]

Technology to hide the metadata created as individuals move about the Web — often called "anonymizing" technologies — emerged in the early 2000s. Anonymizing technologies generally consist of restricted networks within the Internet that use special software to both encrypt metadata headers and move online traffic from computer to computer so that observers can't easily determine where the transmission originated.

One of the first such networks to emerge was Freenet, released publicly in 2000.[3]

Freenet uses volunteered computer power from people running its software to create a decentralized network of computers that store data — such as caches of documents, websites or pirated movies — in encrypted form. Any computer running Freenet software can retrieve stored data from the network and store the computer owner's own data on the network for other users to view.

When a computer running Freenet receives a data request, the software program searches for it. If the information isn't found, the program tosses the request to

When anonymizing networks came on the scene, their users could communicate with other Internet users, visit websites and set up websites accessible only to users of the same network. Buying and selling, however — one of the most popular Internet activities — could not be done without mailing cash or sacrificing anonymity. Electronic money exchanges, such as processing credit cards or the online money-transfer system PayPal, link to payers' real names and locations.

another computer to search in turn. The request bounces onward until the data turn up.

This system keeps network users' online activity private because "if you request a file and another computer gets the request, it has no way of telling if you are the originator of that request or if you are just passing on the request from another computer," explains The Freenet Help Site. "When the data is returned you have no way of telling if the sending computer had the data in its datastore, or if it got [the data] from another computer."[4]

The most commonly used anonymizing technology today is Tor, which stands for "the onion router." Released for public use in 2003, Tor relies on multiple layers of encryption — similar to onion skins — to hide data's original location and its destination information (its metadata) as it bounces through a network of volunteers' computers.[5]

Each intermediary computer in the network deciphers one encryption layer to reveal the next address along the route. No intermediary computer sees both the origin of the data and its final destination. The final node decrypts the message and sends it to its destination, where it arrives bearing the so-called IP (Internet Protocol) address of this last computer — called an "exit relay" — rather than that of the computer where it originated.[6]

Decentralized networks hide online traffic mainly by being so large and diffuse that not even national governments can afford the time and money required to monitor them fully, says Steven Bellovin, a computer network and security researcher at Columbia University in New York City. "It takes a lot of resources to monitor all the possible routes. Nobody really has the resources to do that."

— *Marcia Clemmitt*

American mathematician Whitfield Diffie helped develop a way to prevent online spying that remains the basis of most encryption methods used today.

AFP/Getty Images/Gabriel Bouys

[1] For background, see Stephen Levy, *Crypto: How the Code Rebels Beat the Government — Saving Privacy in the Digital Age* (2001); "Public Key and Private Keys," *Comodo*, http://tinyurl.com/7algdtu.

[2] For background, see "Public Key and Private Keys," *ibid.*

[3] Andy Beckett, "The dark side of the internet," *The Guardian*, Nov. 25, 2009, http://tinyurl.com/p3pa9lk.

[4] "Overview," The Freenet Help Site, Nov. 12, 2004, http://tinyurl.com/zclgbnw.

[5] "Tor FAQ," Tor, http://tinyurl.com/3lgyfa8; "Onion routing," *Tor* blog, April 22, 2012, http://tinyurl.com/gomogwv.

[6] Susan Landau, *Surveillance or Security: The Risks Posed by New Wiretapping Technologies* (2010), p. 139 ff.

That changed in 2009, when a computer programmer using the pseudonym Satoshi Nakamoto invented the Bitcoin network. It uses encryption and a decentralized ledger that records all bitcoin transactions but includes no identifying information about the buyers or sellers, providing more anonymity for financial transactions than anything previously devised online.[56]

As a result, Bitcoin's debut immediately brought commerce — and more crime — to the anonymized Web. For example, The Drugstore market for illegal drug sales

Mark Zuckerberg, the founder of Facebook, has long argued for using only real identities online, but in 2014 the global social media site became one of the most prominent companies to open a website as a Tor hidden service. Tor can provide Facebook access to residents of some countries, such as Iran, that block residents' access to the site.

in 2009 became the first of many such markets among Tor's hidden services.[57]

Anonymity's Enemies

Some governments oppose anonymizing technologies because they allow citizens to bypass state bans on publishing or reading censored information. Some law-enforcement and anti-terrorism agencies have suggested banning anonymizing technologies to prevent crimes such as child-pornography distribution.

In 2008, China, which heavily censors online information, blocked the Tor Project's website, and in 2009 China barred access to many of the computers that carry Tor traffic.[58] The Chinese government justified its strong regulation of online information and services in a 2010 white paper.

"Within Chinese territory the Internet is under the jurisdiction of Chinese sovereignty," said the paper. That being the case, Chinese "laws and regulations clearly prohibit the spread of information that contains content subverting state power, undermining national unity [or] infringing upon national honour and interests," the paper said.[59]

In 2011, the Iranian government blocked or slowed traffic for anonymizing technologies as part of an apparent attempt to muzzle political dissidents.[60] In 2015, Belarus declared that it would ask ISPs (Internet Service Providers) to block users' access to anonymizing technologies.[61] Belarus's longtime president, Alexander Lukashenko, criticized by many for alleged human-rights violations, was facing a contentious campaign for re-election in 2015, which he won.[62]

Some law-enforcement and security agencies have tried to discourage Tor use in general, because the fewer people who use the network in a country the easier it is to discover the identities of those who use it.

In 2013, a panel on cybercrime for Japan's National Police Agency suggested asking websites to block users who came to the sites via the Tor browser.[63]

In 2014, Austrian authorities arrested a volunteer who had allowed Tor traffic to be routed through his computer just as the Kilton Library does in Lebanon, N.H. He was convicted of "contribut[ing]" to the completion" of a cybercrime committed by a Tor user, even though such Tor relay computers capture no record of the traffic that moves through them. The verdict effectively makes it illegal to run a Tor exit node — a Tor network computer through which Tor traffic exits onto a destination website — in Austria, noted a reporter for the website *Techdirt*.[64] Unlike other computers that help anonymize Tor Internet traffic, all traffic passing through exit-node computers carries the IP (Internet Protocol) address of the exit-node computer, potentially implicating the owner in any misdeeds related to the traffic.

The National Security Agency (NSA) has deemed anonymizing technology a key barrier to tackling terrorism and cybercrime. Among the top secret documents leaked by former NSA contractor Edward Snowden was a 2012 NSA slide presentation describing the agency's efforts to discover the identities of Tor users. Its title: "Tor Stinks."[65]

Law-enforcement agencies have scored some major takedowns of Dark Web criminal venues. In August 2013 in Ireland, the FBI arrested Eric Eoin Marques, the suspected owner and operator of Freedom Hosting, a Web hosting service that provided sites to many criminal enterprises operating as Tor hidden services. The FBI called Marques the "largest child porn facilitator on the planet."[66] Marques is currently fighting extradition to the United States, where he is charged with conspiracy to distribute child pornography and other crimes, for which he could face decades in prison.[67]

Also in 2013, the FBI shut down Silk Road, the biggest Tor marketplace and site of some 1.2 million transactions — mostly drug sales — between its early-2011 opening and October 2013 shutdown. The FBI charged then-29-year-old Ross Ulbricht, a former science graduate student from Texas, with running Silk Road under the pseudonym "Dread Pirate Roberts."[68]

Ulbricht built the website — which reportedly earned him tens of millions of dollars in sales commissions — using anonymizing software, but he was caught because he incautiously left tracks on social media, including posting his personal Gmail address.

"People are people, and they tend to still make mistakes" even using Dark Web tools, says the University of Cincinnati's Nedelec. "The takedown of Silk Road was a result of too much sharing of personal information online." Ulbricht was convicted of all charges, including conspiracy to distribute narcotics, and in May 2015 he was sentenced to life in prison without the possibility of parole.[69]

Silk Road's closing did not slow the growth of drug sales on the Dark Web, however. In October 2013, marketplaces — including Silk Road — showed about 18.2 million listings for illegal drug sales. By April 2015, the total stood at 43.6 million, according to the Digital Citizens Alliance, a coalition of businesses and individuals concerned with Internet safety.[70]

Overall, use of anonymizing technologies has continued to rise. Between August 2013 and August 2014, 150 million people worldwide downloaded the Tor browser, and about 2.5 million people used it daily in 2014, according to Tor Project researchers.[71]

Also in 2014, Facebook became one of the most prominent companies to open a website as a Tor hidden service. Facebook founder Mark Zuckerberg has long argued for using only real identities online, but Tor can provide Facebook access to residents of some countries, such as Iran, that periodically block residents' access to the social network.[72]

CURRENT SITUATION
To Block or Not

As anonymizing technologies such as Tor and Bitcoin gain users, governments struggle to balance protection

Michael Chertoff, a security consultant in Washington who served as former President George W. Bush's Homeland Security chief, said criminals are figuring out how to make even better use of the anonymized Internet. Chertoff and Tobby Simon, president of the Synergia Foundation, a research group in Bangalore, India, said new, large Dark Web marketplaces will likely emerge soon that will force government agencies to expend more resources to track increasingly dispersed traffic.

for anonymous speech, considered by many a linchpin of democracy, and fighting cybercrime and terrorism.

In France, for example, the November 2015 terrorist attacks in Paris spurred law enforcement agencies to recommend that the government either block French Internet addresses from connecting to Tor or make downloading Tor software illegal, according to a document leaked to the French newspaper *Le Monde.* Ending Tor use could help keep terrorists from communicating secretly, argued the proposal's champions, who hoped legislation could be introduced early this year.[73]

On Dec. 9, however, French Prime Minister Manuel Valls said the government has no plans to ban or block Tor. "Internet is a freedom, . . . an extraordinary means of communication between people; it is a benefit to the economy," Valls said. "It is also a means for terrorists to communicate and spread their totalitarian ideology. The police must take in all of these aspects to improve their fight against terrorism."[74]

Governments in the United States and elsewhere continue to try to identify and track Tor users, although it's generally easier said than done, says the Electronic

Getty Images/Bloomberg/Andrew Harrer

Should governments curb anonymous markets to fight crime?

YES
Eric Jardine
Research Fellow, Centre for International Governance Innovation

Written for *CQ Researcher*, January 2016

Governments absolutely must curb illegal anonymous markets to help fight crime. There now are anonymous markets for almost everything you can think of. Want an underage family member raped? You can arrange it in an anonymous Dark Web marketplace for around $36,000. Have someone murdered? The cost is between $45,000 and $900,000, depending on the victim's stature and how you want the murder to unfold.

Hiring a network of malware-infected computers from around the world to launch a denial-of-service (DoS) attack against a government, business or not-for-profit website will cost you around $150 for a weeklong barrage. Hacking into someone's email or social media accounts runs about $220. For roughly $550, you can conduct hacks involving espionage or break into a secure website.

Oh, you also can buy guns and drugs on the Dark Web.

Anyone with a computer and an Internet connection can get onto the Dark Web and find anonymous markets like these. You could. I could. A young child could do it without the knowledge of his or her parents.

All you have to do is download a browser like Tor, go to a hidden wiki website and start clicking links until you find the service you're after. With cryptocurrencies like bitcoin, even the final transaction is anonymous. Nefarious goods and services can be purchased without the buyer ever having to leave home.

The problem with anonymous markets is twofold. First, the social costs of the things that can be purchased anonymously online are huge. The cost of DDoS attacks runs upwards of $920 million per day. And, obviously, the individual and social costs of rape and murder are incalculable.

The other problem with these markets is that, more than at any other time in history, they decouple motive and ability. Before the Dark Web, you might have wanted to hack someone's website or hire a hitman, but you likely wouldn't have succeeded because you didn't know how. Now you can do those things — with ease.

Anonymity and free speech are important for democracy, but there is a line that is easily crossed in the Dark Web. The list of nefarious activities that are for sale in anonymous markets, combined with the huge social costs and the disjunction of motive and ability, suggests only one potential response to the proposition: Governments must curb anonymous markets to help fight crime.

NO
Jim Harper
Senior Fellow, Cato Institute

Written for *CQ Researcher*, January 2016

An "anonymous market" is certainly an exotic-sounding beast. Some ill must be afoot when people make no exchange of personal information and use untraceable payment systems to buy and sell.

On the other hand, millions of ordinary Americans engage in commerce like this every day. Buyers whose identities are unknown to merchants, restaurateurs or kiosk operators purchase products and services in exchange for cash and courtesies alone. Yes, some payment systems can be used to trace the actors, and some sales are captured on camera. But it's the exception, not the rule, to gather a stable, useful set of identifiers from daily commerce.

Should governments curb the anonymous markets that exist at fast food restaurants, newsstands and curio shops? Doing so would certainly help fight crime. Thousands of thefts, violent crimes and illegal drug transactions could be thwarted and prosecuted if every real-world commercial transaction required video or digital records of participants.

But such a requirement would defy the sacred principle in American criminal justice that a person is innocent until proven guilty. Americans should be free from surveillance absent suspicion of wrongdoing. Ordinary people participating in ordinary commerce are not obliged to make records of their activities for the benefit of later investigation. The "Dark Web" epithet hardly provides a rationale for a different rule for online transactions.

The Internet allows people to transact more quickly and efficiently and across greater distances than conventional communications. But until recently, such online transactions had to use centralized and fully traceable payment systems. We also have discovered that much of our online life is subject to comprehensive government surveillance.

Exotic name aside, anonymous online markets can recreate the offline status quo. While some early users of the "Dark Web" have employed it for illegal and sometimes nefarious purposes, a broader public will begin to use such tools to transact as they wish, free of prying corporate advertisers and aggressively attentive governments. The vast bulk of future private commerce will be unremarkable, except for the burgeoning economic growth it produces.

There are more than prudential reasons to resist branding anonymous commerce as dangerous. Efforts to stamp it out would suppress good people's use of privacy-protecting technologies while having only a marginal impact on the bad.

Freedom Foundation's Quintin. Agencies such as the FBI and NSA have identified some Tor users by hacking into the network — i.e., looking for software vulnerabilities.

While such hacking "attacks do work, they're not super common," says Quintin. And they are generally usable only once, he says, because Tor's software developers generally learn about a breach quickly and fix the software problem as fast as they can.

"The Tor Project has also come up with some really clever solutions" to attempts by governments such as China's to block Tor, says Quintin.

For example, in addition to the publicly listed Tor entry relay computers through which users connect to the network, new, secret "bridge" relays have been added but not put on the publicly available list of Tor network computers, he says. Instead, one must obtain the IP address of each bridge relay separately through a somewhat time-consuming request process. That's not a big problem for individuals, who need the address of only one accessible bridge relay, which will then connect them to the rest of Tor. For governments hoping to block Tor access nationwide, however, discovering and blocking all the bridges could be a prohibitively resource-intensive and time-consuming process, Quintin says.

"Governments will keep trying to censor Tor, but right now I think Tor is winning. I'm fairly confident that will be the case for a while," Quintin says.

Expanding Networks

All networks likely will have some eavesdroppers, says Columbia University's Bellovin. For example it is assumed that some governments or government-connected ISPs control some Tor relays. Thus, it is crucial for an anonymizing network to have both a large number of computer relays and a large number of users, so identifying an individual user becomes harder, Bellovin explains.

Efforts to increase the number of relays and Tor users are ongoing, such as the Library Freedom Project, a librarian-led effort to inform librarians about online privacy tools and encourage them to volunteer their computers as Tor relays, says Project Director Alison Macrina, a Massachussetts librarian who started the effort about two years ago.

"We travel all over the continental United States and inform librarians about threats to privacy," encouraging them to also educate their patrons about privacy and anonymity, says Macrina. "Libraries have an ethical commitment to privacy and to intellectual freedom. And they also offer the only free computer classes in most communities and provide the only computers that are free and available for the public to use."

Macrina continues, "There's a presumption in the U.S. that people have given up on privacy, but while all I have is . . . a lot of anecdotal evidence, it suggests that that's not true." For example, she says, many people "are creeped out by" commercial websites that profile visitors and then target them with ads as they travel around the Web.

Because Tor keeps websites from learning a visitor's real IP address, using Tor plus limiting how much personal information one shares online can squelch such profiling, she says.

That's especially important for people who hold non-mainstream views or who fear reprisals if their online writings under pseudonyms become known, says Drexel University's Forte, who has interviewed a wide variety of Tor users in her academic research. For example, she has spoken with people who use Tor to thwart tracking of their participation under pseudonyms in online transgender forums because they fear job discrimination if the posts are discovered. She also has interviewed Iranian citizens living in the United States who use Tor to avoid being tracked when they read online political news that's censored in their home country, she says.

Privacy advocates hope to attract members of Congress and their staffs to Tor, says the Tor Project's Krauss. For a government with three independent branches to work as planned, it's vital that legislators and judges, for example, be free to access information and discuss issues online without being spied upon by others, such as executive-branch officials seeking to influence them, she says.

That happened in July 2014, when CIA Director John Brennan admitted — after months of denials — that the agency had spied on Senate staffers' online activities, including their emails, during an inquiry into alleged CIA torture.[75] The incident led congressional staff to ask privacy advocates for training in how to use tools such as Tor, says Krauss.

Whether a lawmaker is in the majority or the minority, freedom to read and write without being spied on is crucial, Krauss says. "This is a nonpartisan issue."

OUTLOOK

Waning Anonymity?

Some technology observers predict that as time goes on, fewer people will value online privacy, and the anonymized Internet may nearly disappear. But many privacy advocates still hope to see anonymizing technology expand its reach.

While privacy advocates hope to see anonymizing software use expand to new populations, it's more likely that its user numbers will shrink under pressure from those who would like to stamp out anonymous activity in cyberspace, declared Luis Villazon, a writer at the technology news website *Techradar*.[76]

Today, the Internet's underlying infrastructure allows small anonymizing networks to be created and to operate online, but an infrastructure could easily be developed that would not allow this, Villazon said. For example, the military might create a high-security network incapable of carrying anonymized traffic, he suggested. Unlike on today's Internet, the underlying technology of that high-security network would verify the true IP addresses of every computer and refuse to move data from anonymized machines, he explained.[77]

Businesses might then embrace the high-security network for making "anonymous net mischief . . . so much harder," eventually bringing the public on board, Villazon said. Ultimately, the no-anonymizing-allowed technology would spread to all or nearly all of the Internet, making privacy advocates' ambition of expanding its use seem "as quaint as a street without [closed-circuit television] cameras," he predicted.[78]

The dream of an Internet where communications privacy is paramount is nearly dead, said Jennifer Granick, director of civil liberties at the Stanford Center for Internet and Society, in Palo Alto, Calif. Internet users prioritize convenience over freedom from surveillance, and governments have played into fears of "terrorists, pedophiles, drug dealers and money launderers" to win support for eliminating privacy and anonymity protections, Granick said.[79]

But "anonymity tools in general may be in a different class" than other privacy-related technologies such as encryption and will probably prove more resistant to governments' desire to squelch them, says the Center for Democracy and Technology's Hall. That's because many law enforcement agencies use anonymity tools and know their value, he says.

Nevertheless, it seems unlikely that anonymizing networks "will ever be really widely used," at least for run-of-the-mill Web surfing, says Hall. Compared with traditional Web browsers' networks, anonymizing software is much slower and can't be used for some popular activities such as video apps, which can compromise anonymity, he says.

However, public discomfort with the degree to which government and corporate entities track and collect personal information online is growing, said Andrew Lewman, former executive director of the Tor Project and now senior vice president of engineering for the Norse Corp., a computer security firm in Boston. "Between . . . data aggregation companies, and now governments spying . . . on users, people are already looking" for technologies that will enhance privacy while being user friendly.[80]

"We're at the beginning of a new wave of privacy-enhancing technology coming into the mainstream," Lewman said. "The first ones to make it easy, sexy and profitable will lead the way."[81]

NOTES

1. Julia Angwin, "First Library to Support Anonymous Internet Browsing Effort Stops After DHS Email," *ProPublica*, Sept. 10, 2015, http://tinyurl.com/zda88cx; Nora Doyle-Burr, "Despite Law-Enforcement Concerns, Lebanon Board Will Reactivate Privacy Network Tor at Kilton Library," *Valley News* [Vermont], Aug. 28, 2013, http://tiny url.com/ne4l5jr.

2. Quoted in *ibid.* (Doyle-Burr)

3. For background, see "Tor: Overview," About Tor, http://tinyurl.com/2a8rnro.

4. "How Big Is the Dark Web?" Tor Project, 2013, http://tinyurl.com/mrvdjsw; "Clearing Up Confusion — Deep Web Vs. Dark Web," *BrightPlanet*, March 27, 2014, http://tinyurl.com/hjszd33.

5. *Ibid.*, "How Big Is the Dark Web?"

6. "Tor Project's struggle to keep the 'dark net' in the shadows," BBC, Aug. 22, 2014, http://tinyurl.com/zj8wd38.

7. asn, "Crowdfunding the Future (of Hidden Services)," *Tor* blog, March 30, 2015, http://tinyurl.com/jwpe2vp.

8. Matt Egan, "What is the Dark Web? How to access the Dark Web. What's the difference between the Dark Web and the Deep Web?" *PC Advisor* [United Kingdom] Nov. 23, 2015, http://tinyurl.com/papxqhz; "What are some cool deep Internet websites?" *Quora*, http://tinyurl.com/pgxowme; Robert W. Gehl, "Power/freedom on the Dark Web: A digital ethnography of the Dark Web Social Network," *New Media & Society*, Oct. 15, 2014, http://tinyurl.com/z78avfc.

9. Murong Xuecun, "Scaling China's Great Firewall," *The New York Times*, Aug. 17, 2015, http://tinyurl.com/hyemd9p.

10. Ibid.; for background, see Jay Michaelson, "Tibet's Monks Are Setting Themselves on Fire Again," *The Daily Beast*, Jan. 20, 2015, http://tinyurl.com/ja8lqhx.

11. Kieren McCarthy, "Bangladesh shuts down its internet during war crimes trial," *The Register* [United Kingdom], Nov. 18, 2015, http://tinyurl.com/zoblxl6; Zara Rahman, "With Messaging Apps Still Banned, Bangladeshis Turn to Tor (and Twitter)," *Global Voices*, Nov. 25, 2015, http://tinyurl.com/zxmtmse.

12. Marc Goodman, *Future Crimes* (2015), p. 198.

13. For background, see Daniel McGlynn, "Digital Currency," *CQ Researcher*, Sept. 26, 2014, 2014, pp. 793-816.

14. Danna Harman, "U.S.-based Isis Cell Fundraising on the Dark Web, New Evidence Suggests," *Haaretz* [Israel], Jan. 29, 2015, http://tinyurl.com/h2vvu2k; Patrick Tucker, "How the Military Will Fight ISIS on the Dark Web," *Defense One*, Feb. 24, 2015, http://tinyurl.com/h4jxjse.

15. Quoted in *ibid.* (Harman).

16. Jamie Bartlett, *The Dark Net: Inside the Digital Underworld* (2015), p. 151; Emily Flitter, "FBI shuts alleged online drug marketplace, Silk Road," Reuters, Oct. 2, 2013, http://tinyurl.com/znxed5s.

17. Ernie Allen, testimony before the U.S. Senate Committee on Homeland Security and Governmental Affairs, Nov. 18, 2013, http://tinyurl.com/j5cvm48.

18. Quoted in Andy Greenberg, "Over 80 Percent of Dark-Web Visits Relate to Pedophilia, Study Finds," *Wired*, Dec. 30, 2014, http://tinyurl.com/mseyabg.

19. asn, "Crowdfunding," *op. cit.*

20. Cited in Greenberg, *op. cit.*

21. Joseph Cox, "The Dark Web As You Know It Is a Myth," *Wired*, June 18, 2015, http://tinyurl.com/zkzw643.

22. For background, see Brian Krebs, "Web Fraud 2.0: Distributing Your Malware," Security Fix blog, *The Washington Post*, Aug. 22, 2008, http://tinyurl.com/6khjfy.

23. Sheera Frenkel, "ISIS Is Using Everything From Encryption To PlayStation To Avoid Being Spied On," *Buzzfeed*, Nov. 16, 2015, http://tinyurl.com/z4cuzpq.

24. John Markoff, *What the Dormouse Said: How the Sixties Counterculture Shaped the Personal Computer Industry* (2005), p. 109.

25. Bartlett, *op. cit.*, p. 136, and Patrick Howell O'Neill, "How the Internet powered a DIY drug revolution," *The Daily Dot*, Aug. 28, 2013, http://tinyurl.com/zyp93zr.

26. Julia Buxton and Tim Bingham, "The Rise and Challenge of Dark Net Drug Markets," Global Drug Policy Observatory, Swansea University, January 2015, p. 6, http://tinyurl.com/jk9cyqe.

27. Bartlett, *op. cit.*, p. 163.

28. "The Global Drug Survey 2015 Findings," Global Drug Survey, June 8, 2015, http://tinyurl.com/hff77og.

29. Bartlett, *op. cit.*, p. 151.

30. *Ibid.*, p. 154.

31. *Ibid.*, p. 163.

32. *Ibid.*, p. 154.

33. Quoted in Buxton and Bingham, *op. cit.*, p. 11.

34. Quoted in David Brill, "How the 'dark web' is changing the face of doctor-shopping," *Australian Doctor*, April 28, 2014, http://tinyurl.com/h6sdybp.

35. Quoted in *ibid.*

36. Allen, *op. cit.*

37. *Ibid.*

38. For background, see Zerocoin Project, http://tinyurl.com/jyvvb26.

39. Michael Chertoff and Tobby Simon, "The Impact of the Dark Web on Internet Governance and Cyber Security," Global Commission on Internet Governance, February 2015, p. 7, http://tinyurl.com/hvn93rn.

40. *Ibid.*

41. *Ibid.*

42. For background, see Bartlett, *op. cit.*, and Steven Levy, *Crypto: How the Code Rebels Beat the Government — Saving Privacy in the Digital Age* (2001).

43. Eric Hughes, "A Cypherpunk's Manifesto," March 9, 1993, http://tinyurl.com/3x8l6b.

44. *Ibid.*

45. For background, see "Public Key and Private Keys," *Comodo*, http://tinyurl.com/7algdtu.

46. For background, see "Beginner's Guide to Internet Protocol (IP) Addresses," ICANN, March 4, 2011, http://tinyurl.com/jhll54e and "Can You Be Tracked Down Just by Your IP Address?" WhatIsMyIPAddress.com, http://tinyurl.com/6pny52x.

47. Hughes, *op. cit.*

48. phobos, "Anonymity by Design versus by Policy," *Tor* blog, Sept. 16, 2009, http://tinyurl.com/j8c9jt5.

49. Quoted in Andy Beckett, "The dark side of the Internet," *The Guardian* [United Kingdom], Nov. 25, 2009, http://tinyurl.com/zhj4c n8.

50. *Ibid.*

51. Susan Landau, *Surveillance or Security? The Risks Posed by New Wiretapping Technologies* (2010), p. 139.

52. *Ibid.*

53. Dune Lawrence, "The Inside Story of Tor, the Best Internet Anonymity Tool the Government Ever Built," *Bloomberg Business*, Jan. 23, 2014, http://tinyurl.com/j6p7u3b.

54. Roger Dingledine, "pre-alpha: run an onion proxy now!" Seul.org archive, Sept. 20, 2002, http://tinyurl.com/yb7wsle; Landau, *op. cit.*

55. "Intro," The Invisible Internet Project (I2P), http://tinyurl.com/nlvgh2r; for background, see Kate Knibbs, "The Super-Anonymous Network That Silk Road Calls Home," *Gizmodo*, Jan. 23, 2015, http://tinyurl.com/pak3umo.

56. Edward V. Murphy, M. Maureen Murphy and Michael V. Seitzinger, "Bitcoin: Questions, Answers, and Analysis of Legal Issues," Congressional Research Service, Oct. 13, 2015, http://tinyurl.com/hjhs7ev; Bartlett, *op. cit.*, p. 74ff & 92ff.

57. Buxton and Bingham, *op. cit.*, p. 6.

58. Anonymous, "Torproject.org Blocked by GFW in China: Sooner or Later?" *Tor* blog, June 21, 2008, http://tinyurl.com/hhvs8ck; phobos, "Tor partially blocked in China," *Tor* blog, Sept. 27, 2009, http://tinyurl.com/ydpsu7o.

59. Michael Bristow, "China defends internet censorship," BBC, June 8, 2010, http://tinyurl.com/aorrz54.

60. Cameran Ashraf, "Iran: Blocking activity, email interception, and renewed pressure on the Green Movement," *Global Voices/Advocacy*, Jan. 11, 2011, http://tinyurl.com/joh7okm.

61. Tetyana Lokot, "Belarus Bans Tor and Other Anonymizers," *Global Voices/Advocacy*, Feb. 25, 2015, http://tinyurl.com/ju8est5.

62. Yuras Karmanau, "Belarus' Lukashenko set for re-election," The Associated Press, Yahoo! News, Oct. 10, 2015, http://tinyurl.com/htjjj5p.

63. Ian Steadman, "Japanese police ask sites to start blocking Tor," *Wired.co.uk*, April 19, 2013, http://tinyurl.com/crayokh; Keiko Tanaka, "Japan: The Police Don't Want You to Use Tor," *Global Voices/Advocacy*, April 23, 2013, http://tinyurl.com/gqb9gup.

64. Mike Masnick, "Austrian Tor Exit Node Operator Found Guilty Because Someone Used His Node To Commit A crime," *Techdirt*, July 2, 2014, http://tinyurl.com/ogex4h7.

65. James Ball, Bruce Schneier and Glenn Greenwald, "NSA and GCHQ target Tor network that protects anonymity of web users," *The Guardian* [U.S. edition], Oct. 4, 2013, http://tinyurl.com/nj28cg8.

66. Meghan Neal, "To Bust a Giant Porn Ring, Did the FBI Crack the Dark Web?" *Motherboard/Vice*, Aug. 5,

2013, http://tinyurl.com/pqaucb7; Patrick Howell O'Neill, "Apparent U.S. crackdown cripples Dark Web's pedophile communities," *The Daily Dot*, Aug. 7, 2013, http://tinyurl.com/jszolf8.

67. "US prisoner writes to judge handling Eric Eoin Marques 'child porn' extradition," *Belfast Telegraph*, Nov. 3, 2015, http://tinyurl.com/zh6hjm2.

68. Nate Anderson and Cyrus Farivar, "How the feds took down the Dread Pirate Roberts," *ars technica*, Oct. 3, 2013, http://tinyurl.com/zwve but; Caitlin Dewey, "Everything we know about Ross Ulbricht, the outdoorsy libertarian behind Silk Road," *The Washington Post*, Oct. 3, 2013, http://tinyurl.com/ho53djk.

69. *Ibid.* (Anderson and Farivar); Andy Greenberg, "Silk Road Creator Ross Ulbricht Sentenced To Life In Prison," *Wired*, May 29, 2015, http://tinyurl.com/gtpxo34.

70. "Silk Road Shutdown Only Temporarily Stifled Online Drug Sales," *Bitcoinist.net*, Aug. 21, 2015, http://tinyurl.com/zyqzo95; "Busted But Not Broken: The State of Silk Road and the Dark Net Marketplaces," Digital Citizens Alliance, http://tinyurl.com/hg9smx9.

71. "Tor Project's struggle to keep the 'dark net' in the shadows," BBC, Aug. 22, 2014, http://tinyurl.com/zj8wd38.

72. Justin W. Moyer, "With Tor, Facebook is the first social media giant to venture into the 'Dark Web,'" *The Washington Post*, Nov. 4, 2014, http://tinyurl.com/z34pl8m; for background, see Arma, "Facebook, hidden services, and https certs," *Tor* blog, Oct. 31, 2014, http:// tinyurl.com/jl58t7c.

73. Joseph Cox, "After Paris Attacks, French Cops Want to Block Tor and Forbid Free Wi-Fi," *Motherboard*, Dec. 6, 2015, http://tinyurl.com/gusmzro; Kari Paul, "Tor and Public Wi-Fi Safe in France, Prime Minister Says," *Motherboard/Vice*, Dec. 10, 2015, http://tinyurl.com/jpn2gtj.

74. Quoted in *ibid.*, Paul.

75. Spencer Ackerman, "CIA admits to spying on Senate staffers," *The Guardian*, July 31, 2014, http://tinyurl.com/oq27rtn.

76. Luis Villazon, "Anonymous Internet use? It's totally over," *Techradar*, Nov. 6, 2008, http://tinyurl.com/grhkv2k.

77. *Ibid.*

78. *Ibid.*

79. Lauren McCauley, " 'The Dream of Internet Freedom is Dying,' Warns Top Civil Liberties Attorney," *Common Dreams*, Aug. 6, 2015, http://tinyurl.com/jqxa4es.

80. Michael Grothaus, "Could The Road To The 'Dark Web' Be The Right One?" *Fast Company*, Dec. 10, 2013, http://tinyurl.com/j876rao.

81. *Ibid.*

BIBLIOGRAPHY
Selected Sources
Books

Bartlett, Jamie, *The Dark Net: Inside the Digital Underworld*, Melville House, 2015.
A London-based analyst of digital social trends examines the benefits and drawbacks of online anonymity, including the development of Dark Web-related phenomena such as Bitcoin and anonymous drug markets.

Goodman, Marc, *Future Crimes: Everything Is Connected, Everyone Is Vulnerable, and What We Can Do About It*, Doubleday, 2015.
A cybercrime analyst describes how current technologies such as the Dark Web are quickly changing the nature of some crimes and the structure of criminal organizations.

Levy, Steven, *Crypto: How the Code Rebels Beat the Government — Saving Privacy in the Digital Age*, Penguin Books, 2002.
A technology writer chronicles the development of digital-privacy technologies.

Articles

Cox, Joseph, "The People Who Risk Jail to Maintain the Tor Network," *Motherboard*, April 27, 2015, http://tinyurl.com/qyo7mhd.
Law-enforcement agencies and some Tor network volunteers have a complicated relationship because some

online crime is linked to the Internet addresses of those volunteers' computers.

Gehl, Robert W., "Power/freedom on the dark web: A digital ethnography of the Dark Web social network," *New Media & Society*, Oct. 15, 2014, http://tinyurl.com/z78avfc.
An associate professor of communication at the University of Utah interviews users of a social-networking site on the Dark Web about topics such as why they prefer to develop their online personas under pseudonyms rather than share personal details and real names.

Lee, Micah, "Edward Snowden Explains How to Reclaim Your Privacy," *The Intercept*, Nov. 12, 2015, http://tinyurl.com/gs4buyb.
In an interview, National Security Agency whistleblower and leaker Edward Snowden argues that Tor is the most important personal-privacy technology in use today.

O'Neill, Patrick Howell, "The real problem with Tor's security," *The Kernel/The Daily Dot*, July 12, 2015, http://tinyurl.com/hcqyapa.
Most arrests and law-enforcement shutdowns of Dark Web sites are carried out because site operators and users employ privacy-protection tools incorrectly.

Schrager, Allison, "The safe, user-friendly way to be a little drug lord: economic secrets of the dark web," *Quartz*, Sept. 16, 2015, http://tinyurl.com/qdj2k5s.
Most of the more than 9,000 Dark Web drug sellers run small, retail operations, and competition in the markets may be driving down drug prices.

Reports and Studies

"Busted But Not Broken: The State of Silk Road and the Dark Net Marketplaces," Digital Citizens Alliance, April 2014, http://tinyurl.com/hg9smx9.
Analysts for a coalition of individuals and businesses concerned with online safety describe the Dark Web markets in the months following the 2013 shutdown of the largest, Silk Road.

Buxton, Julia, and Tim Bingham, "The Rise and Challenge of Dark Net Drug Markets," *Policy Brief 7*, Global Drug Policy Observatory, Swansea University, January 2015, http://tinyurl.com/jk9cyqe.
A university-based research and analysis group on drug policy provides a detailed history of the recent, fast rise of Dark Web drug markets and discusses their potential consequences.

Chertoff, Michael, and Tobby Simon, "The Impact of the Dark Web on Internet Governance and Cybersecurity," Global Commission on Internet Governance, February 2015, http://tinyurl.com/jkj3xfp.
Security analysts give an overview of current activities on the Dark Web and briefly discuss the pros and cons of possible methods for monitoring and regulating it.

Finklea, Kristin, "Dark Web," Congressional Research Service, July 7, 2015, http://tinyurl.com/hlobrje.
An analyst for Congress' nonpartisan research office summarizes the current state of knowledge about the Dark Web.

Murphy, Edward V., M. Maureen Murphy and Michael V. Seitzinger, "Bitcoin: Questions, Answers, and Analysis of Legal Issues," Congressional Research Service, Oct. 13, 2015, http://tinyurl.com/hjhs7ev.
Analysts for Congress' nonpartisan research office explain how the digital currency Bitcoin facilitates online sales transactions that are extremely difficult to trace.

"Report of the Special Rapporteur on the promotion and protection of the right to freedom of opinion and expression, David Kaye," United Nations Human Rights Council, May 22, 2015, http://tinyurl.com/nb33ou8.
An adviser to the U.N. secretary general argues that governments should support anonymizing technologies such as Tor to protect citizens' rights of free speech and political participation.

For More Information

Bitcoin Foundation, bitcoinfoundation.org. Provides information about the cryptocurrency Bitcoin and advocates for its expanded use.

Center for Democracy and Technology, 972 Mission St., Suite 500, San Francisco, CA 94103; 202-637-9805; www.cdt.org. Nonprofit that supports civil liberties online and researches and analyzes digital technologies, including the Dark Web.

Coindesk, Treviot House, 186-192 High Road, Ilford, Essex, England, IG1 1LR; www.coindesk.com. Advertising-supported news and information website about digital currencies such as Bitcoin.

Electronic Frontier Foundation, 815 Eddy St., San Francisco CA 94109; 415-436-9333; www.eff.org. Nonprofit that supports civil liberties in digital media, including the right to use anonymizing technologies.

Freenet, https://freenetproject.org. The home website of Freenet, one of the first anonymizing technologies, has information about how anonymizing software works and why and how Freenet was developed.

Global Commission on Internet Governance, 67 Erb St. West, Waterloo, Ontario, Canada N2L 6C2; 519-885-2444; www.cigionline.org. Independent international think tank that publishes research and analysis on Internet issues, including the Dark Web.

Global Drug Policy Observatory, Research Institute for Arts and Humanities, Room 201, James Callaghan Building, Swansea University, Singleton Park, Swansea, Wales SA2 8PP; 44 (0)1792 295407; www.swansea.ac.uk/gdpo. University-based group that researches drug policy and analyzes Dark Web drug markets.

Global Drug Survey, Fergusson House, 124/128 City Road, London, England EC1V 2NJ; 44 (0)20 7324 3536; www.globaldrugsurvey.com. Independent research group whose annual drug survey covers Dark Web drug-sale issues.

Tor Project, 7 Temple St., Suite A, Cambridge, MA 02139-2403; www.torproject.org. Nonprofit that develops and maintains the Tor network and browser software.

10

Decriminalizing Prostitution

Sarah Glazer

French sex workers and their supporters in Paris oppose passage of a law that makes it illegal to pay for a prostitute's services. On April 6, 2016, French lawmakers adopted the approach known as the Nordic model, joining several other countries and U.S. cities seeking to discourage prostitution by targeting customers.

AFP/Getty Images/Thomas Samson

From *CQ Researcher,*
April 15, 2016

When the human rights organization Amnesty International released a draft proposal last summer urging that the sex trade be decriminalized worldwide, it created a storm of controversy. Prominent feminists and anti-trafficking activists opposed the idea.

Yet the proposal made sense to some women who have worked both where prostitution is legal, such as Australia, and in the United States, where it is a criminal offense in all but a few Nevada counties.

Kimberlee Cline, who identifies herself as an independent sex worker based in California, sees the decriminalized system set up in one state in Australia as the "ideal" scenario, citing its free medical screenings for sex workers, government-backed workers' rights and the ease of setting up appointments with customers.[1]

"When I started work in California," where prostitution is illegal, she said, "none of this support was available."[2]

In its proposal, Amnesty International contends that decriminalizing prostitution, pimping and brothel ownership would strengthen human rights and protect women from violence. Citing police harassment, the organization says "consensual sexual conduct between adults" should be protected from state interference.[3]

That controversial position has highlighted a long-running international debate over whether selling sex is just a contract between two consenting adults or whether it constitutes "paid rape" of vulnerable women — as prostitution researcher Melissa Farley calls it.[4] The debate is occurring amid growing concern over the global trafficking of women and children for sexual

Most Countries Ban Prostitution

A majority of the world's 200 nations outlaw prostitution, but about 70 countries, including Germany and the Netherlands, have legalized it, regulating where and how it can be practiced, such as in licensed brothels. New Zealand and a handful of other countries have fully decriminalized prostitution by removing most laws and regulations against it. Nine countries follow Sweden's so-called Nordic model, in which the buyers of sex, rather than the sellers, are punished. Prostitution is illegal in the United States, but Nevada allows it in brothels in certain counties. In Australia, prostitution is legal and regulated in some states, but the state of New South Wales has completely decriminalized it.

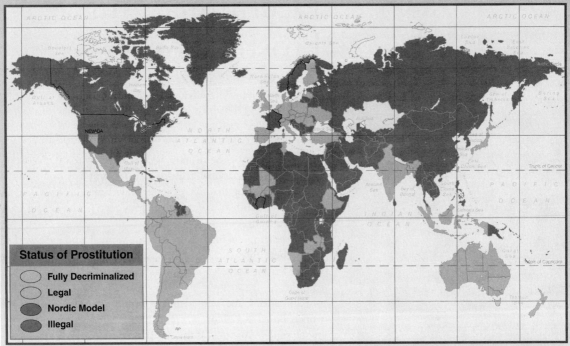

Status of Prostitution

- Fully Decriminalized
- Legal
- Nordic Model
- Illegal

Sources: Asa Bennett, "Prostitution, pimping and brothels: how legal are they across the world?" *The Telegraph*, June 1, 2015, http://tinyurl.com/jcrhjuy; Naomi Grimley, "Amnesty International row: Should prostitution be decriminalised?" BBC News, Aug. 11, 2015, http://tinyurl.com/novjs5f; Rohan Smith, "New Zealand is the best place in the world to work as a prostitute," *New Zealand Herald*, May 22, 2015, http://tinyurl.com/j7m8wcp; Victoria Ho, "Indonesia to shut down all its red-light districts by 2019," *Mashable*, Feb. 24, 2016, http://tinyurl.com/hujx2ts; "The Trouble With Taiwan's New Prostitution Rules," *The Wall Street Journal*, Nov. 16, 2011, http://tinyurl.com/j86w6rr; "France prostitution: MPs outlaw paying for sex," BBC News, April 7, 2016, http://tinyurl.com/jkexgrt

exploitation, which generates an estimated $99 billion a year in illegal profits, according to the International Labour Organization (ILO), the United Nations organization that works to improve working conditions and workers' rights worldwide.[5]

In the United States, some decriminalization advocates speculate that the growing trend toward liberalizing marijuana laws might prompt some jurisdictions to legalize prostitution.[6] But popular support for such a move has yet to materialize. Amnesty's policy announcement did prompt two decriminalization proposals in New Hampshire, but they died in the state legislature this session. And local ballot measures to decriminalize prostitution in California have failed twice.[7]

A recent poll shows Americans about evenly divided on whether prostitution should be legal, but more than half of men said accepting money for sex should be legal, while less than a third of women agreed.[8]

Germany and the Netherlands have legalized prostitution in certain regulated settings, such as state-licensed brothels or designated street zones. Nevada has a similar approach, legalizing prostitution in approved brothels in 10 counties, although it is illegal in the rest of the United States. By contrast, New Zealand and the Australian state of New South Wales have fully "decriminalized" the sex trade, lifting virtually all criminal penalties, with practically no limitations as to where or when it can be practiced.[9]

A third approach, pioneered by Sweden in 1999 and championed by leading feminists such as Gloria Steinem, is a hybrid tactic that is gaining traction around the world and in some U.S. cities.[10] Based on the premise that prostitutes generally are victims of exploitation, such laws make it illegal to purchase sex but not to sell it.

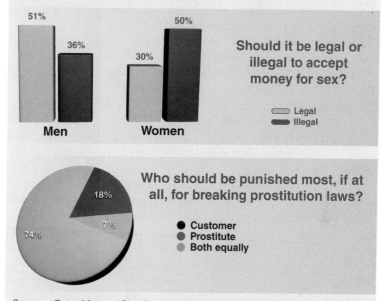

Half of U.S. Men Would Legalize Prostitution

About half of American men say accepting money for sex should be legal, compared with less than a third of women. Among all adults, nearly three-fourths say both prostitutes and customers should be punished for breaking prostitution laws, while nearly a fifth say customers should bear most or all of the punishment.

Should it be legal or illegal to accept money for sex?

Men: 51% Legal, 36% Illegal
Women: 30% Legal, 50% Illegal

Legal / Illegal

Who should be punished most, if at all, for breaking prostitution laws?

18% — Customer
7% — Prostitute
74% — Both equally

● Customer
● Prostitute
● Both equally

Sources: Peter Moore, "Significant gender gap on legalizing prostitution," YouGov, March 10, 2016, http://tinyurl.com/jhsxdyf; Peter Moore, "Country split on legalizing prostitution," YouGov, Sept. 1, 2015, http://tinyurl.com/zolsjuh

Aiming to eliminate prostitution and reinforce Sweden's commitment to gender equality, the so-called "Nordic model" penalizes purchasers of prostitution services with up to one year in jail. The approach has since been adopted by Canada, France, Norway, Iceland and Northern Ireland and is being considered in Britain and the Republic of Ireland.

In the United States, where buying or selling sex is usually a misdemeanor, police traditionally arrest far more prostitutes than customers, who are often let off with a wink and a nod, according to Lina Nealon, founding director of Demand Abolition, an anti-sex-trade group in Cambridge, Mass. But recently many U.S. cities have begun concentrating on arresting buyers, according to Nealon, whose organization is encouraging cities to adopt the Swedish approach.

Compared to women with "little or no choice" but to engage in prostitution to survive, Nealon says, "buyers, by and large, are white, have partners, have jobs in society, have a lot more to lose and therefore are more easily deterred."

The sex trade has become highly polarized between those calling themselves "sex workers" — who say "sex work is work" like any other — and former prostitutes who dub themselves "survivors" of sexual exploitation. Sex workers generally favor New Zealand's decriminalization approach over the regulated systems in Germany and the Netherlands. The Nordic approach, meanwhile is putting "an economic chokehold on the industry and making it more dangerous," according to Savannah Sly, a former Seattle-based sex worker and president of Sex Workers Outreach Project-USA, which advocates decriminalization.

Sly has worked under the legalized system in the Australian state of Victoria, which permits highly regulated brothels, but she prefers the full decriminalization in New South Wales, which allowed her to set up shop independently in a hotel room or anywhere else she wanted to work, and where condom use was optional. In Victoria, condom use is required in brothels, which Sly says was "awesome" for persuading customers to use one. But if a customer says to a woman working on the street, "I'll give you an extra $100 if you ignore that rule," the woman becomes "suddenly illegal" if she agrees, says Sly.

Catherine Murphy, a policy adviser at Amnesty International who helped draft the organization's full decriminalization proposal, says a regulated brothel regime like Victoria's "legalized" system creates "a two-tier system where more marginalized workers on the streets," such as impoverished addicts or illegal migrants, "are still criminalized."

But Taina Bien-Aimé, executive director of the New York-based Coalition Against Trafficking in Women, says whether a country adopts a legalized or decriminalized regime, "culturally and socially it tells society that it is OK to purchase human beings for sex who are vulnerable women and girls. What do men pay for?" she asks. "They don't pay for a date; they pay to humiliate, degrade and act out their sexual fantasies — no matter how dark."

Her organization champions the Nordic model as a way to end demand for prostitution and help reduce international sex trafficking. Anti-trafficking groups claim the burgeoning sex market in places that have legalized prostitution has triggered an increase in sex trafficking and made it easier for brothel owners to hide trafficked and underage women under the cover of a legitimate business.

Millions of women and girls are forcibly trafficked into prostitution worldwide every year, although no widely accepted figures exist.[11] The International Labour Organization (ILO) puts the figure at 4.5 million, but some nongovernmental organizations say it could be as high as 21 million.[12] Valid statistics are difficult to obtain, say some legalization proponents, in part because governments and anti-trafficking groups do not differentiate between trafficking and prostitution that takes place between consenting adults.

Some critics of criminal laws say the international definition of trafficking is so broad it conflates voluntary prostitution and trafficking. The United Nations'

Palermo Protocol, ratified by more than 100 countries, defines trafficking as transporting or harboring someone by threat, force or coercion or by abusing a person in a "position of vulnerability" for the purpose of exploitation; the person's consent is not required.[13]

"There is no clear boundary" between voluntary and involuntary prostitution, argues Janice Raymond, a University of Massachusetts professor emerita in women's studies who calls herself a prostitution "abolitionist" in her 2013 book *Not a Choice, Not a Job*.[14] Opponents of legalization such as Raymond see prostitution as inherently exploitative between a buyer (usually male) and a powerless seller (usually female but sometimes male or transgender), citing the high proportion of marginalized women in the trade.

"It's not so easy" to distinguish those who are forced from those who are willing, says Cherie Jimenez, founding director of the nonprofit EVA Center, which has helped hundreds of women and girls exit prostitution in Boston. "Some of these women brutalized by a pimp will say, 'That's my boyfriend.' You get attached to people — the same as with domestic violence."

Some experts say it is unrealistic to think that demand for the world's so-called oldest profession can be eliminated. "Prostitution doesn't disappear; clients don't go away," even in a country such as Sweden intent on deterring buyers, says Ronald Weitzer, author of the 2011 book *Legalizing Prostitution*.

As human rights organizations, legislators and organizations representing sex workers and survivors of prostitution consider whether to decriminalize or legalize the sex trade, here are some of the questions being debated:

Does decriminalization make the sex trade safer?

In New Zealand's big cities, legal brothels sit next to trendy bars and restaurants. Streetwalkers ply their trade without fear of arrest, and some see police as allies.

Before the government decriminalized prostitution in 2003, police officers were rarely around when needed, said a sex worker named Joyce. Now, "police [are] coming up and down the street every night, and even . . . coming over to make sure that we were all right," she said.[15]

New Zealand eliminated laws against brothel-keeping and pimping (finding customers for a prostitute in exchange for a share of her profits) and imposed no restriction on where or when prostitutes can ply their trade.[16]

The law has succeeded "in making the industry safer and improving the human rights of sex workers," concluded researcher Gillian Abel, who heads the Department of Population Health at the University of Otago, in Christchurch, New Zealand. The freedom from fear of arrest, she wrote, has permitted prostitutes to successfully sue abusive clients and corrupt police who demand sexual favors and to file labor complaints against brothel owners.[17]

By contrast, in New York City, fear of arrest has kept prostitutes from reporting rape, kidnapping and murder, according to a report cited by Amnesty International in its proposal.[18] "Everyone knows prostitution is illegal: If you want to victimize someone who can't go to the cops, it's perfect," says Kate D'Adamo, national policy advocate for the Sex Workers Project at the Urban Justice Center, which provides free legal advice to sex workers and trafficking victims in New York City.

In addition, fear of legal consequences or moral judgment often deters those in the sex trade from seeking crucial health services or makes them unwilling to disclose their sexual practices, several international health commissions have found. In 2010, the U.N. Special Rapporteur on health called for the "decriminalization or legalization of sex work" as a "necessary part of a right-to-health approach."[19]

In Rhode Island, where a fluke in the law legalized indoor prostitution — in massage parlors or independently arranged online — between 2003 and 2009, gonorrhea and rape rates dropped dramatically. Researchers suggested that rapes, which fell by 31 percent, may have declined in part because of increased cooperation between police and prostitutes. And the 39 percent drop in the rate of female gonorrhea, the researchers suggested, may have occurred because prostitutes' legal status gave them increased negotiating power to demand condom use.[20]

Sarah J. Blithe, an assistant professor in communication studies at the University of Nevada, Reno, recently interviewed women in northern Nevada's legal brothels who previously had worked illegally on the street. "Almost unanimously everyone felt the brothel was a better situation. They were getting better customers and were much safer," says Blithe, noting the presence of "panic buttons" and intercoms in every room.

But not everyone sees New Zealand's decriminalization as a desirable model. "The New Zealand women who've contacted us tell us just the opposite" of researcher Abel's contention that it made the industry safer, says Rachel Moran, a former prostitute in Ireland and founder of SPACE International, which advocates criminalizing buyers. "[A]fter decriminalization, men became far pushier, more bullying and demanding," a woman in the trade in New Zealand told Moran, who said she was not surprised because "the state itself has told these men they have entitlement to women's bodies."

Inevitably in decriminalized regimes, Moran contends, "the market massively inflates," competition becomes fierce, "rates drop" and unprotected sex becomes "rampant."

The EVA Center's Jimenez says Amnesty's proposal to decriminalize pimping and prostitution would create an open market for an industry that has become increasingly violent. Many of the women she sees in Boston were in the foster care system when they were younger, have little education, lack family support and live in one short-term hotel after another. Typically, their pimps demand that they earn $600-$700 a day or face reprisals, such as a beating, she says. "We have a huge pimp-driven prostitution industry," which would be allowed to continue under decriminalization, Jimenez says. "No one would be held accountable."

In contrast to New Zealand's approach, the German government took the more limited path to legalizing prostitution in 2002, restricting it to brothels and certain zones in the hope of encouraging safer, cleaner working conditions and equal workers' rights to pay and benefits.

However, Germany's sex industry "was not made safer for women" after legalization, said a letter from anti-trafficking groups criticizing Amnesty's proposal.[21] The Coalition Against Trafficking in Women (CATW), which organized the letter, said Germany's law turned pimps and shady brothel owners into legitimate businessmen and spawned brothel chains offering Friday-night flat-rate specials for men to purchase women for gang rapes and even torture.[22]

"What happens when you are getting gang-raped by buddies who the government says are OK?" asks Bien-Aimé of the Coalition Against Trafficking in Women (CATW). "What recourse would you have with the local police? The money was exchanged; it's a contract."

In the final analysis, some ex-prostitutes say, once the door is closed a woman is powerless against a customer

Cherry Kingsley, who worked as a prostitute in Canada as a teenager, now crusades to help get children out of the sex trade. Estimates of the number of women and girls trafficked into prostitution worldwide range from 4.5 million to as high as 21 million.

determined to have his way with her. "You cannot tell how violent a man is going to be no matter how long you talk to him on the Internet or how long you have him at the door," says Alisa Bernard, 32, of Seattle, who entered prostitution as a runaway teen and left the life in her 20s. She says nothing prevents a buyer from thinking, "I can do anything to you because I've paid for it."

Even in New Zealand, most prostitutes interviewed five years after the law's passage said decriminalization "could do little about violence that occurred." However, many told the government-commissioned researchers they were more likely to report violence under the new law.[23]

The widely differing experiences between high-end "escorts" and those trading survival sex on the street for drugs or food might make this debate seem unresolvable. Sly has worked for 12 years in the United States and Australia as an escort and in other indoor settings, but never on the street. She says she's never had a violent client.

"I've seen thousands of men, and I provide a safe space for people to come in and get their needs met, and they do it on my terms," she says. "And if they don't do it on my terms, I ask them to leave."

Survivors of prostitution consider Sly part of a minority. "Approximately 10 percent of prostitutes "would stay in it if they could," says Bernard, a board member of the

Organization for Prostitution Survivors in Seattle, which helps women exit prostitution. But, "to say, 'Yes, we should listen to this 10 percent' is doing a huge injustice to the other 90 percent."

Does legalizing prostitution increase trafficking?

Since legalizing prostitution in 2002, Germany has become notorious as one of Europe's largest sex markets, nicknamed the "bordello of Europe." By some estimates the number of prostitutes in Germany has doubled over the past 20 years, to 400,000.[24]

Legalization opponents such as the Coalition Against Trafficking in Women, say the sex trade has exploded in Germany, the Netherlands and other countries that have legalized prostitution, triggering a jump in trafficking.[25] An academic study of 150 countries found that places with legalized prostitution tend to report more human trafficking than nations where prostitution is banned. For instance, the researchers found a sharp increase in reported trafficking cases in Germany after it liberalized the sex market in 2002.[26]

"Legalising prostitution appears to boost the market" for global trafficking, because a lot of men will "shy away" from buying sex illegally but "may engage if it's legal," according to Eric Neumayer, one of the study's co-authors and a professor of environment and development at the London School of Economics.[27]

In a society like Germany, where women have good education and job opportunities, there just aren't enough German women to supply the rising demand for legal prostitution, says the CATW's Bien-Aimé, "so you import people. If you look at the Netherlands or Germany, up to 90 percent of women in brothels are undocumented foreign workers, so most likely they've been trafficked."

However, other experts say Neumayer's study used unreliable statistics. For example, it counted all human trafficking cases reported to the United Nations, not just sex trafficking. Labor trafficking accounts for about 40 percent of human trafficking, while sexual exploitation accounts for 53 percent, says the United Nations Office on Drugs and Crime.[28]

Thus, the study doesn't necessarily show a link between legalized prostitution and sex trafficking, says author Weitzer, who is also a professor of sociology at George Washington University.

In fact, trafficking statistics are so unreliable, he says, there is no way to determine whether legalization spurs sex trafficking, partly because trafficking is "such an underground, hidden phenomenon." If a country measures trafficking by an increasing number of cases prosecuted, he points out, "it might be a fluke related to better recording, investigation and enforcement."

Even the Dutch and German government reports cited by anti-trafficking groups have found no increases since legalization, while cautioning that the numbers are inherently unreliable.[29]

Because of the unreliability of conflicting statistics, it's unclear whether trafficking is increasing, decreasing or staying the same in countries where prostitution is legal, most experts say. For example, based on the number of prosecutions, sex trafficking has declined steadily in Germany since 2002. According to federal police statistics, only 636 sex trafficking cases were reported in Germany in 2011, almost a third fewer than before legalization.[30]

However, those numbers may underestimate the actual number of women being trafficked, according to *Der Spiegel*, a German weekly magazine. It is difficult to prove trafficking in court, especially if women rescued in a raid are too frightened to testify, according to a police report quoted by *Der Spiegel*.[31]

When it legalized prostitution in 2000, the Dutch government originally aimed to expose trafficking by carefully monitoring legal brothels. However, a recent evaluation by Dutch researchers said trafficking still thrives behind a legalized façade, particularly when a criminal operator installs a "straw man" to run the brothel. Moreover, according to the two researchers from the Vrije Universiteit (VU University) in Amsterdam, "lawmakers seem to have neglected a very important aspect of human trafficking, namely the exploitation of prostitutes by pimps, particularly in window prostitution" — the windows common in Amsterdam's red light district where women display themselves in their lingerie to attract customers.[32]

University of Oslo Professor of Criminology May-Len Skilbrei, who teaches Norwegian immigration officers how to recognize trafficking cases, says there is "not a clear division" between women who are trafficked into prostitution involuntarily and those who work willingly. "It's difficult to identify because people don't necessarily self-identify as a victim," she says, and countries have different legal thresholds for someone to qualify as a trafficking victim.

For example, the federal trafficking law in the United States is narrower than the definition followed by Norway. For adults, U.S. law describes sex trafficking as inducing someone to commit a commercial sex act by "force, fraud or coercion."[33] But prosecutors acknowledge it is often difficult to prove the existence of such elements, especially if foreign sex workers found in a sting are too frightened to testify in court.

Should more places adopt the "Nordic model"?

In 1999 Sweden became the first country to criminalize the purchase but not the sale of sexual acts. The Nordic model was intended to help fight prostitution by deterring prospective customers both at home and from abroad.[34]

"The rationale was a feminist one and focused on social equality," says University of Oslo sociologist Skilbrei, who has studied the model in Sweden and Norway.

The Swedish experiment was widely hailed as a success after the government reported in 2010 that its new approach had cut street prostitution in half — a trend it confirmed was still holding last year. The share of Swedish men who reported having purchased sex has declined by about 40 percent since 1996, before the law was passed.[35]

By contrast, in nearby Denmark, nine years after prostitution was legalized the government found the number of street prostitutes was three times that in Sweden, even though Denmark has a much smaller population.[36]

According to Stockholm University political scientist Max Waltman, national polls in Sweden also have shown growing support for the sex-purchase ban — from a minority of men before the law's passage to 60 percent in 2014.[37]

The reported success of Sweden's law in reducing prostitution has persuaded other countries to adopt similar laws, including, most recently, France, on April 6. In 2014, the European Parliament recommended that European Union governments adopt the Nordic model.

In the United States, 11 cities are halfway through a two-year effort to demonstrate that focusing enforcement on buyers rather than sellers — an effort organized by Demand Abolition — can reduce demand for prostitution.

Sweden's law also appeared to be deterring trafficking from other countries. "Our law enforcement partners said they have wiretaps of conversations from traffickers saying, 'Don't go to Sweden: The market has dried up and it's high-risk low-reward,' " says Nealon of Demand Abolition.

In 2007, according to Nealon, Sweden had the fewest human trafficking victims moved across its national borders of any country in Europe — 400-600 people, compared to 17,000 in neighboring Finland.[38]

Some researchers cast doubt on the Swedish government's claim that it reduced prostitution, noting that its figures refer only to street prostitution, not the vast hidden arena of prostitution arranged online or by mobile phone. However, a government report last year estimated the size of the online market by counting escort ads on the Web, concluding, "there is nothing indicating that the actual number of individuals engaging in prostitution has increased."[39]

The most serious charge against the Nordic law made by organizations representing sex workers is that it makes their work more dangerous by forcing them to rush their negotiations — about where and what services to provide — because clients fear arrest. In Sweden, even an attempt to purchase sex is punishable by a fine or up to one year in jail, so standing on the street offering to buy a sex act can be risky. Some prostitutes say the law has forced them to provide higher risk sexual services, such as unprotected intercourse, in these hasty negotiations.[40]

However, in interviews with Swedish government and social service agencies, some women say the purchase ban provides a bargaining tool, according to Max Waltman, an assistant professor of political science at Stockholm University. "Some women say they were empowered by the law in negotiating with clients: If the client doesn't want to pay or use a condom, they can threaten to report them to police," says Waltman.

Moreover, since Sweden passed its law, no prostitute has been murdered while working, "and they're still counting the bodies in Germany," where prostitution is legal, says the CATW's Bien-Aimé, who favors the Nordic model.[41]

Prostitutes can still run afoul of other laws in Sweden and Norway, such as laws against pimping, renting to prostitutes or "organizing prostitution" (such as when several women work together). For example, in Norway prostitutes can be evicted by a landlord if they sell sex in their homes, says Amnesty International's Murphy. "The claim that sex workers are not penalized [under the Nordic model] is not the reality."

"The main danger of the Swedish law is it is being pushed . . . in some countries where they have no interest in decriminalizing sex workers," says Luca Stevenson, coordinator of the International Committee on the Rights of Sex Workers in Europe (ICRSE). For instance, Serbia and Lithuania continued to treat prostitutes as criminals after passing Swedish-style purchase bans, with governments using what Stevenson called a "fake gender equality agenda."

In France, which adopted the Nordic model on April 6, a three-year-long debate over the legislation turned ugly, Stevenson says, with prostitutes reporting more violence against them. "Saying sex workers should not exist translates on the ground into more violence, more stigma and discrimination," he says.

In Canada, which adopted a version of the Nordic model in 2014 by making the purchase of sex punishable by up to five years in prison or a $4,000 fine, advocates and critics are split on the law's likely deterrent effects. "There was an initial feeling of fear" among clients who chat online about their purchases of sexual acts, says Chris Atchison, a University of Victoria researcher who studies men who buy sex. After a few months the sellers and clients shifted their online discussions to offshore Web servers to avoid detection, he found. "The sex industry won't go away because of punitive laws," he says.

But Julia Beazley, director of public policy at the Evangelical Fellowship of Canada in Ottawa, which pushed for the new law, says she is convinced by Sweden's experience that the law can reduce trafficking and exploitation in Canada.

"Prostitution is a business, and it's supply and demand like any other, so if you can reduce demand, the supply is not needed," she says.

BACKGROUND
Banning Prostitution

In the United States, prostitution was not broadly criminalized until the two world wars raised concerns about American soldiers' exposure to venereal disease.

In colonial times, prostitution was not a statutory criminal offense, although women could be punished under laws against vagrancy — or "nightwalking," as it was called in colonial Massachusetts.[42] Prostitution as a specific act was not illegal in the United States until 1917, when Massachusetts adopted the first state law banning it.[43]

During the 1849 Gold Rush, Western boomtowns, populated mainly by men, allowed prostitution to flourish.

Starting in the 1870s, some American cities — including San Francisco and St. Louis — legalized prostitution by limiting it to specified "red-light" districts, sometimes in response to residents who wanted to keep disreputable women out of their neighborhoods. In 1897, New Orleans designated a 20-block area known as Storyville as a red-light district. It became the most famous district for prostitutes in the country.[44]

In the early 20th century a widespread panic about an alleged conspiracy to force women into prostitution led to passage of the 1910 Mann Act, or the White Slavery Act, the first federal law to prohibit transporting women across state lines for prostitution or "immoral purposes."[45] After that, many states joined Massachusetts in banning prostitution.[46]

In 1913, the Supreme Court upheld the Mann Act, ruling in *Hoke v. U.S.* that while prostitution is the province of the states, Congress can regulate interstate travel for prostitution.[47] Effie Hoke, who had been convicted under the Mann Act for enticing a woman to cross state lines for prostitution, had challenged the constitutionality of the act, saying it exceeded Congress' powers to regulate interstate commerce because it governed matters of morality. However, the Supreme Court said Congress' power to regulate interstate commerce included commerce that involves moving people across state borders.[48]

Laws against prostitution have remained largely in the hands of the states ever since.

After the United States entered World War I on April 6, 1917, concerns about American soldiers contracting syphilis and other venereal disease from prostitutes led Congress to pass the Chamberlain-Kahn Act of 1918. It specified that women near military bases in the United States (particularly those thought to be prostitutes because they were without escorts) could be detained and quarantined if suspected of having a sexually transmitted disease. At least 20,000 alleged prostitutes were quarantined, and thousands more were incarcerated, in an

Sex workers and sympathizers demonstrate on April 9, 2015, against the closure of some of the "window" brothels in Amsterdam's famous red-light district. Dutch researchers say it is often difficult to detect women who are trafficked into prostitution as opposed to those who work willingly.

attempt to curb the spread of venereal diseases.[49] The act, along with specific local laws, effectively closed the regulated red light districts remaining in the United States.[50]

In 1919, the Volstead Act outlawed the manufacture, sale and import of alcoholic beverages, ushering in the Prohibition era and giving rise to illegal drinking establishments known as "speakeasies," many of which offered both alcohol and prostitution. Prohibition coincided with the criminalization of "bawdy houses," which provided drink as well as sexual acts.[51] In Nevada, while Prohibition closed saloons and other places where prostitutes worked independently, brothels stayed open, claiming to "contain" prostitution.[52]

In 1941, as the United States entered World War II, Congress passed the May Act, making prostitution in military areas a federal offense. Prostitution was generally already illegal in the United States by then, but it "was officially and unofficially tolerated in different places," writes Melissa Hope Ditmore in her history of prostitution, citing a three-week strike by Honolulu's prostitutes during the war.[53]

Sexual Revolution

Starting in the late 1940s and taking hold in the '60s, increasingly liberal attitudes about premarital sex changed men's use of prostitution. By 1948, the frequency with which men had intercourse with prostitutes had declined by up to one-half to two-thirds in two decades, American sexologist Alfred Kinsey reported in his landmark 1948 study *Sexual Behavior in the Human Male.*[54]

For 20 percent of American men born between 1933 and 1942, their first sexual encounter had been with a prostitute. By the 1960s, only 5 percent of men were losing their virginity to a prostitute. Seventy percent were having premarital sex, compared to just a third of their fathers' generation, according to University of Chicago economist Steven D. Levitt and journalist Stephen J. Dubner, authors of *SuperFreakonomics.*[55]

The 1970s saw the proliferation of strip clubs and massage parlors, where prostitution was often offered clandestinely.

In 1971, Nevada passed a law, upheld by a 1980 Nevada Supreme Court decision, creating the only zone in the United States where prostitution is legal. Nevada law permits counties with fewer than 400,000 residents to license brothels. The city of Las Vegas, which wanted to promote a "family" tourism image, historically has opposed legalizing prostitution within its city limits, even though an illegal prostitution market flourishes there, according to Barbara Brents, author of *The State of Sex, a Study of Nevada's Brothels.*[56]

Currently, 10 rural counties in Nevada allow highly regulated licensed brothels, according to Brents, a professor of sociology at the University of Nevada, Las Vegas. Women are required to be checked weekly for venereal disease. Some brothels, along with some local rules, impose "lockdowns," forbidding women to leave the premises during their work contract, typically one to two weeks, on the grounds that outside sexual activity could invalidate their clean bill of health, according to University of Nevado, Reno researcher Blithe.

In the 1970s and the two following decades, two major changes occurred in the world of prostitution — the beginnings of a sex workers' movement and the dawn of the Internet era, which revolutionized how sex purchases were advertised and transacted. In 1973, an organization founded by California prostitute Margo St. James to fight anti-prostitution laws — Call Off Your Tired Old Ethics (COYOTE) — held its first convention. In 1976 St. James and COYOTE sued Rhode Island in federal court, arguing that its ban on prostitution was so broad it could prohibit sex between unmarried adults.

That was followed by a short-lived era when Rhode Island became the only state besides Nevada in which prostitution was legal. In 1980, the Rhode Island legislature made prostitution a misdemeanor, rendering COYOTE's lawsuit moot. But in rewriting the law, drafters inadvertently deleted a section that addressed committing the act of prostitution.[57]

The loophole went unnoticed until 2003, when a lawyer defending four brothels posing as massage parlors argued successfully that no law had been broken because the statute addressed only street prostitution and could not be used to convict someone for activity that occurs in private. By 2007, Providence, R.I., had become a major sex tourism destination, with brothels and strip clubs proliferating. For six years indoor prostitution remained legal in the state, until the legislature explicitly outlawed it in 2009.[58]

The 1990s saw a growing migration from street prostitution to indoors —massage parlors, strip parlors and, with the rise of the Internet, more Web-based transactions such as live, paid sex shows via webcams. Today only 10 to 20 percent of prostitution in the United States is the street variety, according to Weitzer of George Washington University.

Trafficking Concerns

The fall of the Soviet Union in 1991 brought waves of Eastern European women to Western Europe and the United States to work in the sex trade, increasing concerns that women and girls were being duped or forced into prostitution. These concerns prompted new anti-trafficking laws.

In 2000, Congress passed the Trafficking Victims Protection Act, making human trafficking a federal crime with severe penalties. It defines sex trafficking as inducing someone under 18 to perform a commercial sex act or, for adults, a commercial sex act induced by "force, fraud and coercion."[59]

CHRONOLOGY

1800s *Prostitution flourishes in "red-light" districts and the American West.*

1849 Gold Rush brings prostitution to Western boom towns.

1897 Red-light district known as Storyville created in New Orleans.

1910-1941 *Concerns over disease lead to anti-prostitution laws.*

1910 Congress prohibits the transport of women across state lines for prostitution.

1913 U.S. Supreme Court rules that prostitution is the province of the states but allows Congress to regulate interstate travel related to prostitution.

1918 After U.S. entry in 1917 into World War I, Congress passes the Chamberlain-Kahn Act, authorizing women near military bases to be detained if suspected of carrying venereal diseases.

1919 Volstead Act outlawing the production, sale and transport of alcohol, opens era of Prohibition and prostitution at speakeasies.

1941 As the United States enters World War II, the May Act increases penalties for prostitution in military areas.

1948-1973 *Prostitution's popularity declines as sexual mores change.*

1948 In his landmark study, *Sexual Behavior in the Human Male*, sex researcher Alfred Kinsey finds the frequency of men's visits to prostitutes has declined by as much as two-thirds since 1926.

1959 Britain decriminalizes prostitution but bans solicitation and related activities.

1971 Nevada becomes first state to legalize prostitution, allowing brothels in some rural counties.

1973 The California sex workers' organization Call Off Your Old Tired Ethics holds its first convention to protest laws against prostitution.

1999-2016 *Europe and United States pass laws to combat sex trafficking.*

1999 Sweden criminalizes the purchase — but not the selling — of sex in a law that becomes known as the "Nordic model."

2000 Congress passes Trafficking Victims Protection Act, making human trafficking a federal crime. . . . United Nations adopts rule with broader definition of trafficking that includes abusing a person's "position of vulnerability." . . . The Netherlands legalizes prostitution.

2002 Germany legalizes prostitution.

2003 Court case leads to the discovery that Rhode Island accidentally legalized indoor prostitution. . . . New Zealand decriminalizes prostitution.

2008 Norway and Iceland adopt Nordic model. . . . Amsterdam's mayor shuts down "window brothels" featuring prostitutes standing in view of passers-by because of purported involvement of organized crime.

2009 Rhode Island re-criminalizes indoor prostitution.

2014 European Parliament recommends European Union countries adopt Nordic model. . . . Canada adopts Nordic model.

2015 Eleven U.S. cities pledge to curb demand for prostitution by arresting "johns." . . . Sex workers and a disabled would-be client challenge California's law against prostitution in federal court. . . . Northern Ireland adopts Nordic model. . . . Amnesty International proposes decriminalizing sex trade worldwide.

2016 Seattle sting shuts down prostitution review website *The Review Board* (January). . . . New Hampshire Legislature defeats decriminalization proposals (March). . . . German Cabinet proposes to tighten regulations on prostitution (March). . . . Federal judge in California dismisses sex workers' constitutional challenge to state prostitution ban (March). . . . France adopts Nordic-style sex-purchase ban (April 6).

Seattle Shifts Sex Arrests From Sellers to Buyers

Prosecutors deploy a version of "Nordic model."

In King County, Wash., Senior Deputy Prosecuting Attorney Valiant Richey says when he took over sex prosecutions in 2011, "people who worked with victims kept saying, 'Why do you keep arresting women and children instead of going after the buyers?'"

King County — whose largest city is Seattle — was one of the country's fastest-growing commercial sex markets, yet the county's enforcement was "an epic failure," Richey says.

The county was prosecuting about twice as many women for prostitution as buyers, or "johns," Richey discovered. The prosecutor's office has since aimed to shrink the prostitution market by deterring buyers. Last year the county charged three times as many johns as prostitutes.

Prosecutors were emulating Sweden's so-called Nordic model law, which penalizes buyers but not the sellers of sex. Seattle/King County is one of 11 metro areas that last year pledged to reduce demand for prostitution by 20 percent in two years by using Nordic-style strategies.[1]

The national effort was initiated in February 2015 by Demand Abolition, a nonprofit in Cambridge, Mass., committed to eradicating the illegal sex trade in the United States by arresting buyers.[2]

"The laws on the books were being unfairly enforced; in some places it was 11 women in prostitution arrested for every one man," says Demand Abolition's founding director, Lina Nealon. "At the very least, that ratio should be flipped."

Part of the group's strategy is to offer social services to help women exit prostitution. "The beauty of the demand approach is you can levy fines on buyers [that can be used] to help victims," she says.

Halfway through the two-year effort, it's too soon to say how successful the cities have been in reducing customer demand by 20 percent, Nealon says. But she cites Denver as having successfully reversed its arrest ratio from three women arrested for every two "johns."[3]

In Washington state the maximum fine for buying sex is a $1,000 fine or a maximum of 90 days in jail. A bill, supported by the King County and Seattle prosecutors' offices, would have raised the fine to a maximum $5,000 and a year in jail, but it died in this year's legislative session.

King County also went from charging more than 50 juveniles with prostitution in 2009 to none last year. Richey says he would like to see charges for adult sellers take a similar plunge, but that would require persuading all of the county's 38 police agencies as well as prosecutors' offices to change their approach.

Seattle began embracing a strategy similar to the county's in 2012. "We changed our policy . . . and stopped charging the crime of prostitution," shifting the focus to arresting buyers, says Seattle Assistant City Attorney Heidi Sargent. Today, the city charges selected cases of prostitution — if there's been violence or a clear case of drug addiction — but will dismiss the case if the arrestee complies with court-ordered services like drug rehabilitation, according to Sargent.

However, "it is very difficult to prove" coercion under the federal law "because the fraud and force usually happen in the first 24 to 48 hours," says Bien-Aimé of the Coalition Against Trafficking in Women. That's when traffickers, having lured a woman to New York with the promise of a nanny job, may beat or rape her in order to force her to prostitute herself. By the time there's a police raid three months later, the woman is often so beaten

down that, "the force is gone, there's no lock on the door, no gun to her head," she says. "That is a huge challenge for us at the federal level."

By contrast, the U.N. adopted a broader definition of trafficking of women and children in 2000, called the Palermo Protocol. It went into effect in 2003, and has since been ratified by more than 100 countries, including the United States. In addition to threat, force or coercion,

After finding more than 100 websites selling sex in the county, local, county and federal law enforcement officials mounted sting operations against men who buy sex through the Internet. They brought felony charges in January against 12 men in Seattle accused of posting reviews of prostitutes on *The Review Board* website providing information about secret brothels. The men were charged with "promotion of prostitution," punishable by up to five years in prison — a charge usually reserved for pimps and traffickers. Officials closed down a dozen brothels and found 12 South Korean women who allegedly had been forced into prostitution.[4]

However, some sex workers say King County's strategy makes life more dangerous for them because buyers worried about arrest will rush negotiations, make women come to unsecure locations or have sex without a condom. The crackdown "freaks out buyers and weakens a sex worker's ability to screen out clients, which is one of our only tools to stay safe," says Savannah Sly, a former Seattle-based prostitute.

The Review Board provided a good way to screen men online, according to the Sex Workers Outreach Project (SWOP-U.S.A.), representing sex workers in the United States. But fewer customers now are willing to give out personal details because they fear the woman on the other end may be an undercover cop, says Sly, president of SWOP-U.S.A.

Alisa Bernard, 32, said she thought *The Review Board* was a good idea 10 years ago when "my body was being sold on it", but says it's an illusion to think women can screen someone in a profession that puts them at a customer's mercy. "The online boards do not keep women safe," she wrote in *The Seattle Times*. "If a buyer had a bad day, there is nothing stopping him from taking it out on the women they buy, since they see them as an object."[5]

In an interview, Bernard — who says she sold sex on the street as a teenage runaway and left the trade in her early 20s — concedes that an online site can "make you more independent" of a controlling third party like a pimp. "But it makes you more reliant on the buyer, because you have to keep getting good reviews — which means you have to keep pushing your 'No' line [on sexual practices] a lot further away."

Bernard, a board member of Seattle's Organization for Prostitution Survivors, which works with King County to help women leave the trade, says, "more women are getting out" of the prostitution business and "more feel safer knowing the police are less likely to arrest them."

However, in the long run, Bernard says, laws that criminalize women in prostitution should be overturned. A criminal record can keep a woman from finding a legitimate job and starting over.

But Richey says a change in the law is easier said than done. "Our goal is to move toward full implementation of the Nordic model," he says. "If the state legislature passed a law decriminalizing prostitution [for sellers], that could happen overnight. However, much of the state, and indeed the country, is not ready for that."

— *Sarah Glazer*

---

[1] The other 10 metropolitan areas are Atlanta, Boston, Chicago (Cook County, Ill.), Dallas (North Texas), Denver, Houston, Oakland (Alameda County, Calif.), Phoenix, Portland (Multnomah County, Ore.) and San Diego.

[2] "National Initiative to Fight Sex Trafficking Launched," Demand Abolition, Feb. 4, 2015, http://tinyurl.com/joukksg.

[3] Jesse Paul, "Denver shifts prostitution policing to buyers in national initiative," *The Denver Post*, April 29, 2015, http://tinyurl.com/zyqsju3.

[4] "Demand Abolition Applauds Seizure of Sex-Trafficking Websites, and Resulting Felony Charges against Accused Sex-Buyers," news release, Demand Abolition, Jan. 7, 2016, http://tinyurl.com/hjaqkej.

[5] Alisa Bernard, "Shutdown of Sex-trafficking websites long overdue," *The Seattle Times*, Jan. 22, 2016, http://tinyurl.com/zt2vwev.

---

it says abusing someone's "position of vulnerability" can constitute trafficking. The protocol explicitly states that the consent of the trafficking victim is "irrelevant."[60]

Countries that are signatories to the protocol vary in how closely they model their legislation on its definition, with the majority adopting laws with less-expansive definitions of trafficking. The agreement is generally used only as a guideline for national laws and is not enforced.

Scandinavian countries hew closely to Palermo's broader definition and are thus quite generous in awarding assistance to victims found to meet this standard, says University of Oslo sociologist Skilbrei. In Norway, she says, "we've had court cases where victims say they were willingly recruited," but the trafficker is convicted because the victims "were unemployed in their home country and therefore unable to choose freely what to do."

German Government Targets Legal-Prostitution Problems

Only 1 percent of sex workers have signed a work contract.

Marie was a single mother of two in her early 40s when financial desperation drove her to advertise on one of Germany's legal websites offering sexual services.* "I thought, 'No one will pay for a woman in her 40s with a little bit too much weight,'" she says.

Even though she set a high price, the first customer answered her ad within half an hour, she recalls. She made her first appointment in what would become a three-year stretch of prostitution that she says she found "degrading" and sometimes violent without the benefit of protection from either brothel management or the state.

Many Germans, including government officials, assumed that legalizing prostitution in 2002 would lead to clean, safe, regulated brothels; provide government benefits for sex workers and remove a breeding ground for crime.

It didn't turn out that way. The law did not have any "visible" impact on crime, nor did it improve access to social insurance or working conditions for sex workers, a government report concluded five years after the law's passage.[1]

In fact, the Stuttgart brothel where Marie rented a room was "just like a hotel," she says. It had no hygiene standards, and nobody checked on her safety.

---

* Marie is a pseudonym.

As for signing an employment contract with the brothel — which would have provided her with social security and paid sick days — "Forget it," she says. "No one wants to write in stone, 'I'm a prostitute.'" Marie, 53, left prostitution six years ago and now works for a government agency helping refugees.

Indeed, only 1 percent of Germany's sex workers have signed up for a work contract qualifying them for social insurance, according to the only government estimate.[2]

Besides wanting to protect their anonymity, most sex workers prefer the flexibility of working as freelancers and do not want to be subject to an employer's rules on when and where they work, according to Undine de Riviére, a sex worker in Hamburg and spokesperson for the Professional Organisation for Erotic and Sexual Services, representing about 300 sex workers. Brothel operators also prefer to avoid paying the social security taxes required under a contract, the government found.[3]

In March Germany's Cabinet introduced] a bill aimed at tackling some of the most notorious problems in the legalized system. The draft law will require all customers to use condoms starting next year, if, as expected, the law wins parliamentary approval. It would forbid flat rate "gang-bang" parties that simulate group rapes, offered by some brothels. Sex workers will have to register with local authorities — a measure aimed at helping law enforcement find

In Western Europe, concerns about trafficking helped spur new prostitution laws, but they took different approaches. After Sweden adopted its Nordic model in 1999, Norway and Iceland followed suit in 2008, Canada in 2014, Northern Ireland last year, and France on April 6. The Netherlands (2000) and Germany (2002) legalized regulated brothels in hopes that trafficking could be uncovered by making the industry more transparent. In 2003, New Zealand opted for the third path — full decriminalization.

However, after legalization appeared to increase exploitation and trafficking in the Netherlands, Amsterdam began shutting down many of the red-light district's famous window brothels, charging they were run by organized crime.

Amsterdam Mayor Job Cohen initiated the first closures, saying, in 2008, "big crime organizations are involved here in trafficking women, drugs, killings and other criminal activities. . . . We're not banning prostitution, but we are cutting back on the whole circuit: the trafficked women, according to the government. Sex workers over age 21 also will be required to get health examinations at least once a year; those under 21 will have to receive them twice yearly.[4]

However, feminists complain the law is too lenient, while sex-worker organizations have called it too burdensome. "A lot of sex workers will go underground," predicts de Riviére, because they don't want to be "outed" by a government registry, especially those who practice prostitution as a part-time job to supplement their income from conventional jobs. "We're still stigmatized."

Several sex workers are planning to challenge the law in court on the grounds that such information about their sex lives is "sensitive data" protected under European Union law, she says.

Ingeborg Kraus, a psychologist in Karlsruhe who initiated a petition in December 2014 calling for repeal of the 2002 law legalizing prostitution, says the new law will do little to stop the "industrialization" of prostitution in Germany. Women in Stuttgart now charge as little as 25 euros (about $28) for intercourse, but have to pay a daily rent of 180 euros (about $203) for a room in a brothel, she says, requiring them to service seven men a day just to cover their costs.

Although widely accepted figures are hard to come by, experts say most sex workers in Germany are foreigners — with the majority coming from the newer European Union member countries in Eastern Europe, such as Romania and Bulgaria.[5] Critics of the system say up to 90 percent of the women are trafficked.[6]

Kraus would have liked to see the law require monthly health checks so that women, particularly those being trafficked, could develop a relationship with a doctor who could help them get out of prostitution. "What good does it do . . . to say, 'You have AIDS,' " after a year has passed, she asks.

On April 6, the German cabinet agreed to push for another law that would penalize johns with up to five years in jail if they patronize prostitutes forced into the trade. The German government hopes the law will help uncover trafficking, since clients who report suspicions of forced prostitution would not be penalized. However, anti-prostitution and anti-trafficking groups criticized the law as unrealistic, saying it would be difficult to prove a client knew a victim had been forced into the trade.[7]

Speaking on a morning talk show after the government announced its proposal to penalize customers, Sabine Constabel of Sisters e.v., a group that wants to abolish prostitution, said Germany would continue to be "the brothel of Europe."[8]

— *Sarah Glazer*

[1] "Report by the Federal Government on the Impact of the Act Regulating the Legal Situation of Prostitutes (The Prostitution Act)," Republic of Germany, Federal Ministry for Family Affairs, Senior Citizens, Women and Youth, 2007, http://tinyurl.com/zfoh4vg.

[2] *Ibid.*

[3] *Ibid.*

[4] "German cabinet seeks tougher prostitution rules," *Deutsche Welle*, March 23, 2016, http://tinyurl.com/zb4mmyf.

[5] Clare Speak, "Germany may roll back legalized prostitution amid exploitation fears," *Equal Times*, Dec. 17, 2013, http://tinyurl.com/j3ftyrv.

[6] "Germany wins the title of 'bordello of Europe: Why Doesn't Angela Merkel Care?,' " Interview with Ingeborg Kraus by Taina Bien-Aimé, July 19, 2015, http://tinyurl.com/zeuwqzj.

[7] "German plan to jail 'johns' stirs debate on forced prostitution," *Deutsche Welle*, April 6, 2016, http://tinyurl.com/oxwuhmw.

[8] *Ibid.*

gambling halls, the pimps, the money laundering."[61] In the largest such case in 2008, six men were convicted in Amsterdam of trafficking in connection with a network involving more than 100 women.[62]

Nearly one-quarter of Amsterdam's more than 400 windows have been closed. George Washington sociologist Weitzer, who has studied prostitution in Amsterdam, says he thinks the claims of criminal involvement in the red-light district have been exaggerated, although he acknowledges, "You do have low-level pimps who control some of the women who work in the red-light district."

Prostitutes have protested the shutdowns, arguing that renting an individual window is one of the safest, most independent ways for sex workers to operate. "You're just renting space rather than working in a brothel" where you would have to follow a brothel owner's rules, says Yvette Luhrs, a creator of feminist pornography in Amsterdam and spokesperson for PROUD, a Dutch sex workers union.

Luhrs and Weitzer say the city's most recent effort to crack down on organized crime was more of a gentrification effort, aimed at encouraging high-end boutiques and cafes to replace the brothels.

As for crime, Luhrs complains that police don't follow up on rapes and other crime reported by sex workers. "We have stories of people being trafficked," with a pimp who takes all their money, "but when they have gone to police to press charges, the police say, 'You need to stop working as a prostitute; otherwise you have no case,' " she reports.

According to Skilbrei, brothel owners generally eschew trafficking because, "they have everything to lose — their license — if they have a trafficking case." But this safeguard has no effect on the parallel illegal prostitution market, populated by illegal migrants, drug users and others who are not able to work in the regulated brothels, notes Skilbrei.

Increasingly European prostitution has a foreign face, leading inevitably to questions about how many women have been trafficked into the country where they are working. In Germany, Helmut Sporer, Detective Chief Superintendent of the Crimes Squad in Augsburg, said around 80 percent of the prostitutes in Germany are from other countries, mostly from newer European Union (EU) member states in southeastern Europe, such as Romania and Bulgaria.[63]

"Ninety per cent of these women have not freely chosen prostitution, they are subjected to various forms of pressure," he said. Since most have not registered for government benefits, "If a woman goes missing, absolutely no one will notice. Of course, this makes Germany very attractive for traffickers and other profiteers," Sporer said.[64]

In Western and Central Europe, the majority of sex workers are migrants from the EU, China, Nigeria and Latin America, according to Stevenson of the International Committee on the Rights of Sex Workers in Europe. A report last year found that Nigerian and Romanian women were over-represented even among Sweden's estimated 250 street prostitutes.[65]

Some observers worry that the latest deluge of refugees entering Europe, mainly from the Middle East, will exacerbate trafficking. It's a "possibility," says Skilbrei, but "we don't know" if trafficking is increasing.

"With the refugee crisis and lack of economic support for refugees, people are turning to sex work to survive,"

Stevenson says, noting that asylum seekers often receive barely enough to live on from European governments and are not permitted to work legally.[66]

CURRENT SITUATION
United States

Amnesty International's controversial proposal to decriminalize the sex trade has bolstered some advocates' efforts to lift laws banning prostitution in the United States. But the efforts appear unlikely to affect the dominant reform trend in American cities — shifting toward arresting the customers, or "johns," instead of the prostitutes.

Amnesty International expects to finalize its draft proposal in the next few months, according to policy adviser Murphy. But New Hampshire state Rep. Elizabeth Edwards, a Democrat, didn't wait for the final draft. In January she introduced a bill in the state legislature proposing full decriminalization. Edwards said the measure was "in response to" the Amnesty recommendation. She said removing criminal penalties for prostitution would encourage those in the sex trade to report assault and help law enforcement officials refocus on "trafficking and things that aren't consensual."[67]

However the bill ran into strong opposition from the GOP leadership. "Society is just not ready for that," said Majority Leader Dick Hinch, a Republican.[68] At a House hearing on Jan. 28, members expressed concern that decriminalization would encourage more people to become prostitutes, attract an influx of sex tourism and crime to the state and encourage high school football teams to hold "hooker" parties after a victory.[69]

A competing bill introduced by Republican state Rep. J. R. Hoell would adopt the Nordic model by lifting criminal penalties for prostitution but penalizing the buyers. "Criminal penalties [on prostitutes] are used by pimps and traffickers to threaten, 'I'm just going to turn you in,' " he says, strengthening the power of traffickers.

Both bills died in the legislature this session. However, Sex Workers Outreach Project-USA president Sly says her group is contemplating pushing for decriminalization in another state, possibly a liberal one such as Vermont, the first to introduce civil unions and to recognize same-sex marriage by statute.

On March 31, U.S. District Judge Jeffrey White dismissed a federal lawsuit filed a year ago by several women

Should prostitution be decriminalized?

YES
Jerald L. Mosley
Former Supervising Deputy Attorney General,
State of California

Written for *CQ Researcher*, April 2016

Americans enjoy a constitutional right to sexual privacy. Nevertheless, loud voices insist we must criminalize consenting adult prostitution in order to deter nonconsensual and underage prostitution (trafficking). That claim is baseless.

There is no good evidence that Sweden's criminalization of buyers (but not sellers) of sex has decreased trafficking, or that legalization of sex work in Germany, the Netherlands, New Zealand or parts of Australia has increased trafficking. (Of course, if you count as a trafficking victim any sex worker who steps across an international border regardless of how voluntary and intentional her travel is, you may indeed come up with frightening "data.")

The increasingly popular characterization of the sex worker as victim and the customer as the new folk devil also is misguided. Shaming and criminalizing all customers do not protect the sex worker from that one customer looking for an enslaved or underage victim. That criminal is not going to be deterred out of a fear that when he is led to prison as a reviled trafficker, he also will be shamed for buying sex.

Moreover, even if directed only at customers, criminalization of consensual sex for hire hurts the sex worker. In 2012, the United Nations Global Commission on HIV and the Law denounced Sweden's criminalization of buyers, saying it had worsened the lives of sex workers. Criminalization pushes the engagement into the shadows and isolation of the underground, exactly where the killers and traffickers want it. The real criminals are happy to work in those shadows, while law enforcement and prosecutors amass statistics on easy arrests of consenting adults as they claim to be fighting sexual slavery.

In place of analysis the debate often showcases tropes, such as that men are "using" or "buying" a woman. This emotionally charged verbiage tells us nothing, yet it manages to insult the woman who claims a personal right to take money for sex.

In contrast, Thailand's national sex-worker organization, Empower, does tell us something. These workers struck a universal chord in their 2016 statement pleading for understanding that for them, sex work is a way out of generational poverty and that migration is their solution, not their problem. And, most telling, they added, "We want to know, if society were asked to think of us not as criminals, immoral women or helpless victims, but as humans, mothers, workers and family providers, what laws and systems could be imagined?"

NO
Taina Bien-Aimé
Executive Director, Coalition Against Trafficking
in Women

Written for *CQ Researcher*, April 2016

Only prostituted individuals must be decriminalized, as Sweden, Iceland and other countries have enshrined in law.

The system of prostitution is upheld by buyers of sexual acts ("johns"). It is a multibillion-dollar global market where demand for monetized sexual acts generates untold profits for traffickers and pimps, including owners of brothels, strip clubs, massage parlors and pornographers. The law must hold these perpetrators accountable for their crimes.

Many governments continue to promote sexual access to women and girls by law or indifference. Some condone or legalize child marriage, female genital mutilation, polygamy or denial of reproductive rights. Others discriminate explicitly on the basis of sex to exert violent control in the name of culture or religion.

Similarly, some countries and jurisdictions have legalized or decriminalized the harmful practice of prostitution, which in each case has led to a booming sex-trafficking market.

Why do we view prostitution as an exception to gender-based violence? The sex trade has crafted a powerful narrative by co-opting language reverberating deeply held, democratic principles of freedom, agency and choice. Equally evocative concepts are "sex" and "work," each of which resonates with our sense of worth, dignity and rights. By creating the phrase "sex work," the sex trade enlisted the media and entertainment industries to create fantasies of empowered young women gleefully offering "girlfriend experiences" to myriad strangers with no interest in negotiating anything but violence and dehumanization. The exchange of money becomes consent for a "job" whose description allows "clients" to exercise sexual harassment, violence or even torture.

If independent "happy sex workers" exist, they belong to an infinitesimal percentage of the prostituted population, which is overwhelmingly female, of color, disenfranchised and under the brutal thumbs of pimps and traffickers. The handful who see prostitution as "work" cannot dictate public policy. From domestic violence to smoking, we've come to understand society's responsibility to eliminate physical and psychological harms. Under our laws, prostituted people are the only ones punished for their exploitation.

National conversations about economic disparities and equality; incarceration and education; race and opportunity; and terrorism and peace bar us from identifying the sex trade as a viable employer.

Sex workers call for the legalization of sex as work during a demonstration in Rome on April 30, 2015. The sex trade has become highly polarized between those calling themselves "sex workers" — who say "sex work is work" like any other — and former prostitutes who dub themselves "survivors" of sexual exploitation.

who have worked in prostitution and a disabled would-be client challenging the constitutionality of California's prostitution law. The plaintiffs argued the law violates the privacy and free speech rights of consenting adults.

"The intimate association between a prostitute and client, while it may be consensual and cordial, has not merited the protection of the Due Process Clause of the Fourteenth Amendment," White wrote, adding, "the relationship between a client and his or her paid companion may well be the antithesis of the highly personal bonds protected by the Fourteenth Amendment." He sided with the state's arguments that the law promotes public safety and prevents coercion and injury. Lawyers for the plaintiffs have said they will appeal.[70]

"The government has intruded on our privacy — specifically our sexual privacy," says Maxine Doogan, who describes herself as a prostitute for the past 20 years and is president of the Erotic Service Providers Legal, Education and Research Project, which is the lead plaintiff in the case. The San Francisco nonprofit seeks to promote sexual privacy rights on behalf of escorts and others who provide "erotic services."

The plaintiffs' brief cites the Supreme Court's 2003 decision in *Lawrence v. Texas*, which struck down state laws criminalizing sodomy between consenting same-sex adults. The plaintiffs say the Lawrence decision can be interpreted to support the contention that anti-prostitution laws are unconstitutional, since the court clarified that "consensual sexual behavior . . . is protected when it occurs in private between two consenting adults."[71]

In 2008, a ballot initiative launched by the Erotic Service Providers Legal, Education and Research Project aimed to stop enforcement of anti-prostitution laws in San Francisco; it was rejected by 59 percent of voters.[72]

Gaining more traction is an effort by nearly a dozen U.S. cities to use a version of the Nordic model to target johns rather than prostitutes. Denver and Seattle say they have reversed their traditional arrest ratios, which penalized far more prostitutes than customers, and Seattle has even arrested men who share reviews of prostitutes online.[73]

Websites that advertise and promote prostitution also have come under scrutiny from Congress. In March, the Senate voted to hold Backpage.com CEO Carl Ferrer in civil contempt of Congress for failing to comply with a subpoena for documents about the company's business practices, particularly how it screens advertisements for warning signs of sex trafficking and underage girls.[74]

However, D'Adamo of the Urban Justice Center in New York, says such websites have enabled prostitutes to work independently and thus more safely. If such websites are closed down, she says, it will expose more sex workers to trafficking and pimps.

Europe

Prostitution survivor groups are strongly supporting the dominant legislative trend in Europe favoring the Nordic model, while sex worker groups oppose it.

The International Committee on the Rights of Sex Workers in Europe organized a letter to the European Parliament, signed by over 500 sex worker groups and individuals, opposing the Nordic model.[75] The network is pushing for full decriminalization, which the Scottish Parliament is likely to debate next year, says ICRSE coordinator Stevenson.

The Nordic model law adopted by France this month repealed existing laws that penalized prostitutes for soliciting in public. First-time offenders who purchase or attempt to purchase sex will pay a fine of 1,500 euros (about $1,700); repeat offenders will be fined up to 3,750 euros ($4,000).[76]

The law will also help prostitutes gain temporary residence permits and find other work, since most of the country's prostitutes come from outside the country — mostly from Eastern Europe and Africa — and are victims of trafficking, according to France's Minister for Women's Rights, Laurence Rossignol.[77]

However, some prostitutes protested outside the assembly during final debate on the law. And one of the main French police unions, Synergie, said few clients would be caught in the act and that overworked officers had no intention of spying on them.[78]

Ireland's Ministry of Justice has introduced a similar Nordic-style bill, with support from all parties, which advocates predict will become law by this summer.[79]

In Britain, a parliamentary committee is studying the Nordic approach, along with the concept of establishing "managed areas" — specific neighborhoods where prostitution would be allowed during limited hours, modeled after Dutch "tolerance zones." Leeds announced this year it will continue a managed area it piloted after police declared it a success in combating crime. However, a prostitute was murdered in the area last December, and local businesses and residents have complained about the presence of prostitutes.[80]

In Germany and the Netherlands, governments are proposing tighter regulations on legalized prostitution in order to answer criticisms that their laws have failed to stem trafficking, exploitation or the spread of sexually transmitted diseases. The German government is proposing mandated condom use in commercial sex transactions and regular health checks for sex workers, as they are called under German law. It also would require sex workers to register with local authorities so trafficked women can be detected. Sex worker organizations call the law too onerous, and critics of legalization say it does too little to help women in prostitution.

In the Netherlands a pending government-backed proposal would raise the legal age of prostitution from 18 to 21 and punish unlicensed sex workers with up to six months in jail. About a third of the country's sex workers do not have a license, largely because they prefer not to reveal their profession to the government, according to Luhrs of the sex workers union PROUD.

"When there's the 'whore' check mark beside your name, police will pull you out of your car; child services will check if you're a good parent; landlords can legally kick you out of your house," she says.

Canada

After the Canadian Supreme Court declared Canada's ban on brothels unconstitutional in 2014, the Conservative government passed legislation modeled after the Swedish law. However, Canada's law also penalizes prostitutes who ply their trade near schools or community and day care centers.

Police in some cities, including Vancouver and Toronto, have declared they have little intention of actively enforcing the new law, viewing it as a low priority, notes University of Victoria sociologist Atchison. But other cities already are using it to conduct more "john sweeps," reports Beazley of the Evangelical Fellowship of Canada.

Both sides expect sex workers, who mounted the initial constitutional challenge against the old law, to challenge the new one as well. It's unclear whether the new government, whose Liberal party opposed the new law, will initiate any changes.

"The law has a five-year re-evaluation built into it, so I hope they'll let it stand for five years," says Beazley.

OUTLOOK
Debate to Continue

Amid worldwide concern about trafficking and exploitation of women and children in the sex trade, sentiment in Europe appears to be turning away from the legalization approaches embraced by Germany and the Netherlands over a decade ago.

Recent trends suggest that laws focused on penalizing buyers rather than sellers of sex will become increasingly attractive. This movement is likely to gain traction in the United States, where prosecutors and police have become some of the Nordic model's biggest champions as a way to "end demand," say advocacy groups like Demand Abolition and opponents like Sex Workers Outreach Project-USA.

However Americans don't appear ready to wipe out criminal penalties for prostitution anytime soon, judging by the death of bills proposing to do that in New Hampshire this year.

Even in King County, Wash., where police and prosecutors in and around Seattle have embraced the Nordic model by stepping up charges against johns, no one is proposing eliminating the state's criminal laws against selling sex. "I think culturally the community is probably not quite ready for that — even though we are de facto implementing it," says King County's senior deputy prosecuting attorney, Valiant Richey.

In his 2011 book, *Legalizing Prostitution*, George Washington University sociologist Weitzer noted the increasing liberalization of U.S. laws against activities once classified as "vice" — gambling, marijuana use, pornography and gay rights — and asked whether prostitution could become the next area ripe for liberalization. At the time, however, he noted the limited public support for lifting prostitution bans, citing opposition from both the right and the left.[81]

Today, he says, "I think it's premature to imagine we will have legal, regulated prostitution in the United States," although he says there's no reason a city or state couldn't introduce the Dutch form of highly regulated prostitution he favors, requiring licenses and health regulations — while still supporting laws against trafficking.

But prosecutor Richey says ending the demand for prostitution is the only viable way to fight trafficking and the sex trade. He rejects the arguments of Weitzer and sex worker groups that law enforcement should leave consensual prostitution alone and address only trafficking situations. "That's not possible; they're intertwined," he says. "The buying is the cause of all of it — of the market that drives a person into it [for] survival and the pimps who push someone into it because of money."

Two opposite portrayals of prostitution raise the question: Should policy be made for those who say they do it willingly or those who experience prostitution every day as rape? Both sides claim to represent the majority.

"We need to respect diversity: Both the survivors' and sex workers' movements are right," says Skilbrei, of the University of Oslo. "We cannot choose based on a majority vote."

She says policies are needed to help people out of prostitution if they want that and, at the same time, "it might be possible to accommodate sex workers' demands for safety and respect." However, that kind of policy hasn't been adopted anywhere so far, she says. "For some reason, it's difficult for prostitution policies to make room for diversity," she says.

With both sides claiming to be the most authentic representatives of the oldest profession, this debate is likely to divide the American public for many years to come.

NOTES

1. Prostitution is decriminalized in the Australian state of New South Wales; it is legalized in licensed brothels in several states including Victoria. See Coalition Against Trafficking in Women Australia, 2007, http://tinyurl.com/jkeq5pg. In other states, including Western Australia, prostitution is not illegal but operates in a gray zone, with laws against pimping and brothels. See "Australia's Brothel Boom," *Slate*, Jan. 2, 2015, http://tinyurl.com/nhdm9f3.

2. Andrew Breiner, "These three graphs could change your mind about legalizing sex work," Think Progress, July 31, 2015, http://tinyurl.com/hvvbpes.

3. "Summary: Proposed Policy on Sex Work," Position Paper, Amnesty International, 2014, http://tinyurl.com/pbrwzc4.

4. Melissa Farley, "Prostitution, Liberalism and Slavery," *Logos*, 2013, http://tinyurl.com/hj6fvne.

5. "International Labour Standards on Forced Labour," International Labour Organization, undated, http://tinyurl.com/hprp4sv.

6. Ronald Weitzer, *Legalizing Prostitution: From Illicit Vice to Lawful Business* (2012), pp. 213-214. For background, see Ethan McLeod, Legalizing Marijuana, "Hot Topic," *CQ Researcher*, May 22, 2015.

7. Ballot measures to decriminalize prostitution were defeated in San Francisco in 2008 and in Berkeley in 2004. See Weitzer, *op. cit.*, p. 50.

8. Peter Moore, "Country Split on Legalizing Prostitution," YouGov US, Sept. 1, 2015, http://tinyurl.com/zolsjuh.

9. See Weitzer, *op. cit.*, pp. 49-52. In New South Wales, it is an offense to solicit clients or workers near a school, church, hospital or dwelling. See Basil Donovan *et al.*, "The Sex Industry in New South Wales," University of New South Wales, 2012, http://tinyurl.com/htxwbzz.

10. See Jane Kramer, "Road Warrior," *The New Yorker*, Oct. 19, 2015, http://tinyurl.com/pjtsgvl.

11. For background, see Robert Kiener, "Human Trafficking and Slavery," *CQ Global Researcher*, Oct. 16, 2012, pp. 473-496.

12. "Statistics and Indicators on Forced Labour and Trafficking," International Labour Organization, Feb. 29, 2016, http://tinyurl.com/jdug9zk.

13. "Protocol to Prevent, Suppress and Punish Trafficking in Persons, Especially Women and Children, supplementing the United Nations Convention against Transnational Organized Crime," United Nations, Nov. 15, 2000, http://tinyurl.com/h39nnjv. Also see "Guide to the New UN Trafficking Protocol," Coalition Against Trafficking in Women, http://tinyurl.com/zlh9cjt.

14. Janice G. Raymond, *Not a Choice, Not Job* (2013), p. 29. Also see Wim Huisman and Edward R. Kleemans, "Challenges of fighting sex trafficking in the legalized prostitution market of the Netherlands," *Crime Law and Social Change*, Jan. 11, 2014, pp. 215-218, http://tinyurl.com/hj8hj67.

15. Gillian M. Abel, "A decade of decriminalization," *Criminology and Criminal Justice*, Feb. 14, 2014, pp. 580-592, http://tinyurl.com/haqveo3.

16. However some local governments have restricted prostitutes to limited areas. Under the law, failure to use a condom can result in a fine. See, "Prostitution Law Reform in New Zealand," New Zealand Parliament, July 2012, http://tinyurl.com/lwyaatl. Also see "Law," New Zealand Prostitutes Collective, undated, http://tinyurl.com/lmvsu7v.

17. Abel, *op. cit.*

18. "Summary: Proposed Policy on Sex Work," *op. cit.*

19. Anand Grover, Report of the Special Rapporteur, United Nations, Human Rights Council, April 27, 2010, p. 14, http://tinyurl.com/7j2sz62.

20. Scott Cunningham and Manisha Shah, "Decriminalizing Indoor Prostitution," National Bureau of Economic Research, Working Paper 20281, July 2014, p. 24, http://tinyurl.com/hvbf8lm.

21. "CATW Responds," International Coalition Against Trafficking in Women, Aug. 12, 2015, http://tinyurl.com/zjm92tq. Also see "Report by the Federal Government on the Impact of the Act Regulating the Legal Situation of Prostitutes (The Prostitution Act), German Federal Ministry for Family Affairs, Senior Citizens, Women and Youth, 2007, http://tinyurl.com/zfoh4vg.

22. Coalition Against Trafficking in Women letter to Amnesty International, July 17, 2015, http://tinyurl.com/o8whpcb.

23. "Report of the Prostitution Law Review Committee on the Operation of the Prostitution Reform Act 2003," New Zealand Ministry of Justice, 2008, http://tinyurl.com/gun8dr8.

24. Jim Reed, "Mega-brothels," BBC News, Feb. 21, 2014, http://tinyurl.com/luah4h9.

25. Coalition Against Trafficking in Women letter to Amnesty International, *op. cit.*

26. Seo-Young Cho *et al.*, "Does Legalized Prostitution Increase Human Trafficking?" World Development, 41 (1) 2013, pp. 67-82, http://tinyurl.com/zonyrdr.

27. Eric Neumayer, "There is a complex relationship between legalized prostitution and human trafficking," British Politics and Policy Blog, London School of Economics, January 2013, http://tinyurl.com/gmy797v.

28. "Global Report on Trafficking in Persons," United Nations Office on Drugs and Crime, 2014, p. 9, http://tinyurl.com/of4twak.

29. "Report by the [German] Federal Government on the Impact of the Act Regulating the Legal Situation of Prostitutes (The Prostitution Act), *op. cit.*, p. 45. This government report said: "No trend can be observed regarding the number of cases of trafficking . . . following the amendment to the Prostitution Act." Also see A. L. Daalder, "Prostitution in the Netherlands since the lifting of the brothel ban," Research and Documentation Center, Government of the Netherlands, 2007, http://tinyurl.com/h5qnquu.

30. "Unprotected: How Legalizing Prostitution Has Failed: Part 3: Germany's Human Trafficking Problem," *Spiegel Online*, May 30, 2013, http://tinyurl.com/q7zjvgv.

31. *Ibid.*

32. Huisman and Kleemans, *op. cit.*

33. "Federal Law," National Human Trafficking Resource Center, undated, http://tinyurl.com/hkua3x. Anyone under 18 subject to sexual exploitation is considered a trafficking victim.

34. "The Ban against the Purchase of Sexual Services. An Evaluation 1999-2008," Selected extracts of the Swedish government report, Swedish Institute, 2010, http://tinyurl.com/zvv4yeq.

35. "The Extent and Development of Prostitution in Sweden 2014," County Administrative Board of Stockholm, 2015, http://tinyurl.com/jxelxng. See also Coalition Against Trafficking in Women, "Demand Change," p. 12, http://tinyurl.com/jobavdh.

36. "The Ban against the Purchase of Sexual Services. An Evaluation 1999-2008," *op. cit.*, p. 7. For population figures, see "Country Comparison: Population," *CIA World Factbook*, 2015, http://tinyurl.com/6cgwbj.

37. "The Extent and Development of Prostitution in Sweden 2014," *op. cit.*

38. Email from Lina Nealon, citing the Swedish National Rapporteur for Trafficking in Women at the National Criminal Investigation Department, as well as the Finnish Intelligence Agencies. Also see for Swedish trafficking numbers, Gunilla Ekberg, "The Swedish Law that Prohibits the Purchase of Sexual Services," Violence Against Women, October 2004, pp. 1187-1218, http://tinyurl.com/yjbqn8g. Sweden continues to have one of the lowest rates of trafficking in Europe — less than 1 person per 100,000 inhabitants, according the most recent statistics compiled by Eurostat in 2012. See Eurostat, "Trafficking in Human Beings," 2015, p. 23, http://tinyurl.com/jk7rd34.

39. "The Extent and Development of Prostitution in Sweden 2014," *op. cit.*

40. Jay Levy and Pye Jakobsson, "Sweden's abolitionist discourse and law," *Criminology and Criminal Justice*, November 2014, pp. 593-607, http://tinyurl.com/h7axgfs.

41. Michelle Goldberg, "Swedish Prostitution Law Is Spreading Worldwide," *The Guardian*, Aug. 8, 2014, http://tinyurl.com/h643lph.

42. Barbara Meil Hudson, *Uneasy Virtue* (1990), pp. 32-33, http://tinyurl.com/glo9xrs.

43. Lenore Kuo, *Prostitution Policy* (2005), p. 73.

44. Melissa Hope Ditmore, *Prostitution and Sex Work* (2011).

45. Alison Bass, *Getting Screwed* (2015), p. 19.

46. Kuo, *op. cit.*, pp. 53-54.

47. *Hoke v. United States*, 227 U.S. 308 (1913), U.S. Supreme Court, http://tinyurl.com/hso7fq8.

48. "Hoke v. United States," Facts on File, http://inyurl.com/zxvppqx. Also see, Walter F. Pratt, *The Supreme Court Under Edward Douglas White* (1999), p. 93, http://tinyurl.com/jhhhd82.

49. Allan M. Brandt, "The Syphilis Epidemic and Its Relation to AIDS," *Science*, Jan. 22, 1988, pp. 375-380, http://tinyurl.com/jbqjhna.

50. Ditmore, *op. cit.*

51. *Ibid.*, p. 52.

52. Barbara Brents *et al.*, *The State of Sex* (2010), p. 55.

53. Ditmore, *op. cit.*

54. Bass, *op. cit.*, p. 20.

55. Steven D. Levitt and Stephen J. Dubner, *SuperFreakonomics* (2015), pp. 30-31. They cite Charles Winick and Paul M. Kinsie, *The Lively Commerce* (1971) and Edward O. Laumann *et al.*, *The Social Organization of Sexuality* (1994).

56. Brents *et al.*, *op. cit.*, p. 75.

57. Bass, *op. cit.*, pp. 163-164.

58. *Ibid.*

59. "Fact Sheet: Human Trafficking," U.S. Department of Health and Human Services, Office on Trafficking in Persons, Aug. 2, 2012, http://tinyurl.com/hudkm7g.

60. Janice G. Raymond, "Guide to the New UN Trafficking Protocol," Coalition Against Trafficking in Women, 2001, http://tinyurl.com/zlh9cjt.

61. Marlise Simons, "Amsterdam Tries Upscale Fix for Red-Light District Crime," *The New York Times*, Feb. 24, 2008, http://tinyurl.com/h27f7pk.

62. "Six get heavy sentences in Dutch human trafficking trial," The Associated Press, *USA Today*, July 11, 2008, http://tinyurl.com/zgpxacc.

63. Clare Speak, "Germany may roll back legalised prostitution amid exploitation fears," *Equal Times*, Dec. 17, 2013, http://tinyurl.com/j3ftyrv.

64. *Ibid.*

65. "The Extent and Development of Prostitution in Sweden 2014," *op. cit.*

66. For background, see Sarah Glazer, "European Migration Crisis," *CQ Researcher*, July 31, 2015, pp. 649-672.

67. "Repealing Prohibition of Prostitution," New Hampshire Rep. Elizabeth Edwards, press conference, YouTube, Jan. 28, 2016, http://tinyurl.com/hwts8ya.

68. Colleen Shaughnessy, "Manchester rep explains NH Bill to legalize prostitution, other lawmakers vow to kill it," NH1.com, Jan. 5, 2016, http://tinyurl.com/hs82w7v.

69. "First-Ever Bill to Repeal Prohibition on Prostitution — Hearing and Press Conference," New Hampshire House hearing, YouTube, published Jan. 30, 2016, https://www.youtube.com/watch?v=q8Em_DIFa5o.

70. Christi Warren, "Judge upholds prostitution ban in case brought by former Sonoma Country sex worker," *The* [Santa Rosa, Calif.] *Press Democrat*, April 1, 2016, http://tinyurl.com/gs nmm95.

71. Lou Chibbaro, Jr., "Marriage ruling cited in brief to overturn prostitution law," *Washington Blade*, Jan. 22, 2016, http://tinyurl.com/gkvnjjt.

72. "San Francisco Decriminalization of Prostitution: Measure K," *Ballotpedia*, November 2008, http://tinyurl.com/hpcyam6.

73. Jesse Paul, "Denver shifts prostitution policing to buyers in national initiative," *The Denver Post*, April 29, 2015, http://tinyurl.com/jnrdx83.

74. "Portman Continues to Combat Human Trafficking," press release, U.S. Sen. Rob Portman, R-Ohio, March 18, 2016, http://tinyurl.com/zk5r8ql.

75. "560 NGOS and 94 Researchers Demand Members of European Parliament to Reject Ms Honeyball Report," International Committee on the Rights of Sex Workers in Europe (ICRSE), Feb. 18, 2014, http://tinyurl.com/jhn3o7w.

76. Alissa J. Rubin, "To Discourage Prostitution, France Passes Bill that Penalizes Clients," *The New York Times*, April 6, 2016, http://tinyurl.com/ztq87kh.

77. *Ibid.*

78. Charles Bremner, "Paying for sex becomes a crime in France," *The Times* (London), April 6, 2016, http://tinyurl.com/za6xqmb.

79. "Five weeks to put local pimps out of business," *Turn off the Red Light*, Aug. 11, 2015, http://tinyurl.com/ztmnh3d.

80. Sarah Rainey, "Devastating truth about Britain's first 'legal' red light district," *Daily Mail*, Jan. 16, 2016, http://tinyurl.com/z6nglt4.

81. Weitzer, *op. cit.*, p. 214.

BIBLIOGRAPHY

Selected Sources

Books

Bass, Alison, *Getting Screwed: Sex Workers and the Law*, ForeEdge, 2015.
An assistant professor of journalism at West Virginia University combines interviews with sex workers and research on the effects of prostitution laws to argue the practice should be decriminalized.

Brents, Barbara G., Crystal A. Jackson and Kathryn Hausbeck, *The State of Sex: Tourism, Sex and Sin in the New American Heartland*, Routledge, 2010.
Three University of Nevada, Las Vegas, sociology researchers assert that sex workers encounter little violence on the job — a finding frequently cited by proponents of legalizing prostitution.

Moran, Rachel, *Paid For: My Journey through Prostitution*, W.W. Norton, 2015.
In this memoir, the founder of a prostitution survivors' organization explains her support of the Nordic approach of criminalizing sex-buying over other models.

Raymond, Janice G., *Not a Choice, Not a Job: Exposing the Myths About Prostitution and the Global Sex Trade*, Potomac Books, 2013.
A feminist activist and professor emerita of women's studies and medical ethics at the University of Massachusetts, Amherst, Raymond — a self-described

"abolitionist" when it comes to prostitution — argues it is unlike any other job and calls for criminalizing the buying of sexual services.

Weitzer, Ronald, *Legalizing Prostitution: From Illicit Vice to Lawful Business*, New York University Press, 2012.
A George Washington University professor of sociology argues for legalizing brothels but restricting street prostitution.

Articles

Abel, Gillian M., "A decade of decriminalization," *Criminology and Criminal Justice*, Feb. 14, 2014, http://tinyurl.com/haqveo3.
An associate professor who heads the Department of Public Health at the University of Otago in Christchurch, New Zealand, says decriminalization made that country's sex industry safer and improved the rights of sex workers.

Crouch, David, "Swedish Prostitution Law Targets Buyers, but Some Say it Hurts Sellers," *The New York Times*, March 14, 2015, http://tinyurl.com/gpw2pru.
Sweden's law penalizing "johns" has forced women who sell sex into more dangerous situations, critics say, because men who fear getting arrested are pressuring women to make transactions faster and more furtively.

Paul, Jesse, "Denver shifts prostitution policing to buyers in national initiative," *The Denver Post*, April 29, 2015, http://tinyurl.com/zyqsju3.
A journalist describes how Denver officials have shifted their enforcement strategy from rounding up three prostitutes for every two "johns" to the reverse in an effort to deter buyers and reduce demand.

"Prostitution and the Internet: More bang for your buck," *The Economist*, Aug. 9, 2014, http://tinyurl.com/k8v5pwh; "Prostitution: A Personal Choice," *The Economist*, Aug. 9, 2014, http://tinyurl.com/og2ucwm.
An analysis by the weekly news magazine says the expanding online prostitution market will be harder to regulate than street prostitution because it is more hidden and mobile. In an accompanying editorial, the magazine argues that banning prostitution distracts authorities from attacking sex trafficking and modern-day slavery.

"Unprotected: How Legalizing Prostitution Has Failed," *Der Spiegel Online* (Germany), May 30, 2013, http://tinyurl.com/q7zjvgv.
The German magazine finds that the country's legalization of prostitution has failed to stop trafficking and exploitation of sex workers.

Waltman, Max, "Assessing Evidence, Arguments, and Inequality in Bedford v. Canada," *Harvard Journal of Law & Gender*, 2014, pp. 459-544; available at SSRN, http://tinyurl.com/hth3 qp8 or http://tinyurl.com/hl5879q.
A Stockholm University political social scientist argues that Canada's Supreme Court misread the research on decriminalizing prostitution.

Reports and Studies

"Global Report on Trafficking in Persons," United Nations Office on Drugs and Crime, November 2014, http://tinyurl.com/of4twak.
The U.N. office that monitors international crime finds that 53 percent of the global trade in human trafficking is for sexual exploitation.

Farley, Melissa, *et al.*, "Comparing Sex Buyers With Men Who Do Not Buy Sex: New Data on Prostitution and Trafficking," *Journal of Interpersonal Violence*, Aug. 31, 2015, http://tinyurl.com/h6uhaev.
A group of researchers comparing men who buy sex to those who do not concludes that the former had less empathy for prostituted women.

"Summary: proposed policy on sex work," Amnesty International, 2014, http://tinyurl.com/pbrwzc4.
The human-rights group provides arguments for its controversial proposal that the global sex trade should be decriminalized.

For More Information

Amnesty International (USA headquarters), 5 Penn Plaza, 16th Floor, New York, NY 10001; 212-807-8400; www.amnestyusa.org. Global organization working to defend human rights worldwide; supports decriminalizing prostitution.

Coalition Against Trafficking in Women, P.O. Box 7160, JAF Station, New York, NY 10116; 212-643-9895; www .catwinternational.org. Nongovernmental organization seeking to end human trafficking and commercial sexual exploitation of women and children worldwide.

Demand Abolition, 625 Mount Auburn St., Suite 205, Cambridge, MA 02138; 617-995-1900; www.demandabolition .org. Anti-sex-trade organization seeking to combat the demand for purchased sex; created network of 11 cities committed to deterring sex-buyers.

Erotic Service Providers Legal, Education and Research Project, 2261 Market St., # 548, San Francisco, CA 94114; 415-265-3302; http://esplerp.org. Sex workers' group that seeks to advance sexual privacy rights; has challenged the constitutionality of California's anti-prostitution law in federal court.

International Labour Organization, 4 route des Morillons, CH-1211 Genève 22, Switzerland; + (41) 022 799 6111; www.ilo.org/global/lang—en/index.htm. United Nations agency that issues global statistics on human trafficking for sexual exploitation.

Prostitution Research and Education, P.O. Box 16254, San Francisco, CA 94116; 415-922-4555; http:// prostitutionresearch.com. Nonprofit committed to ending prostitution; conducts research and education on prostitution and trafficking.

Sex Workers Outreach Project-USA, 340 S. Lemon St., #7566, Walnut, CA 91789; 877-776-2004, ext. 5; www .swopusa.org. National network that supports people involved in the sex trade; spearheaded unsuccessful 2004 ballot initiative to decriminalize prostitution in Berkeley, Calif.

11

Virtual Reality

Patrick Marshall

A woman at a virtual reality trade show in London last year enjoys a 3-D, 360-degree view of a scene from the film "The Divergent Series: Insurgent" using the soon-to-be-released Oculus Rift headset, which offers high-resolution displays and reduces motion sickness. Facebook, which bought Oculus for $2 billion in 2014, plans to ship the sophisticated, $599 headsets this year, aimed primarily at video-game aficionados.

From *CQ Researcher*,
February 26, 2016

Y ou're shopping online for a six-person tent, but you wonder: Is it really big enough for six people? Instead of guessing, you pop on your virtual-reality headset and click the "VR" button next to an image of the tent on the website.

"Suddenly, you're inside the tent at scale, and you can actually get a sense of how big the thing is," says Bob Berry, CEO of Envelop VR, a virtual-reality startup company in Bellevue, Wash. "VR allows you to see scale in a way that your brain can actually understand it."

No such button yet exists on Internet shopping sites. But Berry, whose company is developing applications that run on Windows 10 software in a virtual-reality environment, predicts one soon will be available. He also predicts that e-commerce will be one of the hottest markets for virtual-reality products.

Virtual-reality experiences aim to provide users with the sense of being immersed in a completely virtual world. While virtual reality has been a staple of hit films such as "The Matrix" and "Avatar," attempts to deliver realistic virtual-reality experiences to individual users so far have fallen far short of consumers' expectations. Heavy headsets, awkward cables, low-resolution video and slow data processing have left many people unconvinced of virtual reality's value. What's more, in many cases users have become literally nauseated from the disorienting sensations caused by the poorly performing technology.

But technology companies say new and improved virtual-reality hardware scheduled to hit the market this year will be a big improvement over existing equipment. Still, as virtual reality advances, experts are debating its psychological and social implications. Some fear virtual reality could be used to torture people by subjecting them to terrifying or disorienting virtual scenes. Others worry whether data collected by virtual-reality systems could compromise users' privacy. And some wonder whether virtual reality needs a tougher rating system than the one used for video games.[1]

Those questions, experts say, could delay how long virtual reality takes to catch on with consumers. But eventually, storytelling via virtual reality will become "as disruptive as cinema was to vaudeville," predicts Forest Key, co-founder and CEO of Pixvana, a Seattle-based startup that is developing tools for handling virtual-reality video streams. He and others say the development of improved virtual-reality hardware, such as goggles and headsets, has reached a turning point.

"For hundreds of dollars, or certainly in the low thousand dollars, you can build a rig that is superb in its capabilities and fully capable of tricking your brain into the effect that virtual reality strives for," Key says.

Industry insiders and investors expect major, if somewhat more gradual, adoption in other market sectors, such as health care, education, business communications, product design and industrial training. Virtual reality already is being used to treat phobias, such as the fear of flying or public speaking, by simulating such environments. And it is being used to lessen trauma by recreating battlefields and crime scenes to give combat veterans and crime victims control over how they respond emotionally to past experiences.[2]

According to SuperData Research, a market research firm that tracks digital games, the worldwide market for virtual-reality gaming alone will reach $5 billion this year and $12 billion by 2018.[3] Globally, the market for all

Game Sales Could Hit $12 Billion in 2018

Global sales of virtual-reality games and accessories could soar from an estimated $5.1 billion in 2016 to $12.3 billion in 2018. Personal-computer-based virtual-reality games are projected to generate the most revenue.

Estimated Revenue for Virtual-Reality Gaming, by Platform, 2016 and 2018

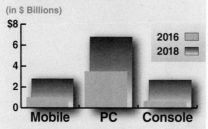

Source: "Virtual Reality Gaming Market Brief," SuperData Research, January 2016, p. 4, downloaded from http://tinyurl.com/h9wlttc

forms of virtual reality is predicted to be nearly $16 billion by 2020, according to MarketsandMarkets, another market research firm.[4]

What's more, some analysts say a related technology known as augmented reality ultimately may be an even bigger market. Augmented-reality experiences do not remove the user from the real world, as in virtual reality. Some products, such as Google Glass, provide information on what the viewer is looking at in a read-out. Other augmented-reality products overlay images and data on a user's view of the real world, such as information about streets, buildings or art in a museum.

Experts foresee an explosion of virtual-reality "experiences" — especially games — after the release of an array of new, better-performing, more comfortable headsets. Sony, HTC and Oculus — which Facebook bought for $2 billion in 2014 — are scheduled to ship the new virtual-reality headsets this year, priced at $350 to $800 and aimed primarily at video-game aficionados. The headsets will offer high-resolution displays and faster refresh rates — the number of frames per second that can be displayed — high enough to greatly reduce motion sickness.

And Microsoft is also expected this year, to introduce its augmented-reality cordless HoloLens headset, which enables viewers to see realistic-looking computer-generated holograms. The devices are expected to be used for such purposes as architects working together on a building design or engineers testing a car design.[5]

Besides games, software developers are hurrying to develop other virtual-reality applications to run on the new equipment, such as applications that support business meetings in which participants can "gather" in the same virtual meeting or conference room. "Any kind of one-to-many or one-to-one communication will be very powerful in VR," Key says.

He also predicts "killer scenarios" for using virtual reality in data analysis and visualization, such as providing a better overall look at how a factory is running. "In an immersive environment, your brain can take in information at a broader scale and at a faster rate than looking at it on a TV screen," Key says.

Virtual reality could also play a big role in product development, experts predict. Changing the size or shape of a car under design — even just making the inside of its roof a little higher — can cost millions of dollars and consume much time. "However, if a digital model is built, changing its height, width, length, color, etc., is relatively cheap and extremely quick," wrote Jim Blascovich, director of the Research Center for Virtual Environments and Behavior at the University of California, Santa Barbara, and Jeremy Bailenson, director of Stanford University's Virtual Human Interaction Lab.[6]

Virtual reality also is increasingly being offered as a new form of journalism. *The New York Times*, for example, released its first virtual-reality project — a report on the global refugee crisis that sought to portray the living conditions for children in several war-torn countries — last November.[7] The newspaper currently has 11 virtual-reality projects that can be viewed using an iOS or Android smartphone and a Google Cardboard headset after downloading a special *New York Times* application.

"You'll see more and more from *The New York Times* on that front," promises Jake Silverstein, editor of *The New York Times Magazine*. "VR is going to be something important going forward."

However, some researchers are concerned that immersive virtual reality may present unforeseen psychological and social challenges. They warn, for example, that virtual-reality experiences can have real physical and emotional consequences. "The brain often fails to differentiate between virtual experiences and real ones," wrote Blascovich and Bailenson. "Walking a tightrope over a chasm in virtual reality can be a terrifying ordeal, even if the walker knows it's virtual rather than physical."[8]

Others have warned that violent virtual-reality video games may be so emotionally powerful that they could have a much greater impact on children than violent video games. "Playing violent video games seems to lead people to *think* of themselves as more aggressive people overall," wrote New York psychologist Mark Koltko-Rivera. Virtual reality could have an even stronger effect,

he fears. "Participating in a violent VR game [produces] more aggressive thoughts than either watching a game or acting out the physical movements," he wrote.[9]

Some analysts have even suggested that virtual reality is powerful enough to be used as an instrument of torture. Just as it can help treat phobias and trauma, "it could be just as powerful in doing the opposite," says technology journalist Doug Bierend. "Virtualized trauma would leave no marks," and like Room 101, a torture chamber in George Orwell's dystopian novel, *1984*, "could confront victims with exactly the worst thing imaginable.[10]

As the industry, researchers and others debate the impact of virtual reality on individuals, society and the economy, here are some of the questions being asked:

Will virtual reality become a mass consumer product?

Virtual reality has been available for decades in niche markets, such as in flight simulators and other training scenarios. However, the expense of the equipment, the amount of space it requires and the fact that virtual-reality experiences caused nausea in some users have kept the technology from reaching mass consumer markets.

But industry insiders say the technology finally is ready for widespread consumer use. "I came to it as a VR skeptic, and I was that way for a long time, [for] well over a decade," says Matt McIlwain, managing director of Madrona Venture Group, a tech-oriented investment firm in Seattle. "That was my mindset up until about 18 months ago."

McIlwain became a booster after visiting virtual-reality companies developing software for the soon-to-be-released Oculus Rift and HTC Vive virtual-reality headsets. "The initial applications . . . were pretty darn good," he says. "Two things . . . were different about them. One was that they were these cool, good experiences. Also, I didn't feel woozy coming out of the experience."

McIlwain describes being on a virtual basketball court with other players and not only being able to shoot baskets, but to talk with the others. "The system knows that I'm hearing your voice in the virtual room," he says, "and so I hear you out of my left ear, not my right ear." After those experiences, his company became a lead investor in several virtual-reality startup companies, including Pixvana and Envelop VR.

Headsets Attract Most Investment

Virtual-reality investors put 60 percent of their money into headset development from 2012 to 2015 and 30 percent into game development. The remainder was allocated among cameras, peripheral accessories, software and social networking platforms.

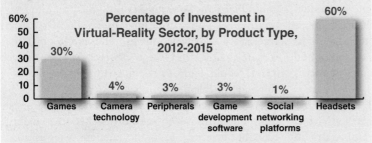

Source: "Virtual Reality Gaming Market Brief," SuperData Research, January 2016, p. 7, downloaded from http://tinyurl.com/h9wlttc

Pixvana CEO Key agrees that new virtual-reality technologies have largely solved the problem of motion, or "simulator," sickness. "VR in the 1990s made me vomit. It made most people vomit," he says. But thanks to recent advances in virtual reality-related technologies — faster processors, better graphics and new methods for tracking movements — the headsets are both more immersive and less likely to result in nausea for the user, Key says.

Of course, affordable, non-nausea-inducing hardware is only part of what is needed to sell virtual reality to large markets. "I think the hardware is here," says Tom Furness, director of the Human Interface Technology Lab (HITLab) at the University of Washington and a virtual-reality pioneer who worked on the technology for the Air Force in the 1970s. "Now it's about the tools to help us develop content easier and better. We don't have those tools right now." Hardware companies such as Oculus and Vive did not return requests for comment.

Key says putting on virtual-reality goggles can be as "uninteresting" as watching a film of a stage presentation. The technology is "not yet exploiting any of the unique capabilities that [eventually] will be exploited," he says. Those innovations will require new kinds of tools. For example, he says, accommodating real-time, multiplayer interactions in virtual-reality scenarios will require new techniques for processing video streams and delivering them to users.

It likely will take time to develop the tools and content that will provide enough applications to attract large numbers of consumers. "Right now this whole industry is in a learning phase," says Berry of Envelop VR. "There is still more that we don't know than we do. A lot of the research . . . done over the last 30 or 40 years has been completely invalidated now that we have really good hardware to test assumptions on, so we are having to learn a lot of new things."

In addition, some analysts are not convinced that researchers have fully resolved the nausea problem. In fact, some manufacturers such as Oculus have acknowledged that whether their equipment causes nausea or eye strain depends on several factors apart from the hardware. Some individuals are more prone to motion sickness than others, and certain scenarios — such as a virtual roller coaster — are more likely to induce such symptoms. As a result, companies reportedly are encouraging game developers to avoid creating virtual environments likely to cause discomfort.[11]

Oculus chief technology officer John Carmack told a conference of game developers in March 2015 that his company is moving cautiously to avoid a "nightmare" scenario in which "people like the demo, they take it home and they start throwing up," he said. "The fear is if a really bad VR product comes out, it could send the industry back to the 1990s."[12]

Ironically, recent research indicates that individuals with the best 3-D vision are most prone to nausea in virtual-reality environments. A recent University of Wisconsin, Madison, study found that nearly two-thirds of people who tested a motion-heavy video using Oculus Rift equipment quit watching the video early due to nausea.[13] They turned out to be the users with the best 3-D vision in the real world.

The cost of virtual-reality equipment also could slow adoption. While the $350 to $800 price tag of a headset may be inexpensive compared with previous generations of VR equipment, it is still beyond the reach of many consumers. And the computer equipment required to use the new headsets is more powerful than what most consumers currently own.

In fact, according to NVIDIA, a graphics device manufacturer in Santa Clara, Calif., fewer than 1 percent of the personal computers currently on the market will be able to handle virtual-reality headsets such as the Oculus Rift.[14] Thus, many consumers will have to spend about $1,000 for a new computer in addition to the cost of the headset before they can experience the new virtual reality.

Will virtual reality's adverse physical and psychological effects outweigh its benefits?

Psychologists and others acknowledge that any tool as powerful as virtual reality can have both beneficial and adverse effects.

On the positive side, researchers say virtual reality can help treat some psychological disorders in addition to boosting the economy, entertaining consumers and enhancing business productivity.[15] For example, virtual reality has been used to place veterans suffering from post-traumatic stress disorder on a simulated Afghanistan battlefield, where they can process their traumatic experience in a safe, therapeutic environment. The virtual experience is so realistic that the users even feels the simulated weight of the rifles they once carried in battle.[16]

In addition, some researchers expect the new generation of virtual reality to be especially effective at sensitivity training. "One of the areas where we are focusing a lot of our energy right now is empathy," says Bailenson of Stanford's Human Interface Technology Lab, where diversity training software creates scenarios in which the user becomes another person, such as a person of a different race or a war refugee.

"You turn around and there's another person in VR with you, and they discriminate against you," he says. "You feel prejudice while wearing the body of someone else. You walk a mile in their shoes."

But some experts worry that being able to deliver powerful, realistic experiences could have unwanted effects that are more potent than motion sickness. In other words, virtual-reality games may be like video games on steroids — not only in their entertainment value but also in their psychological and social impact.

During a demonstration in New York City, a woman tries out the Birdly flight simulator, which mimics the experience of a bird in flight, using a virtual-reality headset.

"You can play eight hours of violent video games a day and still fundamentally be a pretty decent person," says Bailenson. "The research does show that it does make you more aggressive, but in general, there are a lot of really great, wonderful people who play violent video games."

But virtual-reality games are different, according to Bailenson. "Once video games get immersive — where, in order to kill somebody, you literally have to take your hand and saw their throat and get [sensory] feedback as you go through their bones and you're literally going through the muscle memory of killing them — I don't think that's going to work," he says.

Jesse Fox, an assistant professor of communications at Ohio State University who studies virtual reality and other new media technologies, agrees. "We already know that a lot of elements of video games are problematic and . . . that they can have negative effects for certain people in certain circumstances," says Fox. "But the more we get into virtual reality, the more of the senses we're replacing and the more likely we are to really experience it as real. That could completely change the way our brain is processing this information."

Kate Edwards, executive director of the International Game Developers Association, a New Jersey-based group that represents video and computer game developers, says, however, that virtual reality may not have a greater

Demonstrators in New York City's Times Square on Nov. 21, 2015, mourn victims of the ISIS attacks in Paris and condemn the Islamic State's radical interpretation of Islam. ISIS proclaims its devotion to a brutal, apocalyptic version of Islam based on a selective reading of parts of the Quran and other Islamic texts — a reading that mainstream Islamic leaders have denounced as a gross misrepresentation of the faith.

effect on users than do current video games. "The best way to describe the impact is 'different,' " she says, adding that trying to compare the effects of virtual reality and video games is "as useless a concept" as comparing the effects of a short story versus a novel, a film or a television program.

Also, any heightened effects of virtual reality likely will be temporary, she contends. "VR adds a heightened sense of presence, and since that experience is new to many people, it may feel more impactful initially, the way the earliest audiences responded to the first moving pictures," she says.

Edwards agrees that more research is needed on the potential effects of virtual-reality games, but she argues that the research must be unbiased. "We've had far too many studies from people with undisclosed, anti-game biases and methodological flaws," she says.

Concerns should focus on the violence in video games, not on the virtual-reality technology, according to Furness of the HITLab at the University of Washington. "Games aren't bad in themselves; it's the violence in games that is the problem," he says, noting

that adults, not children, design the violent games. After spending years watching children build virtual worlds, he says, he has observed that "when you put them to work building a virtual world, there's no violence in any of them."

Some experts also worry that virtual reality may magnify the addictiveness and social isolation experienced by some individuals with video games and the Internet. "The more that we can simulate experiences [with virtual reality] that we should be having with real people in the real world, that can be a problem," says Fox.

The checks and balances of interactions with the variety of people one meets in real life, she adds, are vastly different than the programmed feedback one gets from digital encounters.

Key, of Pixvana, doesn't buy into the idea that virtual reality is uniquely addictive. "Certainly it will have some compulsive, addictive traits like all media does," he says. "I wouldn't be surprised if in five or six years there is discussion of the intense isolation that virtual reality has. But that's a larger problem in society; it's not a VR-specific problem. And I think we will come to understand the medium and develop best practices."

Furness acknowledges that much is unknown about the long-term effects of either virtual-reality hardware or of yet-to-be-developed content. "Up to this point in time, people have worn [the devices] for maybe an hour at a time or a couple of hours," he says. But as for people spending all day working in a virtual-reality environment, "That's something that requires more research."

Nevertheless, Furness sees far more benefits than risks in virtual reality.

"I believe that it's a way to enhance humans — not only by extending our senses but by actually awakening our senses," he says. Like the blind person who adapts by developing a sharper sense of hearing, he says, "I am hoping that we can retrain capabilities that we've always had but that we shut off because we haven't used them."

Should virtual-reality games be regulated and rated?

Because virtual reality is so immersive and convincing, some analysts have suggested that VR games be regulated to prevent inappropriate material from being sold to certain age groups.

"There are going to be violent games out there, and, let me tell you, it's scary when you take it into VR, because you're now doing it in a way that seems real," says Furness of the Human Interface Technology Lab. "It's got to be numbing the mind and numbing the heart."

As a result, he says, virtual-reality games should be rated just as films and video games are.

But video games are rated through a voluntary system of industry self-regulation, which some experts say may not be enough when it comes to virtual reality.

"We will have to consider the fact that people's brains are going to process VR a little bit differently, and we have to be mindful that people are going to experience things like cybersickness that they may not have experienced before," says Ohio State's Fox.

Virtual reality currently can stir "deep emotional and psychosomatic responses," warns tech journalist Bierend, and be used as a weapon. He wrote in a recent article: "But given how powerful VR is becoming, and how widely used it's evidently going to become, one logical misuse is especially disturbing: torture."[17]

As a result, Bierend calls for greater regulation of virtual-reality applications than video games receive. "There's got to be something higher than an [industry-run] rating system," he says.

Though he did not provide specifics, stricter measures potentially include prohibitions on sales to certain age groups of material considered too violent or otherwise inappropriate.

Seeing the Future

A visitor at the central railway station in Stuttgart, Germany, on Jan. 4, 2016, uses virtual-reality goggles to see what the station will look like when its construction is completed (top). A visitor at the Grand Palais in Paris tests a virtual-reality headset on Dec. 4, 2015, during the United Nations conference on climate change (bottom). Now widely used for gaming, virtual-reality technology is poised to move into other markets, such as health care, education, business communications, product design and industrial training.

Startups Raised Nearly $4 Billion

Facebook, venture capitalists and other investors poured $3.9 billion into virtual- and augmented-reality startup companies from 2010 to 2015. Annual funding peaked in 2014, led by Facebook's $2 billion acquisition of Oculus VR. Magic Leap, a firm developing software for headsets that superimpose virtual content onto real vision, and LENSAR, which is creating technology to help doctors construct models of cataract patients' eyes, raised the most capital.

Investment in Virtual- and Augmented-Reality Companies, 2010-2015 (in $ billions)

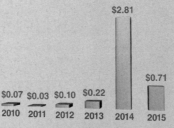

$0.07 — 2010
$0.03 — 2011
$0.10 — 2012
$0.22 — 2013
$2.81 — 2014
$0.71 — 2015

Top-10 Virtual-Reality Companies Ranked by Capital Raised

	Company	Amount Raised		Company	Amount Raised
1	Oculus VR	$2.1 billion	6	Vuforia	$65 million
2	Magic Leap	$593.7 million	7	Matterport	$57.7 million
3	LENSAR	$191.1 million	8	Avegamt	$37 million
4	Jaunt	$101.3 million	9	NextVR	$36 million
5	Blippar	$70.1 million	10	Playful	$33 million

Source: Data for graph provided by *Pitchbook*; table from "Virtual Reality 2015 Analyst Report," *Pitchbook*, December 2015, p. 15, http://tinyurl.com/gqdm7an

Industry associations respond that regulating virtual-reality games is not only unnecessary but unconstitutional. "This . . . was settled by the Supreme Court in 2011, when it ruled that games are protected by the First Amendment, and [it's] not really up for debate," says Dan Hewitt, vice president of media relations and event management at the Entertainment Software Association, a Washington, D.C.-based industry association supporting video and computer game companies.

The court's 7-2 ruling in *Brown v. Entertainment Merchants Association* struck down a California law banning the sale of certain violent video games to children without parental approval.[18] While the court did rule that video games were protected speech, a concurring opinion by Associate Justice Samuel Alito indicated that there might be future limits to that protection as new technologies develop.

"If the technological characteristics of the sophisticated games that are likely to be available in the near future are combined with the characteristics of the most violent games already marketed," Alito warned, "the result will be games that allow troubled teens to experience in an extraordinarily personal and vivid way what it would be like to carry out unspeakable acts of violence."[19]

According to Alito, different media may have different effects on people, and he chided the court's majority for prematurely "dismissing this possibility out of hand."

"I would not squelch legislative efforts to deal with what is perceived by some to be a significant and developing social problem," Alito wrote. "If differently framed statutes are enacted by the states or by the federal government, we can consider the constitutionality of those laws when cases challenging them are presented to us."

Edwards, of the International Game Developers Association, says virtual-reality experiences "are protected speech just as clearly as video games are protected speech, just as clearly as movies are protected speech and just as clearly as books are protected speech." The fear of new technologies "and bad science caused video game developers to suffer a long legal road to the incontrovertible recognition of those rights by the U.S. Supreme Court," Edwards adds. "Our hope and expectation is that VR will be spared a similar, unnecessary legal quagmire."

Some industry insiders argue that fears about virtual reality triggering violent behavior are exaggerated. "I reject that thesis completely," says Key of Pixvana. "My kids are into first-person shooters" — video games in which players aim and fire fake guns — "and I was a gamer. I think people who are into gaming and respect gaming are the last people to suggest that there is any correlation between gaming and violence in society."

Bailenson, of Stanford's Virtual Human Interaction Lab, says he isn't so sure. "Should it be regulated? I don't know. I believe very strongly in free speech," he says, adding, "Personally, I don't let my daughters" play violent video games.

BACKGROUND

Early Entertainment

Two markets have driven the development of virtual-reality technologies: the entertainment industry and the military.

The first device designed to provide a "you are there" feeling was Charles Wheatstone's 1838 stereopticon, an image viewer that offered a 3-D effect.

Wheatstone, a British physician, had discovered that the brain processes two-dimensional images, viewed separately by each eye, into a single image, providing depth perception. Initially, Wheatstone experimented with viewing identical drawings, slightly offset, through two lenses. It wasn't until the mid-1830s, when effective photographic techniques were developed, that Wheatstone's idea produced dramatic results — a realistic 3-D view of subjects viewed through the stereopticon, which became known as a stereoscope.[20]

The device quickly became a craze in Europe and North America, with companies such as Keystone View sending photographers around the globe to capture famous scenes, notable people and major events. The popularity of the stereoscope remained high until a newer technology, motion pictures, captured the public's imagination at the turn of the 19th Century.

It's not known whether Stanley G. Weinbaum, an American science fiction writer, was inspired by the stereoscope, but in 1935 he published a short story, "Pygmalion's Spectacles," which offered the first detailed model for a full virtual-reality experience. In the story, the main character meets a Professor Ludwig, who has invented goggles that deliver a multi-sensation experience, including sight, sound, taste, smell and touch.

"Suppose I make it so that you are in the story, you speak to the shadows, and the shadows reply, and instead of being on a screen, the story is all about you, and you are in it," said Ludwig. "Would that be to make real a dream?"[21]

Four years after the Eastman Kodak Co. introduced Kodachrome color film in 1935, Edwin Eugene Mayer,

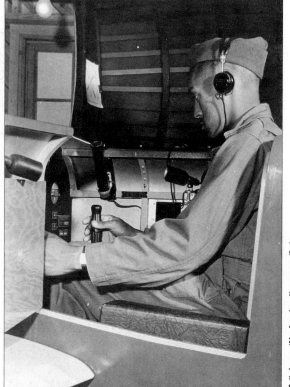

Pvt. James E. Taylor demonstrates the Link Trainer, an early flight simulator, at the Tuskegee Flight School in Alabama on June 6, 1942.

Getty Images/Afro American Newspapers/Gado

a pharmacist and photofinisher in Portland, Ore., introduced a new stereoscopic device, the "View-Master." While not different in concept from the stereoscope, View-Masters offered high-resolution, color 3-D images.[22]

In the mid-1950s, Morton Heilig, a California filmmaker, pushed the stereoscope technology further with his "Sensorama," a theater cabinet featuring stereo speakers, a stereoscopic display, fans to simulate wind, smell "generators" and a vibrating chair. Patented in 1962 under the name "Sensorama Simulator," the device was designed to give users an immersive experience employing four of the five senses. Heilig also invented a 3-D movie camera that featured side-by-side 35mm cameras that was small enough to be used as a handheld device.[23]

CHRONOLOGY

1838-1935 *Key virtual-reality technologies are developed.*

1838 British physician Charles Wheatstone invents the stereopticon, the first 3-D image viewer.

1929 American inventor Edwin Link, a piano-maker training to be a pilot, invents a flight simulator that uses pneumatic bellows to move the cockpit in three directions; it trains 500,000 pilots during World War II.

1935 American science fiction writer Stanley G. Weinbaum publishes "Pygmalion's Spectacles," a short story offering the first detailed model for a full virtual-reality experience. The main character meets a professor who has invented goggles delivering virtual sight, sound, taste, smell and touch.

1960s-1970s *Virtual-reality devices appear and connect to computers.*

1962 California filmmaker Morton Heilig patents "Sensorama," a device intended to enhance the movie-viewing experience in theaters; it features stereo speakers, fans to simulate wind, smell generators and vibrating chairs.

1968 American computer scientist Ivan Sutherland invents the first head-mounted display connected to a computer.

1976 University of Illinois researchers create the first glove using sensors to capture physical data such as the bending of fingers.

1978 Massachusetts Institute of Technology (MIT) researchers develop the Aspen Movie Map, a user-navigable video of the streets of Aspen, Colo., that presages Google's Streetview mapping project.

1980s-1990s *Military development boosts sophistication of virtual-reality systems.*

1982 Thomas Furness, an American engineer working for the Air Force, demonstrates the Visually Coupled Airborne Systems Simulator (VCASS), a head-mounted system for pilot training.

1986 Furness begins developing the Super Cockpit, a headset system allowing pilots to control aircraft with gestures, eye movements and voice commands.

1987 American computer scientist Jaron Lanier coins the term "virtual reality." . . . The Defense Advanced Research Projects Agency (DARPA) and U.S. Army complete SIMNET, a network of simulators connecting ground troops, tanks, helicopters and airplanes in a virtual battlefield. . . . MIT researchers develop a lightweight glove that can communicate gestures to a computer.

1991 The Virtuality Group, a British company, introduces an array of arcade games that offer depth-enhancing 3-D graphics to players wearing goggles and gloves.

1992 University of Illinois, Chicago, researchers create the Cave Automatic Virtual Environment (CAVE), a virtual-reality room in which graphics on walls respond to users' movements.

1993 Japanese company Sega introduces the Sega VR headset for its Sega Genesis game console.

1995 Another Japanese game-maker, Nintendo, releases the Virtual Boy, a portable console with 3-D graphics.

2000s *Smartphone improvements spur virtual-reality headset advances.*

2002 Smartphones begin to appear in U.S. markets.

2010 Microsoft introduces the Kinect motion-sensing game controller for Xbox. Programmers quickly adapt it to control robots and give commands in virtual environments.

2012 Google introduces Google Glass, an augmented-reality device worn like a pair of eyeglasses.

2015 Four companies — Microsoft, Sony, HTC and Oculus — announce plans to ship next-generation virtual-reality headsets in 2016. . . . Google says it will discontinue producing Google Glass but will keep working on a new version.

Military Virtual Reality

The U.S. military didn't build the first flight simulator — the Link Trainer, created in 1929 and patented in 1931 — but it was the simulator's first major customer. Built by American Edwin Link, a former piano maker, the device simulated an airplane's motion by employing motors and pneumatic bellows to rotate the cockpit in three dimensions. Additional motors mimicked turbulence. More than 500,000 allied military pilots used more than 10,000 Link Trainers during World War II.[24]

The original Link Trainer did not include any visual elements. In fact, it wasn't until 1941, when the British government commissioned a version of the trainer known as the Celestial Navigation Trainer, that the system included projected films. The film, however, could not respond to the pilot's actions.[25]

In the mid-1960s, the military moved from arcade-style simulators to head-mounted displays that tracked and responded to the user's orientation.

"One of my jobs was to determine how to best have pilots interact with their very complex machines," says Furness, the Air Force's lead engineer working on head-mounted displays from the 1960s through the '80s. Traditional methods — such as filling the cockpit with gauges and switches — weren't working well, says Furness. "It wasn't a very suitable way to get bandwidth to and from the brain."

In the late 1970s, Furness began developing virtual interfaces — displays the pilots could interact with — for actual flight control. In 1982, he demonstrated the Visually Coupled Airborne Systems Simulator (VCASS), a head-mounted system that offered a 120-degree field of vision. "We didn't call it virtual reality then," he says. "We called it 'visually coupled systems.'"

In the mid-1980s, Furness began work on his most ambitious project — the Super Cockpit. "It was a cockpit that you wear," says Furness. "You put on a magic helmet, a magic flight suit and magic gloves, and you are immersed in a 3-D virtual world in the fighter airplane."

The Super Cockpit was not a simulator. The pilot used it to control his very real aircraft. The system projected information — computer-generated 3-D maps, forward-looking infrared and radar imagery and avionics data — to the pilot. The device's sensors and tracking system, as well as voice-actuated controls, allowed the

pilot to control the aircraft with gestures, eye movements and voice commands, Furness says.

In the 1980s, the military began to employ virtual reality on the ground as well as in the air. In a series of progressively complex demonstrations, the SIMNET program — funded by the Defense Advanced Research Projects Agency (DARPA) and the U.S. Army — connected ground troops, tanks, helicopters and airplanes in a virtual battlefield. When the development program was completed in 1987, a network of 250 simulators at nine training sites and two developmental sites were turned over to the Army.

"The emphasis of SIMNET from the outset was on enhancing tactical team performance by providing commanders and troops an opportunity to practice their skills in a dynamic, free-play environment, in which battle outcomes depend on team coordination and individual initiative, rather than on scripted scenarios controlled by an instructor," wrote Duncan C. Miller and Jack A. Thorpe, two of the principal architects of SIMNET.

Specifically, the program created a virtual world that included thousands of linked devices simulating infantry vehicles, helicopters and fixed-wing aircraft. "In this world, the causal connections among these tactical events, from the individual crew station to the battalion command post, are clear and easily inspectable," they wrote.[26]

Civilian Research

Even as Furness was beginning his work with the Air Force on head-mounted displays, a new surge of research, driven by rapid growth in computing power and DARPA funding, was occurring in academic research labs.

The first head-mounted display connected to a computer instead of a camera was created by Massachusetts Institute of Technology (MIT) computer scientist Ivan Sutherland in 1968. While pathbreaking, the device had obvious limitations: It was monoscopic, rather than stereoscopic, and it could display only monochrome, wireframe objects. What's more, "Sutherland's helmet was so heavy and intimidating that it had to be tethered to the ceiling to alleviate its weight on the user's head and neck," write and Blascovich and Bailenson, virtual-reality researchers at Stanford University and the University of California,

Tech World Gears Up for "Augmented Reality"

"It helps you combine the experiences of real life and digital life."

As you leave your hotel for a walk through Paris, you grab your sunglasses from the dresser. "Take me to the Louvre," you say as you tap the microphone button on the side of the glasses frame. A subtle line appears in your line of sight, directing you to the museum.

As you proceed, you pass a jazz club. You tap the information button on the other side of the frame. As the glasses detect what building you are looking at, information about the club — and tonight's performers — pops into view.

You can't buy those glasses yet. But some analysts predict that such technology — called "augmented reality" because it overlays information, or virtual images, over one's view of the real world — will eclipse virtual-reality products in the marketplace within a few years.

Advocates of augmented-reality technology foresee it doing everything from telling emergency responders the location of the nearest fire extinguisher in a building to helping tourists navigate unfamiliar localities.

Digi-Capital, a market analytics company, predicts that by 2020 augmented-reality products will generate $120 billion in annual revenue worldwide, four times that of virtual reality.[1]

As with virtual reality, however, a lack of affordable, effective hardware so far has kept augmented reality from going mainstream. But that problem will soon be remedied, according to Digi-Capital, which compares augmented reality's market potential to that of smartphones and tablets. Augmented reality "could have hundreds of millions of users," with hardware prices similar to smartphones and tablets, the Digi-Capital report said.

The first augmented reality device to hit the market — Google Glass — was pulled shortly after its release in May 2014. Google Glass, which looked more like a pair of glasses than a headset, tracked the user's location and eye movements,

responded to natural-language voice commands and displayed data on the periphery of the wearer's vision.[2]

Analysts say a variety of factors worked against consumer acceptance of Google Glass, including privacy concerns over the device's onboard cameras. And the device's distinctive look made it easy to spot.

In December 2015, however, Google filed an application with the Federal Communications Commission (FCC) for a new version of Google Glass.[3]

The only other dedicated augmented-reality device in the offing is Microsoft's HoloLens, expected to be released this year.

From media accounts, HoloLens appears more likely than Google Glass to be a commercial success, in part because Microsoft is aiming it at professional markets such as industrial designers and architects rather than consumers. Also, instead of delivering data via a small prism display in the corner of one's field of view, as Google Glass did, HoloLens projects images directly into the user's full field of view. In addition to relying on vocal commands and eye movements, HoloLens — unlike Google Glass — responds to hand gestures.

Augmented reality differs from virtual reality in that it is not completely dependent on new hardware. In fact, some augmented-reality applications run on smartphones.

For example, CivicConnect uses location data from a smartphone and the phone's camera to detect points of interest. Transit schedules, traffic reports and information about local events, emergency facilities or available parking spots can automatically appear on a user's smartphone. The service, a product of Los Angeles-based Civic Resource Group, is available by subscription to municipalities and initially is being deployed by transportation departments and tourism agencies.

Santa Barbara, respectively.[27] As a result, the system was dubbed the "Sword of Damocles."

While not head-mounted or 3-D, the Aspen Movie Map, created by a group of MIT researchers, demonstrated a new level of interactivity with computerized video. Long before Google was founded, the MIT team

sent cars with rooftop cameras through the streets of Aspen, Colo. The resulting footage was correlated with a map of the city, and navigation buttons were provided to allow users to move around in the virtual city.

DARPA funded the Aspen Movie Map because, according to one researcher, "DARPA's hope was that

Hardware designers are working on a number of technologies that experts predict one day will push augmented reality off smartphones while also eliminating the need for clunky headsets. HoloLens, while less bulky than older VR headsets, is still too big for comfortable, all-day wear.

One potential solution: Contact lenses with embedded circuitry that receives signals from, say, a cellphone and projects data, which can be either text or images, to the lens underneath the contact.

"Eventually our plan is to have full-fledged display with reasonable resolution and color that can receive images from an external device and superimpose those images over what you would normally see," Babak Parviz, a professor of electrical engineering at the University of Washington, told a reporter in 2011. "We are very far from that, but are taking small steps in that direction."[4]

Since that interview, Parviz joined the Google Glass team before leaving for Amazon. Amazon did not indicate why Parviz was hired, but industry insiders speculate that the move was part of a long-term Amazon plan to develop wearable technologies.[5]

Meanwhile, the Human Interface Technology Laboratory at the University of Washington is developing virtual retinal displays, which project images directly onto a user's retina. Ultimately, such technology likely would be deployed through a headset or glasses.[6]

Before such technologies can be deployed, however, scientists must figure out how to miniaturize eye-tracking and geolocation systems so data related to objects in a user's field of vision can be correlated accurately.

While augmented-reality technologies are being refined, market analysts are excited about the sector's potential.

"It helps you combine the experiences of real life and digital life," says Stephanie Llamas, research director at SuperData Research, a technology-focused market analysis firm in New York City.

Matt McIlwain, managing director of Madrona Venture Group, a technology-oriented investment firm in Seattle, believes the division between virtual reality and augmented

Stephanie Shine, a nurse at Brigham and Women's Hospital in Boston, is testing whether using Google Glass video streaming could help mothers connect with their newborn babies.

reality is temporary. "We think that those worlds will converge over the next five years," he says, as researchers overcome technological limitations.

— Patrick Marshall

[1] Digi-Capital, "Augmented/Virtual Reality to hit $150 billion disrupting mobile by 2020," *Digi-Capital*, April 2015, http://tinyurl .com/h398v4d.

[2] Aaron Mamiit, "Google Glass is Dead . . . For Now," *Tech Times*, Jan. 21, 2015, http://tinyurl.com/jmcer2l.

[3] Lisa Eadicicco, "See the New Version of Google's Wildest Product," *Time*, Dec. 29, 2015, http://tinyurl.com/juzn9ek.

[4] Larry Greenemeier, "Computerized Contact Lenses Could Enable In-Eye Augmented Reality," *Scientific American*, Nov. 23, 2001, http:// tinyurl.com/ hszyvmw.

[5] Dianne Depra, "Google X director, Glass champion Babak Parviz heads to Amazon," *Tech Times*, July 17, 2014, http://tinyurl.com/hubsvs4.

[6] "How the VRD Works," HITLab, University of Washington, http:// tinyurl.com/ jancnvv.

military personnel could virtually travel to a city before being deployed to familiarize themselves with landmarks, the location of targets and potential threats."[28]

Another important step in the development of virtual-reality infrastructure was the invention of "data gloves," gloves equipped with sensors that feed information about finger and other hand movements to a computer. The first data glove — known as the Sayre Glove — was created in 1976 by a team at the University of Illinois.[29]

Data gloves rapidly improved in the 1980s. In 1987, MIT researchers developed a lightweight Lycra DataGlove, equipped with optical fibers. Like the Sayre

Virtual-Reality Devices on the Horizon

New systems will simulate experiences of space, surgery and fighting.

As consumers await the release of the next generation of virtual-reality headsets, and companies prepare games to run on them, hardware designers are crafting new devices and accessories they hope will enhance the experience.

Among the devices, either available or in the wings, drawing attention:

Google Cardboard

Various manufacturers already are producing this cardboard headset, which is available online for $20. The headset, which holds a smartphone, splits the phone's displayed images between each of the viewer's eyes. Its design is "open source" — in the public domain and available to anyone to sell without needing to pay Google.[1] The headset runs on phones using Google's Android operating system. It also can work with Apple's iPhones, and thanks to a new software developer's kit, iPhones are fully supported by Cardboard apps.[2]

Getty Images/Adam Berry

The Google Cardboard virtual-reality experience is significantly less immersive than that of costlier technologies. The Cardboard doesn't fit snugly against the user's face, and the devices often lack straps to secure the display to the head. What's more, the resolution of smartphone displays can be disappointing. Even though users can turn 360 degrees through displayed content, the devices do not simulate a user's movements through the virtual world, nor can users manipulate objects in the virtual world. Still, Google Cardboard and applications written for it are likely to whet the appetites of virtual-reality enthusiasts.

Tactical Haptics Reactive Grip

Tactical Haptics was founded in 2013 by University of Utah mechanical engineering professor William Provancher to commercialize the Reactive Grip, a device developed at the university's Haptics and Embedded Mechatronics Laboratory. The Reactive Grip, still a prototype, seeks to make any object in a virtual environment, such as a knife or driver's wheel, feel more real. It is compatible with existing motion-based controllers such as Nintendo Wii, Sony Move and Microsoft Kinect. It employs sliding plates in the handle to simulate the feel of holding real objects.[3]

Cyberith Virtualizer

The Austrian company Cyberith is developing the Virtualizer, an omnidirectional treadmill that began as a Kickstarter campaign in July 2014 and is nearing public release. The Virtualizer — which the company said it will sell starting at $599 — allows users to move around inside virtual worlds as characters in games while they get exercise, without tripping over real-world cords or crashing into furniture.[4]

The device features motion sensors and a moveable vertical stabilization ring that holds users in place. The treadmill

Glove, the DataGlove measured the light transmitted through the fibers as the fingers and hand moved.

The DataGlove was better than other manipulators "because it was lightweight, comfortable to wear, unobtrusive to the user, and general purpose," wrote MIT researchers David J. Sturman and David Zeltzer.[30] The DataGlove was commercialized and used widely in research labs as it and similar gloves helped train people for tasks involving hand-eye coordination, such as surgery.[31]

Beginning in the 1990s, gaming companies moved aggressively into virtual reality, although with few results. In 1991, the Virtuality Group, a company based in England, introduced an array of arcade games that, once players donned virtual-reality goggles and data gloves, enables users to walk, run, crouch, jump and kick, and those motions can be moved to a virtual reality game as they actually occur. The Virtualizer also provides a seat for stationary activities, such as operating a virtual vehicle. It features vibration plates under the base that can simulate a floor shake if a virtual "crash" occurs.[5]

YEI PrioVR

Another Kickstarter-funded project, this lightweight sensor suit delivers motion data to a virtual-reality system. YEI Technology says it hopes to ship the product to Kickstarter backers in April.[6] Users strap PrioVR's sensors to key points on the body, and data from the sensors are used to control the movements of an on-screen character in games or other environments.

According to the Portsmouth, Ohio, company's website, PrioVR's sensors track the virtual-reality user's movements as they actually happen without the need for separate cameras or other potentially bulky equipment. Because PrioVR is wireless, it can be used outdoors, and more than one player can participate.[7]

EchoPixel True 3D

Virtual reality also is moving into medicine to help students and surgeons sharpen their skills. In March 2015, the Silicon Valley company EchoPixel received Food and Drug Administration approval for its True 3D Viewer, which allows users to visualize and manipulate images of tissues and organs in 3-D space. The system's software converts two-dimensional images — such as CT scans and MRIs — into stereoscopic 3-D images that can be rotated, sliced and otherwise manipulated as in actual surgery. The company says a True 3D Viewer costs $70,000 but can be leased for $20,000 per year.[8]

SpaceVR Overview One

SpaceVR, another Kickstarter project, wants to send its Overview One virtual-reality camera to the International Space Station to deliver the experience of being an astronaut to consumers who view the resulting films. Overview One consists of 12 modified digital cameras, which the San Francisco company seeks to use in shooting a video stream that would be stitched together into a virtual video sphere and transmitted to Earth.[9]

The project has not yet received NASA approval. The company says it has secured former astronauts and scientists on its board of directors to advise it on space-related matters.[10]

— *Patrick Marshall*

[1] "Get Your Cardboard," Google.com, http://tinyurl.com/k9a7kgs.

[2] Nathan Ingraham, "I just tried Google's new Cardboard with my iPhone," *The Verge*, May 28, 2015, http://tinyurl.com/q2owabl.

[3] Tactical Haptics LLC website, http://tinyurl.com/nlff64g.

[4] Jamie Feltham, "First Cyberith Virtualizers to Cost $599," *VRFocus*, July 22, 2014, http://tinyurl.com/n68bjqd.

[5] Cyberith website, http://tinyurl.com/owp283s; "Cyberith Virtualizer — Immersive Virtual Reality Gaming," Kickstarter.com, http://tinyurl.com/gn779l2.

[6] "PrioVR Update for Jan. 27, 2016," Kickstarter.com, http://tinyurl.com/j8db3m9

[7] YEI Technology website, http://tinyurl.com/lmxlr4d.

[8] Stacy Lawrence, "Startup raising Series A to launch interactive, holographic surgical imaging software," Fierce Medical Devices, March 24, 2015, http://tinyurl.com/zeup2hb.

[9] SpaceVR website, http://tinyurl.com/j6524po.

[10] "SpaceVR Launches Virtual Reality Space Exploration Project on Kickstarter," SpaceVR press release, Aug. 11, 2015, http://tinyurl.com/zdx3865.

offered stereoscopic 3-D graphics. Some of the devices were networked, allowing multiplayer experiences.[32]

The Japanese companies Sega and Nintendo quickly followed with their own virtual-reality equipment. In 1993, Sega introduced its virtual-reality headset for the Sega Genesis game console. The company's virtual-reality wraparound glasses featured head-movement tracking, stereo sound and high-resolution screens. In 1995, Nintendo released Virtual Boy, a portable console with 3-D graphics.[33] Both products were commercial failures because of poor graphics and performance and were soon discontinued.[34]

In 1992, researchers at the University of Illinois, Chicago, tried a different approach, creating the Cave

College students from Great Britain look through stereoscopes at the Australian Museum in Sydney. Invented in 1838 by British physician Charles Wheatstone, the stereoscope was the first device able to provide a 3-D experience. Wheatstone discovered that the brain processes two-dimensional images, viewed separately by each eye, into a single image, creating depth perception.

Automatic Virtual Environment (CAVE). Instead of employing headsets and data gloves, CAVE was a virtual-reality room with graphics displayed on the walls. Users' head and eye movements were tracked to adjust the imagery, and a wand-like device allowed users to interact with virtual objects.[35]

Shrinking Tech

After nearly two decades of slow progress, virtual-reality research picked up steam beginning in 2010, when a number of major manufacturers — including Sony, Google, Microsoft and HTC — began developing light-weight and powerful head-mounted displays.

While the entertainment industry and the military had driven virtual-reality research for decades, some analysts say in the current, new millennium research was reinvigorated by advances in an unrelated product sector: smartphones. According to Pixvana's Key, the components that have been optimized for cellphones — ultra-high-resolution screens, long battery life, lightweight and miniaturized sensors and other components — are just the features needed to make usable headsets.

"That's essentially what a head-mounted display is," says Key. "It's a bunch of the cellphone components attached to a PC."

What's more, he says, the huge market for smartphones has driven down the price of the components.

"When you're producing millions of smartphones a year, the component supply chain has just gotten incredibly optimized," Key says. "We're seeing a 10-fold improvement per year in cost, weight, performance and energy use in all these components."

CURRENT SITUATION
Researching Impacts

As consumers await the imminent release of the next generation of virtual-reality systems, academic research is expanding on the impact of the products. The three largest academic labs are located in the three major hubs for the development of commercial virtual-reality products: Silicon Valley, Los Angeles and Seattle.

Stanford University's Virtual Human Interaction Lab focuses on understanding how humans interact with virtual-reality simulations and how those systems may affect people using them. Specifically, the lab is studying three questions:

- What new social issues will arise from the use of immersive virtual-reality communication systems?
- How can researchers use virtual reality as a basic tool to study the nuances of face-to-face interaction?
- How can virtual reality improve everyday life, such as enhancing conservation, empathy and communications?[36]

Lab director Bailenson says that while his team is technologically savvy, the lab's emphasis is on social science research, not on creating virtual-reality hardware. "Think about how the computer has changed social science," he says. "You can do online surveys and you can measure reaction time. It has completely changed the way we think about research."

Virtual reality may bring even bigger changes, Bailenson says: "With virtual reality, we get all the benefits of the computer, but instead of having you read a paragraph, we can actually put you in a compelling scene and . . . measure what you do, what you say, how you move. It's the most spectacular tool."

Currently, the lab is studying virtual-reality scenarios that teach empathy, integrate virtual reality into educational environments and help individuals understand how human behaviors contribute to climate

Should virtual reality be more regulated than video games?

YES   Doug Bierend
Technology Journalist

Written for *CQ Researcher*, February 2016

Virtual reality appears poised to become at least as widespread, sophisticated, powerful and subversive as any other form of transformative media — television, video games or the Internet. What's in store for virtual reality may be unusually dramatic. Consider that Facebook spent $2 billion on a small headset startup called Oculus and that Magic Leap, a Google-backed outfit engaged in "augmented reality" — a species of virtual reality — describes its upcoming product as "a user interface for reality."

In the probably-sooner-than-we-think future, virtual reality will become a profound bridge between digital and physical realms, connecting people in powerful new ways while making possible unprecedented experiences of significant psychological and even physiological heft. This is what makes virtual reality such a wonderful technology, one that must be respected and, to the extent that it can do harm, regulated.

Effective virtual reality doesn't just create the impression of 3-D images and places. Its goal, as stated by those leading the charge in the field, is to achieve "immersion," the tipping point past which our senses forget they're being "shown" something and instead interpret the stimulus just as they would any other experience. The bar for immersion is surprisingly low and already within reach. This is why virtual-reality technology already has been applied effectively to therapies for such problems as phobias and post-traumatic stress disorder, and why even crudely rendered experiences are enough to create intense and deep psychosomatic effects.

Of course, most people aren't going to use virtual reality to get over a fear of heights, but rather to be entertained, to connect with one another, to have experiences that wouldn't otherwise be possible. As the technology advances, assuming its developers meet their aims, experiences with virtual-reality goggles will become as powerful as those without. The purpose of Entertainment Software Rating Board ratings, to which the video game industry voluntarily submits, is to allow parents to determine if a game's contents are inappropriate. But those ratings simply don't approach the import of virtual reality.

It's easy to imagine regulatory overreach, and any system for virtual reality must be crafted carefully. It's possible that over-regulating this technology could prevent the best it has to offer from reaching people. An acknowledgement of virtual reality's incredible power must be baked into any regulation without standing in the way of its development toward positive ends.

NO   Kate Edwards
Executive Director, International Game Developers Association

Written for *CQ Researcher*, February 2016

Every new media technology has experienced a certain level of caution and critical examination upon its introduction. This has been the case for the printed book, film, radio, television and video games, and now it's the case for virtual reality.

After the initial interest and scrutiny of a new technological medium, society eventually acclimates, and some people opt to consume the medium while some don't. As a society, we now understand that the impact of a medium depends on the artistry of those making it, not on the technology itself. After all, we all will eventually become familiar with this new technology.

Just as we are no longer shocked at the spectacle of television, moving pictures or video games, the same will happen with virtual reality. Once we are as familiar and comfortable with it as we are with film, the real impact of a virtual-reality experience will depend solely on the artistry of those creating it.

A quantitative scale for the "impact" of games and virtual reality is just as useless a concept as measuring the impact of a short story versus a novel, film or television program. A theatrical film can have a very strong impact due to the size of the image (e.g., IMAX) and the proximity of strangers in the audience sharing the experience. But smaller images can be equally impactful when viewed alone at home on TV. Both forms of media can leave a strong impression, but the impacts often are felt quite differently.

The newer artistic mediums of games and virtual reality are no different; they are both impactful, but in different ways.

Every new idea brings risk — not merely of increased liability but of opportunists seeking to capitalize on public perceptions of liabilities that do not exist. We actively encourage research into all aspects of virtual reality, but any research needs to be objective, with all preconceived biases disclosed and with thorough peer review.

It's important to remind ourselves that virtual-reality experiences are products of artistry that the U.S. Supreme Court considers speech protected by the First Amendment — just as clearly as video games, movies and books are protected speech. Thus, any discussion of the regulation of virtual reality as a technology is at best grossly premature and at worst dangerously presumptuous.

A woman tries out a virtual-reality headset during an event sponsored by Stanford University's Virtual Human Interaction Lab in New York City on April 23, 2015. Among other things, the lab is working on virtual-reality software for diversity training and enhancing conservation and communications.

change and how to change those behaviors.

The University of Washington's Human Interface Technology Lab, which Furness founded and directs, also is working on applying virtual reality to educational environments. It is seeking to apply virtual reality to medical and therapeutic goals, such as helping burn victims through games that cancel out pain, overcoming phobias and treating PTSD.

The lab also is developing virtual-reality hardware, especially display technology. Several projects focus on virtual retinal display technologies, which project images from an external source directly onto subjects' retinas rather than onto a screen.[37]

The third major academic virtual-reality research lab, the Institute for Creative Technologies (ICT), is at the University of Southern California, in the heart of the entertainment industry. ICT's virtual-reality research tends to focus on emotional and communications issues in virtual-reality environments. The Virtual Humans group at ICT is working on how to create virtual-reality characters that use language and gestures in natural ways and that can show emotions in reaction to verbal as well as nonverbal stimuli.

The ICT Virtual Worlds Group is studying the potential of using virtual worlds to address real-world issues, such as training, education, health and social support.[38]

In addition to the three West Coast virtual-reality research labs, many smaller labs at universities across the country are focusing more narrowly on applying virtual reality to specific areas. For example, the Virtual Reality Clinical Research Laboratory at the University of Houston is developing applications for treating addictions and mental health disorders.[39]

And the Virtual Reality Design Lab at the University of Minnesota is working on using the technology to create and evaluate product designs. The lab's current focus is on the building industry in general and architectural design in particular.[40]

"Excitement Bubble"

Industry experts say virtual reality finally will be ready for consumers when the new head-mounted displays become available this year. But, they say, the software to go with that hardware is not as far along.

"In three years, no one will be debating whether the hardware is ready," Pixvana's Key says. "It's going to entirely become a question about software, about content."

That need for content and tools has inspired a boom in virtual-reality start-up companies. More than $4 billion has been invested in these startups since 2010, and in 2015 alone 119 deals totaled roughly $602 million.[41]

"We're in a virtual-reality excitement bubble," Adam Draper, CEO of BoostVC, a tech investment firm, told attendees at the Augmented World Expo in Silicon Valley last June. And that bubble is not just the result of hype, he added. "Everything is getting so much better, so much faster," he said.[42]

The startups cover a lot of ground. For example, Florida-based Magic Leap is developing software that "opens up" virtual-reality headsets, allowing content to be overlaid on top of real vision. In October 2014, the company announced it had raised $542 million in "series B" funding — the second round of funding that takes place after a company has met certain milestones — with Google being the lead investor.[43] In February 2016, the company raised $793.5 million in a third round of funding.[44]

Envelop VR, the Bellevue, Wash., startup, is developing a virtual-reality "shell" for the Windows operating system that essentially translates the two-dimensional operating system into 3-D. The company also is developing tools that allow developers to convert 2-D objects — say, objects made in Autodesk's AutoCAD design program — into 3-D objects in the virtual environment. The company raised $2 million in initial funding in June 2015 and then another $4 million in late October.[45]

Seattle-based Pixvana is developing a cloud-based video-processing and delivery platform for virtual-reality applications. The company began operations in December 2015 with $6 million in funding from the Madrona Venture Group.[46]

Emerging Issues

Although enthusiasm is high in academia and among companies and investors for the next generation of virtual reality, some experts worry about possible legal issues and the potential for virtual-reality systems to collect data about those who use the equipment.

Some of those experts say virtual reality raises special liability concerns. "It is immersive, and you will forget your physical surroundings," says Ohio State's Fox. In addition to the physical environment, she says, "you're setting yourself up to hurt yourself if you are not mindful of the space that you're actually in."

And it's not just tripping over cords and banging into furniture that are worrisome. "We are getting pretty closely dialed into people's brains," says Envelop VR's Berry. "We are putting a display an inch away from their eyes and fully consuming their view with a bright light coming from the panel, so you can imagine there are serious health and safety issues around that."

Berry adds that the content for virtual-reality systems also may cause problems. The activities "can make you ill, [either by using a] bad frame rate, or by putting you on a roller coaster when you didn't expect it and you're going up and down and you feel nauseous immediately," he says. "There are some serious issues that we're going to need to address pretty soon, I think."

Daniel Ridlon, a Seattle product liability attorney, agrees that the emerging technology presents potential liability challenges. "We always encourage clients who are manufacturers to analyze the potential hazards of their products and, if they can, to design the products to remove the hazard or, as a final instance, to warn the user against any hazards that might be presented," he says.

"But when you have new technologies, analyzing the risks is, of course, more difficult, because there is less user experience."

Some experts also are concerned about potential privacy issues arising from the data that virtual-reality systems collect.

"In virtual reality, tracking is accomplished not by a satellite but by video cameras, magnetic sensors and other instruments that capture signals from devices worn by users," wrote Blascovich and Bailenson. "The tracking equipment scans users dozens of times per second to determine, for example, if the participant has changed his point of view, if a toe is moved forward, if he or she is leaning sideways and so on."[47]

That tracking data can reveal a lot more about a person than just body position. Digital footprints can reveal much about an individual's physical and psychological identity. "Actions that seem trivial in a virtual world — whether one chooses to walk or run, how quickly one types, or how close one stands to other people — provide clues about the self," wrote Blascovich and Bailenson.[48]

The bottom line, they warn, "is that people's behaviors in virtual reality are tracked, and therefore can be stored, analyzed and used — for good, bad or whatever the person collecting information wants."[49]

OUTLOOK
Benefitting Society?

Marketers expect a major boom in sales of virtual-reality hardware and software in 2016, with gaming systems leading the way.

Global sales will probably be unevenly distributed, however. In fact, according to Stephanie Llamas, SuperData's director of research, European sales ($1.9 billion) will outpace those in North America ($1.6 billion), while Asia will account for $1.1 billion, mostly through sales of low-cost devices such as Google Cardboard.

Llamas sees Google Cardboard as something of a gateway device for virtual reality. Because Google has made Google Cardboard's design freely available to manufacturers, she says it is easy and cheap to manufacture. "For people who are unsure whether they want to spend a significant amount of money entering VR, it's a good starter," she says.

North America and Europe, in contrast to Asia, have more users with the equipment needed for higher-end virtual-reality experiences. "We see the European market as being a little bit bigger," says Llamas. "You have a lot of PC users there, even in emerging markets like Russia and Eastern Europe, that can facilitate the type of hardware that meets the required specs."

At the same time, some experts want to encourage developers to forgo games and work instead on applications that benefit society. "What I'm betting on is that, in the end, we can have an equal or greater share of these vertical markets that eclipse what happens with games," says Furness of the University of Washington's Human Interface Technology Lab. But, she concedes virtual reality ultimately "is going to be about the money, there's no doubt about that."

Specifically, Furness wants to see virtual reality applied to education about social issues. "What I want to do is turn young developers around to working on some things that are really exciting, like developing content that relates to pervasive problems like AIDS in Africa, global warming and renewable energy," he says. "I would like to turn living rooms into classrooms." To that end, Furness recently founded the Virtual World Society, an organization aimed at employing virtual reality to solve pervasive world problems.[50]

Fox, of Ohio State, also would like to see virtual reality's focus shift away from games. "We've been using VR for a long time in the fields of health and education," she says. "I'd like to step that up and not be worrying about playing video games and shooting hyper-sexualized women."

Of course, as with any major new technology, some of virtual reality's biggest effects will take time to become apparent. Indeed, marketers and the media have so far overlooked some of the greatest potential benefits of virtual reality, according to some experts.

For example, Stanford's Bailenson predicts that virtual reality will eliminate the need for unnecessary travel. "Travel should be something that when you want to you should do it, but you shouldn't have to," he says.

"As VR gets better and better, the mediated interaction feels more like face-to-face interaction. It's my hope that we look back 20 years from now, maybe 15 years

from now, and say, 'Can you believe that everybody used to pile into their cars and drive down the same highways an hour each way every day?' Anything that can replace fossil fuel use is great in my book."

NOTES

1. For background, see Alicia Ault, "Video Games and Learning," *CQ Researcher*, Feb. 12, 2016, pp. 145-168.

2. Christina Crouch, "Healing Minds With Virtual Reality," PBS NovaNext, April 2, 2015, http://tinyurl.com/hlawhyj; Karla Zabludovsky, "Virtual Therapy Helps Residents of a Shell-Shocked City," *The New York Times*, May 28, 2012, http://tinyurl.com/c7lmajr.

3. "Virtual Reality Gaming Market Brief," Super Data Research, January 2016, http://tinyurl.com/h9wlttc.

4. "Virtual Reality Market by Technology (Semi & Fully Immersive), Device (HMD, gesture Tracking), Component (Sensor, Display, Software), Application (Gaming, Entertainment, and Industrial), Geography — Trends & Forecasts to 2014-2020," MarketsandMarkets, June 2015, http://tinyurl.com/hwx5bvl.

5. Tim Moynihan, "Hands On With Microsoft's Hololens, One Year Later," *Wired*, Dec. 17, 2015, http://tinyurl.com/nkltcws.

6. Jim Blascovich and Jeremy Bailenson, *Infinite Reality: The Hidden Blueprint of Our Virtual Lives* (2012), p. 193.

7. "NYT VR: How to Experience a New Form of Storytelling From The Times," *The New York Times*, Nov. 5, 2015, http://tinyurl.com/o8ykj89.

8. Blascovich and Bailenson, *op. cit.*, p. 1.

9. Mark Koltko-Rivera, "The Potential Societal Impact of Virtual Reality," 2005, http://tinyurl.com/h2zuvtm.

10. Doug Bierend, "The Dark Age of Virtual Reality-Based Torture is Approaching Fast," *Motherboard*, Jan. 31, 2015, http://tinyurl.com/hfomgnx.

11. Nick Wingfield, "To Bring Virtual Reality to Market, Furious Efforts to Solve Nausea," *The New*

York Times, March 4, 2015, http://tinyurl.com/zxk7yof.

12. *Ibid.*

13. Chris Barncard, "Virtual Reality Makes its Best Users the Most Queasy," University of Wisconsin, Madison, Jan. 29, 2016, http://tinyurl.com/jc5bdts.

14. Chris Neiger, "The Harsh Reality of Virtual Reality: Only 1% of Computers Are Ready for It," *The Motley Fool*, Jan. 5, 2016, http://tinyurl.com/hfcaxcj.

15. Barbara O. Rothbaum *et al.*, "Virtual Reality Exposure Therapy for Vietnam Veterans With Posttraumatic Stress Disorder," *Journal of Clinical Psychiatry*, August 2001, http://tinyurl.com/z8byxon. Also see Barbara O. Rothbaum and Larry F. Hodges, "A Controlled Study of Virtual Reality Exposure Therapy for the Fear of Flying," *Journal of Consulting and Clinical Psychology*, December 2000, http://tinyurl.com/zfd fywn; and E. Klinger *et al.*, "Virtual Reality Therapy Versus Cognitive Behavior Therapy for Social Phobia: A Preliminary Controlled Study," *CyberPsychology & Behavior*, February 2005, http://tinyurl.com/z39qhcx.

16. Couch, *op. cit.*

17. Bierend, *op. cit.*

18. The decision is *Brown v. Entertainment Merchants Association*, U.S. 564 — (2011), http://tinyurl.com/3jh99w8.

19. *Ibid.*

20. Ray Zone, *Stereoscopic Cinema and the Origins of 3-D Film, 1838-1952* (2007).

21. Stanley G. Weinbaum, "Pygmalion's Spectacles" (1935), http://tinyurl.com/j6tjuyd.

22. "The View-Master," OpticalSpy.com, Aug. 2, 2015, http://tinyurl.com/jlyewhd.

23. Jon Turi, "The sights and scents of the Sensorama Simulator," *Engadget*, Feb. 16, 2014, http://tinyurl.com/oupwxfe.

24. "The Link Flight Trainer: A Historical Mechanical Engineering Landmark," American Society of Mechanical Engineers, June 10, 2000, http://tinyurl.com/h9zcndp.

25. Henry E. Lowood, "Virtual Reality," *Encyclopaedia Britannica*, May 14, 2015, http://tinyurl.com/hzzfzwv.

26. Duncan C. Miller and Jack A. Thorpe, "SIMNET: The Advent of Simulator Networking," Proceedings of the IEEE, August 1995, http://tinyurl.com/gukudv9.

27. Blascovich and Bailenson, *op. cit.*, p. 55.

28. Aubrey Anable, "The Architecture Machine Group's Aspen Movie Map: Mediating the Urban Crisis in the 1970s," *Television and New Media*, October 2012, http://tinyurl.com/joeok88.

29. David J. Sturman and David Zeltzer, "A Survey of Glove-Based Input," *IEEE Computer Graphics and Animation*, January 1994, http://tinyurl.com/htfb3y9.

30. *Ibid.*

31. Ali Alaraj *et al.*, "Virtual reality training in neurosurgery: Review of current status and future applications," *Surgical Neurology International*, April 28, 2011, http://tinyurl.com/h58yxpt.

32. Steve Burke, "The History of Virtual Reality & The Future: Rift, Omni, STEM, castAR," *Gamers Nexus*, Oct. 20, 2013, http://tinyurl.com/jgo9fdl.

33. Matt Hill, "The Sega VR Headset That Never Was," *Gizmodo*, Nov. 21, 2014, http://tinyurl.com/jp4udl5.

34. Tim Stevens, "Nintendo Virtual Boy review," *Engadget*, March 21, 2011, http://tinyurl.com/hekgcmg.

35. Brad Grimes, "University of Illinois at Chicago: Virtual Reality's CAVE Pioneer," *EdTech*, Jan. 30, 2013, http://tinyurl.com/zdfe5c8.

36. Stanford University Virtual Human Interaction Lab website, http://tinyurl.com/h7smfws.

37. University of Washington Human Interface Technology Laboratory website, http://tinyurl.com/5jf7ax.

38. University of Southern California Institute for Creative Technologies website, http://tinyurl.com/7rub98m.

39. University of Houston Virtual Reality Clinical Research Laboratory website, http://tinyurl.com/ofdye3k.

40. University of Minnesota Virtual Reality Design Lab website, http://tinyurl.com/hrgzq3a.

41. Jonathan Vanian, "Investors Bet That Virtual Reality is No Illusion," *Fortune*, Nov. 30, 2015, http://tinyurl.com/hl9efx9.

42. Robert Hof, "VC Investments Pour Into Virtual Reality Startups, But Payoff Looks Distant," *Forbes*, June 11, 2015, http://tinyurl.com/jx3vfhw.

43. Jacob Kastrenakes and Ben Popper, "Google leads $542 million funding of mysterious augmented reality firm Magic Leap," *TheVerge*, Oct. 21, 2014, http://tinyurl.com/k54e2gt.

44. Jessi Hempel, "Magic Leap Just Landed an Astounding Amount of VC Money," *Wired*, Feb. 2, 2016, http://tinyurl.com/jd5ug2w.

45. "Virtual Reality Software Company Envelop VR Raises $4 Million in Series A Funding Led by Madrona Venture Group," news release, *BusinessWire*, Oct. 28, 2015, http://tinyurl.com/hm6ggua.

46. John Gaudiosi, "How This Startup Hopes to Improve Virtual Reality Video Delivery," *Fortune*, Dec. 14, 2015, http://tinyurl.com/jml9cjf.

47. Blascovich and Bailenson, *op. cit.*, p. 46.

48. *Ibid.*, p. 159.

49. *Ibid.*, p. 49.

50. Virtual World Society website, http://tinyurl.com/z64a3tf.

BIBLIOGRAPHY

Selected Sources

Books

Blascovich, Jim, and Jeremy Bailenson, *Infinite Reality: The Hidden Blueprint of Our Virtual Lives*, William Morrow, 2012.
Two psychologists examine what they say are virtual reality's subtle but powerful effects on behavior and potential for improving lives.

Hohstadt, Thomas, *The Age of Virtual Reality*, Dahma Media, 2013.
A futurist recounts the pre-digital history of virtual reality and explores benefits and potential challenges of emerging VR technologies.

Nite, Sky, *Virtual Reality Insider, 2nd ed.*, New Dimension Entertainment, 2015.
The CEO of a game company writes about his experiences launching a virtual-reality content company, offering insights about how the industry is structured.

Articles

Bierend, Doug, "The Dark Age of Virtual Reality-Based Torture is Approaching Fast," *Motherboard*, Jan. 31, 2015, http://tinyurl.com/hfomgnx.
A technology journalist warns that virtual-reality experiences can be so realistic and impactful that they could be used in torture.

Hof, Robert, "VC Investments Pour Into Virtual Reality Startups, But Payoff Looks Distant," *Forbes*, June 11, 2015, http://tinyurl.com/jx3vfhw.
A journalist explores the large investments in virtual reality and why the payoff may not come immediately.

Metz, Rachel, "Augmented Reality Study Projects Life-Sized People into Other Rooms," *MIT Technology Review*, Jan. 19, 2016, http://tinyurl.com/ju9z333.
A technology writer describes a Microsoft Research study that uses augmented reality to project the image of a life-sized person into a room.

Neiger, Chris, "The Harsh Reality of Virtual Reality: Only 1% of Computers Are Ready for It," *The Motley Fool*, Jan. 5, 2016, http://tinyurl.com/hfcaxcj.
A technology journalist explains what types of computers will be needed to power the next generation of consumer virtual-reality devices, and how much those computers will cost.

Turi, Jon, "The sights and scents of the Sensorama Simulator," *Engadget*, Feb. 16, 2014, http://tinyurl.com/oupwxfe.
A journalist tells the story of filmmaker Morton Heilig's "Sensorama," a cabinet invented in 1962 for viewing films that provided wind, smells and vibrations.

Westervelt, Amy, "Virtual Reality is Coming to Medical Imaging," *The Wall Street Journal*, Feb. 15, 2016, http://tinyurl.com/jffjxop.
A reporter explores how hospitals and medical schools are starting to use technologies enabling doctors not only to view three-dimensional pictures produced by imaging equipment but to interact with what is pictured — such as a heart or liver — as if those organs were real.

Wingfield, Nick, "To Bring Virtual Reality to Market, Furious Efforts to Solve Nausea," *The New York Times*, March 4, 2015, http://tinyurl.com/zxk7yof.
A reporter looks at how companies developing virtual reality devices are working to overcome "simulator sickness" caused by sensory disorientation.

Reports and Studies

Gerardi, Maryrose, *et al.*, "Virtual Reality Exposure Therapy for Post-Traumatic Stress Disorder and Other Anxiety Disorders," *Current Psychiatry Reports*, 2010, http://tinyurl.com/z4bwwtn.
A team of physicians and computer scientists reviews the evidence on using virtual reality to treat certain phobias and post-traumatic stress disorder.

"Virtual Reality Gaming Market Brief," Super-Data Research, January 2016, http://tinyurl.com/h9wlttc.
A market analysis firm focusing on gaming technologies examines expectations for future sales of virtual-reality games.

"Virtual Reality Market by Technology (Semi & Fully Immersive), Device (HMD, gesture Tracking), Component (Sensor, Display, Software), Application (Gaming, Entertainment, and Industrial), Geography — Trends & Forecasts to 2014-2020," MarketsAndMarkets.com, June 2015, http://tinyurl.com/hwx5bvl.
A market research company assesses the global market for virtual reality for the rest of the decade on the basis of technology, component, device type, application and geography.

Wilson, Clay, "Avatars, Virtual Reality Technology, and the U.S. Military: Emerging Policy Issues," Congressional Research Service, April 9, 2008, http://tinyurl.com/j5cu946.
A specialist in analyzing technology and national security for Congress examines the potential impacts of virtual reality, including cost-benefit implications, future communications infrastructure needs and national-security considerations.

For More Information

Entertainment Consumers Association, 64 Danbury Road, Suite 700, Wilton, CT 06897; 203-761-6180; www.theeca .com. Membership organization representing consumers of digital entertainment in the United States and Canada.

Entertainment Software Association, 575 Seventh St., N.W., Suite 300, Washington, DC 20004; 202-223-2400; www.theesa.com. Industry association representing manufacturers of computer and video games for video game consoles, handheld devices, personal computers and the Internet.

Human Interface Technology Laboratory, University of Washington, Box 352142, Seattle, WA 98195; 206-543-6377; www.hitl.washington.edu. A multidisciplinary research and development laboratory focused on technologies assisting human interaction with the world.

Institute for Creative Technologies, University of Southern California, 12015 Waterfront Drive, Playa Vista, CA 90094; 310-574-5700; ict.usc.edu. Research center focusing on the use of artificial intelligence, graphics and virtual reality.

International Game Developers Association, 19 Mantua Road, Mt. Royal, NJ 08061; www.igda.org. Industry organization representing game creators, including programmers, producers, writers and artists.

Research Center for Virtual Environments, Department of Psychological and Brain Sciences, University of California, Santa Barbara, CA 93106; 805-893-5798; www.recveb.ucsb .edu. Multidisciplinary research organization focused on understanding the interplay of computer-generated virtual environments and human behavior.

Virtual Human Interaction Laboratory, McClatchy Hall, Room 411, Department of Communication, Stanford University, Stanford, CA, 94305; 650-736-8848; vhil.stan ford.edu. Research center exploring interactions among people in immersive virtual-reality simulations and other forms of human digital representation in media, communications systems and games.

Virtual Reality Clinical Research Laboratory, University of Houston, Graduate College of Social Work, 3511 Cullen Blvd., Room 230, Houston, TX 77204-4013; 713-743-2086; www.uh.edu/socialwork/New_research/VRCRL. Researches ways to use virtual-reality technologies to address social behavior, addictions and mental health.

Virtual Reality Design Lab, College of Design, University of Minnesota, 101 Rapson Hall, 89 Church St., S.E., Minneapolis, MN 55455; 612-626-9068; vr.design.umn .edu. Explores ways to use virtual reality in design processes, especially in architecture.

12

Nanotechnology

Patrick Marshall

American nanotechnology pioneer K. Eric Drexler predicts that nanotechnology will transform the world, affecting climate change and global economics. But some scientists and public health advocates warn that nano-sized particles pose potentially catastrophic risks to human health.

From *CQ Researcher*,
June 10, 2016

A doctor injects into a patient's arm synthetic tissue containing electronic sensors too small to see — "nanoelectronic" tissues capable of monitoring the individual's medical condition and alert doctors to possible health problems.

"Ultimately, this is about merging tissue with electronics in a way that it becomes difficult to determine where the tissue ends and the electronics begin," chemist Charles M. Lieber said after announcing that his Harvard University team had embedded the nanoelectronic tissues.[1]

This research could change what it means to be human by connecting "part of the nervous system with a computer, machine or other living body," according to Mihail C. Roco, senior adviser for science and engineering at the National Science Foundation.[2]

No such tissues are on the market yet, but Roco says they will be soon. What's more, he says, nanotechnology will transform not only medicine but also agriculture, manufacturing and the military, among other sectors.*

"The advent of a revolution in nanotechnology will bring capabilities that transform our world, and not in a small way," says longtime nanotechnology engineer K. Eric Drexler, an academic

---

* Nanotechnology generally has been defined as science and engineering conducted with materials between 1 and 100 nanometers (nm) in size, or about 1,000 times smaller than the width of a human hair. According to the National Nanotechnology Infrastructure Network, a nanometer is one-billionth of a meter; a DNA molecule is 2- to 3-nm wide.

visitor at the Oxford Martin Programme on the Impacts of Future Technology at the University of Oxford. "The ramifications [will extend to] climate change, global economic development and the gathering crises of the 21st century."[3]

But others are less optimistic. Some scientists and public health advocates warn that nano-sized particles pose potentially catastrophic risks to human health. Others fear that nanotechnologies could disrupt the global economy, with inexpensive nanomaterials created in labs replacing the natural resources that many developing countries depend on for income. Still others fear nanotechnologies could one day give terrorists and other small groups the ability to produce powerful weapons, including nuclear bombs.

Despite such bold predictions and dire warnings, many experts say nanotechnology is in its early stages and that its full impact will be gradual. Nevertheless, nanotechnology is quickly finding its way into many products. As of March 2015, 622 companies had used nanomaterials in 1,814 consumer products, a thirtyfold increase since 2005, according to the Nanotechnology Consumer Products Inventory, a project of the Woodrow Wilson International Center for Scholars, a Washington think tank, and the Project on Emerging Nanotechnologies, a watchdog founded in 2005 to monitor the development of nanotechnology.[4]

Manufacturers are using nanoparticles to make, among other things, crack-resistant paints that resist graffiti; ceramic coatings for solar cells; scratchproof

Revenue on the Rise

Revenue from nanotechnology-enabled products is projected to more than quadruple from $850 billion in 2012 to nearly $3.7 trillion in 2018. The materials and manufacturing sector is expected to generate nearly half of that projected total. Electronics and information technology products are forecast to account for about a third.

Global Revenue from Nanotechnology-Enabled Products by Sector, 2012 and 2018*

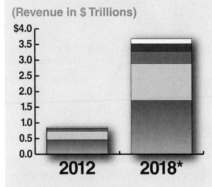

(Revenue in $ Trillions)

- ☐ Energy and environment
- ■ Building materials
- ■ Health care and life sciences
- ☐ Electronics and information technology
- ■ Materials and manufacturing

* *Projected.*

Source: Lux Research Inc., December 2015

eyeglass lenses and super-smooth coatings for a variety of uses, including aircraft fuselages.

In addition, "quantum dots" — spherical nanocrystals made from a core of cadmium selenide inside a shell of cadmium sulfide — enable tablets, computer screens, TVs and medical imaging devices to deliver high-resolution images with pure color reproduction.[5] And nanofibers created from carbon and, more recently, graphene (a form of carbon) are up to 70 percent lighter than copper cables and 20 times stronger than steel.[6]

The nanomaterials market already has passed the trillion-dollar mark, analysts say. Global sales of products that incorporate nanotech materials nearly doubled from $850 billion in 2012 to $1.6 trillion in 2014, according to Lux Research, a Boston-based market research firm, and could reach nearly $4 trillion by 2018.[7]

Still, commercial use of nanotechnology is in its infancy, according to experts. Research emerging from academic laboratories promises a wide range of products that use nanomaterials as well as nanodevices — tiny machines that can, among other things, deliver drugs to individual cells.

Among the products under development are:

- Ultra-efficient solar cells.
- Water desalination and filtration devices that promise to offer inexpensive clean water, even in remote areas.
- Nanoscale sensors that can detect minute levels of toxins and pathogens in the air, water or soil.

Some researchers also believe that nanoscale materials can be manipulated at the molecular level to produce products such as building materials, automobiles and aircraft that are stronger, lighter and much less expensive to manufacture than conventional versions. The process works like a 3-D printer: Molecular-sized machines alter other molecules and reassemble them, layer by layer, to "manufacture" a product. Such nanomanufacturing processes, which have not yet been achieved, are often referred to as "atomically precise manufacturing," or APM.

"What computer systems have done for processing information, APM systems will do for processing matter, providing programmable machines that are fast, inexpensive and enormously flexible — like computers in many ways, but rather than electronic signals, [they will be] producing physical products," Drexler wrote.[8]

Since 2003, when Congress passed the 21st Century Nanotechnology Research and Development Act, the federal government has invested billions of dollars in the field. That legislation created the National Nanotechnology Initiative (NNI), a federal program that coordinates the nanotechnology research efforts of 20 federal departments and agencies.[9] Since the NNI's inception, federal agencies have directed nearly $24 billion to the initiative, and its budget for 2017 is $1.4 billion.[10]

Much of this funding seeks to direct nanotechnology research into specific areas. The U.S. Army, for example, established the Institute for Soldier Nanotechnologies in 2003, a cooperative effort of the Army, the Massachusetts Institute of Technology and the private sector aimed at furthering military-related nanotech research, such as developing materials for lightweight, blast-resistant armor.

Some scientists and environmental groups, however, say nanotechnology presents unknown risks to human health and the environment.

"Over the last 10 or 15 years, there has been a massive amount of research on various types of engineered nanomaterials," says Andrew Maynard, director of the Risk Innovation Lab at the Institute for the Future of Innovation

Federal Funding Targets Research, Projects

The federal National Nanotechnology Initiative plans to spend more than 40 percent of its proposed 2017 budget on foundational research and about one-fourth on developing nanotechnology-enabled applications, devices and systems. The remainder will be used to develop research infrastructure, pursue signature projects in such areas as solar energy and electronics and study nanotechnology's environmental, health and safety effects.

Percentage of National Nanotechnology Initiative Funding Appropriated for Program Areas, Fiscal 2017

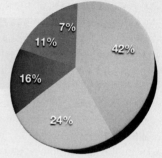

- Foundational research
- Applications, devices and systems
- Infrastructure and instrumentation
- Signature projects
- Environment, health and safety

Source: "Supplement to the President's Budget for Fiscal Year 2017," National Nanotechnology Initiative, March 2016, p. 25, http://tinyurl.com/jq2ofdx

in Society at Arizona State University. "We've learned a little bit, but to date we still don't even know whether we are asking the right questions about nanomaterials."

Maynard compares the potential harm from nanoparticles to that of asbestos, a naturally occurring fibrous material used widely in construction until it was mostly banned in 1989. Asbestos "is a natural nanoscale material, and it causes very serious harm because of its physical structure," he says. "You have a fiber which is very long and thin, and it doesn't dissolve very easily. When it gets in your lungs, it rips your lungs up."

Nanoparticles' tiny size allows them to pass through human tissue and enter individual cells, where they cause damage that is not apparent from their chemical composition, Maynard says. Potentially dangerous engineered nanomaterials have found their way into commercially available baby formulas, according to a May report commissioned by Friends of the Earth, an environmental advocacy group.[11]

"We ended up finding nanomaterials in all six baby formulas that we tested," says Ian Illuminato, the report's author and a health and environmental consultant at Friends of the Earth. One of the ingredients found was nano-hydroxyapatite, a nanomaterial he says was flagged by the European Union's Scientific Committee on

Consumer Safety as unsafe for cosmetics. "That definitely raises concerns for food and infant formula," he says.

According to the report, nanoparticles are being used in foods as nutritional additives and anti-bacterial ingredients as well as for flavoring and coloring. Nanoparticles can also be found in some brands of toothpaste, which use it as a cavity filler, tooth whitener and anti-bacterial agent.[12]

Despite all the positive and negative attention, some experts say nanotechnology has dropped off the public's radar in recent years. "Media coverage, especially traditional print media coverage, peaked in 2007 on nanotechnologies," says Barbara Herr Harthorn, director of the Center for Nanotechnology in Society at the University of California, Santa Barbara. "The lay public has not known much about nano."

Some experts attribute the public's flagging interest to the difficulty of the subject: Laymen can find it hard to understand nanotechnology. Indeed, the term can mean different things to even scientists and engineers.

"As one of my physics professor friends once said, 'Hey, have you heard about nanotechnology? It's the new name for chemistry,' " says Robert D. Rung, executive director of the Oregon Nanoscience and Microtechnologies Institute, a state-funded program to commercialize nanotechnologies. "The idea that it's an all-new concept distinct from physics, chemistry and whatnot never was true."

In fact, "nanotechnology" doesn't refer to a discrete technology, but to an array of existing technologies that are applied at the nanoscale.

Drexler, who popularized the term nanotechnology in his 1986 book, *Engines of Creation: The Coming Era of Nanotechnology*, agrees that the terminology confuses many people. "There are five kinds of nanotechnology," he says. "What the term was originally coined to mean was 'atomically precise fabrication.' " The second kind, he says, is "a bunch of fantasy science fiction and popular-press garbage that grew out of an early version of that picture." The third kind, he says, is what is commonly called "materials science" — science that deals with particles less than 100 nanometers in size. The fourth is nanoelectronics, which used to be called "microelectronics." The fifth, he says, is atomically precise fabrication by chemical and biological means.

"So we have APM, fantasy, materials science, nanoelectronics and advanced molecular sciences," Drexler says. "The last in the list opens the door to the first."

As experts assess the field's future, here are some of the questions they are asking:

Do nanotechnologies threaten human health and the environment?

"Nanobots" — nanoscale robots — destroying the environment. Rogue nanoparticles in the air infiltrating the human body and wreaking havoc in a person's cells. Nanoparticles in sunscreen damaging enzymes that maintain health. The possibilities of harm to humans and the environment caused by nanotechnology and its materials, some say, are many.

But so are the possibilities of good, others say.

One example of the technology's potential benefits are nanomaterials with anti-microbial properties that promise to improve human health.

"Virtually all of today's commercially available hand sanitizers are either isopropyl alcohol or some version of alcohol and/or triclosan or Microban, all of which are toxic chemicals . . . that can be absorbed in your bloodstream and which have been found in groundwater," says Steve Papermaster, co-CEO of NanoGlobal, a startup headquartered in Austin, Texas, that is developing nanomaterials with anti-microbial properties. Apart from being toxic, he says, those chemicals provide short-lived benefits. "If you use them you can get an immediate hygiene effect, yet one minute later you shake somebody's hands or touch a doorknob and it's like there was nothing that ever happened."

In contrast, Papermaster says, the anti-microbial nano-compound his company is about to market is non-toxic and binds safely not only to skin but to hard surfaces. "Instead of being potent for 10 seconds or one minute, it can last for 24 to 48 hours until your skin cells naturally wear off," says Papermaster. "On other surfaces [the benefits] can last for weeks or months."

Recent research also has found that nanomaterials could potentially help people with allergies, asthma, diabetes or other common conditions. Researchers at Northwestern University in Illinois announced in April that they had encased selected allergens in biodegradable nanoparticle shells and injected them in mice. After being treated with the nanoparticle, the mice no longer had an allergic response that could trigger an asthma attack.[13]

Researchers at Seoul National University in South Korea and MC10, an electronics company in Lexington,

Mass., have designed flexible patches that, once attached to the skin of a diabetic patient, can detect excess glucose in sweat and automatically administer drugs by heating up microneedles that penetrate the skin.[14]

Some researchers believe nanotechnologies may turn out to be the strongest weapon against cancer, a disease in which cells grow and divide uncontrollably. According to Oxford's Drexler, nanoscale particles are in development that can detect conditions within a human cell and when appropriate deliver a cell-killing payload. "Devices based on this principle would enable nearly perfect targeting of cancer calls, avoiding significant side-effects," wrote Drexler.[15]

Indeed, some experts say the potential for medical nanotechnology to deliver personalized medicine is virtually unlimited.

Noting that individuals can already obtain their complete DNA code for $1,000, Roco of the National Science Foundation predicts people will soon be able to receive medical treatment at the cellular level tailored to their DNA. "This is no longer speculation. We now have methods to edit DNA," he says. "It will be used for treatment of cancer and other diseases, rebuilding tissue, treating chronic diseases. We are moving effectively in a fast pace."

Nanotechnology also holds great promise, according to many experts, for helping the environment recover from pollution, perhaps even allowing scientists to reverse the accumulation of carbon dioxide in the atmosphere that is driving global climate change. In addition, these experts say, solar cells using nanomaterials could potentially convert sunlight into electricity more efficiently, helping to reduce dependence on fossil fuels and carbon dioxide emissions. Another possibility is the development of an inexpensive, effective treatment of water supplies, they say.[16] Danish scientists recently demonstrated a way to treat water by passing it through a tube with iron nanoparticles that remove traces of pesticides and industrial chemicals.[17]

In the longer term, nanotechnologies will allow nations to clean up existing damage to the environment, experts say. "[Such] technologies can provide new capabilities for capturing and sequestering toxic materials from groundwater and soil, and for more subtle challenges of remediation," wrote Drexler.[18] These technologies, he said, also offer the potential to directly remove CO2 from the atmosphere.

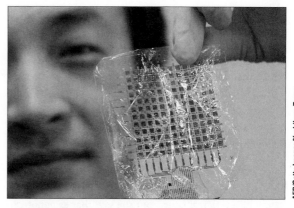

A researcher at the University of Tokyo holds a super-thin, bendable pressure sensor containing carbon nanofibers that could someday be used in special gloves to detect breast cancer lumps and make a digital record of the exam. Nanomaterials are being developed for use in a wide array of medical sensors. While the United States remains the world's leader in nanotechnology, some experts say other countries may be positioning themselves to dominate emerging markets in nanotechnology products.

At the same time, experts generally agree that the same technologies have the potential to harm human health.

"It has been clearly demonstrated that nanoparticles can easily enter the body, for example by inhalation, move around inside us, and sometimes damage cells via various mechanisms," wrote Louis Laurent, research director of the French Agency for Food, Environmental and Occupational Health and Safety. "Appropriate toxicity tests still need to be developed, and for each species of nanoparticle we will need to specify a level of exposure below which there is judged to be no risk."[19]

Recent research indicates that exposure to certain nanoparticles already in use in biomedical products can lead to cardiovascular diseases.[20] Researchers at the Georgia Institute of Technology reported in April 2016 that a nanoparticle widely used in food, cosmetics, sunscreen and other products can harm enzymes that maintain cell health.[21]

The real problem, say some experts, is the dearth of research into the risks of nanomaterials on humans and the environment.

"Welcome to the weird world of nanotechnology safety," says Maynard of the Risk Innovation Lab.

"Researchers have begun to put together some very crude rules that indicate whether something is going to be more or less harmful, depending on what sort of chemicals it is made up of, how large the particles are, what shape the particles are and especially [what] the coating on those particles are. So we are beginning to understand what might make something more or less harmful. But we still are failing miserably to connect that to real-world human exposures."

Christine Peterson, co-founder and past president of the Foresight Institute, a think tank in Palo Alto, Calif., focused on future technologies, agrees that nanoparticle safety is "a very real issue," but she says that as nanotechnology advances, safety will quickly become less of an issue. "Part of why the Foresight Institute is so interested in moving nanotechnologies forward is to get beyond this early stage of relatively crude nanomaterials," she says. "As we move toward real atomically precise controls the nanoparticle safety issue should go away."

Is the federal regulatory framework appropriate for nanotechnologies?

While agencies responsible for regulating nanotechnology products say they are up to the task, and while companies oppose increased regulation, some experts say the regulatory framework needs to be strengthened and better coordinated.

"The basic regulatory mechanisms in the United States — primarily the [Food and Drug Administration] and the [Environmental Protection Agency] — are probably about appropriate right now, and maybe they are on the side of overdone in some cases," says Papermaster of Nano Global. "It's better to be a little bit more cautious than not cautious enough when you're dealing with human health and the environment."

Papermaster says any new technology presents regulatory challenges, but that nanotechnology has been around long enough for regulators to figure out what to do. "There's been time, and there have been tremendous resources poured into understanding" nanoparticles and how to test them, he says. "I think it's on par with any other level of testing of biological drugs, genetic engineering and medical devices."

The private sector widely shares Papermaster's view, according to Harthorn of the Center for Nanotechnology in Society. "We've done surveys that show that industry

is very concerned about engineered nanomaterials from a safety standpoint, but they are still averse to regulation," she says.

Regulatory agencies say they are up to the task of ensuring the safety of nanomaterials, even as they say they want to develop new tools to evaluate the growing number of nano products.

"We know the products coming through, and we know how to evaluate the safety and effectiveness of nanomaterial-based drug products," says Anil Patri, chair of the Nanotechnology Task Force in the Food and Drug Administration (FDA). "Having said that, nanotechnology is an emerging technology with methods and materials being developed. With that in mind, a lot of new instrumentation is being developed."

EPA officials declined requests for an interview, although a spokesperson said that as of April 27, the agency had received more than 170 "new chemical" notices from manufacturers involving nanoparticles and had taken action to limit exposures or to require further testing of health effects in 157 of those cases. The EPA has also proposed rules requiring companies to provide additional details about products with nanomaterials already in the market.

Some experts argue, however, that regulatory agencies need better ways to assess the risk of nanomaterials. The problem, says Maynard of the Risk Innovation Lab, is that current methods assume that a chemical is a chemical and a metal is a metal, regardless of its size. But with nanomaterials, the effects of particles may differ depending on their size and shape. For example, nanosilver, used in cosmetics, disinfectants, food packaging materials and other products, may affect human health and the environment differently than non-nanoscale silver.

"We need a new approach to regulating materials where their physical form can cause harm as well as their chemical composition," says Maynard.

The National Nanotechnology Initiative "has spent 10 years as a cheerleader for any new nanotechnology, and only in the last couple of years has it started to do the environmental health and safety groundwork," says Jaydee Hanson, senior policy analyst at the Center for Food Safety, an advocacy group in Washington. "The NNI needs to complete this change from being a cheerleader for the technology to helping the agencies figure how to better regulate the technology."

Mike Meador, director of NNI's National Nanotechnology Coordination Office, denies the charge, noting that 7 percent of the NNI's annual budget is devoted to environmental health and safety research. "If you look at those and the [environment health and safety] content within those, you're actually looking at a total of about 10 percent of NNI budget," says Meador. "That's a significant investment."

Keeping track of a nanomaterial being used in different products is another problem. "It's easy if you make pristine nanomaterials — nanopowders, nanoparticles, etc. — to do safety assessments," says André Nel, director of the Center for Environmental Implications of Nanotechnology at UCLA, which was founded in 2007 and is funded by the National Science Foundation and the EPA. "But once you start making products out of nanocomposites, it is more difficult to keep track of how nano is used."

Some public safety advocates also say regulatory agencies should adopt a proactive posture and not allow nanomaterials to enter circulation until regulators can ensure their safety in each form and for each use. "I think the FDA is fine with the question marks until something happens, until somebody gets hurt," says Friends of the Earth's Illuminato. "Let's do that work beforehand so we don't even have to go there."

According to the FDA's website, the FDA "encourages manufacturers to consult with the agency before taking their products to market. Such consultation can help FDA to advise companies, review safety information and design any necessary post-marketing safety oversight."[22]

Some in industry say the existing regulatory framework is more than adequate. "Federal agencies have been managing the use of potentially risky materials for years," says Vincent Caprio, chairman of the NanoBusiness Commercialization Association, an industry group based in Connecticut. "They are adjusting to deal with any potential risk [nanotechnology] products might have."

Others in industry warn that current levels of nanotechnology regulation threaten to put U.S. companies at a disadvantage.

"We are killing ourselves," says Rung of the Oregon Nanoscience and Microtechnologies Institute, referring to the impact of federal regulations on nanotechnology industries. "In general, the regulatory burden is very high, and it slows things down. We are choking off our prosperity with regulation that is out of control."

Will nanotechnology disrupt the global economy?

While most if not all market analysts predict the strong growth of nanomaterials in the immediate future, some

---

Federal Funding Declines

Funding for the National Nanotechnology Initiative (NNI) grew more than fourfold from 2001 to 2010 but has fallen during the past five years and is projected to remain flat — at about $1.4 billion — in 2017. The NNI receives most of its funding from the National Science Foundation, National Institutes of Health and Department of Energy. The share it receives from the Department of Defense has declined in all but one of the last four years.

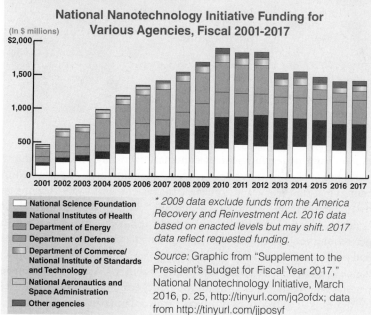

National Nanotechnology Initiative Funding for Various Agencies, Fiscal 2001-2017

(In $ millions)

- ☐ National Science Foundation
- ■ National Institutes of Health
- ▨ Department of Energy
- ▨ Department of Defense
- ▨ Department of Commerce/ National Institute of Standards and Technology
- ☐ National Aeronautics and Space Administration
- ▨ Other agencies

* 2009 data exclude funds from the America Recovery and Reinvestment Act. 2016 data based on enacted levels but may shift. 2017 data reflect requested funding.

Source: Graphic from "Supplement to the President's Budget for Fiscal Year 2017," National Nanotechnology Initiative, March 2016, p. 25, http://tinyurl.com/jq2ofdx; data from http://tinyurl.com/jjposyf

Large Global Nanotech Market Seen

Europe and Asia are expected to continue generating more revenue from nanotechnology-enabled products than the United States in 2018, experts say. Those regions are projected to account for more than two-thirds of global revenue that year, while the United States is expected to represent about a fifth.

Projected Global Revenue from Nanotechnology-Enabled Products, by Region, in $ Trillions, 2018

Projected Total: $3.69 Trillion

$0.27
$0.79
$1.33
$1.3

● Europe
● Asia
● United States
● Rest of world

Source: Lux Research Inc., December 2015

experts say the development of nanomanufacturing could fundamentally transform the global economy by bringing both plenty and upheaval to nations and reshape world trade.

Some experts say nanotechnology will usher in a period of abundance by lowering costs for materials and production, while others warn that that very abundance could present risks to economic stability. "A nanotech revolution could disrupt the global economy by flooding it with cheap products," says a January 2016 report by the Cicero Group, a consultancy in Salt Lake City.[23]

Oxford's Drexler agrees. He says the first wave of disruptions will hit resource-based industries such as mining and manufacturing and then spread to global trade. "Trade relationships that involve international supply chains will be broken down and become much less relevant," Drexler says. And as artificially produced nanomaterials replace natural resources, "the need to import and export raw materials and physical goods after transition of sorts will be radically reduced," Drexler predicts. The impact, he contends, would be devastating to developing countries whose economies depend almost entirely on the export of raw materials.

Peterson of the Foresight Institute says "it's certainly true that there could be and will be employment disruptions from nanotechnology," especially in

manufacturing. And she says "technological unemployment" — unemployment caused by the introduction of a new technology — will add to the disruptions already underway as machine intelligence, including robotics and automation, spreads. "We've already seen the hollowing out of some employment areas [such as manufacturing]. That's only going to continue," she says.

Research on nanotechnology's impact on employment is lacking, noted Noela Invernizzi, a researcher at the Woodrow Wilson International Center for Scholars in Washington. But service-related jobs will likely feel the effects first, she said, since nano products will reduce the need for human labor. She pointed to "nanotechnology innovations such as self-cleaning glass, . . . anti-bacterial hospital materials, anti-scratch and self-repairing paintings, protective coatings for industrial machines, etc., [that] tend to reduce the need for maintenance and repair jobs."[24] Nanomanufacturing will later have broad effects on employment across numerous manufacturing sectors as well, Invernizzi said.

But other experts expect nanotechnologies to create jobs even as some are being lost.

"Changes could be dramatic," says Roco, the National Science Foundation's nanotechnology adviser. "But this is the catch. Yes, there might be less work in one task, but those people can be available to do new jobs that are more advanced." Still, Roco acknowledges that nanotechnology will require workforce adjustments. Society's real challenge, he says, will be to find ways to cushion the blow, such as starting programs to train displaced workers for new jobs created by nanotechnology. "There has to be a way to help this transformation; otherwise it will be very dramatic," he says.

John F. Sargent Jr., an analyst with the Congressional Research Service, a public-policy research arm of Congress, echoed Roco's point. In a December 2013 report, he said nanotechnology over the long term "may deliver revolutionary advances with profound economic and societal implications," but that there is likely to be time to make adjustments. In the short term, he said, the economic impact will be minimal. "Most current applications of nanotechnology are evolutionary in nature," Sargent said, "offering incremental improvements in existing products and generally modest economic and societal benefits."[25]

Even if the United States smoothly transitions to nanomanufacturing, some experts say the changes could disrupt world trade and harm developing countries' economies by reducing — or eliminating — the export markets for their natural resources and manufactured goods. Such disruptions would, of course, also indirectly affect other nations because of the interdependency of the global economy.

The Nanotechnology Industries Association, a Brussels-based industry association, raised another potential problem in a recent report: Countries possessing an advantage in nanotechnology could leave their rivals behind. "Are nanotechnologies going to reduce the rich-poor divide, or will they have the opposite effect?" asks the report.[26]

If countries with advanced nanotechnologies do not take steps to help poorer countries develop their own nanotech capabilities, the report said, the rich will only get richer and the poor poorer. "Alongside their lack of scientists, developing countries lack the required infrastructure: with their R&D capacity inhibited by a lack, or shortage, of high-tech R&D equipment such as clean rooms and analytical equipment, poor countries are not able to become active players in nanotechnology and to effectively close the gap," the report's authors wrote.[27]

But if developing nations receive international aid, nanotechnologies could greatly improve living conditions for their citizens. "Aware of the reported benefits nanotechnologies could have for their populations," the report said, "some countries in the developing world have considered that this technological development could allow them" to leapfrog outdated technologies; "as such they are increasingly investing in [nanotechnology]."[28]

Nanotechnology also could allow poorer nations to grow more food more cheaply by supplanting fertilizer with nanoparticles engineered to increase crop yields, scientists say. Nanotechnology "is part of the evolving

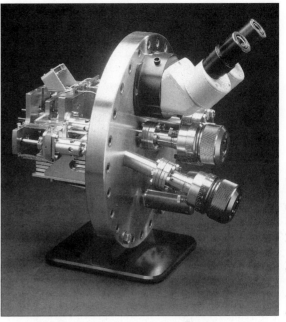

Getty Images/Science & Society Picture Library

The development of the scanning tunneling microscope in 1981 by IBM physicists Gerd Binnig of Germany and Heinrich Rohrer of Switzerland represented a major step in the development of nanotechnology. The instrument can produce a 3-D image of the surface of an object showing its individual atoms.

science of precision agriculture, in which farmers use technology to target their use of water, fertilizer and other inputs," said researchers Ramish Raliya and Pratim Biswas of Washington University in St. Louis. "Precision farming makes agriculture more sustainable because it reduces waste" while increasing productivity.[29]

Nanomaterials also are expected to help developing nations provide inexpensive, cleaner supplies of water to their citizens.[30]

Many leaders of nanotechnology research and development, however, are not focusing on the economic disruptions it will cause; instead they are more concerned about the competitive aspects of the emerging technology. For example, industry, government and academic attendees at a forum on nanomanufacturing "foresaw intense nanotechnology competition on a global scale — with one participant saying that we are already 'in a moon race,'" said a January 2014 Government Accountability Office report.[31]

BACKGROUND

Roots of Nanotechnology

Greek philosophers speculated that matter consisted of invisible particles as early as the 5th century B.C. Philosophers called them "atomos," Greek for "uncuttable" or "unbreakable." And while experiments by chemists and physicists from the early 18th century on supported the concept, it wasn't until 1959 that a scientist publicly said the manipulation of individual atoms and molecules was feasible.[32]

In a lecture to the American Physical Society on Dec. 29, 1959, titled "There's Plenty of Room at the Bottom," Nobel Prize-winner physicist Richard Feynman proposed scientists take on the challenge of "manipulating and controlling things" on a small scale. And by that, he meant a very small scale. "Why cannot we write the entire 24 volumes of the *Encyclopedia Brittanica* on the head of a pin?" he asked.[33]

"It is a staggeringly small world that is below," Feynman told his audience. "In the year 2000, when they look back at this age, they will wonder why it was not until the year 1960 that anybody began seriously to move in this direction."[34]

It's unclear whether Feynman's lecture actually stimulated research, but he was the first to issue a clear challenge for those who would work in what was to be called nanotechnology: "I want to offer another prize — if I can figure out how to phrase it so that I don't get into a mess of arguments about definitions — of another 1,000 dollars to the first guy who makes an operating electric motor — a rotating electric motor which can be controlled from the outside and, not counting the lead-in wires, is only 1/64 inch cube," Feynman said in concluding his lecture.[35]

(In 2014, researchers at the University of Texas announced that they had built a motor small enough to fit inside a human cell.[36])

Seeing the Invisible

The next significant step in the emergence of nanotechnology, though the field was still not known by that name, was the invention of the scanning tunneling microscope in 1981 by IBM researchers Gerd Binnig and Heinrich Rohrer.

Optical lenses in conventional microscopes are useless for viewing objects smaller than the wavelengths of light, which range from 400 to 700 nanometers. But a scanning tunneling microscope employs a sharp metal tip to emit an electrical current to the surface of an object for examination. The variations in the current are then measured to generate a 3-D atomic-scale image of the surface. When Binnig and Rohrer tested the device on a crystal of gold, the resulting images showed neatly arrayed rows of atoms. "I couldn't stop looking at the images," Binnig reportedly said after receiving a Nobel Prize in 1986 for the invention. "It was entering a new world."[37]

A team at Rice University in 1985 used a laser to vaporize carbon, the first direct manipulation of atoms to create a nanomaterial. The process produced a small number of "buckyballs," named after American architect and engineer Buckminster Fuller because the structure of the carbon molecules resembled Fuller's geodesic domes.[38]

Buckyballs were especially interesting because, like Fuller's geodesic domes, they were very strong. In 1991, Sumio Iijima, a scientist working for the Japanese electronics firm NEC, succeeded in producing buckyballs in the shape of long tubes, now called nanotubes and one of the most common nanomaterials on the market today. Nanotubes can be found in products ranging from aircraft fuselages to tennis rackets.[39]

Even as Binnig and Rohrer were putting the finishing touches on their scanning tunneling microscope, Drexler published a paper in 1981 outlining the fundamental principles of molecular engineering and proposed paths for developing what he would soon term "nanotechnologies."

Drexler predicted the development of molecule-sized devices that acted like microscopic tools, arranging atoms and molecules to form tiny machines. Creating such devices — primarily out of protein molecules — "will open a path to the fabrication of devices to complex atomic specifications, thus sidestepping obstacles facing conventional microtechnology," Drexler wrote. "This path will involve construction of molecular machinery able to position reactive groups to atomic precision. It could lead to great advances in computational devices and in the ability to manipulate biological material."[40]

In 1986, Drexler published his *Engines of Creation: The Coming Era of Nanotechnology*, a book for the broader public that popularized the term "nanotechnology." In the book, Drexler developed his ideas for nanomanufacturing, in which he proposed creating nanoscale

CHRONOLOGY

1950s-1990s *Scientists lay the foundation for nanotechnology.*

1959 American physicist Richard Feynman proposes the challenge of "manipulating and controlling things" on extremely small levels.

1981 Physicists Gerd Binnig of Germany and Heinrich Rohrer of Switzerland invent the scanning tunneling microscope, which produces images of objects at the atomic level. . . . American K. Eric Drexler outlines the principles of molecular engineering.

1985 Rice University researchers create the first synthetic nanomaterial called "buckyballs," after engineer and architect Buckminster Fuller's geodesic dome design.

1986 Drexler's *Engines of Creation: The Coming Era of Nanotechnology* popularizes the term "nanotechnology."

1991 Japanese scientist Sumio Iijima invents carbon nanotubes, long, thin molecules of pure carbon now used to strengthen airplane fuselages and other products.

1996 Several federal agencies form what will come to be called the Interagency Working Group on Nanotechnology.

2000-2004 *U.S. government backs nanotechnology development.*

2003 President George W. Bush signs the 21st Century Nanotechnology Research and Development Act establishing the National Nanotechnology Initiative; the law provides $3.6 billion over four years for research grants and establishes a network of research centers. . . . The Army creates the Institute for Soldier Nanotechnologies to further nanotechnology research of interest to the military.

2004 U.S. Department of Health and Human Services and National Institutes of Health begin the NCI Alliance for Nanotechnology in Cancer program, aimed at coordinating multidisciplinary research in cancer nanotechnology.

2005-2010 *Nanotechnology enters the marketplace.*

2005 The Nanotechnology Consumer Products Inventory, a project of the Woodrow Wilson International Center for Scholars and the Project on Emerging Nanotechnologies, begins tracking the growing use of nanomaterial in consumer products.

2006 Rice University researchers build the world's smallest car featuring four spherical buckyball wheels containing 60 atoms apiece. When the temperature rises, the nanocar moves on a gold surface as the buckyball wheels turn.

2010 IBM researchers create a nanoscale 3-D relief map of the world that measures 1/1,000th the size of a grain of salt, demonstrating a powerful methodology for generating nanoscale patterns and structures for fields such as electronics, optoelectronics and medicine.

2012-Present *Nanoelectronics research advances.*

2012 Researchers at Purdue University and three other universities create a transistor — the smallest possible — consisting of a single phosphorous atom.

2013 Stanford University researchers demonstrate a simple computer using 142 transistors made from carbon nanotubes.

2014 Researchers at the University of Texas at Austin's Cockrell School of Engineering demonstrate a three-component nanomotor 500 times smaller than a grain of salt that can fit inside a human cell and deliver medicine. . . . President Obama signs a law creating the National Network for Manufacturing Innovation, aimed at developing advanced manufacturing technologies.

2015 IBM researchers announce they have made nanoscale transistors from parallel rows of carbon nanotubes, allowing for much smaller and faster computer processors. . . . Nanomaterials are used in 1,814 consumer products, a thirtyfold increase since 2005.

2016 Swiss researchers produce a single-atom magnet, allowing for creation of nanoscale data storage devices.

Fears of Nanotechnology Never Materialized

Polls show public is more interested in the technology's job potential.

When nanotechnology first came to the public's attention in the mid-1980s, newspapers and magazines were rife with articles focusing on the safety of the mysterious science of atom-sized objects. Rampant nanobots would destroy the environment, the narrative went, and consumers would ingest food-borne nano-shards that would alter the human genome.[1]

For scientists, nanotech's image was immensely worrying. A public uncomfortable with an emerging technology translates to a federal government unwilling to finance research into it.

But public fears of nanotechnology eventually disappeared. Nanobots did not emerge, no disaster involving nanotechnology occurred and the public did not turn against the technology. Instead, experts say, public attitudes toward nanotechnology now run the gamut, from ignorance of it to excitement about its potential to questions about its impact on jobs and the economy.

Barbara Herr Harthorn, director of the Center for Nanotechnology in Society at the University of California, Santa Barbara, says the public generally is far more focused on nanotechnology's job potential than either the technology's benefits or its dangers.

"The public that we've engaged with here and in the U.K. asked very hard questions about the quality of the jobs that will be created," says Harthorn, who has held focus groups in an effort to learn public perceptions of nanotechnology. "And those who are not elites — which is the majority, since we convene very diverse groups . . . — tend not to see themselves as having the technical knowledge and training to be advanced nanotechnology employees. So they do not see this as creating opportunity for them," says Harthorn, whose center is funded partly by the National Science Foundation and other federal agencies.

Apart from their concern over jobs, Harthorn says, people in the United States and U.K. tend to emphasize nanotechnology's benefits over its risks. In fact, says Harthorn, it was difficult in her focus groups to get individuals to consider or digest information about hazards.

"We could not provide any risk information that would stick," she says. "And we are trying to have these [focus group] sessions balanced, so to provide balance we would keep trying to put more risk messages in. It didn't make any difference."

"assemblers" that could be used to build not only copies of itself but also items of greater complexity, from appliances to automobiles, "from the bottom up." He also warned of the potential for what he called "gray goo," Drexler's term for what might happen if replicating assemblers got out of control and began converting organic material into more assemblers.

Drexler's warning about gray goo, which he said was misunderstood, caused some writers to call for strict limitations on the development of nanotechnologies on the grounds that they could destroy the planet.[41]

National Nanotechnology Initiative

By the mid-1990s, government agencies were beginning to coordinate their efforts to develop nanotechnology. In November 1996, staff from several agencies formed a working group that, in September 1998, was designated the Interagency Working Group on Nanotechnology.[42]

In August 1999 the group completed a draft plan for a federal initiative on nanotechnology, which was sent to the President's Council of Advisers on Science and Technology and the White House Office of Science and Technology Policy. In response, the Clinton administration included $500 million in its 2001 budget request to Congress for a National Nanotechnology Initiative.

Congress followed up by passing the 21st Century Nanotechnology Research and Development Act, which formally established the National Nanotechnology Initiative. The legislation, signed into law by President George W. Bush in 2003, provided $3.6 billion over four years to five primary agencies involved in the initiative — the National Science Foundation, Department of Energy,

Neither was the public particularly interested in potential conservation benefits from nanotechnology. Specifically, "they were not excited by the idea that this lightbulb [using nanotechnology] will last longer and use less energy" than current bulbs, Harthorn says. "They wanted to hear about radical alternatives that would create abundant free energy for everybody in the world so they could use as much as they want and not feel guilty about it."

Much of the public knows little about nanotechnology, surveys show. A 2012 Harris Poll found that 62 percent of American adults had never heard of nanotechnology or, if they had, didn't know what it was.[2] And, unlike in the 1980s, the respondents were not afraid of the technology, with only 6 percent reporting that they believed the risks outweighed the benefits. These results were virtually identical to a 2007 Hart Research poll.[3]

A 2015 survey by the Pew Research Center, a think tank in Washington that studies U.S. trends, found that Americans' knowledge of science in general remains limited and does not extend beyond basic terms and concepts. The same was true of nanotechnology, Pew said: 36 percent of U.S. adults did not know that it "deals with things that are extremely small."[4]

Dietram Scheufele, a professor of science communication at the University of Wisconsin, Madison, attributes much of the evolution in public perceptions of nanotechnology — from fear to limited knowledge — to changes in the media's coverage of it.

"We're losing, even in the big newspapers, people who write regularly about science," Scheufele says. His research shows that most articles about nanotechnology today are written by people who have done only one story on the topic — "people in sports sections who write about new nanosize drugs for athletes, people in fashion magazines who write about some nanoparticles cream," Scheufele says. As a result, he says, "even that handful of people who have written multiple stories who could've rung the alarm bell are no longer there."

Harthorn agrees. "The world has shifted tremendously in the print media," she says. "Science journalists disappeared in the period of time that we were doing this work. It's an interesting societal problem if you have technologies rolling out and you don't have anyone talking about them in the public sphere."

— Patrick Marshall

[1] K. Eric Drexler, *Engines of Creation: The Coming Era of Nanotechnology* (1986); Bill Joy, "Why the Future Doesn't Need Us," *Wired*, April 1, 2000, http://tinyurl.com/jop7nr6.

[2] "Nanotechnology Awareness May Be Low, But Opinions Are Strong," Harris Poll, Sept. 6, 2012, http://tinyurl.com/j4tjqjf.

[3] "Poll Reveals Public Awareness of Nanotech Stuck at Low Level," Hart Research, Sept. 25, 2007, http://tinyurl.com/h8oeu6w.

[4] Cary Funk and Sara Kehaulani Goo, "A Look at What the Public Knows and Does Not Know about Science," Pew Research Center, Sept. 10, 2015, p. 22, http://tinyurl.com/zrurwtx; summary of the report available at http://tinyurl.com/phj4vmr.

NASA, National Institute of Standards and Technology and EPA — to provide research grants and establish a network of research centers.[43]

Other departments involved in nanotechnology research — including the Department of Defense, National Institutes of Health and Department of Homeland Security — were not originally included in the authorizing legislation, although they collectively accounted for 46 percent of NNI funding in 2003. (Today, 20 agencies and departments receive money.)[44]

The National Nanotechnology Initiative also sought to improve collaboration among agencies, with funding directed to and controlled by participating agencies and departments.

For example, the U.S. Department of Health and Human Services and National Institutes of Health in 2004 began the NCI Alliance for Nanotechnology in Cancer, aimed at conducting multidisciplinary research in the public and private sectors in cancer nanotechnology.

Nanotech Schism

Almost as soon as the NNI was established to coordinate research, a schism emerged among researchers.

One faction, with Drexler as its most public voice, charged the NNI with having abandoned its research toward the goal of developing the tools to build objects and devices with molecular "assemblers." These assemblers are now more often called "atomically precise manufacturing," or APM.

"In Washington the promoters of a federal nanotechnology program sold a broad initiative to Congress in 2000 and then promptly redefined its mission to exclude

Countries Pouring Money into Nanotechnology

In China, the effort "has yet to bear fruit."

By all measures, the United States has been and continues to be the world's leader in nanotechnology research, though some experts warn that other countries may be positioning themselves to gain the lion's share of emerging markets in nanotechnology products.

The United States was the global leader in government investments in nanotechnology research in 2014, the most recent year for which comparative global investment figures are available. But the U.S. lead is diminishing.

In 2014, the U.S. government devoted nearly $1.7 billion to nanotechnology research, down 3 percent from the year-earlier total, according to a study funded by the National Science Foundation and the National Nanotechnology Initiative. The 2013 figure, in turn, represented a 17.5% decline from 2012.[1]

Over the same period, according to the report, European and Asian countries were significantly increasing their investments in nanotechnology. European government spending — including by the European Commission and individual country programs — amounted to $2.5 billion in 2014, an increase of nearly 10 percent from 2012.[2]

The report also notes that Asian countries, which represented 30 percent of global government funding in 2014, increased investments by 4 percent over the same period, from $2.2 billion to $2.3 billion.

U.S. corporations have also led global spending by the private sector on nanotechnology research and development, investing $4 billion in 2014, approximately $1.5 billion more than the next country, Japan, according to the report.

What's more, some experts note that such regional figures can hide major shifts by individual countries. Several countries, including China, Korea and Iran, have been increasing their investments by more than 30 percent in recent years, according to Mihail C. Roco, senior adviser for nanotechnology at the National Science Foundation.

Still, Roco says he is not overly concerned about the apparent gap in research investment because other signs point to a continuing strong U.S. lead in basic research.

"The majority of breakthroughs come from the United States," he says. Roco adds that U.S. research accounts for about 67 percent of the citations in the prestigious science and nature journals.

At the same time, Roco acknowledges that being the leading country in nanotechnology research is no guarantee of market dominance.

"In basic research [investment] we are probably comparable," says Roco. "But other countries' governments also invest in platforms for production. In this way, their investments are much larger than what the United States is doing now."

In particular, some experts say China poses a daunting challenge because its government not only is increasing investments in research but also investing heavily in commercializing research results.

"The Chinese government has just pumped huge amounts of money, not just the Beijing government but also regional governments, into nanotechnology," says Richard Appelbaum, a professor at the Center for Nanotechnology in Society at the University of California, Santa Barbara.

the molecular sciences, the fields that comprise the very core of progress in atomic precision," wrote Drexler. "Thus, the word 'nanotechnology' had been redefined to omit (and in practice, exclude) what matters most to achieving the vision that launched the field."[45]

According to Roco of the National Science Foundation and a key architect of the NNI, the initial focus of the

nanotechnology initiative did, indeed, turn toward researching nanoparticles rather than developing APM.

"You have to separate science fiction people from real science," says Roco of Drexler's call to focus the NNI on atomically precise manufacturing. "All of his theories basically were based on a kind of fiction, with imagination and some good connections to reality, but it's not science."

The Chinese government is intent on weaning the country from dependence on foreign technology, according to Appelbaum, who just returned from a research trip to China. In the case of nanotechnology, he says, the effort "has yet to bear fruit."

"They've invested a lot of money, but most of the interviews that we've done there suggest that products are sort of small-scale and in preliminary stages," says Appelbaum. "A lot of the ventures involve partnerships, often with Chinese expats who've been in the United States [and] then have returned to China."

The Chinese government not only has set up research parks but also funded companies to develop products. "China is not shy about placing bets," says Appelbaum. "I was curious to know if that strategy would propel China ahead of the United States."

While actual figures are hard to come by, Appelbaum says "the jury is still out" on whether China's bets will pay off. But, he says, he has seen factors in China that are likely to work against its success.

"One of China's shortcomings is that their research culture, at least based on what we've been able to find out through surveys of faculty and many interviews, is not conducive to innovation," he says. "And there's a huge amount of corruption and cheating."

According to Appelbaum, China is intent on seeing that Chinese students receive training in the United States and then bring their expertise back to China. The problem, he says, is that those students find a different, more repressive intellectual environment when they return to China.

"I think China's main challenge is how can they encourage innovation and creative thinking in science while stifling it elsewhere?" says Appelbaum. "The United States remains by far ahead of China in terms of innovation, there's no question about that."

At least some Chinese nanotechnology researchers also see clear differences in the way the United States and China encourage research and commercialization. "It would be interesting to watch, debate and decide which type of governmental system, the centralized one-party or the almost equally divided two-party system, can more efficiently and effectively utilize public resources to produce nanotechnology products that better serve their own taxpayers, and the worldwide community as well," wrote five researchers at Fuzhou University in China, along with an American professor.[3]

While it's not clear which of the industrialized countries will reap the most rewards from developing the next generations of nanotechnology, some experts say nanotechnology offers both opportunities — especially for water purification and medicine — as well as challenges for developing countries.

Nanotechnology has to overcome a number of obstacles so that its development is fair, according to a recent report by the Brussels-based Nanotechnology Industries Association.

"Problems related to access and patenting issues are significant obstacles to the dissemination of new technologies in the developing world," the report warns.[4] It also says such occurrences as reducing the need of developed countries for the material resources of developing countries, "may result in potential harm for developing economies."

— *Patrick Marshall*

[1] "Nanotechnology Update: U.S. Leads in Government Spending Amidst Increased Spending Across Asia," Lux Research, December 2015, http://tinyurl.com/zkmqb6s.

[2] *Ibid.*, p. 2.

[3] Haiyan Dong, Yu Gao, Patrick J. Sinko, Zaisheng Wu, Jianguo Xu, Lee Jia, "The nanotechnology race between China and the United States," *Nano Today*, Vol. 11, Issue 1, February 2016, pp. 7-12, http://tinyurl.com/hv7syxf.

[4] Guillaume Flament, "Closing the Gap: The Impact of Nanotechnologies on the Global Divide," Nanotechnology Industries Association, Nov. 26, 2013, p. IV, http://tinyurl.com/hr63rf4.

According to Roco, the plan was to begin with researching and developing nanomaterials and then to move to using these materials to develop more complex components. "The initial focus was on particles," he says. "The main challenge is how you build up from elements, and you build systems that exploit completely new elements."

"That's where things stood in 2004," says Adam Keiper, editor of *The New Atlantis*, a journal that focuses on technology and society. "And it was a tense moment, too, because there was this fairly new national nanotechnology initiative that had been given a bundle of money and basically was pouring all of that money into just the more limited vision of nanotech — mostly nanomaterials."

Drexler responds that public fears over nanotechnology, fanned by media reports about the technology's supposed dangers, partly drove the NNI's go-slow approach. The result, he says, was an unfortunate delay in the development of APM.

"[The NNI] wanted to associate themselves with the general vision in a fuzzy way with respect to the positive payoffs, while disassociating themselves from these irrational and inapplicable fears," says Drexler. "It was a process of political and social polarization, a failure to communicate, and what surprised me was a surprising abdication of what I would see as the scientific community's responsibility to evaluate ideas and advise the public on reality."

According to Meador of NNI's National Nanotechnology Coordination Office, there was no coordinated decision to put off research on APM. "Each agency within the NNI carefully looked at what they were going to fund and decided the directions that they wanted to go in," he says.

Once the early debate over NNI's direction died down, Roco says, the first decade was a period of consolidating the basic research on nanomaterials. "In the first 10 years we developed methods to make particle nanotubes for almost all of the elements in the periodic table," he says. "This is just the beginning of nano."

Researchers made progress on a variety of fronts. In 2010, IBM researchers created a nanoscale 3-D relief map of the world that measured 1-1,000th the size of a grain of salt — an achievement with implications for electronics, optoelectronics, medicine and other fields. And in 2013, Stanford University researchers created a simple computer using 142 transistors made from carbon nanotubes.

As the market potential of nanomaterials became more apparent, calls for the NNI to help commercialize products resumed.

Congressional Research Service analyst Sargent noted in 2014 that many in the private sector remained unhappy with NNI's funding decisions. "Some in industry have criticized the NNI for being overly focused on basic research and not being aggressive enough in moving NNI-funded R&D out of government and university laboratories and into industry," he wrote. "Others in industry have criticized the federal government for not providing mechanisms to help advance nanotechnology

R&D to the point where it becomes economically viable for venture capitalists, corporations, and other investors to create products and bring them to market. Some refer to this gap as the 'valley of death.' "[46]

Possibly in response to these pressures, President Obama in his 2013 and 2014 State of the Union addresses called for creating a National Network for Manufacturing Innovation, a network of institutes aimed at developing advanced manufacturing technologies, including nanotechnology.[47]

And on Dec. 16, 2014, he signed into law the Revitalize American Manufacturing and Innovation Act, which created the nationwide network within the National Institute of Standards and Technology, that will seek to develop nanotechnology.[48]

CURRENT SITUATION
New Research Phase

The current state of the field is mixed. The United States remains the global leader in government investments in nanotechnology research, but its lead is diminishing. Other countries — particularly China, South Korea, Iran and Japan — are increasing their investments in nanotechnology research and are starting to catch up to the United States.

On the other hand, the National Nanotechnology Initiative is beginning to push research toward nanomanufacturing and nanoelectronics. "One of the things that we're talking about now within the NNI is atomically precise manufacturing," says Meador of NNI's National Nanotechnology Coordination Office. "You're starting to see agencies and departments like [the Energy Department] investing in that area."

The shift is not an acknowledgment that advocates of atomically precise manufacturing in 2003 were right, Roco of the National Science Foundation says. Rather, it is a natural progression as scientific research advances. "We cannot go directly from foundation to innovation," he says. "The science part is different from the speculative part. The big thing is to have the foundations from which to develop complex systems."

And those foundations have now been laid, says Roco. "We are already building nanomachines now," but building machines based on sound scientific research, he says. Indeed, recent research in academic laboratories

Should federal regulation of nanotechnology be strengthened?

YES
Andrew Maynard
Director, Risk Innovation Lab, Arizona State University

Written for *CQ Researcher*, June 2016

Nanoscale design and fabrication are creating new opportunities for innovation and new approaches to solving challenges, ranging from treating diseases to ensuring access to clean water and energy.

Yet the very properties that make nanotechnology attractive also raise the possibility that they will cause unexpected harm if they are not developed and used appropriately. For instance, particles and fibers that can make materials stronger, more conductive and more versatile may harm people who are exposed to them. And nanostructured materials released into the air, water or soil may damage some species and possibly lead to long-term environmental damage.

Because of the unusual and often dynamic properties of nanomaterials, existing regulations are not necessarily effective at reducing risk or balancing safety and benefits. For instance, a new hybrid nanotechnology-based product designed to act simultaneously as a medical device, a biological sensor and a therapeutic drug will be regulated by the U.S. Food and Drug Administration (FDA). Yet current regulations — which were conceived before such possibilities were dreamed of — cannot ensure the safety or benefits of such products. Similarly, a new nanoparticle-based material would be regulated by the Environmental Protection Agency (EPA) under the Toxic Substances Control Act. However, because the control act is based on an understanding of chemicals that does not reflect the nature of nanomaterials, its application would fall short of ensuring the safe and effective use of the material.

At the heart of this dilemma are two key characteristics of nanotechnology-based products: Risk-relevant properties can vary within and between batches of material and from product to product; and properties vary according to how the product is used, where it is used and how its use varies over time. The majority of regulations relevant to nanotechnology-based products are not responsive to either of these characteristics, and that makes their effectiveness questionable.

Ensuring that nanotechnology products are safe throughout their lifetimes, without unnecessarily impeding beneficial use, requires existing regulations to be enhanced, or in some cases replaced. Nanotechnology-specific regulations are not needed, as the products of nanotechnology do not fit a clear and compellingly unique regulatory category.

But product and domain-specific regulations need to be evaluated to ensure that new materials and products arising from nanotechnology are as safe as possible, while being as beneficial as possible.

NO
Vincent Caprio
Executive Director, NanoBusiness Commercialization Association

Written for *CQ Researcher*, June 2016

The U.S. government's approach to managing potential risks is rooted in regulating "products" and not the technologies that produce them.

Examples of product-specific laws include the Toxic Substances Control Act, the Federal Insecticide, Fungicide, and Rodenticide Act and the Federal Food, Drug, and Cosmetic Act.

The federal agencies charged with implementing these laws, the Environmental Protection Agency (EPA) and the Food and Drug Administration (FDA), respectively, have for years been actively engaged in reviewing and adapting their regulatory powers under the enabling statutes. They've done that to appropriately manage the potential risks associated with the products of emerging technologies, including nanotechnologies.

The NanoBusiness Commercialization Association (NanoBCA) supports the federal government's commitment to fostering nanotechnologies and to leveraging federal research and development investment in nanotechnologies to advance society's goals. Our members have worked closely with policymakers for more than a decade to promote nano innovations.

NanoBCA agrees with the views expressed by the federal government as a whole — including the EPA, FDA and the Organisation for Economic Co-operation and Development (OECD) and its 34 member countries, including the United States — that existing laws and governance systems are sufficient to identify and regulate risks posed by applications of nanotechnology.

The White House Office of Science and Technology Policy in 2011 released a set of principles for the regulation and oversight of applications of nanotechnology. The office said the principles are expressly intended to "achieve consistent approaches across different emerging technologies and to ensure the protection of public health and the environment while avoiding unjustifiably inhibiting innovation, stigmatizing new technologies, or creating trade barriers." NanoBCA strongly endorses these guiding principles.

Given agencies' adaptability and their philosophy of regulating products and not technologies, the federal government is finding the right balance on nanotechnology. It is appropriately managing potential risks from applications of certain nanomaterials, while also promoting the extraordinary benefits that nanotechnologies offer.

If anything is needed, it is more funding to ensure federal agencies possess sufficient resources to do their jobs efficiently and effectively.

The Eternalis Advanced Skin Care System is among the many cosmetics that use nanomaterials to increase the potency of their formulations. Nanotechnology advocates say nanoproducts are safe, but some experts argue the government is not up to the task of ensuring that nanoparticles are safe for public consumption or exposure.

shows great promise for nanomanufacturing and nano-electronics, he says.

Last year, researchers at Stanford University announced they had significantly increased the efficiency of solar cells by using nanowires instead of conventional wires to transfer the electrical charge collected by the cells.[49] According to the researchers, conventional wires block 5 percent to 10 percent of the light that shines on the cell, while the nanowires are effectively invisible.

Researchers at the University of Texas at Austin's Cockrell School of Engineering in May 2014 demonstrated a three-component nanomotor 500 times smaller than a grain of salt that can fit inside a human cell. The motor can rotate for 15 hours and spin at 18,000 revolutions per minute. By comparison, the maximum recommended RPM for a Toyota Prius is 5,200.[50] In experiments, the Cockrell researchers coated the motor's rotor with biochemicals and found that the faster they turned the rotor, the more rapid the delivery of the biochemicals.[51]

Last October, researchers at IBM said they made nanoscale transistors from parallel rows of carbon nanotubes.[52] The method will make it possible to shrink the connections between elements in a processor to 28 atoms, allowing manufacturers to build much smaller and faster computer processors, according to the researchers.

And in April 2016, researchers at the École Polytechnique Fédérale de Lausanne in Switzerland announced they had produced a single-atom magnet, a breakthrough they said will allow creation of nanoscale data storage devices.[53]

Push to Commercialize

Despite the heavy investment in nanotechnology, some experts say a gap in funding between federally sponsored basic research and private-sector funding of commercial ventures persists.

"As a result, U.S. innovators may find it difficult to obtain either public funding or private investment during the middle stages of innovation," the critical point at which the focus is on engineering products based on laboratory research, Timothy M. Persons, chief scientist of the Government Accountability Office, told Congress.[54]

The federal government has been aware of the funding problem since at least the early 1980s, when it began targeting funds — in the form of Small Business Innovation Research grants and, then in 1992, Small Business Technology Transfer grants — to small business in an effort to overcome the gap. In 2013, the most recent year for which data are available, the government granted $1.4 billion in small-business awards and $167.5 million in technology transfer awards. It is not known, however, how many of those dollars were directed to nanotechnology-related projects.[55]

While experts generally agree that these grants have been helpful, some researchers say the funding falls short of the need.

"I've always felt that the United States should expand the [grant] programs and invest more in promising industrial sectors," says Richard Appelbaum, a professor at the Center for Nanotechnology in Society.

Other experts say the lack of federal support for commercialization has given rise to a growing number of public-private efforts that match academic researchers with investors and private-sector companies. "What states will do — what our state has done — is concentrate on local entrepreneurs and universities," says Rung of the Oregon Nanoscience and Microtechnologies Institute. Besides pairing academic researchers with private-sector investors, the institute provides early-stage funding and business counseling.

Similarly, the Center for Nanoscale Science and Technology at the University of Illinois, Urbana-Champaign, not only aims to promote interdisciplinary research in nanotechnologies but also to see research through to commercialization by fostering links with private-sector companies and investors.

"That was a paradigm shift for a land-grant institution like the University of Illinois to move from the traditional model of faculty being engaged in research and education to also being involved in promoting companies on the business side," says Irfan Ahmad, executive director of the nanoscale science center.

Rep. Michael M. Honda, D-Calif., has proposed another type of public-private partnership with his introduction in March of the Nanotechnology Advancement and New Opportunities Act. The bill, which has been referred to committee, would establish a Nanomanufacturing Investment Partnership to provide public funds for pre-commercial nanomanufacturing research and development projects, providing that private-sector companies commit $100 million to the effort.[56]

Safety Concerns

As researchers push nanotechnology research in new directions and proponents look for new ways to commercialize that research, some experts warn that the growing number of nanotechnology products already exceeds regulators' ability to monitor them.

"We always have plenty of work stacked up in the queue that we would like to get to sooner rather than later," says Charles Geraci, associate director at the National Institute for Occupational Safety and Health. The challenge, he says, is to monitor nanomaterials already in the marketplace while keeping an eye on current research. It's important to know "what the next great nanomaterial or variant of it is that will come down in a year or two from now," he says. "Some of these are moving into high-volume commercial applications very rapidly."

Participating experts at a workshop held by the Consumer Products Safety Commission and the NNI warned that the tools available to regulators cannot ensure the safety of products outside the laboratory.

"Assessment methods and tool needs have moved beyond those necessary for fundamental laboratory studies on pristine, as-manufactured" nanomaterials toward real-world conditions, according to the workshop's report.[57]

The report added, "The community cannot afford to evaluate exposures to [engineered nanomaterials] one material at time. It is necessary to develop approaches that rapidly estimate and predict exposures and enable timely decisions about the safe and sustainable design and use of nanomaterials in products."[58]

While regulators and researchers are figuring out how to determine the safety of nanoparticles, safety advocates argue that the government should take a more proactive approach by not allowing nano products on the market until their safety has been determined.

"Agencies, both in the United States and abroad, have not aggressively taken a precautionary approach," says Hanson of the Center for Food Safety. Instead, he says, the government tends to allow nanomaterials to be used until problems arise. "I'm active in my church," says Hanson. "I sometimes joke that being a scientist and being a person of faith, I understand the difference between a faith-based approach and a science-based approach. The administration has largely been using a faith-based approach instead of a science-based approach to regulation."

Patri, of the Nanotechnology Task Force, defends the FDA's approach to nanotechnology, noting the agency has long been dealing with nanomaterials. "FDA has approved hundreds of products containing nanomaterials that are in clinical use right now," he says. "We just didn't call them 'nano' before. We call them 'polymers,' we call them 'liposomes,' we call them 'emulsions.' But now because of their size and unique properties we are calling them 'nano.' So from that perspective, FDA has extensive experience and clinical experience in evaluating safety, effectiveness, and manufacturing quality attributes."

Roco, however, says that nanomaterials are different and that priorities and procedures need to be changed. "The first thing should be coordination to look for potential impacts," he says. "If you have an artificial virus, it cannot be analyzed by the FDA. They don't have the capacity. And this has to be anticipatory."

OUTLOOK

Faster Screening Tools

Experts agree the economic potential of emerging nanotechnologies is huge. One recent study predicts that the global market for nano-enabled products will reach nearly $4 trillion by 2018, up from $1.6 trillion in 2014.[59] However, researchers are unsure how soon methods can be developed for ensuring that those products are safe.

While scientists and engineers are announcing new nanomaterials and nanodevices almost daily, Nel and his team at the Center for Environmental Implications of Nanotechnology are racing to develop ways to more rapidly assess the risks of nanoparticles, nanocompounds and other nano products.

Building on information they have gathered on a wide array of known nanomaterials, the team is developing screening procedures to identify materials most likely to be problematic. "We're developing screening technologies so that instead of doing one material, we can do what we call 'high-throughput or high-content discovery,' " Nel says. "We're working to develop robotic and other high-throughput equipment to be able to do several materials at a time to compare them."

The National Institute for Occupational Safety and Health's Geraci says he is eagerly awaiting the results of Nel's work. "I think André hit it right," he says, "because he is developing what we hope will be an even faster, more efficient ways of testing some of these materials."

Also uncertain is the role nanomaterials and nanotechnologies might eventually play in the military and whether those materials and technologies could also present a threat to national security.

The Global Challenges Foundation, a Stockholm-based nonprofit advocacy group, lists nanotechnology as one of the 12 risks that threaten human civilization. Nanotechnology, it said in a 2015 report, "could lead to the easy construction of large arsenals of weapons by small groups," including terrorists. If nanotechnology allows those groups to extract and process uranium for the construction of nuclear weapons, the report's authors warn, the result could be apocalyptic. "Unlike the strategic stalemate of nuclear weapons, nanotechnology arms races could involve constantly evolving arsenals and become very unstable. These conflicts could lead to mass casualties and potentially to civilization collapse if the world's political and social systems were too damaged."[60]

Nevertheless, discussion about the role of nanomaterials in the military is muted, primarily because, at least for the near future, the U.S. military's nanotechnology goals are similar to those in the civilian world. Indeed, the only major nanotechnology project listed on the website of the Defense Advanced Research Projects Agency is the Atoms to Product project, in which the goal is to develop the technologies and processes required to assemble nanometer-scale pieces for products that are at least 1 millimeter scale in size.[61]

Likewise, the Army-funded Institute for Soldier Nanotechnology is focused on developing strong and light materials, as well as medical nanotechnologies. While these technologies will have battlefield implications — lighter, stronger armor and more effective treatment of wounds — they are not yet of sufficient scale to transform warfare in a fundamental way.

Still, some experts warn that when effective nanomanufacturing technologies are eventually mastered, warring nations and groups will have many more weapons at their disposal.

Oxford's Drexler, a strong advocate of nanomanufacturing, agrees. "Imagine a swarm of unmanned drones — built at low costs and in enormous numbers — pitted against conventional airpower," wrote Drexler. "Air defenses could be saturated if there were sufficient drones — they could simply absorb hits until the defender's munitions ran out."[62]

While Drexler is confident that atomically precise manufacturing will usher in an era of radical abundance, he warns that "unconstrained access to a range of APM-level technologies would place unpredictable capabilities in the hands of hostile nonstate actors, leading to unacceptable and unpredictable risks."[63]

NOTES

1. Peter Reuell, "Merging the biological, electronic Researchers grow cyborg tissues with embedded nanoelectronics," *Harvard Gazette*, Aug. 26, 2012, http://tinyurl.com/9rdhzvm.

2. Mihail C. Roco, "Rise of the Nano Machines," *Scientific American*, April 2013, 308, pp. 48-49, http://tinyurl.com/hf2cs9g.

3. K. Eric Drexler, *Radical Abundance: How a Revolution in Nanotechnology Will Change Civilization, Public Affairs* (2013), p. xi.

4. Marina E. Vance *et al.*, "Nanotechnology in the real world: Redeveloping the nanomaterial consumer products inventory," *Beilstein Journal of Nanotechnology*, Aug. 21, 2015, p. 1771, http://tinyurl.com/zjuokaa.

5. Julie Chaeo, "From the Lab to Your Digital Device, Quantum Dots Have Made Quantum Leaps," Lawrence Berkeley National Laboratory, Jan. 8, 2015, http://tinyurl.com/jdrkw2z.

6. *Ibid.*

7. Ian Kendrick, "Nanotechnology Update: U.S. Leads in Government Spending Amidst Increased Spending Across Asia," Lux Research Inc., December 2015, http://tinyurl.com/zkmqb6s.

8. Drexler, *op. cit.*, p. xii.

9. For background, see David Masci, "Nanotechnology," *CQ Researcher*, June 11, 2004, pp. 517-540.

10. "Supplement to the President's Budget for Fiscal Year 2017, The National Nanotechnology Initiative," Subcommittee on Nanoscale Science, Engineering, and Technology Committee on Technology National Science and Technology Council, March 2016, http://tinyurl.com/hdzryrs.

11. "Nanoparticles in Baby Formula: Tiny New Ingredients are a Big Concern," Friends of the Earth, May 2016, http://tinyurl.com/h55vl4g.

12. Holly Cave, "The Nanotechnology in Your Toothpaste," *The Guardian*, Jan. 13, 2014, http://tinyurl.com/orxox3w.

13. Charles B. Smarr *et al.*, "Biodegradable antigen-associated PLG nanoparticles tolerize Th2-mediated allergic airway inflammation pre- and postsensitization," Proceedings of the National Academy of Sciences, May 3, 2016, http://tinyurl.com/zqo5d76.

14. David Talbot, "Controlling Diabetes with a Skin Patch," *MIT Technology Review*, March 22, 2016, http://tinyurl.com/gwjg8jv.

15. Drexler, *op. cit.*, p. 238.

16. *Ibid.*

17. Kristian Sjøgren, "Scientists are cleaning our drinking water with nanoparticles," *ScienceNordia*, Aug. 26, 2014, http://tinyurl.com/jbre8f5.

18. Drexler, *op. cit.*, p. 233.

19. Jean-Michel Lourtioz *et al.*, eds., *Nanosciences and Nanotechnology: Evolution or Revolution?* (2016), p. 15.

20. Kevin Hattori, "Researchers find exposure to nanoparticles may threaten heart health," Phys. Org., Jan. 9, 2015, http://tinyurl.com/gvne3mm.

21. Sabiha Runa *et al.*, "TiO2Nanoparticles Alter the Expression of Peroxiredoxin Antioxidant Genes," *The Journal of Physical Chemistry*, April 21, 2016, http://tinyurl.com/jhscbcw.

22. "FDA's Approach to Regulation of Nanotechnology Products," Food and Drug Administration, Aug. 5, 2015, http://tinyurl.com/h9uxjdb.

23. "Disruptive Influences: Technology, politics and change in the financial sector," Cicero Group, January 2016, http://tinyurl.com/hhakfyj.

24. Noela Invernizzi, "Nanotechnology between the lab and the shop floor: what are the effects on labor?" *Journal of Nanoparticle Research*, March 7, 2011, http://tinyurl.com/jlqyym9.

25. John F. Sargent Jr., "Nanotechnology: A Policy Primer," Congressional Research Service, Dec. 16, 2013, http://tinyurl.com/zn8bb8k.

26. Guillaume Flament, "Closing the Gap: The Impact of Nanotechnologies on the Global Divide," Nanotechnology Industries Association, Nov. 26, 2013, p. iv, http://tinyurl.com/hr63rf4.

27. *Ibid.*, p. 25.

28. *Ibid.*, p. 4.

29. Ramesh Raliya and Pratim Biswas, "How nanotechnology can help us grow more food using less energy and water," *The Conversation*, May 25, 2016, http://tinyurl.com/jljd72z.

30. Kathy Pretz, "Purifying Water With Nanotech," IEEE The Institute, Dec. 6, 2013, http://tinyurl.com/gnkhddt.

31. "Nanomanufacturing: Emergence and Implications for U.S. Competitiveness, the Environment, and

Human Health," Government Accountability Office, Jan. 31, 2014, p. 16, http://tinyurl.com/zlm27zb.

32. "Plenty of Room at the Bottom," transcript of lecture presented by Richard P. Feynman to the American Physical Society in Pasadena, Dec. 29, 1959, http://tinyurl.com/zn5j58l.

33. *Ibid.*

34. *Ibid.*

35. *Ibid.*

36. "Engineers Build World's Smallest, Fastest Nanomotor," press release, University of Texas at Austin, May 21, 2014, http://tinyurl.com/zscwtqz.

37. "Scanning Tunneling Microscope," IBM, http://tinyurl.com/heauejr.

38. John H. Weaver, "Have buckminsterfullerenes (buckyballs) been put to any practical uses?" *Scientific American*, July 14, 1997, http://tinyurl.com/hk7el4g; "Nanotechnology in sports equipment: The game changer," *NanoWerk*, May 27, 2013, http://tinyurl.com/hf3zk3n.

39. Jennifer Chu, "Taking aircraft manufacturing out of the oven: New technique uses carbon nanotube film to directly heat and cure composite materials," *MIT News*, April 14, 2015, http://tinyurl.com/hrnq7o7.

40. K. Eric Drexler, "Molecular engineering: An approach to the development of general capabilities for molecular manipulation," Proceedings of the National Academy of Sciences, September 1981, p. 5275.

41. Drexler, Radical Abundance, *op. cit.*, p. 201; Bill Joy, "Why the Future Doesn't Need Us," *Wired*, April 1, 2000, http://tinyurl.com/jop7nr6.

42. "Small Wonders, Endless Frontiers: A Review of the National Nanotechnology Initiative," Committee for the Review of the National Nanotechnology Initiative, National Research Council, 2002, p. 11, http://tinyurl.com/hgez7cf.

43. "Public Law 108-153," U.S. Government Printing Office, Dec. 3, 2003, http://tinyurl.com/zaqonwu.

44. John F. Sargent Jr., "The National Nanotechnology Initiative: Overview, Reauthorization, and Appropriations Issues," Congressional Research Service, Dec. 16, 2014, p. 9.

45. Drexler, Radical Abundance, *op. cit.*, p. xiii.

46. Sargent, "The National Nanotechnology Initiative: Overview, Reauthorization, and Appropriations Issues," *op. cit.*, p. 6.

47. For transcripts of President Obama's 2013 and 2014 State of the Union speeches, see http://tinyurl.com/hal3xnj and http://tinyurl.com/jqvac5m.

48. "National Network for Manufacturing Innovation," Manufacturing.gov, http://tinyurl.com/hu5ny7g.

49. Peter Dockrill, "New 'invisible' nano-wires hide from the sun for increased solar cell efficiency," *ScienceAlert*, Nov. 27, 2015, http://tinyurl.com/jacyz43.

50. "Technology File," Toyota, http://tinyurl.com/zjdj8mx.

51. "Engineers Build World's Smallest, Fastest Nanomotor," *op. cit.*

52. John Markoff, "IBM Scientists Find New Way to Shrink Transistors," *The New York Times*, Oct. 1, 2015, http://tinyurl.com/gn7cnsm.

53. F. Donati *et al.*, "Magnetic remanence in single atoms," *Science*, April 15, 2016, http://tinyurl.com/zoocvrl.

54. Timothy M. Persons, "Nanomanufacturing and U.S. Competitiveness: Challenges and Opportunities," testimony before the House Subcommittee on Research and Technology, Committee on Science, Space, and Technology, May 20, 2014, http://tinyurl.com/nfyxqls.

55. "Annual Report, Small Business Innovation Research and Small Business Technology Transfer," U.S. Small Business Administration, Fiscal 2013, p. 5, http://tinyurl.com/jbeg223.

56. Nanotechnology Advancement and New Opportunities Act, Congress.gov, March 23, 2016, http://tinyurl.com/hz48q2o.

57. "Quantifying Exposure to Engineered Nanomaterials (QEEN) from Manufactured Products: Addressing Environmental, Health, and Safety Implications," Workshop Proceedings, Consumer Product Safety Commission in collaboration with the Nanotechnology Initiative, July 7-8, 2015, http://tinyurl.com/jmrkwkn.

58. *Ibid.*, p. 58.

59. Kendrick, *op. cit.*

60. Dennis Pamlin and Stuart Armstrong, "12 Risks that Threaten Human Civilization," Global Challenges Foundation, February 2015, p. 115, http://tinyurl.com/zfk88ff.

61. John Main, "Atoms to Product," Defense Advanced Research Projects Agency, http://tinyurl.com/hy4fhkp.

62. Drexler, Radical Abundance, *op. cit.*, p. 262.

63. *Ibid.*, p. 267.

BIBLIOGRAPHY

Selected Sources

Books

Drexler, Eric K., *Radical Abundance: How a Revolution in Nanotechnology Will Change Civilization*, Public Affairs, 2013.
An MIT-trained engineer who popularized the term "nanotechnology" says coming advances in the technology will revolutionize manufacturing and produce advances capable of healing humans and the environment.

Lourtioz, Jean-Michel, *et al.*, eds., *Nanosciences and Nanotechnology: Evolution or Revolution?* Springer, 2016.
This collection of essays by leading researchers covers the state of nanotechnologies in chemistry, electronics, medicine and materials science. It also covers the history of nanotechnology and the effects of the technology on the environment.

Articles

Cross, Tim, "After Moore's Law," *The Economist Technology Quarterly*, March 12, 2016, http://tinyurl.com/h8dkp3d.
A journalist explains how nanotechnology is helping scientists create smaller transistors and make more powerful computer processors.

Markillie, Paul, "New Materials for Manufacturing," *The Economist Technology Quarterly*, Dec. 5, 2015, http://tinyurl.com/gmb2tor.
A journalist surveys the rapidly expanding use of nanomaterials in a wide array of products.

Prodromakis, Themis, "Nanotechnology is changing everything from medicine to self-healing buildings," *The Independent*, March 23, 2016, http://tinyurl.com/h6caa3j.
The article offers a roundup of the latest advances in nanotechnology research.

Raliya, Ramesh, and Pratim Biswas, "How nanotechnology can help us grow more food using less energy and water," *The Conversation*, May 25, 2016, http://tinyurl.com/jyuykp3.
Two research scientists describe their research using nanoparticles to increase the yield of food crops.

Scheufele, Dietram A., and Bruce V. Lewenstein, "The Public and Nanotechnology: How Citizens Make Sense of Emerging Technologies," *Journal of Nanoparticle Research*, December 2005, http://tinyurl.com/zatkju5.
Two professors of science communication, at the University of Wisconsin, Madison (Scheufele) and Cornell University (Lewenstein), report findings from their national telephone survey on levels of knowledge about and attitudes toward nanotechnology that demonstrate how people make decisions about emerging technologies.

Reports and Studies

"Global Challenges: 12 risks that threaten human civilisation," Global Challenges Foundation, February 2015, http://tinyurl.com/nwrn2fs.
This joint report by the Global Challenges Foundation, which studies the risks facing humanity, and the Oxford Martin School, a research center at Oxford University in Great Britain, lists nanotechnology as one of the 12 major threats to civilization, citing the economic and military disruptions it may cause.

"Nanomanufacturing: Emergence and Implications for U.S. Competitiveness, the Environment, and Human Health," Government Accountability Office, January 2014, http://tinyurl.com/zlm27zb.
The investigative arm of Congress presents the conclusions of a forum of 28 experts from government, academia and the private sector regarding nanomanufacturing and its risks.

"National Nanotechnology Initiative Strategic Plan," National Science and Technology Council Committee on Technology, Subcommittee on Nanoscale Science, Engineering and Technology, February 2014, http://tinyurl.com/h7nw2a8.

The group evaluates the National Nanotechnology Initiative (NNI), a federal program that coordinates nanotechnology research, and discusses the growing focus on environmental health and safety issues.

Sargent Jr., John F., "Nanotechnology: A Policy Primer," Congressional Research Service, Dec. 16, 2013, http://tinyurl.com/zv2dpaw.
An analyst at Congress' research division provides a concise account of the legislative and funding history of the National Nanotechnology Initiative from its founding in 2003. The author also discusses emerging safety issues.

"Supplement to the President's Budget for Fiscal Year 2017: The National Nanotechnology Institute," **Subcommittee on Nanoscale Science, Engineering, and Technology Committee on Technology, National Science and Technology Council, March 2016, http://tinyurl.com/jq2ofdx.**
The NNI's budget request also details progress toward the organization's goals and objectives.

"Tiny Ingredients, Big Risks: Nanomaterials Rapidly Entering Food and Farming," Friends of the Earth, May 2014, http://tinyurl.com/n9ahwup.
An environmental advocacy organization says nanoparticles already are in an array of common foods and that many of these particles are potentially harmful to human health.

For More Information

Center for Nanotechnology in Society, Arizona State University, Tempe, AZ 85281; 480-965-2100; https://cns.asu.edu/. Interdisciplinary academic research program funded partly by the National Science Foundation.

Center for Nanotechnology in Society, University of California, Santa Barbara, CA 93106-2150; 805-893-7743; www.cns.ucsb.edu/. Interdisciplinary academic research program funded partly by the National Science Foundation and the National Nanotechnology Initiative.

Foresight Institute, Box 61058, Palo Alto, CA 94306; 260-338-8873; www.foresight.org/. Think tank and public interest organization that focuses on future transformative technologies.

Friends of the Earth, 1101 15th St., N.W., 11th Floor, Washington, DC 20005; 202-783-7400; www.foe.org/. Environmental advocacy and research organization that examines the health effects of nanotechnology.

NanoBusiness Commercialization Association, 4 Research Dr., Suite 402, Shelton, CT 06484; 203-733-1949; https://www.nanobca.org/. Industry organization advocating for companies involved in nanotechnology research and development, manufacturing and commercialization.

National Institute for Occupational Safety and Health, 1600 Clifton Rd., Atlanta, GA 30329-4027; 800-232-4636; www.cdc.gov/niosh. Research arm of the Occupational Safety and Health Administration that studies the health and safety effects of, among other things, nanoparticles.

National Nanotechnology Initiative, 4201 Wilson Blvd., Stafford II Room 405, Arlington, VA 22230; 703-292-8626; www.nano.gov. Federal interagency organization coordinating efforts in nanotechnology research.

13

Solar Energy Controversies

Kevin Begos

Solar advocates in Los Angeles on Oct. 21, 2015, challenge a proposal by Southern California Edison, the region's major power supplier, to limit the ability of solar users to sell excess solar energy back to the power grid. Known as net metering, the issue is controversial nationwide.

AFP/Getty Images/Frederic J. Brown

From *CQ Researcher*, April 29, 2016

Public utility commission meetings usually attract small audiences — and yawns — but a February [2016] meeting of Nevada's commission was different.

Several hundred demonstrators, carrying signs and pushing wheelbarrows containing more than 30,000 signatures from backers of their cause, protested a move by the commission to gradually increase a monthly surcharge imposed on rooftop-solar energy users from $12.75 to $38.51 and also decrease the amount they get paid for sending excess power back to NV Energy, the state's largest utility.[1]

In its defense, the commission said solar customers were not paying their fair share to maintain the electric grid — the vast system of poles, transformers, wires and other equipment used to supply power to homes, businesses and factories. Solar advocates disagreed, arguing that the state and the utility had promised one set of rates, then retroactively changed the deal.

"Now I feel I'm being penalized for trying to do something better for the environment," says Elizabeth Moore-Barton, a 38-year-old Las Vegas real estate agent who installed solar panels on her family's 3,200-square-foot house in early 2014.

The fracas in Nevada is a sign of the financial stakes — and high emotions — swirling around the fast-growing field of solar energy.

Advocates of renewable energy view solar power as a way to protect the environment by reducing the use of fossil fuels and to save money on electric bills. But many utilities see solar energy as a threat because the ability of homeowners and businesses to

California, New England Lead in Solar Potential

If all suitable rooftops in California had solar systems, they would generate an amount of electricity equal to nearly three-fourths of the electric power sold by utilities in the state in 2013. Rooftop systems in Florida, Michigan and six Northeastern states could offset at least 45 percent of those states' electricity use. Some states with relatively low sun exposure, such as Maine and Vermont, have greater potential than sunny states to offset utility sales of electricity because households in low-sun states tend to consume less utility-generated electricity.

Potential Electricity Generated by Rooftop Solar as a Percentage of 2013 Utility Electricity Sales, by State*

* Excludes Alaska and Hawaii

Source: Pieter Gagnon et al., "Rooftop Solar Photovoltaic Technical Potential in the United States: A Detailed Assessment," National Renewable Energy Laboratory, January 2016, pp. 34-36, http://tinyurl.com/grrs7h3

Potential Amount of Electricity From Rooftop Solar
● More than 65 percent
● 55.1 to 65 percent
○ 45.1 to 55 percent
● 35.1 to 45 percent
● 25.1 to 35 percent
◐ Less than 25 percent

Federal subsidies are boosting solar energy's attractiveness to consumers. In December 2015, Congress extended solar tax credits allowing individuals and businesses to deduct 30 percent of the cost of a solar system from their federal tax bill. The cost of solar panels has declined significantly in recent years — in the 1960s, a panel cost about $100 per watt; in 2016, the price was 57 cents. As prices have dropped, a growing number of environmentally minded consumers have turned to solar because of concerns over climate change and pollution from fossil fuels.[2]

Meanwhile, more companies are using solar energy to save money and to appear environmentally friendly to consumers, according to a 2015 survey by Deloitte Resources, a global consulting firm. The survey found that 39 percent of businesses are installing electricity generation such as solar panels, and that "desire to increase the use of renewables — particularly solar — continues to trend upward among consumers: 64 percent rank 'increasing the use of solar power' among the top three energy-related issues most important to them, up from 58 percent in 2014 and 50 percent in 2013." Deloitte also found that 79 percent of businesses view reducing electricity costs "as essential to staying competitive from an image perspective."[3]

Solar energy use in the United States has more than tripled since 2010, according to the California energy consulting firm GTM Research, and in 2015 the number of residential and commercial solar installations rose by more than 19 percent. Nationwide, some 45,000 businesses and more than 900,000 homes are using solar panels, still a small percentage of the 125 million households in the United States.[4]

Most of those installations are in the sunbaked Southwest, especially California. The U.S. Energy Information Administration (EIA) said that in 2014

generate their own solar power will cut into utility companies' revenue and strain their ability to maintain the electrical grid and build new power plants.

Still, many utilities, businesses, and government agencies are building solar projects or investing in them. Examples include Duke Energy, the nation's largest electric power holding company, the Department of Defense and utilities in Florida, Massachusetts and New Jersey.

"To a certain degree every state is having to worry about" how to help the solar industry without harming the utilities, says Michael Dworkin, director of the Institute for Energy and the Environment at Vermont Law School in South Royalton. Solar is "clearly going from being a fringe [approach] to being a meaningful element" of the power supply, although the solar sector remains tiny compared with oil, coal and natural gas.

California, which requires that 15 percent of roof space on new structures under 10 stories to be solar-ready by being free of or shade and other obstructions, became the first state to generate more than 5 percent of its electricity from solar. And San Francisco's Board of Supervisors passed an ordinance in late April requiring the installation of solar panels on all new residential and commercial buildings built in the city, beginning Jan. 1, 2017.[5]

As solar grows, some electric-industry officials are warning that it could damage the financial underpinnings of the utilities. Under the traditional model, a public commission grants a monopoly to a utility to provide electricity to a service area. In return for that monopoly, the utility is expected to provide reliable, low-cost power to the region. It does so by building power plants that use a generator, often a steam turbine, to create electricity. The steam powering the turbine, in turn, is created by burning coal, oil or natural gas. Utilities also generate or buy power from nuclear plants and hydroelectric dams.

The U.S. electric grid includes about 3,200 utilities, 5,800 power plants and more than 2.7 million miles of power lines, according to Bloomberg.[6] The grid is expensive to build and maintain, and some in the industry argue that monopoly power is essential to maintaining the financial health of utilities and the viability of the electric grid.

Solar energy, they say, undercuts this monopoly because homeowners and businesses are generating their own electricity and thus lowering the utilities' revenues. Yet the demands on the grid remain great because solar users need the grid as a backup supplier or as a place to sell their excess electricity. As a result, supposedly independent solar energy users still need the utilities, said David K. Owens, executive vice president of the Edison Electric Institute, a Washington, D.C.-based utility trade group. And this means, he said, they should have to pay their fair share of the costs of maintaining that grid.[7]

Six New York utilities and three solar companies are seeking a compromise. In late April the two sides proposed a new payment model that would preserve credits for rooftop solar systems while imposing fees on larger solar projects beginning in 2020. In a joint statement, Lyndon Rive, the CEO of SolarCity, the nation's largest solar company, praised the utilities and the compromise.[8]

Still, solar remains a small part of the energy sector. Solar power provided less than 1 percent of the nation's electricity in 2015, while wind power accounted for about 5 percent. By contrast, coal and natural gas each powered 33 percent of nationwide electricity generation, nuclear 20 percent and hydropower 6 percent. All other renewables — including biomass, waste wood and other agricultural products — produced 7 percent.[9]

Two related problems are challenging for the solar industry. Solar power is "intermittent," with daily output spiking when the sun is at its strongest and dropping when at its weakest. Solar energy is generally more feasible in sunny regions such as the Southwest than in cloudy ones such as the Northwest.[10] The vagaries of the weather and the fact that solar systems don't store electricity at night and during cloudy periods mean the industry needs a strong, low-cost storage battery. Although costs have dropped, batteries remain relatively expensive and inefficient, and researchers have achieved no breakthrough comparable to solar panels.

Nonetheless, the allure of the sun as an energy source captivates the public, environmentalists, the business community and many in the energy sector. A 2015 Gallup Poll found that 79 percent of Americans said there should be more emphasis on solar power — the highest number for any form of energy — compared with 28 percent who said the emphasis should be on coal.[11] The Sierra Club and other environmental groups have long backed solar, but now some conservatives, businesspeople and large corporations such as Walmart and major automakers do, too.

"The big picture is that the world and the nation are moving towards a cleaner air portfolio," says Sean Gallagher, who works on state issues for the Solar Energy Industries Association, a trade group in Washington, D.C. "And we're moving that way because we have to, for climate change, but we're also moving that way because clean energy has lots of local benefits." Gallagher says, for example, that jobs installing solar on American roofs or building solar farms can't be outsourced overseas.

The Solar Foundation, an advocacy group in Washington with ties to the industry, estimates that some 209,000 people work in various parts of the industry, up from 100,000 in 2011.[12] And solar will add about 30,000 jobs this year, according to *The Wall Street Journal*, with some laid-off oil workers moving to the solar sector.[13]

Fossil Fuels Provide Most Electricity

Solar energy generated less than 1 percent of U.S. electricity in 2015, while coal and natural gas each provided about a third and nuclear power a fifth. Some experts say solar's share could grow to more than 15 percent in the next 20 years as fossil-fuel generation declines.

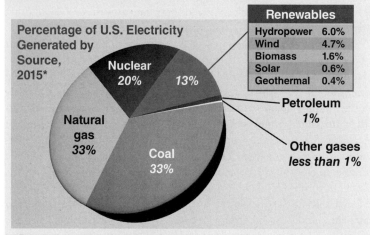

Percentage of U.S. Electricity Generated by Source, 2015*

- Nuclear 20%
- Natural gas 33%
- Coal 33%
- Petroleum 1%
- Other gases less than 1%

Renewables	
Hydropower	6.0%
Wind	4.7%
Biomass	1.6%
Solar	0.6%
Geothermal	0.4%

* Percentages based on preliminary data and do not add to 100 due to rounding.

Source: "What is U.S. electricity generation by energy source?" U.S. Energy Information Administration, updated April 1, 2016, http://tinyurl.com/hf93dfl

Solar is also helping recover some of the lost jobs in the coal industry, where employment is falling because of mechanization and dropping demand for coal. President Obama, in his January 2016 State of the Union message, said, "On rooftops from Arizona to New York, solar is saving Americans tens of millions of dollars a year on their energy bills, and employs more Americans than coal — in jobs that pay better than average."[14]

As solar power continues to expand, here are some of the issues that individuals, utilities, politicians and the courts are debating:

Can solar replace the traditional electric grid?

The electric utility industry and outside experts have begun seriously to discuss a once-remote possibility: In coming decades many people could choose to go "off the grid" by generating and storing their own power.

"[T]here is a perception that customers will always need to remain on the grid," said "Disruptive Challenges," a 2013 report prepared for the Edison Electric Institute. But continued technological advances "could allow customers to be electric grid independent." The report noted that few imagined that cellphones would so quickly replace landlines around much of the nation.[15]

The Rocky Mountain Institute, a Colorado think tank that focuses on the efficient use of resources, examined going-off-the-grid possibilities in 2014 and found even "a growing number of early adopters [of solar power] could trigger" a so-called utility death spiral.

"But what happens when solar and battery technologies are brought together?" the institute asked. "Together they can make the electric grid optional for many customers — without compromising reliability and increasingly at prices cheaper than utility retail electricity."[16]

In that scenario, rapidly declining solar and battery costs would lure customers away from utilities, which then must raise rates to their remaining customers to compensate for lost revenue, resulting in even more defections. The Rocky Mountain report said the possibility of such a scenario is "coming sooner than many had anticipated." As evidence, it said battery costs were about $2,000 per kilowatt hour of storage in 2009, but had fallen to about $750 by 2013.[17]

Other experts say massive utility defections are unlikely.

"There will be thousands in states and tens of thousands nationally. But I don't think there will be millions and tens of millions," says Dworkin of the Institute for Energy and the Environment. He says staying connected to the grid is "a relatively cheap insurance policy" for many Americans.

The average family spends about $14,000 per year on motor vehicles, and about the same on food and clothing, according to Dworkin. "And what do they spend for electricity? They spend $1,400" per year, he says, so the regular grid remains a bargain.

A leading proponent of solar power says utilities should adapt to solar's rise instead of resisting it. "If the utilities were willing to abandon their current business model, they could be the ones who build" the grid that serves rooftop-solar owners, says Bill McKibben, co-founder of the environmental group 350.org, which is pushing for an end to fossil fuel use. In other words, utilities could integrate solar and other renewables in a way that would benefit everybody, he says. "The alternative is to hold off the new technologies as long as possible, which is what they're mostly trying. . . . This is an unwise strategy."

"Since we have a grid, it makes sense to use it as the main storage device. But if the utilities won't adapt to the era of sun and wind, or if they insist on doing it only on their terms," many people will go off-grid, McKibben says.

But utility executes say rooftop-solar owners will still need the electric grid as a backup or as a place to put their excess electricity.

When solar units generate "more power than they need, they need the electrical grid to distribute the excess power" through "net metering," in which a solar customer sells excess power back to the grid, Jonathan Weisgall, a vice president for Berkshire Hathaway Energy, a holding company owned by Berkshire Hathaway of Omaha, Neb., told a congressional committee in 2015. "And when their . . . generation systems aren't generating power — for example with a rooftop solar system, when the sun sets — they will still rely on the utility to provide them with power services."[18]

John Farrell, an energy expert at the Institute for Local Self-Reliance, a think tank in Minneapolis that supports community environmental projects, says there are two ways to look at the grid's future. "One is, it's going to become so easy" to leave it, says Farrell, who adds that even busy families will go off-grid if they can save money by doing so. But Farrell says that from another angle the grid still has value. "Why have a battery [to store power generated by a solar system] in your garage — in every garage — when you can have a big battery in a substation? There are economies of scale in power generation, even with solar," he says.

Rooftop solar may be a small part of total electricity generation now, but some studies show tremendous growth potential, especially in sunny states. A 2016 study by the National Renewable Energy Laboratory, the federal government's primary research facility for renewable energy, nearly doubled previous estimates of the rooftop potential for electricity generation in the United States, albeit with wide variations among states. California could generate 74 percent of the electricity sold by the state's utilities in 2013, the report said. Washington state has among the lowest potential, according to the report, but could still generate 27 percent of the power that was generated in that state in 2013.[19]

Should utilities impose surcharges on solar owners to support the power grid?

Utilities around the nation are seeking or considering new surcharges for owners of rooftop solar systems, arguing that those customers aren't paying their fair share of costs to maintain the electric grid. Solar owners are fighting back, arguing such surcharges are unfair.

"Historically, electric rates have been based on the actual costs incurred by utilities that are then fairly allocated to customers," the Edison Electric Institute said in 2014 testimony to the Energy Department. "Customers should expect to pay for the costs of the generation, transmission and distribution services they receive from their utility."[20]

The institute said that because rooftop solar owners "use the grid in more complex ways than other customers, they are contributing to additional costs that utilities will incur." For example, most customers only receive electricity from a utility. But individual solar owners also send electricity back to a utility, which then has to monitor every unit it receives and mix it into the broader power supply.

In a nationwide survey, the North Carolina Clean Energy Technology Center found 21 instances in 13 states in which utilities proposed higher surcharges on solar power or other forms of renewable energy, but Nevada was alone in enacting major changes.[21]

Brad Klein, a lawyer with the Chicago-based Environmental Law & Policy Center, says that in most cases, state regulators or courts have limited or rejected utility requests for new fees on solar owners. "Just this spring, a state court in Wisconsin reversed the [state utility] commission's decision about solar fees," Klein says. "They found that the commission had no evidence that supports the need for this kind of fee."

Utilities aren't always opposed to solar power or renewable energy. Weisgall told the U.S. Senate

Getty Images/Gamma-Rapho/Eric Vandeville

Getty Images/Bloomberg/Buddhika Weerasinghe

Solar around the World

Solar panels cover the football-field-size roof of the Vatican's Paul VI audience hall; the Basilica of Saint Peter rises in the background. The more than 1,000 photovoltaic panels were installed in 2008 to generate electricity for all heating, cooling and lighting of the huge building (top). Solar panels floating on a reservoir in Kasai, Hyogo Prefecture, Japan, generate 2.3 megawatts (bottom). Many countries, notably Germany and China, see solar power not just as a promising idea but also as a necessity to limit pollution and global warming.

committee in 2015 that Berkshire Hathaway Energy has invested more than $8 billion in recent years for "three very large utility-scale solar projects as well as wind projects."[22]

Weisgall also said that "although the cost of solar power has been declining steadily," utility-size solar makes more economic sense than rooftop solar because it is more cost effective to build one large plant that can supply the same amount of electricity as 1,000 smaller units.

A Massachusetts Institute of Technology report found another problem with smaller solar systems: Current federal subsidies favor residential solar over utility-sized solar, promoting "an inherent inefficiency" in the renewable energy sector.[23] That's because the tax breaks for residential and utility projects are based on installation and construction costs. So a huge solar project, the report said, isn't rewarded for its efficiency of scale, nor are individuals penalized for their smallness and relative inefficiency.

Utilities aren't used to buying back electricity from customers, which is a key issue, says Farrell. Discussions of how to value an individual's rooftop solar energy "gets into the weeds of a lot of really complicated stuff," he says. "The key is for the utility to stop talking just about what costs it has, based on a system that was built for the 20th century."

The debate over solar fees also brings up tricky questions of individual freedom, because public utilities are designed to operate as monopolies. When a Montana utility withdrew a proposal in 2015 to charge solar users extra fees, local ranchers Jean and Floyd Dahlman said, "The people won here today." They argued in their suit against the utility that fees on customers who generate their own power are "unjustified and unnecessary. Individuals have the right to invest in small-scale wind or solar on their property without needless barriers."[24]

The Dahlmans had help in the legal battle from the Alliance for Solar Choice, an advocacy group founded by large rooftop-solar companies that is active in more than 20 states. The group argues that most electric utilities have the power to "dictate prices and limit customer choice."

Monopolistic utilities "in the U.S. are trying to stop the wave of innovation that is rooftop solar" by lobbying for surcharges that make solar less attractive to potential customers, the alliance said.[25] Other observers say many campaigns seeking extra fees on rooftop-solar owners are supported by members of the fossil fuel industry and the American Legislative Exchange Council, a conservative group in Arlington, Va., that accuses solar homeowners of being "freeriders."[26]

For the council, which drafts legislation for conservative lawmakers across the country, the surcharges are a matter of fairness. In a 2014 statement, the council said residential solar owners are often paid the full retail market rate for the excess energy they generate, yet that rate is calculated to include "the fixed costs of the poles, wires, meters" and other infrastructure belonging to utilities. The council said that means the solar owners "effectively avoid paying the grid costs, and these costs for maintaining the grid then are shifted to those customers without rooftop solar."

The council urged state policymakers to impose a surtax on people who generate their own power, and argued that energy policies should "require that everyone who uses the grid helps pay to maintain it."[27]

Should utilities be allowed to charge customers who leave the grid?

For decades the term "going off the grid" has been associated with outdoor enthusiasts or environmentalists

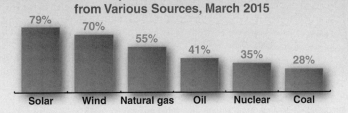

Most Favor Bigger Push on Solar

Almost 80 percent of American adults say the United States should put more emphasis on solar energy production, nearly double the share who want more emphasis on oil. Seventy percent favor more emphasis on wind power.

Percentage of U.S. Adults Who Say the United States Should Put More Emphasis on Domestic Energy Production from Various Sources, March 2015

Solar	Wind	Natural gas	Oil	Nuclear	Coal
79%	70%	55%	41%	35%	28%

Source: Rebecca Riffkin, "U.S. Support for Nuclear Energy at 51%," Gallup, March 30, 2015, http://tinyurl.com/hfdo86a

who seek a natural, self-reliant way of life. Then last year three Las Vegas casinos explored the option, partly in hopes of saving money by installing low-cost solar power. Now the proposed exit from the grid has turned into a legal battle that is spreading as big businesses seek to generate or buy their own power.

MGM Resorts International, Las Vegas Sands and Wynn Las Vegas filed applications with the Nevada Public Utilities Commission to seek their own sources of power. The commission ruled over the summer that they could leave the grid — if they paid a combined exit fee of about $128 million to NV Energy.[28] The exit fees are necessary, the commission said, to make up for the loss of 7 percent of the utility's revenue.

Utilities are required by law to provide long-term forecasts of electricity production and costs. When a major customer leaves the grid, the investments made to meet the power needs under those forecasts are upset, utilities say, and exit fees are needed to offset revenue losses that would have gone toward new power plants and maintenance.[29]

The casino decision came a few months after the utility commission denied an exit request by Switch Communications, a data company. "I really think that given what has happened in the system in the last 15 years, we have to find a better way to make sure that folks who exit aren't harming remaining customers," said Alaina Burtenshaw, the commission chairwoman.[30]

Getty Images/Ethan Miller

Nellis Air Force Base in Las Vegas has a new 102-acre, 15-megawatt solar generating station, dedicated on Feb. 16, 2016. When coupled with another solar array completed in 2007, the new solar facility gives Nellis the largest solar photovoltaic system in the Department of Defense.

The casinos and the tech company based their requests on a rarely used 2001 Nevada law that allows companies to exit the power grid, although the law was unclear on how much of an exit fee they should pay.[31]

The desire to leave the grid has financial and strategic roots, said Wynn Las Vegas President Matthew Maddox. "Exiting bundled service will allow us to continue to invest in our resort and pay employees a living wage, while granting the company the freedom to determine our long-term energy strategy," Maddox said in testimony to the utility commission. He said Wynn is "now contemplating the use of solar energy" and that the exit "will not result in increased costs to either remaining customers or the utility."[32]

The utility commission disagreed and said Wynn would have to pay $15.7 million to leave NV Energy. In January Wynn sued, alleging that the commission "has simply made up rules as it goes along so as to discourage any applicants from exiting bundled retail service."[33]

Switch eventually reached an agreement with NV Energy to pay a premium rate in order to have all its electric needs supplied by renewable energy, and as of late April neither MGM Resorts nor Las Vegas Sands had filed lawsuits. But the battle isn't over. In February a group called Nevadans for Affordable Clean Energy Choices filed a proposed state constitutional amendment

that would let customers choose where to get electricity, without paying exit fees.[34]

Tesla Motors, the electric-car maker, and Switch are among the backers of the ballot initiative. Elon Musk, chairman and CEO Tesla, said "solar energy is the cheapest energy today in the state of Nevada and 'Energy Choice' will enable Tesla and all Nevadans to choose solar."[35]

NV Energy CEO Paul Caudill said the petition didn't surprise him "in light of the dramatic changes in the Western energy markets, including lower natural gas and power prices." He said because of the complexity of the issue, his company is "in no position right now to take a position," but added that NV Energy is open to holding discussions with the various stakeholders.[36]

Farrell of the Institute for Local Self-Reliance says, "I think this [casino challenge] is going to be a landmark case, but there are going to be more of them." These legal challenges, he says, will force utilities to justify how they supply energy and the money they spend on power plants, "given all the different options that it has, and its customers have."

Gallagher of the Solar Energy Industries Association notes that the relationship between the utilities and solar users doesn't have to be adversarial and that the two could find a way to co-exist. He says his association is seeking ways for "the solar industry to work better with utilities."

One idea gaining currency, according to the Rocky Mountain Institute, is community solar installations, where local organizations, utilities and others band together to build a utility-size solar plant. Participants share the costs of constructing the installation, and the benefits. By pooling resources, participants can lower startup costs by as much as 40 percent, the institute said. In addition, the community solar project can "rent" solar-generated power to members without solar-suitable roofs, thus drawing in more customers.[37]

BACKGROUND
Sun Gods

Humans have recognized and puzzled over the sun's power since the dawn of civilization. Sumerians, Egyptians and Romans believed sun gods could deliver wise judgments and bring prosperity, as shown in a 4,000-year-old hymn to Utu, the Sumerian sun god.[38]

Practical applications followed soon after the myths. Around 500 B.C. the Chinese philosopher Confucius wrote that young men "attached a bronze burning mirror" to their belt when dressing for the day. It was used to concentrate the sun's light and kindle fires.[39]

The Greeks and Romans used similar mirrors and also incorporated passive solar heating into their architecture. They also recounted possibly mythical stories about large mirrors used in warfare. The Roman historian Dio Cassius claimed that Archimedes, the path-breaking Greek scientist and mathematician, had helped destroy an invading fleet of Roman ships around 212 B.C.: "For by tilting a kind of mirror toward the sun he concentrated the sun's beam upon it; and owing to the thickness and smoothness of the mirror he ignited the air from this beam and kindled a great flame, the whole of which he directed upon the ships that lay at anchor in the path of the fire, until he consumed them all."[40]

The modern era of solar power began in 1839. French scientist Alexandre-Edmond Becquerel created a rudimentary solar cell and observed that light generated electricity.[41] But Becquerel and other 19th-century scientists still didn't understand why such a process was possible. Many researchers returned to the old idea of using mirrors to concentrate the sun's power, but this time to generate steam and run engines. Augustin Mouchot, another French scientist, was convinced that the world would eventually run out of coal, and he created various solar engines throughout the 1860s and '70s. Mouchot published a book on solar heat and its industrial applications in 1869.[42]

In the United States John Ericsson, who during the Civil War designed the Union ironclad ship *Monitor*, developed a "sun engine" in the early 1870s and published numerous articles about the device, which also generated steam. Then in 1883 Charles Fritts made the first solar power cells, out of selenium (a crystalline nonmetal with semiconducting properties), but they converted less than 1 percent of the sun's power into electricity.[43] That was no competition for fossil fuels and the new boom in oil wells that began in 1859 in western Pennsylvania.

A theoretical turning point came in 1905. Albert Einstein explained the science behind what he called photovoltaics, and he later won the Nobel Prize for the discovery. Decades later NASA succinctly explained the

Solar Impulse 2, a solar-powered plane piloted by Swiss adventurer Bertrand Piccard, soars over the Golden Gate Bridge as it arrives in San Francisco on April 23, 2016, after a three-day, more than 2,000-mile flight from Hawaii. The plane was expected to reach New York in June as it continues on its around-the-world journey. San Francisco made its own headlines in late April when it required the installation of solar panels on all new residential and commercial buildings in the city beginning in 2017.

Getty Images/Jean Revillard

revolutionary insight: "Photovoltaics is the direct conversion of light into electricity at the atomic level. Some materials exhibit a property known as the photoelectric effect that causes them to absorb photons of light and release electrons. When these free electrons are captured, an electric current results that can be used as electricity."[44]

After World War I several prominent scientists in the United States, Germany and elsewhere did extensive research, seeking practical applications for solar energy. In a 1929 feature for *Popular Science Monthly*, Robert H. Goddard, now remembered as the father of the U.S. rocket program, said "time and money are being spent in huge quantities to dig coal from mines, to pump oil from wells, and to harness streams for power, when more than a hundred thousand times as much power is constantly being delivered free right on the Earth's surface."[45] Charles Greeley Abbot, an astrophysicist and secretary of the Smithsonian Institution from 1928 to 1944, obtained numerous patents for solar cookers, boilers and engines.[46]

A 1931 *New York Times* headline proclaimed that "Use of Solar Energy Is Near a Solution." The article said, "The new photocell developments promise an entirely new method of power production."[47]

CHRONOLOGY

1839-1905 *Scientists discover photovoltaics and later explain how it works.*

1839 French scientist Alexandre-Edmond Becquerel discovers photovoltaics, the conversion of sunlight into electricity.

1905 Albert Einstein explains how a current flows through metal when it is exposed to sunlight. He wins the Nobel Prize for this work.

1954-1973 *Use of solar power gathers momentum.*

1954 Scientists at Bell Labs make the first solar panels.

1955 Western Electric begins to sell solar-powered products, such as a dollar bill changer.

1958 Satellites begin to use solar cells.

1963 Solar energy is used to power a Japanese lighthouse.

1973-1990 *After the Arab oil embargo, interest in solar power grows, then fades, as world oil prices plummet in early 1980s.*

1973 Members of the Organization of Petroleum Exporting Countries (OPEC) impose an embargo against the United States, drawing attention to the need for alternative energy.

1979 President Jimmy Carter installs solar panels on the White House.

1983 Six-megawatt solar substation in California supplies power to the grid.

1986 President Ronald Reagan removes solar panels from the White House.

1991-2009 *Solar research grows again as foreign countries begin large-scale solar installations.*

1991 President George H. W. Bush expands the federal Solar Energy Research Institute, renamed the National Renewable Energy Laboratory.

1994 The National Renewable Energy Laboratory develops a solar cell that exceeds 30 percent efficiency.

2000 Germany's Renewable Energies Sources Act takes effect; backers seek a long-term transition from fossil fuels.

2003 Tesla Motors is founded by Silicon Valley investors with a goal of making electric vehicles commercially successful. Elon Musk joins the company in 2004.

2004 Republican California Gov. Arnold Schwarzenegger calls for the state to have 1 million solar systems by 2017.

2005 Congress approves a 30 percent investment tax credit for solar systems.

2006 California Public Utilities Commission approves a $2 billion program to promote solar power.

2010-Present *Solar panel costs fall sharply, leading to a worldwide increase in solar use.*

2010 Chinese factories start reducing solar panel manufacturing costs. That leads to increased sales but also trade lawsuits and numerous solar-company bankruptcies in the United States and Europe, including the U.S. solar firm Solyndra.

2011 Germany accelerates its transition to renewable power after the Fukushima nuclear disaster in Japan in which a tsunami caused equipment failures that resulted in the release of radioactivity.

2014 Germany produces 50 percent of its electricity from solar on one day, but the ongoing transition to clean energy causes serious financial problems for some established utilities.

2015 Congress and the Obama administration extend solar tax credits for five years.

2016 Tesla Motors shocks industry experts by receiving 325,000 advance orders for a new electric car in the first seven days after it is announced.

But the widespread availability of cheap fossil fuels tempered enthusiasm for solar as a major fuel source. So did the rise of atomic energy following Einstein's discovery of the theory of relativity, which helped lay the foundation for modern physics. After World War II, scientists and governments around the world spent vast amounts of time and money building atomic bombs and nuclear reactors, pushing solar research into the background.

Amory Lovins, an American physicist and authority on energy at the Rocky Mountain Institute, later saw a pattern. "Diverse societies around the world have repeatedly invented and refined solar energy, only to have it scuttled, even forgotten, as discoveries of apparently cheap new fuels — coal, oil, gas, nuclear — distracted customers, diverted providers, and befuddled policy makers."[48]

Modern Solar Power

In the early 1950s researchers at Bell Labs in New Jersey made a breakthrough that laid the foundation for today's boom in solar power. The scientists discovered that receptor cells made of silicon (the main element in sand) were far more efficient in converting sunlight into electricity than previously used materials, and the addition of tiny concentrations of gallium to the cell surface further improved efficiency. When Bell held a demonstration of the new solar device in April 1954, *The New York Times* put the news on its front page.

"Vast Power of the Sun Is Trapped By Battery Using Sand Ingredient," the headline read, and the story said the discovery "may mark the beginning of a new era, leading eventually to the realization of one of mankind's most cherished dreams — the harnessing of the almost limitless energy of the sun for the uses of civilization."[49]

Earlier solar cells had converted about one-half of 1 percent of the sun's power into electricity. The Bell scientists significantly improved that and determined that silicon cells could theoretically reach a conversion rate of about 25 percent. Today new records are set regularly, with some residential solar panels rated at 21 or 22 percent. Laboratory tests of experimental panels have recorded efficiencies of nearly 50 percent.[50]

After the Bell discovery RCA Labs, Western Electric and Soviet scientists began working on silicon cell efficiency. Solar had two promising markets: the emerging space industry, and remote locations such as lighthouses that were difficult and costly to supply with conventional power. In 1958 the *Vanguard I* satellite used a solar array for its radios, as did the Soviet *Sputnik 3* satellite. By 1962 rapid improvements in efficiency led to the first telecommunication satellite, *Telstar*, sending TV and radio signals under solar power.[51]

However, solar was still far from competitive with fossil fuels. In 1956 Daryl Chapin, one of the Bell scientists involved with the breakthrough research, calculated that it would cost about $1.4 million to build a solar array powerful enough for an average house, and that "clearly, we have not advanced to where we can compete . . . commercially."[52]

The next breakthrough came from an unexpected source. In the late 1960s Elliot Berman, an American chemist, began looking for ways to reduce the cost of solar power. Berman persuaded the oil-industry giant Exxon to finance his research, and he was soon able to lower costs from $100 per watt to $20, in part by using recycled silicon.[53] Many oil platforms in the Gulf of Mexico were outfitted with the new solar panels, and Berman also explored the idea of producing thin solar films, which can be produced in rolls.[54]

The 1973-74 Arab oil embargo helped set the stage for major government support for solar power. Americans were angry about rising gas prices and long lines at gasoline stations, and many were ready to consider alternative forms of energy to heat and cool their homes.

Republican President Gerald Ford signed a bill to fund solar research in 1974, and Democratic President Jimmy Carter began regularly to discuss solar power and a transition to renewable energy after he entered the White House in 1977. "The oil and natural gas we rely on for 75 percent of our energy are simply running out," he said.[55]

In 1978 Carter signed the Energy Tax Act, which for the first time gave residential and commercial solar installations a 30 percent tax credit. In a May 1978 address about the founding of a national Solar Energy Research Institute, Carter said, "The question is no longer whether solar energy works. We know it works. The only question is how to cut costs so that solar power can be used more widely. . . . The government will speed this program by increasing demand for solar hardware, so that mass production can help to bring

Homeowners Look to Solar to Save Money — and the Environment

But many factors determine whether it's a good investment.

Brian Urbaszewski installed solar panels on the roof of his modest story-and-a-half Chicago bungalow in late 2014, but he had been dreaming of them for a long time.

"Honestly, since I was about 11," says Urbaszewski, 48, who had imagined powering a room in his boyhood home. Now Urbaszewski works on air pollution issues for the Respiratory Health Association of Metropolitan Chicago, and he says he "wanted to do something in my own way to fight back [against pollution], but I wanted to do it in a way I can afford."

After he bought his bungalow in 2002 he says he had to figure out how to fulfill his solar dream. "The cost was the big leap," Urbaszewski says. He did not want to lease solar panels and then have to worry about what would happen if he sold the house. Leases for a solar system often run 15 or 20 years, and either a new buyer has to take over the payments or the seller has to buy out the lease and try to price that into the sale.

Several developments persuaded Urbaszewski a few years ago that "the stars were all sort of lined up." Solar panel prices fell sharply after 2011. In addition, a 30 percent federal solar tax credit, along with some similar state and local programs, lets people deduct a portion of the total purchase and installation cost directly from their tax bill. Chicago also had a program allowing individual homeowners to pool orders to get further discounts. And Illinois was granting tax rebates on solar installations of up to 25 percent.

The programs covered a little more than half of the $14,000 total cost, and Urbaszewski borrowed the remainder. His system has 14 solar panels.

Urbaszewski's home was one of 904,000 nationally with solar as of the end of 2015, according to the Solar Energy Industries Association, a trade group in Washington, D.C. Lyndon Rive, co-founder of SolarCity, the nation's biggest provider of solar systems, said the company installed panels on a roof at a rate of every three minutes last year. "My goal is to get it to one home every three seconds," he said.[1]

Numerous factors determine whether homeowners are making a good investment in solar. One is government regulation. Kelly Schwarze leased a solar system for his one-story house in Las Vegas in November 2015, expecting to save $50 or $60 per month on his electric bill — only to see Nevada's Public Utilities Commission raise utility rates for solar users a month later, after utility NV Energy claimed solar owners were not paying their fair share of total costs for the electric grid.[2]

prices down." He set a goal of using solar energy in 2.5 million homes by 1985.[56]

Carter and his allies promoted the economic, environmental and foreign policy benefits of solar power. In 1979 a congressional study claimed "a massive shift from oil and coal use to solar energy by 1990 would create almost three million new jobs for Americans," according to an Associated Press report.[57]

The public relations highlight of the era came in June 1979, when Carter had solar water heating panels installed on the White House roof. "Today, in directly harnessing the power of the sun, we're taking the energy that God gave us, the most renewable energy that we will ever see, and using it to replace our dwindling supplies of fossil fuels," Carter said.[58] "I'm proposing major tax credits to speed the development and the commercialization of solar energy. This strong federal commitment to solar energy will be sustained year after year after year after year. It will not be a temporary program."

But it was temporary. Oil and natural gas didn't run out, and when Republican Ronald Reagan took office in 1981 his administration slashed funding for solar.

"Heavy reliance on these sources is still in the future," Reagan said in 1982.[59] Reagan's administration

"I'm obviously upset because of what our state leaders have done," Schwarze says. "I think it's completely irresponsible. . . . It was my understanding that if I got in, I would be protected."

Urbaszewski notes that solar costs vary widely by state because of the presence or absence of rebate programs, so he urges homeowners to carefully research all the issues before buying. He says that while he received the 25 percent state rebate, some people who bought solar panels after he did were denied a rebate, partly because of a state budget standoff.

Another kind of problem also upended Urbaszewski's price calculations: A neighboring homeowner built an extension that blocks some sun during the winter, reducing Urbaszewski's solar system's productivity and the monthly savings on his electric bill. Still, he says, he expects solar to be a good long-term investment.

Anne Linehan and her husband installed solar in the Cape Cod-style house they built in 2007 in Tunbridge, Vt., for practical and environmental reasons. They wanted to help the environment by using renewable energy, and connecting to the conventional electric grid would have been costly: Their home is last on a dead-end road, and they would have had to pay major fees to bring an underground power line to the house. So they turned to solar.

Linehan, 43, who works in administration at Vermont Law School, says she "was a little nervous at first" about living off the grid, but she now has no regrets. "It's just two of us. I think for people with kids it might be different," she says of their power needs.

They have a wood-fired boiler, propane heat and solar hot water, as well as a backup generator that they rarely

Solar panels cover part of the roof of a home in Pittsfield, Maine.

need to use. After tax rebates the 28-panel solar system, which is mounted on the ground, not the roof, cost about $15,400, and they have no electric bills, Linehan says.

Now she loves to brag about being off-grid. Linehan says so many people have gone off-grid in Vermont that their boasting has inspired a wry Yankee joke. "How do you find out if somebody lives off the grid?" the joke asks. "Oh, they'll tell you" is the reply.

— Kevin Begos

[1] Bill McKibben, "Power to the People," *The New Yorker*, June 29, 2015, http://tinyurl.com/olht8rw.

[2] Daniel Rothberg, "Warren Buffett discusses NV Energy, solar rates and Elon Musk in CNBC interview" *Las Vegas Sun*, March 1, 2016, http://tinyurl.com/jsucj6b.

cut federal funding and tax credits for numerous solar programs, suggesting the free market should take charge.[60] In 1986 the president had the solar water panels removed from the White House, and a Reagan spokesman said "'putting them back up would be very unwise, based on cost."[61]

Germany and China

Despite Reagan's shunning of solar, some research continued during the 1980s and '90s, although installations remained a tiny part of the total electricity mix. Then other countries began to see solar power not just as a

promising idea but as a necessity to limit pollution and global warming. In 2000 Germany began a wide-ranging program to support renewable energy, noting that "in the long term, the use of solar radiation energy holds the greatest potential for providing energy supply which does not have an adverse impact on the climate."[62] By mid-2003, some 100,000 German roofs had solar installations, and in 2004 the government passed laws that encouraged even more growth in the industry. For years regional and national Chinese officials and banks offered significant subsidies to solar companies, including loans and tax breaks.[63]

Solar Energy, Electric Cars Share Sunny Outlook

The two industries can help each other grow, experts say.

In the Nevada desert, billionaire Elon Musk is pursuing his vision of a sustainable future featuring solar energy and electric cars.

As CEO of Tesla Motors, an electric-car company, and as chairman of SolarCity, the nation's largest solar company, Musk is building a huge battery factory that aims to lower costs and attract customers for both companies.

Parts of the "gigafactory" are already operating, and Musk said that when it is finished by 2020, it will be the world's largest manufacturer of lithium ion batteries, a type of rechargeable battery used in electric vehicles and other items such as battery-driven power tools. That scale of production is expected to lower costs for Tesla's electric cars, but it also could benefit SolarCity because the batteries can be used to store solar-generated electricity for nighttime use.[1]

The idea of pairing solar homeownership with electric car ownership resonates with many people. A 2012 study by the California Environmental Protection Agency found that 39 percent of electric vehicle owners also have home solar systems, and another 17 percent planned to install panels. Homeowners with solar, according to the study, use it "to 'fuel' their vehicles with renewable solar energy," providing a "potentially strong link between the two markets."[2]

Other car manufacturers besides Tesla are linking the solar and automobile industries in innovative ways. In 2015 the Ford Motor Co. created the second-largest solar carport in the Midwest when it placed a solar canopy over 360 parking spaces at its headquarters in Dearborn, Mich. The carport is expected to generate 1.13 million kilowatt hours annually — enough to power 30 electric-vehicle charging stations at the site while supplying electricity to Ford's headquarters. Ford also installed a 500-kilowatt solar system at an assembly plant in Wayne, Mich., in 2010, to help power the production of electric and hybrid vehicles.[3]

Still, the outlook for electric vehicles is mixed, some analysts say. Car sales are growing, but technological challenges remain. "I don't think we can get [to a low-cost battery] without major technological advancements," says Jeremy Michalek, director of the Vehicle Electrification Group at Carnegie Mellon University in Pittsburgh, adding that although there "certainly could be" a breakthrough, where it will come from is unknown.

Until a few years ago, electric vehicles were significantly more expensive to produce than regular cars. The price has dropped steadily, but the question is how much further it can drop with current battery technology.

Jay Apt, co-director of the Carnegie Mellon Electricity Industry Center in Pittsburgh, says batteries are improving, but the costs of materials such as cobalt keep prices high.

Other analysts are more bullish about electric cars. A 2016 study by Bloomberg New Energy Finance, a research and consulting firm, found that global yearly electric vehicle sales could reach 41 million by 2040, or about 35 percent of new light-duty car and truck sales.[4] In 2015, about 540,000 electric vehicles were sold worldwide — less than 1 percent of the global auto market.[5]

Recent advance orders for Tesla's Model 3 mid-market sedan were startling, said Jessica Caldwell, an analyst at Edmunds.com, an online database of car prices and other automobile-related information. In early 2016 Tesla received 325,000 worldwide reservations for the Model 3 in seven days, and company officials hope to be producing 500,000 electric cars a year before 2020. "We've never seen

During the same era, China rapidly expanded solar panel production. China-based Suntech, once the world's largest solar panel maker, was listed on the New York Stock Exchange in 2005. Wholesale solar panel costs declined and then crashed after the market was saturated, leading to bankruptcies and industry consolidation around the world. The Silicon Valley startup Solyndra collapsed in 2011 and defaulted on more than $500 million in federal loan guarantees, leading to widespread media anything quite like this in the auto industry," Caldwell said of the surge in orders. "It is unprecedented."[6]

But in addition to producing cheaper and better batteries at its Nevada gigafactory, Caldwell said, Tesla must prove that it can reliably manufacture large numbers of cars. "Tesla is great at design and great at technology and marketing," she said, "but production has kind of been their Achilles' heel."[7] Tesla has struggled with parts shortages and delivery delays, but says it is addressing those problems. It also conducted its largest-ever recall last year over a seatbelt connection issue.[8]

Some experts said it is important to remember that the Model 3 isn't the modern equivalent of a Ford Model T. "This is not a mass-market car. It's not bringing electric vehicles to the masses; it's bringing electric vehicles to the next step in the luxury chain," said Sam Jaffe of Cairn Energy Research Advisors, a research and consulting firm in Boulder, Colo.[9]

When options are included, the Model 3's base price of $35,000 will climb significantly for many purchasers.. Buyers put down $1,000 to reserve a car, but they can cancel and get a refund. Model 3 production won't begin until late 2017. Tesla said the advance orders could ultimately generate $14 billion in sales.

Michael Dworkin, an electric-industry expert at Vermont Law School, says he sees much progress in the electric car industry. He cited Chevrolet, which after tax credits now sells a car for $26,000 that will travel 50 miles on an electric battery, but by next fall is expected offer one traveling 200 miles on a battery while selling for under $30,000.

Musk shares this optimism. At the Model 3's launch, he said the ultimate goal is to spur a transition away from gasoline-powered cars. "Why are we making electric cars? Why does it matter?" Musk asked. "It's because it's very important to accelerate the transition to sustainable transport" given rising carbon-dioxide levels from burning fossil fuels. "This is really important for the future of the world."[10]

— *Kevin Begos*

Tesla Model S cars at the electric car maker's factory in Tilburg, Netherlands, await delivery on Oct. 8, 2015.

Getty Images/Bloomberg/Jasper Juinen

---

[1] "Tesla Gigafactory," Tesla Motors, http://tinyurl.com/jj3ek28.

[2] "California Plug-in Electric Vehicle Survey," California Center for Sustainable Energy, 2012, http://tinyurl.com/howlz58.

[3] "Ford, DTE Energy to Build Michigan's Largest Solar Array," Ford Motor Co., Aug. 14, 2014, http://tinyurl.com/zmnqu6x.

[4] "Electric vehicles to be 35% of global new car sales by 2040," Bloomberg New Energy Finance, Feb. 25, 2016, http://tinyurl.com/gqevroj.

[5] "Global Electric Sales Surpass Half a Million in 2015," Clean Technica, March 8, 2016, http://tinyurl.com/h27w99h.

[6] Brian Fung and Matt McFarland, "The car industry has never witnessed what Tesla is about to go through," *The Washington Post*, April 4, 2016, http://tinyurl.com/j4g5bnf. "Tesla Gigafactory," *op. cit.*

[7] Neal Boudette, "Tesla Recalls Model X S.U.V.s," *The New York Times*, April 11, 2016, http://tinyurl.com/hg4lf4g.

[8] Dana Hull, "Tesla Recalls All 90,000 Model S Cars to Check Seat Belts," *Bloomberg News*, Nov. 20, 2015, http://tinyurl.com/ozjlzyk.

[9] Julia Pyper, "Tesla's Model 3 Won't Change the World. And that's OK," Greentech Media, April 1, 2016, http://tinyurl.com/j5uhdmj.

[10] "Tesla Unveils Model 3," March 31, 2016, http://tinyurl.com/hfs974d.

coverage and to criticism of the Obama administration, which had touted the company and approved the guarantees.[64]

The long-term question about the solar boom and bust is "whether governments and private investors that helped fuel the go-go first stage of the global clean-energy drive can exercise enough discipline to put it on a more economically sustainable path," said a 2013 article from the Stanford Graduate School of Business.[65]

A technician checks equipment at a Solyndra manufacturing facility in Fremont, Calif., on Nov. 23, 2010. The much-touted Silicon Valley startup collapsed in 2011 and defaulted on more than $500 million in federal loan guarantees, leading to widespread media coverage and to criticism of the Obama administration, which had approved the guarantees.

But the manufacturing turmoil settled down, and large and small customers began to benefit from a stable supply of low-cost solar panels.

CURRENT SITUATION
Plunging Costs

Solar prices now run about 57 cents per watt, down from $100 per watt in the 1960s. The steep drop has opened new markets worldwide, including in impoverished communities in Africa and Asia that previously lacked electricity. The consulting firm IHS predicts that revenue from global sales of solar modules — the components that go into panels — will reach $41.9 billion this year, up from $30 billion in 2013.[66]

The bullish outlook is inspiring new research that aims to make solar panels even cheaper and more efficient. Crystalline solar — panels made out of crystal silicon — is still used in most installations, but scientists are experimenting with thin-film systems and organic photovoltaics — an advanced photovoltaic that uses organic (carbon-based) electronics. These new panels have the "potential to provide electricity at a lower cost than first- and second-generation solar technologies," according to the Department of Energy.[67]

But all is not sunny in the solar industry. Falling prices for oil and natural gas in 2015 and early 2016 have fueled concerns on Wall Street that the demand for solar energy will weaken this year. Investors also worry that a few solar companies have over-expanded. On April 21 renewable energy company SunEdison filed for Chapter 11 bankruptcy protection. The company, based in Maryland Heights, Mo., spent billions of dollars buying solar and wind projects all over the world in 2014 and 2015 but struggled to manage the debt it took on. Wall Street investors and the U.S. Justice Department began to question company accounting, and when trading was stopped recently SunEdison's stock price was 34 cents, down from about $33 less than a year ago.[68]

The net metering issue, in which solar users sell excess electricity to the utility, also has been controversial. Utilities and regulators across the nation have been unable to agree on how to compensate a solar customer who sells excess power back to the grid, according to the Clean Energy Technology Center. Solar firms and environmentalists want net metering laws expanded so that more people can sell more power, but lawmakers and regulators are struggling to find a balance utilities can live with. In New Hampshire an 8.5 megawatt solar project, which would be the largest in the state, is on hold until net metering limits are raised.[69]

Under the payment compromise between several solar companies and utilities that was announced in New York in late April, residential solar users would still get money back from utilities that purchase power from them under "net metering," but only until 2020, when the net metering rates would start to decline for new customers. Developers of larger solar projects and community systems would also pay extra fees to utilities, based on how much power they generate.[70]

More utilities are embracing solar energy, according to GTM Research. It predicts that by the end of this year, more than half of utility solar installations will exceed the targets set by 36 states and the District of Columbia for renewable energy use.[71]

And more corporations, including Amazon, Google and Cisco, are using solar for power. Whole Foods Market, a national grocery chain, plans to install solar on up to 100 stores around the country.[72] Walmart is No. 1 among corporate solar users, according to the Solar

AT ISSUE

Should governments give tax breaks to promote solar energy?

YES Michelle Kinman
Clean Energy Advocate, Environment California Research & Policy Center

Written for *CQ Researcher*, April 2016

NO Katie Tubb
Policy Analyst, Heritage Foundation's Thomas A. Roe Institute for Economic Policy Studies

Written for *CQ Researcher*, April 2016

Every two minutes, another American family or business goes solar, helping to clean our air, fight climate change, improve the reliability of our electricity grid, boost the economy and create jobs. The explosive growth of solar power in recent years is a result of a number of forward-thinking public policies, not the least of which are tax incentives.

Solar energy tax credits support a clean, pollution-free resource. Offering solar tax credits provides families and businesses with help on the high, but declining, upfront costs of going solar and provides lenders and investors with long-term certainty. According to the Environment America Research & Policy Center in Boston, tax-credit programs are almost twice as common in the top 10 solar states as in the rest of the country.

What's more, tax credits can work in tandem with other proven policies to expand solar opportunities for all, as in California. While California does not have state solar tax credits, our state has become the nation's solar leader thanks to strong federal solar tax credits combined with thoughtful state and local policies, such as requiring increased production of renewable energy, crediting solar-energy producers for energy they add to the grid, and providing incentives for the development of renewable-energy technology.

As such, I breathed a sigh of relief — and cleaner air — when Congress extended the Solar Investment Tax Credits last year. The Solar Energy Industries Association has calculated that solar generation in the United States will offset more than 100 million metric tons of carbon dioxide annually by 2021, with a quarter of those emissions resulting from the extension of the federal solar tax credit. According to the Environmental Protection Agency, this is the equivalent of taking 20 million passenger vehicles off our roads.

We need solar energy to solve the climate crisis and create healthier communities. Yet the burgeoning solar industry is competing with the fossil fuel industry, which enjoys billions in subsidies annually and whose prices do not include the external costs they impose on the society of today and tomorrow, such as air pollution and global warming. Tax credits have a clear track record of success in stimulating the growth of solar energy, helping to level the playing field.

Solar tax credits are an effective, proven tool for increasing the growth of solar power, a key component of the 100 percent clean energy future demanded by the climate crisis.

the solar industry itself has made the case for why we should not continue doling out tax credits. It installed a record 7.3 gigawatts of solar capacity in 2015 — a 16 percent increase from the previous year. The United States ranks in the top five globally for solar capacity and new installations.

Modern, more efficient solar power now makes good economic sense in certain parts of the country. Bloomberg New Energy Finance forecasts the industry in America will likely triple by 2022, even without federal tax credits. The Institute for Local Self-Governance estimates: "In 22 states, at least one gigawatt of solar (and often much more) could be installed at a comparable cost to retail electricity prices by 2017, tax credit not included."

Even the CEOs of some solar companies say tax credits are unnecessary. Noting that the industry has had six years to plan for the phase-out of the federal investment tax credit, Sunnova Energy Corp. CEO John Berger informed Congress: "We do not believe an extension of this credit is necessary for the continued health of the solar industry. In fact, quite the opposite is true. If the credit is allowed to step down as planned, the industry will remain more robust in both the long and short term."

Despite solar's apparent health, robustness and maturity, some in the industry still lobbied Congress for yet another extension of solar tax credits last year. That should raise red flags.

The fact is, tax credits and other subsidies reward the wrong things. They do not just prop up uncompetitive companies. A marketplace crowded with companies dependent on subsidies makes it harder for truly productive, solvent companies to compete.

Nor do tax credits make solar energy less expensive. They just make more people (taxpayers, many of whom aren't customers) pay for it.

Worse, subsidies remove the incentive for companies to innovate and build better business models that actually reduce costs and increase the efficiency of solar energy. Instead, tax credits tie the solar industry to boom and bust cycles induced by political decisions made in Washington, not by real market demand. Such crony capitalism serves consumers poorly.

Solar companies who say they do not need the credit are labeled "outliers." But what the market needs are more "outliers," not more companies whose business model depends on perpetual subsidies from taxpayers.

Bill McKibben is co-founder of the environmental group 350.org, which supports solar energy development and is pushing for an end to fossil fuel use. McKibben says utilities should adapt to solar's rise instead of resisting it.

Energy Industries Association, with 142 megawatts of solar photovoltaic capacity at 348 installations.[73]

In 20 states, rooftop solar power costs about the same as electricity bought from the grid, and the total could reach 42 states by 2020, according to GTM Research. But GTM also said that future surcharges could drastically alter the outlook. For example, if all rooftop solar owners had to pay an additional $50 per month, solar would be cost-competitive in just two states. "The future of rate design and net metering rules will shape the residential solar economic outlook," the report said.[74]

Political Debates

Congress' decision in December 2015 to extend the solar tax credit for five years means that the most significant federal policy question is settled for the near future. Solar proponents have long defended the credits as fair, noting that the oil industry has received special tax credits to encourage production since 1916.[75] They also note that the worldwide playing field is still heavily tilted toward fossil fuels. The International Energy Agency estimates that global fossil fuel subsidies totaled $490 billion in 2014, compared with about $112 billion for renewable-energy subsidies.[76]

A wide swath of the public supports solar power and other renewable energy, Gallup found. "In a time of notable partisan polarization, growing support for alternative energy among Republicans and Democrats represents a rare instance where a bipartisan coalition could form," the polling firm said in March.[77]

Still, the presidential candidates in both parties offer a wide range of opinions on solar and renewable energy, according to a League of Conservation Voters analysis.

Sen. Ted Cruz, a Texas Republican and candidate for the GOP presidential nomination, said he supports an "all of the above" energy strategy that includes solar, coal, oil, gas and nuclear. But Cruz voted in 2015 against legislation that aimed for a national goal of 25 percent of electricity from renewable sources by 2025.[78] Cruz opposes most federal energy subsidies and says competition should determine who succeeds.

Republican presidential front-runner Donald Trump hasn't made recent detailed comments about solar power, but in 2012 he told Fox News that "solar, as you know, hasn't caught on because, I mean, a solar panel takes 32 years — it's a 32-year payback. Who wants a 32-year payback? The fact is, the technology is not there yet."[79] (Solar advocates dismiss his claim that users need 32 years to recover the cost of their investment, as well as his assertion that solar technology remains unproven.[80])

Republican Gov. John Kasich of Ohio — a coal and natural-gas producing state — has defended fossil fuels because of their importance to employment and the economy. But presidential candidate Kasich, who trails Trump and Cruz in the GOP delegate count, also has said that "I believe in wind and solar" and that the United States needs to be energy independent.[81] Environmentalists, however, have criticized his record as Ohio governor, noting that in 2014 he signed a two-year freeze on clean-energy standards that required the state to generate 25 percent of its energy from "advanced" energy sources, half of them renewables, by 2025.[82]

The two Democratic candidates are urging major investments in solar. "I want to have half a billion more solar panels deployed in the first four years [of my presidency]," former Sen. Hillary Clinton of New York said in February. Her energy platform calls for "modernizing North American energy infrastructure" and setting "coordinated targets for clean energy."[83]

Sen. Bernie Sanders of Vermont said in January that "we need to keep fossil fuels in the ground and move to 100 percent renewable energy." In 2015 he sponsored legislation to put solar panels on 10 million roofs by 2025, but the measure failed in the Senate.[84]

In some states pro- and anti-solar groups seek to give voters the final say on a variety of issues. When Florida solar advocates campaigned for a constitutional referendum that would let individuals or businesses lease or sell power independently, utilities created a competing ballot proposal that critics said maintained the status quo. Then the Florida Legislature added a different solar constitutional amendment to this year's primary vote in August that would give property tax exemptions for solar installations. Pro- and anti-solar forces in Nevada are seeking to put referendums on the ballot, too.

In the Courts

Numerous court cases on the local, state and federal levels could affect solar power's growth, says Klein, the Environmental Law & Policy Center lawyer, and some pending national rulings could help settle recurring controversies.

The U.S. Supreme Court's review of the Obama administration's Clean Power Plan affects solar growth nationwide, Klein says. The Clean Power Plan seeks to wean the energy sector from coal and replace it with cleaner sources, including solar. More than 24 states and several industry groups and utilities sued last fall, arguing the plan is illegal.[85]

Klein says he expects the Supreme Court to uphold the plan, though a timeline for the court to review the issue remains unclear in the wake of Associate Justice Antonin Scalia's death in February. If the plan is upheld, it would remove "one of the typical excuses for states to hold back" from solar and other renewables, Klein says.[86]

Experts and renewable energy advocates had feared that an unrelated Supreme Court case, *Hughes v. Talen Energy Marketing*, could indirectly slow solar energy growth. A coalition of electric power companies argued Maryland had wrongly infringed on the Federal Energy Regulatory Commission's authority to regulate interstate electricity transmission by subsidizing the construction of new power plants.

In April the court sided with the utilities, striking down the Maryland program in a unanimous ruling.

However, Associate Justice Ruth Bader Ginsburg wrote for the majority that "nothing in this opinion should be read to foreclose Maryland and other states from encouraging production of new or clean generation" in a number of other ways.[87]

Steven Ferrey, a Massachusetts lawyer and professor who specializes in energy law, says several state laws encouraging renewable energy have been challenged on constitutional grounds. Although the courts recognize that states can provide tax credits to in-state renewable energy projects, he says, states that provide or deny incentives to projects that cross state lines may be encroaching on federal authority under the Constitution's Commerce Clause. Ferrey says he doubts the *Talen* case will have a huge impact on renewable energy but adds that states have to make sure their programs don't infringe on federal authority.

OUTLOOK
Boom to Continue?

Despite the political and legal uncertainties surrounding the solar industry, the boom in both utility scale and rooftop solar installations is expected to continue. The Solar Energy Industries Association predicts that by 2020 the industry will be employing 220,000 more workers in manufacturing, installation, sales and other jobs, and that solar will be generating about 3.5 percent of the nation's electricity, up from about 1 percent in 2016.[88]

Bloomberg New Energy Finance, which produces reports and provides research to businesses, said the federal tax credits will drive about $38 billion of investment in U.S. solar through 2021 and that when the credits expire, "solar and wind will be the cheapest forms of new electricity in many states across the U.S."[89]

Dworkin of Vermont Law School says solar generation in the United States will catch up to wind at some point, and he is more optimistic than the Solar industries association about solar's potential growth: Rooftop solar will be supplying 10 or 15 percent of the nation's power, he predicts. Utility-owned solar will grow, too, he says.

"I think the battery storage is going to be less of a problem than we thought it would," so the nation could transition from fossil fuels to more than 50 percent renewable energy by about 2035, Dworkin says. "I don't know whether we can do it in 10 years. But I think within 15 to 20."

There is broad agreement that utilities will face continuing pressures to adapt. "If you look 10 years out, we're going to have to come up with some solutions" for utilities, so they can properly value solar production and allow "the new utility business model to also work," says Gallagher of the Solar industries association.

The Department of Energy's SunShot program, which seeks to make solar energy fully cost competitive with traditional energy sources before 2020, provides funding for research and training projects that encourage solar manufacturing and use. The department estimated that continued cost reductions could result in solar energy meeting 14 percent of U.S. electricity needs by 2030 and 27 percent by 2050."[90]

The Solar industries association projects that there will be 394,000 new rooftop solar installations this year; 479,000 in 2017; 539,000 in 2018, 628,000 in 2019; and 686,000 in 2020. If those estimates hold true, 3.6 million homes could have solar in five years, up from 904,000 in 2015.

Radha Adhar, who works on federal policy for the Sierra Club says the group is "thrilled by the record-breaking growth in the solar industry. And, frankly, we're not surprised. Solar energy delivers triple-line benefits. It's good for our economy, it's good for public health, and it's good for the environment. Now that Congress has finally provided the industry with the policy certainty they need, we know the solar industry will have a bright future."

Big utilities are trying new approaches, too. Duke Energy is participating in community solar projects, supplying grants to help schools and other nonprofits install solar. Duke spokesman Ryan Mosier said the company is "looking at the business case for shared solar for customers in each of the states we serve."[91]

Still, the growth of solar and other renewables can still cause major headaches for many utilities, some energy experts say. Weisgall of Berkshire Hathaway Energy said utilities and regulators in areas that have seen tremendous growth in renewables, such as Western states, have also seen real turmoil. The growing number of suppliers in solar and other renewable energy sources are joining an outdated, fractured grid that can border on chaotic. "To call the Western grid Balkanized is an insult to Macedonia," Weisgall said.[92]

NOTES

1. Sean Whaley, "Worries over firearms surface in rooftop solar debate," *Las Vegas Review-Journal*, Feb. 10, 2016, http://tinyurl.com/znrr3xr; Sean Whaley and Alex Corey, "Utility regulators OK phased-in rate hikes," *Las Vegas Review-Journal*, Feb. 12, 2016, http://tinyurl.com/z3frmeq.

2. Mike Munsell, "Solar Module Prices Reached 57 Cents per Watt in 2015," GreenTech Media, March 10, 2016, http://tinyurl.com/gthvym9.

3. "Energy management passes the point of no return," Deloitte Resources, 2015, http://tinyurl.com/zv82st9.

4. James McBride, "Modernizing the U.S. Energy Grid," Council on Foreign Relations, Jan. 26, 2016, http://tinyurl.com/phw5hwp, and interview with the Solar Energy Industries Association; total household numbers are from Statista, 2015, http://tinyurl.com/hcdk3t7.

5. "Solar, natural gas, wind, make up most 2016 generation additions," Today in Energy, March 1, 2016,http://tinyurl.com/gtw3fak; Gina-Marie Cheeseman, "San Francisco to Require Rooftop Solar On New Construction," *TriplePundit*, April 25, 2016, http://tinyurl.com/joywkk9.

6. "Why the U.S. Power Grid's Days Are Numbered," Bloomberg, Aug. 22, 2013, http://tinyurl.com/hcox7je.

7. Herman K. Trabish, "EEI's David Owens on Utility Business in an Age of Distributed Generation," GTM, July 23, 2013, http://tinyurl.com/znxs56d.

8. William Opalka, "Utility-Solar Partnership Proposes Net Metering Overhaul," *RTO Insider*, April 25, 2016, http://tinyurl.com/zp362gn.

9. "What is U.S. electricity generation by energy source?" U.S. Energy Information Administration, http://tinyurl.com/hf93dfl.

10. Pieter Gagnon *et al.*, "Rooftop Solar Photovoltaic Technical Potentialin the United States: A Detailed Assessment," National Renewable Energy Laboratory, January 2016, http://tinyurl.com/grrs7h3.

11. Rebecca Riffkin, "U.S. Support for Nuclear Energy at 51%," Gallup, March 20, 2015, http://tinyurl.com/hfdo86a.

12. "2015 National Solar Jobs Census," The Solar Foundation, http://tinyurl.com/zyyrz3y.

13. Lynn Cook, "As Oils Jobs Dry Up, Workers Turn to Solar Sector," *The Wall Street Journal*, April 21, 2016, http://tinyurl.com/zf85eyw.

14. President Obama, "State of the Union Address," The White House, Jan. 13, 2016, http://tinyurl.com/zaw6f6e.

15. Peter Kind, "Disruptive Challenges: Financial Implications and Strategic Responses to a Changing Retail Electric Business," Edison Electric Institute, March 2013, http://tinyurl.com/khjxbfx.

16. Peter Bronski *et al.*, "The Economics of Grid Defection," Rocky Mountain Institute, 2014, http://tinyurl.com/jm6kume.

17. "Chevrolet Bolt battery cells to cost 'industry-leading' $145 per kWh," *Electric Vehicle News*, Oct. 3, 2015, http://tinyurl.com/hak553y.

18. Jonathan Weisgall, statement to the Senate Energy and Natural Resources Committee, May 14, 2015, http://tinyurl.com/zrfxm83.

19. "Rooftop Solar Photovoltaic Technical Potential," *op. cit.*

20. "Net Benefits and Costs of Distributed Solar Energy and Innovative Solar Deployment Models, DOE-EERE," Edison Electric Institute, http://tinyurl.com/zv2cox6.

21. "The 50 States of Solar," North Carolina Clean Energy Technology Center, February 2016, http://tinyurl.com/hk8lfbh.

22. Weisgall, statement to the Senate Energy and Natural Resources Committee, *op. cit.*

23. "MIT Study on the Future of Solar Energy," May 5, 2015, http://tinyurl.com/jfwxole.

24. "Montana-Dakota Utilities Drops Contested Solar Fee," Alliance for Solar Choice, Nov. 19, 2015, http://tinyurl.com/obhn275.

25. "Core Issues," The Alliance for Solar Choice, undated, http://tinyurl.com/zftut3y.

26. "The Koch Attack on Solar Energy," *The New York Times*, April 26, 2014, http://tinyurl.com/kd9alpw; Suzanne Goldenberg and Ed Pilkington, "ALEC calls for penalties on 'freerider' homeowners in assault on clean energy," *The Guardian*, Dec. 4, 2013, http://tinyurl.com/mbng4qe.

27. "Updating Net Metering Policies Resolution," American Legislative Exchange Council, Jan. 9, 2014, http://tinyurl.com/gsufyfk.

28. Kyle Roerink, "Estimates are in for NV Energy Exit fees for MGM, Sands, Wynn," *Las Vegas Sun*, Aug. 19, 2015, http://tinyurl.com/nn5k98p.

29. *Ibid.*; Patrick Walker, "Switch denied to leave NV Energy; PUC may want Switch to pay $27M to exit," Las VegasNOW.com, June 10, 2015, http://tinyurl.com/j2twcq5.

30. Walker, *ibid.*

31. Roerink, *op. cit.*

32. Revised Direct Testimony of Matt Maddox, Public Utilities Commission of Nevada, Sept. 9, 2015, http://tinyurl.com/zmu42yg.

33. Carri Geer Thevenot, "Wynn Las Vegas challenges fee for leaving as retail customer of Nevada Power," *Las Vegas Review-Journal*, Jan. 26, 2016, http://tinyurl.com/hssokck.

34. Sandra Chereb, "Initiative proposes breaking up NV Energy monopoly," *Las Vegas Review-Journal*, Feb. 4, 2016, http://tinyurl.com/jyy2u7y.

35. Daniel Rothberg, "Tesla, Switch backing effort to end NV Energy monopoly," *VegasInc*, March 25, 2016, http://tinyurl.com/gptakbe.

36. Daniel Rothberg, "Group proposes ballot measure to break NV Energy's monopoly," *VegasInc*, Feb. 3, 2016, http://tinyurl.com/ha5vpo5; and Chereb, *op. cit.*

37. Herman K. Trabish, "How utility collaboration can cut community solar costs by up to 40%," *Utility Dive*, March 28, 2016, http://tinyurl.com/jhesros.

38. "A hymn to Utu," The Electronic Text Corpus of Sumerian Literature, http://tinyurl.com/j5lremh.

39. John Perlin, *Let It Shine: The 6,000-Year Story of Solar Energy* (2013).

40. Dio Cassius, "Roman History," http://tinyurl.com/z738zcr.

41. "Becquerel Prize for Outstanding Merits in Photovoltaics," http://tinyurl.com/jotmca9.

42. *(La) Chaleur solaire et ses applications industrielles* (1869).

43. "This Month in Physics History," The American Physical Society, http://tinyurl.com/hu4b94z.

44. Gil Knier, "How do Photovoltaics Work?" *NASA Science News*, http://tinyurl.com/2aj7mgy.

45. R.H. Goddard, "A new invention to harness the sun," *Popular Science Monthly*, November 1929, http://tinyurl.com/z3s8wv5.

46. "Obituaries, Charles Greeley Abbot," *Quarterly Journal of the Royal Astronomical Society*, http://tinyurl.com/hookfaf.

47. "Use of Solar Energy Is Near a Solution," *The New York Times*, April 4, 1931, http://tinyurl.com/hlvlura.

48. Perlin, *op. cit.*

49. "Vast Power of the Sun Is Tapped By Battery Using Sand Ingredient," *The New York Times*, April 26, 1954, http://tinyurl.com/z9yqzky.

50. "Best Research-Cell Efficiencies," National Renewable Energy Lab, undated, http://tinyurl.com/82y64w7.

51. "The History of Solar," U.S. Department of Energy, http://tinyurl.com/ntjqyzm.

52. Perlin, *op. cit.*

53. "The History of Solar," *op. cit.*

54. Perlin, *op. cit.*

55. Jimmy Carter, "Address to the Nation on Energy," The American Presidency Project, http://tinyurl.com/zs96tq9.

56. Jimmy Carter, "Golden, Colorado, Remarks at the Solar Energy Research Institute on South Table Mountain," The American Presidency Project, May 3, 1978, http://tinyurl.com/jzhmzcj.

57. "Solar Energy Use, Job Boom Tied," The Associated Press, April 23, 1979, http://tinyurl.com/hect3a8.

58. Jimmy Carter, "Solar Energy Remarks Announcing Administration Proposals," The American Presidency Project, June 20, 1979, http://tinyurl.com/guf2gb3.

59. Ronald Reagan, "Remarks at the Opening Ceremonies for the Knoxville International Energy Exposition (World's Fair) in Tennessee," The American Presidency Project, May 1, 1982, http://tinyurl.com/hml6w8j.

60. Michael deCourcy Hinds, "U.S. Assistance Wanes for the Solar Industry," *The New York Times*, Nov. 4, 1982, http://tinyurl.com/gsvgn47.

61. "White House Will Not Replace Solar Water-Heating System," The Associated Press, *The New York Times*, Aug. 24, 1986, http://tinyurl.com/yf5buwu.

62. Perlin, *op. cit.*

63. Jeffrey Ball, "China's Solar-Panel Boom and Bust," *Insights by Stanford Business*, June 7, 2013, http://tinyurl.com/pqv4542.

64. "Solyndra Scandal," *The Washington Post Special Reports*, Dec. 25, 2011, http://tinyurl.com/h9ou94x.

65. Ball, *op. cit.*

66. "Global PV Module Revenue to Reach Record $41.9 Billion in 2016, IHS Says," press release, IHS, Sept. 21, 2015, http://tinyurl.com/hhmlxgw.

67. "Organic photovoltaics research," U.S. Department of Energy, http://tinyurl.com/zywr3qz.

68. "SunEdison files for bankruptcy protection," Reuters, April 21, 2016, http://tinyurl.com/zgatrh8.

69. "Franklin Mayor: Solar Project Stalled Until Metering Cap Raised," New Hampshire Public Radio, Feb. 29, 2016, http://tinyurl.com/hgn9fzb.

70. "NY Energy Utilities And Solar Providers File Joint Proposal To Encourage More Renewables," press release, ConEdison, April 19, 2016, http://tinyurl.com/hvemxx9.

71. Colin Smith, "The Next Wave of U.S. Utility Solar: Procurement Beyond the RPS," GTM Research, March 2016, http://tinyurl.com/zf5rpkf.

72. "SolarCity to Work with Whole Foods Market to Install Solar Power Systems Across the U.S.," press release, SolarCity, March 8, 2016, http://tinyurl.com/j7fjnaw.

73. "Solar Means Business 2015: Top Corporate Solar Users," Solar Energy Industries Association, 2015, http://tinyurl.com/hpxwzr6.

74. "Cory Honeyman, "U.S. Residential Solar Economic Outlook 2016-2020, GTM Research, February 2016, http://tinyurl.com/zh3jb7z.

75. Molly Sherlock, "Energy Tax Policy: Historical Perspectives on and Current Status of Energy Tax Expenditures," Congressional Research Service, May 2011, http://tinyurl.com/pcczolx.

76. "World Energy Outlook 2015," International Energy Agency, 2015, http://tinyurl.com/hu4sjrw.

77. "In U.S., 73% Now Prioritize Alternative Energy Over Oil, Gas," Gallup, March 24, 2016, http://tinyurl.com/h4rj7bo.

78. "2016 Presidential Candidates on Renewable Energy," League of Conservation Voters, March 25, 2016, http://tinyurl.com/glmlxwt.

79. Rich Dana, "Trump: Obama an economic 'ignoramus,' energy policy a 'complete and total disaster," Fox News, March 16, 2012, http://tinyurl.com/7vszq8s.

80. "Where Does Trump Stand on Solar?" *Solar Tribune*, Aug. 10, 2015, http://tinyurl.com/hkebgvg.

81. "2016 Presidential Candidates on Renewable Energy," *op. cit.*

82. "Gov. Kasich Admits Renewables Are the Future, So Why Did He Freeze Ohio's Clean Energy Mandate?" *EcoWatch*, Feb. 10, 2016, http://tinyurl.com/z87fpkx.

83. "2016 Presidential Candidates on Renewable Energy," *op. cit.*

84. *Ibid.*

85. Alan Neuhauser, "Supreme Court Blocks Signature Obama Climate Rule," *U.S. News & World Report*, Feb. 10, 2016, http://tinyurl.com/zljocda.

86. For background on the Clean Power Plan, see Jill U. Adams, "Air Pollution and Climate Change," *CQ Researcher*, Nov. 13, 2015, pp. 961-984.

87. The Supreme Court ruling can be found at http://tinyurl.com/jm4eskz.

88. "SEIA Celebrates Extension of the ITC," Solar Energy Industries Association, Dec. 18, 2015, http://tinyurl.com/jm2ud7x.

89. Tom Randall, "What Just Happened in Solar Is a Bigger Deal Than Oil Exports," Dec. 17, 2015, Bloomberg Business, http://tinyurl.com/h8x7asv.

90. "SunShot Vision Study," U.S. Department of Energy, February 2012, http://tinyurl.com/zktnynb.

91. Trabish, "How Utility Collaboration Can Cut Community Solar Costs," *op. cit.*

92. Katherine Tweed, "5 quotes we love from BNEF's Future of Energy Summit," *GreenTech Media*, April 6, 2016, http://tinyurl.com/jdrjh8m.

BIBLIOGRAPHY

Selected Sources

Books

Levine, Steve, *The Powerhouse: America, China, and the Great Battery War*, Penguin Books, 2016.
A journalist details the two years he spent following researchers at a federal battery laboratory in depicting the technical and political forces that were behind the race to develop a new generation of low-cost batteries.

Perlin, John, *Let It Shine: The 6,000-Year Story of Solar Energy*, New World Library, 2013.
A historian who oversaw multiple solar installations at the University of California, Santa Barbara, chronicles the use of solar energy from ancient times to the space age.

Yergin, Daniel, *The Quest: Energy, Security and the Remaking of the Modern World*, Penguin Books, 2012.
A leading energy expert chronicles how technology, natural resources and politics interact to drive global change.

Articles

Buhayar, Noah, "Who Owns the Sun?" *Bloomberg Businessweek*, Jan. 28, 2016, http://bloom.bg/1ZUi7mY.
Warren Buffett and Elon Musk, billionaires with competing interests in the solar-power boom, face off in Nevada.

Cardwell, Diane, "Patagonia to Help Fund Residential Solar Installations," *The New York Times*, March 10, 2016, http://nyti.ms/1RD4pAx.
An outdoor-clothing company invests in a program to put solar panels on 1,500 homes in eight states.

Cardwell, Diane, and Julie Creswell, "SolarCity and Other Rooftop Providers Face a Cloudier Future," *The New York Times*, Feb. 10, 2016, http://tinyurl.com/j53ak7d.
Uncertainty over the rate that utilities pay for solar power has hurt the stock price of leading solar manufacturers.

Helman, Christopher, "Disney Taps Solar Power With Mickey Mouse PV Project," *Forbes*, Feb. 29, 2016, http://tinyurl.com/gsvmxo4.
Duke Energy builds a large new solar farm next to Disney World in Florida as part of a deal with a local entity that manages utilities for Disney and other nearby businesses.

McKibben, Bill, "Power to the People," *The New Yorker*, June 29, 2015, http://tinyurl.com/olht8rw.
An environmental writer and activist explains why the growth of rooftop solar threatens utility companies.

Stephens, Joe, and Carol D. Leonnig, "Solyndra Scandal," *The Washington Post*, Dec. 25, 2011, http://wapo.st/1Q6jtq8.
A series of articles focuses on the Silicon Valley solar company Solyndra, which collapsed after receiving large federal clean-energy grants, prompting congressional investigations. In the 2012 presidential election, Republicans made an issue of the Obama administration's decision to award the grants.

Reports and Studies

"The 50 States of Solar, 2015 Policy Review," North Carolina Clean Energy Technology Center, Feb. 23, 2016, http://tinyurl.com/jahlnj8.
A center affiliated with the College of Engineering at North Carolina State University examines how different states are regulating and discussing solar power.

"The Future of Solar Energy," MIT Energy Initiative, May 5, 2015, https://mitei.mit.edu/futureofsolar.
Massachusetts Institute of Technology researchers examine solar energy technical, business, and policy questions and make recommendations for federal and state support of the industry.

Kind, Peter, "Disruptive Challenges: Financial Implications and Strategic Responses to a Changing Retail Electric Business," Edison Electric Institute, January 2013, http://bit.ly/1pEzp7z.
A study funded by the utility industry examines the potential long-term impacts of solar power.

"New Energy Outlook 2015," Bloomberg New Energy Finance, June 23, 2015, http://tinyurl.com/ntlqu6n.
An energy consulting firm presents long-term forecasts for global trends in solar power and other forms of energy, including fossil fuels, along with an analysis of projected future carbon dioxide emissions.

"Solar," U.S. Energy Information Administration, updated continuously, http://1.usa.gov/1RDTQNO.
This list includes articles and reports on solar energy from U.S. government analysts.

"Solar on Superstores, How the Roofs of Big Box Stores Can Help America Shift to Clean Energy," Environment America Research & Policy Center, Feb. 16, 2016, http://bit.ly/1ToeDub.
An environmental group estimates the national potential for installing solar panels on the rooftops of superstores and shopping malls.

"Top Solar Power Industry Trends for 2015," IHS, Jan. 8, 2015, http://bit.ly/1DDSHhv.
An energy consulting firm based in Englewood, Colo., analyzes global solar power trends.

For More Information

American Solar Energy Society, 2525 Arapahoe Ave., Suite E4-253, Boulder, CO, 80302; 303-443-3130; www.ases.org. Association of solar professionals, established in 1954.

Edison Electric Institute, 701 Pennsylvania Ave., N.W., Washington, DC 20004-2696; 202-508-5000; www.eei.org/Pages/default.aspx. Association representing investor-owned U.S. electric companies.

National Renewable Energy Laboratory, 15013 Denver West Parkway, Golden, CO 80401; 303-275-3000; www.nrel.gov/about/golden.html. Federal center for renewable-energy research.

Solar Energy Industries Association, 600 14th St., N.W., Suite 400, Washington, DC 20005; 202-682-0556; www.seia.org. Trade group representing solar energy manufacturers, installers and advocates.

U.S. Energy Information Administration, 1000 Independence Ave., S.W., Washington, DC 20585; 202-586-8800; https://www.eia.gov/todayinenergy/index.cfm?tg=solar. Federal agency that collects, analyzes and publishes national and state data on energy, including solar.

Vermont Law School Institute for Energy and the Environment, 164 Chelsea St., South Royalton, VT 05068; 802-831-1151; www.vermontlaw.edu/IEE. Offers courses, research and training on legal, policy, and environmental aspects of energy use.

14

Arctic Development

Reed Karaim

A tourist photographs a Polar bear from their ship in the Arctic Ocean. As climate change shrinks polar ice at an unprecedented rate, northern sea lanes are opening to increased shipping and tourism, even as environmentalists warn that the region's disappearing ice sheet threatens the survival of the polar bear population.

Courtesy of Kent Haffer

From *CQ Researcher*,
December 2, 2016

This September [2016], the *Crystal Serenity* did something that would have been unimaginable only a few years earlier. It became the first large luxury cruise ship to voyage through the once impassable Northwest Passage. Nearly 1,100 passengers paid between $22,000 and $120,000 for the privilege of seeing up close the legendary Arctic sea route that courses through the top of the world, connecting the Atlantic Ocean to the Pacific.[1]

The trip, widely criticized by environmentalists for its adverse carbon footprint, is a symbol of the dramatic changes occurring in the Arctic — a vast, frigid region that encompasses the Arctic Ocean and the adjacent waters and coastal areas of eight countries. Climate change is warming the region twice as fast as the rest of the globe. It also is causing polar ice to disappear at an unprecedented rate, opening new mineral resources to development and northern sea lanes to increased shipping and tourism.[2]

Some Arctic inhabitants see the warming as a potential economic boon that can improve residents' lives by creating more and better jobs through the exploitation of the region's oil, gas and minerals. But others believe the drilling, mining and industrialization associated with development will despoil the fragile Arctic environment, destroy indigenous lifestyles and accelerate the global warming already remaking the Earth's northernmost region, one of the most untrammeled parts of the globe.

"When you look at rural Alaska, any sort of economic development that creates jobs is critically important," says Gail Schubert, CEO and president of the Bering Straits Native Corp., a nonprofit based in Nome that manages the land, resources and tribal businesses

Arctic Holds Vast Oil, Natural Gas Reserves

The Arctic's 8.2 million square miles hold an estimated 13 percent of the world's undiscovered oil and 30 percent of its undiscovered natural gas. The West Siberian Basin is estimated to have the most natural gas and Arctic Alaska the most oil. Disputes over development and ownership of the region and its resources have erupted regularly.

Estimated Oil and Gas Reserves, 2008

Arctic Region	Oil (million barrels)	Natural Gas (billion cubic feet)
Amerasia Basin	9,732.58	56,891.21
Arctic Alaska	29,960.94	221,397.60
East Barents Basin	7,406.49	317,557.97
East Greenland Rift Basins	8,902.13	86,180.06
West Greenland-East Canada	7,274.40	51,818.16
West Siberian Basin	3,659.88	651,498.56
Yenisey-Khatanga Basin	5,583.74	99,964.26

Sources: "Circum-Arctic Resource Appraisal: Estimates of Undiscovered Oil and Gas North of the Arctic Circle," U.S. Geological Survey, U.S. Department of the Interior, 2008, p. 4, http://tinyurl.com/7tufxej; "Arctic oil and natural gas resources," U.S. Energy Information Administration, http://tinyurl.com/jfna7gy

of Native peoples in parts of northern Alaska. "I just think that the opportunities are really tremendous."

"[People] keep using the word development. I use the word exploitation," says Robert Thompson, chairman of REDOIL (Resisting Environmental Destruction On Indigenous Lands), a grassroots organization with members in several Native Alaskan villages. "We recognize that we need an economy, but what we need is renewable energy and a sustainable economy, activities that can happen without harming the Earth."

The resources potentially available for development are globally significant. A review conducted by the U.S. Geological Survey in 2008 estimated that the Arctic territories contain 90 billion barrels of undiscovered oil and 1,669 trillion cubic feet of natural gas, or 13 percent of the world's oil reserves and 30 percent of its untapped natural gas.[3]

The Arctic also has large deposits of copper, nickel, zinc and other valuable minerals, according to a 2016 report by Paavo Lipponen, a former prime minister of Finland. Russia alone is estimated to have as much as $2 trillion worth of minerals in its Arctic region, the world's largest untapped mineral reserves. The United States, Sweden, Finland, Norway and Canada have significant mineral resources in their northern territories as well.[4] As the Arctic opens up, the regional nations have been eyeing opportunities for expanded development.

Two shipping routes — the Northwest Passage and the northern route above Russia, which shortens the sea route from Europe to Asia by more than 4,000 miles — are expected to become navigable for

Arctic Temperatures Rising Fast

Air temperature increases in the Arctic region have outpaced average increases worldwide since 2003. The second-warmest Arctic temperature was recorded in 2015, when large swaths of the region were more than 3 degrees Celsius (5 degrees Fahrenheit) warmer than average for the region.

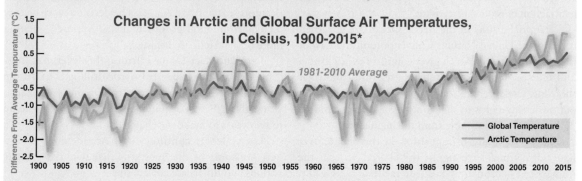

* The graph represents differences between average Arctic and global land surface air temperatures from 1900-2015 relative to the 1981-2010 average. Each year runs from October of one year to September of the next. There were few weather stations in the Arctic, particularly in northern Canada, before 1940.

Source: Rebecca Lindsey, "2015 Arctic Report Card: Visual Highlights," Climate.gov, Dec. 8, 2015, http://tinyurl.com/z59vqzg

more ships and for longer periods of the year as the polar ice retreats. New fisheries could also become accessible.

But these opportunities face growing regional and global environmental concerns. Environmentalists and local activists worry about oil spills, which are almost impossible to clean up in the remote and treacherous waters of the Arctic Ocean, and about protecting the ecosystem on land, which is already changing due to global warming. Polar ice, which has been shrinking at a rate of 12 percent a decade since the late 1970s and stood at a record low in October, has altered and reduced the habitat for various Arctic species, including polar bears, walruses, seals and migratory birds. The thawing of permafrost — the frozen soil beneath the tundra — is also adversely affecting the Arctic.[5]

The Arctic plays a vital role in the Earth's climate. Scientists say Arctic ice moderates global warming by reflecting a significant part of the sun's rays back into space. As the Arctic ice sheet shrinks, solar energy that would have been reflected is instead absorbed by the ocean, warming the water and further exacerbating climate change.[6]

Potentially even more catastrophic, say climate researchers, is the release of huge amounts of methane, a greenhouse gas that had been frozen beneath the sea floor and in permafrost. The release of the methane in the atmosphere "would be a catastrophe for mankind" because it would greatly accelerate global warming, according to Peter Wadhams, a professor of ocean physics at Cambridge University in England, who is among the world's foremost expert on polar ice.[7]

The shifts in the Arctic environment were dramatically illustrated in November, when scientists discovered the air temperature was about 36 degrees Fahrenheit warmer than normal, a development scientists attribute to a shift in the jet stream and to warmer ocean water. Daniel Swain, a climate scientist at the University of California Los Angeles (UCLA) described the unexpectedly higher temperature as "extraordinary."[8]

Complicating the situation in the region, which has 4 million people, are the many countries and indigenous groups claiming jurisdiction over, or rights to, parts of the Arctic.[9] In addition to the United States, seven nations have territory that extends into the Arctic: Canada, Denmark (which includes Greenland), Finland, Iceland, Norway, Russia and Sweden. Meanwhile, population in the Alaskan and Canadian Arctic grew by nearly

15 percent between 2000 and 2013, according to a report by a Nordic research group, although the overall Arctic population fell by 1.4 percent in that same period, primarily due to a population decline of nearly 10 percent in the Russian Arctic resulting from "its post-Soviet contraction of economic activity."[10]

Territorial claims in the Arctic Ocean are governed through the United Nations Convention on the Law of the Sea (UNCLOS), which gives countries the right to a 200-mile economic zone stretching seaward from their shoreline. Under certain conditions, UNCLOS also spells out ownership rights to the Continental Shelf extending 350 nautical miles or more from the mainland.[11]

Due to Republican opposition in the Senate over issues of national sovereignty, the United States is the only Arctic nation that has not ratified UNCLOS, although it generally follows its provisions. Many observers say Russia has been the most aggressive, seeking to extend its territorial rights along part of the Arctic seabed all the way to the North Pole.[12] Russia also is building up its military presence in the Arctic, sparking concern about a regional arms race as other nations respond.

The eight Arctic nations meet and talk through the Arctic Council, an international advisory forum created 20 years ago to improve collaboration on Arctic issues. U.S. Ambassador David A. Balton chairs the council's Senior Arctic Officials group, which coordinates council activities. Promoting environmental protection is a priority, Balton says, but when it comes to the risks from development, "each country in the Arctic will assess those risks differently."

The United States and Canada announced a new Arctic partnership at a summit meeting last March between President Obama and Canadian Prime Minister Justin Trudeau. The two leaders pledged their countries would work with the region's indigenous peoples to protect Arctic biodiversity, incorporate traditional knowledge into decision-making and build a sustainable Arctic economy.[13]

The two also promised to help create "low impact shipping corridors," taking into account important ecological and cultural areas in the region and to call for international agreements to prevent the opening of unregulated fisheries in the Arctic Ocean. In addition, they said they will work for a "science-based approach to oil and gas" development to ensure adequate environmental safeguards are in place before proceeding.[14]

But the declaration did not specify the conditions under which the countries would support resource development. In mid-November, the Obama administration announced it would ban the sale of new oil drilling leases for five years, from 2017 to 2022, in the Chukchi and Beaufort seas north of Alaska. The decision was a victory for environmental groups that had opposed opening more of the Arctic to drilling.[15]

President-elect Donald Trump, however, has indicated he supports expanded Arctic drilling. The Trump administration could overturn Obama's decision, although regulatory requirements mean it could take up to two years to make the change.[16]

As the debate continues over Arctic development, here are some of the questions that scientists, Arctic nations and others are considering:

Will further oil and gas development harm the Arctic ecosystem?

A global oil gut has dropped the price of crude oil by nearly 50 percent in the last four years to below $50 a barrel in late 2016.[17] Analysts say the low price has dampened oil companies' enthusiasm to undertake expensive and difficult exploration or development of untapped oil. Last year, Royal Dutch Shell ended a nine-year, $7 billion search for oil off the coast of the Alaskan Arctic, citing both the high costs and "the challenging and unpredictable federal regulatory environment."[18]

A series of accidents and delays plagued the Shell effort, including a drilling rig that became unmoored and ran aground in stormy seas. The oil company's decision followed decisions by Conoco, the Norwegian oil company Statoil and at least five other companies to suspend their offshore Alaskan oil explorations; between July 2012 and April 2016. Oil companies relinquished 376 leases in the Chukchi and Beaufort seas, according to the Interior Department's Bureau of Ocean Energy Management.[19]

Environmentalists have hailed these decisions as proof of the unfeasibility of drilling in the often treacherous waters of the far north. "There really is no worse place to drill for oil. It's incredibly remote. It's incredibly challenging," says Niel Lawrence, a senior attorney at the Natural Resources Defense Council, a Washington-based environmental group, who oversees preservation efforts in Alaska. "There's a tiny little window each year to drill, and there's really no way to clean up an oil spill" in Arctic waters because of the ice and harsh conditions.

Nevertheless, other oil companies are continuing their search. Caelus Energy recently announced a find in Smith Bay, off the coast of Alaska's North Slope, the petroleum-rich wilderness on the northern slope of the Brooks mountain range, that it says could total 6 billion barrels. Of that amount, Caelus believes about 2.4 billion barrels are recoverable, enough to supply the needs of the United States for some four months.[20]

Kara Moriarty, president and CEO of the Anchorage-based Alaska Oil and Gas Association, says existing oil wells on North Slope lands prove that drilling can proceed safely. "We have produced over 17 billion barrels of oil from [Alaska's] North Slope and counting," she says. "I will hold our track record on the North Slope up against anybody's. Can [the Caelus Energy find] be developed safely? We absolutely believe so."

Moriarty defends the federal and state environmental regulations governing both onshore and offshore oil development in the state as among the most stringent in the world. "This project is not going to be approved without diligent oversight," she says.

Some proponents of oil and gas drilling say that it would improve critical infrastructure, helping to ensure the United States can protect its interests in the region.[21]

But Cathleen Kelly, a senior fellow at the Center for American Progress, a liberal public policy and advocacy group based in Washington, says offshore drilling increases the chances of a devastating oil spill in the Arctic. She points to a 2014 draft environmental impact statement on opening part of the Arctic Ocean to drilling. The study by the Bureau of Ocean Energy Management concluded that over the 77-years it would take to fully exploit the Arctic Ocean leases, the chance of at least one oil spill of more than 1,000 barrels was 75 percent, with up to 800 smaller spills likely.[22]

When the Interior Department puts the odds of a large spill at 75 percent, says Kelly, "that's a clear signal that it's utterly irresponsible to pursue offshore oil and gas development."

An underwater blowout, such as the explosion of the *Deepwater Horizon* oil rig in the Gulf of Mexico in 2010, would be the most devastating type of accident, according to Cambridge University's Wadhams. He served on a panel for the U.S. National Research Council that examined the consequences of a blowout in the Arctic. Oil would spread throughout the ocean by attaching itself to the underside of floating ice, the panel determined, endangering wildlife in a wide area.

"We concluded that if a blowout occurs from the seabed there is no known method of cleaning it up," Wadhams wrote.[23]

However, Alaska Gov. Bill Walker, an independent, called the Caelus discovery "good news for the state of Alaska," noting that the trans-Alaskan pipeline is running at only 25 percent of capacity because of declining production in North Slope fields. He and other proponents favor more drilling to help make up the shortfall.[24]

In addition, Gwen Holdmann, director of the Alaska Center for Energy and Power at the University of Alaska, Fairbanks, says developing offshore oil resources in the U.S Arctic could be the environmentally responsible choice. "Our world depends on fossil fuels. That's just a reality, and I think, in general, the U.S. has done a pretty good job of trying to take into consideration the environmental impacts," says Holdmann. "If we're not developing our own resources, they're probably going to be developed in other places where there's less attention paid to those issues."

Russia is developing three potentially large onshore oil fields in the Arctic region, fields one analysis says could help Russia surpass Saudi Arabia as the world's largest oil producer.[25] Norway also has offered new oil drilling leases to expand oil production in its Arctic waters.[26]

But the challenges of drilling in the region mean Arctic oil fields can take two decades or more to move from discovery to production.[27] The obstacles, including regulatory hurdles, are many, according to the U.S. Energy Information Administration. Besides stormy seas and remote wilderness, drillers need specially designed equipment to withstand the cold temperatures; must recruit workers at higher pay willing to live and work in an inhospitable region; and must overcome long supply lines and limited transportation access that raise production costs.[28]

Lawrence says the global push to switch to renewable energy sources to slow climate change means such a timeline doesn't make sense. "By the time that oil can make it into American energy plans, we have to be very largely off fossil fuels," he says.

Smelt fishing is important to the economy of Russia's Murmansk region, just north of the Arctic Circle. Environmentalists say global warming already has seriously disrupted hunting and fishing in the Arctic, particularly among indigenous peoples, who have long depended on these activities for survival. Some Native peoples, however, embrace industry and development, saying traditional pursuits are no longer sufficient to support their economies.

"Anybody looking at what the economic future of Alaska is has to be concerned about people getting their hopes built up around an industry that we know has to be ramped down pretty quickly if we're not going to overheat the globe," he says.

Should more ship traffic be allowed through northern Arctic routes?

In 2007, when reduced floating ice first opened up the Northwest Passage in summer months for a few ships, optimism ran high among some in the media that the passage would provide a new, significantly shorter northern shipping route, particularly for oil and gas tankers.[29] At the time, scientists were predicting the passage could be ice-free by midcentury. Some researchers now believe that will happen even sooner than expected.

Cambridge University's Wadhams says the Arctic Ocean could be largely ice-free for five months out of the year by 2018. This does not mean all Arctic ice will be gone, he stresses, but the main body of ocean ice will have disappeared.[30]

Nevertheless, some Arctic experts believe conditions in the Northwest Passage, roughly 900 miles long, remain hazardous enough that it's unlikely to become a major shipping route anytime soon.[31] "The new conditions are described as ice-free, but what you get is a lot of ice floating around," says the Natural Resources Defense Council's Lawrence. "The Northwest Passage is not commercially viable at this point because of the floating ice. It's a novelty, and a couple of ships going through on a novelty basis isn't a major threat to the ecosystem."

In recent years, only a handful of cargo ships, specially reinforced to deal with scattered ice, have carried cargo through the Northwest Passage.[32] Twelve cargo-carrying ships used the northern sea route in 2015, although the number has been higher in previous years. In comparison, 17,483 ships went through Egypt's Suez Canal, the principal sea route from Europe to Asia.[33]

Shipping is more likely to occur first on the northern sea route above Russia, says Arctic Council Ambassador Balton. "Russian development of the northern sea route is a key priority for them," he says. "The northern route is likely to develop first, if only because of the ice considerations. Yes, the *Crystal Serenity* [cruise ship] went through the Northwest Passage, but it's really the other side of the Arctic that's warming sooner."

The two routes present an opportunity to cut shipping costs and could even bring environmental benefits, some analysts say. "A shorter path via the northern sea route . . . means fewer emissions of pollutants and greenhouse gases" compared with ships forced to take the longer route, wrote Vladimir Mednikov, president of the Russian International Maritime Law Association, and Henry Huntington, science director for Arctic Ocean projects at the Pew Charitable Trusts, a nonprofit research center based in Philadelphia.[34]

While the Arctic passages have risks, they note the northern sea route has had fewer accidents so far than the global average for shipping. They also believe ships can avoid the most environmentally sensitive areas. "With sound planning, effective rules and frequent communication among all involved parties, Arctic shipping can lead to more economic opportunity, better international cooperation and sustainable environmental protection throughout the region," Mednikov and Huntington wrote.[35]

But other experts believe increased shipping carries large environmental risks. The Center for

American Progress's Kelly says it will be necessary to eliminate the use of heavy fuel oil by ships traversing the Arctic seas and also to reduce engine emissions, particularly black carbon, which is essentially soot that can coat the ice and speed its melting.

"The spill risks [from ships] are great, and heavy fuel oil is basically like pouring asphalt into the sea. It's very destructive," she says. "If shipping is going to happen, and estimates say it will increase dramatically as we see less ice, we need to have the right environmental protections in place."

Ships traversing the northern sea route or the Northwest Passage will need to pass through the Bering Strait, the narrow passage between Russian Siberia and Alaska. Some tribal officials in Alaska say increased shipping could help spur infrastructure development and badly needed economic growth in the area. Port Clarence, a village along the Bering Strait, has a natural 12-mile-deep harbor that the Bering Straits Native Corp. says could be developed to provide a port for ships using the Arctic routes. Or Nome, which is about 70 miles farther south but has more facilities, could be dredged to become a deep-water port.

Melting Ice Opens Arctic Sea Lanes

Accelerated melting of Arctic Ocean ice has opened new sea lanes to shipping and tourism during much of the summer. Scientists predict that by 2030 the Arctic Ocean will be largely ice-free during the summer. The transpolar sea route, currently hindered by ice, would become the most direct route between Asia and Europe if global warming continues.

Source: Malte Humpert and Andreas Raspotnik, "The Future of Arctic Shipping along the Transpolar Sea Route," Arctic Institute, Nov. 27, 2012, http://tinyurl.com/cm4mcs3

"We're excited for both possibilities," says Schubert, the Bering Straits Native Corp. CEO. "Any economic development that happens in the region is good for the people of the region."

Given the vastness of Alaska's undeveloped areas along the Bering Strait and across the state, Schubert says limited growth will not cause significant environmental damage. "You're looking at basically a postage stamp area of development," she says.

But Dune Lankard, senior Alaskan representative for the Center for Biological Diversity, a Tucson-based environmental organization, says increased shipping will harm wildlife, much of which is already suffering from climate change. "Building the ports and increasing maritime traffic in the region will only further threaten endangered species such as the whales and [other] marine mammals," he says.

Potential fuel spills, sewage and the increased risk of collision all endanger native species, Lankard notes, as does the increased noise that comes with human activity, which research has found to significantly disrupt whale communication.[36]

An oil-soaked seabird is taken to a rescue center in Valdez, Alaska, in April 1989, soon after the tanker *Exxon Valdez* ran aground in Prince William Sound, spilling 11 million gallons of crude oil. An estimated 2,000 sea otters, 302 harbor seals and 250,000 seabirds died immediately after the spill. Critics cite the devastating accident as a reason to oppose further Arctic oil drilling, but supporters of development note that the spill occurred more than 25 years ago.

However, Holdmann, of the Alaska Center for Energy and Power, says increased ship traffic could help Alaska develop industry by providing greater access to shipping, and much of that industry could be powered by alternative energy sources, such as wind, which is plentiful in the Arctic but currently make little sense because the extra power isn't needed.

"We want to make sure we're selecting industries in keeping with local values," she says, "but if we're careful, we have this golden opportunity to think ahead about what kind of industries we can attract if we're in a great position from shipping."

Could further Arctic development accelerate climate change?

Most climate scientists agree the Arctic plays a significant role in climate change and its consequences. As the polar ice shrinks, there is less ice to reflect sunlight back into the atmosphere, accelerating the melting of ice and the warming of the ocean. This creates what Mark Serreze, head of the National Snow and Ice Data Center in Boulder, Colo., calls "the Arctic death spiral."[37]

Melting ice sheets cause sea levels to rise, one of the consequences of climate change. And the thawing permafrost releases methane, one of the most destructive greenhouse gases. Methane traps heat in the atmosphere, further worsening Arctic thawing and melting.

Under these conditions, environmentalists say, oil and gas drilling exacerbates the situation because it results in more fossil fuels being burned and thus more carbon dioxide and other greenhouse gases being released into the atmosphere.

"Experts estimate that if the oil and gas recoverable in the Arctic is extracted and burned, it would emit nearly 16 billion metric tons of CO2 — more than double the total U.S. CO2 emissions in 2013," says the Center for American Progress's Kelly. "That needs to be part of the equation when you're talking about Arctic development."

But Charles Ebinger, a senior fellow specializing in energy policy at the centrist Brookings Institution, said U.S. government and industry estimates indicate global oil use will continue to rise through 2030 to 2040, in part because of growing demand in the developing world. The question is not whether the world will still be burning oil, he said, "but where will this oil come from."[38]

In that equation, supporters of Arctic drilling say it's no worse for the planet to drill in the far north than it is to drill elsewhere if sufficient environmental protections are in place. And they deny that development will worsen climate change in the Arctic.

"However, climate change is a global issue, and any specific impact on the Arctic region is more likely to be determined by global emissions of greenhouse gases rather than Arctic development alone," stated the London-based International Association of Oil and Gas Producers, whose members produce about one-third of the world's oil and gas.[39]

But other experts say oil and gas drilling and increased shipping or industrial expansion could worsen Arctic warming and global climate change. Black carbon, emitted when fossil fuels or wood are burned, can cover the ice, causing it to absorb the sun's heat instead of reflect it, accelerating the melting. Recognizing the problem, the Arctic Council has been working on an agreement among Arctic nations to reduce black carbon emissions in the region.

Any development that heats up the permafrost just below the Arctic soil and sea floor could also increase methane releases, says Kevin Schaefer, a permafrost expert with the National Snow and Ice Data Center at the University of Colorado, Boulder. "The development can promote thawing, which accelerates the process," he says.

Roads, buildings and industrial development that do not take the permafrost temperature into account contribute to the problem, Schaefer says. However, he adds, development can be done without damaging the permafrost. "For example, [some] people who live on permafrost actually raise their house on stilts so the air flows underneath their house and you don't melt the permafrost," he says. He also cites the trans-Alaskan pipeline, much of which was built above ground to minimize damage to the permafrost.

But even if development is done responsibly, global warming is already thawing permafrost, which researchers believe will contribute to warming by releasing methane. Projections range from a "catastrophic" additional rise in temperatures of 0.6 Celsius by 2040, according to Cambridge University's Wadhams, to a much slower rise in temperature that won't peak until 2300, according to research by Schaefer and colleagues.

Ted Schuur, a professor of ecosystem ecology at Northern Arizona University in Flagstaff who has focused much of his research on the Arctic, says this thawing is already shifting the Arctic landscape, rendering the soil less stable.

Buildings in Russian Arctic communities have been buckling as the permafrost thaws beneath them. Reports from Russia's Arctic even indicate anthrax spores may have been released as old graves, dug shallow in the frozen soil, have opened as the permafrost thawed near the town of Salekhard. Experts believe the released bacteria may have infected 72 people and killed a child in 2016.[40]

Development in the region, Schuur says, is going to be more a victim than a cause of global warming, which is largely triggered elsewhere. Rising temperatures are causing changes in the topography and the ecosystem that are going to complicate further development, he explains, even if it is environmentally responsible.

"The best thing we can do for the Arctic is focus on emissions coming out of our power plants," says Schuur. "More than anything we can do in the Arctic, controlling human emissions elsewhere is No. 1 on the list if we want to slow climate change."

BACKGROUND
Early Settlements

Humans made their way into the far north in Europe and Asia as early as 28,000 to 40,000 years ago. They arrived in the North American Arctic sometime between 14,000 B.C. and 12,000 B.C., migrating from Russian Siberia to present-day Alaska over a vast land bridge across today's Bering Strait.[41]

Far larger than its name implies, the bridge was 600 miles wide, north to south, and twice the size of Texas, but it was low-lying and prone to flooding. Between 10,000 and 9,000 B.C., it sank below the waves for good after melting glaciers caused sea levels to rise at the end of the last ice age.[42]

Despite its remoteness, evidence suggests that ancient Middle Eastern and European explorers traveled to the region. In 330 B.C., Pytheas, a Greek geographer and explorer, wrote of a voyage into a far northern sea where his ship reached pack ice — floating ice that combines to form a larger ice mass. Ptolemy II of Egypt, who ruled in the third century B.C., was reported to have kept a polar bear as part of his court menagerie.[43]

In Northern Europe, nations such as Norway, Sweden and Russia extended their presence and authority in the Arctic region through the Middle Ages. But in North America, the Inuit, Inupiat and other indigenous Arctic peoples were left largely undisturbed by the West until the 18th century.

Vitus Bering, a Danish seafarer employed by the Russian czar, is credited with Westerners' discovery of Alaska. Bering led two expeditions to the Arctic. The first, in 1728, was to determine whether Siberia was connected to Alaska. Bering sailed far enough north up the strait eventually named after him to determine that Asia and North America were not joined by land.[44]

On his second, larger expedition to the region, Bering reached Alaska in 1741. Battling inclement weather and the debilitating effects of scurvy, a disease caused by the lack of vitamin C, Bering took harbor on Bering Island about 120 miles from the Siberian coast. The expedition was marooned after a storm wrecked the explorers' ships, and Bering and nearly half his crew died from malnutrition before the survivors were able to build a small vessel and return to Russia the following year.[45]

George Vancouver, an officer in the Royal Navy, followed up with a voyage exploring the west coast of Canada, concluding that if a Northwest Passage did exist, it was so far north that it would be impassible due to polar ice, a supposition that proved correct until the 21st century.[46]

By the time of Vancouver's voyage, Russian fur traders had already started visiting the territory that would become Alaska. The first Russian colony, known as Three Saints Bay, was founded on Kodiak Island in 1784.[47] The search for furs sent Russians to the mainland, where they established several small forts and settlements along the coast, sparking clashes with indigenous peoples who resisted the incursion. The Russian population in Alaska never reached more than 500, however, and inland Alaska remained largely unknown to the West.[48]

In the 1850s, after losing the Crimean War to a coalition of British forces and others, a nearly bankrupt czar offered to sell Alaska to the United States, which had been expanding its own fur trade and exploration in the far north. The purchase was delayed by the U.S. Civil War, but in 1867, Secretary of State William Seward signed a treaty with Russia to purchase Alaska for $7.2 million, or about 2 cents an acre.[49]

The purchase was widely ridiculed in the United States as "Seward's folly," and the Senate ratified the treaty by only one vote.[50] The deal was driven by a belief that Alaska contained untapped resources, but white settlement remained sparse until the discovery of gold along Canada's Klondike River, near Nome, and in other locations sparked gold rushes that brought thousands of people to boomtowns.

"In all these places and others, the gold fever eventually passed, but large white populations were now in the North to stay," noted historian John McCannon.[51]

20th-Century Oil Boom

In the early 20th century, all the Arctic nations moved to expand their authority in the far north as they began stepping up exploration for valuable resources beyond gold.

Between the two world wars, Scandinavian countries began mining for nickel, iron ore and other metals north of the Arctic Circle. For example, Norway began developing its zinc and aluminum mines around Glomfjord.[52]

Coal mining had begun on a limited basis, but early in the 20th century it became a significant industry in several Arctic nations, particularly in the Soviet Union.[53] Overall, the Soviets had "a cornucopia of mineral wealth throughout the north," including in its Siberian gold fields, noted McCannon, and the country moved to exploit its Arctic resources in the first half of the 20th century, often using forced labor from camps established to hold political dissidents and common criminals.[54]

Expanded development brought greater disruption to long-established native Arctic cultures. In the 1930s, the Soviet Union collectivized the reindeer herds of Natives, which were used for meat, furs and transportation.[55] Canada, the United States and the Scandinavian countries all pushed the Native populations to adopt a Western lifestyle, discouraging local languages and traditions.[56]

Despite these changes, much of the Arctic wilderness remained largely untouched, and the overall population was sparse. Alaska's population stood at only 226,000 in 1960, the year after statehood.[57]

Oil would spur the next round of Arctic development. The Soviet Union had developed the first oil field in the Arctic at Chibyuskoe in 1930. Two years later Soviet geologists discovered a large oil field at Yarega, which began production in 1935. More oil and gas were found in western Siberia in the 1950s and '60s.[58]

In Alaska, a U.S. military buildup that began during World War II and continued into the Cold War contributed to infrastructure development and economic growth. Tourism and commercial fishing also helped bring people and jobs to the region. "But the true monarch of Alaska's economy was and remains oil," wrote McCannon.[59]

In the 1950s, oil fields opened on the Kenai Peninsula and Cook Inlet. However, "the most successful strike and the one that most fundamentally transformed the state, came in early 1968, when the Atlantic Richfield Company . . . tapped into the deposits beneath Prudhoe Bay, on the North Slope," McCannon said.[60]

The Prudhoe Bay oil field turned out to be the largest oil reserve at that time in North America, holding at least 13 billion barrels of recoverable petroleum.[61] The discovery transformed Alaska's economy and state budget. State tax revenues from North Slope oil reached $50 billion in the first 25 years, providing more than 80 percent of the state's revenues. One-third of Alaska's economy is tied to oil production, and

CHRONOLOGY

1740s–1780s *Europeans and Anglo-Americans move into the Arctic.*

1741 Danish seafarer Vitus Bering "discovers" Alaska.

1778 British explorer James Cook seeks a Northwest Passage above Alaska but is blocked by Arctic sea ice.

1784 First Russian settlement in Alaska is established on Kodiak Island.

1860s–1910s *Arctic exploration continues as Anglo settlement takes hold.*

1867 U.S. buys Alaska from Russia for $7.2 million, about 2 cents an acre. The purchase by U.S. Secretary of State William Seward is ridiculed as "Seward's folly."

1897 The discovery of gold along the Klondike River kicks off the largest of several gold rushes in the Arctic that eventually lure 100,000 people to the region.

1902 Alaska's first oil well begins operating on the southern coastline.

1909 An expedition led by American naval officer Robert Peary claims to be the first to reach the North Pole, but some analysts doubt the accomplishment.

1930s–1960s *World War II and the discovery of major oil fields in the Arctic transform the region.*

1930 The first Arctic oil field is developed at Chibyuskoe in the Soviet Union.

1942 Japan invades the Aleutian Islands, spurring U.S. construction of the Alaska-Canada highway to transport troops in Alaska.

1945 President Harry S. Truman extends U.S. control to all natural resources off America's continental shelf. Other nations follow suit.

1959 Alaska becomes the 49th state.

1968 Major oil and gas fields are discovered in Alaska's Prudhoe Bay.

1970s–1990s *Oil continues to power the Arctic economy.*

1971 President Richard M. Nixon signs the Alaska Native Claims Settlement Act, turning over 44 million acres and $963 million to Native Alaskans.

1974 Construction begins on the trans-Alaskan pipeline, which will carry oil 800 miles from Prudhoe Bay to Valdez, when completed in 1977.

1989 The tanker *Exxon Valdez* spills 11 million gallons of oil into Alaska's Prince William Sound, polluting more than 1,000 miles of coastline.

1994 U.N. Convention on the Law of the Sea (UNCLOS) takes effect, giving nations rights 200 miles out to sea and to their continental shelves. Senate Republicans block U.S. ratification of the convention, saying it limits U.S. sovereignty.

1996 The eight nations with territory in the Arctic establish the Arctic Council to promote cooperation in the region.

2000s–Present *Climate change and the potential for new development dominate debates over Arctic policy.*

2007 Northwest Passage opens for the first time on record, although floating ice continues to make the transit perilous.

2012 Greenpeace begins a campaign to ban Arctic oil drilling; it is one of several environmental groups opposed to further oil and gas development in the region.

2015 Royal Dutch Shell announces it's abandoning its nine-year, $7 billion search for oil in the Arctic, reflecting a decline in oil prices and continuing difficulty of Arctic exploration.

2016 Luxury cruise liner *Crystal Serenity* takes passengers through the formerly impassable Northwest Passage, illustrating the impact of global warming on the Arctic. . . . Caelus Energy says its newly discovered oil field off Alaska's North Slope could contain 2.4 billion barrels of recoverable oil.

West Keeps Eye on Russia's Arctic Buildup

"This is a place where Putin can flex his muscle."

A Russian military buildup in the Arctic has alarmed many Western analysts, sparking fears of a new Cold War in one of the coldest parts of the globe.

The increased military activity has accompanied Russia's claim to seabed territorial rights reaching all the way to the North Pole, a claim that will be decided under the United Nations Convention on the Law of the Sea (UNCLOS), which adjudicates underwater territorial claims. Russia maintains it has rights along two underwater ridges, which it says extend from its continental shelf to the pole, thus giving it a claim under UNCLOS.

But regardless of the UNCLOS decision, many observers say Russia is intent on expanding its influence and capabilities in the Arctic. The Russians have or are building 19 military bases in the region.[1] The country is also reportedly establishing an Arctic command that will include four new brigades and 50 airfields by 2020, and it has staged elaborate war games in the far north.[2]

"I don't think anybody can deny that Russia has begun the process of remilitarizing territories in the Arctic," says Alan Dowd, a senior fellow who specializes in defense and security issues with the Fraser Institute, a think tank in Vancouver, Canada.

Russia insists its buildup is defensive in nature and relatively modest. Some analysts say Russia's economic dependence on oil revenues for its economy makes it vital for the country to protect its interests in the Arctic, which is believed to hold vast untapped resources, including oil and gas. Russia also wants to make sure it can safeguard the northern sea passage, which can dramatically shorten the distance between Europe and Asia and which has become more easily navigable as polar ice retreats.[3]

But Dowd says the buildup is also part of Russian President Vladimir Putin's larger geopolitical strategy to seize the advantage where possible in a larger contest with the West. "This is a place where he can flex his muscle," Dowd says. "He knows that in certain areas of the world, he can play to his strengths and U.S. weaknesses, and this is one of those areas."

The United States has troops in Alaska, but its military presence in the Arctic is significantly smaller than Russia's. The U.S. Coast Guard, for example, has two icebreakers, both older vessels, while Russia maintains a fleet of 40 icebreakers with 11 more planned.[4]

Dowd notes that the other seven Arctic nations have begun responding to Russia's buildup. Congress recently authorized a new icebreaker, the first in 25 years.[5] The United States also has announced plans to post a small number of U.S. Marines in Norway, which is creating a military headquarters on its lands north of the Arctic Circle.[6]

Denmark, too, has created an Arctic command, Dowd says, and is beefing up its forces in Greenland, an autonomous country within the kingdom of Denmark. Canada is modestly expanding its military presence in the Arctic by building up a training center at Resolute Bay and improving its ability to rapidly move forces into the far north.[7]

in 1982 residents began receiving annual checks from an oil royalty fund.[62]

The discovery also led to construction of the trans-Alaska pipeline, an 800-mile-long network of pipes and pumping stations that moves oil from the North Slope to the ice-free port of Valdez on Alaska's southern coast. After the project was authorized by Congress in 1973, oil companies began transporting oil through the $8 billion, 48-inch pipeline in 1977 — the nation's largest private infrastructure project in history at the time.[63]

At the peak of construction, more than 28,000 people worked on the pipeline, further boosting the Alaskan economy.[64] But the project aroused strong environmental opposition, with opponents contending breaks could damage the Arctic habitat and that the line would interrupt migration of caribou and other wildlife.[65]

Environmental groups and the oil industry disagree on the pipeline's impact. The industry maintains it is one of the cleanest in operation, while environmentalists say it has had a sucession of smaller leaks and other problems.[66]

Dowd believes the other Arctic nations need to show a united front to prevent Russia from leveraging its expanded military power to gain advantage in the competition for the region's natural resources. "If you don't start to posture yourself for cooperative defense in the Arctic," he says, "Russia will win by fait accompli and quite literally divide and conquer."

But other Arctic experts don't view the relationship between Arctic nations in the same terms. U.S. Ambassador David A. Balton is chair of the Senior Arctic Officials, the group coordinating the activities of the Arctic Council, a forum set up for international collaboration between the eight Arctic nations.

"It's no secret that the United States and Russia, really Russia and other countries in the Arctic, do not see eye to eye on any number of issues outside the Arctic," Balton says. "But for the most part, the eight countries, including Russia, are finding ways to continue to cooperate in the Arctic in general and the Arctic Council in particular." For example, he says, the two nations have worked closely together on a proposal to increase scientific cooperation across borders.

Balton says Russian leaders have an interest in maintaining that cooperative relationship. "The Russians who come to the Arctic Council meetings clearly have instructions from home to work with us to try to find common ground," he says. "It's a spirit of collaboration I am hopeful will continue."

— *Reed Karaim*

Russian President Vladimir Putin awards a medal to the captain of a nuclear cruiser in Severomorsk, the main administrative base of the Russian Northern Fleet. Russia's claim to seabed territorial rights reaching to the North Pole has been accompanied by an increased military presence in the Arctic.

[1] Yasmin Tadjdeh, "Russia Expands Military Presence in Arctic," *National Defense*, December 2015, http://tinyurl.com/glu9zo5.

[2] "Arctic Attracting New Military Scrutiny," Agence France-Presse, *Defense News*, Nov. 1, 2015, http://tinyurl.com/h42odla.

[3] Kenneth Yalowitz and Vincent Gallucci, "Can the U.S. and Russia Avoid an Arctic Arms Race?" *The National Interest*, April 8, 2016, http://tinyurl.com/h2h63th.

[4] "Arctic Attracting New Military Scrutiny," *op. cit.*

[5] "U.S. to build first icebreaker in 25 years," *NavalToday.com*, May 30, 2016, http://tinyurl.com/hhmtuhn.

[6] Jamie Crawford, "Norway welcomes US Marines amid Russian tensions," CNN, Oct. 24, 2016, http://tinyurl.com/z8x7dgt.

[7] David Pugliese, "Canadian Military Looks to Expand Arctic Footprint," *Defense News*, May 23, 1016, http://tinyurl.com/h4lblm3.

In 1980, Congress set aside 104.3 million acres of federal lands through the landmark Alaska National Interest Lands Conservation Act, which imposed restrictions on the exploitation of oil, gas and minerals in those areas.[67]

The biggest environmental disaster connected to North Slope oil did not happen on land but at sea in 1989, when the tanker *Exxon Valdez* ran aground on Bligh reef in Prince William Sound, spilling 11 million gallons of crude — the worst oil spill in U.S. history up to that point. It contaminated more than a thousand miles of shoreline and killed an estimated 2,000 sea otters, 302 harbor seals and 250,000 seabirds in the days immediately after the spill.[68]

Scientists believe the spill continued to damage wildlife for more than a decade, increasing mortality rates for salmon, wild ducks and sea mammals as oil remained in ocean sediments and contaminated the food chain. Critics of further development cite the *Valdez* spill as an example of the dangers of expanded oil drilling and shipping in the Arctic, while supporters point out it occurred more than 25 years ago. But Greenpeace, the

For Indigenous Peoples, Climate Change Hits Home

"The whole ecosystem is caving in."

The Native Alaskan village of Shishmaref has become a dramatic example of the way global warming is upending life in the Arctic.

Faced with rising seas and a crumbling shoreline, villagers voted in August to abandon their traditional home on a barrier island north of the Bering Strait and relocate about five miles inland on the mainland.[1] At least 30 other Native Alaskan villages likely face a similar fate.[2]

The decision to leave Shishmaref, where the Native population has lived for centuries, was difficult, with 78 villagers voting to stay and 89 to move. "It's been really hard for me and my family to really discuss this, because Shishmaref is our home," resident Esau Innok told *The New York Times*. "It's where our heart is. It's where I want to be buried."[3]

The traditional lifestyle of Native Alaskans has always been tied to the land and sea in the Arctic's unique environment. Hunting and fishing not only provide food but also hold deep cultural significance for the Inuit and other peoples in the far north. Both activities depend on an intimate relationship with the natural world.

As they deal with an environment already changing because of climate change, many Native Alaskans worry about the potential consequences of expanded mineral extraction, shipping and industrial development that a warmer climate will enable. Others, however, embrace industry and development, saying fishing and hunting are no longer sufficient to support the Native population and pay for sorely needed public works.

Among those siding with tradition is Robert Thompson, an Inupiat in Katovik, who is chairman of REDOIL (Resisting Environmental Destruction on Indigenous Lands), a grassroots organization that opposes further oil and gas drilling. He says environmental changes already have seriously disrupted hunting and fishing.

"We used to hunt musk ox. They're all gone. We're catching new types of fish, which most people don't even like to eat. Saffron cod have moved on," Thompson says. "Eider ducks, we used to hunt them along the coast, and now there's open water along the shore. The whole ecosystem is caving in, not dramatically at every moment, but if you watch it and analyze it, you can see it happening."

Thompson says more development, particularly oil and gas drilling in the remote Arctic waters, is risky because of the region's vast distances, rough weather and ice, which oil can cling to after a spill. "If they have an oil spill, there's no technology to really clean it out of the water," Thompson says. "How long is it going to be toxic in the water? You could wipe out our polar bears. You could wipe out our whales. You could wipe out our fish."

Dune Lankard, an Athabaskan Native, is a commercial fisherman and Alaskan representative of the Center for Biological Diversity, a group that works to protect international environmental organization, said spills continue to be a serious danger. They point to ongoing problems in Russia, with up to 500,000 metric tons of oil leaking into the Arctic Ocean annually.[69]

Climate Change Impact

Since the 1970s, researchers have tracked a steady reduction in Arctic ice. Much of the research on Arctic climate change has focused on the shrinking pack ice because of its potential to raise sea levels and accelerate global warming. "The most salient fact about the Arctic since the end of the Cold War has been its disappearing act — or at least its changing state of matter from solid to liquid," wrote McCannon.[70]

The polar ice pack expands in the winter and shrinks in the summer, and the longer-term retreat is not uniform. Some years see more loss than others, and some see modest increases. But overall, the area covered by ice in the Arctic was down in September by 48 percent since the 1970s, according to data from the National Snow and Ice Data Center.[71]

endangered species. He says he began opposing oil and gas drilling after seeing the consequences of the spill that occurred in 1989 when the *Exxon Valdez* oil tanker ran aground in Alaska's Prince William Sound. Herring, which provided half the income for area fishermen, have never recovered from the spill, he says. "When we think about our native way of life, it all depends on a pristine habitat that replenishes itself. We have a saying in the fishing business: It's a renewable economy as long as we protect our habitat. But if we destroy that, there goes everything."

However, other Native Alaskans believe development, including environmentally responsible drilling, could help economically struggling communities that are poorer than the rest of Alaska. "People think of our villages as quaint, but we have real needs: schools, power plants," said Richard Glenn, a whaling captain and executive vice president of the Arctic Slope Regional Corp., which manages the land and business interests of Inupiat on the North Slope.[4] The corporation owns nearly 5 million acres that hold rich mineral deposits, including oil and coal.[5]

Gail Schubert, CEO and president of the Bering Straits Native Corp., which handles the resources and tribal businesses of Native peoples in parts of northern Alaska, says the jobs and increased income that could come with development would be a boon to many Natives who lack the financial resources to improve their lives.

She believes they can take advantage of the economic opportunities without losing their identity.

"I'm an Inupiat Eskimo born and raised in Unalakleet, one of our coastal communities. We've actually had contact [with the outside world] for more than 100 years, and I think we're really adaptable people," Schubert says. "We've managed to adapt to changes, a lot of them positive, like

AFP/Getty Images/Gabriel Bouys

Increased wave action caused by climate change is affecting indigenous villages, including this home in the Alaskan barrier island town of Shishmaref. Faced with rising seas and a crumbling shoreline, villagers voted in August 2016 to relocate to the mainland.

running water and sewer systems and electricity, but at the same time hold on to our culture and heritage."

— *Reed Karaim*

[1] Steve Visser and John Newsome, "Alaskan village votes to relocate over global warming," CNN, Aug. 18, 2016, http://tinyurl.com/zvm5pgm.

[2] "Alaska Native Villages: Limited Progress Has Been Made on Relocating Villages Threatened by Flooding and Erosion," U.S. Government Accountability Office, June 2009, http://tinyurl.com/nz3as2d.

[3] Christopher Mele and Daniel Victor, "Reeling From Effects of Climate Change, Alaskan Village Votes to Relocate," *The New York Times*, Aug. 19, 2016, http://tinyurl.com/jpna4o2.

[4] Craig Welch, "Why Alaska's Inupiat Are Warming to Offshore Oil Drilling," *National Geographic*, May 22, 2015, http://tinyurl.com/jg84eff.

[5] "Lands," Arctic Slope Regional Corp., http://tinyurl.com/zrjnflw.

Climate change has been having a wide-ranging effect on land in the far north, say residents. "If you're somebody who lives in the Arctic, or even the sub-Arctic, it's pretty difficult to deny that climate change is happening," says Holdmann, director of the Alaska Center for Energy and Power. "You can see it with your own eyes."

In the Alaskan interior near Fairbanks, where Holdmann lives, "our growing season has increased by 30 percent over the last 100 years. That's measurable frost-free days," she says.

The shift has led to the encroachment of invasive plant species that thrive in the warmer weather, which in turn affects native wildlife. "In Nome, there's a huge degree of shrubby vegetation that's coming in where the tundra used to be," Holdmann says. "When I work with indigenous people there, they will point out to me how this whole hillside is now covered with willows and shrubs, and they will say, 'When I was a child, there was where we had reindeer, and now there's no reindeer. Now there's moose.'"

In northern Finland on Feb. 5, 2016, experts test an oil skimmer attached to an icebreaker that can help remove oil after a spill. Environmentalists say that as climate change makes more Arctic shipping and drilling possible, the chances of spills increase. In Alaska's Arctic waters, the discovery of a major oil field has stoked hopes among many in the state that mineral and industrial development could boost the region's economy.

Polar bears have received the most attention, but environmental groups note that the changing environment is threatening other species, too. The Arctic fox has faced competition from the larger red fox as that species has moved north into Arctic habitats.[72]

Coastal erosion already has forced some Native villages to move. "As the Arctic Ocean becomes more ice-free, the wave action is increasing. The ice acts like a lid. It calms down the ice. Remove the ice and the waves are more powerful and that promotes erosion," says Schaefer of the National Snow and Ice Data Center. "The coastal erosion rates are very high now, as high as 10 meters per year."

Schuur, the ecosystem professor at Northern Arizona University, says the changes likely to occur on land as the Arctic warms will be significant. "People talk about the opening of a new ocean," he says, "but one thing that's perhaps underappreciated is that the terrestrial landscape will also be in transition to a new state that we can't quite fathom yet."

CURRENT SITUATION
Curbing Carbon

In May the United States turns over to Finland the two-year Arctic Council chairmanship, which rotates between member states. The council operates primarily through working groups that tackle specific areas of concern, such as environmental protection, and several of the groups are developing plans to present at the May meeting in Fairbanks, Alaska.

Among the most critical for the health of the Arctic could be forging a consensus on limiting black carbon. "The U.S. chairmanship started in the spring of 2015. It was agreed that over these two years we would develop an ambitious target for the reduction of black carbon emission in the Arctic," says Senior Arctic Officials Chairman Balton. "The group we set up to do this is still working. Whether we get there or not, I can't say yet."

Balton says most council members are committed to reducing black carbon, but Russia has objected to the plan for reasons that he says are unclear. "I'm less confident that Russia is committed to do this," he says.

However, he adds, Russia and the United States continue to work together on other areas. For instance, the two countries are cooperating on developing a binding agreement among the Arctic nations to reduce red tape and other hurdles preventing scientists from operating across borders.

"The effort to negotiate this treaty has been led jointly by the U.S. and Russia," Balton says. "They have co-chaired this exercise, and the treaty that will be signed next May is basically done. I'm quite confident that it will be ready."

The council also is promoting renewable energy in the Arctic, Balton says, in part to reduce reliance on diesel generators for electricity in many remote villages. Representatives of six indigenous groups — the Aleut, Athabaskan, Gwich'in, Inuit, Saami and an association of Russian indigenous peoples — are permanent participants in the council.[73]

Promoting renewable energy is part of the council's commitment to sustainable Arctic development, which Balton points out involves protecting the region's wildlife and natural resources. "For a lot of the people who live north of the Arctic Circle, their ways of life are subsistence based," he says. "For them, sustainable development means protecting the natural environment so they can continue to harvest fish, marine mammals, elk and the other things they live on."

At a Senior Arctic Officials meeting in Portland, Maine, in October, member states agreed to continue collaborating on ways to advance environmental protection and mitigate the effects of Arctic climate change.[74]

Is further oil drilling good for the Arctic?

YES

Kara Moriarty
President and CEO, Alaska Oil and Gas Association

Written for *CQ Researcher*, December 2016

The Arctic is much more than a source of energy resources and natural beauty. It is home to thousands of Alaska Natives who understand the link between energy resource development, infrastructure needs and the vibrant ecosystem that supports a subsistence lifestyle. Not to mention, the Alaskans who live here overwhelmingly support developing our Arctic resources — more than 70 percent want to see more oil and gas development in the Arctic, including offshore.

The United States and Alaska are uniquely positioned to capitalize on the emerging opportunities becoming available in the Arctic, but they can do so only if vibrant private-public partnerships can flourish. As other Arctic countries like Russia rush to develop the Arctic for their own benefit, America is in danger of being left behind.

The Arctic desperately needs infrastructure as more activity comes to the region. Fortunately, companies that want to do business in the Arctic stand ready to spend the billions of dollars required to develop infrastructure. Oil and gas companies are experts at developing world-class infrastructure in sensitive environments. These companies regularly spend billions in Alaska building roads and bridges, health and safety facilities, search-and-rescue operations, airstrips and hangars and other facilities that improve the quality of life in a remote and underdeveloped part of the world. This infrastructure provides immense benefit to Arctic communities that would not otherwise enjoy such amenities.

As engagement in the Arctic becomes urgent, accelerating energy development will expand the nation's footprint in an area that is strategically important. The newly open waters are multiplying U.S. security concerns, prompting Coast Guard Rear Adm. Daniel Abel to state, "Just the amount of new open water I have to deal with is the size of 45 percent of the continental U.S."

The choice for the United States is whether to lead in the Arctic or sit on the sidelines and watch as other countries pursue the opportunities offered in the region. With one-third of the nation's oil and gas reserves, Alaska is poised to support Arctic development for decades and in turn continue to be an energy heartland to the United States. By using proven technology to safely and responsibly drill for oil and gas in the Arctic, America stands to benefit from economic growth, development of robust infrastructure and improved national security.

NO

Dune Lankard
Alaska Representative, Center for Biological Diversity

Written for *CQ Researcher*, December 2016

I've been hearing about drilling in the Arctic all my life. For Native Alaskans, it's one of those discussions that never seems to end. But the truth is, there's no way to make drilling safe — and it's time to finally put an end to it.

More drilling will only push us deeper into the very climate crisis that's driving the tragic transformation of the Arctic, where sea ice has hit record lows and polar bears and ice seals that rely on that ice for survival face the very real prospect of disappearing forever. It's profoundly depressing to bear witness to what's happening in the Arctic because of climate change. We have a moral obligation to make sure it doesn't get worse.

If a major offshore oil spill occurred, there would be no way to clean it up. If you thought the 2010 *Deepwater Horizon* disaster was bad, imagine the same scenario in a place that's prone to hurricane-force storms, 20-foot swells, sea ice, frigid temperatures and seasonal darkness. In some cases the nearest Coast Guard facility is 1,000 miles away.

Alaska, sadly, already knows the damage that the oil industry can do.

Prince William Sound has never fully recovered from 1989's *Exxon Valdez* oil spill, an event that changed my life and that of my Native Alaskan fishing community forever. I've been a commercial and subsistence fisherman for decades, so everyone should know that the herring have yet to recover from the spill.

An oil spill in the Arctic could destroy the livelihoods of the people who depend on a clean environment for hunting and fishing. The Arctic is a national treasure that supports a rich diversity of wildlife, but oil drilling and infrastructure would put caribou, polar bears, birds, whales, ice seals, salmon and the traditional communities that depend on them in harm's way. My brothers and sisters in Arctic communities are already being displaced by rising seas and depleted hunting and fishing grounds.

A recent study found that carbon emissions from current drilling projects would take us beyond 2 degrees Celsius of warming. And scientists have warned that all Arctic oil must be left untapped if we are to meet our climate goals.

Arctic drilling just doesn't make sense — not for the planet and not for those of us who call Alaska home.

Territorial Disputes

Russia continues to press a claim that would greatly expand its territory beneath the Arctic sea. Denmark has filed a similar claim, and Canada is expected to follow suit. In each case, the claims, which overlap in some instances, could extend national sovereignty to the North Pole and give the country access to trillions of dollars' worth of oil, gas and other mineral resources.[75]

Under UNCLOS rules, nations can claim economic sovereignty over the continental shelf beneath the sea extending out from its territory up to 350 miles or farther if they can show a natural geological extension of the shelf.[76]

Russia says several underwater ridges extend its rights to the North Pole, giving it an additional 460,000 square miles of territory. Russia first submitted the claim to the United Nations in 2002, but it was rejected for lack of scientific support. In August 2015, Russia resubmitted the claim with additional scientific research.[77]

In between the two submissions, Russia symbolically staked out its right to the North Pole by sending a small submarine to plant a titanium Russian flag on the seabed two miles below the surface of the pole. The act was derided by Peter MacKay, Canada's then-foreign minister. "This isn't the 15th century," said MacKay. "You can't go around the world and just plant flags and say, 'We're claiming this territory.' "[78]

Denmark's claim to seabed territory is based on an extension of its continental shelf from Greenland, an autonomous country within the Kingdom of Denmark. And Canada is expected to file a claim by 2018 based on an extension of its own Arctic continental shelf.[79]

"Everybody knows the North Pole is Canadian," Canadian Prime Minister Trudeau said jokingly in response to a question during a public forum earlier this year about Russia's claims.[80]

The potential stakes for development are huge. About one-third of the Arctic consists of these continental shelves, scientists say, and the vast underwater region likely contains large mineral resources.[81] Russia's Ministry of Natural Resources estimates its shelf — the world's largest — could hold up to 5 billion tons of oil and natural gas. Russian scientists also believe it could contain 90 percent of Russia's remaining nickel, cobalt and platinum, and 70 to 90 percent of the country's reserves of gold and diamonds.[82]

Offshore Discoveries

Caelus Energy's oil discovery in Smith Bay could provide a huge boost for Alaska's economy. Jim Musselman, Caelus CEO, estimates the field could produce 200,000 barrels a day once it's in operation. However, it is expected to take at least five years and cost up to $10 billion to develop the field, which will have up to 400 wells on four drilling pads.[83]

Environmental groups vow to fight development of the field. But Moriarty, head of the Alaska Oil and Gas Association, says the Smith Bay find could provide a "huge shot in the arm" to Alaska's economy, which has suffered from the fall in oil prices over the last few years.[84]

"Alaska needs the revenue such a huge field would provide," she says. "Alaskans need the hundreds of jobs required to develop a large-scale project; the economy needs the hundreds of millions of dollars that will be spent to pursue this development."

President-elect Trump is expected to try to overturn Obama's decision to ban drilling for five years in the Chukchi and Beaufort seas. But several Republicans on Capitol Hill, including Sen. Lisa Murkowski, R-Alaska, who chairs the Energy and Natural Resources Committee, believe the government should be opening even more Arctic waters to drilling. On the other side of the aisle, Democrats in both the House and Senate have opposed further oil development in the area.[85]

The United States is not the only Arctic nation debating whether to drill. Norway's Statoil has been aggressively seeking additional Arctic oil reserves to compensate for low prices and declining production projected from its existing oil fields.[86] But Norway recently backed off plans to open part of its Arctic waters for oil development. Local fishermen and environmental groups fiercely opposed the proposal to allow drilling near the Lofoten Islands, an area that has the world's largest cold-water coral reef and is crucial to fish spawning.[87]

Trump's Plans

If he holds to his campaign positions, Trump's ascension to the White House will mean a dramatic shift in U.S. policies toward Arctic drilling and climate change.

In a speech in North Dakota last May, Trump attacked the Obama administration's policy toward the Arctic, saying, "He's taken huge percentages of the

Alaska petroleum — and you take the reserve — he's taken it off the table."[88]

However, the Obama administration has allowed limited drilling in the National Petroleum Reserve in Alaska, a federally owned 22.8-million-acre tract on the North Slope managed by the Department of the Interior. Observers suspect Trump was referring to the Arctic National Wildlife Refuge, which has long been off limits to drilling. Congress would have to vote to open the refuge to oil drilling.[89]

Trump also has referred to climate change as a "hoax" perpetrated by the Chinese to make the United States uncompetitive in manufacturing.[90] (China is a participant in U.N. led climate change efforts and has announced it will sign the Paris agreement to limit global warming.[91])

Trump's opponent, Democrat Hillary Clinton, had supported a ban on drilling in the Alaskan Arctic, calling it "a unique treasure."[92] In contrast, Trump's website says he will "unleash America's $50 trillion in untapped shale, oil and natural gas reserves, plus hundreds of years in clean coal reserves."[93]

Trump has yet to announce who will head the Interior Department or the Environmental Protection Agency (EPA), which he has vowed to dramatically downsize. But former Republican Gov. Sarah Palin of Alaska, who has used the phrase "drill, baby, drill" to describe her position on oil development in the state, is rumored to be under consideration for Interior secretary.[94]

Trump has also appointed one of the leading climate-change skeptics, Myron Ebell, to head his EPA transition team. Ebell, who directs environmental and energy policy at the Competitive Enterprise Institute, a libertarian advocacy group in Washington, has called the scientific consensus on climate change "phony," is considered a possible choice to head the agency.[95]

Environmental groups are vowing to fight any effort by the new administration to weaken the nation's environmental standards or reduce its effort to limit greenhouse gas emissions.

"The next four years will not be easy, but we have fought hostile administrations before," said Erich Pica, president of Friends of the Earth U.S., an environmental group based in Washington. "Under President George W. Bush, the environmental community took the battle to the courts and Congress . . . ; we galvanized the public to take action. After the more recent fights to kill the Keystone XL

pipeline, ban fracking and shut down coal plants, the environmental movement is stronger than we have ever been."[96]

OUTLOOK
Embracing Renewables

The Arctic's future depends in part on how fast the ice sheet melts and the permafrost thaws as a result of climate change.[97]

Accelerated melting will open underwater resources to development more quickly but will also give Arctic inhabitants less time to adapt to a rapidly changing environment. Matt Ganley, vice president for media and external affairs for the Bering Straits Native Corp., says several communities in the region already face eroding shorelines and other challenges associated with climate change.

Over the next five years, he hopes those communities will take advantage of the situation to improve their infrastructure. "It's an awful situation, but rather than just moving communities and then doing things the same old way, it gives us an opportunity to do things in new ways, such as embrace renewable energy sources," he says. "We're at ground zero for global warming, but we can also be at ground zero for really innovative ways of dealing with it."

Over the longer term, Holdmann, head of the Alaska Center for Energy and Power, says the state has significant renewable energy resources it can exploit, including wind, geothermal and tidal energy. However, as the climate changes, she also sees the opportunity for more traditional economic development, including pursuing more manufacturing and increasing industrial capacity.

"If all of a sudden the coastal areas and the Arctic are opening up, that's where we can see opportunities for places like Nome to become hubs of economic opportunity," she says. "I'd like to see opportunities for people to have careers and businesses in these remote areas where they don't have to move down south to big cities to be part of the modern global economy."

The Natural Resources Defense Council's Lawrence says the state has to free itself from its economic dependence on oil and gas. "The route that Alaska is clinging to right now is just not viable over the long term, and it has to find a way to diversify its economy in this digital era," he says, "just as Washington state had to move on from [dependence on] the timber industry or Maine had to move on from the fishing industry."

On an international scale, Balton says the Arctic Council hopes to expand its policy-making role to deal with the consequences of increased development.

Alan Dowd, a senior fellow specializing in security issues at the Fraser Institute, a research think tank in Vancouver, Canada, says the region's future will depend on the other Arctic nations adopting a policy, perhaps through NATO, to back each other against Russian expansionism. Taking such a stance, he says, could "promote peaceful development that would be beneficial to all parties involved."

REDOIL's Thompson says looking five or 10 years ahead is shortsighted. As an Inupiat Native, he wants to see the region preserved and protected much longer than that. "I'm looking seven generations down the road," he says, and the critical move for future generations is to protect the wildlife and plants so Arctic natives can continue to practice their traditional lifestyle.

If the development of oil and other mineral resources is limited, Thompson says, "we'll find out who the real Alaskans are. This area got by fine for 10,000 years without oil, so we can be just fine without it now."

NOTES

1. Will Oremus, "The Upside of Global Warming: Luxury Northwest Passage" Cruises for the Filthy Rich, *Slate*, Aug. 17, 2016, http://tinyurl. com/jgsqeaq; Mark Thiessen, "Thanks to Melting Ice, Cruise Ship Travels Northwest Passage," *U.S. News & World Report*, Sept. 9, 2016, http://tinyurl.com/h3n2vjs.

2. Florence Fetterer, "Guest Post: Piecing together the Arctic's sea ice history back to 1850," *CarbonBrief*, Aug. 11, 2016, http://tiny url.com/jj7v3cw; Chris Mooney and Jason Samenow, "The North Pole is an insane 36 degrees warmer than normal as winter descends," *The Washington Post*, Nov. 17, 2016, http://tinyurl.com/htekzdc.

3. Kenneth Bird *et al.*, "Circum-Arctic Resource Appraisal: Estimates of Undiscovered Oil and Gas North of the Arctic Circle," U.S. Geological Survey, 2008, http://tinyurl.com/7tufxej; "Arctic oil and natural gas resources," Energy Information Administration, Jan. 20, 2012, http://tinyurl.com/jfna7gy.

4. Paavo Lipponen, "Arctic Development Opportunities," *Pöyry*, April 2016, http://tinyurl.com/gmqne5t.

5. Fetterer, *op. cit.*; Shaye Wolf, "Extinction. It's Not Just for Polar Bears," Center for Biological Diversity and Care for the Wild International, September 2010, http://tinyurl.com/h8dsku7; and Brandon Miller, "Amid higher global temperatures, sea ice at record lows at poles," CNN, Nov. 19, 2016, http://tinyurl.com/hywyebf.

6. Fetterer, *ibid.*

7. Peter Wadhams, "A Farewell to Ice: A Report from the Arctic," Allen Lane, Kindle edition, location 126, Sept. 1, 2016.

8. Mooney and Samenow, *op. cit.*

9. "Arctic People," National Snow and Ice Data Center, 2016, http://tinyurl.com/z7zx8mz.

10. "Arctic Human Development Report," *Tema Nord*, 2014, pp. 53-55, http://tinyurl.com/jy4zjq4.

11. "United Nations Convention on the Law of the Sea of 10 December 1982, Overview and full text," United Nations, Aug. 12, 2013, http://tinyurl.com/53hdl.

12. Carol Williams, "Russia claims vast Arctic territory, seeks U.N. recognition," *Los Angeles Times*, Aug. 4, 2015, http://tinyurl.com/q8eel9l.

13. "U.S.-Canada Joint Statement on Climate, Energy, and Arctic Leadership," The White House, March 10, 2016, http://tinyurl.com/zhjsrbl.

14. *Ibid.*

15. William Yardley, "Obama administration bans Arctic offshore oil drilling through 2022. But will Trump reverse it?" *Los Angeles Times*, Nov. 18, 2016, http://tinyurl.com/gsy5aal.

16. *Ibid.*

17. "U.S. gasoline and crude oil prices," Short-Term Energy Outlook October 2016, U.S. Energy Information Administration, Oct. 13, 2016, http://tinyurl.com/hsmuvk9.

18. Clifford Krauss and Stanley Reed, "Shell Exits Arctic as Slump in Oil Prices Forces Industry to Retrench," *The New York Times*, Sept. 28, 2015, http://tinyurl.com/nuogtey.

19. Yereth Rosen, "Shell isn't the only oil company leaving Alaska's Arctic," *Alaska Dispatch News*, May 10, 2016, http://tinyurl.com/go7cnmj.

20. Elwood Brehmer, "The 6 billion barrel oil discovery," *Alaska Journal of Commerce*, Oct. 4, 2016,

http://tinyurl.com/jl5z3z7; "How much oil is consumed in the United States?" U.S. Energy Information Administration, March 17, 2016, http://tinyurl.com/h7tgdfq.

21. Jennifer A. Dlouhy, "Obama's Offshore Oil Plan Forces Drillers to Focus on Gulf," Bloomberg, Nov. 18, 2016, http://tinyurl.com/z8bs7jx.

22. Krista Langlois, "Drilling the Arctic comes with a 75 percent chance of a large oil spill," *High Country News*, Dec. 10, 2014, http://tinyurl.com/zhluj7b.

23. Wadhams, *op. cit.*, Kindle edition, location 99.

24. "Governor Walker Applauds Caelus Discovery," Office of the Governor Bill Walker, State of Alaska, Oct. 4, 2016, http://tinyurl.com/jpyoyxl.

25. Irina Slav, "Russia Ramps Up Arctic Oil Production," Oilprice.com, July 21, 2016, http://tinyurl.com/huenx43.

26. Christina Nunez, "Norway Offers New Energy Leases, Stoking Polar Arctic Rush," *National Geographic*, Jan. 24, 2015, http://tinyurl.com/qey6ocj.

27. Jon Marsh Duesund, "Arctic Offshore Oil, Gas Outlook, Figure 2," Rystad Energy, *E&P magazine*, March 2, 2015, http://tinyurl.com/ht2ju8z.

28. "Arctic oil and natural gas resources," *op. cit.*

29. Brian Beary, "Race for the Arctic," *CQ Researcher*, August 2008, pp. 213-242.

30. Wadhams, *op. cit.*, Kindle edition, location 83-84.

31. "Northwest Passage," *Encyclopedia Britannica*, 2016, http://tinyurl.com/gmorlzr.

32. R.K. Headland, "Transits of the Northwest Passage to End of the 2015 Navigation Season — Atlantic Ocean — Arctic Ocean — Pacific Ocean," Americanpolar.org, Oct. 5, 2015, http://tinyurl.com/zor3qfa.

33. "Northern Sea Route Shipping Statistics," Protection of the Arctic Marine Environment, 2016, http://tinyurl.com/gwcsmcy; "Monthly Number & Net Tone by Ship Type, Direction & Ship Status," Suez Canal Traffic Statistics, Suez Canal Authority, http://tinyurl.com/ju9a83c.

34. Henry Huntington and Vladimir Mednikov, "Arctic Shipping: Creating Good Governance Based on Truth, not Myth," Pew Charitable Trusts, Aug. 2, 2016, http://tinyurl.com/hhdn9mm.

35. *Ibid.*

36. Sonia Van Gilder Cooke, "Turn It Down: How Human Noise Is Disturbing the Whales," *Time*, March 1, 2012, http://tinyurl.com/hqcboje.

37. Wadhams, *op. cit.*, p. 83.

38. Charles Ebinger, "6 years from the BP Deepwater Horizon oil spill: What we've learned, and what we shouldn't misunderstand," Brookings Institution, April 20, 2016, http://tinyurl.com/j9r9a3q.

39. "Arctic Environment," International Association of Oil and Gas Producers, 2016, http://tinyurl.com/zoqgofw.

40. Alec Luhn, "Arctic Cities Crumble as Climate Change Thaws Permafrost," *Wired*, Oct. 20, 2016, http://tinyurl.com/hp4ahhy; Alec Luhn, "Anthrax outbreak triggered by climate change kills boy in Arctic Circle," *The Guardian*, Aug. 1, 2016, http://tinyurl.com/gl95vej.

41. John McCannon, *A History of the Arctic, Nature, Exploration and Exploitation* (2012), p. 28.

42. *Ibid.*, p. 35.

43. *Ibid.*

44. Aleksey Malyshev, "Prominent Russians: Vitus Bering," Russiapedia, http://tinyurl.com/z8cr7q5.

45. *Ibid.*

46. "James Cook North-West Passage expedition 1776–78: What prompted Cook out of retirement for one last expedition?" Royal Museums Greenwich, http://tinyurl.com/h7wtuvl.

47. "1784, Russians Settle Alaska," History.com, http://tinyurl.com/3k3and5.

48. "Alaska's Heritage, Chapter 3-2: Settlement and Population Patterns," Alaska Humanities Forum, Alaska History & Cultural Studies, 2016, http://tinyurl.com/jxeahjo.

49. "1784, Russians settle Alaska," *op. cit.*

50. *Ibid.*

51. McCannon, *op. cit.*, p. 158.

52. *Ibid.*, p. 204.

53. Rachel Nuwer, "A Soviet Ghost Town in the Arctic Circle, Pyramiden Stands Alone," *Smithsonian*, May 19, 2014, http://tinyurl.com/q6bz2pu.

54. McCannon, *op. cit.*, p. 207.

55. "Arctic History," *Arctic-Info*, March 2, 2016, http://tinyurl.com/hqq5e2d.

56. McCannon, *op. cit.*, pp. 200-205.

57. *Ibid.*, p. 253.

58. Alexey Kontorovich, "Oil and Gas of the Russian Arctic: History of Development in the 20th Century, Resources, and Strategy for the 21st Century," *Science First Hand*, Aug. 30, 2015, http://tinyurl.com/hvxrtc7.

59. McCannon, *op. cit.*, p. 253.

60. *Ibid.*

61. *Ibid.*

62. "Oil Discovery and Development in Alaska," Alaska Humanities Forum, 2016, http://tinyurl.com/zglnbht.

63. "Trans-Alaska Pipeline History," American Oil & Gas Historical Society, 2016, http://tinyurl.com/ja94shg.

64. *Ibid.*

65. "The Alaska Pipeline, The Environmental Movement and the Oil Industry," American Experience, PBS, April 4, 2006, http://tinyurl.com/gsvbn5l.

66. *Ibid.*

67. "Congress Clears Alaska Lands Legislation," *CQ Almanac*, 1980, http://tinyurl.com/gnxvaov.

68. Sarah Graham, "Environmental Effects of Exxon Valdez Spill Still Being Felt," *Scientific American*, Dec. 19, 2003, http://tinyurl.com/jg839wg.

69. *Ibid.*; "Russian Oil Disaster, the ongoing Arctic oil spill crisis," Greenpeace International, 2016, http://tinyurl.com/d54y855.

70. McCannon, *op. cit.*, p. 280.

71. "2016 ties with 2007 for second lowest Arctic sea ice minimum," National Snow and Ice Data Center, Sept. 15, 2016, http://tinyurl.com/j6tvnde.

72. Wolf, *op. cit.*

73. "The Arctic Council: A Backgrounder," Arctic Council, May 23, 2016, http://tinyurl.com/7wez p4e.

74. "Arctic Council advances environmental protection and sustainable development in Portland, Maine," Arctic Council, Oct. 6, 2016, www.arctic-council.org/index.php/en/our-work 2/8-news-and-events/425-sao-oct-2016-post-release.

75. "Frozen Conflict, Denmark claims the North Pole," *The Economist*, Dec. 20, 2014, http://tinyurl.com/gpetm4p.

76. *Arctic Ocean: The Unexpected Frontier* (May 2009).

77. Williams, *op. cit.*

78. C.J. Chivers, "Russians Plant Flag on the Arctic Seabed," *The New York Times*, Aug. 3, 2007, http://tinyurl.com/hl3hnwm.

79. Levon Sevunts, "Canada to submit its Arctic continental shelf claim in 2018," Radio Canada International, May 3, 2016, http://tinyurl.com/gkppvzm.

80. Zi-Ann Lum, "Justin Trudeau: 'Everybody Knows The North Pole Is In Canada,'" *The Huffington Post Canada*, March 3, 2016, http://tinyurl.com/hu9jzxa.

81. "Oil and Natural Gas Resources of the Arctic," *op. cit.*

82. Williams, *op. cit.*; Betsy Baker, "Law, Science, and the Continental Shelf: The Russian Federation and the Promise of Arctic Cooperation," *American University International Law Review*, 2010, http://tinyurl.com/gtcssf7.

83. Brehmer, *op. cit.*

84. Kirk Johnson, "Alaskans Brace for Spending Cuts as Oil Prices Tumble," *The New York Times*, July 15, 2016, http://tinyurl.com/hx6jakb.

85. Devin Henry, "Obama weighs big Arctic decision," *The Hill*, July 3, 2016, http://tinyurl.com/hysyd2l.

86. Nick Cunningham, "Norway Forced To Cancel Arctic Drilling Plans," Oilprice.com, Sept. 9, 2016, http://tinyurl.com/jyp4796.

87. *Ibid.*

88. Erica Martinson, "Trump energy plan calls for more drilling, fewer environmental protections," *Alaska Dispatch News*, July 14, 2016, http://tinyurl.com/j6bamnc.

89. *Ibid.*

90. Louis Jacobson, "Yes, Donald Trump did call climate change a Chinese hoax," *PolitiFact*, June 3, 2016, http://tinyurl.com/jgrkft5.

91. Tom Phillips, Fiona Harvey and Alan Yuhas, "Breakthrough as US and China agree to ratify Paris climate deal," *The Guardian*, Sept. 3, 2016, http://tinyurl.com/gsf2eck.

92. Juliet Eilperin, "Hillary Clinton breaks with Obama to oppose Arctic drilling," *The Washington Post*, Aug. 18, 2015, http://tinyurl.com/grkf979.

93. "An American First Energy Plan," Trump Pence, Make America Great Again, 2016, http://tinyurl.com/zetcnut.

94. Nancy Cook and Andrew Restuccia, "Meets Trump's Cabinet-in-Waiting," *Politico*, Nov. 9, 2016, http://tinyurl.com/p39o6tr.

95. Julia Boccagno, "Climate change denier is leading Trump's EPA transition team," CBS News, Nov. 11, 2016, http://tinyurl.com/zdg82oa.

96. Erich Pica, "The environmental resistance will stand against Trump," Friends of the Earth, Nov. 9, 2016, http://tinyurl.com/gungw24.

97. Jason Samenow, "Arctic sea ice is at a record low and could, in spurts, disappear within our lifetimes," *The Washington Post*, Oct. 27, 2016, http://tinyurl.com/z8ku8of.

BIBLIOGRAPHY

Selected Sources

Books

McCannon, John, *A History of the Arctic: Nature, Exploration and Exploitation*, Reaktion Books, 2012.
A history professor and Arctic expert at Southern New Hampshire University explores the region from prehistoric times, including its indigenous cultures, the era of Western exploration and today's debate over the development of Arctic resources.

Struzik, Edward, *Future Arctic: Field Notes from a World on the Edge*, Island Press, 2015.
A journalist and explorer who has traveled extensively through the Arctic examines the region's unfolding transformation and looks ahead to the impact it is likely to have on the local culture and environment.

Wadhams, Peter, *A Farewell to Ice: A Report from the Arctic*, Allen Lane, Kindle edition 2016.
An English scientist considered one of the world's leading experts on sea ice predicts the Arctic could be effectively free of ice in the next few years because of global warming, which he says could have catastrophic consequences for the entire planet.

Watt-Cloutier, Sheila, *The Right to Be Cold: One Woman's Story of Protecting Her Culture, the Arctic and the Whole Planet*, Penguin Canada, 2016.
A foremost Canadian environmental and human rights activist links the safeguarding of the Arctic to the survival of her Inuit culture.

Articles

Mooney, Chris, "The Arctic is being utterly transformed — and we're just starting to grasp the consequences," *The Washington Post*, Sept. 28, 2016, http://tinyurl.com/huzulv8.
Scientists at a special White House conference on the Arctic say the region is warming faster than any other because of global climate change but that research is lacking on the full consequences of this change.

Myers, Steven Lee, "U.S. Is Playing Catch-Up With Russia in Scramble for the Arctic," *The New York Times*, Aug. 29, 2015, http://tinyurl.com/j76m4zf.
Analysts and government officials say the United States is lagging behind other Arctic nations, particularly Russia, in adjusting to the region's changing environment and emerging opportunities.

Thiessen, Mark, "Thanks to Melting Ice, Cruise Ship Travels Northwest Passage," *U.S. News & World Report*, Sept. 9, 2016, http://tinyurl.com/h3n2vjs.
The voyage of the luxury cruise liner *Crystal Serenity* through the once impassible Northwest Passage raises questions about the economic and environmental impact of melting Arctic ice as a result of global warming.

Yalowitz, Kenneth, and Vincent Gallucci, "Can the U.S. and Russia Avoid an Arctic Arms Race?" *The National Interest*, April 8, 2016, http://tinyurl.com/h2h63th.
The United States and Russia have largely cooperated on issues concerning the Arctic, but increasing tensions between the two nations and the decision by both to hold large-scale military maneuvers in the area have raised the possibility of an Arctic arms race.

Reports and Studies

"Arctic Marine Strategic Plan, 2015-2025, Protecting Marine and Coastal Ecosystems in a Changing Arctic," Arctic Council, April 2015, http://tinyurl.com/zvgm2r7.
An intergovernmental forum that works to manage Arctic resources and promote sustainable development looks at the challenges facing Arctic marine and coastal

ecosystems from climate change and increased development and outlines ways to deal with them.

"Arctic Potential, Realizing the Promise of U.S. Arctic Oil and Gas Resources," Committee on Arctic Research, National Petroleum Council, 2015, http://tinyurl.com/zwxytcb.
The council, an oil and gas industry advisory committee to the U.S. secretary of Energy, concludes that with careful environmental stewardship, oil and gas resources in the Arctic can be safely developed.

Hamilton, Neil, "Arctic Sanctuary, Global Commons, Environmental Protection and Future-Proofing," Greenpeace International, June 2014, http://tinyurl.com/hat5etv.
Greenpeace, the international environmental group, looks at the development ongoing and proposed in the Arctic region and calls for the creation of an Arctic sanctuary of 2.8 million square kilometers (roughly 1.08 million square miles) to protect the area's endangered species and ecosystem from further destruction.

"Opportunities and Challenges for Arctic Oil and Gas Development," Woodrow Wilson International Center for Scholars, 2014, http://tinyurl.com/zabpcrk.
A report for the Wilson Center, a nonpartisan policy forum in Washington, considers the opportunity for expanded oil and gas drilling in the Arctic, predicting that $100 billion could be invested in the region in the next decade.

O'Rourke, Ronald, "Changes in the Arctic: Background and Issues for Congress," Congressional Research Service, Oct. 14, 2014, http://tinyurl.com/zpa4qnh.
The nonpartisan research arm of Congress looks at the potential economic benefits, environmental costs and heightened international competition and tensions that arise from climate change in the Arctic, which is opening more areas to potential development.

For More Information

Alaska Oil and Gas Association, 121 W. Fireweed, Suite 207, Anchorage, Alaska 99503; 907-272-1481; www.aoga.org. Trade group representing companies exploring, producing, refining or marketing oil and gas in Alaska and its offshore areas.

Arctic Council, Fram Centre, Postboks 6606 Langnes, 9296 Tromsø, Norway; 47-77 75-01-40; www.arctic-council.org. Intergovernmental forum promoting cooperation among the Arctic nations, including the United States, and Arctic indigenous communities on issues of common concern.

Center for Biological Diversity, 378 N. Main Ave., Tucson, AZ 85701; 866-357-3349; www.biologicaldiversity.org. Works to protect endangered species, including polar bears and other Arctic wildlife, threatened by climate change or development.

International Association of Oil and Gas Producers, City Tower, 40 Basinghall St., 14th Floor, London EC2V 5DE, United Kingdom; 44-0-20-3763-9700; www.iogp.org/About-IOGP. Membership association for oil and gas producers active in the Artic and other parts of the world.

Inuit Circumpolar Council-Alaska, 3900 Arctic Blvd., Suite 203, Anchorage, Alaska 99503; 907-274-9058; http://iccalaska.org. Represents approximately 160,000 Inuit from Alaska, Canada, Greenland and Chukotka (Russia).

National Resources Defense Council, 40 W. 20th St., 11th floor, New York, NY 10011; 212-727-2700; www.nrdc.org. Environmental advocacy group with more than 2 million members that focuses on protecting natural habitats, plants and wildlife.

United States Arctic Research Commission, 4350 N. Fairfax Drive, Suite 510, Arlington, VA 22203; 703-525-0111; www.arctic.gov. Federal agency that establishes or recommends policies and priorities for Arctic scientific research.

15

Fighting Cancer

Barbara Mantel

Kent Haffer, a computer professional from Missouri, was diagnosed with advanced stage 3 melanoma in 2005. But today, thanks to a new drug, his cancer is in remission. While rapid advances in cancer treatment are helping patients like Haffer, experts caution that the new drugs can be prohibitively expensive and may have limited effectiveness.

From *CQ Researcher*,
January 22, 2016

E leven years ago [in 2005], Kent Haffer learned he had advanced stage 3 melanoma after seeing a cancer specialist for two black bumps on his calf. Biopsies showed the skin cancer had spread to eight nearby lymph nodes.

"I was 44 at the time, and I was thinking, 'Why me?' I was never a sun worshiper," says Haffer, a computer professional from St. Peters, Mo. Only about a quarter of patients with Haffer's diagnosis are still alive 10 years later. In contrast, 95 percent of patients survive at least that long when melanoma is caught in its earliest stage.[1]

Thrice-weekly shots of the protein interferon, multiple surgeries to remove cancerous lumps and chemotherapy directly into his leg could not halt the disease's progression, which migrated to his thigh.

So in 2007, his oncologist at Washington University's Siteman Cancer Center in St. Louis entered Haffer in his clinical trial for ipilimumab, a drug that helps the body's immune system recognize and attack melanoma cells. Two-thirds through a two-year course of 26 doses, Haffer was in remission.

"The main side effect is, my hair turned white. I didn't care; it could have turned pink," says Haffer. To reduce the risk of recurrence, a few years ago Haffer received three doses of a vaccine tailored to his tumors' genetic makeup.

Next month, he will mark six years in remission.

Patients such as Haffer are benefiting from rapid advances in cancer treatment, including immunotherapy, which stimulates the body's immune system to fight cancer, and targeted therapy, which

Cancer Survival Rising

The five-year survival rate for Americans diagnosed with cancer rose by nearly 40 percent since 1975, according to the National Cancer Institute.

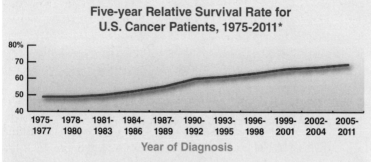

Five-year Relative Survival Rate for U.S. Cancer Patients, 1975-2011*

Year of Diagnosis

* Based on data from federal registry of patients in Atlanta, Connecticut, Detroit, Hawaii, Iowa, New Mexico, San Francisco, Seattle and Utah.

Source: "Table 2.8, All Cancer Sites (Invasive), 5-Year Relative and Period Survival by Race, Sex, Diagnosis Year and Age," National Cancer Institute, accessed Jan. 12, 2016, http://tinyurl.com/zb7qomp

takes aim at precise molecules on the surface of cancer cells. The U.S. Food and Drug Administration (FDA) designates many of these new drugs "breakthrough" therapies and approves them in a streamlined process established in 2013. A breakthrough therapy must address a life-threatening condition and seem highly likely to help patients.[2]

Yet exuberant media reports and direct-to-patient advertisements for these techniques may be creating false hope. At least at the moment, the FDA has approved immunotherapies for only a few kinds of advanced cancer. And targeted therapies, while more numerous, often stop working as tumors develop resistance to the drugs.

In addition, the newest cancer medicines can be prohibitively expensive, costing more than $100,000 a year per patient. Congress has held hearings, and oncologists are speaking out against the high prices, which drug makers defend, citing the tremendous cost and risky nature of research and development.

Meanwhile, insurers and drug makers blame each other for the growing financial burden on patients. "Cancer patients face higher out-of-pocket costs for their medicines than any other patients," says Holly Campbell, a spokeswoman for the Washington-based Pharmaceutical Research and Manufacturers of America, a trade association for drug makers. "That has to do with their insurance benefit design, not with the launch price of a medicine." Most insurers have tiered systems for reimbursement, and the majority place oral cancer drugs, which patients take at home and purchase through a pharmacy, in the highest cost-sharing tier, meaning patients have to pay more.[3]

But insurers say they have no choice, given the high cost of cancer drugs. "If insurance plans were going to cover every single cancer drug at zero cost sharing or at the one- or two-level tier, premiums would skyrocket, and no one would be able to afford insurance," says Clare Krusing, spokeswoman for America's Health Insurance Plans, an industry trade association in Washington.

At the same time, cancer screening guidelines are changing, with some experts recommending that screening be done less often and later, in the case of breast cancer, or not at all, in the case of prostate cancer. But these changes are prompting sometimes rancorous debate.

In his State of the Union address this month, President Obama said he wanted to make "America the country that cures cancer once and for all" and put Vice President Joe Biden in charge of the effort, although details were scarce.[4] Biden, whose son Beau died of brain cancer in May, pushed Congress in December to approve a substantial increase in federal dollars for medical research, including for cancer, after more than a decade of funding stagnation.

But the idea of a single cancer cure is misleading, say experts, because cancer is not one disease but a collection of more than 100 complex and related diseases, in which some of the body's cells divide without stopping and spread to surrounding tissue.[5]

Cancer is the second-leading cause of death in the United States after heart disease. Lung cancer is the biggest cancer killer by far, followed in descending order by colorectal, pancreatic, breast, liver and prostate cancers.[6]

Nevertheless, reductions in smoking and advances in prevention, early detection and treatment have resulted in a 23 percent decline in the cancer death rate between its 1991 peak and 2012, the latest year for which data are available. In 2012, 582,623 people died of cancer.[7] Experts say the number of deaths could be cut further, possibly in half, because many cancers are linked to preventable risk factors, such as tobacco use, obesity, lack of exercise, infection and exposure to ultraviolet light from the sun or tanning beds.[8]

Cancer groups warn that demand for cancer care will grow to record levels over the next 15 years, pushed by three trends:

- More people are being covered by insurance;
- As treatment improves, the ranks of cancer survivors are growing, and many will need continuing care; and
- The number of new cancers is projected to increase 38 percent between 2015 and 2035 as the U.S. population grows and ages.[9]

Cancer, after all, is predominantly a disease of older age because the body accumulates cancer-causing cellular abnormalities over time.

Meanwhile, the number of oncologists — doctors who specialize in treating cancer — is projected to grow far more slowly. As a result, "more than 400,000 Americans may have difficulty getting critical cancer care," said the American Society of Clinical Oncology (ASCO), based in Alexandria, Va.[10]

Racial and ethnic minorities may bear the brunt of the crisis. Disparities persist in cancer patients' outcomes across racial and ethnic lines, and access to quality care is a factor, along with geography, culture, income level, education and genetics. It's a complex mix that defies "easy solutions," according to ASCO. African-Americans, for example, are nearly 20 percent more likely to die from cancer than whites.[11]

Disparities are even more pronounced in particular cancers. Black men are twice as likely to die from prostate cancer as white men.[12] Researchers don't yet understand why, says L. Michelle Bennett, director, of the Center for Research Strategy at the National Cancer Institute (NCI) in Bethesda, Md. Biological factors are a possibility, Bennett says.

The same could be said of breast cancer. Genetics and biology may explain why African-American women are more likely to have larger tumors and a more aggressive type of cancer than white women. But blacks and Hispanics also are more likely to receive their diagnoses later than whites and to get inappropriate treatment, a recent study found. These last disparities "have more to do with social, cultural and economic factors," said Lu Chen, the study's lead author and a researcher at Seattle's Fred Hutchinson Cancer Research Center.[13]

To better understand the racial disparities, Bennett says, clinical trials need to enroll more minorities. Nationally, fewer than 2 percent of cancer clinical trial participants are black and Hispanic.[14] So the NCI has developed a network of researchers, doctors and hospitals that is making clinical trials more accessible to diverse populations. Minorities now account for about 20 percent of patients recruited into trials at some sites. "That's quite an amazing statistic," says Bennett.

As the fight against cancer continues, here are some of the questions that patients and their advocates, oncologists, researchers, drug makers and insurers are debating:

Is cutting back on cancer screening a good idea?

Early detection saves lives. That has been the medical establishment's mantra for decades. But research is calling that logic into question, and cancer screening guidelines are changing as a result.

Medical experts now agree that women don't need their first Pap smear screening for cervical cancer until age 21 and then only every three years, later and less frequently than prior recommendations.[15] Breast and prostate cancer screening guidelines also have been narrowed but with far less agreement and much more controversy.

In 2012, the U.S. Preventive Services Task Force, an independent, government-selected panel of experts, recommended against routine prostate cancer screening in men of any age, giving it a D grade. (The task force assigns each preventive service a letter grade from A to D, based on the strength of the evidence for benefits versus harm.) Previously it had recommended against screening only in men 75 years and older. The blood test screens for prostate-specific antigen (PSA), a protein associated with the disease.[16]

Cancer Deaths Highest for Blacks

African-Americans were more likely to die from cancer than any other racial or ethnic group during the 2008-12 period, according to the latest available data. Whites had the second-highest mortality rate, followed by Hispanics and Native Americans.

Age-Adjusted Cancer Mortality Rate per 100,000 Population, by Race/Ethnicity, 2008-2012

Black	202.0
White	170.9
Hispanic	119.3
American Indian/Alaska Native	117.4
Asian/Pacific Islander	106.6

Source: "Table 2.15, All Cancer Sites (Invasive), Age-adjusted Rates and Trends by Race/Ethnicity and Sex," National Cancer Institute, accessed Jan. 12, 2016, http://tinyurl.com/jbkg6yc

The task force said the benefit of PSA screening was, at most, small. "And I emphasize 'at most,'" says Dr. Michael LeFevre, the task force's immediate past chair and a University of Missouri professor of medicine. The test saves few lives, he says, and "the harms are more substantial."

Those harms are related largely to overdiagnosis. As many as half of detected prostate cancers never advance or grow so slowly that they pose no health threat in a man's lifetime. But evidence shows that nearly all men opt for treatment, so many are receiving unneeded surgery, radiation or hormone therapy, which can lead to impotence, urinary incontinence and bowel-control problems.[17]

The task force has its critics.

"I am very concerned about the change in the task force guideline," says Dr. Richard Wender, the American Cancer Society's chief cancer control officer. Since the task force issued a draft guideline in 2011, prostate cancer screening has declined, and fewer early-stage cancers are being detected, he says.

Wender agrees that reduced screening is resulting in less overdiagnosis. "But I'm also fairly certain that we will see more men diagnosed at an advanced stage over time," he says, and, as a result, "we'll see a slowing of the rate of decline in prostate cancer deaths."

The American Cancer Society recommends that men begin discussing with their doctor whether to undergo routine PSA testing at age 50 and continue that discussion until they no longer have a 10-year life expectancy.[18]

But predictions that reduced screening will negatively impact the prostate cancer death rate is "very premature," says LeFevre.

The debate about breast cancer screening has been even more heated. In 2009, the task force caused an uproar when it recommended that women of average risk between ages 40 and 49 no longer have routine mammography screening but instead make up their own minds. It gave such screening a C grade. It also recommended that women between ages 50 and 74 switch from annual to biennial mammograms, which got a B. Updated guidelines this month kept these recommendations essentially unchanged.[19]

As with all its guidelines, the task force tried to balance benefit — a lower chance of dying from breast cancer — and harms. "The most serious potential harm is being diagnosed with a cancer that would not become a threat during your lifetime," said Dr. Kirsten Bibbins-Domingo, the task force's vice chairperson and professor of medicine and of epidemiology and biostatistics at the University of California, San Francisco.[20]

The American College of Radiology, a professional medical society, continues to recommend annual mammography screening starting at age 40 and says the task force's guideline "would result in thousands of additional and unnecessary breast cancer deaths each year."[21]

The task force underestimated mammography's benefits, the radiology group says. It gave too much weight to randomized controlled clinical trials, most of which were decades old and used outdated technology, says Dr. Debra Monticciolo, chair of the American College of Radiology's breast imaging commission and a Texas A&M University professor. And it gave short shrift to observational studies of women who had mammography that showed as much as 40 percent reductions in mortality, she says.

But LeFevre says, "It's easy to cherry pick and decide which study shows what you want it to show. I can pick out observational studies that show no benefit at all." The task force looked carefully at randomized trials, observational studies and computer models, he says.

Monticciolo also says the task force overestimated screening's harms. No one can accurately measure overdiagnosis, she says: "The estimates are all over the map."

The radiology group has its own critics. "I don't think the American College of Radiology should be issuing guidelines on mammography screening. There is no objectivity there" because its members are the ones administering the screening, says Fran Visco, president of the Washington-based National Breast Cancer Coalition, an advocacy group that supports the task force's guidelines. "We spend billions of dollars a year on mammography screening that could be better spent on people without access to treatment or on research."

Adding to the confusion, the American Cancer Society revised its breast cancer screening guidelines late last year, favoring less frequent screening and a later start, but it did not go quite as far as the task force. The society recommends women start discussing screening with health care providers at age 40, begin yearly mammograms at age 45 and switch to biennial screening at age 55.[22]

The Affordable Care Act requires private insurers to fully cover preventive services that are assigned an A or B grade by the task force. But the task force's breast cancer screening recommendations won't affect insurance coverage anytime soon, because Congress passed legislation late last year requiring insurers to ignore the latest guidelines, at least through 2017. Until then, insurers should rely on the task force's 2002 recommendation for annual mammograms starting at age 40.[23]

In any case, screening would be less controversial, experts say, if doctors knew which detected breast cancers, mostly ductal carcinoma in situ, an early breast cancer confined to the milk ducts, are likely to be harmless. Such cases could be carefully watched instead of being treated unnecessarily, says Wenders. But that tool does not yet exist. Doctors can measure the aggressiveness of prostate cancer, however, and more men are opting for "active surveillance" when appropriate, he says.

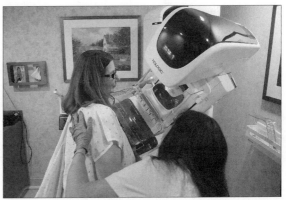

Getty Images/Sun Sentinel/Amy Beth Bennett

A patient undergoes three-dimensional digital mammography at the Women's Imaging Center at Memorial Regional Hospital in Hollywood, Fla. Recommendations vary widely on what age to begin breast cancer screening. The U.S. Preventive Services Task Force, an independent panel of experts, does not recommend routine mammography for women of average risk between ages 40 and 49 but says screening in this age group should be an individual decision.

Is precision medicine a game changer for cancer?

Personalized genomic testing has been "heralded as the next big weapon in the war on cancer," according to *ScienceNews*.[24] The DNA of a patient's tumor is tested for genetic mutations that cause a cancer to grow and spread, and a drug is prescribed that precisely targets those abnormalities.

Cancer Treatment Centers of America frequently advertises its use of genomic testing on television and in print. And journalists often use superlatives such as "game changer," "miracle" and "revolutionary" to describe targeted therapies.[25]

But FDA-approved targeted therapies exist for only a small minority of patients, says Dr. Theodora Ross, director of the cancer genetics program at the University of Texas Southwestern Medical Center in Dallas. "I would say it's probably about 5 percent." These therapies work against only a handful of known mutations and are approved for a limited number of cancers.

They are improving care and extending survival for patients with chronic myelogenous leukemia, a blood cancer, and some advanced lung, gastrointestinal and breast cancers with mutations that can be targeted. However, with the exception of lung cancer, most of these drugs are approved for use only after other treatments, such as chemotherapy, have failed or stopped working.

There have been some notable successes. The pill Gleevec has transformed chronic myelogenous leukemia into a manageable disease, and Herceptin is allowing some breast cancer patients to live cancer-free for more than a decade.

But, typically, the effects of targeted medicines wear off relatively quickly, even though more than 80 percent of treated patients respond initially, says Elaine Mardis, director of technology development at Washington University's McDonnell Genome Institute in St. Louis. "Patients have a durability of response that can be a few months, where they remain tumor-free, and then advance with more aggressive disease. Or it can be a few years," she says. That's because tumor cells evolve and develop resistance to these drugs.

As a result, targeted therapy can be a roller coaster for patients and their families. Phyllis Merchant of Ashland, Mass., watched her sister, who had lung cancer, try five different targeted therapies, enjoying relatively good health until each drug stopped working. Merchant said when further genetic testing revealed another mutation that might be a target for yet a sixth therapy, her sister refused. "We all accepted her decision, knowing it'd be too hard for her to come back from the brink again," said Merchant. Her sister died in July.[26]

It's now standard procedure to test patients with the kinds of cancers for which approved therapies exist and prescribe the matching drugs if the target mutations are found. And health insurance pays for it.

Cancer Cases to Grow

The number of U.S. cancer cases diagnosed annually is projected to rise 38 percent by 2035, to almost 2.4 million, according to the World Health Organization's cancer research agency. An aging population will be the key factor in the increase, according to the American Association for Cancer Research. Tobacco use and obesity also will contribute to the rise, the group said.

Projected Annual Number of New Cancer Diagnoses, 2015-2035

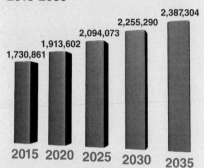

Source: "GLOBOCAN 2012" Database, International Agency for Research on Cancer, accessed Jan. 12, 2016, http://tinyurl.com/kjodu7h; caption information from "AACR Cancer Progress Report 2015," American Association for Cancer Research, September 2015, p. 13, http://tinyurl.com/j5qxo9z

But some doctors are going further and ordering the sequencing of hundreds of tumor genes in all sorts of patients who have run out of options, seeking mutations that can be targeted with drugs not yet approved for those cancers. For example, a patient with pancreatic cancer might have the same mutation that has been successfully treated in lung cancer.

Doctors affiliated with Ross' hospital have sent tumor tissue from about 600 patients to labs for this kind of broad sequencing. "It's a desperate last-ditch effort," says Ross. "And it's not going to help the patient." The hospital's preliminary review has found that about 2 percent of these patients had a mutation that matched a targeted therapy, but none responded to treatment.

"Doctors send these tests, and they're extremely expensive, and they're not covered by insurance," Ross says. The price is about $5,000, she says. This kind of broad sequencing of a tumor's DNA should not be done outside of a clinical trial, she says. "Without data, it's kind of like snake oil."

Dr. Maurie Markman, president of medicine and science at Cancer Treatment Centers of America, strongly disagrees. For the past two years, the network of five hospitals has been offering advanced genomic testing of between 300 and 500 cancer genes to any individual who has failed to respond or is no longer responding to standard medical treatment; who has a cancer where the standard care hardly ever works; or who has an unusually aggressive cancer.

"I care deeply about patients," says Markman. "What would you do if this were your mother, your sister or your child or your wife?"

Targeted therapy has been prescribed in more than 10 percent of the network's tested patients, he says. When asked how they have responded to treatment, Markman replied, "This is not a research study; this is a clinical effort. We are evaluating it as we go along."

Even when there is no known drug to treat a cancer's mutations, patients may still benefit from genomic testing, says Markman. They could be referred to participate in a "basket" trial, a new kind of clinical trial in which patients with different cancers with the same mutation are studied together. Or perhaps an appropriate drug will come to market a few months down the road, he says.

"If I were diagnosed with cancer today, the first thing I would do is to get a genetic test of that tumor," says Mardis. Her hospital does not offer such testing; it offers only the narrow genetic testing that is FDA-approved and reimbursed by insurance. In addition to Cancer Treatment Centers of America, several other hospitals offer broad genetic testing of cancers, and some are paying for it.

One is Memorial Sloan Kettering Cancer Center in New York City, which pays for genomic testing for patients with metastatic cancer — cancer that has spread to other body sites. "The results of the test are unlikely to influence clinical treatment," says Dr. Charles Sawyers, chair of the hospital's human oncology and pathogenesis programs. But the testing will allow researchers at the hospital to gather enough patient data to find new mutations, especially rare ones, that might lend themselves to treatment, he says. "People are not going to stop generating this data," he says. "There's just too much enthusiasm for it."

A Glossary of Terms

Term	Definition
Adoptive T-cell (or cellular) therapy	Treatment in which scientists collect a patient's cancer-fighting T cells and amend them in a lab to recognize and attack tumors; they then place the cells back in the patient's bloodstream in hopes of overwhelming the cancer.
Biosimilars	Drugs that closely resemble biologics, complex medicines that are made from living organisms.
BRCA1/BRCA2	Genes that help suppress cell growth but can contain mutations that heighten a patient's risk of breast, ovarian, prostate or other cancers.
Genomic testing	Test that analyzes a patient's tumor DNA to identify changes linked to cancer's growth and spread.
HER2-positive	Type of breast cancer in which cells have too much HER2 protein, which helps control cell growth; excessive protein allows cancer cells to grow faster and makes cancer more likely to spread.
Immunotherapy	Treatment that uses substances to stimulate the body's immune system to fight cancer, infection and other diseases.
Liquid biopsy	Test of patient's blood, urine or other bodily fluids to search for DNA shed by cancer cells to help assess whether cancer is responding to treatment or is in remission.
Monoclonal antibody	Lab-made protein that binds to cancer cells and is used alone or to carry drugs, toxins or radioactive substances to fight cancer.
Targeted therapy	Treatment that uses drugs or other substances to identify and attack specific types of cancer cells while minimizing harm to normal cells.

Sources: "NCI Dictionary of Cancer Terms," National Cancer Institute; "Adoptive T Cell Therapy," University of Washington School of Medicine, undated; "Biosimilars," U.S. Food and Drug Administration, updated Aug. 27, 2015; "Tumor Assessments at CTCA," Cancer Treatment Centers of America, undated; and Melinda Beck, "A Blood Test for Early Cancer Detection Sparks Debate," *The Wall Street Journal*, Sept. 28, 2015

Are the high prices of new cancer drugs justified?

Last August, 118 leading oncologists wrote an editorial in the journal *Mayo Clinic Proceedings* protesting the high prices of cancer drugs, which, they said, are "affecting the care of patients with cancer and our health care system." All newly approved cancer drugs in 2014 had prices exceeding $120,000 a year per patient, they said. The physicians called on patients and health care providers to sign an online petition demanding that federal officials intervene.[27]

Christian S. Hinrichs, a researcher at the National Cancer Institute's Center for Cancer Research, is working on new ways to fight cervical and other forms of cancer. Congress increased federal cancer research funding by $264 million in 2016, money scientists say is needed to build on promising treatments that use the body's immune system to fight cancer or that target molecules on cancer cells to destroy them.

"Cancer drug prices have gone beyond any reasonable expectation," says Dr. Hagop Kantarjian, leukemia department chair at MD Anderson Cancer Center in Houston and a co-author of the editorial. Insurers, who foot most of the bill, agree. A drug's price "is essentially what drug makers choose for it to be," says Krusing of America's Health Insurance Plans. "And that's unsustainable."

The average launch price for 58 cancer drugs approved between 1995 and 2013 increased by 10 percent a year, after adjusting for inflation and health benefits, according to one study.[28] "That is very high," says health economist David Howard, a study co-author and professor at Atlanta's Emory University. Put another way, patients and their insurers paid $54,100 for a year of life in 1995, $139,000 a decade later and $207,000 by 2013, after accounting for inflation.[29]

Those prices force some patients to make drastic choices, Kantarjian says: " 'Am I going to buy the drug to prolong or save my life, or will I forgo it so I can save money for food and lodging and educating my kids?' "

Although Medicare, the federal health insurance program for people age 65 or older, and private insurance pay the lion's share of drug costs, patients have co-pays, co-sharing (where they pay a percentage) and deductibles. Experts say cancer patients can easily reach the maximum out-of-pocket costs allowed under the Affordable Care Act, which is $6,850 for an individual health insurance plan in 2016.[30] And out-of-pocket cost for a cancer patient with Medicare coverage can exceed $10,000 a year for a single drug, according to the Kaiser Family Foundation, a nonprofit in Menlo Park, Calif., that focuses on national health issues.[31]

"All of our member companies have patient assistance programs that help uninsured and underinsured patients," says Campbell of Pharmaceutical Research and Manufacturers of America.

But Kantarjian says assistance programs are not the answer. "Patients should not have to be beggars," he says. "Give us a transparent price that is decent and reasonable, and we'll pay for it."

The impact extends beyond cancer patients, says Dr. Clifford Hudis, breast medicine chief and vice president for government relations at New York's Memorial Sloan Kettering Cancer Center. "Everybody will ultimately bear the cost of rising drug prices because they will ultimately have to be reflected in premiums."

Howard cites several reasons for high prices. "The people who decide what drugs to use, mainly oncologists, are not the ones who are paying for it," he says. In addition, patent protection for new drugs insulates manufacturers from competition and gives them monopoly power to set prices, he says. Once approved by the FDA, a drug typically has 12.5 years of patent protection remaining.[32]

But Campbell says drug pricing is complex and reflects billions of dollars spent on research and development each year and "the clinical benefits that a drug provides patients."

Critics dispute such rationales. Price "isn't linked to how effective the drug is. It isn't linked to what therapies it displaces. It isn't linked to how long people live. It isn't linked to their side effects," says Hudis. Instead, a *JAMA Oncology* study showed prices of newly approved cancer drugs "simply reflect what the market will bear."[33]

Kantarjian and his co-authors offered several proposals to rein in prices. They include allowing the importation of cancer drugs from Canada, where medications are cheaper, and permitting Medicare to negotiate drug prices with manufacturers. Hospitals, private insurers and the pharmacy benefit managers they both hire negotiate with drug makers. So do Medicaid — the federal health insurance program for low income people — and the Veterans Administration. But Congress has forbidden Medicare, the largest spender on cancer drugs, from direct negotiations.

Howard says allowing greater competition from generic and biosimilar medications might be a more effective strategy. Biosimilars are lower-cost versions of biologics, complex medicines made from living cells, many of which are used to treat cancer. The federal government only recently created a process for approving biosimilar drugs and has approved just one.[34]

But perhaps the oncologists' most controversial proposal is to convene an expert panel that would "propose a fair price for new treatments," based on the value of health benefits to patients and to the health care system.[35]

"Policy makers and doctors pushing for price controls believe they can reduce the return for a successful new drug while still preserving the incentive to innovate. This is a dangerous form of magical thinking," said Dr. Thomas Stossel, a hematologist and Harvard Medical School professor. Controlling prices would scare away investors from the risky process of developing drugs, he said.[36]

Not true, said Dr. Peter Bach, director of Sloan Kettering's Center for Health Policy and Outcomes. The current system discourages innovation because it allows drugs with little extra value to command the same high prices as truly novel drugs, Bach said.[37]

Whatever the case, value-based pricing is proceeding slowly through private-sector initiatives. Express Scripts, a St. Louis-based pharmacy benefit manager, will start using disease-specific value-based pricing this year. So if a drug extends life by four months for one kind of cancer but only two months in another cancer type, reimbursement would reflect that difference: a higher reimbursement for the former than the latter.[38]

Pharmaceutical companies and insurers also are discussing tying drug reimbursement to individual patient outcomes, measured against benchmarks. However, experts say establishing benchmarks would be difficult for cancer because patients' responses to a drug can be so variable.

President Richard M. Nixon signs the National Cancer Act on Dec. 23, 1971. The compromise legislation kept the National Cancer Institute (NCI) within the National Institutes of Health and drug approval at the Food and Drug Administration but provided unprecedented funding to the NCI. It left unresolved a growing tension within the cancer establishment: Which should get more NCI funding — basic research or clinical testing of drugs to find a cure?

In the meantime, the American Society of Clinical Oncology is developing an online tool that assigns each drug a "net health benefit" score to encourage doctors and patients to talk about a drug's value. And Sloan Kettering has created an interactive online tool, called DrugAbacus, that allows users to compare prices for 54 cancer drugs with hypothetical prices that result when users assign monetary values to side effects, extra months of life, a drug's novelty and other measures.

"The goal is to influence the people who set prices," says Sloan Kettering's Hudis. It's beginning to work, he says. "One company with a product coming out soon recently phoned me up unpaid, just to ask my opinion about pricing," says Hudis. "This has never happened to me before."

BACKGROUND
Early Treatment

In 1937, President Franklin D. Roosevelt signed legislation establishing the National Cancer Institute, the government's principal agency for cancer research and training.[39] A little more than a year later, construction began on the institute's state-of-the-art laboratory in

Bethesda, where it was hoped scientists would lead a national effort to understand and overcome cancer.

But World War II intervened. "Congress's promised funds for a 'programmatic response to cancer' never materialized, and the NCI languished in neglect," wrote cancer physician and researcher Siddhartha Mukherjee in *The Emperor of All Maladies: A Biography of Cancer.* "The social outcry about cancer also drifted into silence."[40]

So did many private conversations. In the 1940s, cancer's "assaults were so unyielding, so unsparing, that the disease was considered too dark a subject for most people to discuss — even doctors," wrote physician Paul Marks, president emeritus of Memorial Sloan Kettering Cancer Center, in *On The Cancer Frontier: One Man, One Disease, and a Medical Revolution.*[41]

Nevertheless, researchers made some notable advances during the decade. The Pap test was introduced in 1943, enabling doctors to test a sample of a woman's cervical cells for abnormalities that could lead to cancer if left untreated. In 1947, Boston physician Sidney Farber reported the partial remission of pediatric leukemia in 10 children, using the drug aminopterin, a derivative of folic acid. Until then, children usually died within weeks of diagnosis. And in 1949, the FDA approved the first chemotherapy drug: nitrogen mustard, stockpiled as a weapon in World War II, to treat Hodgkin lymphoma — cancer of the immune system.[42]

After a renewed focus on the battle against cancer following the war, a series of important developments ensued in the 1950s and '60s:

- In 1954, Congress authorized the National Cancer Institute to build a focused program to find effective chemotherapy drugs; in the next 10 years, the institute tested more than 200,000 compounds.[43]
- In 1955, the NCI established a nationwide cancer research network to conduct clinical trials.[44]
- In 1958, institute scientists demonstrated that combination chemotherapy, the use of multiple drugs together, could produce remissions in patients with acute leukemia.
- In 1964, the U.S. surgeon general officially linked smoking to lung cancer and other serious health problems.[45]

- And in 1965, a new combination chemotherapy regimen was found to cure up to half of patients with advanced Hodgkin lymphoma.[46]

Despite these advances, at the start of the 1970s, "we had few clues as to how to develop effective new cancer treatments," said Marks.[47]

War on Cancer

Mary Lasker was a philanthropist and the widow of advertising magnate Albert Lasker, who had made a fortune devising campaigns touting Lucky Strike cigarettes. She had already spent decades lobbying U.S. presidents and members of Congress on health issues, using her influence to help establish the National Cancer Institute and other institutes within the National Institutes of Health. It was Lasker who persuaded Congress to fund NCI's chemotherapy screening initiative in 1955, a "hugely controversial" program that moved the institute away from its exclusive focus on basic research to include applied research, wrote physician and former NCI Director Vincent DeVita in *The Death of Cancer.*[48]

By the spring of 1970, "Mary decided that the country that had put a man on the moon . . . was ready to declare war on cancer," said DeVita. Lasker again worked behind the scenes, this time to forge bipartisan support for legislation that would substantially increase NCI's funding, remove it from NIH jurisdiction, require a comprehensive plan for vanquishing cancer and move approval of anti-cancer drugs from the FDA to a new independent cancer agency to which the NCI would report.[49]

Academic researchers, the NIH and the American Medical Association, the largest association of doctors and medical students, attacked the bill when it was introduced in the Senate. They argued that pumping money into cancer research would siphon money from other medical research and that every other institute within the NIH would want such independence.[50]

On Dec. 23, 1971, President Richard M. Nixon signed the National Cancer Act, a compromise bill that kept the NCI within the NIH and drug approval at the FDA but provided unprecedented funding to the NCI: an annual budget of $600 million by 1974.[51]

But it left unresolved a growing tension within the cancer establishment: Which should get more NCI

CHRONOLOGY

1930s-1960s *National Cancer Institute (NCI) established; early chemotherapy advances.*

1937 NCI, the government's principal agency for cancer research and training, is created.

1943 Pap test enables doctors to examine cervical cells for abnormalities that could lead to cancer.

1947 American physician Sidney Farber reports the partial remission of deadly childhood leukemia in 10 children using the drug aminopterin, a derivative of folic acid.

1949 Food and Drug Administration (FDA) approves nitrogen mustard as the first chemotherapy drug.

1954 Congress authorizes NCI to build a drug-testing program; over 10 years, it tests more than 200,000 compounds.

1955 NCI establishes nationwide research network to conduct clinical trials.

1964 U.S. surgeon general links smoking to cancer.

1965 A chemotherapy drug combination cures up to half of patients with advanced Hodgkin lymphoma, a disease of the white blood cells.

1970s-1980s *Government declares war on cancer; progress is made in breast cancer.*

1971 President Richard M. Nixon signs National Cancer Act and declares a war on cancer.

1976 Research shows that chemotherapy after surgery prolongs the lives of women with early-stage breast cancer.

1977 Studies show that lumpectomy — removal of only the tumor — followed by radiation therapy is as effective as mastectomy for women with early-stage breast cancer.

1980 Cancer death rate climbs to 207 per 100,000 population, from 199 per 100,000 five years earlier.

1981 Epidemiologists Richard Doll and Richard Peto conclude that most cancer is avoidable and that cancer deaths are due, in descending order, to diet, tobacco use, infections, sexual behavior, manmade carcinogens, sun exposure and unknown origin.

1985 Nearly one-third of U.S. women older than 40 are screened for breast cancer; by 2008, the rate approaches 70 percent.

1986 Epidemiologists John Bailar and Elaine Smith conclude that the war on cancer is being lost and recommend shifting money from treatment research to prevention. . . . FDA approves the first prostate cancer screening test, plus the anti-cancer drug Tamoxifen to prevent relapse in post-menopausal women after breast cancer surgery.

1990s-Present *Cancer death rate declines; FDA approves targeted cancer drugs and immunotherapies.*

1992 Cancer death rate falls from its 1991 peak as a result of reduced smoking, earlier detection of colorectal cancers and improved prostate and breast cancer treatments.

1997 FDA approves rituximab, a drug for B-cell non-Hodgkin lymphoma that targets a cancer surface protein. . . . Researchers discover that BRCA1 and BRCA2 mutations raise ovarian and breast cancer risk.

1998 FDA approves the drug Herceptin to treat a subtype of advanced breast cancer.

2006 FDA approves Gardasil, a vaccine against two strains of the human papillomavirus (HPV) that cause most cervical cancers.

2011 FDA approves the immunotherapy drug ipilimumab for advanced melanoma, a cancer of the skin.

2012 Cancer death rate has declined 23 percent since 1991 peak.

2015 Congress gives NIH $200 million in 2016 for President Obama's precision medicine initiative to accelerate research.

2016 Government has approved dozens of targeted drug therapies and several immunotherapies to fight cancer. . . . President Obama calls for "a new national effort" to cure cancer.

Scientists Seek Big Answers From "Big Data"

"This has the potential to transform the way we do routine care."

Doctors and hospitals generate a tremendous amount of data on patients that is stored electronically or on paper, accessible only to a patient's health care providers, the patient and the patient's family. Stripped of its identifying facts and pooled into vast databases, say cancer specialists and data experts, this information could be analyzed to find new uses for existing drugs, uncover harmful drug side effects, provide clues for treating patients with rare diseases and suggest promising avenues for drug research.

"This has the potential to transform the way we do routine care," said Dr. Clifford Hudis, a breast cancer specialist at Memorial Sloan Kettering Cancer Center in New York City.[1]

But some researchers believe that carefully controlled clinical trials should remain the primary way to develop new treatments, arguing that big-data approaches are too anecdotal to yield much useful information.

One "big-data" project underway is led by the American Society of Clinical Oncology, a professional organization of cancer doctors in Alexandria, Va., that is developing a system called CancerLinQ. Participating oncologists will eventually contribute millions of patient records to the system, says Dr. Richard Schilsky, the society's chief medical officer. Cancer doctors will be able to measure their patients' outcomes against a dozen or more quality measures and turn to CancerLinQ when stumped by a difficult case or a patient with a rare cancer, he says.

In that situation today, a doctor might call a colleague for advice, "and maybe that doctor has seen one or two similar cases or maybe none at all," says Schilsky. In contrast, CancerLinQ will allow the doctor to learn about "every other doctor's experience in the system."

Currently, researchers rely on clinical trials of experimental therapies to develop treatment options and obtain Food and Drug Administration (FDA) approval. But trials have problems, says Schilsky. Only about 5 percent of adult cancer patients participate, and they tend to be younger, healthier and less representative of the U.S. population, he says. "We don't really know how applicable the clinical trial data is to the people we have to treat every day."

In addition, researchers are dividing cancers into smaller and smaller subtypes that share genetic mutations or cellular abnormalities. So instead of recruiting all lung cancer patients into a clinical trial, for example, they might want to study only patients with squamous cell lung cancer with a particular genetic profile. "But it's hard to find enough patients who have the relevant molecular subtype," Schilsky says.

For these reasons, analyzing the data of the 95 percent of patients who don't participate in clinical trials is critical, he says.

But the task of pooling this data is daunting, not least of all because many software programs that handle electronic

funding — basic research or clinical testing of drugs to find a cure? Many argued that it was premature to focus a large part of the budget on a potential cure before the biology of cancer was better understood. Others argued that cancer patients deserved a bigger effort to find better treatments, even if cancer's mechanics remained mostly a mystery. In fact, both Nixon and Lasker had promised the public a "cure" for cancer by 1976 if Congress passed the National Cancer Act, which even those pushing for more applied research knew was an "absurd" goal, said De-Vita.[52]

The rest of the 1970s witnessed several milestones, particularly regarding breast cancer. Studies showed that lumpectomy — the removal of only the breast tumor — followed by radiation therapy was as effective as a mastectomy for women with early-stage breast cancer. Mammography screening for breast cancer was becoming more common, as were fecal tests and colonoscopies for colon cancer, detecting disease at an earlier and more treatable stage.[53]

In addition, after convincing reluctant breast cancer surgeons that it was worth studying adjuvant chemotherapy, or the use of chemotherapy after surgery, researchers demonstrated that it prolonged the lives of women with early-stage breast cancer. This finding set "the stage for research on adjuvant therapy in other common cancers, health records don't talk to one another. CancerLinQ is working with the German software company SAP to overcome the hurdles. The clinical oncology society hopes to have the system fully operational sometime after June.

Dr. Charles Sawyers, chair of Sloan Kettering's human oncology and pathogenesis program, is leading another big-data project on behalf of the American Association for Cancer Research. Cancer centers routinely test the tumors of a minority of cancer patients, looking for the handful of mutations that can be treated with approved drugs. But several centers go further and sequence hundreds of tumor genes in their most-advanced cancer patients, hoping that a few might benefit. Mostly, however, the centers are trying to further research in the field of targeted drug therapy.

Seven cancer centers around the world have begun to pool the huge amounts of data they generate from such sequencing. The database, called GENIE (Genomics, Evidence, Neoplasia, Information, Exchange), will have several uses, says Sawyers.

By pooling the sequencing results of millions of patients, researchers may discover known mutations in cancer types not yet approved for treatment by a targeted drug. These patients could be given the drug, and GENIE would then capture "the outcomes of all of those cases" for researchers to study, says Sawyers.

In addition, the outcomes could lead a drug developer to say, " 'Hey, we should do a clinical trial,' " says Sawyers. And the data in GENIE could help researchers find more cancer mutations that determine why drugs work well in some patients and not in others. Doctors could then give a drug to only patients for whom it will likely work.

The participating institutions will get six months of exclusive use of their patients' records from the time they submit them to GENIE. After that, the records will be available to all members of the consortium for another six months and to the broader research community after that. Sawyers hopes to have 100,000 patient records in the system within five years.[2]

Both Sawyers and Schilsky say patients should not worry about privacy because the data are stripped of all identifying information before being broadly shared.

Some observers doubt that major advances will result from data collected outside of randomized clinical trials. "It's an open question as to how much we can learn from big compilations of data collected without experimental design," where one treatment is tested against another, said Dr. John Ioannidis, a professor of medicine and health research and policy at Stanford University.[3]

"Is it all anecdotal? Yes," says Schilsky. But sacrificing some of the accuracy and precision of clinical trial data is necessary to get a large number of cases that are more representative of the cancer population, he says. "That's a trade-off, but we'll still get useful information."

— *Barbara Mantel*

---

[1] Marie McCullough, " 'Big data' coming soon to cancer care in Philly," *The Philadelphia Inquirer*, Jan. 22, 2015, http://tinyurl.com/hsk48nh.

[2] Jocelyn Kaiser, "Cancer researchers band together to pool tumor genome data," *Science*, Nov. 6, 2015, http://tinyurl.com/h3gexnc.

[3] Miguel Helft, "Can Big Data cure cancer?" *Fortune*, July 24, 2014, http://tinyurl.com/zg2e32u.

---

including colon and lung cancer, making it one of the most important advances in modern cancer care," according to the American Society of Clinical Oncology (ASCO).[54]

As a result, surgeries became less radical. But these new approaches "had yet to be widely implemented outside the NCI and certainly not enough to affect national mortality statistics," De-Vita said.[55]

In 1973, the government's Surveillance, Epidemiology and End Results Program (SEER) began to collect incidence and mortality data from state cancer registries. The U.S. cancer mortality rate climbed from 199 per 100,000 population in 1975 to 207 in 1980. (These rates are age-adjusted, because cancer is more likely to be found in an older population.)[56] The increase was due largely to soaring lung cancer rates from smoking.[57]

Changing Mortality Rates

In 1986, epidemiologists John Bailar and Elaine Smith studied rising mortality statistics dating back to 1950 and concluded that "we are losing the war against cancer." In their widely cited 1986 article in the *New England Journal of Medicine*, Bailar and Smith recommended shifting research from treatment to prevention "if substantial progress against cancer is to be forthcoming."[58] Only 20 percent of NCI grants were going to prevention research.[59]

Researchers Focus on Why Cancers Grow and Return

"Cancer stem cells are driving the tumor growth."

When it comes to devising cancer drugs, scientists treat all cells in a cancer as more or less the same and target them all for destruction. The idea is that any one of these cells could cause the cancer to grow and spread. But many patients relapse after treatment, and their cancer returns.

An increasing number of researchers are pursuing a different theory: Inside each tumor or blood cancer are a small number of so-called cancer stem cells that are responsible for a cancer's growth, spread and resistance to treatment. If the theory is correct, it would have large implications for cancer treatment.

CQ Researcher *correspondent Barbara Mantel interviewed a leading cancer stem cell researcher, Dr. Max Wicha, a professor of oncology at the University of Michigan and the founding director emeritus of its Comprehensive Cancer Center. An edited version follows.*

CQ Researcher: What is a stem cell?

Dr. Max Wicha: A stem cell is a cell that has two properties: It can make identical copies of itself, and it can differentiate and produce other cells that comprise an organ.

CQR: What kind of stem cells are there?

M.W.: One type are the embryonic stem cells, and those are the cells that are produced early during embryo formation. They can virtually form any cell in the body. Then there are adult stem cells, which you have in every organ of your body, and they're specific to that organ. So, for example, a stem cell in the lung makes only other lung cells, and it makes all the cells in the lung.

CQR: And what are cancer stem cells?

M.W.: We think many cancers originate from an adult stem cell that becomes mutated. Normally an adult stem cell divides in a very controlled way, but when the adult stem cell becomes mutated, it no longer has normal control mechanisms.

CQR: How do you know cancer stem cells exist?

M.W.: If you take a tumor, say a breast tumor, we can isolate cells that we know are the stem cells because we've identified certain proteins on these cells. If you take these stem cells out of a breast cancer and put them in a mouse that has no immune system — so it can't reject the tumor — the stem cells will grow into a tumor. But if you take the 98 percent of the cells in that breast cancer that are not stem cells and put them into a mouse, they won't form any tumor.

CQR: Why is that?

M.W.: Because only the stem cell can reproduce itself the number of times required to make a tumor. The other cells in a tumor have only a very limited capacity to reproduce. Those other cells have the same mutations as the cancer stem cell because they come from the cancer stem cell. But only the cancer stem cells are essentially immortal.

By this time, the cancer institute was funding "enormous, expensive, multi-institutional trials" of drugs that were often horrifically toxic, with side effects that included vomiting, infections, shock and organ damage, wrote cancer physician Mukherjee. Yet combination chemotherapy by itself was producing only modest or minimal gains in survival, often measured in months.[60]

One drug stood out, however. In 1986, the FDA approved Tamoxifen, a hormone, for post-menopausal women following breast cancer surgery. Studies showed that Tamoxifen dramatically increased survival rates for women with estrogen receptor-positive breast cancer, where cancer cells receive signals from estrogen that could promote

CQR: Do cancer stem cells play a role in a cancer's spread to other parts of the body?

M.W.: When you have these cancer stem cells traveling through the blood, they can go to different organs and form metastases [or cancer growths] in those organs. If you have other cancer cells that aren't the stem cells in the blood, they don't have the capacity to renew themselves at the distant site. So the cancer stem cells are not only driving the tumor growth but are driving the metastasis.

CQR: In which cancers have researchers found cancer stem cells?

M.W.: Almost all cancers now.

CQR: What role do cancer stem cells play in drug resistance?

M.W.: We've found that these cells are much more resistant to treatment. So, for instance, when we give patients chemotherapy, often the cancer will shrink, which is good. But we're largely killing the bulk cells in the tumor, and we're leaving the seeds [the cancer stem cells] behind. So the seeds can grow back, and that's why the cancer comes back.

CQR: What makes cancer stem cells resistant to treatment?

M.W.: It's a number of things. One is that these cells can actually sometimes exist in a dormant state, and when a cell is dormant, it's not dividing or doing much, and it's very hard to kill. But then it can come out of its dormant state after you finish the therapy. But it's more complicated than that. These stem cells also have the capacity to repair any damage to their DNA, any damage that chemotherapy does.

CQR: Are researchers trying to find drugs that work against the cancer stem cells?

M.W.: Yes, there are now 100 clinical trials going on around the world, with at least a dozen different drugs that target

Courtesy of Dr Wicha and the University of Michigan Comprehensive Cancer Center

Dr. Max Wicha, a leading cancer stem cell researcher, is a professor of oncology at the University of Michigan and founding director emeritus of its Comprehensive Cancer Center.

the specific pathways that regulate cancer stem cells. We have to be very careful when we develop drugs that could target cancer stem cells because some of these pathways may be used by normal stem cells. And your body needs the normal stem cells.

CQR: Do we know if these drugs are working?

M.W.: It looks like most of them are quite safe. So those are the early phase trials, called Phase I. A number of these trials have moved to what's called Phase II. And I think in the next couple of years, we'll really know whether this first group of drugs that targets cancer stem cells really affects patient outcomes. To definitely show that, it usually goes to the next phase of a trial, called Phase III, in which you compare the standard therapies to the standard therapies plus a cancer stem cell therapy. All of these cancer stem cell therapies are going to be combined with a standard therapy to hit the bulk of a cancer.

their growth. In addition, the drug had few significant side effects.[61]

That same year, the FDA approved the first test for a prostate-specific antigen (PSA) in men age 50 or older. Its widespread use eventually led to a significant increase in early-stage prostate cancer diagnoses, "sparking debate about whether such screening improves survival or simply leads to diagnosis and unnecessary treatment of slow-growing cancers that would never have become life-threatening," said ASCO.[62]

By the early 1990s, a reduction in smoking, earlier detection of colorectal cancers and improved prostate and breast cancer treatments began to lower the cancer mortality rate.[63] In 1992, the rate declined for the first time since SEER began collecting data, after peaking in 1991 at 215 cancer deaths per 100,000 population.[64]

Targeted Therapies

Between 1990 and 2005, the cancer mortality rate dropped by nearly 15 percent, "a decline unprecedented in the history of the disease," wrote Mukherjee. Changes in behavior, such as a continued decline in smoking, contributed, as did expanded screening for colon, cervical and breast cancers and successful chemotherapy treatment for leukemia, lymphoma, testicular and breast cancers. But these victories were "the results of discoveries made in the '50s and '60s," Mukherjee said. They rarely made use of the discoveries that began in the 1980s into the genetic mutations and cellular pathways of cancer.[65]

That began to change in the late 1990s, as the FDA began approving drugs that target mutated or overabundant surface proteins on cancer cells and drugs that actively stimulate the body's immune system to fight cancer. In 1997, the FDA approved rituximab, a new kind of drug called a monoclonal antibody, to treat patients with B-cell non-Hodgkin lymphoma that no longer responded to other treatments. Rituximab coats the surface of cancerous lymphoma cells and allows the body's immune system to destroy them. In addition, researchers discovered that women with mutations in the BRCA1 and BRCA2 genes have a much higher risk of developing breast and ovarian cancers. Soon after, studies showed that preventive surgery to remove breasts and ovaries may significantly lower that risk.[66]

Then in 1998, the FDA approved another monoclonal antibody, trastuzumab, known commercially as Herceptin. Adding it to chemotherapy dramatically increased survival rates for women with an advanced breast cancer that overproduces the HER2 protein. Herceptin blocks the protein's chemical signals that stimulate uncontrolled cell growth. Eight years later, the FDA approved it for use after surgery in women with early-stage HER2-positive breast cancer.[67]

Other drugs that have been developed through a better understanding of the mechanics of cancer cells include:

- Imatinib, known as Gleevec, approved in 2001 for chronic myelogenous leukemia and now the standard of care for this blood cancer.[68]

- Gefitinib and erlotinib, approved in 2003 for advanced lung cancer, which block a protein found on the surface of cancer cells that encourages uncontrolled growth. The drugs work only for patients with specific protein mutations, found most often in nonsmokers.[69]

- Bevacizumab, known as Avastin, approved in 2004 to treat colorectal cancer. It was the first of a new type of targeted drug that blocks the growth in blood vessels needed for tumors to expand.[70]

- Cetuximab and panitumumab, approved between 2004 and 2008 to treat colon cancer that has spread to other parts of the body.[71]

- Gardasil, a vaccine approved in 2006 to prevent infection from two strains of the human papillomavirus (HPV16 and HPV18), which cause about 70 percent of all cervical cancers.[72]

- Ipilimumab, approved in 2011 for patients with advanced melanoma that is not responding to other therapies. It boosts the immune system's ability to destroy cancer cells.[73]

Dozens of targeted drugs have been approved for many different kinds of cancers, including head and neck, cervical, kidney and liver; in addition, several immunotherapy agents have been approved for advanced melanoma, lung and kidney cancer.[74]

In addition, genetic testing of tumors for the genes that control cell growth is helping patients avoid unnecessary therapies. A study released last fall showed that women with early stage, hormone-positive, non-HER2 breast cancer who were classified as low risk could receive the usual hormone therapy and skip chemotherapy with very little risk of relapse.[75]

Meanwhile, the overall cancer mortality rate declined to about 166 per 100,000 population in 2012, the last year of available data.[76]

CURRENT SITUATION
Immunotherapy's Promise

Jimmy Carter appears to be cancer free. Last August, the former U.S. president announced that he had stage 4 metastatic melanoma. He then underwent surgery and radiation and began periodic treatments with the immunotherapy drug pembrolizumab, sold as Keytruda. In

December, the 91-year-old Carter announced that there were no longer signs of the lesions that had spread to his brain.[77]

"I don't think we know yet how much of the success is related to Keytruda," but the drug is showing remarkable promise, said Dr. Leonard Lichtenfeld, deputy chief medical officer for the American Cancer Society.[78]

Keytruda and similar new drugs are a radical departure from chemotherapy, which directly kills cancer cells. Instead, the new drugs harness the body's immune system to do the job. And unlike some targeted drugs that alter cancer cells so the immune system can better attack them, Keytruda directly fires up the immune system, an approach called "active" immunotherapy.

Although researchers have been studying immunotherapy for decades, the field only recently began generating excitement among physicians, says Jill O'Donnell-Tormey, CEO of the New York-based Cancer Research Institute, a nonprofit that funds immunotherapy research. A few years ago, nobody came to the immunotherapy sessions at meetings of the American Society of Clinical Oncology, she says. "But last year at ASCO, it was standing room only."

The year 2011 was the inflection point, she says, when the FDA approved the active immunotherapy ipilimumab, sold as Yervoy, to treat metastatic melanoma. "Here was a disease, metastatic melanoma, for which no drug had ever extended life, and this was the first drug to do that," says O'Donnell-Tormey. "It was very exciting." In fact, some patients with advanced melanoma who took Yervoy in trials have been alive for 10 years.

Lately, there has been a flurry of immunotherapy approvals. In 2014 the FDA approved Keytruda and Opdivo, the brand name for nivolumab, to treat advanced melanoma. Last year, the agency also approved both drugs for use in advanced squamous non-small cell lung cancer, and, in the case of Opdivo, for treating advanced kidney cancer.[79]

All three drugs are known as "immune checkpoint blockers." "Normally, our immune system is highly regulated because we want it to see foreign invaders, but we don't want it to attack our own tissues," says Dr. Stanley Riddell, a researcher at the Fred Hutchinson Cancer Research Center in Seattle. These three drugs interfere with that regulation by releasing the brakes, or checkpoints, on the immune system. They do it by binding to

Former U.S. president Jimmy Carter announced in August 2015 that he had stage 4 metastatic melanoma. He then underwent surgery and radiation and began periodic treatments with the immunotherapy drug pembrolizumab, sold as Keytruda. In December 2015 Carter announced there were no longer signs of the lesions that had spread to his brain.

certain molecules on the surface of the immune system's T-cells, a type of white blood cell, unleashing them to attack the cancer.

The drugs work for melanoma and for lung and kidney cancers because those tumors have hundreds, even thousands, of genetic mutations caused by sun exposure, smoking or toxins passing through the body's filtering system, respectively. These mutations cause the cancer cells to make abnormal proteins, alerting the immune system.

"So the greater the mutational burden, the more likely a tumor is viewed by the immune system as being foreign," says Riddell.

The results of immunotherapy can be long-lasting, at least in advanced melanoma. "These treatments can potentially hit a home run because the immune system can adapt to whatever the tumor does and stay on top of it," said Dr. Mark Faries, a melanoma expert at the John Wayne Cancer Institute in Santa Monica, Calif. The beneficial results from targeted therapy, on the other hand, are often short-lived because the cancer figures out how to outwit those drugs. The same can be true of conventional chemotherapy.[80]

Patients with advanced lung or kidney cancer are also surviving longer with immunotherapy, although the data are not as far along as in melanoma. And the drugs are shrinking tumors in trials of other cancers, such as head and neck, bladder and some ovarian cancers.

Should all women over 30 be screened for the inherited mutations that raise breast and ovarian cancer risk?

YES
Steven Narod, M.D.
Senior Scientist, Women's College Research Institute, Toronto

Written for *CQ Researcher*, January 2016

Any woman over 30 wishing to be tested for inherited mutations in the BRCA1 and BRCA2 genes, which raise ovarian and breast cancer risk, should be able to do so at a reasonable cost.

Approximately one in 200 women carry a mutation, and the information contained in a report of a positive BRCA1 or BRCA2 mutation is important, accurate and clear. The risk of ovarian cancer exceeds 5 percent in women with a BRCA1 or BRCA2 mutation, and these women should be offered a preventive oophorectomy, or removal of their ovaries.

The risk of breast cancer associated with mutations in BRCA1 and BRCA2 are 70 percent and 40 percent, respectively, and a preventive mastectomy merits discussion.

I am familiar with arguments against universal screening. Many of the risks associated with susceptibility genes other than the BRCA genes are not well defined and may never be. Those ambiguous genes should not be included in the test. At present only four genes should be: BRCA1, BRCA2, PALB2 and RAD51C. Women with a mutation in RAD51C also face an increased risk of ovarian cancer, and a mutation in PALB2 carries a 30 percent risk of breast cancer.

Others are concerned that the cost of universal testing will be very high considering the counseling that goes with it. But if a woman at average risk has a negative test, she will not need personalized post-test counseling.

Her breast cancer risk is then a bit lower than it was before testing. She is not a candidate for preventive surgery; she won't take the anti-breast cancer drug Tamoxifen, which is prescribed to high-risk women, and mammography is not particularly effective. So we can focus on the rare women with a mutation.

Approximately 15 percent of all ovarian cancer cases are due to mutations in BRCA1, BRCA2 and RAD51C. These are theoretically preventable by preventive surgery, providing the woman is aware of her mutation status in time. That is to say, up to 15 percent of ovarian cancers can be prevented through robust genetic programs. Currently, only 1 to 2 percent of ovarian cancers are being prevented.

Many of the patients who present evidence of cancer do not have a family history that would qualify for testing. For others, the physician neglects to make the referral.

Two percent is a start, but we could do much better.

NO
Karuna Jaggar
Executive Director, Breast Cancer Action

Written for *CQ Researcher*, January 2016

This year, 40,000 women in the United States will die of breast cancer. And that is heartbreaking and unacceptable. However, the proposal to screen all American women over age 30 for inherited mutations linked to breast and ovarian cancers falls short as a matter of public health and fails to recognize the significant limitations and harms of mass genetic testing in the current health care environment.

BRCA testing is currently recommended for women believed to be at risk due to their personal and family medical histories. Testing is limited because mutations in the BRCA genes, which raise the risk of breast and ovarian cancer, are rare in the general population and because only 5 percent to 10 percent of breast cancers are linked to such mutations.

Genetic testing brings with it a wide range of medical, ethical and scientific issues, and responsible testing requires trained genetic counselors before and after testing. Patients and their families with knowledge of a genetic mutation face a complex set of choices challenging to navigate.

Currently, between 3 percent and 10 percent of those who undergo testing learn they have a variant of unknown significance, a mutation on the BRCA gene that may or may not be harmful.

The proposal to introduce genetic testing to the general population would mean that up to 1 million women would get this type of complex and difficult result, placing greater demands on genetic counselors who cannot meet existing patient demand.

Yet it is wrong to subject people to testing without providing them with professional counseling to explain their test results.

Initiating mass genetic testing for a rare genetic mutation linked to only a fraction of all breast cancers will unfortunately not stem the breast cancer epidemic. At an approximate cost of $1,000 per person, initial BRCA testing for the current population of women over 30 would run $105 billion.

I recognize the value and importance of genetic testing when it is medically warranted. In fact, Breast Cancer Action was the only breast cancer organization to join a lawsuit challenging Myriad Genetics' patent stranglehold on genetic testing, a case we won in June 2013 when the U.S. Supreme Court unanimously ruled that human genes cannot be patented.

And there is no question that all women need better risk-assessment tools for breast cancer, one piece of which includes genetic and inherited risk screening for some women.

But the answer to the breast cancer epidemic does not rest with mass genetic testing given the current shortcomings.

But while immunotherapy can yield dramatic results, only about 20 to 30 percent of patients respond, mystifying researchers. "We fund an awful lot of research trying to understand that," says O'Donnell-Tormey.

Research is beginning to uncover clues. Patients who respond to the checkpoint blockers have cancers with more mutations, says Riddell. But at the same time some mutations prevent patients from responding to the drugs.

Researchers are developing strategies to get around the low response rate. "The future is in combinations" of immunotherapy drugs, says O'Donnell-Tormey. Last fall, the FDA approved the first combination treatment, Yervoy and Opdivo together, for patients whose advanced melanoma lacked a particular mutation that is present in about half of melanomas. In a trial, the drug combination shrank tumors in 60 percent of such patients.[81] It's too early to say whether the treatment will extend their lives.

But using more than one immunotherapy at a time raises the likelihood of side effects, such as diarrhea, colitis and lung inflammation. That's because when the immune system is unleashed, it can damage normal tissue as well as cancer cells. However, such side effects "are very controllable now by steroids," says O'Donnell-Tormey.

Riddell's lab and others are working on another kind of immunotherapy, still in trials but showing promise in melanoma and in cancers with far fewer mutations, such as cancers of the blood. It's called adoptive T-cell therapy, which involves taking some of the patient's own cancer-fighting T-cells, growing or altering them in the laboratory, and then placing them back in the patient in hopes of overwhelming the cancer.

Researchers have several ways to do this. Some are culturing T-cells called tumor infiltrating lymphocytes, and others are engineering T-cells by attaching to them a conventional cancer-specific receptor that targets a molecule on the cancer cell. Riddell's team is attaching to T-cells a synthetic receptor created in the laboratory. These "chimeric antigen receptors," as they're called, tell the T-cells to proliferate and kill the cancer.

It's "incredibly potent," says Riddell. "You can get really tiny, tiny numbers of T-cells into the patient, and they eradicate massive" tumors that have resisted all other forms of therapy. Ninety-three percent of patients with acute lymphoblastic leukemia in a trial at his center,

Getty Images/Toronto Star/Tara Walton

Many cancers are linked to preventable risk factors, such as exposure to ultraviolet light from the sun or tanning beds, tobacco use, obesity and lack of exercise. Advances in prevention, early detection and treatment have resulted in a 23 percent decline in the cancer death rate between its 1991 peak and 2012, the latest year for which data are available. Experts say the number of deaths could be cut further, possibly in half.

who have failed all other treatments, are in "complete remission," Riddell says. The key question is, will it last?

Liquid Biopsy

Determining how someone's cancer is responding to treatment or whether a cancer in remission has returned can involve expensive scans and invasive biopsies. The dream of oncologists is to use a simple blood or urine test instead. Companies around the world are developing and evaluating such tests, called a liquid biopsy, and recent studies are promising.

"This could change forever the way we follow up, not only response to treatments but also the emergence of [drug] resistance, and down the line could even be used for really early diagnosis," said Dr. José Baselga, chief medical officer at Memorial Sloan Kettering Cancer Center.[82]

As a tumor grows, some cancer cells die, rupture and release DNA fragments into the bloodstream. A liquid biopsy test detects this circulating DNA.

In a study of 126 lymphoma patients, liquid biopsy found evidence of recurrent cancer three months before it showed up on CT scans.[83] Another study found that a liquid biopsy could detect genetic mutations in prostate cancer that might cause the cancer's drug resistance. A third study compared liquid and tissue biopsies in a breast cancer patient over time and found that the blood test accurately detected her tumor's developing mutations.[84]

But these studies are small and preliminary. "What is really missing at the moment is the hard evidence that using liquid biopsy and treating patients on that basis improves hard endpoints, like how long the patient lives," said Dr. Nicholas Turner, a researcher at the London-based Institute of Cancer Research. "The field really needs those studies to change practice."[85]

Nevertheless, one U.S. company released two liquid biopsy tests in September. Pathway Genomics offers one test for doctors to monitor cancer patients and another test to detect cancer in high-risk individuals who are showing no symptoms.[86] A few weeks after the launch, the company received a letter from the FDA, stating that it could not find "any published evidence that this test or any similar test has been clinically validated as a screening tool for early detection of cancer in high risk individuals." The FDA requested a meeting.

Initially, the company allowed consumers to order the $699 liquid biopsy detection test directly, in consultation with an online doctor provided by the company. Now a patient's licensed physician or oncologist must order it.[87] And the company says it is conducting more studies on the test's efficacy.[88]

Many experts agree with the FDA and say using liquid biopsy to detect traces of cancer in healthy individuals is years away. The risks for such a test include finding DNA fragments for a cancer but then being unable to find the cancer site. "Do we give the patient chemotherapy or some other form of therapy?" said the American Cancer Society's Lichtenfeld. "We just don't know."[89]

OUTLOOK
Funding Uncertainty

Cancer groups have been celebrating since President Obama signed an omnibus spending bill in December that keeps the government running until the end of September and includes a $264 million increase for cancer research at the National Cancer Institute this year. The NCI budget had fallen nearly 25 percent since 2003, after adjusting for inflation.[90]

"We're ecstatic to get cancer research back on track," says Jon Retzlaff, head of science policy and government affairs at the American Association for Cancer Research.

The 12-year decline in real funding has meant fewer research grants into the basic science of cancer, fewer

opportunities for young scientists, "fewer clinical trials being started, and fewer patients having a chance to enroll in trials," says Dr. Richard Schilsky, chief medical officer at the American Society of Clinical Oncology.

The NIH also received $200 million for President Obama's Precision Medicine Initiative to accelerate treatment of diseases, including cancer, based on an individual's genes, environment and lifestyle.[91]

But funding in the years ahead is "a big unknown," says Retzlaff. Unless Congress works out more onetime deals like this year's, overall federal spending will revert to budget caps that Congress put in place in 2011. "We'll have to be working hard every year at this," he says.

"The vast majority of recent advances stem from basic biomedical research funded by the government 10 or 15 or 20 years ago," says Schilsky. "The big question is, will there be any fruit to harvest 15 years from now if we don't continue to maintain investment in biomedical research?"

Meanwhile, researchers say promising new advances are being tested in ongoing clinical trials. In the field of immunotherapy, "checkpoint blockers are being tested in all sorts of combinations, and that will be an increasingly fertile area," says Riddell of the Fred Hutchinson Cancer Research Center. And while the FDA has not yet approved any adoptive T-cell therapies, he anticipates some will be approved within 18 months to two years.

In addition, "there are all sorts of trials going on now combining immunotherapy with radiation and with chemotherapy," says the Cancer Research Institute's O'Donnell-Tormey. "And it would probably mean using a lower dose of chemotherapy than in standard treatment," she says.

Washington University's Mardis anticipates immunotherapy and targeted medicines being used together in coming years. "It would take advantage of the dramatic early clearance of tumors that is available from targeted therapies," but which is often short-lived as the cancer develops resistance, says Mardis. "And then following up with the more durable response of immunotherapy when the patient is at a lower tumor burden. Sort of a one-two punch."

In the meantime, health economist Howard predicts that prices of these new cancer drugs will continue to climb, although at a lower rate, over the next five years.

"The same factors that have caused prices to go up in the past are present today," says Howard. "However, doctors are more sensitive to prices today than they were in the past, and that will temper companies' ability to set higher prices to some degree."

NOTES

1. "What are the survival rates for melanoma skin cancer, by stage?" American Cancer Society, March 20, 2015, http://tinyurl.com/lhqro3k.

2. "The State of Cancer Care in America 2015," American Society of Clinical Oncology, 2015, http://tinyurl.com/zsmqbfd.

3. "ACS CAN Examination of Cancer Drug Coverage and Transparency in the Health Insurance Marketplaces," American Cancer Society Cancer Action Network, Nov. 18, 2015, pp. 8-9, http://tinyurl.com/oene6zm.

4. "State of the Union 2016: President Obama's Full Prepared Remarks," ABC News, Jan. 12, 2016, http://tinyurl.com/joywuha.

5. Gina Kolata and Gardiner Harris, "'Moonshot' to Cure Cancer, to Be Led by Biden, Relies on Outmoded View of Disease," *The New York Times*, Jan. 13, 2016, http://tinyurl.com/zegtwz6.

6. Rebecca L. Siegel *et al.*, "Cancer Statistics, 2016," *CA: A Cancer Journal for Clinicians*, January/February 2016, p. 9, http://tinyurl.com/ j96nkox.

7. *Ibid.*, pp. 20-23.

8. "AACR Cancer Progress Report 2015," American Association for Cancer Research, 2015, p. 4, http://tinyurl.com/j5qxo9z.

9. "GLOBOCAN 2012" Database, International Agency for Research on Cancer, accessed Jan. 12, 2016, http://tinyurl.com/kjodu7h.

10. "First-Ever Comprehensive Analysis of U.S. Cancer Care Exposes Threats to Patients' Access," American Society of Clinical Oncology, http://tinyurl.com/pjf7usw.

11. "The State of Cancer Care in America 2015," *op. cit.*, pp. 16, 17.

12. *Ibid.*, p. 16.

13. "Disparities in Breast Cancer Persist Across All Subtypes and Stages," American Association for Cancer Research, Oct. 13, 2015, http://tinyurl.com/j2sr9d3; Alice Park, "What Race Has to Do With Breast Cancer," *Time*, Oct. 13, 2015, http://tinyurl.com/zc2m276.

14. Mary Elizabeth Dallas, "Still Too Few Minority Participants in U.S. Clinical Trials, Study Finds," *U.S. News & World Report*, March 21, 2014, http://tinyurl.com/j687o7u.

15. "Cervical Cancer Screening," The American College of Obstetricians and Gynecologists, December 2015, http://tinyurl.com/ocxwfd6; "Cervical Cancer: Screening," U.S. Preventive Services Task Force, March 2012, http://tinyurl.com/zxphswd.

16. "Prostate Cancer Screening: Consumer Guide," U.S. Preventive Services Task Force, May 2012, http://tinyurl.com/ocp2jxf.

17. Virginia A. Moyer, "Screening for Prostate Cancer: U.S. Preventive Services Task Force Recommendation Statement," *Annals of Internal Medicine*, July 17, 2012, pp. 121, 122, http://tinyurl.com/jusqfmp.

18. "American Cancer Society recommendations for prostate cancer early detection," American Cancer Society, Jan. 6, 2015, http://tinyurl.com/p6aoebw.

19. "Breast Cancer: Screening," U.S. Preventive Services Task Force, Dec. 4, 2015, http://tinyurl.com/pdbgcme; "Breast Cancer Screening Draft Recommendations," USPSTF, April 20, 2015, http://tinyurl.com/hgq6bfq.

20. Kirsten Bibbins-Domingo, "New breast cancer screening guidelines explained," *The Washington Post*, April 29, 2015, http://tinyurl.com/hmcp53h.

21. "USPSTF Breast Cancer Screening Recommendations Would Cost Thousands of Lives and Could Eliminate Mammography Insurance Coverage for Millions of Women," American College of Radiology, April 20, 2015, http://tinyurl.com/kxh5scs; "ACR and SBI Continue to Recommend Regular Mammography Starting at Age 40," American College of Radiology, Oct. 20, 2015, http://tinyurl.com/jfnbkpk.

22. "American Cancer Society Guidelines for the Early Detection of Cancer," American Cancer Society, Oct. 20, 2015, http://tinyurl.com/4yh7owd.

23. Lena H. Sun, "New breast cancer screening guidelines at odds with Congress," *The Washington Post*, Jan. 11, 2016, http://tinyurl.com/hbby57h.

24. Rachel Ehrenberg, "Year in review: Cancer genetics grows up," *ScienceNews*, Dec. 15, 2015, http://tinyurl.com/hzdf6fh.

25. Matthew V. Abola and Vinay Prasad, "The Use of Superlatives in Cancer Research," *JAMA Oncology*, January 2016, http://tinyurl.com/hl9vefq.

26. Bob Tedeschi, "For cancer patients, breakthrough drugs are saving lives but wrenching souls," STAT, Nov. 4, 2015, http://tinyurl.com/hhln6rm.

27. "In Support of a Patient-Driven Initiative and Petition to Lower the High Price of Cancer Drugs," *Mayo Clinic Proceedings*, August 2015, http://tinyurl.com/zwdanfm.

28. David H. Howard *et al.*, "Pricing in the Market for Anticancer Drugs," *Journal of Economic Perspectives*, Winter 2015, p. 140, http://tinyurl.com/hmodj33.

29. *Ibid.*, p. 149.

30. "Out-of-pocket maximum/limit," HealthCare. gov, http://tinyurl.com/hpjadej.

31. "Although a Small Share of Medicare Part D Enrollees Take Specialty Drugs, A New Analysis Finds Those Who Do Can Face Thousands of Dollars in Out-of-Pocket Drug Costs Despite Plan Limits on Catastrophic Expenses," Henry J. Kaiser Family Foundation, Dec. 2, 2015, http://tinyurl.com/hf77wpu.

32. Austin Frakt, "How the patent system and the FDA discourage study of cancer prevention," *The Incidental Economist*, Dec. 30, 2015, http://tinyurl.com/gwma3p9.

33. Sham Mailankody and Vinay Prasad, "Five Years of Cancer Drug Approvals: Innovation, Efficacy, and Costs," *JAMA Oncology*, July 2015, http://tinyurl.com/j3hsz79.

34. "What are 'Biosimilar' Drugs?" *The Wall Street Journal*, March 6, 2015, http://tinyurl.com/hprcz4u.

35. "In Support of a Patient-Driven Initiative and Petition to Lower the High Price of Cancer Drugs," *op. cit.*

36. Thomas P. Stossel, "What Cancer Doctors Don't Know About Cancer Drugs," *The Wall Street Journal*, Sept. 22, 2015, http://tinyurl.com/otfnwc2.

37. Peter B. Bach, "Could High Drug Prices Be Bad for Innovation," *Forbes*, Oct. 23, 2014, http://tinyurl.com/znms9nq.

38. Joyce Frieden, "Value-Based Pricing Will Help with High Rx Costs," *MedPage Today*, Nov. 23, 2015, http://tinyurl.com/juhf8qz.

39. "National Cancer Act of 1937," National Cancer Institute, http://tinyurl.com/cednc5r.

40. Siddhartha Mukherjee, *The Emperor of All Maladies: A Biography of Cancer* (2010), p. 26.

41. Paul A. Marks and James Sterngold, *On the Cancer Frontier: One Man, One Disease, and a Medical Revolution* (2014), p. 5.

42. "Progress & Timeline," American Society of Clinical Oncology, http://tinyurl.com/jc685kv.

43. Mukherjee, *op. cit.*, p. 122.

44. "Progress & Timeline," *op. cit.*

45. *Ibid.*

46. *Ibid.*

47. Marks and Sterngold, *op. cit.*, p. 55.

48. Vincent T. DeVita and Elizabeth DeVita-Raeburn, *The Death of Cancer* (2015), p. 129.

49. *Ibid.*, pp. 131-132.

50. *Ibid.*, p. 133.

51. "Progress & Timeline," *op. cit.*

52. DeVita and DeVita-Raeburn, *op. cit.*, p. 149.

53. "Progress & Timeline," *op. cit.*

54. *Ibid.*

55. DeVita and DeVita-Raeburn, *op. cit.*, p. 162.

56. "Fast Stats," Surveillance, Epidemiology, and End Results Program, National Institutes of Health, http://tinyurl.com/ha4dk5w.

57. Marks and Sterngold, *op. cit.*, p. 113.

58. John C. Bailar III and Elaine M. Smith, "Progress against Cancer?" *The New England Journal of Medicine*, May 8, 1986, http://tinyurl.com/hdwo8sb.

59. Mukherjee, *op. cit.*, p. 234.

60. *Ibid.*, pp. 207-208.

61. "Progress & Timeline," *op. cit.*

62. *Ibid.*

63. Sherri L. Stewart *et al.*, "Cancer Mortality Surveillance — United States, 1990-2000," Centers for Disease Control and Prevention, June 4, 2004, http://tinyurl.com/772rvoo.

64. "Fast Stats," *op. cit.*

65. Mukherjee, *op. cit.*, pp. 401-402.

66. "Progress & Timeline," *op. cit.*

67. *Ibid.*

68. *Ibid.*; "Leukemia — Chronic Myeloid — CML: Treatment Options," Cancer.Net, http://tinyurl.com/j76qyxa.

69. *Ibid.*, "Progress & Timeline;" "Lung Cancer — Non-Small Cell: Treatment Options," Cancer. Net, http://tinyurl.com/p4cunrx.

70. *Ibid.*, "Progress & Timeline."

71. *Ibid.*

72. *Ibid.*

73. *Ibid.*

74. "Targeted Cancer Therapies," National Cancer Institute, http://tinyurl.com/jkzwuwe.

75. "Big change ahead for early breast cancer treatment?" The Associated Press, CBS News, Sept. 28, 2015, http://tinyurl.com/jadx7mu.

76. "Fast Stats," *op. cit.*

77. Keith Collins, "All The President's MABS," *Quartz*, Dec. 10, 2015, http://tinyurl.com/zafp fwz; "What are the survival rates for melanoma skin cancer, by stage?" *op. cit.*

78. David Mills, "Drug Used in Jimmy Carter's Cancer Treatment Among a New Generation of Immune Therapies," *Healthline*, Dec. 8, 2015, http://tinyurl.com/j5jydrh.

79. "Opdivo Approval History," Drugs.com, http://tinyurl.com/jcbwrbl; "Keytruda Approval History," drugs.com, http://tinyurl.com/hfbcp9c.

80. Linda Marsa, "Immunotherapy's Promise Against Cancer," *U.S. News & World Report*, Oct. 6, 2015, http://tinyurl.com/q5txj4m.

81. Karen Honey, "FDA Approves Combination of Immunotherapeutics," American Association for Cancer Research, Oct. 2, 2015, http://tinyurl.com/jjv78a7.

82. Gina Kolata, "New Blood Test Shows Promise in Cancer Fight," *The New York Times*, April 19, 2015, http://tinyurl.com/lhs4m4e.

83. *Ibid.*

84. Julie Steenhuysen and Ben Hirschler, "Case for testing cancer in blood builds, one study at a time," Reuters, Nov. 4, 2015, http://tinyurl.com/zdk7mto.

85. *Ibid.*

86. "CancerIntercept Detect: pricing," *Pathway Genomics*, http://tinyurl.com/gwm4hll.

87. Antonio Regalado, "Why You Shouldn't Bother with a $699 Cancer Test," *MIT Technology Review*, Sept. 10, 2015, http://tinyurl. com/zt6rctc; "CancerInterceptTM Test Requisition (USA — Domestic)," *Pathway Genomics*, http://tinyurl.com/j23bjey.

88. "Pathway Genomics' response to FDA Letter on CancerIntercept Detect," *Pathway Genomics*, Sept. 24, 2015, http://tinyurl.com/jf5rhnr.

89. Ariana Eunjung Cha, "Healthy people can now order a $299 'liquid biopsy' blood test for cancer. Should you get it?" *The Washington Post*, Oct. 15, 2015, http://tinyurl.com/zjygzp4.

90. "NCI Budget and Appropriations," National Cancer Institute, http://tinyurl.com/jpxct8o.

91. David Nather, "It's official: The NIH budget is getting an extra $2 billion," STAT, Dec. 18, 2015, http://tinyurl.com/hzggkty.

BIBLIOGRAPHY
Selected Sources
Books

DeVita, Vincent T., and Elizabeth DeVita-Raeburn, *The Death of Cancer: After Fifty Years on the Front Lines of Medicine, a Pioneering Oncologist Reveals Why the War Against Cancer is Winnable — and How We Can Get There*, Sarah Crichton Books, 2015.
A former National Cancer Institute director examines the history of cancer research, treatment and politics.

His co-author (and daughter) DeVita-Raeburn is a science writer.

Johnson, George, *The Cancer Chronicles: Unlocking Medicine's Deepest Mystery,* **Knopf, 2013.**
A science writer explores the most recent advances in cancer research and treatment.

Marks, Paul A., and James Sterngold, *On the Cancer Frontier: One Man, One Disease, and a Medical Revolution,* **Public Affairs, 2014.**
A president emeritus of Memorial Sloan Kettering Cancer Center (Marks) discusses his career fighting cancer. His co-author is a *Wall Street Journal* business reporter.

Mukherjee, Siddhartha, *The Emperor of All Maladies: A Biography of Cancer,* **Scribner, 2010.**
A cancer physician and researcher traces the long history of cancer research and treatment in this Pulitzer Prize-winning book.

Articles

Collins, Keith, "All the President's MABS," *Quartz,* **Dec. 10, 2015, http://tinyurl.com/zafpfwz.**
Former President Jimmy Carter was declared cancer-free after surgery, radiation and immunotherapy.

Frieden, Joyce, "Value-Based Pricing Will Help with High Rx Costs," *MedPage Today,* **Nov. 23, 2015, http://tinyurl.com/juhf8qz.**
Linking cancer drug prices to the value of health benefits they generate can lower high drug costs, some experts say.

Kolata, Gina, "New Blood Test Shows Promise in Cancer Fight," *The New York Times,* **April 19, 2015, http://tinyurl.com/onmeyk6.**
A blood test may help doctors manage cancer patients' treatment without expensive scans or invasive biopsies.

Marsa, Linda, "Immunotherapy's Promise Against Cancer," *U.S. News & World Report,* **Oct. 6, 2015, http://tinyurl.com/q5txj4m.**
Harnessing the body's immune system to fight cancer is helping some patients live longer.

Schattner, Elaine, "Precision Medicine Is a Needed Goal That Will Benefit Cancer Patients," *Forbes,* **Nov. 9, 2015, http://tinyurl.com/hycnzvv.**

Targeted pharmaceutical treatments are improving survival rates for patients in the United States with certain cancers, although the tumors that are targeted often develop resistance to the prescribed drugs.

Shute, Nancy, "Treatment Changes For DCIS Haven't Affected Breast Cancer Deaths," **NPR, Nov. 6, 2015, http://tinyurl.com/q2ayo64.**
A fraction of women with noninvasive cancer of the milk duct, called stage-zero breast cancer, choose watchful waiting, while an increasing number are opting for a double mastectomy.

Reports and Studies

"Cancer Facts & Figures 2015," American Cancer Society, 2015, http://tinyurl.com/kf48j3h.
Cancer is the second-most common cause of death after heart disease, according to the latest report from a leading cancer research and advocacy group.

Hoadley, Jack, "It Pays to Shop: Variation in Out-of-Pocket Costs for Medicare Part D Enrollees in 2016," Henry J. Kaiser Family Foundation, Dec. 2, 2015, http://tinyurl.com/hgg5pd9.
Medicare patients can pay more than $10,000 a year for a single cancer drug, a nonpartisan group that studies health policy finds.

Howard, David H., *et al.,* **"Pricing in the Market for Anticancer Drugs,"** *Journal of Economic Perspectives,* **Winter 2015, http://tinyurl.com/hmodj33.**
The average price for 58 new cancer drugs has increased by 10 percent a year, after inflation.

Mailankody, Sham, and Vinay Prasad, "Five Years of Cancer Drug Approvals: Innovation, Efficacy, and Costs," *JAMA Oncology,* **July 2015, http://tinyurl.com/j3hsz79.**
Prices of new cancer drugs are not related to health benefits but instead reflect what the market can bear, according to two National Cancer Institute researchers.

"The State of Cancer Care in America 2015," American Society of Clinical Oncology, 2015, http://tinyurl.com/zsmqbfd.
The aging population of the United States and subsequent increase in the number of cancer patients and survivors is straining the delivery of high quality cancer care, an oncologists' group says.

For More Information

American Association for Cancer Research, 615 Chestnut St., 17th Floor, Philadelphia, PA 19106; 215-440-9300; www.aacr.org. Fosters cancer research, publishes medical journals and convenes scientific conferences.

American Cancer Society, 250 Williams St., N.W., Atlanta, GA 30303; 404-320-3333; www.cancer.org. Community-based nationwide organization that sponsors cancer research and public education and advocates for policies and laws.

American Society of Clinical Oncology, 2318 Mill Rd., Suite 800, Alexandria, VA 22314; 571-483-1300; www.asco .org. Medical society that supports professional education for oncologists and cancer research.

America's Health Insurance Plans, 601 Pennsylvania Ave., N.W., South Building, Suite 500, Washington, DC 20004; 202-778-3200; www.ahip.org. Represents the health insurance industry.

National Cancer Institute, 9609 Medical Center Drive, GB 9609 MSC 9760, Bethesda, MD 20892; 301-496-4000; www.cancer .gov. Principal federal agency for cancer research and training.

Pharmaceutical Research and Manufacturers of America, 950 F St., N.W., Suite 300, Washington, DC 20004; 202-835-3400; www.phrma.org. Represents biopharmaceutical researchers and biotechnology companies.

U.S. Preventive Services Task Force, 5600 Fishers Lane, Rockville, MD 20857; 301-427-1584; www.uspreventive servicestaskforce.org. Independent expert panel that makes evidence-based recommendations about clinical preventive services.

16 Mosquito-Borne Disease

Alan Greenblatt

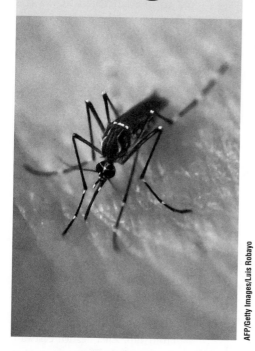

Aedes aegypti, known as the yellow fever mosquito, carries viruses that can cause a number of devastating illnesses, including dengue, chikungunya and Zika, a fast-moving virus now spreading throughout the Americas. Experts say Zika offers the latest evidence that the mosquito threat will grow as Earth's climate warms and the insect's habitat expands.

From *CQ Researcher*, July 22, 2016

AFP/Getty Images/Luis Robayo

They weigh a fraction of an ounce and live, at most, a month or two. But mosquitoes have been called the "most dangerous animal" on Earth, and the unfolding crisis over the Zika virus is only the latest example of why.[1]

Most mosquitoes are merely a nuisance. But bites from some species can have deadly consequences. Mosquitoes — or more accurately the viruses they carry — kill about 725,000 people a year, mostly in tropical and subtropical regions where the insects thrive. By contrast, sharks, perhaps the most feared animal on the planet, kill about 10.[2]

Despite recent progress, malaria remains the deadliest mosquito-borne disease, killing more than 400,000 people each year and sickening at least 200 million.[3] Yellow fever, once the most feared mosquito-borne illness in North America, has recently broken out in Africa, and China has seen its first cases. West Nile virus, chikungunya and dengue fever — mosquito-borne diseases that were not serious threats in the Americas until recently — are making significant inroads in the United States.

And now mosquitoes are spreading Zika, a virus that has emerged in at least 60 countries. Brazil, site of the 2016 Summer Olympics, is the epicenter of the disease in the Americas, recording close to 500,000 cases since the outbreak began in late 2014 — some 100,000 cases alone this year, including several thousand involving pregnant women whose babies were born with birth defects.[4]

"Everything we look at with this virus seems to be a little scarier than we initially thought," said Anne Schuchat, principal deputy director of the Centers for Disease Control and Prevention (CDC).[5]

Selected Mosquito-borne Diseases

Chikungunya

Symptoms: Fever and joint pain and possibly muscle aches and headaches.

Where it occurs: Africa, Asia and Europe. It first appeared in the Americas in Caribbean countries in 2013; the first locally acquired case in the continental United States was reported in Florida in 2014.

Species that spread it: Most often *Aedes aegypti* and *Aedes albopictus*.

Dengue

Symptoms: Fever and at least two of the following: severe headache, severe eye pain, joint pain, muscle and/or bone pain, rash, mild bleeding, low white-cell count.

Where it occurs: Endemic in more than 100 countries, primarily in tropical urban areas; the Americas, Southeast Asia and Western Pacific most affected. Dengue is endemic in Puerto Rico; outbreaks have occurred in Hawaii and South Texas.

Species that spread it: Mainly *Aedes aegypti* but also *Aedes albopictus*.

Malaria

Symptoms: Typically fever, headache, chills and vomiting. Left untreated, those infected may develop more severe complications and die.

Where it occurs: More than 100 countries and territories, including large areas of Africa and Asia. Most deaths occur among African children. About 1,500 cases are reported annually in the United States among immigrants and returning travelers.

Species that spread it: *Anopheles*, particularly *Anopheles gambiae*.

West Nile Virus

Symptoms: Often, none. About one in five of those infected develop a fever accompanied by headache, body aches, joint pains, vomiting, diarrhea or rash; weakness and fatigue can last for months. About 10 percent of those who develop neurological symptoms such as seizures will die.

Where it occurs: Africa, Europe, Middle East, North America, West Asia, U.S.

Species that spread it: Numerous, particularly *Culex*.

Yellow Fever

Symptoms: Initially, fever, chills, severe headache, back pain, body aches, nausea, vomiting, fatigue or weakness, but most people have mild or no symptoms. About 15 percent develop severe illness and up to half may die.

Where it occurs: Tropical areas of Africa and Central and South America. In a few cases, returning travelers from Africa carried it to China this year.

Species that spread it: *Aedes* and *Haemogogus*.

Zika

Symptoms: Fever, rash, joint pain, but most people have mild or no symptoms. In some cases, the virus can cause birth defects and neurological disorders.

Where it occurs: Pacific islands, Africa, Latin America, the Caribbean. No locally acquired cases have yet occurred in the continental United States.

Species that spread it: Primarily *Aedes aegypti*.

Mosquito Species

Aedes aegypti: The yellow fever mosquito bites mainly humans.

Aedes albopictus: The Asian tiger mosquito is larger and blacker than *Aedes aegypti* and feeds on humans, pets and wild animals.

Anopheles: The common malaria mosquito; females taking blood meals to boost egg production pose biggest threat to humans.

Culex: Breeds prolifically; preys on birds and humans.

Sources: Centers for Disease Control and Prevention; World Health Organization

Public health officials warn that the outbreaks of Zika and other viruses are signs that mosquitoes pose a greater threat to humans as the climate warms and the insects' habitat expands into more temperate climes. In fact, scientists fear more disease outbreaks of all types due to global commerce, human encroachment into animal habitats and climate change. "We're seeing a whole new set of viruses that either were very rare or were thought to be limited to one particular area," says Marten Edwards, an entomologist at Muhlenberg College in Pennsylvania. "We're all one airplane flight away" from getting infected, he says.

Until a year ago, Zika was little known and rarely diagnosed. Scientists first identified it in the Zika Forest of Uganda in 1947, but it was hardly studied because of its rarity — scientists knew of only 14 cases before 2007 — and because it didn't appear to kill humans or farm animals.[6] Then, in 2007, a Zika outbreak hit 500 of the 7,000 residents on the Pacific Island of Yap, near the Philippines. As would occur elsewhere, Zika spread rapidly, then seemingly disappeared as the local populace built up immunity. No one in that epidemic died.[7]

From Yap, Zika headed eastward to French Polynesia, near New Zealand, where a 2013 outbreak reached all 76 inhabited islands. Since then it has struck the Americas. In Brazil, which has been hardest hit, Zika has led to the births of about 5,000 microcephalic babies in the past year.[8] Microcephaly, a condition in which a baby's head and brain are smaller than normal, can lead to developmental problems and vision and hearing loss. In severe cases, a shortened lifespan can result.[9]

Researchers have linked Zika to other birth defects and more serious conditions, such as the neurological disease Guillain-Barré Syndrome, a rare, potentially fatal disorder in which the body's immune system attacks the nerves.

Scientists expect Zika eventually to reach every country in the Western Hemisphere except Canada, plus mainland Chile, according to the Pan American Health Organization, the Americas branch of the World Health Organization (WHO).

"Zika is very much on the move," writes Donald G. McNeil Jr., a *New York Times* global health reporter, in his new book about the disease. "Transmission is increasing in Central America and the Caribbean and will keep doing so at least until the fall."[10]

No one has yet contracted Zika from a mosquito bite within the continental United States. But about 1,305 people have become infected while traveling abroad, and in U.S. territories another 2,905 people have gotten Zika, according to the CDC. On July 19, the Florida health department announced it is investigating a possible first locally transmitted Zika case.[11]

In February, the WHO declared Zika a global health emergency. With Brazil set to host the Summer Olympics and Paralympics, there have been calls to postpone, move or cancel the Games, but health officials say the presence of tourists during Brazil's winter season, when mosquitoes are mostly dormant, will not increase the disease's spread.

Scientists blame Zika's spread on the *Aedes aegypti* mosquito, the primary vector, or carrier, of the virus. The Asian tiger mosquito (*Aedes albopictus*), which causes chikungunya, has a wider range within the United States and might also carry Zika, but it is not known to be an effective carrier.

Disease-Carrying Mosquitoes Range across U.S.

The *Aedes aegypti* mosquito, the primary carrier of Zika, dengue, chikungunya and other viruses, typically is found during the warmer months in 28 mostly Southern states, stretching from California to Florida, and as far north as the southern tip of New York. The Asian tiger mosquito (*Aedes albopictus*), which ranges as far north as southern Maine and across the Midwest, may also carry Zika, but that connection is uncertain, scientists say.

Range of Disease-Carrying Mosquitoes in U.S., 2016

Source: Centers for Disease Control and Prevention, 2016, www.cdc.gov/zika/vector/range.html

Zika is especially troublesome, scientists say, because it is the first mosquito-borne virus that can be spread via sex and is known to spread between pregnant women and their fetuses. On July 15, the CDC reported the first known case of a woman infecting her male partner through sex. The agency said women should use protection if their partners have traveled to Zika-infested regions, regardless of whether their partners are male or female.[12]

In most cases, Zika appears to be harmless. Four out of five people infected with the virus aren't even aware of it because they have no symptoms. Others may experience mild problems, such as fever, rash or headache. Once exposed to Zika, humans are believed to be immune to the virus. However, an infected person can spread it through sexual contact or by being bitten by a mosquito that then goes on to bite others.

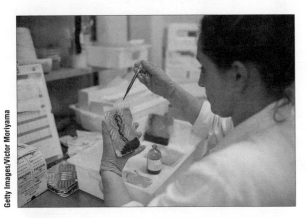

A technician prepares blood for feeding genetically modified mosquitoes at a laboratory operated by the British biotechnology firm Oxitec in Campinas, Brazil, on Feb. 11, 2016. Oxitec recently received tentative approval for the trial release in the Florida Keys of genetically altered mosquitoes, whose offspring would not survive.

What's more, because Zika has emerged so rapidly — and the virus is mutating as it travels — scientists still are determining its full effects.

In areas where Zika is present, the question of whether to advise women to delay pregnancy is controversial within public health circles. Many doctors have told patients they should wait, but the CDC and the WHO have not taken a formal position, although they have urged pregnant women or the partners of women trying to get pregnant not to travel to areas with high prevalence for Zika. Officials in some Latin American countries have warned women that they should postpone pregnancy.[13]

In February, President Obama asked Congress to approve nearly $2 billion to fight the virus, but disagreements over how to pay for the funding have so far stymied congressional action. Republicans fear giving the administration a "blank check" and the flexibility to move money around without accountability, while Democrats have objected to provisions attached to the GOP's Zika bill. In July, Senate Democrats blocked a $1.1 billion GOP package because it would have cut health care funding, barred money for Planned Parenthood's birth control efforts, changed non-health-related environmental regulations and altered a rule allowing Confederate flag displays at veterans' cemeteries.[14]

Public health agencies have shifted funds from other programs to ramp up anti-Zika efforts, but many officials fear they will not have enough money to combat the virus vigorously. "Right now, in the continental U.S., we are not prepared to handle Zika if we start seeing transmission," says Peter Hotez, dean of the National School of Tropical Medicine at Baylor College of Medicine in Houston.

Areas of the Gulf Coast, from Florida to Texas, are fertile breeding grounds for *Aedes aegypti* mosquitoes. Urban areas with high concentration of poverty may be especially vulnerable, Hotez says. Poor people tend to be exposed to mosquito-borne illnesses more frequently because they may live in areas with inadequate sanitation, mosquito abatement programs and access to health care. In addition, many do not have air conditioning or screens, so they leave doors and windows open, letting in more mosquitoes.

"Some of the poorest counties in Texas, for example, . . . are probably at the highest risk for the Zika circulation and have the least resources to do anything about it," said Scott C. Weaver, director of the Institute for Human Infections and Immunity at the University of Texas Medical Branch in Galveston.[15]

And the disease may spread elsewhere. "No one who has studied *Aedes aegypti* is really surprised at all that it would spread a disease rapidly as a vector," says Edwards, the Muhlenberg entomologist. The mosquito is "a problem that's been there all along, waiting for a virus to spread."

Because of the way *Aedes aegypti* has evolved, it is particularly hard to kill off. Spraying campaigns don't work well because the mosquito can lay its eggs in tiny bodies of water, including indoors. Female mosquitoes suck blood to nourish their eggs. "It can lay eggs in a bottle cap with a couple of drops of water, or the cellophane wrapper of a cigarette pack," says Daniel Epstein, a communications officer with the Pan American Health Organization.

Scientists are experimenting with genetic engineering techniques to kill off mosquitoes, but the approach is controversial because of fears it could affect the larger ecosystem. The urgency of the Zika crisis, however, is lending momentum to their efforts.

As people wait to see whether Zika will become prevalent in the United States and other countries, here are some of the questions scientists, public health officials, lawmakers and the public are debating:

Is the U.S. public health system prepared for Zika?

Many doctors and health officials worry that Zika could overwhelm the public health system.

"We are underfunded, under-resourced and outgunned by the mosquito," says LaMar Hasbrouck, executive director of the National Association of County and City Health Officials.

A recent study by the Trust for America's Health, a nonprofit advocacy group, found that public health spending remains below the levels before the 2007-09 recession. The nation ramped up public health spending in response to the terrorist attacks of 2001, partly in fear that terrorists might attack the United States with chemical or biological weapons. But funding for the CDC, as well as the federal program that provides grants to states and localities for response to public health emergencies, is down from its peak levels more than a decade ago. Many states have cut their own funding in recent years as well.[16]

Money aside, other experts say, the public health system has a number of attributes. The United States has advanced health care facilities and personnel ready to treat Zika, and health officials say they have been preparing for months to contain the virus should it appear locally, including readying plans to isolate patients. The CDC is already monitoring hundreds of patients with Zika.

Local education campaigns and other efforts have helped prevent dengue and other viruses from spreading in recent years, experts say. "We have been very successful so far in controlling epidemics," says José Szapocznik, who chairs the Public Health Services Department at the University of Miami.

"If you were to ask any state health official, they would probably say at this point in time they're generally pleased with the progress they're making to respond to and contain Zika, should it become a locally acquired and transmitted disease," says James Blumenstock, chief program officer for public health at the Association of State and Territorial Health Officials.

But because the U.S. public health system is decentralized and fragmented, Blumenstock and other health officials say Zika could pose a serious test in terms of response. "If we really need to ramp up and respond to

larger numbers," Blumenstock says, "we could be reaching a tipping point on resources where there's a limit to how much the nation's public health system can offer protection."

The United States has no single public health system. States and localities carry out much of the work of educating the public and combating epidemics. The picture varies so much from state to state — and within states — that a coherent or consistent response to health threats isn't always possible, according to Celine Gounder, an infectious disease specialist and former New York City assistant health commissioner.

The number of personnel at state health departments ranges from several hundred to just a few. And at the county level, the amount of resources and personnel devoted to public health depends on how much politicians are willing to spend on what sometimes seem like distant threats.[17]

But those in public health circles like to say that a town doesn't wait until a fire breaks out to build a firehouse, and the town doesn't shut down the firehouse if no fires occur. But many health officials feel that's exactly what happens in public health. The urgency of a new threat can bring additional money, but it's purely reactive. Communities do not prepare in advance, and after a threat ebbs, funding and attention do so as well.

Public health professionals decry this pattern of lurching from crisis to crisis. "We can't just keep running from one fire to the next, whether the current most pressing threat is Zika, Ebola, Legionnaire's disease or lead in the water supply," Gounder writes. "Yet historically, there's been little long-term political will to sustain public health funding."[18]

Blumenstock and other public health officials worry that, with Zika, the nation isn't even lurching effectively, because Congress has failed so far to respond. Congressional inaction has forced the Obama administration to shift money meant to deal with the Ebola virus, for which Congress appropriated more than $5 billion in emergency funds in 2014, to the Zika threat.[19]

They say that even if state and local health departments effectively respond to Zika, they'll have done so by raiding funds meant to address other problems. Then they may be stretched too thin to effectively deal with severe problems such as a measles outbreak, a severe flu season or a bad hurricane season, Blumenstock and Gouder say.

"Preparedness money has been cut, so the core capacity of the public health system has diminished to the lowest I've seen in many, many years," says Bryan Callahan, a senior program officer at the Bill & Melinda Gates Foundation, which is the largest nongovernmental funder of anti-malaria efforts. "The public health folks always do what they can with what they have, but they're teetering dangerously close to being unable to deal with this crisis in any meaningful way."

"I'm confident that certain public health agencies are able to respond to Zika, but this is not uniform," says Amesh Adalja, an expert on infectious disease at the Center for Health Security at the University of Pittsburgh Medical Center (UPMC). "It's basically a lottery [as to] whether you have a county health department that has the capacity to respond to infectious diseases."

Should mosquitoes be eradicated?

A couple of years ago, billionaire philanthropist Bill Gates called mosquitoes the "most dangerous animal on earth," noting that "when it comes to killing humans, no other animal even comes close."[20]

But officials disagree over whether governments should attempt to eradicate the mosquitoes that carry deadly viruses. According to the American Mosquito Control Association, which represents mosquito control agencies, 174 different mosquito species are prevalent in the United States. Most are harmless, and no one suggests trying to wipe them all out. But some scientists consider *Aedes aegypti*, the primary carrier for Zika, dengue and yellow fever, a tempting target for eradication.

"Eradicating *Aedes aegypti* would be a good thing," says Crystal Boddie, a senior associate at the UPMC Center for Health Security and a former program manager with the federal Department of Homeland Security. "It carries all these diseases and poses a big risk to our public health."

Mosquito larvae are a food source for fish, and bats and birds eat adult mosquitoes. Mosquitoes can also act as pollinators for plants. Boddie says because *Aedes aegypti* is not native to the Western Hemisphere, wiping out the species shouldn't cause huge disruptions in the food chain. But other experts warn that targeting a species for elimination, particularly through heavy use of pesticides, can have unintended consequences on the ecosystem.

"You cannot reverse this epidemic through pesticides alone," says Szapocznik. "There's just so much we can fumigate. All those pesticides have adverse consequences for other animals and humans."

Killing mosquitoes with pesticides could damage animal habitats, particularly if poisonous chemicals are used in mass quantities. International efforts to wipe out mosquitoes to prevent malaria in the 1950s and '60s led to environmental poisoning stemming from widespread use of the chemical DDT, which eventually was banned in the United States.[21]

Mosquito control experts have long tried to use natural predators against the insects. For example, they have distributed fish that eat mosquito larvae and encouraged residents to build houses for bats, which can eat 1,000 mosquitoes per hour.[22]

Although insecticides remain a primary tool, scientists today are looking at newer methods. The Gates Foundation is sponsoring studies in Brazil and Colombia to release mosquitoes infected with Wolbachia, a bacteria that severely limits mosquitoes' ability to transmit viruses. Once a mosquito has the bacteria, it will be passed on to its offspring. Earlier studies were promising, says Callahan, the foundation official. "Wolbachia works not only in dengue but a whole host of viruses, including Zika, chikungunya, West Nile and yellow fever," he says.

Scientists also are experimenting with genetic modifications to limit mosquito populations. In March, the Food and Drug Administration (FDA) gave tentative approval to Oxitec, a British biotechnology company, to run a trial study in the Florida Keys. Oxitec wants to release genetically modified *Aedes aegypti* males, whose offspring would not survive.

Local residents and critics of releasing genetically modified mosquitoes into the wild have expressed concerns about potential dangers, including toxic or allergic effects on humans and other wildlife, that they claim Oxitec has not addressed. "The company has been criticised by independent scientists for the poor quality of its risk assessments for the Cayman Islands and Malaysia [experiments] and lack of transparency and public consultation," according to GeneWatch UK, a nonprofit public interest group.[23]

Oxitec insists its technology is safe and says it is the result of extensive research.[24]

Scientists also are exploring "gene drive" systems that can cause mutations, such as resistance to malaria, to be inherited by mosquito offspring.[25] But this technique also has drawn claims that it upsets ecosystems or alters the spread of disease in potentially harmful ways. "We don't know whether the elimination of malaria specifically won't somehow have genetic effects that cause a super-virulent pathogen to be released or to bring in much greater catastrophic consequences," New York University bioethicist Brendan Parent said.[26]

Combating *Aedes aegypti* mosquitoes requires a special effort, say mosquito-control experts, with house-to-house inspections and efforts to persuade people to clean up all containers that can allow the species to breed — which means attempting to get rid of objects as small as bottle caps.

But that's a daunting task, and even public health officials who believe mosquito eradication might be worthwhile doubt localities possess the resources for such an effort.

It is possible to eradicate particular species of mosquitoes from large areas. By 1970, 18 Latin American nations had eliminated *Aedes aegypti* within their borders. But countries have to get their neighbors to do the same or the mosquitoes will return over time. The United States ignored requests from other countries to participate in the eradication effort until 1965 and dropped its own effort just four years later as interest in the project waned.[27]

Because yellow fever and dengue had largely disappeared from the United States, few public officials worried about *Aedes aegypti*. As a result, the Gulf Coast gave the mosquito a base from which to replenish and spread. "The U.S. kind of gave up its effort and stopped funding," says Epstein of the Pan American Health Organization. "*Aedes aegypti* came roaring back and reinfested the rest of the hemisphere."

Hotez, the tropical disease dean at Baylor, believes Zika's emergence may revive the question of *Aedes aegypti* eradication in the United States. With enough resources, he says, the species can be eradicated.

Malaria Deaths Fall as Spending Increases

The number of malaria deaths worldwide fell by nearly half between 2000 and 2015, from more than 839,000 to fewer than 438,000, with most of the 2015 deaths occurring in Africa and Southeast Asia. Spending by the Global Fund to Fight AIDS, Tuberculosis and Malaria to reduce malaria deaths rose from $200 million in 2004 to more than $7 billion in 2015.

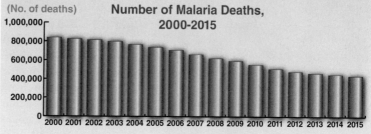

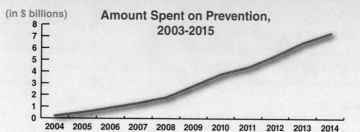

Sources: "World Malaria Report 2015," World Health Organization, http://tinyurl.com/zd2jvvy; "Results Report 2015," Global Fund to Fight AIDS, Tuberculosis and Malaria, p. 17, http://tinyurl.com/q3odyhl

And that may be something people want because of the harm *Aedes aegypti* is causing humans.

"Zika has engendered a renewed interest in mosquitoes as being a vector and not just a nuisance," says Joe Conlon, technical adviser to the American Mosquito Control Association. "People who were against pesticides, now they just want them dead and don't care how you do it."

Should pregnant women with Zika have access to abortion where it is restricted or outlawed?

Because of the severity of microcephaly and other birth defects linked to Zika, many women's rights and health care advocates argue that pregnant women should have access to abortion. But many countries most severely affected by Zika do not allow abortions: El Salvador and

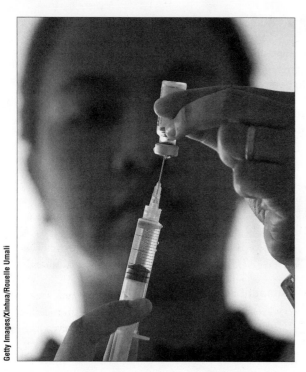

A health worker prepares to inject the world's first dengue vaccine at a public school in Marikina City, Philippines, on April 4. Dengue is found in more than 100 countries, primarily in tropical urban areas. The virus is endemic in Puerto Rico; outbreaks have occurred in Hawaii and South Texas.

Nicaragua outlaw abortion entirely, while Brazil and Venezuela prohibit abortion except when necessary to save the pregnant woman's life.

In February, the U.N. High Commissioner for Human Rights said that to respond effectively to the Zika threat, nations must repeal "laws and policies that restrict access to sexual and reproductive health" services.[28]

Anis, a Brazilian bioethics group, has petitioned that country's Supreme Court to allow women infected with Zika to have abortions. In El Salvador, the health minister has argued that his nation must revise its abortion laws because of the risk of severe birth defects, but his efforts have been unsuccessful.

"It has made the issue more salient and has highlighted the cruelty behind some of these restrictive abortion laws," said Francoise Girard, president of the International Women's Health Coalition, a New York-based nonprofit that promotes reproductive rights. "There is an incredible amount of anxiety, fear and stress among women that are pregnant."[29]

Women's rights groups and public health advocates note that within the United States, states have passed more than 200 laws restricting abortion over the past five years. Many of these laws have passed in Southern states where Zika is expected to be most prevalent.[30]

After Texas enacted a law in 2013 that forced abortion providers to meet higher safety standards, half of the abortion clinics in the state closed.[31] The Supreme Court, in a 5-3 vote in late June, overturned that law, saying the restrictions were merely cover for making abortions harder to obtain.[32]

In addition, about a dozen states — most recently South Carolina in May — have banned most abortions after 20 weeks of pregnancy. Microcephaly is not detected through normal pregnancy screenings such as ultrasounds, and it can't be diagnosed even through more sophisticated tests such as CT scans and MRIs until at least 19 weeks into a pregnancy.

"The microcephalic development is not visible early on," says Szapocznik, the Miami public health professor.

But abortion opponents say Zika's spread is no reason to promote greater access to the procedure. They argue that abortion supporters have used other medical conditions in the past as reasons to increase access to abortion.

Not all pregnant women infected with Zika have children with birth defects. Abortion opponents stress that Zika's effects are still unknown, so governments should not rush to increase abortion rights.

"The kneejerk reaction of, 'We need more abortion,' to a relatively unknown occurrence is alarming," says Mike Gonidakis, president of Ohio Right to Life, which opposes abortion. "Of course, no one wants their unborn child to have Zika, but babies that are born with Zika, that's not a death sentence. What is a death sentence is abortion."

At a February hearing on Zika, Rep. Christopher Smith, R-N.J., a leading congressional opponent of abortion, recounted the story of a Brazilian woman born with microcephaly whose doctors predicted she would not walk or talk but who has been able to work as a journalist. "[W]e must work harder to prevent maternal infections and devise compassionate ways to ensure that any child born with disabilities from this or any other infection is welcomed, loved and gets the care he or she needs," Smith said.[33]

In recent decades, many families have made it a point to try to adopt children with special needs or other disabilities, notes John Stonestreet, president of the Colson Center for Christian Worldview, a religious organization in Lansdowne, Va. "We've seen societies that consider individuals with disabilities to be less valuable than other members of society," Stonestreet says. "We've rightly condemned that as being heartless, inhumane and wrong."

Health officials hope that the Zika threat will stem the push against contraceptives in some states. In February, Pope Francis drew headlines when he suggested that contraceptives, which violate Catholic doctrine, might be permissible as part of the effort to combat Zika. But he underscored that abortion is "an absolute evil" and would not be justifiable in the Zika fight.[34]

And the current version of the congressional funding bill for Zika died in the Senate in July after Democrats complained it blocked money to pay for contraceptives or condoms and didn't provide money for family-planning groups such as Planned Parenthood. Republicans and Democrats have since traded charges over which side is being more irresponsible.[35]

The political maneuvering has exasperated some health officials. "Public health has always been a partnership between the federal, state and local levels," says Georges Benjamin, executive director of the American Public Health Association, a trade group for professionals in the field. "Congress has failed to do its job, frankly."

Cindy Pellegrini, a lobbyist for the March of Dimes, which advocates for maternal and fetal health, said the GOP's bill was "doomed from the start" because it was loaded with provisions that Democrats opposed.[36]

BACKGROUND
Breaking Yellow Fever

Although malaria has been the major killer among mosquito-borne illnesses worldwide, yellow fever has done more to shape history in the Americas.

Yellow fever first broke out in the Americas in 1648, in Barbados, Havana and Yucatán, Mexico. By the 1690s, it was present in North America, notably in the port cities of Charleston, New York and Philadelphia.[37]

Although it didn't kill as many people and wasn't as contagious as cholera or smallpox, it created more panic, journalist Molly Caldwell Crosby writes in her history of the disease, *The American Plague.* "Yellow fever became the most dreaded disease in North America for two hundred years," she said.[38]

In 1793, some 5,500 people died during an outbreak in Philadelphia, which was then the U.S. capital.[39] Over a 35-year span during the 1800s, New Orleans suffered a dozen outbreaks, each causing more than 1,000 deaths.[40]

Yellow fever also helped reshape the continent. The French dictator Napoleon, who dreamed of building an empire in the Americas, saw thousands of his troops die from yellow fever in Haiti during a failed attempt to end a slave rebellion. Discouraged by the setback and other problems, he sold millions of acres to the United States in 1803 in what became known as the Louisiana Purchase.

Yellow fever was associated with the slave trade. Steam power and other navigational improvements cut the time crossing the Atlantic Ocean from 30 days to seven during the 19th century, meaning people infected with yellow fever could travel before its symptoms showed.[41] Although the disease could affect anyone, its spread contributed to prejudice against blacks and immigrants, as well as to the view that the American South was a distinct region within the country.

"Carolina is in the spring a paradise, in the summer a hell, and in the autumn a hospital," a German commentator wrote during the colonial period, an observation that still applied in the 19th century.[42]

A warm, wet winter in 1878 helped create perfect conditions for the *Aedes aegypti* mosquito. That year, a yellow fever epidemic spread from Brazil and killed 20,000 in the Mississippi Valley. The population of Memphis, Tenn., in July 1878 was 47,000. By September, only 19,000 people remained in the city, and 17,000 of them had yellow fever.[43]

In the late 19th century, scattered physicians — the Scottish doctor Patrick Manson, working in China, and Alphonse Laveran, a French army physician stationed in Algeria — made the first connections between insects and disease. Their findings, and those of other pioneering scientists, were generally greeted with ridicule. *The Washington Post* wrote in 1890, "Of all the silly and nonsensical rigmarole of yellow fever that has yet found its way into print . . . the silliest beyond compare is to be found in the arguments and theories generated by the mosquito hypothesis."[44] Laveran was ultimately awarded a Nobel Prize for his work in 1907.

When French teams failed to complete the Panama Canal after one-third of the workers died from yellow fever or malaria, the U.S. Army prepared to take over. It created a Yellow Fever Commission in 1900, headed by Maj. Walter Reed, after whom the Army later named its flagship medical center.

To test the hypothesis that mosquitoes were responsible for spreading the disease, Reed paid human volunteers $100 to be exposed to yellow fever, with another $100 paid as a bonus if they contracted the disease. As Crosby noted, before World War I, soldiers were more likely to die from diseases than from bullets, "so volunteering for human experiments" that might determine the cause of disease "might not seem as much of a psychological departure as it would today."[45]

Reed proved the link between mosquitoes and disease. Using a process of elimination, he exposed his subjects to every manner of filth, thus showing that germs, infected clothing or air did not spread yellow fever. After a subject named John Moran, who was housed among mosquitoes in one of Reed's buildings, came down with a high fever, Reed smiled and said, "Moran, this is one of the happiest days of my life."[46]

William Gorgas, the Army's chief sanitary engineer, introduced draconian anti-mosquito measures in Havana, which the Army still occupied following the Spanish-American War. His targets were puddles and broken flower pots and drained or oiled pools of standing water. Cases dropped from 1,400 in 1900 to zero in 1902.[47] Residents were fined if mosquito larvae were found on their property — a policy still in place in Havana today.[48]

Gorgas soon exported his sanitation methods to Panama, but many, including Secretary of War (and future President) William Howard Taft, remained skeptical about mosquitoes being the root cause of disease. Taft lobbied to remove Gorgas from his post. A doctor friend convinced President Theodore Roosevelt that fighting mosquitoes was the best way to combat yellow fever.

"You must choose between the old method and the new," the doctor, Alexander Lambert, told the president. "You must choose between failure with mosquitoes or success without them."[49]

After being stymied at first, Gorgas was given a staff of 4,100 workers and the entire U.S. supply of sulphur, kerosene and pyrethrum to use as insecticides.[50] They worked — at least where Gorgas deployed them. Where an earlier French dig had failed, largely due to death and disease, the Americans succeeded, with only 350 deaths among the white American canal workers, the focus of Gorgas' sanitation efforts.

In 1937, microbiologist Max Theiler and other scientists funded by the Rockefeller Institute developed a cheap and effective vaccine for yellow fever. By 1942, 7 million doses were given to American and British soldiers fighting in Africa. Not one case of yellow fever occurred among them.[51]

Attacking Malaria

Malaria remained a major problem. "People forget today, but even as recently as World War II, every country in the world had endemic malaria transmission within its borders, even inside the Arctic Circle," said Richard Feachem, the first executive director of the Global Fund to Fight AIDS, Tuberculosis and Malaria.[52]

For more than a century, humans had taken quinine, an extract of cinchona bark, to help prevent parasites that cause malaria from growing in the gut. By the 1940s, researchers had developed the first synthetic antimalarial treatments, chloroquine and amodiaquine. The U.S. Army was heavily involved in anti-malaria research during World War II because of the number of soldiers who contracted the disease while fighting in the Pacific jungles.

By 1944, the Army had begun using dichlorodiphenyltrichloroethane, or DDT, as an insecticide.

Some strains of malaria became resistant to chloroquine. Other treatments followed, but despite billions of dollars invested in research no vaccine has been developed.

Malaria was less of a problem in rich countries such as the United States and Britain than in Asia and, especially, Africa. For one thing, mosquitoes preferred to feed on herds of cattle instead of humans. In addition, as swampland was drained for pasture and increasing numbers of people moved from farms to cities, the disease declined. Malaria was eradicated in the United States by 1952, although cases have occurred sporadically among travelers.[53]

CHRONOLOGY

1940s-1970s *Efforts to wipe out mosquitoes result in environmental damage.*

1947 Zika virus first identified in Uganda's Zika Forest.

1951 American researcher Max Theiler wins Nobel Prize in medicine for his role in developing yellow fever vaccine.

1951 Malaria temporarily eradicated in the United States.

1954 Zika first identified in a human in Nigeria.

1955 The World Health Organization (WHO) initiates Global Malaria Eradication plan.

1962 Eighteen Latin American countries succeed in eradicating *Aedes aegypti* mosquitoes. . . . American biologist Rachel Carson's influential book *Silent Spring* tells how the pesticide DDT wreaked environmental havoc.

1963 Dengue fever outbreak in Puerto Rico marks the disease's first appearance in the Western Hemisphere in 20 years.

1969 WHO largely abandons its mosquito eradication campaign, recommending that countries adopt control strategies.

1972 U.S. bans use of DDT.

1990s-2000s *Malaria and other mosquito-borne illnesses re-emerge as major concerns.*

1995 Europe records 90,000 cases of malaria.

1999 Outbreak of West Nile virus in New York state represents the disease's first appearance in the Western Hemisphere.

2001 Maui sees its first case of dengue in more than 50 years.

2002 A malaria case in Virginia is the first in the U.S. in several years. . . . Global Fund to Fight AIDS, Tuberculosis and Malaria, a public-private partnership, is established and becomes the main conduit for Western aid.

2005 President George W. Bush announces the U.S. will spend $1.2 billion over five years to fight malaria.

2007 In the first major outbreak of Zika, dozens of residents are infected on Yap, a Pacific island. . . . . Scientists detect separate Asian and African strains of the virus.

2008 Aid from governments and foundations devoted to fighting malaria increases to more than $1 billion, up from $100 million in 1998.

2010-Present *Zika and other mosquito-borne diseases become prevalent in the Americas.*

2010 Campaigns succeed in halving malaria cases in 10 African countries over the past decade.

2012 West Nile virus kills 89 people in the Dallas-Fort Worth area, part of a record U.S. death toll of 286.

2013 Zika outbreak reaches all 67 inhabited islands of French Polynesia. . . . First known Zika case appears in the U.S.; the disease is diagnosed in a New York man who had been in French Polynesia.

2014 Chikungunya spreads in Florida, Puerto Rico and U.S. Virgin Islands.

2015 Brazil records 1.6 million cases of dengue, nearly triple the number in 2014. . . . As Zika spreads rapidly in Brazil, more than 3,000 babies are born with microcephaly. . . . The first locally transmitted U.S. case of Zika is reported in Puerto Rico.

2016 WHO declares Zika a global health emergency (Feb. 1). . . . President Obama requests $1.9 billion in emergency supplemental funding for Zika (Feb. 22) . . . . Centers for Disease Control and Prevention says Zika virus in pregnant women can cause microcephaly in fetuses (April 13). . . . Vaccine shortages force WHO to approve yellow fever vaccinations of one-fifth strength (June 17). . . . Inovio Pharmaceuticals announces first trial of a Zika vaccine (June 20). . . . Senate Democrats block passage of a $1.1 billion funding package to combat Zika out of concern about its restrictions on birth control (July). . . .

Experts Differ on Zika Threat at Summer Olympics

Some athletes are staying away from the Games in Brazil.

NBC will be sending hundreds of people to Brazil to help with coverage of the Summer Olympics, but the "Today" show's Savannah Guthrie won't be one of them. Guthrie was set to co-host the broadcast of the Games' opening ceremonies on Aug. 5, but she is pregnant and on the advice of her physician will not be attending.

Both the Olympics and the Paralympics, which starts Sept. 7, are being held in Rio de Janeiro. The World Health Organization (WHO) has said the Olympics will not substantially worsen the spread of Zika. But with Brazil at the center of the disease's outbreak, many have questioned whether the Games should have been postponed, canceled or moved.

"[W]hile Brazil's Zika inevitably will spread globally — given enough time, viruses always do — it helps nobody to speed that up," Canadian immunologist Amir Attaran wrote in a widely cited article in the *Harvard Public Health Review.* "In particular, it cannot possibly help when an estimated 500,000 foreign tourists flock into Rio for the Games, potentially becoming infected, and returning to their [homes]."[1]

Several top golfers and American cyclist Tejay van Garderen are among the athletes skipping the Games due to health concerns. Britain's Greg Rutherford will be going to Rio in hopes of earning another gold medal in the long jump, but his partner won't be coming along, and they have frozen his sperm as a precaution.[2] Hope Solo, the goalkeeper on the American women's soccer team, says she will participate but only "grudgingly."

"I'm not sure I'm even going to be leaving the hotel room, outside of practice," Solo told CNBC in May. "I strongly believe that no athlete should be put into this position — to decide between your Olympic dreams and your own health."[3]

The National Institutes of Health announced on July 5 that it will fund a study to monitor the health of U.S. athletes and coaches for up to two years after the Games.[4] But while it may make intuitive sense that it's a bad idea to hold a global gathering at the center of an epidemic — 160,000 Brazilians have been infected with Zika this year — the WHO and other health officials insist the risk of infection is minimal.

For one thing, the Games are taking place during winter in the Southern Hemisphere, when mosquitoes are least active. Already, the number of new cases has dropped from more than 3,000 per week earlier in the year to about 30 per week in June.[5] "There's little mosquito-borne disease at that time," says Daniel Epstein, a communications officer with the Pan American Health Organization, a regional office of WHO.

Epstein adds that Brazilian officials will make every effort to ensure that Olympic venues are well sprayed. And, he says, substantial travel between Brazil and the rest of the world already occurs. "The number of people who are going to the Olympics and coming back are less than

The Rockefeller Foundation had led the charge against mosquito-borne illnesses for decades, but after World War II primary responsibility for fighting malaria internationally switched to the World Health Organization, established in 1948.

Following the war, DDT was widely adopted for civilian use, replacing earlier pesticides, such as Paris green, a highly toxic compound powder that includes arsenic. DDT did not directly harm human health but was fatal to mosquitoes, and the chemical became the foundation for an eradication campaign begun by the WHO in the 1950s.

In 1958, Congress allocated $100 million for the anti-malarial program. By 1963, Congress had spent nearly $500 million, with 93 countries around the world using U.S. dollars to finance spraying campaigns.[54]

Initial results were spectacular. In Sri Lanka, the number of malaria cases plummeted from 3 million in

1 percent of the people who are traveling back and forth to Zika-infested countries," Epstein says.

One epidemiological model projects that, at most, 16 foreign tourists will contract Zika at the Olympics.[6] At a news conference in June, Brazilian health minister Ricardo Barros said the chances of catching the Zika virus at the Games is "almost zero."[7]

"There isn't a public health or Zika rationale to move the Olympics or delay the Olympics," says Thomas V. Inglesby, director of the Center for Health Security at the University of Pittsburgh Medical Center.

Foreign travel always has risks. Whether it is worth taking a chance on attending this particular Olympics, Inglesby says, is a personal choice.

A fair number of people are choosing not to go, whether due to Zika, Brazil's ongoing corruption and political turmoil or other reasons. Sixty-three percent of travel agents surveyed in June said they were seeing less interest in trips to Rio than there had been for recent Games in London and Beijing.[8]

As a result, travelers who do head to this year's Games will get a better deal, said Julia Carter, sales director for Brazil Nuts, a South American tour operator based in Naples, Fla. "There are certainly more deals than there were six months ago," she said.[9]

— *Alan Greenblatt*

Standing water in a slum near the site of the Summer Olympics in Rio de Janeiro is a potential breeding ground for Zika-carrying mosquitoes.

[1] Amir Attaran, "Off the Podium: Why Public Health Concerns for Global Spread of Zika Virus Means That Rio de Janeiro's 2016 Olympic Games Must Not Proceed," *Harvard Public Health Review*, May 2016, http://tinyurl.com/hsmlav2.

[2] Susie Verilli, "Why I'm Not Flying Down to Rio," *Standard Issue*, June 7, 2016, http://tinyurl.com/zomln43.

[3] Matthew J. Belvedere, "Soccer star Hope Solo decides to go to the Rio Olympics despite Zika concerns," CNBC, May 10, 2016, http://tinyurl.com/hnvkbl8.

[4] Bill Berkrot, "U.S. to fund Zika virus study of U.S. Olympic team," Reuters, July 5, 2016, http://tinyurl.com/j9o95rm.

[5] Dom Phillips, "Brazil says there is 'almost zero' risk of Zika during Olympics. Really?" *The Washington Post*, July 6, 2016, http://tinyurl.com/jlcfhla.

[6] Marcello Nascimento Burattini *et al.*, "Potential exposure to Zika virus for foreign tourists during the 2016 Carnival and Olympic Games in Rio de Janeiro, Brazil," *Epidemiology & Infection*, July 2016, http://tinyurl.com/j59r7xg.

[7] Shasta Darlington, "Risk of catching Zika during Olympics is 'almost zero,' Brazilian official says," CNN, June 11, 2016, http://tinyurl.com/z72ol56.

[8] Nell McShane Wulfhart, "Zika Fears and Political Chaos Keeping Rio Olympics Affordable," *The New York Times*, June 13, 2016, http://tinyurl.com/h8g9zdz.

[9] *Ibid.*

1946 to just 18 in 1963. India, which saw 75 million infections and 800,000 deaths in 1947, had fewer than 100 malaria deaths in 1965. All told, 18 countries that were home to nearly one-third of the world's population were declared malaria-free.[55]

"The sudden lifting of the malarial burden brought about by liberal use of DDT in the years immediately after World War II was one of the most dramatic and abrupt health changes ever experienced by humankind," wrote historian William H. McNeill.[56]

But victory was short-lived. DDT destroyed a wide spectrum of insects and also poisoned animals. Nature writer Rachel Carson's landmark 1962 book, *Silent Spring*, warned that DDT and other pesticides had endangered ecosystems and threatened extinction of the bald eagle. Carson's book and her Capitol Hill testimony helped persuade Congress to cut off funding

Major Success: Malaria Deaths on the Decline

But limited donor interest, poverty inhibit further progress.

Public health experts call the fight against malaria, an ancient and deadly parasitic disease that attacks the liver and is spread by mosquitoes, one of the great global health success stories of the century. Deaths and transmissions have fallen sharply in recent years, an incredible achievement, experts say, given a lack of international attention to the disease a couple of decades ago.

But malaria remains a stubborn foe because both the malaria parasite and the mosquitoes that carry it have repeatedly developed resistance to pesticides and drugs used to fight the disease. Public health officials say more eradication tools — and money — are needed if progress is to continue.

Since 2000, annual malaria cases worldwide have dropped from an estimated 262 million globally in 2000 to 214 million in 2015, while malaria deaths have declined by nearly half, from about 839,000 to 438,000, with most of the deaths occurring in Africa and Southeast Asia, according to the World Health Organization.[1] And over the next couple of years, the number of countries considered malaria-free, meaning the disease is not transmitted locally, could grow considerably. South Africa, Botswana, Nepal and Ecuador are among the countries on track to join that list.

"In 1900, just about every country in the world had endemic malaria," says Bryan Callahan, a senior program officer with the Bill & Melinda Gates Foundation, the largest nongovernmental funder of anti-malaria efforts. "Now, half the member states of the United Nations don't have it. That's a huge public health achievement."

Nevertheless, malaria remains a scourge, killing a child in Africa every two minutes.[2] Earlier efforts to beat back malaria fell short, largely because anti-malaria efforts became a victim of their own success. Once eradicated from an area, malaria can return within a single transmission season, so the disease requires constant vigilance. Thus, perversely, the more success achieved, the less likely donors were to remain interested in combating the disease, says Scott Filler, senior malaria coordinator for the Global Fund to Fight AIDS, Tuberculosis and Malaria, a public-private organization that is the primary international conduit for anti-malaria efforts.

"Malaria falls off people's list of priorities when fewer kids are dying," Filler says. "As we get more successful, unfortunately, people punish success by forgetting how bad it was."

Although efforts to find a vaccine have been underway for decades, none exists yet. And the malaria-carrying mosquitoes — about 40 species of *Anopheles* — and the malaria-causing parasite have proven adaptable to insecticides and drugs. Chloroquine was once the most common anti-malaria drug, but drug-resistant strains of the disease have developed in many countries. Today's drug of choice is ACT (artemisinin-based combination therapies), but resistant parasites have developed in several Southeast Asian countries.[3]

"We're reaching an inflection point where our tools won't be effective if we don't bring in new tools," Filler says.

Currently, insecticide-treated bed nets, which protect individuals — especially children — from being bitten while they sleep, are an important weapon against the disease. But some mosquitoes in Africa are developing resistance.

Filler says a new combination of insecticides will be used to treat bed nets in the next year or two, but he warns this will drive up costs. Progress against malaria will require continued financial investment, especially since most health gains have occurred in places where malaria is less severe. Plus, it remains a major killer in several West and Central African countries, many of them impoverished.

for the mosquito eradication campaign in 1963.[57] Abroad, DDT spraying had become controversial among the public; many people didn't want their properties treated because DDT can kill farmyard animals and pets, so some bribed sprayers to bypass them.[58] By 1972, the United States had banned the use of DDT.[59]

However, by the time DDT was banned, the surviving mosquitoes had developed resistance to the chemical. As a result, the legacy of the DDT campaign — which never got underway in Africa for political reasons having to do with colonialism and the Cold War — was DDT-resistant mosquitoes. By 1969, Sri Lanka was

In the past, malaria has been beaten back, only to re-emerge as a major threat. A global eradication effort in the 1950s and '60s was eventually abandoned, in large part due to environmental problems with DDT, the primary chemical used for spraying, plus the mosquitoes developed resistance to the chemical. In addition, donors lost interest when deaths declined, and fighting malaria was not coordinated on an international basis.[4]

Then, in 1999, the United Nations made fighting malaria a priority as part of its Millennium Development Goals.[5] A highly influential 2001 paper argued that treating malaria was not only a health issue but a prerequisite for ending poverty in many nations, largely because of the millions of people in the developing world who are debilitated by the disease each year.[6]

Around the turn of the 21st century, the Gates Foundation and the Global Fund were established. The fund's efforts received major help from rich nations, including the United States. In addition, President George W. Bush began a billion-dollar initiative in 2005, with the goal of reducing malaria-related mortality by 50 percent in 15 countries in sub-Saharan Africa.[7] The Obama administration has continued to support the initiative.

"We know exactly what it takes to prevent and treat the disease," Bush said at a White House summit on malaria in 2006. "The only question is whether we have the will to act."[8]

Serious obstacles, such as fraud and corruption, hamper the distribution of bed nets and other aid in some countries, experts say.[9]

"Where malaria is worst is where health systems are weakest," says Filler. "The fight against malaria is a long, hard fight."

— *Alan Greenblatt*

[1] "Results Report," The Global Fund to Fight AIDS, Tuberculosis and Malaria, Sept. 18, 2015, http://tinyurl.com/nmeg2yr; "World Malaria Report 2015," World Health Organization, p. 9, http://tinyurl.com/zd2jvvy.

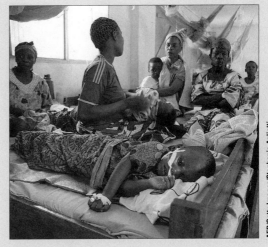

A child with malaria lies on a bed at a hospital in the Nyarugusu refugee camp in northwest Tanzania on June 11, 2015. The disease kills a child in Africa every two minutes.

[2] Jon Greenberg, "Malaria's toll: Close to one African child killed every 2 minutes," *Politifact*, April 25, 2016, http://tinyurl.com/hou62ew.

[3] "Q&A on artemisinin resistance," World Health Organization, February 2015, tinyurl.com/mbaup5l.

[4] Sonia Shah, *The Fever* (2010), p. 215.

[5] For background, see Danielle Kurtzleben, "Millennium Development Goals," *CQ Global Researcher*, Sept. 4, 2012, pp. 401-424.

[6] John Luke Gallup and Jeffrey D. Sachs, "The Economic Burden of Malaria," *American Journal of Tropical Medicine and Hygiene*, January 2001, www.ncbi.nlm.nih.gov/books/NBK2624/

[7] For more information, see "Background," President's Malaria Initiative, https://www.pmi.gov/about.

[8] Alex Perry, *Lifeblood: How to Change the World One Dead Mosquito at a Time* (2011), p. 92.

[9] *Ibid.*, p. 190.

back up to 500,000 malaria cases, while India saw 1 million.[60]

Despite these setbacks, the campaign did eradicate malaria in many places and helped build a public health infrastructure that contributed to the fight against other diseases, such as smallpox.[61]

Western Outbreaks

By the late 1990s, other mosquito borne-illnesses began to crop up in the Americas. The hemisphere's first case of West Nile encephalitis, which had been identified in Uganda in 1937, occurred in New York City in 1999. The CDC originally misidentified it as St. Louis encephalitis,

Garbage in the streets of Luanda, capital of Angola on the West African coast, can catch rainwater and become mosquito-breeding grounds. Along with Congo, Angola is suffering an outbreak of yellow fever, which is carried by the *Aedes aegypti* mosquito.

which was first identified in 1933 in that city and occurred primarily in the Mississippi Valley and Gulf Coast.

Tracey McNamara, a veterinarian and pathologist at the Bronx Zoo, determined that the same virus was responsible for bird deaths, and researchers subsequently identified it as West Nile.[62] By 2002, West Nile had spread to Louisiana and other Southern states and was responsible for 4,161 cases and 284 deaths in the United States.[63] About 2,000 cases are diagnosed in the United States each year, typically resulting in some 50 deaths, although there were 119 in 2015.[64]

Mosquitoes of the genus Culex spread West Nile; these carriers like to breed in stagnant and dirty (or organic rich) water. By contrast, the *Aedes aegypti* mosquito prefers clean water, laying eggs in manufactured containers such as barrels, tires or bottles. *Aedes aegypti* mosquitoes, in fact, typically don't breed in bodies of water with natural bottoms of sand or mud.[65]

"*Aedes aegypti* evolved on the borders of what became the Sahara Desert," says Edwards, the entomologist at Muhlenberg College. "It became adapted to live in our stored water. If it didn't have humans providing water for it, it would not have been able to survive."

Non-experts once knew *Aedes aegypti* as the yellow fever mosquito, but in recent years it has been spreading

other diseases, including dengue, chikungunya and Zika. Dengue, which was barely considered a problem in the Western Hemisphere during the 1950s, has become an increasing concern in the Americas, with the number of cases growing thirtyfold from the 1960s to the 2010s, according to the WHO. In 2010, the Americas had 1.7 million cases.[66] Last year, Brazil alone saw 1.6 million dengue cases, nearly triple the country's rate in 2014.[67]

"Dengue doesn't have a high mortality rate but causes huge health costs," says Callahan of the Gates Foundation. "People often wind up having extreme symptoms of bone ache, backache, high fever. People feel that their muscles are contracting so severely it will break their back." In fact, dengue is sometimes called "breakbone fever" because of the severe pain it causes in the joints and muscles.

Since 2001, dengue outbreaks have occurred in Hawaii, Texas and Florida. Public health officials have warned that the spread of dengue — and more recently, chikungunya — shows that the United States needs to step up its mosquito and surveillance efforts.

Since 2014, chikungunya, which rarely infected U.S. travelers even a decade ago, has been transmitted locally in the Caribbean and Florida.[68] Last year, 44 states recorded cases of chikungunya.[69]

"There was a perception that mosquito-borne diseases were not a problem, because we'd overcome yellow fever and malaria," says Thomas V. Inglesby, director of the Center for Health Security. "With cases of chikungunya in Florida and Texas and Hawaii, now we can't ignore a problem that makes visible the mistakes we make in vector control."

CURRENT SITUATION
Zika's Challenges

In Congress, the debate continues over how to provide funding to fight Zika.

President Obama asked the House and Senate in February for $1.9 billion to prevent the spread of Zika in the United States. The money would be used to bolster efforts among federal agencies and offer grants to states for treatment, disease prevention and vaccine research, Obama said.[70]

Congress was slow to respond to the president's request. Republicans, who control both chambers, said

Should genetically modified mosquitoes be used to fight disease?

YES Nina Fedoroff
Professor Emeritus of Biology, Penn State University

Written for *CQ Researcher*, July 2016

NO Jaydee Hanson
Senior Policy Analyst, Center for Food Safety

Written for *CQ Researcher*, July 2016

The Zika virus, like the dengue, chikungunya and yellow fever viruses, is transmitted by mosquitoes, most commonly *Aedes aegypti.* Vaccines can protect people but take time to develop. Until a Zika vaccine is available, attention remains on reducing the mosquito population. Insecticides are used widely but work inefficiently, indiscriminately and only temporarily.

Hence attention has turned to biological approaches, which deserve serious consideration. The first, simplest and most extensively tested of these is the release of male mosquitoes endowed with a lethal gene. The laboratory-reared mosquitoes, developed by the British biological engineering firm Oxitec, are sex-sorted, and the males are released to find and mate with females. The lethal gene becomes active and the offspring die, rapidly reducing mosquito numbers. People are not affected because male mosquitoes don't bite them.

The Oxitec mosquito has been tested in the Cayman Islands, Malaysia and Brazil since 2009 and has reduced mosquito populations by as much as 99 percent. However, because these insects are genetically modified, they are heavily regulated, and the approval process can take years. In the United States, the Food and Drug Administration is regulating the Oxitec mosquito as a "new animal drug," an odd use of regulations designed to ensure that a new drug is safe and effective.

A second biological approach is based on the observation that infection of mosquitoes with certain Wolbachia bacteria interferes with their fertility and their ability to transmit viral diseases. If an uninfected male mates with a Wolbachia-infected female, most of the eggs won't hatch and the infected mosquitoes will take over the population. Wolbachia infection also reduces the mosquitoes' ability to transmit dengue and Zika. While preliminary evidence shows that transmission is blocked at least transiently, some scientists are concerned about the long-term effects of replacing uninfected mosquitoes with Wolbachia-infected ones.

A recently developed gene-editing system that goes by the unwieldy acronym of CRISPR/Cas9 has considerable potential. For examples, the CRISPR/Cas9 system can be designed in a test tube to promote the rapid spread of a fertility-reducing gene in the mosquito population. Male mosquitoes genetically modified with such a gene construct would be released to mate with wild females, as described for the Oxitec mosquito. By reducing fertility, this approach might result in the complete elimination of the targeted species of this invasive pest.

Many countries are able to control mosquito transmitted disease without wiping out all mosquitoes. Before attempting to control mosquito populations via genetic engineering, we should consider the risks and alternatives.

Mosquitoes provide a food for animals and help pollinate plants. Genetically engineering mosquitoes to die off could threaten species that rely on them, including already at-risk amphibians, bats and birds. Likewise, eliminating one mosquito species may open more space for another that carries the same diseases.

The lack of independent research on the impact of genetically engineered mosquitoes constitutes a troubling factor in the drive to release billions of these insects. Few studies, if any, have been done to understand the unintended evolutionary effects of introducing new genes into a species. While the public duty to control viral diseases such as Zika and dengue is paramount, Oxitec, the company manufacturing the genetically engineered mosquitoes, has not demonstrated that its release of the mosquitoes in Brazil, the Cayman Islands and Malaysia has reduced disease, or that these mosquitoes will not have unintended effects on humans or animals. In addition to potential threats to ecosystems and a lack of evidence about the efficacy of using genetics to minimize diseases' spread, there is little information about what ingesting these insects could do to people.

Furthermore, genetically engineered mosquitoes are an expensive biotech "fix" to a problem of diseases related to poverty. Areas with the highest rates of mosquito-borne illness are those with inadequate housing and lack of resources for insecticides. But genetically engineered insects are costly and, like the pesticides they are intended to replace, must be used over and over again — even as communities still have to pay for pesticides on the non-genetically engineered species.

The risks of releasing genetically engineered mosquitoes are clear, but the benefits are not. We need independent, transparent ecological risk and safety assessments and a regulatory system equipped to deal with the novel risks from these experimental mosquitoes before they are released into our environment. The release of genetically engineered mosquitoes must be compared to other methods used to reduce mosquito populations, such as infecting mosquitoes with Wolbachia bacteria, as well as vaccines. When vaccines keep people from getting disease, mosquitoes can't pass it on.

When a thorough assessment is done, genetically engineered mosquitoes will likely be shown to be an unproven and expensive gamble in the effort to reduce diseases such as Zika and dengue.

Fumigation targets *Aedes aegypti* mosquitoes in Jakarta, capital of Indonesia, on Feb. 6. Environmentalists say using pesticides to kill virus-carrying mosquitoes can damage animal habitats. Instead, some experts advocate using natural predators against the insects, such as fish that eat mosquito larvae, and bats, which gorge on mosquitoes.

they were concerned that the administration's plan was not well thought out and lacked specifics.

"It doesn't take a lot of thought to realize that this is a request for a blank check," Senate Majority Whip John Cornyn of Texas said in April. "What they want to do is play a shell game with this money. They want to get the money and if they don't need it to deal with Zika, they can transfer it for other purposes, again without any transparency, without any real political accountability."[71]

Indeed, the Obama administration did shift funds previously appropriated to fight Ebola to get its Zika response up and running. On the local level, the change meant health departments had to do shifting of their own: A survey in April found that two-thirds of local health departments cut their preparedness budgets, while more than 40 percent reduced their medical staffing and supply budgets.[72]

On May 17, the Senate passed a bipartisan compromise to provide $1.1 billion for mosquito control, public education and vaccine development. The next day, the House passed a bill to provide $622 million for the Zika fight, limiting spending to the current fiscal year and shifting leftover Ebola funding to Zika to offset the cost.

A deal was then worked out in June between the House and Senate, with input primarily from Republicans. It would provide $1.1 billion, equaling the Senate version, but $750 million of the funding would have to come from cuts in other programs. In addition, the bill included provisions that Democrats opposed, such as a stipulation that no funding in this legislation go to Planned Parenthood or other family-planning groups. Another would allow the display of Confederate flags in veterans' cemeteries.[73]

The House passed the bill on June 23 along party lines. But the White House issued a veto threat. "This plan from congressional Republicans is four months late and nearly a billion dollars short of what our public health experts have said is necessary to do everything possible to fight the Zika virus and steals funding from other health priorities," White House press secretary Josh Earnest said in a June 23 statement.[74]

On June 28, Senate Democrats blocked the bill's passage, criticizing Republicans for the unrelated provisions.[75] Democrats have tried, unsuccessfully, to get Senate Republicans to reconsider their stance but Senate Majority Leader Mitch McConnell, R-Ky., said on July 12 that he will not bring a new bill to the floor.[76] Instead, on July 14, he brought up the same package Democrats had rejected, leading to the same result.

Local Response

With Congress deadlocked, local and state health officials worry that they may be unable to ramp up their efforts in time to prevent Zika outbreaks. At this point, Congress won't appropriate funds until September at the earliest. Even then, the money has to reach state and local officials, who must hire personnel to carry out public education campaigns and surveillance, prevention and treatment efforts.

"It's sobering to think that going into this mosquito season, half of the counties in the United States didn't have a mosquito-control effort in place, including counties in Texas," says Inglesby of the Center for Health Security. "In some places, it's clearly one person who is driving around with a fogger on the truck, who switches to snow plowing in the wintertime."

Experts say public health departments cannot easily hire a number of new people and expect them to be up to the task, which in the case of Zika may require delicate interviews with possible victims about their sexual history. Many of those interviews will likely have to be conducted with people with limited English skills.

Health departments at the local level are hoping to increase their laboratory capacity as well, so they can quickly monitor and detect outbreaks. That, in turn, will allow a state to rapidly and aggressively direct resources toward an affected area.

Response to an outbreak will also allow mosquito abatement efforts to go into overdrive. In 2009, in response to only three dengue cases in Key West, the Florida Keys Mosquito Control District brought out its helicopters to spray. It also sent teams door to door to encourage residents to chlorinate their pools and use larvicides where rainwater collected.[77]

But few jurisdictions have that kind of mosquito control infrastructure in place.

What's more, blanket spraying won't be much of a help against *Aedes aegypti* mosquitoes, which often hide in small containers, including in people's homes. The species has "become ubiquitous and hard to get rid of," says the Pan American Health Organization's Epstein.

Getting rid of *Aedes aegypti* may be particularly difficult in high-poverty areas where governments have fewer resources than in richer areas. They may also have poorer garbage collection, with more refuse piling up and becoming rain catchers and mosquito-breeding grounds.

"Our whole infrastructure for controlling mosquitoes has been depleted over the years," says Hotez of Baylor. "Right now, we're not in a position to control *Aedes aegypti*, which is the only way you can prevent Zika, because we're not going to have a vaccine in time."

At least 18 public and private labs are working on a Zika vaccine.[78] In June, Inovio Pharmaceuticals, a company based in Plymouth Meeting, Pa., announced that it will start the first initial, small-scale trial of a Zika vaccine.[79] But no vaccine is expected to reach the market before 2018, at the earliest.[80]

Vaccines that are promising in the lab must first undergo clinical tests, in which human volunteers receive the vaccine. In the case of Zika, the disease's spread might complicate efforts because scientists may find it harder to determine whether patients developed immunity due to the vaccine or natural exposure to the disease. For these reasons, vaccine development is focusing on pregnant women and women of child-bearing age, said Anthony Fauci, director of the National Institute of Allergy and Infectious Disease.[81]

The hit-and-miss nature of mosquito control in the United States also has Hotez and some other public health experts concerned about the resurgence of yellow fever and the possibility of its reappearance in this country.

Angola and Congo in western Africa, with more than 900 confirmed cases, currently have yellow fever outbreaks. Although a vaccine is available, health care workers and doctors may run short of doses if yellow fever continues spreading. With stockpiles depleted, the WHO in June approved "fractional dosing," or vaccinations of just one-fifth the normally prescribed strength, a dosage it says can work in patients for 12 months or longer.[82]

"We are vulnerable to yellow fever," Hotez says, noting that globalization means the disease can travel with humans and then be spread by local *Aedes aegypti* mosquitoes.[83] "Yellow fever could return to the U.S., in the same areas where we're worried about Zika."

OUTLOOK
Emergency Fund Needed?

Many public health experts agree that Zika is going to be a scourge in the Americas for the foreseeable future, and a vaccine likely won't be ready for years.

And Zika is not the only challenge scientists face. They have been working on a vaccine for dengue for more than a decade, and millions of dollars have been spent over the years in search of a successful vaccine against malaria.

Public health officials also fear the emergence of a new, unknown virus. Given the combination of climate change, globalization and human encroachment into animal habitats, fresh epidemics are taken almost as a given. "The world's getting smaller, so we're more likely to have sporadic outbreaks of diseases no one's ever heard of," says Conlon, the American Mosquito Control Association adviser.

The litany of outbreaks in recent years, including Ebola, the H1N1 flu virus, and severe acute respiratory syndrome, or SARS, should have acted as wakeup calls to policymakers — but that hasn't been the case, says Benjamin of the American Public Health Association, pointing to the slow response to Zika.[84] "I was a perpetual optimist, but Congress has shown me that even in a major crisis they're unable to respond in a timely way," he says. "We're not even lurching effectively from crisis to crisis, and that's got to change."

Given how Congress has responded — or failed to respond — to public health crises, many public health professionals would prefer a standing reserve fund that could be tapped when an emergency arises, such as those available for responding to natural disasters.

"The nation's public health system is no different from any other system that's critical to national security," says Blumenstock of the Association of State and Territorial Health Officers.

The idea has some appeal even to members of Congress, who don't particularly like the pressure or the criticism they come under when having to craft an emergency supplemental spending bill from scratch. Rep. Rosa DeLauro, a Connecticut Democrat, has introduced a bill that would authorize $5 billion for a public health emergency fund. And Sen. Bill Cassidy, a Louisiana Republican, introduced similar legislation on July 15.

But it may be a stretch to expect Congress to set aside $5 billion to cope with future emergencies, when members were reluctant to provide less than $2 billion for Zika, a threat already at hand. Some members, such as Senate Majority Whip Cornyn, say Congress must ensure the executive branch spends the funding wisely; others are hesitant to set aside money on something that may not happen.

Nevertheless, Conlon says the nation cannot afford to wait. "I know this is a hard sell when there's not an immediate threat," he says, "but if you think of 'immediate' as two to three years, rather than two to three weeks, then there is an immediate threat."

The Center for Health Security's Inglesby says the problems Zika is creating, following a series of other public health crises, might generate "enough momentum now, so we could at least have a new system put in place in a year or two, related to a disaster relief fund."

Like other health experts, Inglesby underscores the importance of having a more robust public health system in place, one that not only can respond quickly to outbreaks but continually monitors threats and educate the public about them, especially by retaining experienced lab personnel and maintaining surveillance systems.

Public officials have long had a mind-set that mosquito-borne illnesses and other "tropical" diseases are more of a problem in Africa and Asia than in the United States and Europe. But Zika and the recurrence of diseases, including yellow fever and dengue, should give the lie to that notion, says Hotez of Baylor.

Hotez suggests that poverty is a prime indicator when trying to predict the course of an infectious disease. Rather than thinking in terms of separate outcomes for developed and developing countries, he says, "we find that most of the world's neglected and emerging infections are happening among the poor in developed countries."

Thus, policymakers in the United States and other rich nations cannot assume that infectious diseases are someone else's problem, or that they can easily be contained before becoming endemic at home.

"No one is forecasting that these types of threats or emergencies are going to go away," Blumenstock says. "They're going to become faster and more furious."

NOTES

1. Bill Gates, "The Deadliest Animal in the World," GatesNotes, April 25, 2014, http://tinyurl.com/zqef7cn. Gates compiled the mosquito figure from World Health Organization statistics and said "all calculations have wide error margins."

2. *Ibid.*

3. "The Reality of Malaria," UNICEF, undated, www.unicef.org/health/files/health_africamalaria.pdf.

4. "Zika Situation Report," World Health Organization, Feb. 5, 2016, http://tinyurl.com/zfea3ov.

5. Debra Goldschmidt, "Zika virus 'scarier than initially thought,' " CNN, April 12, 2016, http://tinyurl.com/hjfy9ez.

6. McNeil, *op. cit.*, p. 25.

7. Mark R. Duffy *et al.*, "Zika Virus Outbreak on Yap Island, Federated States of Micronesia," *The New England Journal of Medicine*, June 11, 2009, http://tinyurl.com/jyreb56.

8. "Brazil says Zika-linked microcephaly cases stable at 4,908," Reuters, April 26, 2016, http://tinyurl.com/hgamv9a.

9. "Facts about Microcephaly," Centers for Disease Control and Prevention, http://tinyurl.com/haslh6z.

10. McNeil, *op. cit.*, p. 159.

11. "Zika Virus," Centers for Disease Control and Prevention, http://tinyurl.com/jjj5bcw; Daniel Chang, "Miami may have Florida's first locally acquired case of Zika virus," *Miami Herald*, July 19, 2016, http://tinyurl.com/hg3waw5.

12. "About Zika," Centers for Disease Control and Prevention, http://tinyurl.com/z4n69st; "New York sees first documented case of a woman spreading Zika via sex," The Associated Press, July 15, 2016, http://tinyurl.com/zeqdruj.

13. McNeil, *op. cit.*, p. 144.

14. Burgess Everett and Jennifer Haberkorn, "Democrats block Zika funding bill, blame GOP," *Politico*, June 28, 2016, http://tinyurl.com/zwxxdvl.

15. Vikas Bajaj, "How Zika Became a Global Threat," *The New York Times*, June 13, 2016, http://tinyurl.com/gopxaae.

16. Richard Hamburg, Laura M. Segal and Alejandra Martín, "Investing in America's Health: A State-by-State Look at Public Health Funding and Key Health Facts," Trust for America's Health, April 2016, http://tinyurl.com/zeaqmpx.

17. Lisa Rapaport, "U.S. Public Health Funding On The Decline," Reuters Health, *The Huffington Post*, Nov. 19, 2015, http://tinyurl.com/gnnbafh.

18. Celine Gounder, "Zika is a warning to the US public health system to stop rushing from fire to fire," *Quartz*, April 18, 2016, http://tinyurl.com/j2zpc89. For background on lead contamination, see Jill U. Adams, "Drinking Water Safety," *CQ Researcher*, July 15, 2016, pp. 577-600.

19. Jennifer Kates *et al.*, "The U.S. Response to Ebola: Status of the FY2015 Emergency Ebola Appropriation," Kaiser Family Foundation, Dec. 11, 2015, http://tinyurl.com/ob45ebk.

20. Gates, *op. cit.*

21. "DDT Ban Takes Effect," Environmental Protection Agency, Dec. 31, 1972, http://tinyurl.com/jo6cc64.

22. Arielle Dollinger, "Devouring 1,000 Mosquitoes an Hour, Bats Are Now Welcome Guests as Zika Fears Rise," *The New York Times*, July 4, 2016, http://tinyurl.com/zc7tkvu.

23. "Oxitec's Genetically Modified Mosquitoes: A Credible Approach to Dengue Fever?" *GeneWatch UK*, March 2015, http://tinyurl.com/zjw9zor.

24. Flavio Devienne Ferreira, "Inside the Mosquito Factory That Could Stop Dengue and Zika," *MIT Technology Review*, Feb. 17, 2016, http://tinyurl.com/h9jet7m.

25. Andrew Hammond *et al.*, "A CRISPR-Cas9 gene drive system targeting female reproduction in the malaria mosquito vector Anopheles *gambiae*," *Nature Biotechnology*, Dec. 7, 2015, http://tinyurl.com/jy3q5qd.

26. Rob Stein, "Powerful 'Gene Drive' Can Quickly Change An Entire Species," NPR, Nov. 5, 2015, http://tinyurl.com/otoefrk.

27. Peter J. Hotez, "Zika in the United States of America and a Fateful 1969 Decision," PLOS Neglected Tropical Diseases, May 26, 2016, http://tinyurl.com/zv64thq.

28. "Upholding women's human rights essential to Zika response," U.S. High Commissioner for Human Rights, Feb. 5, 2016, http://tinyurl.com/jbenko4.

29. Ann M. Simmons, "Zika fears increase demand for abortions in countries where it's illegal to have one," *Los Angeles Times*, http://tinyurl.com/hffgrpw.

30. "In Just the Last Four Years, States Have Enacted 231 Abortion Restrictions," Guttmacher Institute, Jan. 5, 2015, http://tinyurl.com/jq2x43t.

31. Abby Goodnough, "Texas Abortion Law Has Women Waiting Longer, and Paying More," *The New York Times*, March 18, 2016, http://tinyurl.com/gpx3z96.

32. Robert Barnes, "Supreme Court strikes down Texas abortion clinic restrictions," *The Washington Post*, June 27, 2016, http://tinyurl.com/z73q3us; the court ruling is at http://tinyurl.com/zremwx2.

33. Christopher H. Smith, "The Global Zika Epidemic," Office of Rep. Christopher H. Smith, Feb. 10, 2016, http://tinyurl.com/z6kjvrq.

34. Sarah Pulliam Bailey and Michelle Boorstein, "Pope Francis suggests contraception could be permissible in Zika fight," *The Washington Post*, Feb. 18, 2016, http://tinyurl.com/zvyjom2.

35. David M. Herszenhorn, "Zika Bill Is Blocked by Senate Democrats Upset Over Provisions," *The New York Times*, June 28, 2016, http://tinyurl.com/zu7jez9.

36. Everett and Haberkorn, *op. cit.*

37. Irwin W. Sherman, *Twelve Diseases That Changed Our World* (2007), p. 144.

38. Molly Caldwell Crosby, *The American Plague* (2006), p. 11.

39. Andrew Spielman and Michael D'Antonio, *Mosquito: The Story of Man's Deadliest Foe* (2001), p. 61.

40. *Ibid.*

41. Mark Harrison, *Contagion: How Commerce Has Spread Disease* (2012), p. 107.

42. Sonia Shah, *op. cit.*, p. 47.

43. Crosby, *op. cit.*, pp. 47, 55.

44. Sherman, *op. cit.*, p. 151.

45. Crosby, *op. cit.*, p. 173.

46. *Ibid.*, p. 181.

47. Sherman *op. cit.*, p. 152.

48. Crosby, *op. cit.*, p. 204.

49. *Ibid.*, p. 205.

50. Shah, *op. cit.*, p. 182.

51. Crosby, *op. cit.*, p. 228.

52. Alex Perry, *Lifeblood* (2011), p. 20.

53. *Ibid.*, p. 23.

54. Shah, *op. cit.*, p. 207.

55. Perry, *op. cit.*, p. 23.

56. William H. McNeill, *Plagues and People* (1977), p. 249.

57. Perry, *op. cit.*, p. 25.

58. Shah, *op. cit.*, p. 210.

59. *Ibid.*, p. 216.

60. Perry, *op. cit.*, p. 26.

61. Shah, *op. cit.*, p. 216.

62. Mark Jerome Walters, *Six Modern Plagues* (2003), p. 133.

63. *Ibid.*, p. 145.

64. McNeil, *op. cit.*, p. 162.

65. McNeill, *op. cit.*, p. 188.

66. Olivia Brathwaite Dick *et al.*, "Review: The History of Dengue Outbreaks in the Americas," *The American Journal of Tropical Medicine and Hygiene*, Oct. 3, 2012, http://tinyurl.com/go6apdl.

67. McNeil, *op. cit.*, p. 15.

68. "Chikungunya virus in the United States," Centers for Disease Control and Prevention, http://tinyurl.com/pkl7jou.

69. "2015 provisional data for the United States," Centers for Disease Control and Prevention, Jan. 12, 2016, http://tinyurl.com/hcbrhcj.

70. President Obama, letter to Congress, Feb. 22, 2016, http://tinyurl.com/jeheodu.

71. Mike DeBonis, "Why Republicans are opposing President Obama's request for Zika funding," *The Washington Post*, April 28, 2016, http://tinyurl.com/hlu8e5u.

72. "Impact of the Redirection of Public Health Emergency Preparedness (PHEP) Funding from State and Local Health Departments to Support National Zika Response," National Association of County and City Health Officials, May 2016, http://tinyurl.com/hcylw8o.

73. Erin Kelly, "House approves $1.1 billion deal to combat Zika virus," *USA Today*, June 23, 2016, http://tinyurl.com/jyv9wdq; Herszenhorn, *op. cit.*

74. Kelly, *ibid.*

75. Herszenhorn, *op. cit.*

76. Laura Barron-Lopez, "Senate Still At Odds Over Zika Funding With Only 3 Days Left Before Summer Break," *The Huffington Post*, July 12, 2016, http://tinyurl.com/zf6vd5r.

77. McNeil, *op. cit.*, p. 160.

78. *Ibid.*, p. 163.

79. Gillian Mohney, "What We Know About the First Zika Vaccine Trial by Inovio Pharmaceuticals," ABC News, June 21, 2016, http://tinyurl.com/h93rmnu.

80. Tulip Mazumdar, "Zika vaccine possible 'within months,'" BBC, March 4, 2016, http://tinyurl.com/jsdvpst.

81. *Ibid.*

82. "Lower doses of yellow fever vaccine could be used in emergencies," World Health Organization, June 17, 2016, http://tinyurl.com/z4j2fts.

83. Peter Hotez and Kristy Murray, "Could Yellow Fever Return to the United States?" Public Library of Science, Dec. 5, 2013, http://tinyurl.com/z4c2boc.

84. For more on these outbreaks, see Marcia Clemmitt, "Emerging Infectious Diseases," *CQ Researcher*, Feb. 13, 2015, pp. 145-168.

BIBLIOGRAPHY

Selected Sources

Books

Crosby, Molly Caldwell, *The American Plague: The Untold Story of Yellow Fever, the Epidemic That Shaped Our History*, Berkley Books, 2006.
A journalist notes that yellow fever caused more than 100,000 deaths in this country, making it the most feared disease in North America for 200 years.

McNeil Jr., Donald G., *Zika: The Emerging Epidemic*, Norton, 2016.
The global health reporter for The New York Times documents the early spread of the disease and describes conflicts within public health organizations about how to respond.

Perry, Alex, *Lifeblood: How to Change the World One Dead Mosquito at a Time*, PublicAffairs, 2011.
A former *Time* Africa bureau chief focuses on renewed efforts by Western governments and charities to combat malaria.

Shah, Sonia, *The Fever: How Malaria Has Ruled Humankind for 500,000 Years*, Sarah Crichton Books, 2010.
A science journalist recounts the history of a disease that predates humans and has shaped history.

Articles

Attaran, Amir, "Off the Podium: Why Public Health Concerns for Global Spread of Zika Virus Means That Rio de Janeiro's 2016 Olympic Games Must Not Proceed," *Harvard Public Health Review*, May 2016, http://tinyurl.com/hsmlav2.
In a widely cited article, a Canadian public health professor argues that the Olympic and Paralympic Games should be moved, postponed or canceled because of the Zika outbreak in Brazil.

"Breaking the Fever," *The Economist*, Oct. 10, 2015, http://tinyurl.com/h536kt3.
The cost of fighting malaria is escalating and might double to $6 billion by 2025, but the rewards in health and economic productivity would far outpace that expense, experts say.

Caplan-Bricker, Nora, "The GOP's War on Abortion May Have Cleared the Way for a Zika Disaster," *Slate*, June 14, 2016, http://tinyurl.com/j4q7gud.
Southern states such as Texas and Florida, where Zika will likely do the most damage, have restrictive abortion laws and haven't accepted the federal Medicaid expansion, so they are among the least prepared to confront the virus.

Picciuto, Elizabeth, "I'm Raising a Kid With Microcephaly. Here's What the Media Gets Wrong," *The Daily Beast*, Feb. 23, 2016, http://tinyurl.com/zqxnd7u.
The author's son has microcephaly. He's non-verbal, uses a wheelchair and requires a feeding tube. But Picciuto says media outlets do a disservice by describing microcephalic children as nightmarish burdens.

Pillinger, Mara, "Mosquitoes don't just spread the Zika virus. They may be helping an older killer reemerge," *The Washington Post*, June 16, 2016, http://tinyurl.com/h7ftg5q.
A shortage of vaccines and lack of attention to yellow fever mean the disease might stage a comeback in the Americas.

Regalado, Antonio, "Bacteria-Laden Mosquitoes May Be the Cheapest Way to Stop Dengue and Zika," *MIT Technology Review*, Feb. 26, 2016, http://tinyurl.com/zpjh5zf.
The Gates Foundation is investing millions of dollars in an effort to release bacteria-laden mosquitoes into Latin American cities. Because the bacteria prevent mosquitoes from passing on viruses, this method holds promise for reducing the spread of disease at a low cost.

Simmons, Ann M., "Zika fears increase demand for abortions in countries where it's illegal to have one," *Los Angeles Times*, March 9, 2016, http://tinyurl.com/hffgrpw.
Abortion rights activists and health professionals worry that bans on abortion in many Latin American countries will lead more women to undergo dangerous

clandestine abortions due to fears about the birth defects caused by Zika.

Reports and Studies

"Draft Interim CDC Zika Response Plan," Centers for Disease Control and Prevention, June 2016, http://tinyurl.com/h9txuux.
The federal agency outlines its plans for responding to local transmission of Zika and the steps states and localities should take in areas such as surveillance, lab work, mosquito control and outreach to pregnant women.

"Gene Drives on the Horizon: Advancing Science, Navigating Uncertainty, and Aligning Research with Public Values," National Academies of Science, Engineering, and Medicine, June 8, 2016, http://tinyurl.com/j3xe5dt.

A panel of scientists concludes that altering genes to prevent mosquitoes from reproducing is potentially dangerous, and it recommends further, tightly controlled studies of creatures outside of laboratories.

Hamburg, Richard, Laura M. Segal and Alejandra Martín, "Investing in America's Health: A State-by-State Look at Public Health Funding and Key Health Facts," Trust for America's Health, April 2016, http://tinyurl.com/zeaqmpx.
Public health has been chronically underfunded for decades, but the situation has gotten worse in recent years, a health advocacy group argues. As a result, the public health system is not properly equipped to carry out core functions such as enacting programs to prevent diseases and prepare for health emergencies.

For More Information

American Mosquito Control Association, 1120 Route 73, Suite 200, Mount Laurel, NJ 08054; 856-439-9222; www.mosquito.org. Provides expertise and assistance to mosquito-control authorities primarily in the public sector.

American Public Health Association, 800 Eye St., N.W., Washington, DC 20001; 202-777-2742; www.apha.org. Lobbies policymakers, publishes research and conducts the world's largest annual public health meeting.

Annenberg Public Policy Center, University of Pennsylvania, 202 S. 36th St., Philadelphia, PA 19104; 215-898-9400; www.annenbergpublicpolicycenter.org/. Conducts regular polling about American attitudes and understanding of the Zika virus.

Association of State and Territorial Health Officials, 2231 Crystal Drive, Suite 450, Arlington, VA 22202; 202-371-9090; www.astho.org. Represents state-level public health agencies and helps them formulate policies.

Center for Infectious Disease Research and Policy, University of Minnesota, 420 Delaware St., S.E., Minneapolis, MN 55455; 612-626-6770; www.cidrap.umn.edu/. Targets infectious disease threats through research and the translation of scientific information for general audiences.

Centers for Disease Control and Prevention, 1600 Clifton Rd., Atlanta, GA 30329; 800-232-4636; www.cdc.gov. Federal agency that researches and provides information on infectious diseases and other threats to public health and safety.

Global Fund to Fight AIDS, Tuberculosis and Malaria, Chemin de Blandonnet 8, 1214 Vernier, Geneva, Switzerland; +41-58-791-1700; www.theglobalfund.org/en/. Coordinates global aid from governments, nonprofits and the private sector; acts as the main international coordinator of the fight against malaria.

National Association of County and City Health Officials, 1100 17th St., N.W., 7th Floor, Washington, DC 20036; 202-783-5550; www.naccho.org. Represents more than 2,800 local health departments across the United States.

UPMC Center for Health Security, 621 E. Pratt St., Suite 210, Baltimore, MD 21202; 443-573-3304; www.upmchealthsecurity.org/. Examines how scientific and technological innovations can protect people's health from challenges including emerging infectious diseases; affiliated with the University of Pittsburgh Medical Center.

World Health Organization, 525 23rd St., N.W., Washington, DC 20037; 202-974-3000; www.who.int/en/. Arm of the United Nations concerned with international health, including outbreaks of infectious disease.